MW01121764

CHARLES THE BOLD AND ITALY (1467–1477)

Politics and Personnel

Plate 1. Oil on panel portrait, 60 × 45 cm, of Charles, duke of Burgundy, copied c. 1570 by Cristofano Altissimo (died 1605) from a lost original, perhaps from life, in the portrait gallery of Paolo Giovio, Borgovice, near Como. No. 461, Uffizi Gallery, Florence. Photograph supplied by Cecil H. Clough.

CHARLES THE BOLD AND ITALY (1467–1477)

Politics and Personnel

R. J. Walsh

With a Postscript and Bibliographical Supplement by
Werner Paravicini
and an Editorial Preface by
Cecil H. Clough

LIVERPOOL UNIVERSITY PRESS

First published 2005 by
Liverpool University Press
4 Cambridge Street
Liverpool L69 7ZU

British Library Cataloguing-in-Publication data
A British Library CIP record is available

ISBN 0-85323-838-3

Typeset by Servis Filmsetting Ltd, Manchester
Printed and bound in the European Union by Bell and Bain Ltd, Glasgow

Contents

List of Abbreviations

AB	*Annales de Bourgogne*
ADNB	Archives départementales du Nord, Lille, Série B
AG	Archivio di Stato, Mantua, Archivio Gonzaga
AGR	Archives Générales du Royaume (Algemeen Rijksarchief), Brussels
AGR, CC	Archives Générales du Royaume, Chambre des Comptes
AKG	*Archiv für Kulturgeschichte*
AOGV	Archiv des Ordens vom Goldenen Vliesse, Vienna: registers of the proceedings of the chapter meetings of the Order of the Golden Fleece (Toison d'Or)
AS	Archivio di Stato
ASF	Archivio di Stato, Florence
ASF MAP	Archivio di Stato, Florence, Mediceo avanti il Principato
ASI	*Archivio storico italiano*
ASL	*Archivio storico lombardo*
ASM	Archivio di Stato, Milan, Fondo Visconteo-Sforzesco, Potenze Estere
ASPN	*Archivio storico per le province napoletane*
ASV, P	Archivio di Stato, Venice, Collezione del Cardinale Lodovico Podocataro, Atti della Curia Romana
ASV, SS	Archivio di Stato, Venice, Senato Secreta, Deliberazioni
BCRH	*Bulletin de la Commission royale d'histoire*
BEC	*Bibliothèque de l'École des Chartes*
BIHBR	*Bulletin de l'Institut historique belge de Rome*
BL	British Library (London)
BMGN	*Bijdragen en mededelingen betreffende de geschiedenis der Nederlanden*

BNMV	Biblioteca Nazionale Marciana, Venice
BZGA	*Basler Zeitschrift für Geschichte und Altertumskunde*
CSP Milan	*Calendar of state papers and manuscripts existing in the archives and collections of Milan*, ed. A.B. Hinds, one volume only published (London, 1912)
CSP Venice	*Calendar of state papers and manuscripts, relating to English affairs, existing in the archives and collections of Venice and in other libraries of northern Italy*, 38 vols (London, 1864–1947)
DBI	*Dizionario biografico degli italiani*, in progress, Rome, 1960–
EHR	*English Historical Review*
GSLI	*Giornale storico della letteratura italiana*
IMU	*Italia medioevale e umanistica*
JMH	*Journal of Medieval History*
MA	*Le Moyen Age*
MAHEFR	*Mélanges d'archéologie et d'histoire de l'École française de Rome*
MOG	*Mitteilungen des Instituts für österreichische Geschichtsforschung*
PCEEB	*Publications du Centre européen d'études bourguignonnes (XIVᵉ–XVIᵉ s., formerly burgondo-médianes)*
RIS	Rerum Italicarum Scriptores
RSI	Raccolta degli storici italiani
RSI	*Rivista storica italiana*
SR	*Studies in the Renaissance*
TG	*Tijdschrift voor geschiedenis*

List of Illustrations

Maps

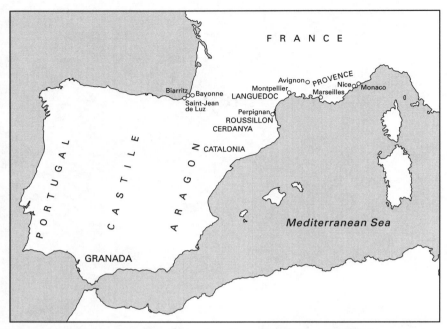

The Western Mediterranean in the time of Charles the Bold

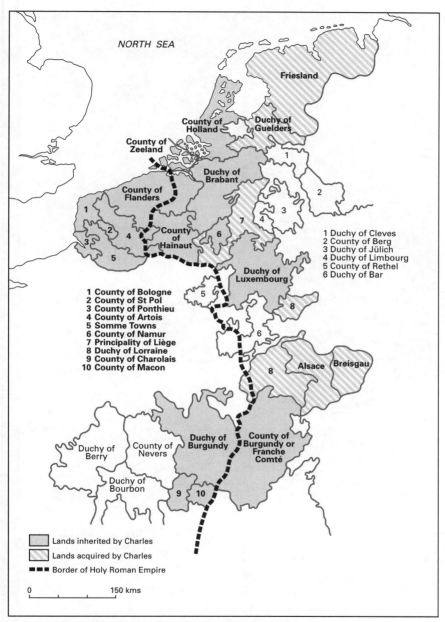

NORTH SEA

Friesland

County of Holland

Duchy of Guelders

County of Zeeland

Duchy of Brabant

County of Flanders

1

2

3

4

5

County of Hainaut

6

7

5

Duchy of Luxembourg

8

6

8

Alsace

Breisgau

1 Duchy of Cleves
2 County of Berg
3 Duchy of Jülich
4 Duchy of Limbourg
5 County of Rethel
6 Duchy of Bar

1 County of Bologne
2 County of St Pol
3 County of Ponthieu
4 County of Artois
5 Somme Towns
6 County of Namur
7 Principality of Liège
8 Duchy of Lorraine
9 County of Charolais
10 County of Macon

Duchy of Berry

County of Nevers

Duchy of Burgundy

County of Burgundy or Franche Comté

Duchy of Bourbon

9

10

Lands inherited by Charles

Lands acquired by Charles

Border of Holy Roman Empire

0   150 kms

Valois Burgundy in the time of Charles the Bold

Towns and cities in and around Valois Burgundy in the time of Charles the Bold

Italy in the time of Charles the Bold: states

Italy in the time of Charles the Bold: towns and cities

Editorial Preface

This preface aims to place Dr Richard Walsh's remarkable researches on the history of the final decade of the duchy of Burgundy in the broader historical perspective of Western Christendom in the second half of the fifteenth century. Attention is also drawn to several unusual features likely to be misunderstood or overlooked. All in all this will enable the proper appreciation of the importance of this book. Publication has long been delayed by misfortunes, so the appearance at last of Dr Walsh's study, with its vital scholarly apparatus in an appropriate format, and illustrations, is welcomed *cum laude*.

The duchy of Burgundy warrants a prime slot in the Department of Dead-Ends, as suggested perhaps by Charles the Bold's other epithet: the Rash. Charles came to rule Burgundy in his own right on 15 June 1467, following the death of his father, Duke Philip, having acted as lieutenant on the latter's behalf for the previous two years. On accession Charles, like his ducal forebears, was immediately faced, theoretically at least, with paying homage for his territories to two overlords: to Louis XI, king of France, for French lands, and to Frederick III, the emperor, for those imperial.[1] These invidious obligations, even if they could apparently be neglected with impunity, had their dangers: should these two overlords war with each other, and each demand from Charles his feudal obligation of military service, clearly he could not fulfil both obligations in person, thus theoretically could expect to be legally deprived of his holdings by the dissatisfied overlord. Furthermore, the English monarchy had in 1453 lost all French territory save Calais, while on 22 July 1461 there followed the accession of a very able and totally unscrupulous monarch – Louis XI – to the French throne, both factors which ensured that French power in Western Christendom would increase, thereby reversing those very circumstances that had enabled the dukes of Burgundy before Charles to consolidate their state, particularly at the expense of France. Fortunately for Charles the rule of Frederick III marked an imperial nadir and overlordship claims had long been forgotten.

Charles was head of probably the wealthiest state in Western Christendom, but unusual in having two overlords. Only on the Italian peninsula did the Este dynasty face a parallel situation, holding from both pope and emperor. The Marquis Borso d'Este raised the status of the dynasty when on 18 May 1452 he and his successors were elevated dukes by the emperor for the holdings of Modena, Reggio and Rovigo; moreover, from 14 April 1471 Borso and his successors were elevated dukes by the pope for the vicariates of Ferrara and those associated. It should not be overlooked that rank or status might be involved, as well as feudal obligations and homage to the overlord, as Charles appreciated. An overlord could reject a successor who was illegitimate (though sometimes did not) and certainly would a female (though ways might be found to get round even this problem). Accordingly, for the underlord his fertility and that of his wife were prime considerations. If his wife failed to produce a male heir, he could look to a mistress for a son, and then seek a papal bull of legitimisation (which might prove acceptable). Borso's father, the Marquis Niccolò III d'Este, had three wives; the second, Parisina, he had executed after she was caught *in flagrante delicto* with his then only legitimate son, Ugo, likewise beheaded; eventually by his third wife, married late in life, he had two sons, Ercole and Sigismondo.[2] By then he had somewhat overdone illegitimate children, conservatively numbered as thirty, giving rise to the quip: 'Di quà, di là, sul Pò; tutti figli di Niccolò'.

A typical result was rivalry for the succession. This the marquis had sought to resolve following Ugo's execution by choosing Leonello (illegitimate but legitimised) for that role, and having him trained for the task. Following Leonello's early death, despite the existence by then of legitimate claimants, Ercole and Sigismondo, Leonello's brother, Borso, was chosen to succeed by popular election. The succession of these (or any future) legitimate children had been specifically excluded by Niccolò III in the marriage contract drawn up with his third wife. For his part, Charles of Burgundy had lost two wives by the age of 34 and was left with but a daughter, Mary. His third marriage in 1468 to Margaret of York, sister of Edward IV, king of England, was politically shrewd but proved barren, hence effectively a catastrophe. Charles had no mis-

tresses and no male heir – testimony to his Christian morality, yet suici-
dal for his dynasty and such territorial achievements as he attained, a
problem that dual overlordship exacerbated.

In spite of his exceptional wealth and pre-eminent 'magnificence', to
adopt a contemporary term, the consequence of overlordship, however
ineffective, was to reduce Charles's rank among European powers. As
mentioned, this concept of rank or status should not be minimised, and
was reflected by Charles's feudal position, which placed him merely at
the head of the Italian states. England and Scotland were sovereign
powers in their own right, like the major continental powers: France,
Bohemia, Poland and Hungary. It is true that in the first half of the
fifteenth century Bohemia had broken with the Roman Catholic faith,
surviving as a Hussite kingdom, an anachronism within Western
Christendom. Poland was another anomaly, its Lithuanian half being
Greek Orthodox, looking to Moscow as the third Rome, with a sovereign
in Lithuania who professed that faith. All the other Roman Catholic
states, including the duchy of Burgundy, were under the authority of the
pope in all ecclesiastical matters – the key concerns of matrimony,
divorce and legitimacy, as will be examined further below.

The German empire was not a unified state, the numerous cities and
fiefs comprising it being essentially tied to the emperor in origin by
feudal obligations. Though convention placed the emperor below the
pope only, his authority in his state rendered him ever weaker vis-à-vis
monarchs of Western Christendom as they consistently consolidated
their power at home. On the Italian peninsula, unusually, there remained
vestiges of those once dominant dual institutions of Western
Christendom, pope and emperor; in the centre and south of the Italian
peninsula papal claims to overlordship were a serious matter, in part
because they were bolstered by ecclesiastical authority. It was not simply
a case of the latter determining matrimony and legitimacy of birth – it
held the keys to heaven. Moreover, aside from the fief of Naples, most
vicariates were comparatively modest in size and individually no match
for a papal army. From the election of Martin V in 417 the popes had
the undying objective of recovering the papal states conceded to vicars
in fief during the times of papal political weakness in the previous
century. In this regard the granting of Ferrara to the Este, as dukes, mentioned above, was untypical.

In the south of the peninsula the kingdom of Naples (including Sicily,
hence known as the Kingdom of the Two Sicilies) had been a papal fief
since 1265 following its creation by Pope Clement IV and the agreement

to the terms the next year by Charles, duke of Anjou, the brother of King Louis IX of France. King Ferrante was illegitimate and as such specifically excluded by his grandfather's will from inheriting Sicily, which on his accession to Naples had passed to the king of Aragon, his relative. Being illegitimate Ferrante had difficulties in obtaining enfiefment with Naples from certain popes, indeed from several he failed to receive it. Furthermore René I (1409–1480), duke of Anjou and of Lorraine and count of Provence, claimed to be the rightful king of Naples, though after a protracted military campaign against Ferrante's father, Alfonso I (V of Aragon), he had been driven from the peninsula.[3] Ferrante's perpetual fear was a further military campaign from René or his heirs, with support from the king of France. It was these circumstances that stimulated Charles of Burgundy to look to Ferrante for support against Louis XI, electing him to his prestigious Order of the Golden Fleece in 1473, an issue meriting further examination below.

While the emperor claimed to be overlord of the northern Italian peninsula, his pretensions were largely ignored. The republic of Venice and the Tuscan republics of Florence, Siena and Lucca in no way recognised imperial jurisdiction; yet there always remained the possibility of a powerful emperor bringing an army into Italy and enforcing his authority, as was to be the case with Charles V in the sixteenth century. The Visconti did hold the duchy of Milan in fief from the emperor. Following the line's extinction and Francesco Sforza's subsequent overthrow in 1450 of the short-lived Ambrosian republic, he and his Sforza successors ruled the duchy with an assumed title of duke until 1494 without imperial authority. Among the smaller states there were rulers who took satisfaction in an imperial privilege for their authority; the largest was the marquisate of Mantua, held by the Gonzaga dynasty, consistently with imperial authority supporting its rule. Such a privilege, in theory at least, gave some protection against the over-mighty subject within and the expansionist aims of neighbours, above all the Sforza of Milan and the republic of Venice.

Charles the Bold's ambition was to establish as a sovereign state a kingdom totally independent of the king of France and the emperor. Its territory would extend from the North Sea to the Mediterranean, where by 1473 the ruler of Savoy was his client, while René I had promised Charles's accession to the Comté of Provence on his death. This kingdom would broadly conform territorially to a resuscitated Middle Kingdom of Lothar as it existed in 843. Illustrated maps depicting its scope are provided by Christopher Cope's book (1986).[4] To counter

Louis XI, who sought to frustrate him, Charles had an ally in Edward IV of England, who became his brother-in-law; Edward had reasserted that he was king of France and intended to recover his rightful French territory. In 1473 at Trier the duke sought to negotiate with Frederick III for a crown, which he thought he had. He also desired election as king of the Romans and eventual succession as emperor on Frederick's death: this too came to nothing. The failure of his schemes, together with his critical alienation of the Swiss Confederation, has been plotted in considerable detail over almost a century and a half, from John Foster Kirk's three-volume history, first published in Philadelphia between 1863 and 1868 (Kirk, 1824–1904, was a Canadian-born American scholar who is now undervalued and neglected) to Richard Vaughan's authoritative biography (1973). This path was charted by way of Toutey (1902), Cartellier (1926) and Bartier (1970); the latter's book, though undocumented, is notable for its iconographical contribution provided by Ann Rouzet.[5] Werner Paravicini's bibliographical supplement to this book provides vital information on relevant contributions published after Dr Walsh's researches had terminated. As an adjunct it should be recalled that Charles, eager to win general approval from the powers of Western Christendom, in the face of Ottoman expansion in the Mediterranean after the fall of Constantinople in 1453, proclaimed his zeal for a crusade. This facet of the duke's policy has been clarified admirably by Richard Walsh's 1977 article, 'Charles the Bold and the Crusade: Politics and Propaganda'.[6]

At the time that he was working on his volume on Charles the Bold Vaughan appreciated that a significant lacuna in the available research was information on the duke's international relations with the states of the Italian peninsula; presumably he had in mind the pope as a political power, and the major states. It is this entirely new dimension which Dr Walsh's volume provides. It is scrupulously based on primary documents, in the main drawn upon for the first time, often quoted *in extenso* and always precisely. The archives consulted are detailed in the introduction; those of lesser states, such as Genoa, Siena and Lucca, remain to be explored and may furnish missing pieces of the jigsaw. However, this volume provides a largely complete picture and a distinct one; it represents an extraordinarily complex undertaking and a contribution to knowledge which will stand the test of time.

The duke's dealings, essentially ecclesiastical in nature, with the two popes in authority during his rule have been outlined in previous studies and typify those of any ruler of the period. The most important for

Charles the Bold concerned dispensations associated with projected marriage alliances. Since he had no illegitimate children, as already mentioned, he did not require bulls of legitimisation such as were commonly sought by rulers on the Italian peninsula. As already indicated, healthy children, particularly if legitimate, were considered as wealth and an investment for the family's perpetuation. In the case of a ruling dynasty on the Italian peninsula, certainly, daughters were educated like their brothers so that, should they marry into a ruling family, they would know how to govern in the absence of their husband or in the event of his death during the heir's minority (under sixteen), which would necessitate a regency.[7] As contemporaries were wont to remark, children were merchandise, for the interest of the dynasty was paramount; this is reflected in this volume in the case of the tuppenny-coloured career of Prince Federico d'Aragona.

Often a key feature of a treaty or alliance was a projected marriage, sometimes dual, between families of the two major signatories. Today canon law in this connection tends to be unfamiliar and 'betrothal' misunderstood.[8] There were two stages to be differentiated in the process that achieved the actual marriage ceremony. The first was largely posturing, or diplomatic bluff. Betrothal, which was before witnesses and legally documented, was *per verba de futura*, made by the parent or parents on behalf of the couple, who might be babies. The second stage was the actual marriage before witnesses in a church and sanctified by a priest. This was *per verba de praesenti*, the couple individually declaring their willingness to marry. This consent was the essential feature, as until then any original contract could be broken. A woman who married into a ruling family was expected to be of like status to her husband – on these grounds Edward IV's marriage to Elizabeth Woodville was a matter of concern, and she was also a widow.[9] Shortly before marriage the woman would have been examined by doctors for any malformity, for evidence of virginity, and for evidence that she was likely to be able to bear children. These were basic considerations for succession, inheritance and feudal holdings. The actual consummation of the marriage was witnessed, and recorded by notarial documents, since impotence was grounds for release from the marriage contract, as was refusal to consummate. In the case of a woman marriage was usually not before the age of fourteen. It was most exceptional for a woman to refuse the eventual marriage, but it was within her power: after the betrothal, however, such a breach on her part brought disgrace upon her family and would result in the rest of her life being passed in a nunnery, as was the case with Cecilia Gonzaga (1426–1456).[10] It should be remembered that these considerations would have been common knowledge among the upper classes, who in the fifteenth century negotiated marriage accordingly.

The pope was overlord on the Italian peninsula of the papal states and the fief of the kingdom of Naples; beyond this latter he held Sicily in fief, and in the north an enclave of Avignon, surrounded by French lands, known as the Comté de Venaissin, adjoining Dauphiné and Provence. Hence, apart from the pope's authority in international affairs through his ecclesiastical powers, in his own right he had political ambitions and even power beyond the Italian peninsula. Dr Walsh probably excludes Avignon as being beyond Italy, but his volume makes an original contribution, providing in depth the divergent aims of the two popes with whom Charles negotiated, and explaining how their different temporal objectives interacted with the duke's quest for papal support in his manoeuvres directed at Louis XI. Original, likewise, is the discussion of the issue of the papal alum monopoly in the Burgundian state. Charles's looking to King Ferrante as an ally was also dominated by his desire to obtain support against Louis XI, since he was aware that Ferrante feared that the duke of Anjou's claim to the kingdom of Naples might be backed militarily by the French king. There was the complication that Ferrante countered by seeking Provence for Alfonso, duke of Calabria, his eldest son and heir; Charles believed that he was half-promised this territory and that it was essential for his kingdom.

The dukes of Milan and of Ferrara were long-standing allies of the king of France, ties which Charles sought to render inoperative. He also saw the opportunity to obtain for cash payments the service of those rulers of Italian states who were also in 1474 *condottieri* captains, notably the marquis of Mantua, the duke of Ferrara and the count (then duke) of Urbino; he negotiated the purchase of military equipment and horses, the former from Milan, the latter from Mantua. One of the results of the Peace of Lodi of 1454, whereby the five major powers on the Italian peninsula undertook not to expand through military aggression, was to channel the accomplishment of this objective into other means: principally marriage alliances, diplomacy, and the creation of what amounted to satellite localities. In this latter regard one thinks of Caterina Sforza's marriage to Girolamo Riario, the dowry being Imola and Forlì, effectively the eyes for the Sforza of Milan in the Romagna, where (in Cotignola) the Sforza had originated. The relatively peaceful conditions on the Italian peninsula during Charles's reign as duke meant that its *condottieri* tended to be under-employed, and so service even beyond the peninsula for financial survival was more acceptable.

States sought to negotiate in secret, planning to confuse the enemy as to their real objectives. An illustration throws a sidelight on bids for Italian troops by Charles which were followed up, probably unknowingly, by King Edward IV and which were part of the combined Anglo-Burgundian invasion of France planned for the summer of 1475.[11] The trail of clues is by way of Orders of Chivalry, a theme meriting attention regarding connections with the Italian peninsula. An alliance between Ferrante, king of Naples, and Charles the Bold was proclaimed in November 1471. In May 1473 the king was elected to Charles's Order of the Golden Fleece (founded 1432); the following September marked the reciprocal election of Charles to Ferrante's Order of the Ermine (founded by him in 1465); thereby the 1471 alliance was strengthened. Early in 1474 Charles, ever needful of troops, approached his ally Ferrante to this end. The response was an offer of a force of one thousand men-at-arms, the *quid pro quo* required being marriage between Ferrante's son, Prince Federico, and the duke's only daughter, Mary. Charles did not respond favourably, so in late October the prince was sent by his father with the insignia of the Ermine to promote the scheme by his own initiative – without success.

By October 1474 Edward IV had become involved, perhaps independently. Orders of Chivalry were, however, a mainstay of the negotiations: Ferrante had been elected to the Garter on 21 March 1462, and one may suspect that he reciprocated by electing Edward to the Ermine in 1465 or shortly afterwards (no substantial records of the knights remain). At the February 1474 election to the Garter Federico da Montefeltro was nominated but not elected. What is significant is that at the 18 August election he was elected by all sponsors, among them the most intimate of the royal circle; one supposes royal pressure had been exerted. An undated letter from Federico to the king, most likely written before the 18 August election, promised him his devotion. By the summer of 1474 Edward IV was actively seeking allies and supplies, as his brother-in-law Charles had been in the previous months, for the war planned for the following summer. Federico da Montefeltro was in the protection of King Ferrante and held his vicariates from the pope. One can believe that the king saw the advantages of the Garter for furthering a bid for Montefeltro troops in 1415. The English knight Bartelot de Rivière, who had taken the Garter insignia to Ferrante, probably in 1463, was sent at the end of August 1474 with those for Federico. With Rivière was John

Sant, abbot of Abingdon, who was to be the new royal proctor at the papal curia. Federico was invested in late September and Rivière conferred secretly with Ferrante; Sant had access to the pope. Presumably the objective was the acquisition of Montefeltro troops for 1475; Edward IV was no more successful in his scheme than Charles had been.

Edward IV was taken in by Italian chicanery. Save for the year 1473–74, from 1460 until his death in 1482 Federico da Montefeltro, count and then duke of Urbino, was general of the king of Naples and the Italian League, which included the pope, whose authority gave him priority claims. In mid-1473 Federico's contract expired and was not renewed; as a result, early in 1474 the republics of Florence and Venice legitimately made bids for his military service. Accordingly Edward IV, who was well informed on Italian matters, believed that he might be successful with a similar bid. In fact Federico's objectives in his approaches to Edward were essentially a means of strengthening his hand in negotiations with the king of Naples and the pope.

At the very time he was elected to the Garter, and as yet unbeknown in England, Federico's contract as general was renewed. On 20 August he was appointed Gonfaloniere of the Church and the following day invested a papal duke, receiving the golden rose. He had already been elected to the Order of the Ermine. Further, his negotiations with the pope concerning his daughter's betrothal to the pope's brother were advancing and divulged, as agreed, on 10 October. Federico had all he wanted and not only would he have been misguided to agree to military service with Edward IV, he would have been legally unable to do so without authority from the pope and the king of Naples, as doubtless the royal envoys discovered. There is some evidence that the king of Naples, out of self-interest, fostered Edward IV's hopes that there could be an attack on France launched from the Italian peninsula in support of that from England and Burgundy projected for the summer of 1475.

Dr Walsh's volume provides fascinating information relating to Edward IV's endeavours as they directly concerned Charles, further revealing how complicated issues were and the difficulty of conciliating Italian allies and their interests. Genoa had been under direct rule from the Sforza of Milan since 1464. In consequence, early in 1473 a number of Genoese nobles living as exiles at Charles's court urged him to lead an army into the Italian peninsula and restore Genoa to self-rule, which could only mean war on the duke of Milan. One such exile, Agostino Fregoso, probably by 1474 had military command of a modest force in the Burgundian army. That year he became involved in an internal plot in Genoa, sponsored by King Ferrante, for a rebellion to drive out the Sforza. The link with Ferrante was strengthened by Fregoso's betrothal to Federico da Montefeltro's beautiful (if illegitimate) daughter, Gentile. Dr Walsh clearly reveals that Ferrante's aim was to control Genoa, which he claimed had been promised to his father, Alfonso V, by the last Visconti duke of Milan; Genoa was to be the launching pad for his campaign against Provence, which he coveted; in this his ambitions clashed directly with those of Charles.

Obviously exiles from several Italian states were a factor in influencing Charles's thinking about the Italian peninsula. Just as important, if not more so since they were permanent, were the colonies of Italians resident in his domain, notably in the cities of the Low Countries, particularly Bruges. This topic warrants further investigation. These Italians, usually merchants forming confraternities determined by the locality of their origin, had close contacts with the Italian peninsula and the commercial centres of Western Christendom. In order to conduct profitable business they depended on knowledge of existing and likely future affairs. They were a source of wealth as merchants and bankers, quite apart from the luxury goods, such as Lucchese silk, which they sold. Something of the potential of this field of study is suggested by a recent study of members of the Gigli family of Lucca, some of whom were residents of Bruges, with a base in London.[12]

Finally, Italian art as a feature of Charles's 'magnificence' is covered by Dr Walsh's volume, yet it seems there is the potential for further interesting discoveries, perhaps on the evidence of Burgundian loot after Charles's defeat at Nancy. Frustratingly, though, the link with Italy, even when likely, may not convincingly be Charles the Bold.

In conclusion, to encourage future scholars in the field, it should be remarked that it is now easier to locate materials in Italian archives than it was in Dr Walsh's day: basic research tools are in the course of publication by the Ministero per i Beni Culturali e Ambienali, Rome. Exceptionally useful is the *Guida Generale degli Archivi di Stato italiani* (4 volumes to date, Rome, 1981–94, with a Cumulative Index promised). Likewise fundamental is *Le Fonti Archivistiche: Catalogo delle Guide e degli Inventari Editi (1861–1991)* (Rome, 1995). There are volumes of importance for the period of Charles the Bold: the series *Carteggio degli oratori mantovani alla corte sforzesca*, commencing in 1450 (I, 1999) is in progress, with volume VII for 1466–67 (Rome, 1999, edited by Maria Nadia Covini), and volume VIII for 1468–71 (Rome, 2000, same editor). Equally useful is the three-volume critical edition of Jacopo

Ammannati Piccolomini, *Lettere (1444–1479)* (Rome, 1997, edited by P. Cherubini).

Cecil H. Clough
1995, 2004

Notes

1. If there was an overlord, a state's loyalty and obedience to its ruler, the under-lord, could be seriously affected. In the case of the duke of Burgundy those towns of which the French king was overlord never forgot that they were ulti-mately dependent on the French crown, with consequences for ducal attempts at unification, taxation, and war against the overlord. See A. Leguai, 'The Relations between the Towns of Burgundy and the French Crown in the Fifteenth Century', in *The Crown and Local Communities in England and France in the Fifteenth Century*, ed. J.R. Highfield and R. Jeffs (Gloucester, 1981), 129–45; F. Cusin, 'Impero, Borgogna e politica italiana', *Nuova Rivista Storica*, 19 (1935), 137–72; 20 (1936), 34–57.
2. For what follows on the Este, see W.L. Gundersheimer, *Ferrara: The Style of a Renaissance Despotism* (Princeton, NJ, 1973).
3. A. Ryder, 'The Angevin Bid for Naples, 1380–1480', in *The French Descent into Renaissance Italy 1494–95: Antecedents and Effects*, ed. D. Abulafia (Aldershot, 1995), 55–69.
4. C. Cope, *Phoenix Frustrated: The Lost Kingdom of Burgundy* (London, 1986).
5. J.F. Kirk, *History of Charles the Bold, Duke of Burgundy*, 3 vols. (Philadelphia, 1863–68); R. Vaughan, *Charles the Bold, the Last Valois Duke of Burgundy* (London, 1973); E. Toutey, *Charles le Téméraire et la Ligue de Constance* (Paris, 1902); O. Cartellieri, *Am Hofe der Herzöge von Burgund: kulturhistorische Bilder* (Basel, 1926); J. Bartier, *Charles le Téméraire*, with *Documentation iconographique* by Anne Rouzet (Brussels, 1970), a *de luxe* edition of the previously published text (Brussels, 1944).
6. *JMH*, 3 (1977), 53–86.
7. C.H. Clough, 'Daughters and Wives of the Montefeltro: Outstanding Blue-stockings of the Quattrocento', *Renaissance Studies*, 10 (1996), 31–55.
8. A useful introduction to the issue is provided by L. Seidel, *Jan van Eyck's Arnolfini Portrait: Stories of an Icon* (Cambridge, 1993), Chapter 1, 19–74, and E. Hall, *The Arnolfini Betrothal: Medieval Marriage and the Enigma of Van Eyck's Double Portrait* (Berkeley, CA, 1994), Chapters 2 and 3, 13–94, and Appendix, 131–3.
9. Cf. G. Brucker, *Giovanni and Lusanna: Love and Marriage in Renaissance Florence* (Berkeley, CA, 1986), which concerns an otherwise valid marriage, nullified at Rome on the grounds that the woman, being of artisan class, was not of status sufficient to marry a husband of patrician class.
10. The case of Cecilia Gonzaga is described in all its aspects by F. Tarducci, *Cecilia Gonzaga e Oddantonio da Montefeltro: Narrazione e Documenti* (Mantua, 1897).
11. For what follows concerning Edward IV's objectives, as those of Federico da Montefeltro and King Ferrante, see C.H. Clough, 'Federico da Montefeltro and

the Kings of Naples: A Study in Fifteenth-Century Survival', *Renaissance Studies*, 6 (1992), in particular pp. 134, 138, 146. For the Order of the Ermine, see D'A.J.D. Boulton, *The Knights of the Crown: The Monarchical Orders of Knighthood in Later Medieval Europe, 1325–1520* (Woodbridge, 1987), 397–426, with known knights at pp. 414–15, and p. 416 for the probability of Edward IV having been elected. The second edition of this work (Woodbridge, 2000) adds nothing concerning this Order.

12. C.H. Clough, 'Three Gigli of Lucca in England in the Fifteenth and Early Sixteenth Centuries: Diversification in a Family of Mercery Merchants', in *'Tant d'Emprises' – So Many Undertakings: Essays in Honour of Anne F. Sutton, The Ricardian*, 13 (2003), ed. L. Visser-Fuchs, 121–47.

Introduction

When the 33-year-old Charles the Bold became duke of Burgundy in succession to his father Philip the Good on 15 June 1467, the territorial conglomerate he inherited was a major European power. The nucleus of Burgundy had been formed, through the dynastic union of the duchy and county of Burgundy with the county of Flanders, by his great-grandfather Philip the Bold (1363–1404), youngest son of King John II of France, as a result of an attempt by the French monarchy both to provide for its cadet branches and to extend by this means its own power. But as the decades passed the links between Burgundy and France became less close and often more strained. Philip the Bold and his son John the Fearless (1404–1419) laid the foundations for the dramatic expansion of Burgundian rule (into much of what are now the Benelux countries) which took place in the reign of Duke John's son Philip the Good (1419–1467). The centre of the Burgundian dukes' interests, power and wealth shifted decisively northwards.

This change was masked for a time by the courtly deference to the French monarchy shown by the ostensibly Francophile Philip the Good, but a new clarity emerged during the reign of his son Charles the Bold (1467–1477). If the Hundred Years War had provided an opportunity for Burgundy to take advantage of the weakness of her neighbour to expand, then the recovery of France after the effective end of that conflict presented her with an obvious potential threat. Charles did not feel bound by any of the ties of sentiment which had caused his father sometimes to overlook the danger from France. He aimed to convert *de facto* into *de jure* independence of France, to keep French power in check while seeking to increase the power of Burgundy. To this end he gathered allies wherever he could. Though he was indefatigable in trying to maintain the concessions of French territory gained by his father, power in France itself was not his priority, and the scope of his ambitions lay elsewhere, particularly in the lands of the Empire, where he negotiated to succeed Frederick III on the imperial throne.

This change of emphasis was reflected not only in his diplomacy but also in his very blood. He was half-Portuguese in parentage and, through his mother, Isabel of Portugal, descended from John of Gaunt. Though a native French speaker, he made an alliance with France's traditional enemy, England. He could, in fact, speak the language of his third wife Margaret of York, the sister of the first Yorkist king Edward IV, and he was conscious too of his Lancastrian ancestry and quietly nurtured his own not-so-tenuous claim to the English throne.

One area of Europe with which Charles the Bold maintained much closer relations than had any of his three predecessors was Italy or, rather, with the various states that then made up what we know today as Italy. His relations with the Italian states were not merely formal or decorative. They arose from his abiding suspicion of his feudal overlord, King Louis XI of France, and from his search for security against the growing power of a neighbour whom he never trusted. But the duke's relations with Italy were not confined to politics. The influx of Italians to the Burgundian court in his reign was unprecedented. The size of the Italian contingent in his entourage impressed contemporaries and has continued to fascinate historians. The Italians, moreover, did not constitute just another foreign group in what had always been a cosmopolitan environment, for they were looked on with special favour by the duke himself. He could speak to them in their own language and his outlook was influenced by them to an extent which, though historians find difficulty agreeing in their precise assessment of it, has led some to consider him a proto-Renaissance prince.

Aspects of his relations with Italy have been written about by many historians over the last century and a half, but none has considered them all together at any length. It was half a century ago that the late John Bartier drew attention to the need for such a study.[1] This book attempts to meet that need and to provide an overall study which not only places Charles the Bold's relations with Italy in both an Italian and a European context, but also explains and illuminates the presence of Italians at his court. In examining the course and character of the last Valois duke of Burgundy's relations with Italy, it addresses itself to the following questions: why, in comparison with his predecessors, was Charles the Bold so interested in Italy? What did he expect to obtain, and what *did* he obtain, from his relations with Italian rulers? Why were there so many Italians in his entourage? What did they do there and what sort of people were they? To what extent and in what ways was the duke himself influenced by them? The arrangement of chapters reflects this approach. The first two chapters are mainly concerned with the course of Charles the Bold's Italian relations. The last five deal in more detail with the Italians around him and with his behaviour towards them, while providing further illustration of his diplomatic policies regarding the peninsula.

In gathering material I have aimed (within, of course, the usual limits of time and opportunity) both to read as much as possible of the vast amount of pertinent published work and to extend archival research in this field. The archives of Milan and Venice have for many years been extensively searched by others, but in Milan, the well worked *Borgogna e Fiandra, Francia, Savoia e Piemonte* and *Venezia* series in the Archivio di Stato still proved fruitful, as did also the less used *Napoli* and *Roma* series. In Venice, in the Biblioteca Nazionale Marciana, I read through the dispatches of Zaccaria Barbaro, Venetian ambassador to Naples, which, to the best of my knowledge, had previously been used only by Karl Bittmann. In the Archivio di Stato, the Cardinal Podocataro collection provided some significant documents. The once comparatively neglected Archivio Gonzaga in the Archivio di Stato in Mantua provided much of interest; not only, naturally, for Rodolfo Gonzaga's visit to the Burgundian court but also for Charles the Bold's relations with Mantua in general, as well as with other Italian states. The Archivi di Stato in Modena and Florence also provided useful material, if to a lesser extent. Italian archives obviously constitute a major source for a work such as this. Indeed, the survival of so much Italian evidence is itself testimony to the closeness of the last Valois duke of Burgundy's relations with Italy and to the impact he made on the peninsula. But Italian sources also tell us much about other aspects of his reign, and this is a useful reminder that one should view his relations with Italy in the context of his diplomacy as a whole.

In addition to this Italian material, I have investigated carefully the great series of Burgundian accounts preserved in the Archives Départementales du Nord at Lille. These are an invaluable source for the presence of Italians at Charles the Bold's court and in his army and for payments to Burgundian ambassadors sent to Italy. Also useful are the Burgundian accounts preserved in the Archives Générales du Royaume in Brussels.

For the convenience of the reader I have, wherever possible, cited the published version of a document, especially with regard to Italian diplomatic dispatches.

I have been working on this study of Charles the Bold, on and off, for a period considerably longer than the ten years he reigned. It started out as a thesis and was subsequently revised and updated for publication at the invitation of a university press that subsequently decided not to go ahead. When, perforce, I left academic life in 1985, I feared it might never see the light of day, so it is with a great deal of satisfaction and relief that I place my research in the public domain at last. I am indebted to the Liverpool Historical Studies series, to its sponsor (the School of History, University of Liverpool), to Liverpool University Press for giving me this opportunity and, further, to the editor of the series, the late Professor Paul Hair, for guiding me through the processes of publication.

Much fine work in pertinent fields has been published in the years since I was professionally engaged in research. Professor Werner Paravicini, who explains the genesis of this book in his postscript and bibliographical supplement, has been kind enough to provide an invaluable bibliographical update. I still wish, however, to emphasise certain points, elaborated in the pages that follow. If we are to elucidate the processes and practices of diplomacy at this period, we need to study diplomatic correspondence and not just treatises. If we are to understand the diplomatic history of the times, we need to explore as wide a range of sources as possible. The dispatches of the Milanese ambassadors in Burgundy, France and Savoy have substantially influenced and improved historians' understanding of the period because they survive in such numbers and many have been published. However, several series of Milanese diplomatic correspondence have been comparatively neglected, especially Venice, Rome and Naples. Equally, much can be learnt from the Gonzaga archives, in the correspondence of the Mantuan ambassadors in Milan, Venice, Naples, Rome and elsewhere. And, of course, other sources almost certainly remain to be discovered. Finally, while Milan, for the reasons cited, looms large in the diplomatic history of the third quarter of the fifteenth century, the role of Naples should not be overlooked simply because so much less source material survives.

In the course of my research I have received much help from those who showed me the generosity characteristic of true scholarship. In particular, my indebtedness to Professor Werner Paravicini, Professore Alfredo Parente, Professor Elisabeth Swain and Dr Michael Mallett is acknowledged below, in Chapters 1, 5, 6 and 7 respectively. I should also mention, among others, Professor Ralph Giesey, who provided much information on Ernst Kantorowicz's research into Charles the Bold's relations with Italy; Dr Ronald Lightbown, who was kind enough to let me see a chapter of his book on Mantegna before publication; Dr John A. F. Thomson, who advised me on some points of ecclesiastical history; Dr Lorne Campbell, who generously provided information on a member of Rodolfo Gonzaga's entourage; Dr Sabine Eiche, who kindly assisted me with illustrations; and Mr Ian Moxon, who has helped me in a variety of ways over a long period of time. I am indebted to the staff of the libraries and archives where I have worked and/or from which I have been allowed to obtain reproductions of documents.

Over the years I have been fortunate in receiving help and encouragement from those who were not just colleagues but also friends. The late John Armstrong, my tutor at Oxford, first encouraged my interest in Burgundian history; his erudition has been an inspiration to me ever since. My supervisor at Hull, Professor Richard Vaughan, gave unsparingly of his time and knowledge. I owe a great debt to Professor Vincent Ilardi for allowing me to tap his incomparable expertise in Italian Renaissance diplomacy, not to mention his unrivalled collection of Quattrocento diplomatic documents on microfilm; his advocacy behind the scenes has been invaluable. Dr Cecil Clough has assisted me in innumerable ways, not least by the personal encouragement and kindness which are his hallmarks. It is thanks to him, ultimately, that this book came to be published. Finally, I could not have completed this project without my wife Gill, who not only supported me over many years in what might have seemed at times an obsession but also, in the crucial pre-publication stage, provided invaluable guidance in the realm of IT, so essential to present-day publishing.

Note

1. J. Bartier, in the bibliography (p. 453) to his chapter 'Karel de Stoute' in *Algemene geschiedenis der Nederlanden*, ed. J. A. van Houtte, J. F. Niedermeyer, J. Presser, J. Romein and H. van Werweke, 12 vols (Utrecht–Antwerp–Brussels–Ghent–Louvain, 1949–58), III: *De late Middeleeuwen 1305–1477* (1951), 272–98. In the same sentence Bartier called for a similar overall study of Charles the Bold's relations with Spain, but none has yet been written. The comments of the duke's best modern biographer, Richard Vaughan, are valuable and in many respects pioneering but also, of necessity, brief (R. Vaughan, *Charles the Bold, The Last Duke of Burgundy* (London, 1973), especially pp. 154–56, 214–16).

Addendum

The dispatches of Zaccaria Barbaro from Naples have now been published: *Dispacci di Zaccaria Barbaro (1 novembre 1471–7 settembre 1473)*, ed. G. Corazzol, in the series Corrispondenze diplomatiche veneziane da Napoli, Istituto Italiano per gli Studi Filosofici (Rome, 1994). The dispatches of the Mantuan ambassadors in Milan for the second half of the fifteenth century are in the process of being published by the Ministero per i Beni e le Attività Culturali, Ufficio Centrale per i Beni Archivistici, under the general editorship of F. Leverotti. Volumes I–III, which cover the period 1450–1461, have been published (Rome, 1999–2000), edited by I. Lazzarini, as have Volumes VII and VIII, which cover the period 1466–1471, edited by M.N. Covini (Rome, 1999–2000).

CHAPTER 1

Aims and Achievements of Charles the Bold's Relations with Italy

The basic outlines of Charles the Bold's diplomatic relations with Italy have been fairly clearly established by a succession of historians over the last hundred years and more,[1] and, though it would be foolish to give the impression that nothing further remains to be discovered, the intention in this chapter is to concentrate more on analysis than on narrative.

As will be argued later in this chapter, perhaps controversially, the duke's interest in territorial expansion in Italy was probably never more than fleeting. To anticipate the argument, therefore, it seems safe to say that for most of his reign Italy occupied basically a subordinate, if still important, position in his diplomatic schemes; in other words, his main reason for entering into close relations with the rulers of the peninsula was to help to further his plans elsewhere. This chapter, then, will try to show how his dealings with Italy fitted into the wider framework of his diplomatic activity; to explain why his relations with the peninsula's largest states were both far closer and more continuous than those maintained by his predecessors; and to assess the aims and achievements of these relations in terms of his success in obtaining the diplomatic and material assistance which he clearly hoped to extract from his Italian partners.

Such an analysis, moreover, will help to set the scene for some of the themes of the later chapters, which will investigate both the activities of the Italians at the Burgundian court and the extent of their many-sided influence on the duke himself. The presence of these men at court cannot be understood without reference to the events outlined in this chapter, because the unprecedentedly high number of Italians attached to the entourage and service of Charles the Bold is explicable largely in terms of the intimacy of his relations with the peninsula's rulers. This observation applies particularly to the diplomats accredited to the duke.

It applies also, if less directly, to the even more numerous group of exiles and expatriates. The Burgundian court had traditionally afforded a refuge to such men; but this attraction was immeasurably reinforced by the last Valois duke's deep interest in and involvement with Italian politics, a state of affairs which encouraged their hopes that they might be able to use his power for their own ends in their homeland. Finally, the largest group by far of Italians in the ducal service — the soldiers — was brought by Charles to Burgundy from the peninsula as a result of his admiration of their prowess. It is true that these contingents were obtained mainly as a result of direct Burgundian recruiting in the peninsula, but the duke's original hope that he would be able substantially to augment his army through the good offices of his Italian partners — though only partially fulfilled, as we shall see later — was, nonetheless, one of the basic motives behind his eagerness to secure Italian allies.[2]

Italy in Charles's diplomatic strategy: the quest for security against Louis XI

The recovery of France in the latter years of King Charles VII and under King Louis XI from the abasement suffered during the Hundred Years War posed a grave threat to those of her neighbours who had reason to fear the Most Christian Kings' growing power. In regard to England, for example, Charles VII used his influence to support Henry VI in the face of the Yorkists' challenge during the crisis years of 1460–1461, while Louis XI played a large part in the deposition of Edward IV and the re-adoption of Henry VI in 1470. In Aragon the 1460s and 1470s were marked by John II's bitter struggle against Louis XI to establish control over the key provinces of Catalonia, Cerdaña (Cerdanya/Cerdagne) and Roussillon. In Italy the Aragonese dynasty of Naples felt that its survival depended largely on the attitude of the king of France, who could decide whether to help or hinder the claims of the rival house of Anjou to the Neapolitan throne. In the same period, likewise, the dukes of Burgundy had cause to fear the growing self-assertiveness of France, since it seemed to be aimed at ending their quasi-independence or even at bringing about their total destruction.

The third quarter of the fifteenth century was marked also by the gradual interlocking, all over western Europe, of pre-existing but discrete sets of alliances. Indeed, it has been claimed that the origins of the state-system of early modern times can be found in this process.[3] These developments were aided considerably and to some extent caused by the increasing sophistication of diplomatic techniques and by the regularity and frequency of diplomatic intercourse which emerged at this time; the influence of these technical refinements owed much to the example and practice of Italy and to the place of Italy in the European state-system.

Yet this web of alliances was primarily the response to a deeply felt need, and the major dynamic force in western Europe was provided by many separate rulers' reactions, whether of hope or of dread, to the reinvigoration of the French monarchy. Moreover, the ill-concealed desire of Louis XI to dominate his neighbours and destroy his enemies drove all those who felt threatened to join forces in a spirit of mutual self-preservation. This deliberate taking of sides was apparent throughout western Europe: not only in France and Burgundy but also in Germany, Italy, England and the Iberian peninsula.

The significance of the hostility between Louis XI and Charles the Bold as the major feature of the last Valois duke's reign has been influentially and authoritatively challenged. Karl Bittmann has shown that the much cited passages of Commynes' *Mémoires* most crucial to this interpretation are unreliable; in fact, he has argued, the French king had many other enemies to worry about, which made confrontation with Charles only intermittent, so that on occasions he sought a lasting settlement of the differences between them. As for the duke of Burgundy, Richard Vaughan argued convincingly that the enmity between Charles and Louis, though very real, should be kept in perspective: the duke found himself more consistently in conflict with the towns of the Low Countries and of the Rhine valley than with Louis XI, while expansion in Germany and a desire to win the imperial crown took a far higher place among his priorities than did wielding influence, or gaining territories, in France.[4]

Nevertheless, the balance should not be tilted too far in this direction. Charles certainly did have specific territorial objectives in France which motivated his campaigns there from 1465 onwards, namely the possession (or repossession, following the loss of Saint-Quentin and Amiens in 1471) of the so-called Somme towns, for these, together with Roye, Montdidier and Péronne, gave him a strategic line of defence on the frontier with northern France.[5] Conversely, his attempts to extend his influence outside the kingdom of France, as in the case of the neighbouring lands of Savoy and Provence, could also bring him into conflict with Louis, because Louis too sought to extend his influence there. Again, the duke's quest for the imperial crown arose in part from his desire to establish Burgundian juridical independence of the French monarchy, while it was his ambition to secure at least *de facto* independence by strengthening Burgundy territorially through expansion in Lorraine, Alsace and Savoy that helped to provoke the fatal clash with the Swiss and their German allies. Moreover, on occasions (as, for example, in the winter campaign of 1470–1471), Louis XI talked not only of effectively imposing his suzerainty on those Burgundian territories feudally subject to the French crown, but also of totally defeating and dismembering the Burgundian state. It was against threats such as these, above all, that Charles the Bold sought alliances wherever he could find them. In fact, some of the alliances he made committed him to further confrontation with France, for he was not prepared to agree to the type of settlement which Louis repeatedly offered him that would have allowed the French king a free hand against the duke's other allies, such as Duke Francis II of Brittany in 1469–1470 or King John II of Aragon in 1473.

As far as Charles the Bold's relations with Italy are concerned, the theme of conflict with France is particularly striking. For a start, the longest series of dispatches sent by an Italian ambassador from the Burgundian court, those of the Milanese Giovanni (or Giovan) Pietro Panigarola, is studded with evidence of what has been termed the duke's 'almost paranoiac suspicion of the king of France'.[6] We find Charles repeatedly denouncing the king's congenital inability to resist the temptation to intrigue against all and sundry; in particular, the duke was convinced that, behind the hostile actions of his foes, he could invariably detect the guiding hand of Louis XI. Moreover, it was in Italy that the process of taking sides for and against France could best be seen in microcosm. Diplomatic interchange was more regular and frequent there than elsewhere; the creation of alliance-systems was more common and formalised; and above all, the alignment of states in relation to France took place with greater ease through the fact that such alignments could readily be superimposed on the pattern of relationships, whether of amity or animosity, already in existence among the Italian states.

When Charles the Bold became duke of Burgundy in June 1467, the Italian state-system was dominated by a triple alliance consisting of the duchy of Milan, the republic of Florence and the kingdom of Naples. The alliance was, in effect, a bulwark of French influence in the peninsula, for Milan and Florence were firmly committed by ties of both interest and affection to Louis XI, while King Ferrante of Naples had not yet allowed his latent suspicions of the French king to develop into outright hostility. Faced by this Francophile grouping, Charles the Bold's first task was to break it up or, at least, to encourage the formation of a bloc of Italian powers friendly to himself which would act as a counterpoise. By this means he endeavoured to raise Burgundy to the position of dominant influence in Italy, thereby supplanting that of France. His intention was to deprive Louis of any diplomatic, military or financial assistance which his Italian partners might give him. Ultimately, Charles hoped to derive such assistance from his own friends in the peninsula, and, as we shall see, it was largely against France that he wanted this help to be given.

Italy in Charles's diplomatic strategy: the rise and fall of Burgundian influence

There was little continuity between Charles the Bold's relations with Italy and those maintained by his predecessors. The interventions of Philip the Bold and John the Fearless, the first two Valois dukes, in the politics of the peninsula had been peripheral to their main concerns, while the interest in Italy of Charles the Bold's father, Philip the Good, was motivated primarily by his desire to further the cause of the crusade. In his latter years, Philip the Good was on amicable terms both with the rulers of the larger states of the peninsula, such as Milan, Venice and Naples, and with lesser princes like the marquises of Mantua and Ferrara; he did not, though, make general and binding alliances with them.[7]

But in the new situation of growing danger from France which faced Charles the Bold, there was little room for mere neutrality, however friendly. In fact, Burgundian policy towards Italy passed through a phase of marked discontinuity in the mid-1460s, as Charles let the good relations established by his father slip noticeably in the years between 1464, when he first began to assert himself politically, and 1467, when he acceded to the ducal throne. Relations with Venice cooled after the fiasco of the 1464 crusading scheme, for which the republic had held such high hopes of help from Philip the Good. During the War of the Public Weal in France in 1465 Charles sided with the Angevin party, which was hostile not only to Louis XI but also to his Italian allies, the duke of Milan and the king of Naples. Moreover, Duke Francesco Sforza of Milan at that time showed clearly, by sending military help to Louis XI, on which side the balance would fall if there were any conflict of loyalties between his French ally and his other friends, such as Burgundy. Certainly, the warmth that had characterised the relationship between

Philip the Good and Francesco Sforza was regarded by both their respective successors as being a desirable state of affairs and as one worth restoring,[8] but until 1475 circumstances rendered such a *rapprochement* impossible. When, however, Charles the Bold reasserted Burgundian influence in Italy, he did not, unlike his father, refrain from entering into written treaties of alliance, which specified commitments and obligations binding on both himself and his allies.

The strengthening of the Burgundian connnection with Italy in the early years of the duke's reign was the result of pressures which came from several directions, though none was totally divorced from his general strategy of buttressing his inheritance against potential enemies by diplomatic means.

The first set of pressures came from the duchy of Savoy. From the time of Philip the Bold, the Valois dukes of Burgundy had been on intimate terms, and had intermarried, with the house of Savoy. In addition, Savoy was one of the neighbours over whom Louis XI hoped to assert his control, so that Charles the Bold's alliances with Duke Amadeus IX and his influential brother Philip in the summer of 1467 added another link to the chain of alliances forged among those French princes who were determined to resist the French king. Moreover — especially in the first half of the fifteenth century — the dukes of Savoy had extended their rule for a considerable distance over the Alps into Piedmont, with the result that by 1467 the state of Savoy was almost half-Italian. The duchy had one major territorial claim in Italy, which was to regain the lands in northern Italy lost in earlier wars to Francesco Sforza and his Visconti predecessors. Charles was thus brought, through his close relations with Savoy, into a vicarious conflict with Milan, the keystone of French influence in the peninsula. Through Savoy he also came into contact with the republic of Venice, which had made an alliance with Savoy in 1467 that was aimed essentially against Milan. Venice, moreover, because of her old hostility towards the Sforza and because of long-standing ties with the Low Countries — particularly those of a commercial nature — was predisposed to align herself with the duke of Burgundy rather than with the king of France.

At the opposite end of the peninsula the king of Naples was another potential ally, even though he appeared in 1467 to be inclined more towards France. One of Francesco Sforza's conditions for his alliance with Louis XI in 1463 had been that the French king should not support John of Anjou, duke of Lorraine (and titular duke of Calabria), who was then trying, on behalf of his father René, to wrest the Neapolitan throne from King Ferrante. Louis accepted the condition, and Ferrante had for a time joined Milan and Florence in adopting a friendly posture towards France. From 1467 onwards, however, Louis XI's attempts to master Catalonia by using the Angevins as his agents there were seen by the king of Naples as constituting an act of overt hostility, for not only was the king of Aragon a close relative and ally (John II was the brother and successor in Aragon of Ferrante's father Alfonso the Magnanimous, king of Aragon, Naples and Sicily), but also the conquest of Catalonia, he felt, would merely serve as the prelude to, and provide the springboard for, a further Angevin attack on Naples. Consequently, Ferrante increasingly looked to friendship with Burgundy as a means of security. His treaty of alliance was signed on 15 February 1471.[9] Like that with Savoy, Charles the Bold's treaty with Naples added to the widespread series of anti-French alliances already in existence, for Ferrante was an ally of Edward IV of England and of John II of Aragon, both of whom were allied to each other as well as to Burgundy.

While these contacts progressively embroiled the duke in Italian affairs, they also brought home to him the urgent necessity to set his relationship with Milan on a satisfactory footing. Milan was the major pillar of French influence in the peninsula. As an ally the duchy of Milan had many advantages. It was geographically the most accessible of the Italian states to France and Burgundy; its armaments industry enjoyed a European reputation; and the Sforza dukes were renowned for their wealth and power. The dispatch of Milanese troops to France in 1465 earned Louis XI's undying gratitude towards Francesco; and, although its military influence on the outcome of the War of the Public Weal had been small, the Milanese expedition had profound psychological results, since the simple fact of an Italian intervention in transalpine affairs aroused great fear and hostility among the king's foes.[10] Moreover, Louis on several later occasions (1468, 1471, 1472 and 1474) was to ask again for military assistance from Milan.[11] Milan became even more closely attached to France in the spring of 1468 when Galeazzo Maria Sforza (who succeeded his father Francesco in 1466) married Bona of Savoy, Louis's niece.

By this time the duke of Burgundy regarded Galeazzo Maria as 'son adversaire'; for example, he protested strongly against the duke of Milan's attack on Piedmont, undertaken on the instructions of Louis XI in the autumn of 1468 as a diversionary measure against Burgundy.[12] On the other hand, because of the potential value of Milan as an ally and because he wanted to deprive Louis XI of his most powerful friend in Italy, Charles never gave up hope of reaching a compromise with

Galeazzo Maria; in 1470, for instance, he tried to persuade him to adhere to the league he was then negotiating with the king of Naples.[13] Such hopes were encouraged by the duke of Milan's wish to remain on good terms with all,[14] rather than to commit himself firmly — and hazardously — to one or other of the two conflicting rulers. Consequently, the duke of Burgundy's attitude towards Milan in ensuing years was somewhat ambivalent, and confrontation alternated with periods of friendly exchanges. It was not until January 1475, however, that Charles could entice Galeazzo Maria away from Louis XI, and in the meantime he concentrated on encircling Milan in Italy and on so paralysing Galeazzo Maria with fears of Burgundian intentions against him that he would render no assistance to the king of France. Eventually this persistent diplomatic pressure had its effect and the duke of Milan changed sides. In this sense, the treaty of Moncalieri, concluded on 30 January 1475, represented the culmination of Charles the Bold's Italian policy, although in practical terms the alliance did not represent quite the triumph that he would have wished, as we shall see in due course.

Charles the Bold's formation of a bloc of allies in Italy was curiously slow, for it was not until 1471 that his first Italian alliance, that with Naples, was negotiated, ratified and proclaimed. Perhaps this hesitation was due to the fact that in these years his interest focussed at least as much on the Empire (marital negotiations with Fredrick III and extensions of influence or territory in Liège, Frisia, Ferrette (Pfirt) and Alsace) as on France. His lingering hopes for a league with Galeazzo Maria may also have had a delaying effect, for an alliance with Milan — given the significance Charles attached to such a prospect — would have made treaties with other Italian powers less essential; indeed, the chances of an understanding with Milan could actually have been prejudiced by leagues with Italian rulers who were Galeazzo Maria's enemies.

During this period of uncertainty contacts were maintained between Burgundy and Naples. A Neapolitan ambassador attended the chapter meeting of the Order of the Golden Fleece held at Bruges in the spring of 1468, a Burgundian poursuivant was in Naples in the late summer of 1469, and at about the same time a Neapolitan envoy visited the Burgundian court.[15] But nothing definite resulted for the time being. Equally, Charles the Bold's proposals for an alliance with Venice, made through the Venetian ambassador Antonio Dandolo (who was at the Burgundian court in the early months of 1468 and again from the early summer of 1469 until the first half of 1470) did not meet with the republic's approval. The duke seems to have envisaged a grand league subsuming the existing alliances between himself and Savoy, and Savoy and the republic, perhaps with the informal adherence of Pope Paul II.[16] Yet these diplomatic moves, if mainly unfruitful, did at least have the effect of frightening the duke of Milan into a more conciliatory attitude.[17]

The mounting tension between Burgundy and France in 1469 and 1470 which followed Louis XI's rejection of the articles of Péronne agreed in October 1468 injected a greater measure of urgency into the duke's relations with Italy. Charles remained unable to persuade Galeazzo Maria to make an alliance, but, by encouraging the *entente* which blossomed between Naples and Venice during 1470,[18] thereby detaching King Ferrante from his recently renewed alliance with Milan and Florence, he struck a valuable blow against Louis XI. The duke's negotiations with Ferrante now began in earnest. In March 1470 his Milanese councillor Raimondo Marliani (or de Marliano) was in Rome to arrange a league ('*alcuna strecta intelligentia*') between the two rulers.[19] A few months later a Messer Antonello arrived at the Burgundian court from Naples, ostensibly to bring Charles some horses sent by Ferrante as a gift but probably also in order to further the discussions; certainly, Ferrante issued on 4 August a procuration for his ambassador at the Burgundian court, Francesco Bertini, to conclude and sign an alliance.[20] On 14 February 1471 a treaty was signed by the proctors of the two rulers (for Charles, Guillaume Hugonet and Guy de Brimeu, and for Ferrante, Francesco Bertini, then bishop of Andria but shortly to become bishop of Capaccio) at Arras, ratified by Charles at Abbeville on 15 August, and proclaimed at Saint-Omer and at Naples on 1 November, to be published elsewhere in the duke's lands later that month.[21]

The treaty was a general defensive alliance designed to last for sixty years.[22] Although declared to be motivated by the need to combat the advance of the Turks, it was aimed, as far as Charles was concerned, particularly against Louis XI and Galeazzo Maria. Against Louis it allowed him to lengthen the list of allies for the campaign which the following summer seemed bound to bring, although Louis professed indifference, saying that Ferrante was too far away to harm him.[23] Galeazzo Maria felt much more gravely threatened. He was aware that the king of Naples professed to regard him now as his '*capital inimico*'; indeed, as Charles later argued, when recommending Ferrante's election to the Order of the Golden Fleece in May 1473, the king of Naples was a useful friend because he could help keep Galeazzo Maria in check.[24] The fact that Naples was allied to both Burgundy and Venice and that the Venetians now maintained an ambassador at the Burgundian court (Bernardo

Bembo, who arrived in August 1471) served only to increase the duke of Milan's alarm. Moreover, even though he had achieved a reconciliation with Savoy through the treaty of Mirabello in July 1471, he had offended his foremost ally in doing so, for Louis XI viewed Savoy as belonging to his own sphere of influence, while at the same time that threat had in no way altered Savoy's alignment with Burgundy.

These pressures had the desired effect on the duke of Milan. Frightened of provoking Ferrante and of committing himself too far to Louis XI, he politely refused in the early months of 1472 to send help to the French troops fighting against the king of Aragon. At the same time he discreetly made some friendly overtures to the duke of Burgundy. These moves did not greatly allay Charles the Bold's hostility; nor did they fail to come to the attention, and provoke the anger, of Louis XI.[25] The duke of Burgundy was able to tighten the screw a little more by sending an agent to Rome in the spring of 1472 in order to spread rumours of an imminent Burgundian attack on Milan.[26] All this time he was fostering his relations with Mantua and Ferrara, which, though minor states, were strategically situated neighbours of Milan.[27]

The Neapolitan alliance had further repercussions. In August 1471 the Venetian ambassador Bernardo Bembo arrived at the Burgundian court at Abbeville.[28] It was not until 20 March 1472 that the Venetian senate decided to empower him to make an alliance with Burgundy, but this decision owed much to the urging and advice given by Ferrante, who wanted to see his two allies united by treaty themselves.[29] The negotiations were concluded in midsummer, and the treaty itself, which was scheduled to last for five years, was proclaimed by the Burgundian chancellor, Guillaume Hugonet, on his master's behalf in the camp at Roye on 20 June 1472.[30] Like the Neapolitan alliance, that with Venice was aimed primarily against France and Milan; its proclamation came only two weeks after the duke of Burgundy's declaration of war on Louis XI on 6 June, while, in Italy, Venice left little doubt that the alliance was directed against Galeazzo Maria.[31]

The duke of Burgundy completed the circle of his Italian alliances by reasserting his influence in Savoy. His encouragement towards the end of 1472 of the proposed marriage between Ferrante's daughter Beatrice and the young Duke Philibert of Savoy (who had succeeded his father Amadeus IX a few months earlier) was not only a means of drawing his allies into a closer unity, but also a blow against Galeazzo Maria, who had hoped to increase his own influence in Savoy by wedding a daughter to Philibert.[32]

The duke of Milan was now more exposed than ever and his reaction was similar to that of the previous year. Already before the conclusion of the Franco–Burgundian truce on 3 November 1472, he had made covert approaches to Charles the Bold through their common ally Yolande, mother of Duke Philibert and, following the death of her husband Duke Amadeus IX earlier that year, regent of Savoy. The duke of Burgundy treated these overtures favourably, since he was preparing to enlarge his army with Italian mercenaries and would have welcomed passage for them through Lombardy.[33] This was, in fact, almost exactly the situation which was to bring about the treaty of Moncalieri just over two years later, when Galeazzo Maria, threatened by the encircling allies of Burgundy, was to take advantage of the willing mediation of Yolande of Savoy, in a time of Franco–Burgundian truce, to make an alliance with Charles the Bold.

On this occasion, however, he was still too cautious to take the decisive step, for at the same time as he was making overtures to Burgundy he was negotiating with Louis XI for the renewal of the treaty which had originally bestowed Genoa and Savona on his father as fiefs of the French crown. That treaty was renewed at Lyon on 16 January 1473, at the cost to Galeazzo Maria of a 'loan' of 50,000 ducats.[34] Charles the Bold's inclusion of the duke of Milan as an ally when he renewed his truces with Louis just over three months later could have been the result either of misinformation or of cunning. In any case, the gambit rebounded on him. Sforza immediately repudiated the inclusion, of which, he said, he had had no prior knowledge and to which he had certainly not consented, and his protestations of innocence were eventually accepted by Louis XI.[35]

The duke of Burgundy's actions during the period of truce, however — especially his recruiting of Italian mercenaries and his apparent acceptance of invitations made by a number of Italian exiles to attack Milan — were designed in part to warn Galeazzo Maria against sending help to his French ally in preparation for the campaigns of the coming spring. He achieved his purpose. If one condition of the renewal in January 1473 of the Franco–Milanese alliance was that Galeazzo Maria should have no more dealings with Charles, another was that he should not be required to send any material assistance to Louis XI during the next three years.[36] This 'strania liga', as Ferrante described it,[37] could easily be interpreted as a declaration by Galeazzo Maria of neutrality henceforth in the struggle between France and Burgundy.

In the spring of 1473 the truce between Louis XI and Charles was renewed until July 1474. The two rulers' mutual fear and suspicion did not diminish, for it seemed likely that this respite would be used by each merely to strengthen his own diplomatic and military position in preparation for the beginning of the following year's campaigning season. The attitude which Milan would take therefore remained crucial. In January 1474 a French embassy arrived in Pavia to ask the duke of Milan to lend Louis the services of his two leading captains, Roberto Sanseverino and Donato del Conte, together with two hundred soldiers. Whilst not wishing to give Louis further cause for complaint, Galeazzo Maria was even more anxious to avoid becoming too deeply embroiled in the Franco–Burgundian conflict, and he was glad when the further renewal in June 1474 of the truce between Charles and Louis seemed to resolve his dilemma. Louis's eagerness to borrow Sanseverino did not diminish in succeeding months, but the duke of Milan found no shortage of plausible excuses which enabled him politely to refuse; one such was the state of Italy, a reference to the bloc of Burgundian allies in the peninsula whose existence severely curtailed his freedom of action.[38]

Galeazzo Maria's reticence was undoubtedly to a large extent the result of Charles the Bold's diplomatic offensive against him. The continuing rumours of a Burgundian attack on Milan encouraged Sforza to keep his troops at home. Charles aimed to achieve the same effect by continuing his negotiations with the Venetian captain-general Bartolomeo Colleoni — however futile these negotiations, begun in 1471, had now become in themselves; the Venetians told the duke of Milan the following year that they, together with the king of Naples, had allowed these contacts to proceed in order to frighten him.[39]

The duke of Burgundy's carrot and stick policy towards Milan was completed, as had happened during previous periods of truce with Louis XI, by friendly gestures designed to weaken Sforza's attachment to France.[40] This time, however, the exchanges did not end after the further renewal of the Franco–Burgundian truce. Galeazzo Maria propositioned Charles in the summer of 1474 through the Burgundian representatives in Venice and Rome and, in the meantime, he withdrew his naval support from the French army about to begin campaigning in Roussillon, an action which significantly hindered French attempts to recover Perpignan from the duke of Burgundy's ally, the king of Aragon.[41] For his part, Charles the Bold gradually became persuaded that the duke of Milan was now sincere, while, on the other side, Galeazzo Maria was sufficiently emboldened by his improving relations with Venice (which was becoming estranged from Naples) — culminating in an alliance at the beginning of November — to make a firm commitment to Burgundy. Negotiations were set in motion in the second half of November when Galeazzo Maria authorised Yolande of Savoy to mediate an alliance with Burgundy on his behalf;[42] after some delay caused by the late arrival of instructions for the Burgundian representative Guillaume de Rochefort and by the inevitable haggling over terms, a treaty was concluded at Moncalieri in Piedmont on 30 January 1475.[43]

On the Burgundian side, the treaty of Moncalieri was welcomed with great rejoicing; it was said openly that an alliance with Milan was fundamental because only through Milan could Burgundy obtain help from her other friends in Italy.[44] Louis XI, however, was gravely perturbed by the news, whose importance he fully recognised.[45] The Milanese alliance was a triumph for the duke of Burgundy not only for its own intrinsic value but also because it completed the series of compacts which established him as the dominant ultramontane influence in the peninsula. As far as Italy was concerned, Charles had turned the tables decisively on the French king. Three of the four major secular powers of the peninsula — Naples, Venice and now Milan — were committed to him by treaty. Even the fourth of these powers, the republic of Florence, which had so long been undeviatingly loyal to the French monarchy, was by 1475 prepared to offer Charles, through their common ally the Venetians, a stance of neutrality in the event of further Franco–Burgundian conflict.[46] The fifth of the major Italian powers, the papacy, could hardly become a declared ally, but in 1475 and 1476 the actions of Pope Sixtus IV or, at least, of his legates in France and Germany, tended to have favourable effects for the duke of Burgundy as far as his relations with the emperor and the king of France were concerned.[47]

If, through these arrangements, Charles had now achieved the main objective of his Italian policy — to prevent Louis XI obtaining military or diplomatic help against him from his friends in the peninsula — his fear of France nonetheless remained central to that policy, even after January 1475. In the summer of 1475 and again shortly after the battle of Grandson in March 1476, for example, he urged Galeazzo Maria to join with him in giving guarantees to René, duke of Anjou (and titular king of Naples), sufficient to embolden that ineffectual monarch to resist Louis's pressure to gain control of Provence (which Charles himself coveted). In April 1476 he requested the duke of Milan to use his influence in Rome to strengthen Sixtus IV's rumoured resolve to place Avignon under a Burgundian protectorate, a plan which the pope was said to have adopted as a means of keeping the city out of the hands of the king of France. Just before this, the fall of Vaudémont (occupied by Burgundian forces, along with the rest of Lorraine, in the second half of 1475) to the supporters of Duke René II of Lorraine, which Charles attributed to the malevolent influence of the French king, so enraged him that he expressed the intention of immediately declaring war on Louis XI — thus leaving the Swiss campaign to one side — and he asked his Milanese ally to lend him troops for this purpose.[48]

It is true that, from November 1472 until his death in January 1477, Charles the Bold's relations with Louis XI were governed by truces, apart from a brief period of warfare between June and September 1475; and further, that the main enemy against whom his troops actually fought in the last two and a half years of his reign were German and Swiss; this strategic alignment too — as well as the anti-French posture — being reflected in his Italian policy. Thus, in 1474 he asked Venice (unsuccessfully) to help him by attacking Duke Sigmund of Austria, his former ally who had recently been reconciled with the league of Constance (an alliance between the Swiss and certain Upper Rhine powers concluded in the spring of 1474), Burgundy's declared enemy.[49] Similarly it was the Swiss against whom Charles first invoked the treaty of Moncalieri, by asking the duke of Milan early in July 1475 to send to the defence of the Franche-Comté the four hundred lances specified in the treaty as the support which was to be sent by either party to the help of the other when requested to do so.[50]

Yet the priority Charles gave to defeating the Swiss in the last part of his reign should not blind us to the hostility towards Louis XI which continued to motivate his actions, for behind the enmity of all his foes he believed he could detect the malevolent guidance of the French king. Just over a week before the battle of Grandson in March 1476 he ascribed his determination to seek a decisive encounter with the Swiss, despite the manifest dangers, largely to his conviction that they, the Swiss — as successors in this respect of the Liégois, Emperor Frederick III and Duke René of Lorraine — were the last aggressors Louis could conjure up against him.[51] Defeat at Grandson in no way weakened this conviction, as he explained three weeks before the battle of Murten. Besides a burning desire to avenge his sorely wounded pride, he was motivated by the knowledge that defeating the Swiss would make him master of Savoy, thereby preventing it falling to Louis, as well as enabling him to regain Alsace and Ferrette, lost in 1474. But in order to achieve lasting security he intended, with the Swiss defeated, to chase Louis to Paris and force an advantageous settlement out of him. So great, therefore, were the benefits he envisaged as proceeding from a successful campaign against the Swiss that he would insist on doing battle with them even if the reward for making an honourable peace instead were the imperial crown itself.[52]

If these were the objectives which the treaty of Moncalieri was in part designed to facilitate, it did not, unfortunately, match his expectations. His hopes of extracting now from Galeazzo Maria the diplomatic and military aid which he had intended by his policies of the previous four years to deter the duke of Milan from sending to Louis XI were completely disappointed. His requests to Galeazzo Maria to meet his treaty obligations, whether against the Swiss or against the king of France, were simply evaded, despite the dispatch to Milan of several Burgundian envoys and even of letters from Charles himself.[53] The duke of Milan showed no willingness to commit himself firmly to the Burgundian cause at the risk of exposing himself to the hostility of Charles the Bold's enemies. Instead he maintained contacts with Louis XI, while his relations with the Swiss remained ambiguous.[54]

The effect on the outcome of Charles the Bold's campaigns of his Milanese ally's timidity is difficult to assess. He himself does not seem to have let himself be disheartened by it, although some of his close advisers, such as Guillaume de Rochefort, voiced their bitter disillusionment with Sforza.[55] Charles was not held back from his determination to seek out the Swiss, although he did confess himself unable, without Milanese backing, to turn his attention in the spring of 1476 from the Swiss to Louis XI.[56]

Waiting fruitlessly for Milanese assistance which never came was one of the reasons why he delayed so long in the camp at Lausanne before again setting out against the Swiss. To this extent the unreliability of Galeazzo Maria exerted a tangible negative effect on the duke of Burgundy's endeavours. Conversely, had Galeazzo Maria fulfilled his obligations as requested, then the outcome of the duke's plans might well have been more favourable. It was perhaps with deliberate pointedness that Charles remarked to the Milanese ambassador at the beginning of June 1476 that, if he defeated the Swiss, the victory would be all the more meritorious because it would have been gained by his own efforts alone ('*a Dio solo sarà obligato*').[57]

His gradual disillusionment with the practical benefits of the treaty of Moncalieri must have been increased by the fact that, in effect though not in intention, the Milanese alliance did not so much complement as replace those with Naples and Venice. The latter were still in force in

1475 but had by then lost much of their meaning. Charles felt that both the king of Naples and the Venetians had let him down after the initial honeymoon periods which followed the conclusion of his alliances with them. For this reason, which was strengthened by the unhappy effects of the Milanese alliance on his relations with Venice and particularly with Naples, the treaty of Moncalieri for Charles was, so to speak, a case of placing all his diplomatic eggs in one basket. With regard to Ferrante, the Burgundian cardinal, Philibert Hugonet, was letting it be clearly understood in Rome by the end of 1474 that his master felt deceived by, and dissatisfied with, him.[58] Charles did not even observe the courtesy of informing Ferrante of the conclusion of the alliance with Milan, although he informed the pope and the Florentines; he refused to show the Neapolitan ambassador at his court (Francesco Bertini, bishop of Capaccio) a copy of the treaty before the alliance was officially proclaimed in mid-April 1475; and even then the king of Naples complained that no reservations had been made in it for him.[59] A similar coolness had developed in relations with Venice. Charles soon found that the republic had little intention of diverting resources to help him fight the French king as long as the Turkish menace remained so pressing. He was particularly annoyed when, at the beginning of November 1474, the Venetians entered into an alliance with Milan and Florence, two powers still formally committed to France, for it seemed — though only briefly, as it proved — that they had defected to the side of his enemies. The fact that they had not given prior notification of their intentions added to his displeasure. He retaliated by neglecting to give them advance notification of his Milanese alliance.[60] The repercussions of this estrangement were still being felt two months later when one of Charles the Bold's leading advisers, Guy de Brimeu, lord of Humbercourt, told the Milanese ambassador that privately his master set little store by the Venetians.[61]

A final reason why the results of the treaty of Moncalieri were less felicitous than Charles had envisaged was that the treaty, while it completed the block of Burgundian allies in Italy, at the same time, paradoxically, helped to weaken it and hasten its dissolution. The Italian allies of Burgundy were united in little else but their common attachment to Charles the Bold. Savoy, for example, had for some years been on cool terms with Venice both as the price of her alliance with Milan and because she opposed the republic's ambitions in Cyprus, to which Savoy also laid claim. The Venetian alliance with Naples had foundered in 1473 on the rock of clashing interests in the Mediterranean as well as in Italy itself. Savoy's rapprochement with Naples in 1475 and 1476 did not endear either power to Galeazzo Maria. These instances could be multi-plied but we may note in particular the effects on Charles of the friction between Milan and Naples. Ferrante's fear of isolation following the con-clusion of the so-called Triple Alliance (Milan, Florence and Venice) and of the league of Moncalieri in the winter of 1474–1475 stimulated his willingness to attempt *détente* with Louis XI, while Galeazzo Maria used the excuse of Neapolitan hostility to Milan to refuse the duke of Burgundy's requests to send Milanese troops against the Swiss.[62]

By the beginning of 1476 these contradictory forces could no longer be ignored. Burgundy was still the predominant ultramontane influence in Italy but the appearance was more imposing than the reality. Venice, for example, sent no replacement throughout 1476 after her ambassa-dor Marcantonio Morosini left the Burgundian court at the end of 1475.[63] Again, by January 1476 the duke's bastard half-brother Anthony of Burgundy was proclaiming that the Neapolitan alliance was doomed, while Don Federico, Ferrante's second son who had arrived at court just five months earlier with hopes of marrying the duke's heiress Mary, was talking as if his departure was merely a matter of time.[64] It was becom-ing clear too that little reliance could be placed on the duke of Milan. Not only would he not fulfil his treaty obligations, but also there was ample evidence to suggest that he was simply awaiting a suitable oppor-tunity to break with Burgundy and return to his French alliance — pro-vided only that Louis XI would be merciful enough to accept the prodigal's return — so obsessed had he become by the fear that Charles was bent on the conquest of Milan.[65]

The only real comfort for the duke of Burgundy was his virtual annex-ation, in the first half of 1476, of the duchy of Savoy. He needed to control Savoy both to forestall Louis XI's designs there and in order to maintain communications with Italy, where he was still attempting to recruit troops. He did not disguise his determination not to allow the regent Yolande and, in particular, her eldest son, the young Duke Philibert, to escape from his clutches, even if it necessitated force, an eventuality which he considered in advance.[66]

If his defeat at the battle of Grandson in March 1476 weakened his influence in Italy, it was the defeat at Murten in June that shattered it. The immediate result of that battle was to place Savoy in the hands of forces friendly to Louis XI. Shortly afterwards, a *sauve-qui-peut* state of mind began to grip the Burgundian allies in the face of the French king's recovery of influence relative to that of Charles the Bold; such an attitude, incidentally, suggests that balance-of-power considerations were far from uppermost in their thoughts. Naples led the way. On his father's instructions, Don Federico had already left the duke of Burgundy less than 48 hours before the battle of Murten; he arrived at the French court in mid-July, and from this visit stemmed his marriage to Louis XI's niece Anne of Savoy (Duke Philibert's sister), which took place two years later. As for Galeazzo Maria, he continued after the battle to ply Charles with advice and promises of assistance, but his actions belied his words. In the first week of July he empowered Francesco Pietrasanta to go to Louis to negotiate the renewal of the old Franco–Milanese alliance; the renewal was completed by the end of August, and shortly before this, as a sign of the new alignment, Giovani Pietro Panigarola left the Burgundian court despite Charles the Bold's pleas to his master to let him stay.[67] Venice hastened to adapt herself to the new political realities and to follow her Milanese ally's example: an ambassador was dispatched to the French court in August, ostensibly to protest at French harassment of the republic's shipping but really to sweeten the king's attitude towards a power so long associated with the defeated duke of Burgundy.[68]

The minor powers friendly to the duke, who in any case were neither so compromised nor so conspicuous as their larger neighbours, took slightly longer to change course. Towards the end of 1478, Duke Ercole d'Este of Ferrara sent an ambassador to the French court, where he remained for over a year and a half, while in June 1480 Gilbert de Bourbon, count of Montpensier and dauphin of Auvergne, led an embassy to Mantua to ask successfully for the hand in marriage of Chiara, daughter of Marquis Federico.[69]

By the end of 1476 Charles the Bold's influence in Italy was as weak as it had been at his accession, if not weaker, for he was seen as a ruler whose star was waning. His rivalry with the king of France for dominance in the peninsula had now come full circle. For Italians it was almost as if, even before the battle of Nancy, he were already dead.[70] His death at Nancy on 5 January 1477 served only to clarify the situation, for, as Ferrante's secretary Antonio Cincinello remarked, apparently regretfully, when he heard the news, with Louis XI having now complete control of Savoy and thus also free passage into Italy, he would henceforth be as irresistible in the west as the Grand Turk was in the east; and another erstwhile Burgundian ally, the republic of Venice, expressed a similar fear that Italy was now menaced by two dragons from east and west — Sultan Mehmed II and King Louis XI — to whom the peninsula was doomed to fall prey unless its rulers united in the face of the common peril.[71]

The Burgundian hegemony in Italy was a short-lived phenomenon. Burgundian influence competed strongly with that of France from about the middle of 1472 and, with the treaty of Moncalieri in January 1475, it largely displaced French influence. It continued uneasily to hold sway in the peninsula until the battle of Murten but crumbled rapidly in the latter part of 1476, largely as a result of Charles the Bold's decline north of the Alps, until it disappeared with his death at Nancy. Nor were his successors, his daughter Mary and her husband Maximilian of Habsburg, in any position to attempt to restore it until a good many years had elapsed, so that, almost by default, Louis XI again found himself the apparent arbiter of Italy.

Yet the expected French dominance in the peninsula was not established so completely during the last years of Louis XI's reign as had been feared, or hoped, in the aftermath of the disappearance of the Burgundian leviathan. Political events both in Italy and beyond the Alps prevented this. In Italy the value to France of Milan and Florence as allies declined as a result of the internal dissension and external warfare that plagued those states following the assassination of Galeazzo Maria and the upheavals of the Pazzi conspiracy in December 1476 and April 1478 respectively. In any case, the power of the Sforza and of the Medici in Italy was increasingly challenged by the growing influence of King Ferrante of Naples, whose attitude towards France was inevitably more wary. On the other side of the Alps, Louis XI could spare little attention for Italian affairs while he was engaged in the several wars of conquest with Charles the Bold's successors which arose from his attempt to turn the sudden death of the last Valois duke to his own territorial advantage. French pressure on Italy was further eased for a few years after 1483 through the introspection forced on the French monarchy by the minority of Charles VIII, although ironically it was eventually Charles VIII's expedition to Naples in 1494 that was to change the course of Italian history.

The material value of the Italian alliances: provisions

Although there was an element of ostentation in the way Charles collected allies,[72] it is clear also that he proceeded on the assumption that they should be more use than ornament. This can easily be seen, first of all, in the timing of the alliances he made in Italy. The treaty with Naples in 1471 was negotiated during a period of open — and, for Charles, desperately threatening — war between France and Burgundy.[73] Negotiations for the Venetian alliance took place during a period of truce but the treaty was eventually concluded only a matter of days after the duke had declared war on the French king in June 1472. The treaty of Moncalieri with Milan was drawn up in January 1475, halfway through a one-year truce with France, in preparation for the joint Anglo–Burgundian attack on Louis XI which was planned for the summer of 1475. In addition, Charles the Bold's immediate concern with this alliance — at least in the short term, since he himself seemed irretrievably embroiled in the siege of Neuss — was to find a means of protecting his flanks and especially the Franche-Comté (which his expedition to the Rhine had forced him to leave somewhat exposed) from the attacks of his enemies and from those of the League of Constance in particular.

The provisions of the treaties reveal even more clearly than their timing the duke's expectations of benefits from them. The alliance with Naples stipulated that if one party were attacked, the other must help until the war was ended, either by peaceful compromise or by victory, and at his own expense. Each would be obliged to provide either men — Ferrante to provide Charles with 1,000 three-man Italian lances or 600 lances plus infantry equal to 400 lances, Charles to provide Ferrante with 500 three-man Gallic lances and 1,000 mounted archers or crossbowmen (the lance was a cavalry unit whose composition varied over time and from country to country) — or money, paying for each year of the war 120,000 gold ducats in two instalments. The choice of men or money lay with the party attacked — men were to be sent within five months of being requested, money within three — unless geographical reasons made it impossible to send men. Peace could not be made by either party without the agreement or inclusion of the other. Pending the customary reservation of each party's allies, the treaty was applicable to any aggressor without exception, although according to the Neapolitan ambassador in Venice a place was left for the republic to join the alliance if she wished.[74] The essence of the treaty between Charles and Venice was the clause agreed by their respective proctors, Guillaume Hugonet and Bernardo Bembo, at Arras on 4 June 1472: each party promised, if he was at peace and the other at war, to pay his ally 100,000 crowns (each of 24 *gros*) in four instalments.[75] As Ferrante remarked shortly afterwards, the Venetians had made a far narrower commitment to help the duke than he himself had given the previous year.[76] As for the treaty of Moncalieri, it stipulated that, if either party were attacked, the other was to send him either 400 lances, each consisting of six soldiers, or the sum of 60,000 gold ducats in the period of one year; the choice of soldiers or money lay with the party sending help.

All these treaties differed slightly in the degree of commitment accepted by the contracting parties. None of them initially made any reservations of rulers against whom they might not be invoked. Naples and Milan were bound to help Charles only when he was the aggrieved party, while the Venetians undertook to help whenever their ally was at war, whoever was the aggressor. The Venetians, on the other hand, were not bound to help if they themselves were already engaged in hostilities, a limitation which did not apply to Milan or Naples. Indeed, probably contrary to the duke's expectations, the republic tried to get, rather than give, help. Since Charles usually had a truce with Louis XI after June 1472, while his Venetian allies continued to be at war with the Turks, the republic persisted in the hope that the duke might help her against the infidel or even emulate his father Philip the Good and plan a crusade.[77] Or perhaps this merely underlines that, whatever the fine print of the treaties with his allies, Charles intended that he alone should be on the receiving end of any assistance due.

The attitude to be adopted by the non-aggrieved party to his ally's attacker also differed in the three treaties. According to the summary of the Neapolitan treaty given by Charles the Bold's minister Jean le Gros when it was proclaimed at Saint-Omer on 1 November 1471, Ferrante was expected not only to send help to Charles but also to declare war on any who attacked him;[78] since the aggressor envisaged was presumably Louis XI and since Ferrante for reasons of geography would have found it difficult to strike at France, he was probably meant to fulfil this obligation by attacking Louis XI's ally in Italy, Galeazzo Maria. As we have just seen, Venice was reportedly offered a place in the Burgundian–Neapolitan treaty but she preferred to negotiate her own terms, since she clearly disliked the possibility of incurring an obligation to attack Milan.[79] Finally, Galeazzo Maria was asked in 1475 to pledge himself only to lend no aid or comfort to his new ally's enemies.

As regards the level of material assistance to be given, the terms for Ferrante were the most onerous, perhaps because, as the weakest and least secure of the three Italian powers here considered, he was obliged to agree to such terms as Charles chose to offer. Jean le Gros's summary of his obligations even implied that he was both to supply men and money *and* to attack the aggressor, although the treaty itself neither mentioned a requirement to declare war nor stipulated the sending of both men and money. The duke of Milan was simply required to send material aid and, in his case, the choice between sending men or money lay with the party sending that help, not, as in the Neapolitan treaty, with the party requesting it. The Venetians limited themselves to a promise to give financial aid. They also made their alliance for a period of only five years, whereas the Neapolitan treaty was meant to last for sixty. By contrast, the treaty of Moncalieri bound not only Charles and Galeazzo Maria but also their children, heirs and successors in perpetuity; and yet it was the most short-lived of the three alliances.

The material value of the Italian alliances: fulfilment

Experience was to show Charles that the value of the elaborate provisions outlined above was greater in theory than in practice. Let us begin by considering financial aid. In the second half of 1473 he received from the king of Naples 20,000 ducats. This sum represented a small part of the proceeds from the sale in his lands of the stockpile of Neapolitan alum which had built up because of his commercial treaty with the pope (discussed more fully in the next chapter); that treaty, concluded in May 1468, had forbidden the sale in the Low Countries of any alum other than that from the papal mines at Tolfa, and its abrogation was a precondition for Charles to extract a subsidy from his Neapolitan ally.[80] The duke, however, showed very muted gratitude. In the first place, he came to feel that he had been duped in allowing himself to be persuaded to take an action offensive to Pope Sixtus for such a relatively small sum. Moreover, this was the first subsidy Ferrante had paid since their treaty had been concluded almost two years before. It is true that when the Burgundian embassy led by Philippe de Croy had arrived in Naples in February 1472, Ferrante had offered his ally 160,000 ducats on condition that he renewed the war against Louis XI; at that time, however, Charles had declined the offer because he felt a renewal of the truce was imminent. But when war broke out in the summer, he sent another embassy to ask for money, and Ferrante seemed willing to pay, as he wanted by this means to evade any obligation to make his own declaration of war on France (or Milan). In November the duke made a truce with Louis which lasted throughout the winter of 1472–1473; it was then prolonged into the summer of 1473, and Ferrante refused any subsidy now on the grounds that he was not obliged to pay one during a period of truce. The excuse may have been justified technically but, as Charles had used this respite to conquer the duchy of Guelders, he felt his ally was being unreasonable: could Ferrante not see, he protested, that the conquest of

[22]

Guelders was just as severe a blow to the power of the French king as if he had actually attacked him directly?

The situation repeated itself in the spring of 1474 when Charles sent his councillor Pierre (or Pieter) Bogaert to request Ferrante's assistance so that he could prepare for the hostilities with France which were expected to follow the expiry of the truce in the summer. This time he was reported to have asked for the huge sum of 120,000 ducats stipulated in the treaty.[81] The request went unanswered and Charles does not seem during the rest of his reign to have bothered asking Ferrante for money again.

He had little more success over money with his other allies. Those who had reason to fear the Burgundian alliance with Venice, notably the duke of Milan and the king of France, suspected that the republic was providing Charles with an annual subsidy.[82] But there is no evidence of this from the Burgundian side, and indeed, in view of what has been said above about the Venetians' attitude, it seems inherently improbable.

From Milan Charles preferred to request troops rather than money. There were several reasons for this. He admired the Milanese army and wanted some of its contingents among his own forces. He may also have felt that, because Milan was more accessible than Venice or Naples, it was just as easy for Galeazzo Maria — and more useful to himself — to send men. Finally, although Sforza, renowned as a splendid ruler, had on occasions given Louis XI the benefit of his riches, there were still limits to his generosity, and Charles may have been aware that one of the reasons adduced in Naples (by Ferrante's leading adviser Diomede Carafa) for Galeazzo Maria's defection from the French alliance in 1475 was his irritation at Louis's persistent requests for 'loans'.[83] In the event, the one financial appeal he made was after the battle of Murten had hastened the dissolution of the league of Moncalieri. His plea (expressed in a letter to his ally carried by the returning ambassador Panigarola) that the duke of Milan should help with money via the Medici bank, secretly and at a certain time,[84] was probably designed as much to test Galeazzo Maria's changed attitude towards him as to elicit the money itself.

The financial resources of the famous bank of the Medici family, or, at least, of its subsidiary in Bruges whose manager Tommaso Portinari was a ducal councillor, might be thought to have been an obvious quarter to which Charles would turn for aid. Portinari certainly helped provide the duke with the liquidity so necessary for prompt payments, for example, to his large army. But, as will be argued later (Chapter 3), Portinari was by no means as reckless as some historians have alleged.

Nor should his intimacy with Charles be interpreted as a sign that Florence herself sided with the duke rather than with the French crown, her traditional ultramontane ally, for the republic kept her distance and her relations with Charles were never really cordial.

Charles even managed to obtain a certain amount of income, at least until 1473, from Rome, through the alum agreement made with Pope Paul II in 1468, since this granted him a fee of 5.55 per cent of the price of all papal alum sold in his lands. Nor did he necessarily lose by the abrogation of the treaty in the summer of 1473, because he continued to levy this fee on the non-papal alum which only then did he allow to be imported and sold; moreover, the ending of the irksome papal monopoly enabled him to receive not only, as we have seen, a subsidy of 20,000 ducats from the king of Naples but also, from the States General meeting at Brussels in March 1473, a grant of 500,000 crowns per annum for six years.[85]

In addition to a source of finance, Charles also saw Italy as a storehouse of various kinds of military and naval equipment which he hoped either to beg or to buy. Two Venetian and two Florentine ships of no mean specification were among the vessels which he requisitioned to provide a fleet to combat the earl of Warwick in the summer of 1470.[86] The early draft of his treaty with Naples contained a clause dealing with naval assistance — if one party sent ships rather than money, then he should also provision them at the standard rate — but it was omitted from the final treaty.[87] At the beginning of 1473 he even went as far as appointing a Genoese exile, Giangaleazzo Fregoso, as his admiral.[88]

Military equipment, however, was his priority, and, as in so much else, he laid greatest store by Milan, whose arms industry enjoyed a European reputation. Like his father, Charles regularly bought armour from Genoese and Lombard dealers in the Low Countries.[89] The first time that he seems to have attempted to purchase military equipment in the duchy of Milan itself was in the early months of 1473, when a number of his recently recruited Italian captains were sent to the peninsula to enlist their allotted quota of troops. Giacomo Galeota went to see the duke of Milan at Pavia in February and was granted permission to buy a certain amount of suits of armour and horses. Galeazzo Maria explained that he felt he could thus show his goodwill towards the duke of Burgundy — without at the same time offending Louis XI — because a truce was then in force between the two ultramontane rulers. The following month, however, he became apprehensive about the implications of this concession and ordered Galeota to leave the duchy of Milan;

Galeota had apparently been hoping to purchase between 200 and 300 suits of armour, which Sforza found excessive.[90] A few months later Charles the Bold's Piedmontese captains, the brothers Antonio and Pietro dei Corradi di Lignana, complained to Yolande of Savoy that the duke of Milan had confiscated some military equipment which they had bought in his lands.[91] This incident led during the next 18 months to repeated requests by Charles for restitution, since, he said, the goods seized belonged to him, having been bought with his own, and not the captains', money; he implied that Galeazzo Maria's action was that of a declared enemy and could provoke reprisals. The duke of Milan justified himself on the grounds that, while he had every respect for the duke of Burgundy, the Corradi di Lignana brothers were old enemies who, in this manner, were being punished as such. The altercations and correspondence were temporarily ended only by the conclusion of the treaty of Moncalieri, something which this incident seemed at one stage likely to prevent.

But once that treaty had been concluded, Charles hoped mainly for Milanese troops rather than equipment. The heavy material losses suffered at the battle of Grandson made the problem of re-equipping his army more pressing and, at the end of March 1476, he sent his Italian secretary Anselmino da Prato to Milan (all the available military equipment in Geneva having already been bought up for this purpose) to buy 20,000 ducats' worth of munitions.[92] Anselmino met the duke of Milan two weeks later. He asked him to assign him an official who could show him the best and most honest manufacturers; to forbid them to work on other contracts until his mission was complete; and, in general, to do all in his power to expedite his mission. He did manage to purchase over 7,000 livres' worth of equipment but, as Galeazzo Maria pointed out to Panigarola at the beginning of May, the capacity of the Milanese arms industry was far less now when Italy was at peace than in former, more troubled days, so that Anselmino's requirements could not speedily be met, especially as the duke of Burgundy had not given advance warning. But Anselmino, who left Milan at the end of April and had arrived back in the Burgundian camp on 17 May, felt that the duke of Milan had deliberately frustrated him, and this allegation finds some support in Galeazzo Maria's confession to Panigarola that he had not let the Burgundian envoy buy up all the Italian munitions that were for sale (it was a different matter with those of French or German manufacture, which were regarded as inferior), since he had not wished to be left unprotected himself.

The second part of Anselmino's mission, to bring about the restoration of the goods seized from the Corradi di Lignana brothers three years before, was no more successful, although Galeazzo Maria prevaricated rather than refused outright. His decision in both cases was no doubt influenced by the fear that those weapons could be turned against him by his Burgundian ally, whom he increasingly suspected at this time of planning an attack on Milan.

Even if Charles had obtained from his allies sufficient quantities of money and military supplies, these would have been of little use without the troops they were designed to pay and equip. He certainly hoped his Italian allies would send him contingents from their own armies or, at least, allow him to recruit in their lands. It was here that he probably cherished the greatest hopes, and experienced the greatest disappointments, in his relations with Italy. Although his friends among the minor rulers, such as the marquis of Mantua and the duke of Ferrara, proved helpful, and Yolande of Savoy placed no hindrance in the way of those of her subjects who wished to enlist in the Burgundan army, Charles found Naples, Venice and Milan more recalcitrant.

From Naples he did not seriously request troops until the early months of 1474, in preparation for the expiry of his truce with France.[93] Ferrante's response was far from unconditional. In the autumn of 1474 he sent his son Don Federico to the Burgundian court accompanied by an entourage some 500 strong, the bulk of whom could be classed as fighting men. This glittering Neapolitan contingent undoubtedly played a not unimportant part in Charles the Bold's campaigns between September 1475 and June 1476, but its presence in the Burgundian camp lasted only so long as Ferrante continued to believe in the possibility of success attending his son's courtship of the Burgundian heiress Mary, so that Charles could not really dispose of these troops as freely as he would have wished.[94] His attempts to rouse Galeazzo Maria to observe the obligations of the treaty of Moncalieri occasioned, as has been mentioned, much diplomatic activity but bore little fruit. As for Venice, she had prudently omitted from her 1472 treaty with Charles any reference to sending him soldiers.

Nor were his partners particularly helpful with regard to allowing Burgundian recruiting in their domains or of their subjects. For example, in the early months of 1473 Ferrante, for the sake of his own peace of mind, instructed his ambassador at the Burgundian court to persuade the duke to dismiss those Neapolitan exiles whom Charles had recently enlisted; at the same time, in response to the requests of

Galeazzo Maria, he ordered one of his captains stationed in the Romagna, Don Carlo da Faenza, to cease his contacts with the Genoese malcontents who were then flocking to Burgundy.[95] During the period between about October 1472 and the middle of 1475 when the bulk of Burgundian recruiting in the peninsula was carried out, the Venetians too showed little desire to help their ally at the cost of impairing relations with their Italian neighbours. The senate refused to allow Cola di Monforte, count of Campobasso, and Giacomo Galeota to lodge their recruits in the Terraferma and it was only after much haggling that it granted this permission to Troilo da Rossano.[96] The Venetians, while not forbidding their subjects to enlist in the Burgundian army, did not exactly encourage them to do so. Their attitude was well illustrated by their actions concerning one Leonello del Nievo (or Mevo) of Vicenza, who had been banished to the Venetian lands beyond the River Piave for eight years for his many misdeeds. Leonello's request to be allowed to join the Burgundian army was granted by the Council of Ten, which made the concession that his period of service there could count towards his term of banishment.[97]

From Venice, however, Charles was eager to obtain the services of just one man in particular: the republic's captain-general, Bartolomeo Colleoni, who still enjoyed a great reputation even though he was some-what past his prime and now virtually semi-retired. Already at the end of 1471, even before the conclusion of an alliance between Burgundy and Venice, the duke's envoys (Guillaume de Rochefort and Antonio dei Corradi di Lignana) had arrived in Venice to ask for Colleoni's release. Contact was renewed the following year and at the beginning of 1473 Charles seemed at last to have succeeded in recruiting the great captain, for a contract was actually signed by both parties. Unfortunately, the Venetians vetoed all such dealings, and, despite the continuation of negotiations right up to his death in the summer of 1475, Colleoni was in fact never to leave home to fight for Charles. But these complicated manoeuvres did, at least, have a useful intimidatory effect on the duke of Milan.[98]

As far as recruiting was concerned, the duke of Burgundy probably received as much help from the comparatively minor states of Ferrara and Mantua as from Naples and Venice, for Ercole d'Este and Lodovico Gonzaga not only allowed their lands to be used as bases for the Italian captains recruiting in the peninsula on Charles the Bold's behalf, but they also permitted and even encouraged their subjects to enlist in the Burgundian army. Giacomo Galeota was at Reggio in the lands of the duke of Ferrara from the second week of April 1473 until at least the middle of the following month. While he was there he officially enrolled the troops gathered elsewhere by his colleagues, the count of Campobasso and Troilo da Rossano;[99] the latter had arrived in Ferrara, where he was well known, in the second half of March.[100] Meanwhile, while Galeota was staying at Reggio, he briefly visited Lodovico Gonzaga in Mantua certainly once and possibly twice.[101]

Subjects of these rulers were without doubt recruited during this time. At the beginning of March 1473 Burgundian ambassadors arrived in Modena and reportedly persuaded many of the town's citizens to enlist.[102] One of the most splendid of the recruits from the lands of the Este was Count Giberto da Correggio, son of Manfredo. By letters patent dated Ferrara 26 March 1473 and signed with the great seal, Duke Ercole gave his promise that Giberto would keep his contract with the count of Campobasso, which he had agreed with him in the person of the count's envoy, Barnabo dei Crotti; he remained three years in the Burgundian army, returning to Italy in April 1476, disillusioned above all by arrears of pay.[103] Three other subjects of Duke Ercole whom we know to have been among such recruits were an unnamed son of Count Uguccione Rangone, lord of Spilamberto, who probably enlisted about the same time as Giberto da Correggio; Simone Malaspina, an illegitimate nephew of the marquis of Fosdinovo, who was in Charles the Bold's army in 1473 but who had returned to the service of the Este by 1474; and a Marco da Ferrara, who was serving in the Burgundian army in Savoy in April 1476 when he was condemned to death by Charles for disobedience.[104]

Subjects of Lodovico Gonzaga, marquis of Mantua, were recruited, although it is difficult to estimate their numbers. But they did not lack their master's encouragement. For instance, Lodovico declared himself delighted to give one Giacomo da Mantua permission to join the company of Galeota in June 1473, for, he said, in serving Charles Giacomo was equally serving the marquis himself. Within two years this Giacomo seems either to have died on active service or perhaps to have returned home, judging by the fact that his son Biagio took over in May 1475 the two hundred lances previously commanded by his father.[105]

Good relations with Savoy too enabled Charles to augment his army. It is probable that his army included subjects of the Italian territories of that duchy from the beginning of his reign. In the accounts of the receiver-general for 1470, for instance, we find records of payments made to a Jehan de Piedmont;[106] Piedmontese troops may have accompanied Philip of Savoy to the Low Countries in 1468 when he took up residence at the Burgundian court; and certainly Giacomo dei Vischi of the counts of San Martino (usually referred to in Burgundian sources as 'le comte de Saint Martin') had long maintained friendly contacts with the Burgundian court before he was given a military command by Charles in 1471.[107]

More Piedmontese must have been recruited in the first half of 1473, for Yolande of Savoy placed no restrictions on Burgundian recruiting either in her lands or of her subjects. In May 1473 she claimed, in reply to Galeazzo Maria's protestations, to have allowed no more than a hundred of her subjects to be recruited, but several times this number were enlisted in Piedmont by just one of Charles the Bold's captains, Antonio dei Corradi di Lignana.[108] In subsequent years, moreover, she gave free passage through her lands to troops travelling north from Italy to the Burgundian army, much to the annoyance, and despite the repeated protests, of her neighbours in the Swiss cantons and in the towns of the Upper Rhine.[109] The hundred men-at-arms whom Guillaume de Rochefort was commissioned to recruit in the lands of Savoy in December 1474[110] could have included Piedmontese, as too could those enlisted during the first half of 1476 by Hugues de Chalon when, as we shall see shortly, he set up his recruiting headquarters at Turin. In 1476 many Savoyard troops fought in the Burgundian army against the Swiss and these also must have included some Italians; it is hard to estimate their numbers but ten days after the battle of Grandson Panigarola wrote that the Savoyard reinforcements expected to arrive shortly in the camp at Lausanne were said to total between four and six thousand men.[111]

It could not be expected that the duke of Milan would greatly assist the Burgundian recruiting of 1473 since he was still allied to the French king and, indeed, Louis XI wrote in January that year asking him to waylay the count of Campobasso or any other of Charles the Bold's Italian mercenaries who tried to pass through his lands.[112] Charles sought to counter this pressure by sending letters to Galeazzo Maria asking for safe-conducts for Campobasso and Galeota.[113] Charles's desire to facilitate his recruiting in Italy was probably one of the main reasons for his overtures to Galeazzo Maria during the period of truce with Louis XI. His requests placed the duke of Milan in a quandary, because, while he did not wish to offend the French king, the fact of the truce would have given him an excuse for obliging Charles should any friendly gesture towards Burgundy be misinterpreted by his ally.

Characteristically, he sought a compromise. He proclaimed a sentence of outlawry against any of his subjects who joined Charles to fight against Louis.[114] He seized munitions purchased in his lands by some of the duke of Burgundy's Italian captains.[115] He tried to prevent Milanese arms traders leaving the city to supply the Burgundian recruits, but had second thoughts when he realised there might be damaging economic effects (by giving away business to the Venetian city of Brescia), especially now that there was talk of a lasting Franco–Burgundian settlement.[116] He made no attempt to seize Campobasso, although he did refuse his request for a personal interview; on the other hand, he granted an audience to Galeota at Pavia in February 1473.[117] Finally, there is no doubt that he did allow passage — from Piedmont through Lombardy to the Veneto, where they were to assemble and be paid — to some of the Burgundian recruits; his justification was that he was really doing Charles no favour, since the recruits would have more difficulty reaching him from the lands of the Venetian republic than if they had stayed in Piedmont.[118]

By 1476 Charles the Bold's expectations must have been higher, for Galeazzo Maria was now his ally; moreover, since in 1471 and again in 1474, Sforza, while he was still allied to France, seems to have allowed troops to be recruited in Lombardy to fight for Louis in Catalonia and Roussillon,[119] Charles must have hoped that the same facilities would now be extended to him. Already by February 1476 a sufficient number of Milanese troops had left their posts to join the Burgundian army for Galeazzo Maria to feel compelled to ask his ally to refuse to accept them into his service unless they could produce written permission from the duke of Milan for their departure.[120] After the battle of Grandson Charles sought to reinforce his army, depleted more by desertions than by casualties, through fresh recruiting in Italy. On 17 April 1476 Hugues de Chalon, lord of Châteauguyon, arrived in Turin to start recruiting;[121] and within days he was assessing the merits of scores of often penniless Italian mercenaries who had flocked thither from all over northern Italy. Galeazzo Maria had already promised before Hugues' arrival to proclaim throughout his lands that all who wished might freely enlist, providing they had the necessary papers,[122] but as usual his actions belied his words. He vetoed the enlistment of several of the captains who had gone to Turin from Milan, partly to secure better conditions and partly to escape from Milan.[123] He could hardly be blamed for taking precautions but his attitude certainly delayed matters, and it was partly for this reason that Hugues' mission was overtaken by events: during the chaos which engulfed the duchy of Savoy in the aftermath of the battle of Murten all Burgundians became suspect and Hugues was for a time detained in Piedmont and his recruiting funds seized.[124]

Another disappointment was the strategic effects of the alliance. Charles must have hoped that with Milan on his side he could defeat the Swiss by means of a pincer movement, with Galeazzo Maria providing the thrust from the south. The duke of Milan, however, soon made it clear that he had no intention of declaring war on the Swiss. Moreover, when Charles asked him in the second half of March 1476 to send troops to the Burgundian camp in Savoy, Galeazzo Maria in effect refused by referring to the clause in the treaty of Moncalieri which obliged the party requesting military aid to ensure that the troops would have safe passage.[125] The problem was that, since the duke of Milan was, not unreasonably, suspected of harbouring designs on Piedmont, Yolande of Savoy was unwilling to allow Milanese troops though her lands. Partly in order to resolve this dilemma and partly to extend his own influence in Savoy, Charles decided to garrison the main passages across the Alps from Piedmont into Savoy — the Col d'Agnello, the Val d'Aosta, Castel Delfino and Susa among other key points — with his own men.[126] His prompt action, however, contradicted a promise he had made to his ally in an unguarded moment immediately after the battle of Grandson that he would allow Galeazzo Maria himself to garrison the passes,[127] a proposal which, naturally, had delighted the duke of Milan. Charles now sought to explain why he had gone back on his word by saying that, as soon as he had the passes under his own control — which was a necessary first step, since Yolande trusted him but not the duke of Milan — he would then place them in his ally's hand. In the weeks before the fateful battle of Murten the Milanese ambassador Panigarola relentlessly badgered Charles to carry out his pledge. Whatever his reasons, however, whether because he was reluctant to betray Yolande to Galeazzo Maria or because he intended to make himself master of Savoy, the duke of Burgundy proceeded no further in satisfying his ally before his second defeat at the hands of the Swiss in June, after which the matter became irrelevant.

We may conclude this discussion of the specific obligations laid on the duke's Italian allies by observing that they were by no means discharged to the letter — Charles would have been foolish, it is true, if he had ever expected they would be, although there is no evidence that he did allow his hopes completely to outstrip his sense of probability — and that the military and financial help which he received from Naples, Venice and

Milan was, though not negligible, arguably of less importance than the actual diplomatic influence obtained through the conclusion of the alliances themselves. In other words, while his diplomacy in Italy won him the upper hand over his enemies — notably the king of France — especially between the end of 1472 and the middle of 1476, the material assistance he was able to elicit from his partners in the peninsula did not decisively increase his ability to overpower his foes on the field of battle. In general, perhaps, he was too much, though understandably, inclined to mistake the eagerness of his Italian partners to seek, by means of alliance with Burgundy, some security for themselves against ultramontane threats — and, in the case of Venice especially, but also to some degree Naples, against the Turks — for a willingness on their part to support him in his personal ambitions to the extent of direct assistance and intervention.

Charles the Bold's territorial ambitions in Italy

Even during the supposed golden age between the Peace of Lodi in 1454 and the descent of King Charles VIII in 1494, Italy could never be totally isolated from transalpine Europe. Too many ultramontane princes harboured territorial designs in Italy for her rulers to be able to live without fear of invasion. Traditionally the major claimant in this context was the Empire, although by the second half of the fifteenth century it had lost the power to enforce its will in many areas of northern Italy to which it nonetheless never relinquished its pretensions. In particular, Frederick III could not forgive what he regarded as the usurpation of the imperial fief of Milan by Francesco Sforza in 1450. The house of Orléans also laid claim to Milan, regarding itself as the rightful heir — being descended through the female line — after the demise of the last Visconti duke without male heirs in 1447. To the south, the house of Anjou resorted to arms on several occasions during the fifteenth century in attempts to make good its claim to the throne of Naples. By the end of the century, the claims of the houses of Orléans and Anjou would be integrated with those of the French Crown itself. But already in the reign of Louis XI France had a potential foothold in northern Italy — Asti, owned by the duke of Orléans — while, in addition, she had obtained from the Sforza dukes of Milan the recognition of Genoa and Savona as French fiefs through the bestowal of them on Francesco Sforza in 1463 (although French suzerainty in Genoa did not have the strongest legal justification and was disputed by the emperor). Finally, the crown of Aragon was firmly in possession of Sicily by this time and, after 1458, retained residual claims also to the kingdom of Naples.

Yet the Valois dukes of Burgundy had no established place in this welter of territorial ambitions and disputed legal titles. This helps to explain the comparative lack of interest shown by Charles the Bold's predecessors in the affairs of the peninsula.[128] But Burgundian involvement became much more marked in the reign of the last Valois duke, and there are several reasons for investigating whether this involvement arose from the possibility that Charles, like so many other ultramontane princes of his day but unlike his Burgundian predecessors, hoped for or planned an expansion of his dominions into the peninsula. Throughout his reign he sought to enlarge his territorial patrimony both in the Empire (Guelders, Frisia, Liège, Alsace and Ferrette) and along the borders of France (the Somme towns, Lorraine, Savoy and Provence). Nor did his appetite end there. The fact that Edward IV was his ally, albeit a somewhat inconstant one, did not lessen his conviction that he himself had a better claim to the English throne. Yet at the same time as he was assessing the advantages of possessing England, he was dallying with the pleasant thought of deposing Louis XI and making himself king of France; and towards the end of his reign he even had some encouragement to envisage acquiring titles still further afield, those of emperor of Constantinople and/or Trebizond.[129]

Consequently, there is a *prima facie* case for supposing him to have been capable of harbouring ambitions in Italy also. This is true especially if, as some have suggested, he really did envisage re-establishing the old Middle Kingdom, or Lotharingia, stretching from the North Sea to below Rome.[130] In fact, his actions in regard to Italy — notably his Italian alliances and his Italian recruiting — together with his campaigns in Savoy towards the end of his reign, his known appetite for conquest, and his obvious imperial ambitions, provoked repeated rumours of a Burgundian descent on the peninsula. In the 1470s it was from the direction of Charles the Bold, more than from any other interested ultramontane ruler, that an invasion was expected.

There was no shortage of targets at which, had he so desired, he could have struck. Many places invited conquest though their insecurity. Genoa, for example, was restive under Milanese rule. The Sforza dynasty in Milan was itself threatened at times by the hostility of Naples and Venice and menaced by the dual claims of the emperor and the duke of Orléans. The Aragonese dynasty in Naples faced a similar predicament in respect of the house of Anjou. The Medici regime in Florence could not fail to be aware of the sympathy extended to its exiled opponents by hostile rulers in other parts of Italy.

Charles was well informed about this state of affairs, both from the accounts given by the diplomats sent to him by rival Italian powers and from the exiles and expatriates who flocked to his court in the hope of persuading him to take up the cudgels on their behalf. A particularly large influx of such malcontents and adventurers occurred in the winter of 1472–1473, at the time of — and, no doubt, partly as a result of — his major recruiting drive in the peninsula, which had provoked rumours of a Burgundian invasion.

At one date or another Milan and Genoa, Florence, Naples and Venice were all mentioned by observers as possible targets.[131] But overall the name of Charles the Bold was connected mainly with Milan. The king of Naples was an ally;[132] so was Venice, and the duke of Burgundy's relations with Florence were in general, whether in amity or hostility, of a rather tenuous and remote nature. There were several reasons why Milan should have been considered the prime target. The most obvious was that it was not only a rich duchy but also the Italian state geographically easiest to attack. This fact would have lost much of its force had Charles possessed no reason for hostility to Galeazzo Maria. During the bulk of his reign, however, as we have seen, the duke of Milan was regarded by Charles with great enmity because he was closely associated with Louis XI, and this enmity was fanned by the anti-Milanese exiles at his court, most of whom were of Genoese or Piedmontese origin, such as Giangaleazzo Fregoso and his cousin Agostino and the Corradi di Lignana brothers, Antonio, Pietro and Agostino.

Moreover, Galeazzo Maria's occasional diplomatic isolation provided the circumstances necessary to embolden the duke of Burgundy to act against Milan. The great weakness of the Sforza regime was its failure to obtain imperial recognition, so that in periods of good Burgundian relations with Frederick III Charles could have justified an attack on Milan as a fulfilment of imperial policy, while in periods of less cordial relations he could have used the conquest of Milan as a means of strengthening his claim to be considered a fit candidate for the imperial crown by showing himself to be capable of enforcing imperial rights. Imperial hostility tended to force Milan into reliance on France but that was no absolute guarantee of protection. Galeazzo Maria's attachment to Louis XI could easily have provided Charles with a *casus belli*, while at times of disillusionment with his ally Louis XI showed (or, at least, pretended to show) a disposition not to defend Milan in the event of a Burgundian attack. Finally, Charles might have hoped in such an event for the help or compliance of Galeazzo's Italian foes, Venice and Naples.

The force of these arguments was lessened only slightly by the existence of an alliance between Burgundy and Milan from January 1475 to August 1476. After all, the value of the duchy of Milan as a potential conquest remained, as did the presence at the Burgundian court of the anti-Milanese exiles and the continuation of the non-recognition of the Sforza dynasty by Frederick III.[133] The fact that the duke of Milan was an ally did not exclude him absolutely from the range of Charles the Bold's potential victims. Moreover, Charles's loyalty towards his Milanese ally was severely strained by Galeazzo Maria's behaviour in that period, so that he might eventually have come to feel himself released from any sense of obligation towards him.

The recurrence of rumours of a Burgundian expedition against Milan was one of the features of Charles the Bold's reign. This was noticed over a century ago by the great Jacob Burckhardt; indeed, his Swiss compatriot Emil Dürr, who made such an important contribution to the study of the duke's diplomacy, devoted to this theme a long and still unsurpassed essay in passages of which he suggested that the conquest of Milan was the long-intended culmination of efforts Charles made from his accession onwards to re-establish the old Middle Kingdom.[134] Another seminal historian of Valois Burgundy, Hermann Heimpel, also expressed the view, no doubt influenced in part by Dürr, that Charles, from 1474 onwards, devoted his energies towards creating a territorial block stretching from Frisia to Milan.[135] More recently, Richard Vaughan concluded that the duke, for example in 1469, seriously toyed with the idea of a military expedition to north Italy and the conquest of Milan.[136]

The value as historical evidence for the duke's intentions of the quantity and persistence of rumours of a Burgundian attack on Milan is not necessarily nullified by the fact that neither he nor his army ever got as far as actually crossing the Alps into Italy. Nevertheless, it would be foolish to deny that interpreting the evidence presents difficulties. The historian is naturally grateful for the survival of so much diplomatic correspondence from this period, but it should be recognised that the wealth of detail contained in ambassadorial dispatches consists as much of hearsay and speculation as of hard fact and direct observation. Much of the evidence for the duke's Italian schemes derives from the Milanese chancery and its provenance is reflected in its content. Galeazzo Maria was painfully aware that events beyond the Alps could have repercussions in Italy and that, for both diplomatic and geographical reasons, Milan would be the first to feel them.[137] But, in addition to this simple realism, Galeazzo Maria was led by his own deviousness (which he projected on to other rulers when interpreting their actions), timidity and almost paranoid insecurity, pessimistically to foresee all imaginable dangers even when none existed. He could feel threatened both when his ally Louis XI was in a situation of hostile confrontation with the duke of Burgundy and when these two rulers attempted reconciliation; the vicissitudes of imperial–Burgundian relations caused similar disquiet. His assiduous efforts, through the dispatch to all quarters of agents and spies, to obtain notice of possibly menacing developments sometimes resulted only in a flood of conflicting rumour which reduced him to a state of chronic indecision.[138]

Conversely, sources for the manner in which Charles the Bold's external relations were decided and shaped are, for a variety of reasons, extremely scanty.[139] No reports survive, for instance, of discussions at his council meetings. This is probably as much a reflection of his manner of government as the result of losses of source material, for, as the Mantuan prince Rodolfo Gonzaga noticed in 1469, the duke's affairs proceeded as secretly as could be and he confided in very few.[140] Consequently, the historian who wishes to penetrate to the heart of the duke's intentions regarding Italy has little to guide him beyond deductions from the movements of the duke's armies, the direction of his diplomatic activity and the scope of his supposed ambitions.

The closest we can get to his inner thoughts is the opinions of those around him. Many of them, though, particularly the exiles and expatriates with a grudge against the duke of Milan, had a personal interest in propagating reports of the imminence of a Burgundian descent on Italy, even when they amounted to little more than wishful thinking. Charles found it difficult to turn away such men, however disreputable, and he sometimes gave the impression of being favourable to their fanciful schemes.[141] But it is more likely that, while unmoved by their pretensions, he affected to lend them an ear because this had the effect of frightening those concerned, such as the duke of Milan, whom Charles, as argued earlier, wished to immobilise with apprehension in order to nullify the advantage to Louis XI of the French king's alliance, until 1475, with Galeazzo Maria.

Another source of information on the duke's Italian plans, though of equally uncertain reliability, was the circle of Louis XI: the king himself, his courtiers, the Italian ambassadors at his court and his agents abroad, especially in Italy itself. This source has to be treated with caution because 'the universal spider' was adept at propagating misinformation. In March 1476, for example, he boasted of how he had disseminated rumours of an impending Burgundian descent on Italy in order to spread confusion there and, above all, to arouse suspicion between Galeazzo Maria and Charles the Bold and thus to help undermine the treaty of Moncalieri which had been such a blow to his influence in the peninsula.[142] Louis had probably had a hand in spreading similar canards before 1475, designed in that case to frighten the duke of Milan into greater reliance on his French partner by raising the spectre of foreign conquest and deposition. The merit of such rumour-mongering lay in the very ambiguity of its implications, for the insecure Galeazzo Maria was sure to choose the most pessimistic interpretation.[143]

The difficulties attending this type of evidence can be easily illustrated. Early in 1472, for example, Charles told the Neapolitan ambassador at his court, doubtless in the knowledge that the report would eventually reach Galeazzo Maria, that Louis XI had offered to help him to attack Milan.[144] Considered in isolation, his words could be interpreted in several different ways: that Louis really had made this offer; that the king's offer was insincere and designed not so much to encourage Charles as to warn off Galeazzo Maria from his flirtation with Burgundy by showing him the danger of losing French support; or that Charles had invented, exaggerated or misinterpreted the king's overtures in order to divide Galeazzo Maria from his ally by sowing the seeds of doubt in his mind about Louis's reliability. And even if Louis's offer was genuine, there is no reason automatically to assume that Charles was tempted to act on it.

Perhaps the best method of finding a way through such a morass of rumour is to examine in turn each period when the duke was reported to be contemplating an attack on Milan.

Even before his accession, his name was linked with schemes aimed against Galeazzo Maria. In the spring of 1467 the king of Bohemia tried unsuccessfully to secure an alliance with Louis XI on the grounds of their common interests. His envoy alleged, among other things, that Charles and his father Philip the Good were in league with the emperor, the pope, the duke of Savoy and the Venetians to implement an imperial restoration in Milan. The assertion derived its credibility from the fact of Burgundian negotiations with the emperor for some sort of royal or even imperial crown as a reward for their assistance.[145]

Yet it was not through his imperial ambitions that Charles, now duke, first became seriously implicated in plans for a campaign in Lombardy.

In January 1469 Galeazzo Maria received reports from his agents in France that Philip of Savoy (brother of Duke Amadeus IX and recently elected member of the Order of the Golden Fleece) was boasting of having secured promises of Burgundian support for an attack on Milan. The support was to consist of between 4,000 and 8,000 archers and between 400 and 600 lances (the accounts differed over the exact figures) and the command of the expedition was to be shared jointly by Philip and by Anthony of Burgundy.[146] The reaction of the threatened Galeazzo Maria is interesting. Whilst he affected to be unconcerned by what he pretended to regard merely as Philip's braggadocio, nonetheless he hastened to seek assurances from Louis XI that the king of France would try to prevent such an attack or at least give armed assistance if it did take place. Louis readily gave these assurances, although he endeavoured to comfort his ally that Philip's high hopes had scant basis in reality.[147]

It is difficult to ascertain exactly how far Charles went in his promises of support to Philip. The evidence for this support comes ultimately from Philip himself or from sources close to him, and it was naturally in his interest to exaggerate the value of any promises received. We have no evidence of any specific discussions which the duke of Burgundy may have held with him on the subject, but the fact that actual numbers of soldiers to be lent emerged could be a significant pointer. On the other hand, Charles had cause to raise Philip's hopes without fulfilling them. As a focus for anti-French feeling in Savoy, Philip, whose hostility to Louis XI went back to at least 1462, was an important ally whom the duke was anxious to keep. At the Péronne interview in October 1468 Charles had not been able, or willing, to obtain satisfaction for the full extent of Philip's financial and political grievances against Louis, and the hint of help for an expedition against Milan may, therefore, have suggested itself to the duke as an easy way of satisfying Philip in the short term without incurring obligations of too specific a nature; at the same time, he was aware that he must not let himself be outbid by the French king, as Louis too was prepared to make all sorts of promises in order to restore his influence in Savoy by means of a *rapprochement* with Philip.[148]

This is not to say that the duke's encouragement of Philip was necessarily deceitful. In the winter of 1468–1469 Charles found himself being pushed into confrontation with Galeazzo Maria from a number of directions. Philip's requests for help against Milan arose not only from a youthful spirit of adventure but also from a grudge of some years' standing against the Sforza regime. He had deliberately placed himself at the head of the irredentists who wished to win back lands lost to Milan earlier in the century; he had already, for example, led such a campaign against Lombardy in 1467, when he claimed that Charles had promised him Burgundian support in the form of 800 cavalry and 500 infantry.[149] It was also about this time in the winter of 1468–1469 that the Venetian pope, Paul II, was striving to erect a series of alliances to facilitate the overthrow of the three main pillars of French influence in the peninsula: the Sforza in Milan, the Medici in Florence and the Aragonese in Naples. Charles was connected indirectly with this scheme, which was based in Italy largely on Savoy and Venice, because he was allied to Savoy, because he was then negotiating for an alliance with Venice, the ally of Savoy, and because the papal legate at his court, the Dalmatian Lucas de Tolentis, whom he greatly trusted, was widely regarded by Milanese sympathisers not only as the representative of the pope but also as an agent of the Venetians.[150] As for Charles himself, we saw earlier that by this time he had his own reasons for hostility towards Galeazzo Maria and, following the short-lived Franco–Burgundian settlement made at Péronne in October 1468, he may have felt that a favourable time had arrived to settle accounts with him.

All in all, though, it would seem that Charles was not prepared to take the final step of ordering a possibly risky attack on Milan, despite his own grievances and those of his allies, unless it fitted in with his own priorities. Probably he did seriously consider the project in the early weeks of 1469 but eventually he thought better of it. Indeed, the mere appearance of lending his support to the various anti-Milanese elements served the purpose of rendering Galeazzo Maria more conciliatory and, to that extent, undermining the Milanese alliance with France: the summer of 1469 saw the arrival at his court of an embassy from Galeazzo Maria which attempted, unsuccessfully as it happened, to patch up their differences.

Between 1470 and 1472 the Burgundian threat to Milan receded. In that time the temporary replacement of Burgundian by French influence in Savoy, the flight of Philip of Savoy to the French court and the improvement in relations between Savoy and Milan removed the set of circumstances which had rendered the 1469 invasion rumours plausible. Moreover, Charles the Bold's preoccupation with the threat from France in those years gave him little leisure to contemplate adventures beyond the Alps, while, at the same time, a rift was opening to his advantage between Galeazzo Maria and Louis XI.

One small cloud, however, did briefly emerge on the political horizon in this period. In the spring of 1472 the duke's Piedmontese councillor Antonio dei Corradi di Lignana, who had been sent to Rome on official business, talked openly of an imminent Burgundian descent on Italy; this story was also circulated in Venice by his brother Agostino, who was there as ambassador of Savoy; and it was duly relayed back to Galeazzo Maria. The essence of the story was that Charles had decided to marry his heiress Mary to Frederick III's son Maximilian, not only in order to strengthen himself against Louis XI but also to increase his influence in Italy. Fortified by this match, the emperor intended to raise his standard in Italy and proclaim both the old imperial rights and the liberties formerly enjoyed by the communes. Then, with Charles's blessing, he would march into Italy. He intended to recruit an army in advance which would assemble at Mirandola and he hoped for the support or acquiescence of Venice, the duke of Ferrara and the marquis of Mantua. He felt his task would be facilitated by the opposition to Galeazzo Maria existing in the Lombard towns subject to Milanese rule, notably Genoa, in his army and even in the ducal family circle itself. Moreover, he was sure Louis XI would place no obstacle in his path.[151] One of Galeazzo Maria's correspondents attributed the initiative for the scheme — which, he reassured him, was mere talk — to Charles, who, he wrote, was goading on the irresolute emperor because of his fervour for the imperial marriage.[152]

What are we to make of this curiously detailed report (which has lain hitherto unnoticed)? It is the only evidence we have that at this time Charles was again considering a Milanese campaign, and that fact alone might serve to cast some doubt on its authenticity. Moreover, on one point of chronology it is less than convincing, for the duke of Burgundy's *rapprochement* with the emperor, which was to lead in the following year to the dramatic interview at Trier, did not begin to bloom until the late summer of 1472.[153]

In this light the story put about by Antonio dei Corradi di Lignana might be dismissed as just another instance of wishful thinking by an Italian expatriate in the Burgundian service, were it not for the fact that Antonio was in Rome as duke's official representative. Perhaps he was indeed acting in some sense as the duke's mouthpiece. His master, after all, was on the verge of war with France in the spring of 1472 and he did not want Milanese help to be sent to Louis as had almost happened the previous year.[154] Certainly, if he had wished to alarm Galeazzo Maria into inaction, he could not have devised a scenario better calculated to frighten him, for Antonio's report played cruelly on the duke of Milan's known fears: his fear of the emperor, whose opposition to the Sforza now appeared to enjoy the support of Burgundy necessary for its enforcement; his fear of Venice, which had always shown such hostility to him and his father; his fear of betrayal by Louis XI, on whom his diplomatic isolation forced him to rely more than his political instinct told him was wise; fear of his Mantuan and Ferrarese neighbours, whom he had tried to treat as satellites; fear of his subjects, some of whom, especially in Genoa, resented the loss of former liberties enjoyed before subjection to Milanese rule; and lastly, fear even of his own family.[155] If the whole story was basically an elaborate bluff, then that interpretation receives some justification and corroboration from the fact that Charles employed a similar ruse to deceive Galeazzo Maria and Louis XI not long afterwards, as we shall see.

In the early months of 1473 reports of the duke's designs on Italy began to multiply, just as they had in 1469. On this occasion Milan was not the only, but certainly seemed the most likely, target for him. Several of his actions at this time caused observers to arrive at that conclusion. The main one, undoubtedly, was his recruiting of thousands of Italian soldiers in the north of the peninsula. Why, it was asked, did he need so many more troops and why was he assembling them in Piedmont and the Veneto unless he intended using them against Galeazzo Maria? Moreover, his recent alliance with Venice and his increasingly cordial relations with Savoy gave him the means to attack Milan from two directions. His negotiations with Venice for the services of her captain-general Bartolomeo Colleoni, who, though his best years were past, remained a bitter foe of the Sforza, added weight to the view that Milan was the target. Furthermore, his efforts to improve relations with Frederick III could be interpreted as an attempt to secure imperial approval for the end of the Sforza usurpation in Milan. A scheme such as this was certainly canvassed by several of the Italians in his entourage, many of whom joined him at this very time, some doubtless precisely because they hoped he would be sympathetic. Finally, Charles himself had been snubbed and deceived by Galeazzo Maria in the last months of 1472 after friendly exchanges, which he perhaps hoped would have led to an alliance but which were ended by Galeazzo Maria's renewal instead of the league with France; and this disappointment could have implanted thoughts of revenge in his mind.

On the other hand, these plausible extrapolations from the duke's behaviour to his supposed intentions — made by observers in Italy, Savoy, France and the Low Countries and preserved mostly in the Italian diplomatic correspondence of the period[156] — could equally be dismissed as little more than intelligent but inaccurate guesswork, since not all the duke's actions indicated an attack on Milan. The exiles' confident talk of a probable expedition was largely the result of wishful thinking, and the fact that Charles gave them a friendly reception did not mean he was under their influence. For example, his envoy to Venice, the Venetian Francesco Querini, told the Milanese ambassador at the court of Savoy that Charles had replied to the offers of Antonio and Agostino dei Corradi di Lignana to overthrow Sforza rule in Milan, Pavia and Genoa with the help of Colleoni, by saying that he was more concerned with France than with Italy and that, as for Italy, he preferred to have Galeazzo Maria as a friend rather than otherwise.[157] Similarly, the army he had recruited in the peninsula was clearly intended to be employed not there but against Louis XI, for it was ordered to assemble when complete in the duchy of Burgundy, as if in preparation for a campaign in France.[158]

Yet if the most striking clues for a Burgundian attack on Milan at this time were not the most reliable ones, there *is* evidence that the duke did at some stage contemplate military action in the peninsula and this evidence, at least, is more or less direct information about the way his mind was working during the period of truce with Louis XI that lasted through the winter of 1472–1473. At the end of March 1473 King Ferrante told the secretary of the Venetian ambassador in Naples that in recent months his Burgundian ally had urged him to make an agreement to make changes ('*novità*') in Italy; Charles intended to arrange his affairs with Louis so as to leave himself free to turn his attention to the peninsula. Ferrante did not divulge when this proposal had been made nor what his response had been, but it was presumably not encouraging, for much as Ferrante disliked the duke of Milan, he had a personal interest in preventing ultramontane interference in Italian affairs. Moreover, this attitude was shared by the duke of Burgundy's other Italian ally, Venice.[159]

Since Charles could not have hoped to proceed without the consent of Naples and Venice, the clear lack of it probably helped tip the balance against invasion. But the rumours continued, for the simple reason that the duke was putting out a diplomatic smokescreen with a skill which the artful Italian rulers of the day might themselves have envied.[160] During the winter truce of 1472–1473 he had hoped to finalise his long-cherished plans for a joint Anglo–Burgundian campaign against Louis XI to be set in motion when the truce expired at the end of March. But when Edward IV made it clear that he could not cross the Channel that year, Charles contented himself with prolonging the truce for a further twelve months. He now had to find a way of putting the coming campaigning season to good use. Two possible targets seemed open to him: Guelders or Milan. In fact, his efforts in the months following his decision not to attack France were directed almost exclusively towards preparing militarily and diplomatically for the conquest of Guelders, which promised the lesser risk and the greater benefit. Some informed observers still held the view that he would choose Milan, and Louis himself seemed prepared to encourage Burgundian embroilment in Italy. Charles probably deliberately fostered this misconception in order to obtain the advantage of surprise; and when he marched into Guelders in June 1473 he left the French king completely fooled ('*ingannato*').[161]

Despite the alarms caused, firstly, by the meeting between Charles and the emperor at Trier in October and November 1473, a meeting which Galeazzo Maria did his best to undermine and whose failure he greeted with relief;[162] and, secondly, by the arrival of Charles at Dijon from the Low Countries in January 1474 with an armed escort whose size was sufficient to frighten more than just the duke of Milan,[163] there is little evidence to justify Dürr's assertion that by now the duke of Burgundy's designs on Milan could no longer be doubted.[164]

The conclusion of an alliance between the two rulers, at Moncalieri on 30 January 1475, should have put an end once and for all to Galeazzo Maria's fear of Burgundian attack, and, for a time at least, he was able to enjoy an unwonted feeling of security. But, even before the end of the year, his old suspicions had returned. Indeed, they continued to grow to a new level of intensity up until the battle of Murten in June 1476, which was to put a speedy end to what Dürr termed Charles the Bold's apparently inexorable push across the Alps towards the south.[165] Far from reassuring Galeazzo Maria, the fact of his Burgundian alliance came to seem to him to be little more than a cruel deception which masked the duke's true intentions towards him. Moreover, on this occasion and unlike earlier occasions, other Italian powers, such as Naples, Florence, Venice and Rome, shared his fears and began to see in the duke of Burgundy a threat to the peace and prosperity of the peninsula as a whole.

The fervour of the early months of the alliance was doomed, in the nature of things, not to last and it gradually evaporated amidst misunderstandings and an awareness of some conflict of interests. But what made Galeazzo Maria regard Charles as a direct threat, rather than merely as an ally with whom he did not see entirely eye to eye, was Charles's determination to seek out and defeat the Swiss and the consequent marshalling of the bulk of the Burgundian army in Savoy, whence the western Alpine passes led straight into Lombardy. Galeazzo Maria could not envisage any worthwhile advantage accruing to Charles from defeating the Swiss; all he could foresee was the danger to his ally's person, state and allies in the event of a Burgundian defeat. Why, therefore, he argued, did Charles press on so resolutely and ignore his ally's repeated warnings, even after his first defeat at Grandson in March 1476, unless it was because he secretly regarded the success of the Swiss campaign as a necessary prelude to a descent on Italy? Moreover, his fears were increased by his conviction that, in his second encounter with the Swiss, Charles would emerge victorious.[166]

Once this interpretation had recommended itself to him, he began to find no shortage of corroborating evidence. The duke of Burgundy's truce with Frederick III after the siege of Neuss, the negotiations which followed and eventually led to an alliance proclaimed in April 1476, and the fact that he himself was not specifically reserved by Charles as an ally in any of these agreements led Galeazzo Maria to fear he was about to be sacrificed — as had been rumoured earlier, in 1467 and 1472 — on the altar of his ally's imperial ambitions. Similarly, the proposals for a reconciliation made to Charles by Louis XI both before and after the battle of Grandson were construed by the duke of Milan as leading the way to a settlement which would leave Charles free to satisfy his ambitions in Italy at the expense of Louis XI's former ally, towards whom the French king still felt bitter as a result of the defection represented by the treaty of Moncalieri. Other Burgundian actions in the first half of 1476 seemed to be part and parcel of this developing threat: Charles the Bold's attempts to gain access to the Mediterranean through the acquisition of Provence; his garrisoning of the passes leading from Savoy into Piedmont and Lombardy with his own troops; his efforts to assemble a force of Italian soldiers at Turin under the supervision of Hugues de Chalon; and his continued harbouring of Sforzaphobes in his household and army.

Yet if we examine the evidence impartially, which Galeazzo Maria was never in a position to do, it certainly does not lead inexorably to the conclusion that the duke of Milan's premise, an impending Burgundian attack, was correct; and, if so, that deprives the argument also of the force of much of the corroborating detail outlined above. Charles always claimed — and the sheer repetition of his views must carry some weight, unless one believes, with Galeazzo Maria, that he was capable of unremitting deception — that he had undertaken the Swiss war for defensive reasons, not as the prelude to new schemes of conquest beyond the Alps. He wanted to destroy at source the Swiss threat to the security of the Franche-Comté, which had been repeatedly ravaged by the Swiss and their allies since 1474, and to maintain his political credit by defending his ally, Savoy, against them. Nor, judging by his declared intentions, would his energies in the event of a victory over the Swiss have been directed thereafter towards major new acquisitions of territory; rather he envisaged, once the Swiss hydra had been tamed, being free to re-establish his authority in Lorraine and Alsace, and also to settle old scores with Louis XI.[167]

Had he not been defeated at Murten, it seems on balance more likely that he would have continued the policies of previous years — designed to hold and increase Burgundian territory in the Empire, to bring about his elevation to the imperial throne and to strike a lasting blow at the power of the French crown — than that he would have embarked on the hazardous path of Italian adventure. His declared intentions in the first half of 1476 certainly lead to this conclusion. As for his actions, they can be convincingly portrayed as having been intended to lead up to an expedition across the Alps as the climax of long-held ambitions only if it can be shown at the same time that those ambitions were the continuation of earlier projects regarding Italy and, especially, Milan. But while the earlier invasion scares of 1469, 1472, 1472–1473 and 1473–1474 were caused by the fact that Charles did undeniably display a fleeting interest in the Italian scheme, this interest was nonetheless an aberration from his more consistent concern with France and the Empire; indeed, it was often more apparent than real and sometimes deliberately feigned in order to disguise his plans elsewhere. It is, of course, quite possible that, had the duke once attained his ends in France and the Empire, he would *then* have turned again to Italy to seek the culmination of his life's work. That type of consideration, however, takes us into an area of pure speculation. If we limit our inquiry to the period under review, we find that the notion that he persistently regarded territorial expansion in Italy as a necessary adjunct of his known ambitions, and consequently gave it a high priority, has yet to be demonstrated. It would be asking a good deal actually to disprove that notion, because it is always hard to prove a negative. But it does seem more reasonable to accept that, as an area for possible territorial expansion, Italy for Charles was neither that important nor that tempting, and this view is in no way novel, for, as John Foster Kirk wrote over a century ago when describing the duke's advance into Savoy early in 1476, 'he as little dreamed at present as he had ever done of scaling the Alps in pursuit of a fantastic glory . . . he was in quest, not of adventure, but of security'.[168]

* * *

Since at least the time of the publication of Philippe de Commynes' memoirs, the degree to which hostility to Louis XI was a determining influence on the foreign policy of Charles the Bold has been a matter of dispute by historians. Richard Vaughan and Karl Bittmann, two major figures in post-war Burgundian historiography, have, in their studies of respectively Charles the Bold and Commynes, strongly and authoritatively challenged the polarisation viewpoint. The analysis offered in this chapter is to some extent revisionist in arguing that, at least in his relations with Italy, Charles was motivated primarily by a concern with Louis XI. His first priority in his relations with Italy was to counter the French influence which he found predominating there at his accession. In this he succeeded, and the treaty of Moncalieri in January 1475 represented the zenith of Burgundian influence in the peninsula. But this achievement was already in doubt by the end of that year and by the end of 1476 it had disappeared almost completely. His second priority was again the result of his hostility to Louis XI, namely to obtain military, material and financial support from his Italian allies for campaigns fought north of the Alps. His success in this respect was small compared with the extent of his hopes, but neither was it minimal, an illustration of the maxim that a man's reach is often greater than his grasp. Finally, it might be said that the aims and perhaps also the conduct of the duke's Italian policy were coherent and rational, in complete contrast to the epithet of 'the Rash'. This applies particularly to his attitude towards territorial expansion in the peninsula. Italy provided many a tempting target for conquest, notably Milan, and there were those who strongly encouraged him to try his luck there. But, while he certainly did on occasion seriously contemplate taking their advice, yet he stepped back each time in order to concentrate on more easily attainable and more immediately beneficial goals closer to home. Charles the Bold, all agree, was motivated to a marked degree by a desire for conquest and glory; but, at least as far as Italy was concerned, he tempered this desire with a measured assessment of his actual resources and real needs.

Notes

1. There has been no previous monograph on Charles and Italy but of particular importance are E. Dürr, 'Galeazzo Maria Sforza und seine Stellung zu den Burgunderkriegen. Eine Untersuchung über die südfranzösisch-italienische Politik Karls des Kühnen', *BZGA*, 10 (1911), 259–415; and, more recently, the *Excursus* by R. Fubini in Lorenzo de' Medici, *Lettere*, ed. R. Fubini, N. Rubinstein and M. Mallett, 8 vols so far published (Florence, 1977–2001), II

(1977), 491–535; T. Zambarbieri, 'Milano e la Borgogna tra 1474 e il 1477: le loro relazioni diplomatiche nel contesto dell'Europa mediana', *Libri e documenti*, 8/1 (1982), 33–69, and 8/2 (1982), 1–36; and R. Fubini, 'I rapporti diplomatici tra Milano e Borgogna con particolare riguardo all'alleanza del 1475–1476', *PCEEB*, 28 (1988), 95–114. For the reign as a whole R. Vaughan, *Charles the Bold* (London, 1973) is still the standard work. Much of the diplomatic correspondence from the *Borgogna e Fiandra* series in ASM 515–521 (covering the period of Charles the Bold's reign) has latterly been published as *Carteggi diplomatici fra Milano sforzesca e la Borgogna*, Fonti per la storia d'Italia pubblicate dall'Istituto storico italiano per l'età moderna e contemporanea, ed. E. Sestan, 2 vols (Rome, 1985–7). I worked with the original documents because at that time they had not been published but, for the convenience of the reader, I have cited them according to the document number in Sestan's edition (hereafter referred to as *Carteggi*). However, an older work, the collection *Dépêches des ambassadeurs milanais sur les campagnes de Charles-le-Hardi, duc de Bourgogne, de 1474 à 1477*, ed. F. de Gingins La Sarra, 2 vols (Paris–Geneva, 1858), remains useful because it publishes dispatches from series other than *Borgogna e Fiandra*, e.g. *Savoia*.

2. Below, 'The material value of the Italian alliances', and, in general, Chap. 7.

3. The word *Staatensystem* is used by M. Matzenauer, *Studien zur Politik Karls des Kühnen bis 1474* (Zürich, 1946), 7, 222, who emphasises the crucial role played by Charles the Bold's Burgundy, while, for the role of France and Italy, see V. Ilardi, 'The Italian League, Francesco Sforza and Charles VIII (1454–1461)', *SR*, 6 (1959), 129–66; 'France and Milan: the uneasy alliance, 1452–1466', in *Gli Sforza a Milano e in Lombardia e i loro rapporti con gli stati italiani ed europei (1450–1535)* (Milan, 1982), 415–47 [both articles reprinted in V. Ilardi, *Studies in Italian Renaissance diplomatic history*, Variorum Collected Studies, 239 (London, 1986), nos. II and III]; G. Pillinini, *Il sistema degli stati italiani 1454–1494* (Venice, 1970).

4. K. Bittmann, *Ludwig XI. und Karl der Kühne. Die Memoiren des Philippe de Commynes al historische Quelle*, vols I/1-2 and II/1 [the only parts published] (Göttingen, 1964–70); Vaughan, *Charles the Bold*. More recently, Charles's interest in the Empire, as against the rivalry with Louis XI, has been emphasised by J.-M. Cauchies, *Louis XI et Charles le Hardi. De Péronne à Nancy (1468–1477): le conflit*, Bibliothèque du Moyen Age, 8 (Brussels, 1996).

5. Vaughan, *Charles*, 42–3, 68, 289, 346, 352.

6. Vaughan, *Charles*, 83.

7. R. Vaughan, *Philip the Bold* (London, 1962), 55–6, 108–9, to which add J.J.N. Palmer, 'English foreign policy 1388–99', in *The reign of Richard II*, ed. F.R.H. du Boulay and C.M. Barron (London, 1971), 75–107 (pp. 86–107); *John the Fearless* (London, 1966), 260–1; *Philip the Good* (London, 1970), 161–2, 216–20, 274, 358–9, 368; also Zambarbieri, 'Milano e la Borgogna. I', 34; R.J. Walsh, 'Relations between Milan and Burgundy in the period 1450–1476', in *Gli Sforza*, 369–96 (pp. 370–3, 379–80, 381–2, 389).

8. For example, by Marquis Gian Lodovico Pallavicini and Tommaso Tebaldi, the Milanese ambassadors sent to the Burgundian court in the summer of 1469 at their public audience (see the memorandum they made out for chancellor

Cicco Simonetta on their return: *Carteggi*, I, no. 163), and in the preface to the treaty of Moncalieri between Charles and Galeazzo Maria in January 1475. To some extent, though, this was just a standard diplomatic formula, for the alliance made in 1471 between Charles and King Ferrante of Naples was similarly described in its preface as restoring the amity previously obtaining between the parties' fathers.

9. ADN B 334 (Trésor des Chartes)/16206.

10. Walsh, 'Relations between Milan and Burgundy', 373. The Milanese ambassadors who visited the Burgundian court in 1469 felt obliged to make their excuses for the 1465 expedition: see their memorandum cited above.

11. Bittmann, *Ludwig XI und Karl der Kühne*, I/1, 311, 314–15, 326; I/2, 561, 613.

12. G. Chastellain, *Oeuvres*, ed. J.B.M.C. Kervyn de Lettenhove, 8 vols (Brussels, 1863–8), V (= *Chronique*), 352; Charles to the duke of Milan, Péronne, 11 September 1468, *Carteggi*, I, no. 152 (another protest by Charles, made when he received the Milanese ambassadors in 1469, is contained in their memorandum in *Carteggi*, I, no. 163).

13. Sforza (dei) Bettini, Milanese ambassador in France, to Galeazzo Maria from Le Mans, 23 August 1470 (ASM 537), and Giovanni Andrea Cagnola, Milanese ambassador in Naples, to the same, 23 May and 14 June 1471 (ASM 220). Charles in 1469 had already unsuccessfully pressed Pallavicino and Tebaldi at their public audience to commit their master to an alliance with him.

14. '*stare cum tutti sul generale*' was the Italian translation of Louis XI's contemptuous description of this policy: Cristoforo da Bollate, Milanese ambassador in France, to Galeazzo Maria from Chartres, 23 December 1473 (ASM 540).

15. J. Molinet, *Chroniques*, ed. G. Doutrepont and O. Jodogne, 3 vols (Brussels, 1935–7), I, 171 (citing a lost portion of Chastellain's chronicle); *Fonti aragonesi a cura degli archivisti napoletani*, III, ed. B. Mazzoleni (Naples, 1953), part 2 (= *Il registro 'Sigillorum Summarie Magni Sigilli XLVI' (1469–70)*, 45 no. 3; AGR CC 1924, f.204ᵛ ('Messire Jehan Durmont').

16. ASV, SS, reg. XXIII, f. 60ᵛ, and reg. XXIV, ff. 23ᵛ–4, 27, 27ᵛ, 34, 34ᵛ, 57ᵛ, 61, 61ᵛ, 105ᵛ; Bittmann, *Ludwig XI. und Karl der Kühne*, II/1, 315–16; *Deutsche Reichstagsakten unter Kaiser Friedrich III. Achte Abteilung, erste Hälfte 1468–1470*, ed. I. Most-Kolbe (Göttingen, 1973), 62, 64–5; Vaughan, *Charles*, 130.

17. For example, Galeazzo Maria's instructions to his ambassadors to Burgundy in May 1469 (*Carteggi*, I, no. 157) reveal his fears of the anti-Milanese influence supposedly exerted on Charles by the Venetians and by Philip of Savoy.

18. ASV, SS, XXV, 43ᵛ, and XXVI, 169ᵛ; see also M. Jacoviello, 'Relazioni politiche tra Venezia e Napoli nella seconda metà del XV secolo', *ASPN*, 96 (1978), 67–133 (pp. 82–3).

19. *Carteggi*, I, no. 168.

20. Rodolfo Gonzaga to his mother, Marchioness Barbara of Mantua, from Saint-Omer, 10 July 1470 (AG 2100); *Fonti aragonesi*, III/2, 127 (no. 863).

21. ADN B 334 (Trésor des Chartes)/16206. It is worth emphasising that this document lay apparently unnoticed for five centuries until brought to light by W. Schulz, *Andreaskreuz und Christusorden. Isabella von Portugal und der burgundis-*

che Kreuzzug (Fribourg, 1976), 258. A draft of the treaty is in AGR, Trésor des Chartes, no. 2007. For further material relating to its negotiation and proclamation see J. Bartier, *Légistes et gens de finances au XVe siècle. Les conseillers des ducs de Bourgogne Philippe le Bon et Charles le Téméraire* (Brussels, 1955), 442–7; W. Paravicini, *Guy de Brimeu* (Bonn, 1975), 464 and note 68. Some controversy has arisen because of the possibility for confusion of nomenclature in the documents between Ferrante of Naples and Ferdinand of Aragon and because of the nearly simultaneous conclusion and proclamation of the Burgundian–Aragonese and Burgundian–Neapolitan alliances. Joseph Calmette was incorrect in postulating a triple alliance between Charles the Bold, John II and Ferrante proclaimed at Saint-Omer on 1 November 1471, for there was no triple alliance as such, although all three rulers were allied by bilateral treaties. What actually seems to have happened was that at Abbeville on 6 or 7 August 1471 Charles accepted the inclusion in his existing treaty with John II of the latter's son Ferdinand and of Ferdinand's wife Isabella of Castile, and this inclusion, along with the Burgundian–Neapolitan treaty, was proclaimed at Saint-Omer on 1 November 1471. This revised view is the work of Torregrosa and, latterly, Vicens Vives. Compare G. Passero, *Storie in forma di giornali*, ed. V.M. Altobelli and M.M. Vecchioni (Naples, 1785), 29; J. Calmette, *Louis XI, Jean II et la révolution catalane (1461–1473)* (Toulouse, 1903), 319; *La question des Pyrénées et la marche d'Espagne au moyen-âge* (Paris, 1947), 175; E. Dürr, 'Ludwig XI., die aragonesisch-castilianische Heirat und Karl der Kühne', *MIÖG*, 35 (1914), 297–332 (p. 327); J. Calmette and G. Périnelle, *Louis XI et l'Angleterre (1461–1483)* (Paris, 1930), 143; A.M. Torregrosa, 'Aspectos de la política exterior de Juan II de Aragón', *Estudios de historia moderna*, 2 (1952), 99–132 (pp. 129–30); J. Vicens Vives, *Historia crítica de la vida y reinado de Fernando II de Aragón* (Zaragoza, 1962), 301–3; Vaughan, *Charles*, 75 note 2.

22. And not ten years, as Guillaume de Rochefort told the Milanese ambassador Panigarola in January 1476: *Carteggi*, II, no. 393.

23. Vaughan, *Charles*, 73; Emanuele de Iacopo, Milanese ambassador in France, to Galeazzo Maria from Tours, 18 January 1472 (ASM 539).

24. BNMV (= Classe Italiani VII, cod. 398 — this manuscript comprises six separately paginated registers of the dispatches sent from Naples by the Venetian ambassador Zaccaria Barbaro between 1 November 1471 and 7 September 1473 to Doges Niccolò Tron (died 28 July 1473) and Niccolò Marcello), reg. I, f. 4 (Barbaro to the doge, 5 November 1471); AOGV, III, 31, summarised by F.A.F.T. de Reiffenberg, *Histoire de l'Ordre de la Toison d'Or* (Brussels, 1830), 73.

25. P.M. Perret, *Histoire des relations de la France avec Venise du XIIIe siècle à l'avènement de Charles VIII*, 2 vols (Paris, 1896), I, 586–8; M.C. Daviso di Charvensod, *La duchessa Iolanda* (Turin, 1935), 98–102; Calmette, *La question des Pyrénées*, 179–86.

26. Letter (signature missing) to the duke of Milan from Rome, 18 April 1472 (ASM 69).

27. These relations are treated more fully in Chapter 6.

28. BL, Additional MS 41068A (Bembo's commonplace book), f. 101[v]/142[v]

(old/new foliation). The exact day of his arrival is not recorded, although we know that the Burgundian court was at Abbeville on 1–5, 9–17 and 26–31 August: H. Vander Linden, *Itinéraires de Charles, duc de Bourgogne, Marguerite d'York et Marie de Bourgogne (1467–1477)* (Brussels, 1936), 32–3.

29. ASV, SS, XXV, 77ᵛ, 81, 85, 96–7, 113; BNMV 8170/I, 11, 39 (Barbaro to the doge, 14 November 1471 and 1 January 1472).
30. ASV, Libri Commemoralia, XVI, 64–73.
31. Nicolaus Bononiensis, Milanese ambassador in Venice, to the duke of Milan, 23 July 1471 (ASM 357); D. Malipiero, *Annali veneti dall'anno 1457 al 1500*, ed. F. Longo and A. Sagredo (Florence, 1843), 238.
32. For Charles the Bold's part in this match see, for example, Giovanni Arcimboldi, bishop of Novara, and G.A. Cagnola, Milanese ambassadors in Rome, to Galeazzo Maria, 4 November 1472 (ASM 71).
33. Bittmann, *Ludwig XI und Karl der Kühne*, II/1, 492 and n. 309; H. Brauer-Gramm, *Der Landvogt Peter von Hagenbach* (Göttingen, 1957), 193–4.
34. Perret, *Histoire des relations de la France avec Venise*, II, 3–5; M.C. Daviso di Charvensod, *Filippo II il Senza Terra* (Turin, 1941), 101–3; E. Fumagalli, 'Nuovi documenti su Lorenzo e Giuliano de' Medici', *IMU*, 23 (1980), 115–64 (pp. 117–19).
35. Cristoforo da Bollate to Galeazzo Maria, Tonnay-Charente, 10 April 1473 (ASM 540); Galeazzo Maria to Charles the Bold, April 1473 (*Carteggi*, I, no. 200); *Lettres de Louis XI*, ed. J. Vaesen, E. Charavay and B. de Mandrot, 11 vols (Paris, 1883–1909), V, 140–2.
36. A copy of the treaty is in ASM 540.
37. Barbaro to the doge, 17 February 1473 (BNMV 8170/V, 11).
38. Galeazzo Maria to Cristoforo da Bollate, Milan, 28 June 1473 (ASM 540); Zaccaria Saggio, Mantuan ambassador in Milan, to Marquis Lodovico Gonzaga, 18 January 1474 (AG 1624); C. Simonetta, *I Diarii*, ed. A.R. Natale (Milan, 1962), 82–4; Galeazzo Maria to Cristoforo da Bollate from Villanova, 1 April 1474, and from Pavia, 13 June 1474, and his reply to the French ambassador (the bishop of Senlis) dated Pavia, 12 October 1474 (all in ASM 541).
39. Walsh, 'Relations between Milan and Burgundy', 375. It seems that the feud between Colleoni and Galeazzo Maria was no less personal than political: L. Fumi, 'Una farsa rappresentata in Parigi contra Bartolomeo Colleoni' [1474], in *Miscellanea di studi storici in onore di Antonio Manno*, ed. P. Boselli, 2 vols (Turin, 1912), II, 589–94.
40. The duke of Milan to Cristoforo da Bollate, Pavia, 18 August 1473 (ASM 540); Giovanni Palomar, Neapolitan ambassador to Burgundy, to the duke, Thionville, 6 December 1473 (ASM 490); the duke to Antonio d'Appiano, Milanese ambassador to Savoy, Pavia, 25 January 1474 (ASM 491); Cristoforo da Bollate to the duke, Senlis, 1 March 1474 (ASM 541); Simonetta, *Diarii*, 84.
41. Bittmann, *Ludwig XI. und Karl der Kühne*, II/1, 196–9, 201, 222–3, 243–6; *Lettres de Louis XI*, V, 296–7.
42. Antonio d'Appiano to the duke of Milan, Moncalieri, 19 November 1474 (ASM 491); the duke to Antonio '*manu propria*', Villanova, 21 November 1474 (*Carteggi*, I, no. 225).

43. The course of the negotiations can be studied in the correspondence between Galeazzo Maria and his ambassadors in Piedmont (the resident, Antonio d'Appiano, and the three special envoys Orfeo dei Cenni da Ricavo, Giovan Angelo Talenti and Alessandro Colletta) in *Carteggi*, I, nos. 227–38; see also Dürr, 'Galeazzo Maria und seine Stellung zu den Burgunderkriegen', 291–2. The treaty itself is in Turin, Archivio di Stato, Protocolli, XVII, 267, and has been published several times; by J. Dumont, *Corps universel diplomatique de droit des gens*, 8 vols in 16 parts (Amsterdam, 1726–31), III/1, 496–71; in P. de Commynes, *Mémoires*, ed. D. Godefroy and N. Lenglet du Fresnoy, 3 vols (Paris–London, 1747), II, 356-62; by S. Guichenon, *Histoire généalogique de la royale maison de Savoie*, 4 vols, 2nd edtn (Turin, 1778–80), IV/2, 425–8 [the version cited in following pages]; by U. Plancher, *Histoire générale et particulière de Bourgogne*, 4 vols (Dijon, 1739–81), IV, cclv–vii.
44. Walsh, 'Relations', 377.
45. See, for example, Saggio to the marquis of Mantua, Milan, 30 March 1475 (AG 1625).
46. AS, SS, XXVI, 176^v–7, and XXVII, 4^v. Charles the Bold's relations with Florence are considered at greater length below, in Chapter 3.
47. Below, Chapter 2, 'Papal mediation in disputes'.
48. For these examples see *Carteggi*, I, no. 327, II, nos. 479, 532.
49. Perret, *Histoire*, II, 44–51; H. Knebel, *Diarium*, ed. J. Vischer and H. Boos, 2 vols (Leipzig, 1880–7), I, 144–5.
50. Saggio to the marquis of Mantua, Milan, 10 and 28 July 1475 (AG 1625).
51. *Carteggi*, II, no. 481.
52. *Carteggi*, II, no. 592; see also Vaughan, *Charles*, 387; J.F. Kirk, *History of Charles the Bold*, 3 vols (London, 1863–8), III, 347.
53. For example, Charles to the duke, Namur, 27 August 1475 (AS 537 — misfiled, this *carteggio* being for France in the late 1460s).
54. See especially Dürr, 'Galeazzo Maria', 293–413; L. de' Medici, *Lettere*, II, 497–522 (*Excursus* IV, by R. Fubini); Zambarbieri, 'Milano e la Borgogna. II', 2–4.
55. *Carteggi*, II, nos 431, 541, 573.
56. *Carteggi*, II, nos. 511, 512, 556.
57. *Carteggi*, II, no. 592.
58. Sacramoro, Milanese ambassador in Rome, to the duke of Milan, 20 December 1474 (ASM 78); the full name of this ambassador, which appears to have been Antonio Sacramoro dei Chiozzi or dei Mengozzi, seems to have been seldom used.
59. Francesco Maletta, Milanese ambassador in Naples, to the duke of Milan, 20 February and 1 and 8 March 1475 (ASM 227); *Carteggi*, I, nos. 262, 327.
60. Leonardo Botta, Milanese ambassador in Venice, to the duke of Milan, 24 June 1474 and 10 February 1475 (ASM 359); Perret, *Histoire*, II, 38–40, 46; *Carteggi*, I, no. 256; ASV, SS, XXVII, 4, 4^v.
61. *Carteggi*, I, no. 262.
62. He used this excuse, for example, in his letter to Panigarola of 30 July 1475 (*Carteggi*, II, no. 334); see also Zambarbieri, 'Milano e la Borgogna. I', 41.
63. Below, pp. 203–4.

64. *Carteggi*, II, nos. 393, 395.
65. 'Il dubio nostro è del duca e non del re': *Carteggi*, II, no. 428 (Galeazzo Maria's instructions for his ambassadors at the Burgundian court, Pierfrancesco Visconti and Giovanni Pallavicino de Scipiono, 23 February 1476); see also Zambarbieri, 'Milano e la Borgogna. II', 2–3.
66. *Carteggi*, II, nos. 532, 544, 592, 599.
67. Perret, *Histoire*, II, 83; and, on Panigarola's departure, *Carteggi*, II, nos. 648–50.
68. Perret, *Histoire*, II, 84–9.
69. G. Périnelle, 'Dépêches de Nicholas de' Roberti, ambassadeur d'Hercule Ier duc de Ferrare auprès du roi Louis XI (nov. 1478–juillet 1480)', *MAHEFR*, 24 (1904), 130–203, 425–77; S. Brinton, *The Gonzaga* (London, 1927), 95; *Lettres de Louis XI*, IX, 20, and X, 426–7 (the original of the latter is in AG 626).
70. Walsh, 'Relations', 377.
71. Antonio Donato, Mantuan ambassador in Naples, to the marquis of Mantua, 7 February 1477 (AG 805); E. Motta, 'Spigolature d'archivio per la storia di Venezia nella seconda metà del Quattrocento (dall'Archivio di Stato milanese).1. Cassandra nel 1477?', *Archivio veneto*, 36 (1888), 377–8.
72. Vaughan, *Charles*, 179–80.
73. Later in the year Charles thanked Ferrante profusely for having stood by him at this critical juncture when, as he said, everyone else was abandoning him: Barbaro to the doge, Naples, 8 December 1471 (BNMV 8170/I, 25); Molinet, *Chroniques*, I, 87. Ferrante had tried to help him by urging Louis to lay down his arms and resort instead to the mediation of the pope to compose their differences: Sforza Bettini to the duke of Milan, Ham, 5 May 1471 (ASM 538).
74. Nicolaus Bononsiensis to the duke of Milan, Venice, 24 November 1471 (ASM 357) who also reported the slightly different figures given by the Neapolitan ambassador: 3,000 cavalry and 2,000 infantry or 80,000 ducats per annum.
75. ASV, Libri Commemoralia, XVI, 64^v.
76. Barbaro to the doge, Naples, 27 June 1472 (BNMV 8170/III, 26).
77. R.J. Walsh, 'Charles the Bold and the crusade: politics and propaganda', *JMH*, 3 (1977), 53–86 (pp. 57–9). The main additions and corrections I wish to make to this article are: (1) p. 68: the former councillor of Charles the Bold who relayed the duke's intention to go on crusade to his grandson Philip the Handsome was Olivier de la Marche (see his *Mémoires*, ed. H. Beaune and J. d'Arbaumont, 4 vols (Paris, 1883–8), I, 145, a reference I owe to the kindness of Prof. Werner Paravicini); (2) pp. 68–9: the original text of the account of Anselme Adournes' journey to the Holy Land has since been published, edited and translated by J. Heers and G. de Groer, *Itinéraire d'Anselme Adorno en Terre Sainte (1470–1471)*, Sources d'histoire médiévale publiées par l'Institut de Recherche et d'Histoire des Textes (Paris, 1978), and, on his connection in this context with King James III of Scotland, see now A.D. Macquarrie, 'Anselm Adornes of Bruges: traveller in the East and friend of James III', *Innes Review*, 33 (1982), 15–22 (pp. 16–17, 19); (3) pp. 70–2: on Lodovico da

Bologna's connection with Charles in 1473 and on his mission to Uzun Hasan see now also J. Richard, *La papauté et les missions d'Orient au moyen âge* (Rome, 1977), 274–8; (4) pp. 72–4: on the schemes to invest Charles with the titles of emperor of Constantinople and emperor of Trebizond see now also the editorial *Excursus* by R. Fubini in L. de' Medici, *Lettere*, II, 504–6; (5): the whole theme has been re-examined by H. Taparel, 'Le duché Valois de Bourgogne et l'Orient ottoman au XIV et XV° siècle' (Thèse de 3° cycle, Université de Toulouse le Mirail, U.E.R. d'Histoire, annéee 1981–2), but he has little to say about Charles the Bold.

78. Bartier, *Légistes*, 446.

79. Nicolaus Bononsiensis to the duke of Milan, Venice, 24 November 1471 (ASM 357); ASV, SS, XXV, 36ᵛ–7.

80. For this paragraph see Maletta to the duke of Milan, Naples, 27 January 1472 (ASM 221); Barbaro to the doge, Naples, 12 February, 11 October and 5 November 1472 and 21 March 1473 (BNMV 8170/II, 5, IV, 6, 20, and V, 9); Cristoforo da Bollate to the duke of Milan, Vendôme, 10 October 1473 (ASM 540, summarised by Bittmann, *Ludwig XI. und Karl der Kühne*, II/1, 117); R. Gandilhon, *Politique économique de Louis XI* (Paris, 1941), 383.

81. Maletta to the duke of Milan, Naples, 28 February and 11 May 1474 (ASM 225).

82. *Carteggi*, I, no. 183; J. de Roye, *Journal, connu sous le nom de chronique scandaleuse 1460–1483*, ed. B. de Mandrot, 2 vols (Paris, 1894–6), I, 301; Cristoforo da Bollate to the duke of Milan, Paris, 15 January 1475 (ASM 542); Knebel, *Diarium*, I, 200.

83. Maletta to the duke of Milan, Naples, 20 February 1475 (ASM 227).

84. Galeazzo Maria to Francesco Pietrasanta, his ambassador in France, Galiate, 10 September 1476 (ASM 542).

85. Below, Chapter 2, pp. 96–7.

86. Rodolfo Gonzaga to the marchioness of Mantua, Saint-Omer, 10 July 1470 (AG 2100); on the Burgundian fleet of 1470 see Vaughan, *Charles*, 61–4, 227.

87. AGR, Trésor des Chartes, 2007 (unfoliated but see f. 3). Ferrante did, however, send naval help to his and Charles the Bold's ally, the king of Aragon, against Louis XI in Catalonia and Roussillon: J. Vicens Vives, *Fernando el Católico* (Madrid, 1952), 206 note 236; *Juan II de Aragón* (Barcelona, 1953), 351; I. Schiappoli, *Napoli aragonese* (Naples, 1972), 109–10.

88. *Carteggi*, I, no. 185; L. de' Medici, *Lettere*, II, 101, n.3; the duke of Milan to Maletta in Naples, Abiate, 26 March 1473 (ASM 223). Fregoso is not mentioned by R. Degryse, 'De admiraals en de eigen marine van de Bourgondische hertogen, 1364–1488', *Mededelingen der Akademie van Marine van België*, 27 (1965), 139–225. I have not seen J. Paviot, *La politique navale des ducs de Bourgogne (1384–1482)* (Lille, 1995).

89. Walsh, 'Relations', 384–5, 396. Shortly before the battle of Murten Charles told Panigarola to ask his master to send him a suit of armour made in Milan. It was to be light and made to his own design; this was important, Panigarola pointed out to Galeazzo Maria, because the duke donned his armour nearly every day, so it had to be comfortable. The reason he needed a new suit of armour was that, owing to the loss of weight caused by his recent illness, his

old one no longer fitted: *Carteggi*, II, no. 582. Perhaps this explains why he took such a long time to prepare himself for battle — with dire results — when the Swiss made a surprise attack a few days later: P. Ghinzhoni, 'La battaglia di Morat', *Archivio storico lombardo*, 2nd ser., 9 (1892), 102–9; *Carteggi*, II, no. 612.

90. Simonetta, *Diarii*, 11–12; the duke of Milan to d'Appiano, Abiate, 12, 16 and 19 March 1473 (ASM 490).

91. Antonio d'Appiano to the duke of Milan, Turin, 16 August 1473 (ASM 490).

92. For this and the next paragraph see *Carteggi*, I, nos 476, 485–6, 538, 544; Simonetta, *Diarii*, 199–200; Saggio to the marquis of Mantua, Milan, 29 April 1476 (AG 1625); d'Appiano to the duke of Milan, Geneva, 25 May 1476 (ASM 495); AGR CC 25543, ff. 119, 261 (payments to Anselmino da Prato by the ducal *trésorier des guerres*). It will be noticed that the Italian munitions Charles wanted were mainly hand weapons and suits of armour; as regards artillery, his own lands could provide that, as well as the men with the skill necessary to work it.

93. Ferrante to Antonio Cincinello, his ambassador in Milan, Sarni, 4 March 1474 (ASM 225).

94. But had he consented to Federico's suit, then the case would probably have been different, for by a mandate of 18 October 1474 Ferrante empowered his son to offer any amount of men or money that might be necessary to secure the match: J. Calmette, 'Le projet de mariage bourguignon-napolitain en 1474 d'après un acquisition récente de la Bibliothèque Nationale', *BEC*, 72 (1911), 459–72 (p. 466). Federico's suit is dealt with in more detail below, Chapter 6, 'Federico d'Aragona'.

95. Barbaro to the doge, Naples, 25 April 1473 (BNMV 8170/VI, 3); the duke of Milan to Maletta in Naples, Abiate, 8 March 1473, and Maletta to the duke, 26 March 1473 (ASM 223).

96. Galeota to Guillaume de Rochefort, Brescia, 31 March 1473 (ASM 358); ASV, SS, XXV, 166, 183ᵛ; XXVI, 1ᵛ, 5ᵛ.

97. ASV, Consiglio dei X: Misto, vol. XVII, ff. 146, 153ᵛ, vol. XVIII, f 10ᵛ, and Capi dei Consiglidei X: Lettere, vol. I, ff 22, 32, 369.

98. B. Belotti, *La vita di Bartolomeo Colleoni* (Bergamo, 1923), 463–74, 487–90, 502–7.

99. *Carteggi*, I, no. 199; Vaughan, *Charles*, 216; Galeota to the duke of Milan, Reggio, 16 May 1473 (ASM 323).

100. See the letter lacking signature and addressee dated Ferrara, 21 March 1473 in ASM 323.

101. Lodovico Gonzaga to Saggio in Milan, 6 April 1473 (AG 2187, f. 898) and to Galeota, 10 June 1473 (AG 2892, lib. LXXI, f. 36ᵛ).

102. J. de' Bianchi, *Cronaca modenese* (Parma, 1861), 44.

103. Modena, Archivio di Stato, Epistolae, vol. III, f. 108; *Carteggi*, I, no. 199; *Dépêches . . . Charles-le-Hardi*, II, no. 161.

104. *Carteggi*, I, no. 199; L. de' Medici, *Lettere*, II, 360–1; *Carteggi*, II, no. 528; *Dépêches . . . Charles-le-Hardi*, II, no. 180. According to the unreliable Knebel (*Diarium*, I, 158–9), Ercole sent troops to fight for Charles at the siege of Neuss in 1474–1475.

105. Lodovico to Galeota, Mantua, 8 April 1473, and Lodovico's letters of credence for Giacomo da Mantua, 10 June 1473 (AG 2892, lib. LXXI, ff. 11, 38ᵛ); *Carteggi*, I, no. 199; AGR CC 25542,f. 41 (payments to Biagio by the *trésorier des guerres*).

106. AGR CC 1925, ff. 339, 358ᵛ, 394.

107. Below, Chapter 4, 'Factions' and Chapter 7, 'Chronology of recruitment'.

108. F. Gabotto, *Lo stato sabaudo da Amadeo VIII ad Emanuele Filiberto II*, 3 vols (Turin, 1893), II, 106 n. 3.

109. Bittmann, *Ludwig XI. und Karl der Kühne*, II/1, 461 n. 272; *Inventaire sommaire des Archives Communales de la ville de Strasbourg antérieurs à 1790*, ed. J. Brucker, 4 vols (Strasbourg, 1878–86), I, 90–2; E. Bauer, *Négociations et campagnes de Rodolph de Hochberg* (Neuchâtel, 1928), 66; E. Colombo, *Iolanda duchessa di Savoia (1465–78): studio storico* (Turin, 1893), 127; A. Grand, *Der Anteil des Wallis an den Burgunderkriegen* (Brig, 1913), 68–71, 82–3, 100.

110. J. Mangin, 'Guillaume de Rochefort' (unpublished dissertation, thèse de licenciat ès lois et lettres de l'École des Chartes, Paris, 1936), 30.

111. Vaughan, *Charles*, 386; *Carteggi*, II, no. 466.

112. *Lettres de Louis XI*, V, 103–5.

113. B. Croce, 'Il conte di Campobasso', in his *Vite di avventure di fede e di passione*, 2nd ed. (Bari, 1947), 47–186 (p. 104 n. 1); Simonetta, *Diarii*, 11–12 (Galeota).

114. Cristoforo da Bollate to the duke of Milan, Amboise, 6 July 1473 (ASM 540).

115. Apart from Antonio dei Corradi di Lignana and Galeota mentioned already, another victim of these confiscations was Francesco Achilles dei Conti (one of Campobasso's men): see his letter to the duke of Milan asking for restoration two years later, from Reggio, 9 April 1475 (ASM 323).

116. Saggio to the marquis of Mantua, Milan, 26 February and 22 March 1473 (AG 1624).

117. The duke of Milan to Marco Trotto and Cristoforo da Bollate, his ambassadors in France, Milan, 10 January 1473 (ASM 540); Simonetta, *Diarii*, 11–12.

118. Brauer-Gramm, *Der Landvogt Peter von Hagenbach*, 188; Barbaro to the doge, Naples, 6 April 1473 (BNMV 8170/V, 28).

119. For 1471 see P.M. Perret, 'Boffille de Juge, comte de Castres, et la république de Venise', *Annales du Midi*, 3 (1891), 159–231 (pp. 165–6); *Histoire*, I, 576; and for 1474 see F. Pasquier, *Un favori de Louis XI, Boffille de Juge* (Albi, 1914), 10–12, 21–2, 173–4, 181–3. See also P. Contamine, *Guerre, état et société à la fin du Moyen Âge. Etude sur les armées des rois de France 1337–1494* (Paris–The Hague, 1972), 284 and note 39, 457 and note 38.

120. *Carteggi*, II, no. 406.

121. Francesco Pietrasanta to the duke of Milan, Turin, 17 April 1476 (ASM 495).

122. *Carteggi*, II, no. 513.

123. For example, Don Francesco da Castiglione and Ugo di Sanseverino: d'Appiano to the duke of Milan, Lausanne, 17 and 18 May 1476 (ASM 495) and *Carteggi*, II, no. 534.

124. He, but apparently not his money, was released probably at the beginning of July: Giovanni Bianchi to the duke of Milan, Turin, 2 and 4 July 1476 (ASM 496); *Carteggi*, II, no. 640; P. de Commynes, *Mémoires*, ed. J. Calmette and G. Durville, 3 vols (Paris, 1924–5), II (1925), 112.

125. For this clause see the text of the treaty in Guichenon, *Histoire*, IV/2, 427; and for Galeazzo Maria's excuses see *Carteggi*, II, nos. 477, 492, 504.

126. *Carteggi*, II, nos. 492, 505.

127. *Carteggi*, II, no. 468.

128. We might, however, mention the brief acceptance by Pisa for a few months in 1406 of the joint suzerainty of John the Fearless and Louis, duke of Orleans, and the attempt by Philip the Good in 1445 to persuade Filippo Maria Visconti, duke of Milan, to cede Genoa to him: Vaughan, *John*, 38, 146, 200–31; A. Grunzweig, 'Un plan d'acquisition de Gênes par Philippe le Bon', *MA*, 42 (1931), 81–110.

129. Vaughan, *Charles*, 72; *Calendar of state papers and manuscripts existing in the archives and collections of Milan*, ed. A.B. Hinds [one volume only published] (London, 1912), I, no. 221; Walsh, 'Charles the Bold and the crusade', 72–6.

130. E. Dürr, 'Karl der Kühne und der Ursprung des habsburgisch-spanischen Imperiums', *Historische Zeitschrift*, 113 (194), 22–55 (pp. 47–8), and *La politique des Confédérés au XIV ᵉ et au XVᵉ siècle* (Bern, 1935), 282.

131. All five were mentioned in the letter of Francesco Bertini, Neapolitan ambassador in Burgundy, to Ferrante from Brussels, 26 February 1473, which was summarised by Maletta to the duke of Milan, Naples, 30 March 1473 (ASM 223).

132. Although, as with England, Charles was not above trying to gain a title to the Neapolitan throne: Walsh, 'Charles the Bold and the crusade', 82, note 26.

133. During the final eighteen months of his life Galeazzo Maria made extremely persistent attempts to secure this recognition. The fate of the negotiations, however, depended very much on Charles, who was asked to mediate between his Milanese and imperial allies. By the time they came to an end with the dissolution of the Milanese–Burgundian alliance, they had reached an advanced but still incomplete stage: F. Cusin, 'I rapporti tra la Lombardia e l'impero dalla morte di Francesco Sforza all'avvento di Ludovico il Moro', *Annali della R. Università degli Studi Economici e Commerciali di Trieste*, 6 (1934), 213–322 (pp. 293–305).

134. Dürr, 'Galeazzo Maria', 262–3, 280. Dürr seemed to modify this view slightly in later works where he concluded that Charles the Bold's attention was directed towards the Mediterranean only from about 1474 onwards, although he still felt Charles harboured designs on the duchy of Milan: Dürr, 'Karl der Kühne', 48–9, and *La politique des Confédérés*, 281–6. For Burckhardt see W. Kaegi, 'Ein Plan Jacob Burckhardts zu einem Werk über Karl den Kühnen', *BZGA*, 30 (1930), 393–8 (p. 396).

135. H. Heimpel, 'Karl der Kühne und der burgundische Staat', in *Festschrift für Gerhard Ritter*, ed. R. Nürnberger (Tübingen, 1950), 140–55 (pp. 151–3).

136. Vaughan, *Charles*, 184.

137. Fumagalli, 'Nuovi documenti', 130–1.

138. L. de' Medici, *Lettere*, II, 519.

139. Dürr, 'Galeazzo Maria', 263–4.

140. Rodolfo to his mother, the marchioness of Mantua, Ghent, 23 January 1470 (AG 2100).

141. The remarks of Francesco Bertini quoted by F. Cusin, 'Impero, Borgogna e

politica italiana (l'incontro di Treviri del 1473)', *Nuova rivista storica*, 19 (1935), 137–72, and 20 (1936), 34–57 (p. 41) were echoed by Panigarola: *Carteggi*, II, no. 508.

142. *Carteggi*, II, no. 482 (Panigarola's source was one of Louis XI's chamberlains who had just visited Charles).

143. Edward IV employed a similar ruse against Galeazzo Maria in 1476: *CSP Milan*, I, no. 326.

144. Bittmann, *Ludwig XI. und Karl der Kühne*, I/2, 571.

145. J. Pažout, 'König Georg von Böhmen und die Concilfrage im Jahre 1467', *Archiv für österreichische Geschichte*, 40 (1869), 323–71; F.G. Heymann, *George of Bohemia* (Princeton, N.J., 1965), 426–7; J. Maček, 'Le mouvement conciliaire, Louis XI et Georges de Poděbrady', *Historica* [Prague], 15 (1967), 5–63 (pp. 46–8); see also A.M. and P. Bonenfant, 'Le projet d'érection des états bourguignons en royaume en 1447', *MA*, 45 (1935), 10–23 (p. 22 note 2); Vaughan, *Charles*, 42.

146. Zannono Coiro to the duke of Milan, Lyon, 12 and 15 January 1469 (the first is used by Vaughan, *Charles*, 184), and Sforza Bettini to the same, Tours, 19 January 1469 (all in ASM 536).

147. See Galeazzo Maria's instructions for Emanuele de Jacopo, ambassador to France, dated Vigevano, 14 January 1469, and his letter to Emanuele and Bettini dated 21 (January?) 1469 (ASM 536), and *Lettres de Louis XI*, III, 317; IV, 343–4.

148. Vaughan, *Charles*, 243; Daviso, *Iolanda*, 32–4, 43.

149. Gabotto, *Lo stato sabaudo*, II, 112, note 1.

150. On Paul II and Tolentis see below, Chapter 2, section 'Relations with the papacy . . .'.

151. Letter to the duke of Milan, Rome, 18 April 1472 (ASM 69). The signature is missing but the author may have been the Ardilas Pannatinis mentioned in the next note.

152. Ardilas Pannatinis to the duke of Milan, Rome, 9 May 1472 (ASM 70).

153. Vaughan, *Charles*, 135–6.

154. Galeazzo Maria had offered Louis XI troops in 1471: Bittmann, *Ludwig XI. und Karl der Kühne*, I/2, 562.

155. On, for example, his brothers Sforza Maria and Lodovico il Moro compare A. Dina, 'Lodovico il Moro prima della sua venuta al governo', *ASL*, 2nd ser., 3 (1886), 737–76 (pp. 764–6) with R. Fubini, 'Osservazioni e documenti sulla crisi del ducato di Milano nel 1477', in *Essays presented to Myron P. Gilmore*, ed. S. Bertelli and G. Ramakus, 2 vols (Florence, 1978), I, 47–103 (pp. 59 and 67, note 3) and Fubini's *Excursus* in L. de' Medici, *Lettere*, II, 525, 531, 534.

156. There are some general traces of the Milan rumours also, though not relating specifically to 1473, in Commynes, *Mémoires*, II, 8, 102, and P. Wielant, *Recueil des antiquités de Flandre*, in *Collection de chroniques belges inédits*, IV, ed. J.J. de Smet (Brussels, 1865), 1–442 (p. 53).

157. D'Appiano to the duke of Milan, Vercelli, 10 January 1473 (ASM 490).

158. Vaughan, *Charles*, 214–15.

159. Barbaro to the doge, Naples, 29 March 1473 (BNMV 8170/V, 21); see also Bittmann, *Ludwig XI. und Karl der Kühne*, II/1, 85.

160. What follows is based on Bittmann, *Ludwig XI. und Karl der Kühne*, II/1, 59–105; see also Vaughan, *Charles*, 117–18.

161. This word was used by the Milanese ambassador in France, Cristoforo da Bollate: Bittmann, *Ludwig XI. und Karl der Kühne*, II/1, 99 note 120.

162. Cusin, 'I rapporti', 255–70; Dürr, 'Galeazzo Maria Sforza', 279–80. On relations between Charles and Frederick III see also L. Boehm, 'Burgundy and the Empire in the reign of Charles the Bold', *International History Review*, 1 (1979), 153–62, which is basically a translation of Chap 11 of her *Geschichte Burgunds. Politik — Staatsbildungen — Kultur*, 2nd ed. (Stuttgart, etc, 1979).

163. Saggio to the marquis of Mantua, Milan, 12 February and 2 March 1474 (AG 1624); Bittmann, *Ludwig XI. und Karl der Kühne*, II/1, 191–2; Vaughan, *Charles*, 276.

164. Dürr, 'Galeazzo Maria', 280.

165. Dürr, 'Galeazzo Maria', 263.

166. He even made a bet on it with his captain Donato del Conte: A. Bertolotti, 'Spedizioni militari in Piemonte sconosciute o poco note di Galeazzo Maria Sforza', *ASL*, 10 (1883), 548–646 (p. 575).

167. *Carteggi*, II, nos. 481, 592.

168. Kirk, *History of Charles the Bold*, III, 251–2. More recently Zambarbieri, 'Milano e la Borgogna', I, 40, and II, 2–3, 4, 9, is sceptical of the view that Charles had designs on Milan, arguing instead that Galeazzo Maria's fears were the result more of his own timidity and duplicitous mentality and of Louis XI's intrigues than of any real intention on the part of the duke of Burgundy. The opposite view, however, is taken by Fubini, 'I rapporti diplomatici tra Milano e Borgogna' (see especially pp. 99, 111), who argues that Charles's designs on Milan were both a consistent aim of his foreign policy and an essential component of his imperial ambitions. He cites as proof of this a document of May 1476, published by Sestan (*Carteggi*, II, no. 578), in which Charles gives powers to Antonio Mattia da Iseo to act as his deputy in the duchy of Milan. One wonders, though, whether this single testimony can bear the weight that Fubini, a fastidious historian, places on it. Is not the document, like many others at the time, simply evidence of the duke's campaign at this time to recruit Italian soldiers to rebuild his army for the forthcoming campaign against the Swiss? Was da Iseo, the person thus empowered, a significant enough figure to be entrusted by Charles with such a major task as being the duke's deputy in a political manner? Was he not, rather, simply one of the many plotters and malcontents at the Burgundian court, like the abbot of Casanova, the Fregoso and Francesco Querini, who, as Italian ambassadors repeatedly complained, mistook the duke's hospitality to visitors for support for their schemes?

CHAPTER TWO

Charles the Bold and the Papacy

As Charles the Bold's relations with the papacy were inevitably somewhat more *sui generis* than those with the purely temporal Italian rulers
of Naples, Venice, Milan and the other states discussed in the previous
chapter, they will be dealt with separately here.

The duke's relations with Rome were affected both by the papacy's
universal role and, in the half-century before the Reformation, by its
increasingly Italian characteristics. During the reigns of the two pontiffs
in question — Paul II (1464–1471) and Sixtus IV (1471–1484) — the
universal role of the Holy See affected Charles very closely in certain
areas. Papal taxation and appointments, for example, could have diplomatic repercussions; the pope's power to grant or refuse dispensations
from the canonical prohibition on marriages within certain degrees of
consanguinity might make or mar marital diplomacy; and the pope's duty
to intervene between warring rulers in the interests of peace and for the
furtherance of the crusade was a political fact that could not be ignored.
In other senses, though, the duke's relations with Rome were much more
directly connected with Italy. The numerous legates who visited his
court, whether as peacemakers or as tax-collectors, were nearly all
Italian. The pope's standing as the temporal ruler of the Papal States had
a bearing on the papacy's attitude towards its neighbours in Italy, and
hence on its attitude to Charles himself, as a result of his relations with
those neighbours. The degree of influence that certain Italian rulers had
in Rome was a factor to which Charles gave serious thought before
making alliances in the peninsula, and his attempts to render Paul II and
Sixtus IV more pliable led him to attempt to assemble a pro-Burgundian
party at the curia. Finally, the value of undertaking a general survey of
his relations with the Holy See is emphasised by the consideration that,

in this respect, he has been less well served by historians than his predecessor, Philip the Good, or his contemporary, Louis XI;[1] this should be borne in mind when reading what follows, because more research is clearly still needed.[2]

Relations with the papacy as an Italian temporal power

Regardless of the person of the papal throne's incumbent, some measure of consistency in its external relations was forced on the papacy by the regard successive pontiffs were bound to have for their traditional powers and prerogatives. Yet there is a sense in which the papacy could also be regarded as a temporal power like Milan, Naples and Venice. For example, the possession of the States of the Church, which for financial reasons were perhaps more important to the Holy See in the fifteenth century than they had been for a long time previously, gave the vicars of Christ a recognised place within the Italian state-system, while, to the south, the kingdom of Naples was a reluctant fief of Rome. In this context the differing geographical origins of successive popes, and the political preferences which arose from them, could result in important variations in the Holy See's attitude towards her neighbours. Certainly, it is not hard to detect a contrast in outlook between Paul II and Sixtus IV.

Pietro Barbo, who reigned from 30 August 1464 until 26 July 1471 as Pope Paul II, came from a Venetian patrician family and tended to view Rome's neighbours as a Venetian would; this implied hostility to Milan and Florence and, beyond the Alps, hostility also to Louis XI but a friendly attitude towards Charles the Bold. His attempts to secure Burgundian intervention in the peninsula against King Ferrante in 1469[3] could be construed as a part of the traditional policy of enforcing Rome's suzerainty over its fief, although, as the fate of Naples was then bound up also with that of the Medici and Sforza regimes in Florence and Milan, the call for Burgundian intervention might equally be interpreted in an anti-French light. Certainly, some idea of his feelings towards Charles at this time can be gleaned from a letter he wrote to him on 18 October 1469 in which he declared himself ready to grant the duke anything within reason.[4]

His actions during the following year more openly favoured Burgundy, for in 1470 he helped mediate an alliance between Venice and Naples, which, as far as he was concerned, was clearly meant to balance that recently concluded by Milan and Florence with Louis XI. Louis was not slow to recognise the danger and declared the pope a Burgundian.[5] His fears were justified, for the Venetian–Neapolitan alliance marked an important stage in the emergence of a pro-Burgundian bloc in the peninsula to oppose that aligned with France. Towards the end of his life Paul II became a little disillusioned with Charles, mainly as a result of the duke's hesitations in fully implementing their agreement over the papal alum monopoly; but shortly before his death he was still sufficiently favourable to create provisionally a Burgundian cardinal, a creation which, not having been fully formalised, was to cause his successor much trouble; and it was around this time that Louis XI accused him of being the most perfidious Burgundian alive.[6]

By contrast, Francesco della Rovere, who was elected pope as Sixtus IV on 9 August 1471, was born near Savona in Liguria, a region subject for some time past to strong French and Milanese influence. The importance of the part played by Galeazzo Maria in securing della Rovere's election has been clearly demonstrated by historians.[7] The duke of Milan clearly expected the new pope to be pliable to his wishes and he was not disappointed; equally, Sixtus was regarded by the duke of Milan's enemies as little more than his mouthpiece. In general, Sixtus IV's Milanese sympathies worked to Charles the Bold's disadvantage in the period between his election and the conclusion of the treaty of Moncalieri. In Italy, for instance, he did not disguise his displeasure at the Neapolitan alliance with Burgundy proclaimed in November 1471 and he refused to bless it when so requested by Ferrante, partly because, despite its ringing crusading declarations, he suspected Ferrante of trying to use it to escape his vassalage to the Holy See, while others at the curia were alarmed because Ferrante had not reserved in the treaty his erstwhile allies, Milan and Florence.[8] In the following summer Sixtus annoyed Charles by helping to bring about, albeit only briefly, a fragile reconciliation between Ferrante and Galeazzo Maria; this action seemed to presage the return of Naples to the French camp.[9] Beyond the Alps this period witnessed also growing difficulties over the implementation in the Low Countries of the papal alum agreement, leading to its abrogation in June 1473, and over Charles the Bold's refusal to submit himself to papal mediation in his disputes with Louis XI,[10] while ill-feeling continued over the duke's demand for the creation of two Burgundian cardinals, an issue which was only half-settled by the promotion of Philibert Hugonet in May 1473. Indeed, in June 1474 Charles complained that Sixtus IV was even more contrary than the king of France.[11]

The adverse effects on Charles of the replacement on the papal throne of the pro-Venetian Paul II by the pro-Milanese Sixtus IV were graphically illustrated by the fate of the papal legate at his court, Lucas de Tolentis. Lucas had been first sent to the Low Countries during the papacy of Calixtus III (1455–1458);[12] he returned again at the end of 1463 on behalf of Pius II (1458–1464) and stayed for two years. In 1466 he was back again, this time in the service of Paul II. Originally his powers were limited to the collection of papal taxes, but were gradually extended to the sale of indulgences, the supervision of the papal alum monopoly (which he negotiated in 1468), and to a wide variety of legatine functions. In 1469 he was rewarded by promotion to the see of Šibenik (in Croatia, formerly Sebenico). Above all, Lucas was a Venetian subject, having been born in Korčula (formerly Curzola), the main town of the Croatian island of the same name situated a few miles off the Dalmatian coast. This fact greatly disturbed the duke of Milan, who regarded the legate as little more than an agent of the hated Venetians, especially during the latter part of Paul II's reign when Lucas was rising steadily in Charles the Bold's esteem and when Paul II's hostility to Milan was reflected in his friendly attitude towards Burgundy.

The death of Paul II and the election of Sixtus IV weakened Lucas's position. He was recalled to Rome at either the end of 1471 or the beginning of 1472, ostensibly for discussions about the alum monopoly but probably also, we may surmise, in order that the new pope might apprise himself of the value of a legate appointed by his Venetian predecessor. For the time being at least, the pope must have been satisfied, and Lucas had arrived back at the Burgundian court by the second half of March 1472.[13] But while his acceptability to Charles remained undiminished, his credit in Rome declined. The ground was cut from under his feet not only by the deterioration in papal–Burgundian relations caused by the actions of Sixtus IV and his legates, which Lucas was powerless to prevent, but also by the insidious and sometimes outright hostility towards him of two pro-Milanese legates, Pietro Aliprandi and Andrea dei Spiriti of Viterbo. Aliprandi, *nuncius apostolicus Anglie*, arrived in Flanders from England towards the end of 1472, and his letters to the duke of Milan at that time accused Lucas not only of neglecting papal interests — as a result, he alleged, of Lucas being in receipt of a pension from both the duke of Burgundy and the Venetians (who had recently made an alliance with Charles) — but also of positively harming them, by encouraging the duke's intransigent attitude towards Rome. Consequently, in order to remedy the situation, he urged Galeazzo Maria to use his influence at the curia to secure Lucas's recall and his replacement as legate at the Burgundian court by Aliprandi himself.[14]

This denigration was continued by Andrea dei Spiriti (or de Spiritibus), who travelled to the French and Burgundian courts in the spring and summer of 1473. Andrea quoted Charles as having said (during their meeting in the Burgundian camp outside Nijmegen in July 1473) that Sixtus had his detractors even among the clergy, and he reported that Charles, when asked to be more specific, had pointed to Lucas, who was then in the room with them. Moreover, as a friend of Galeazzo Maria, Andrea was worried by the dangers which would face Rome and Milan if Charles's forthcoming interview with the emperor proved successful; he accused Lucas of being the prime mover behind this scheme, motivated, he claimed, by hopes of future rewards from the Venetians and the duke of Burgundy.[15] It may be, of course, that the embattled legate gave the appearance of neglecting his duty, whether because he genuinely had his doubts about the course of papal policy towards Burgundy or because his Venetian sympathies, together perhaps with an unmistakable admiration of the duke, clouded his judgement. Lucas himself, however, protested that he had always done his best, and in a letter written, significantly, just two months after Andrea dei Spiriti's stormy visit, he asked the pope to pay no heed to his rivals and detractors.[16] But by this time it was being said in Rome that Sixtus himself had formed a poor opinion of the legate for being Venetian in his outlook, and the Milanese representative in Rome was instructed to exploit these suspicions and ensure that Sixtus had Lucas replaced by someone more reliable.[17] By the spring of 1474 this concerted opposition seems to have achieved its aim. Lucas left for Italy probably not long after Charles had signed letters of credence, at Vesoul on 23 March, addressed on Lucas's behalf to Cardinal Francesco Gonzaga, who, on 9 May, wrote from Rome to his father, the marquis of Mantua, to report that Lucas had just visited him that day.[18] The letters of credence complained that Lucas was being persecuted by enemies in Rome simply because he was inclined in the duke of Burgundy's favour. In view of all this, it seems likely that the legate's return took place under the shadow of disgrace. It seems probable also that Pietro Aliprandi fulfilled his desire to replace Lucas; he was described by the Milanese chancellor towards the end of 1473 as 'oratore del papa in Borgogna' and, after returning to Rome in September 1474, he was again at the Burgundian court in the summer of the following year.[19]

By the treaty of Moncalieri in January 1475 the duke of Milan crossed from the French to the Burgundian camp, and this change of sides was reflected by Sixtus IV in a far more friendly attitude towards Charles than he had displayed for the past three and a half years. Galeazzo Maria now instructed his agents in Rome to help rather than hinder Burgundian requests to the pope. The return to the Burgundian court in the spring of 1476 of Lucas de Tolentis, who was so much *persona grata* there, was a clear sign of this new outlook. At the same time, the activities of the papal legates in Germany and France in mediating in disputes involving Charles the Bold tended to facilitate rather than obstruct his plans. Papal blessings seemed to flow right up to the end of his reign; for example, it was on 1 December 1476 that Lucas issued at Antwerp the dispensation necessary for the fateful marriage between Mary of Burgundy and Maximilian of Austria.[20]

On the other hand, Sixtus seems never to have been fully reconciled to Burgundy, even after the treaty of Moncalieri. The favourable attitude of his legates towards Charles should not necessarily be taken as a faithful reflection of that of their master; for example, despite the grant of a dispensation for the marriage between Mary and Maximilian, the attitude of the pope himself is unclear. Perhaps a truer guide to his feelings is offered by the letter he wrote to Lucas on 28 December 1476 in which he declared himself most willing to satisfy the duke's wishes but regretted that in his recent creation of cardinals he had once again been unable to grant the red hat to the duke's nominee, Ferry de Clugny.[21] Moreover, as far as Italy was concerned, the pope shared the growing alarm of Galeazzo Maria in 1476 that Italy, and particularly Milan, were gravely threatened by Charles and by Louis XI. The dispatches sent from Rome by the Milanese ambassador give a clear picture of the pope's fears not only on his Milanese friend's account but also on his own. He was afraid lest the peace of Italy and the authority of the Holy See should fall victim to a reconciliation between the king of France and the duke of Burgundy, but he was alarmed also that Charles might attempt an expedition across the Alps even without the help or compliance of Louis XI. It is not without interest to find him talking in the language of an as-yet rudimentary Italian nationalism, if such a term may be used; he spoke of the natural opposition between Italians and ultramontanes and called for the rulers of the peninsula to stand together against the common foe.[22] As for Charles himself, Sixtus predicted as early as November 1476 that the duke's ambition and cruelty would lead him to disaster.[23]

Papal dispensations and Charles the Bold's marital policy

At this period marriages within at least the first four degrees of consanguinity were forbidden by canon law, although exemptions could be obtained from Rome; and, since so many of Europe's ruling houses were interrelated to some extent, special permission was not infrequently required. But because, at the same time, many of these marriages were designed to further policies of princely dynasticism, papal grants of the necessary dispensations could have far-reaching diplomatic repercussions, and this made it difficult for successive popes to preserve the appearance of neutrality amid the political struggles and rivalries of their time. This was particularly true of the later Middle Ages when dynasties such as the Habsburgs raised marital diplomacy to the level of a fine art; but the history of Valois Burgundy provides similar illustrations, a good example being Urban V in 1369 granting a dispensation for the marriage between the first duke, Philip the Bold, and the Flemish heiress Margaret of Male, while refusing a dispensation for a marriage between Margaret and Philip's rival for her hand, Edward III's son Edmund Langley.[24]

Charles himself became aware of this particular papal prerogative quite early in his reign, when he sought to marry Edward IV's sister Margaret, a match which was designed to cement previous treaties of friendship with England and to bolster Burgundy against France. Negotiations had proceeded fitfully for several years but were speeded up with Charles the Bold's accession in June 1467, and by October that year sufficient progress had been made for the duke to write to Paul II requesting the dispensation required by his and Margaret's consanguinity.[25] For the next few months, however, there was deadlock. Louis XI, naturally, was aware of the dangers posed by the projected marriage. His requests to both Edward and Charles not to go ahead with it fell on deaf ears, but at the same time he took more positive action in sending envoys to Rome to prevent the dispensation being granted by deploying the argument that the Franco–Burgundian treaty of Arras, made in 1435, forbade any separate Burgundian dealings with England which had not been approved by the king of France. He also asked the duke of Milan and, less successfully, the king of Naples to use their influence in Rome on his behalf.[26]

These intrigues, though unsuccessful, did cause delay, which in turn caused some friction between Charles and Edward. Another delay may have been the work of the pope himself. Shortly before the marriage treaty was concluded on 16 February 1468, Charles had been informed of Paul II's intention to satisfy his requirements, but it was not until 17 May that the dispensation was finally granted at Westminster by the papal legate in England, Dr Stefano Trenta (or Trento), bishop of Lucca.[27] This timing suggests that Paul's delay may have been deliberate, in order to put pressure on Charles, and the most probable aim of such pressure was to obtain the duke's agreement to a monopoly in his lands for papal alum; this agreement was reached on 5 May although not confirmed by the duke until 24 June.[28] Still, the marriage could now go ahead, being celebrated on 3 July and representing a considerable diplomatic triumph. But had the pope in question been Sixtus IV rather than Paul II, the outcome might well have been different.

The marriage which took place in 1470 between the duke's illegitimate half-sister Anne and his cousin Adolf of Cleves, lord of Ravenstein, was a continuation of the marriage policy which had enabled his Valois predecessors to extend their influence over the neighbouring duchy of Cleves.[29] This was, again, a marriage with political overtones. But it has not previously been noticed that this time too a papal dispensation was required; and that, as in 1468, the duke's good relations with Paul II enabled him to achieve his objective. His councillor Guillaume de Rochefort had asked for papal approval when he had been in Rome on various matters of ducal business in the early summer of 1469. Paul wrote to Charles on 18 October expressing a willingness to satisfy his requests. But on the same day he wrote to Lucas de Tolentis instructing him to impress on the duke the magnitude of this favour, for, he said, previous popes had seldom permitted marriages of couples related in the second degree; on this occasion, however, he had decided to make an exception in view of the devotion to Rome and the crusading cause shown by the duke and his predecessors. Nonetheless, he wanted something in return and made it clear to Lucas that he expected the alum agreement concluded in the previous year to be implemented more effectively in future.[30]

Of all the projects connected with the duke's marital diplomacy it was the matrimonial prospects of his daughter and heiress Mary (born on 13 February 1457) that lay closest to his heart. For much of his reign, though, he was less interested in finding Mary a husband than in gaining political advantage from the numerous princes who bid for her hand: a policy, as Louis XI described it, of trading.[31]

Few of these schemes reached such an advanced stage that an application for the usually necessary papal dispensation was called for, but the suit made by Louis XI's brother Charles proved to be an exception. It illustrates perfectly both the duke of Burgundy's calculating use of his daughter as an instrument of policy and the political embarrassment which requests for dispensations could cause the Holy See. The political importance of Charles of France lay in the fact that he was Louis XI's heir-apparent until the birth of the future Charles VIII on 30 June 1470; and even afterwards, since the dauphin was a sickly child who might not, it seemed, survive to adulthood (like two earlier sons born to Louis), and because Charles of France was both a natural focus of loyalty for the dissident French princes and a man of weak character easily influenced by others, it was vital for Louis to control his brother's actions. The suggestion of a match between Charles of France and Mary of Burgundy seems to have originated on the Burgundian side. The duke sent an embassy to Charles of France in October 1469; it was, however, unsuccessful. His sincerity at this time is difficult to assess but it is certain that the overture was prompted largely by his desperate need for allies against the anti-Burgundian coalition then being engineered by Louis XI. It may be also that he hoped to divert the attention of Charles of France away from the marriage with Juana of Castile, daughter and potential heiress of Henry IV,[32] which Louis had for some time been urging on him. This match could have led to the dominance of French influence in the Iberian peninsula. It would without doubt have been detrimental to the duke's ally (since February 1469), King John II of Aragon, and to the prospects of John's son Ferdinand, who hoped to unite the kingdoms of Aragon and Castile through his marriage, on 17 October 1469, to Henry IV's sister Isabel.[33]

The project re-emerged in the early months of 1471 during and after the brief war between Louis XI and Charles the Bold. Philippe de Commynes' view that Charles of France urged his royal brother to start this war, in order to force the duke of Burgundy to give him his daughter in marriage, is highly suspect. In fact, it was the duke who took the initiative, by reviving his earlier offers in order to exploit the growing division already apparent between the king and his brother and thus to break the most important link in the circle of the king's allies, which recently had almost enabled Louis to inflict on him a decisive defeat. On this occasion, the duke was certainly insincere, for he was simultaneously offering Mary's hand to Duke Nicholas of Lorraine; moreover, in the autumn he showed himself not averse in principle to accepting a peace treaty with the king, one of whose major conditions was that he should have nothing to do with a match between Mary and Louis' brother. By now, however, the project was virtually dead anyway. In the summer Charles had sent envoys to Rome to request both a dispensation and his release from oaths sworn in 1469, under duress, that he would renounce the Burgundian match. As might have been expected, Louis too sent envoys to persuade the pope to refuse. These rival pressures resulted in papal inaction, which suited Louis' purposes, and the king's worries were effectively ended by the death of Paul II in July 1471 and his succession in August by the more amenable Sixtus IV.

The most persistent of these schemes revolving around Mary of Burgundy was the match between her and Maximilian of Austria, son of Emperor Frederick III. Maximilian was, by rank at least, the most splendid suitor available — although others wielded more effective power — and it was through some sort of arrangement with Frederick that Charles the Bold hoped to realise his own imperial ambitions by being accepted as King of the Romans after Frederick's death. The first time negotiations reached such a stage as to involve Rome was in 1469 when Paul II seemed to favour a match between Mary and Maximilian — second cousins, sharing a common great-grandfather in King John I of Portugal, father of Mary's grandmother Isabel of Portugal and grandfather of Maximilian's mother Eleonore of Portugal — as a means of obtaining Burgundian support in Italian affairs.[34] By the autumn of 1473 the prospect of an imperial–Burgundian marriage seemed even closer when Charles arranged to meet Frederick at Trier. This time, however, the pope was Sixtus IV. Before Charles left the recently conquered duchy of Guelders in the summer of 1473, he had asked the pope to appoint the newly promoted Burgundian cardinal, Philibert Hugonet, as legate *a latere* for the meeting at Trier in case it should prove necessary to issue a dispensation on the spot. Sixtus refused on the grounds that such a marriage was neither in his interests nor in those of the duke of Milan and the king of France. In an attempt at compromise, Charles's Venetian allies proposed Marco Barbo, cardinal of San Marco, as a candidate for the office of legate, but he too was rejected.[35]

After the failure of the Trier summit, the imperial–Burgundian marriage project did not re-emerge until the middle of 1475, but thereafter Charles made firmer commitments to Maximilian than he ever gave to any other suitor, including Don Federico, son of the king of Naples, who was then at his court.[36] The marital negotiations proceeded step by step with the re-establishment of amity between the duke and the emperor. It may have been at the time of the truce ending the siege of Neuss at the end of May 1475 that Charles gave the emperor his oral agreement to the marriage;[37] and henceforward Frederick, who was now as eager for the match as was the duke, badgered him to keep his word. The truce was enlarged into a perpetual peace treaty on 17 November 1475 and at this time Charles committed his promises to paper. The peace treaty was not formally proclaimed by him until 14 April 1476, but shortly afterwards, on 6 May, he signed the treaty of engagement between Mary and Maximilian. The marriage was scheduled to be celebrated in November but in the event it did not take place until after Charles the Bold's death.

Yet it is difficult to discover the attitude of the pope himself at this decisive juncture. The improvement in relations between Charles and the emperor which led to the marriage alliance had been considerably facilitated by the papal legate in Germany, the bishop of Forlì. The restoration of peace to such a substantial area of Christendom must have been welcome to Sixtus IV, yet there is no evidence that he directly encouraged the bishop's subsequent efforts. The same problem arises in attempting to ascertain his views on the marriage itself. Again, it was a legate, Lucas de Tolentis, rather than Sixtus himself, who expedited matters by issuing on 1 December 1476 a dispensation that the pope confirmed on New Year's Day 1477.[38] In this respect it may be significant that, according to the wording of the document itself, the legate had made no prior reference to his superior before issuing it. Moreover, none of the Italian diplomatic correspondence surviving from the period embracing the last months of the duke's life which the author has consulted so much as hints at any diplomatic activity being undertaken in Rome by either of the interested parties; this silence is all the more striking when one recalls the amount of evidence surviving on the intrigues at the curia in 1467–1468 and 1471–1472 over the marriages of, respectively, Charles the Bold and Charles of France. Sixtus may perhaps have found himself faced with a *fait accompli* which would have been both difficult and embarrassing to disown; but it does also seem reasonable to refrain from concluding that the pope, in confirming a dispensation which was on purely technical grounds unobjectionable, was in any way consciously promoting the Burgundian cause.

Papal mediation in disputes

The popes had traditionally been looked to as the ultimate arbiters of quarrels between Christian princes, but the pressure on them to act as peacemakers increased sharply during the fifteenth century when a united Christian front came to be seen as the *sine qua non* for successful resistance against the advancing Turks. Because of the frequency of Charles the Bold's wars in France and the Empire and the wide areas of western Europe affected by them, the number of papal legates who travelled to, or had dealings with, the Burgundian court during his reign was comparatively high. These legates were Stefano Nardini, archbishop of Milan, and Onofrio di Santa Croce (or Onofrio Santacroce), bishop of Tricarico, who were required to deal with the affairs of France and Liège in 1467 and 1468; Cardinal Basil Bessarion and Andrea dei Spiriti, who attempted to make peace between France and Burgundy in 1472 and 1473; Niccolò Sandonnino, bishop of Modena, and Cardinal Giuliano della Rovere, whose business in France in 1475 and 1476 brought them into contact also with Charles the Bold; and Alessandro Nanni (or Numai), bishop of Forlì, who as legate *ad partes Germaniae* was instrumental in reconciling the duke and the emperor in 1475 and 1476. Nor should we overlook Lucas de Tolentis, resident legate in the Low Countries for the bulk of the duke's reign.

Of all the Italian diplomats who appeared at the court of Charles the Bold, one can most readily sympathise with these papal legates. Unlike their colleagues — the representatives of lay powers, who, at that time, were usually sent for protracted periods only to those ultramontane rulers who were already at least friends, if not allies of their masters — legates could not be sure of their reception, and, if they were welcomed by one of the parties to a dispute, this did not necessarily hold good for the other; indeed, a warm reception by one of the parties could ensure for the legate a cool reception or even none at all by the other. Moreover, the legate had few diplomatic weapons at his disposal other than moral pressure and exhortations, which seldom proved sufficient. The main problem, however, was simply the intractability of the disputes themselves, and the popes in Rome, the legates often felt, frequently failed to appreciate fully the difficulties they faced. As a result, the effects of papal mediation were slight and virtually no legate returned to Italy with his reputation enhanced.

As far as Charles the Bold was concerned, few legates were able to persuade him that peace was desirable in itself, for he tended to raise objections to, or place conditions on, their initial proposals. In the winter of 1467–1468 his opposition to the peace suggested by Nardini seems to have been based on a suspicion that it might merely allow Louis XI a free hand against his enemies and the duke's allies while preventing Charles from intervening. Onofrio's desire to arrange a peaceful settlement at

Liège in 1468 ran counter to the duke's intention to enforce his own solution there, if necessary by military means. The mediation of Bessarion and Spiriti in 1472 and 1473 was rejected by Charles because he was not prepared to ratify a *status quo* which accepted Louis XI's seizure in 1471 of the important towns of Saint-Quentin and Amiens; he refused to lay down his arms permanently until they were restored.

Nor did he regard legates as impartial merely because they represented the Holy See. He suspected Nardini, Bessarion and Spiriti of pro-Milanese or pro-French sympathies, if not both, and he reposed real confidence only in Tolentis and Nanni. Moreover, he repudiated Rome's conception of the conflict between himself and Louis XI as one between a fractious prince and his liege lord; on the contrary, he justified his wars in France as based on natural justice and the right of self-defence against an incorrigible intriguer. What he regarded as the papacy's misconception of the true state of affairs resulted in legates visiting the French court before they visited his. He objected to this too, not only because he suspected the legates would be misled by propaganda but also because he felt the status he claimed as a prince independent of and equal to the French king was thereby brought into question. Only in the last years of his reign did Charles take a less jaundiced view. Nanni's legation in Germany enabled him to extract himself with honour from the siege of Neuss, to make a settlement with the emperor by which Frederick promised not to hinder his planned campaigns against the duke of Lorraine and the Swiss, and to achieve a reconciliation subsequently which was to blossom into an alliance based on the projected marriage of Mary and Maximilian. In addition, he was able to exploit the quarrel between Sixtus and Louis in the spring of 1476 over the legation to the papal enclave of Avignon and other matters, almost to the point of establishing a Burgundian protectorate over the city, which could also have furthered his plans to secure the legacy of Provence from King René. But these later events should not blind us to what had gone before, and it is certainly a mistake to regard Sixtus as having favoured the Burgundian cause all along;[39] even five years after the duke's death, Sixtus was accused by the conciliarists of having stirred up war between Louis and Charles.

The first of the legates was Stefano Nardini, archbishop of Milan. He had arrived in France in April 1467 empowered to collect a papal tithe, to discuss the Pragmatic Sanction of Bourges (which had been regarded as an infringement of papal rights ever since it had been formulated in the conciliarist climate of 1438), and to try to make a lasting peace between the king and the princes — especially the dukes of Burgundy,

Berry and Brittany — and between the duke of Burgundy and the bishop and city of Liège.[40] According to the chronicler Chastellain, Louis had detained the legate for some months in France, apparently for fear of possible intrigues with the duke of Burgundy, but then, when he saw that Charles might make some significant gains in his conflict with Liège, which had previously been offered French protection, he allowed him to go to the Burgundian court in an attempt to mediate and, in effect, to delay the duke through procrastination. Nardini arrived in Brussels in October 1467, the day after Cardinal Jean Balue, who came as Louis's emissary. By this time, however, the duke entertained the gravest doubts about his impartiality. The long delay between his arrival in France and his departure for the Low Countries made him suspect the legate of French sympathies, and he regarded him as more the king's agent than the pope's. He also distrusted his connection with Milan. Above all, he was suspicious of anything that might deflect him from his planned campaign against Liège. At first he refused to receive the legate and told him to consult instead with his officials, but soon relented and granted an audience at Louvain. Nardini, conducting himself with much dignity, told the duke his mission was to make peace between him and Charles of France on the one hand and between him and Louis XI on the other; the blame for his failure to come earlier he cast firmly on Louis. Charles replied politely but firmly that he could not talk of such matters until his return from Liège.

There matters apparently rested. Nardini seems to have left before Charles returned from Liège on Christmas Eve.[41] In any case, another papal envoy, Onofrio di Santa Croce, had now been appointed specifically to deal with the Liège problem. Having returned to France, Nardini was able to arrange a settlement between the king and the duke of Brittany in the early months of 1468, and Louis was so pleased that he recommended him to the pope for a red hat. But his subsequent attempts at mediation caused Louis to accuse him of intriguing with his enemies, so that the legate left France in June having been virtually expelled. His failure could not be attributed to incompetence, ambition or deviousness. In fact, rather as in the case of his successor Onofrio, the intractability of the problems he faced was itself the obstacle; a solution was impossible without the full cooperation of all parties concerned and this was never forthcoming. The mutual distrust between Louis and Charles prevented him enjoying the confidence of both simultaneously and, as it transpired, he came to be viewed by each of them as partial to the other; he was not to be the last papal envoy who suffered this fate.

He was surely glad to leave the troubled affairs of Liège to his successor; they had, after all, defied a lasting solution for over half a century.[42] The geographical position of this ecclesiastical principality — almost completely surrounded by Burgundian territories and lying across the route between the Burgundian Low Countries and the Rhine — had inevitably led to disputes with earlier Valois dukes; and the conflicts usual in such cases between the ecclesiastical rulers and their subjects had provided an opportunity for neighbours, especially the dukes of Burgundy and the kings of France, to interfere. The installation in Liège as bishop of Louis de Bourbon in 1465 was a clear attempt by Philip the Good to impose his rule on the city and territory through a young and weak relative (his nephew) who might be expected to act as a Burgundian agent. Louis's role, however, was not accepted by powerful sections of his subjects and the ensuing conflicts only resulted, after open warfare in which Burgundian forces participated and despite the attempts of Louis XI to intervene at the request of the dissidents, in an increase of Burgundian influence. It was as a result of Philip the Good's request to Paul II for a legate to be sent to ratify the treaty of Saint-Trond of 22 December 1465, which appointed the duke hereditary protector of the city and principality of Liège, that Onofrio di Santa Croce, bishop of Tricarico, was sent to the Low Countries. Although he was not sent as legate specifically to Burgundy, it was inevitable that he should have dealings with the duke, for it was the Burgundian claims in Liège which threatened the rights and privileges of the Church that it was Onofrio's job to uphold. Fortunately, we know more about this legation than most because Onofrio wrote his own (unfinished) account to explain and justify his failure to achieve a peaceful settlement.[43] His task was almost impossible. His original mandate was dated 28 August 1467 but by the time he left Rome on 27 February 1468 the situation in Liège had altered significantly. In November 1467 the peace of Saint-Trond had been succeeded by that of Brusthem, imposed on the city by Charles the Bold after a brief military campaign, which stopped not far short of incorporating the principality within the Burgundian state. Onofrio's job now was to persuade Charles to modify the treaty of Brusthem insofar as it infringed the prerogatives of the Church and to reconcile the bishop of Liège with his subjects.

Onofrio arrived in Liège on 30 April 1468, when Nardini was still in France. There can be no doubting either the indefatigable efforts he made over the next six months to bring about a peace acceptable to all, or the compassion he showed in carrying out his task. He travelled repeatedly between Liège and the bishop (who for some time had not dared reside in the city) and he twice visited Charles, in June and August. Nor was he new to the problems of Liège, having accompanied Pedro Ferriz there in 1463 in an earlier attempt at mediation. But he received a severe setback in the return to the city, on 9 September, of the anti-Burgundian exiles (who had fled or been expelled shortly before the treaty of Brusthem), because they now began to prepare for war on the assumption that Charles would soon be otherwise engaged in hostilities with France; they may even have had Louis XI's assistance. The chances of a non-military solution were finally dashed by the Liègeois' attack on a Burgundian force at Tongres (Tongeren) during the night of 9–10 October. Charles was determined to punish what he saw as an outrage and, as a result of undertakings received from Louis XI during their meeting at Péronne which was then in progress, he was able to throw his whole might against Liège without having to worry about the possibility of a French attack in the rear. This marked the total failure of Onofrio's mission, for not only had he been unable to reconcile the bishop with the townspeople and protect the rights of the Church but also he had failed to halt this new Burgundian campaign which ended in the sack of Liège and the virtual annexation of the principality by Charles the Bold.

Philippe de Commynes' assertion that Onofrio — allegedly motivated by an ambition to replace Louis de Bourbon as bishop — actually hindered a peaceful solution by stirring up the Liègeois against Charles has long been discredited.[44] In fact Guillaume Fichet, writing to Cardinal Bessarion in March 1472 that legates to 'Gallia' needed to be free from avarice and ambition and that too many in the past had ignored this, regarded the bishop of Tricarico as a shining exception and stated that, for his abstinence from these vices, he was revered in France to that day.[45] Nonetheless, Onofrio does reveal in his apologia characteristics which may not have made him the ideal man for the job. Although in the exordium he professed to have forsaken elegance in the interests of truth and clarity, his subsequent text rather belies this. There is undoubtedly an element of self-dramatisation in the narrative, which is written in the Caesarean third person singular and which has a further Caesarean characteristic: a neglect of specific dates. We are given to believe that his speeches were so eloquent that audiences were moved to tears, attributing the power of his words to divine inspiration. His clear predilection for facetious irony was probably less endearing than irritating to those with whom he had to deal; but a more important disadvantage must have been the fact that he could not speak French.[46]

Basically, though, the root of the problem lay elsewhere, in the objective circumstances of the conflict. In this sense, Onofrio's fate illustrates perfectly the difficulties experienced by all the legates called on to mediate in quarrels involving Charles the Bold. Onofrio had too many conflicting parties to bring together. Although some Liègeois were prepared to meet the duke halfway, provided the most objectionable parts of the treaty of Brusthem were amended, events soon gave the initiative to the hardliners who would have been satisfied only by the eradication of all traces of Burgundian rule. As for the bishop of Liège, he showed himself willing at times to acquiesce in the legate's efforts but in general he was too indecisive, or perhaps he was too frightened of the duke of Burgundy, to reject openly the treaty of Brusthem. Finally, the attitude of Charles himself, which was the decisive factor, was one averse to compromise. He put pressure on Louis de Bourbon not to return to Liège, since a reconciliation between the bishop and his flock would have removed the main reason, or excuse, for Burgundian intervention; at the same time he insisted that the treaty of Brusthem was not to be renegotiated and that Louis accept it in its entirety. In the event, it has been said, Onofrio's efforts served only to hinder effective resistance by the Liègois to Charles.[47] He returned to Rome early in 1469 only to find that Paul II refused to receive him, apparently believing that the legate alone was responsible for the unhappy outcome to events at Liège; possibly the pope had already been influenced against him by the Burgundian version of those events. It was in order to remedy this injustice, as he saw it, that Onofrio set about dictating his own account. Unfortunately Paul died before the work was completed, and although his successor Sixtus IV showed more sympathy, Onofrio died a broken man shortly afterwards, in Rome on 20 October 1471, before he could clear his name.

In contrast with Liège, the duchy of Guelders gave an instance of how cooperation between Burgundian and papal policy was possible.[48] In September 1470 Paul II wrote to Charles urging him to intercede for the release of Duke Arnold of Guelders with Arnold's son Adolf, who was holding his father captive. Prompted but not motivated solely by this letter, Charles did intercede; more effectively, he sent a body of his troops to Guelders in January 1471 to release the duke and bring him to Hesdin. Shortly afterwards, it was Adolf's turn to be imprisoned, by Charles, so that Duke Arnold was able to return to Guelders as ruler. Thereafter Charles turned the situation to his own advantage. In his will made three days before his death on 23 February 1473 Arnold named Charles his heir; Charles made good this claim against the supporters of

Adolf by armed force in the summer; and Adolf was not released until after the duke's death in 1477. In this case no special emissary was sent from Rome, matters being dealt with on behalf of the Holy See by the resident legate, Lucas de Tolentis. Lucas had earlier been empowered by Paul II to intervene in the neighbouring region of Utrecht between Bishop David, Charles the Bold's natural half-brother, and his rival Gijsbrecht van Brederode, but his exact role is unclear.[49]

As for peace between Burgundy and France, several years passed after the legation of Stefano Nardini before another attempt was made. Just before Christmas 1471 Sixtus IV held a secret consistory in which five special legates were chosen to bring peace to the most troubled areas of Christendom and, at the same time, to promote the crusade against the Turks (their conquest in 1470 of the Venetian stronghold of Negroponte (Khalkís) in Euboea having aroused almost as much of a stir as the fall of Constantinople in 1453, particularly in Italy, where fears now grew of a possible Turkish landing). The legate chosen to go to France and Burgundy was himself an exile from the east (born in Trebizond) and a lifelong Turcophobe, Cardinal Basil Bessarion.[50] The pope's hopes for a settlement were impossibly high. He wrote to Charles on 16 March 1472 urging him to lay down his arms (in fact a truce was already in force) and negotiate with Louis XI so that, when Bessarion arrived, the legate would have no more to do than confirm a treaty already made.[51] Bessarion, however, did not leave Rome until the second half of May, and by the time he arrived in Lyon about a month later Charles had already declared war on Louis.

The renewal of hostilities after more than twelve months of truces made Bessarion's task more difficult but not impossible, for in the negotiations conducted intermittently with Louis since the ceasefire of April 1471 Charles had not been totally averse to the idea of a long-term settlement with the king.[52] But he insisted on the restoration of Amiens and Saint-Quentin, seized by the French in January 1471, before he would agree to serious talks.[53] Moreover, he wanted the pope to provide firm guarantees against what he had come to regard as Louis's wilful perfidy. His list of grievances against the king, on which he expatiated to Lucas de Tolentis, stretched back to the years following Louis' accession in 1461, when, according to the duke, the king had shown nothing but ingratitude for the favours showered on him at the Burgundian court by Philip the Good during his self-imposed exile from France. Since then, Charles claimed, Louis had tried to turn Philip against him when he was still count of Charolais and to seduce those around him, and had even attempted to procure the assassination of his friends. He accused Louis of stirring up the towns of Dinant and Liège against him; of unjustly depriving his own brother, Charles of France, of the duchy of Normandy; of shamelessly breaking the treaty of Péronne, particularly by his seizure of Saint-Quentin and Amiens, whose earlier cession to Burgundy had been confirmed by that treaty; of trying to force the duke of Brittany to renounce his alliance with Burgundy; of intriguing against Charles's brother-in-law Edward IV; and, finally, of causing the death of Charles of France, this being the duke's immediate *casus belli* in June 1472.

Moreover, if he was suspicious of Louis's trustworthiness, he was also far from certain of Bessarion's impartiality. He felt insulted by the legate's omission to inform him of his appointment in writing. He claimed that Bessarion wrote to him only once during the time he spent in France. He disliked the warmth of the reception which Louis initially gave him; in his opinion, this meant that Bessarion had become the king's creature, and he refused to consider even a truce unless the legate at least did him the courtesy of coming to see him first in order to convince him otherwise; but in fact Bessarion never did visit the Burgundian court. The duke's fears regarding Bessarion's supposedly pro-French attitude were not ungrounded. Bessarion himself had at one stage urged his appointment as legate to France because, he said, he believed he would be acceptable to the king, while Louis had apparently welcomed his appointment at first and had written to him to hasten his departure from Rome. Gradually, however, Louis's attitude changed. He had wanted a peace with Burgundy in order to be able to concentrate his forces against Charles of France, but his brother's death in May enabled him to recover Guienne without making any concessions to the duke. It also eased the pressure on him in another way because, by ending the possibility of a marriage between Charles of France and Mary of Burgundy, it made it less necessary for him to be conciliatory towards Rome to prevent the grant of the dispensation which his brother had not given up hopes of obtaining. Bessarion did not arrive in Lyon until the latter part of June and by now Louis was reluctant to discuss the Pragmatic Sanction of Bourges and the legation of Avignon to which his mission was also related. Above all, the king was displeased by the legate's attitude towards Charles the Bold. He complained that Bessarion's household was full of Burgundians and refused to grant him an audience until the last week of August. He was angered too when the legate refused his plea to excommunicate the dukes of Burgundy and Brittany as a means of forcing them to make peace.[54]

Thus Bessarion now found himself (as, before him, had Nardini) in the unenviable position of being suspected by each party of inclining towards the other. His mission came to a premature end. He probably left France in the second half of September; to the displeasure of Charles and Louis he now added that of Sixtus IV, who had not given him permission to return. Back in Italy, he was overtaken by fatigue, illness and old age and died at Ravenna on 18 November. By way of an epitaph, a contemporary noted that he had gone to France with his reputation high but had returned with it sadly diminished because of the failure of his legation, though this was attributable, the writer thought, mostly to the ill-will and fickleness of Louis XI.[55]

Even before Bessarion's death Sixtus had, towards the middle of October, appointed his successor, Guillaume d'Estouteville, cardinal-bishop of Rouen. A choice less acceptable to Charles could hardly have been made, for he was a subject of, and on good terms with, the king of France. Edward IV was no less irritated, for he had just formally rendered his obedience to the pope and now saw him displaying openly his sympathy for Louis. When the news reached Charles, he furiously threatened to end the papal alum monopoly in his lands and made dark hints about taking his complaints against Sixtus before a general council of the Church, a move then considered as the ultimate sanction against Rome.[56]

Whether from a genuine desire to further the crusade or in an attempt to please Louis, Sixtus continued with his efforts at mediation; and, if he allowed d'Estouteville's appointment in effect to be quashed by Burgundian resistance, his choice for d'Estouteville's successor, the Viterbese protonotary apostolic, Andrea dei Spiriti, was to prove even less acceptable to Charles, for this legation culminated in the fulmination against him of a bull of excommunication.[57] Andrea was appointed legate to France and Burgundy in January 1473. To help him in his task, he was granted a power none of his predecessors had enjoyed, namely the power to excommunicate any of the French princes who refused his call to make peace; but this did not apply to Louis, significantly. He arrived at the French court in May 1473 and quickly entered the king's good graces because Louis thought he could use him for his own ends. Louis was as keen as ever for a lasting settlement with Burgundy, because the repeatedly renewed but short truces which were all Charles had consented to since April 1471 had allowed him no peace of mind, while, conversely, they had permitted his adversary to build up his own military, diplomatic and territorial power against France. At this time Louis particularly wanted security on his northern borders so that he could safely turn his attention to the pressing problems of the South, where the king of Aragon was striving to regain the counties of Cerdaña and Roussillon mortgaged to France a decade earlier. Andrea seems to have been predisposed towards Louis by his Milanese sympathies.[58] Moreover, the pope too was now more inclined towards France because the concordat agreed in August 1472 had settled many of their outstanding differences, while the alum agreement with Burgundy, which had once been a similar means of gaining favour, had already fallen into desuetude before it was actually abrogated by the duke in the summer of 1473.

Andrea visited Charles in the Burgundian camp outside Nijmegen on 3 July. What happened next was described by him to the Milanese ambassador in France after his return. Four times the duke refused to receive him and, when at last he did, it was in a public audience, not in private as requested; this distinction was important because the duke then publicly humiliated him by saying he regarded him as the envoy not of the pope but of Louis XI. The account of the resident legate in the Low Countries, however, is significantly different. Lucas de Tolentis wrote to the pope a month later that through his good offices Andrea had quickly obtained an audience and that, to start with, the duke had listened to him respectfully. But all this changed when Andrea produced a *breve monitionis*. Nothing is known about the exact wording of this document, which has not itself survived; but although, as we shall see shortly, Charles later stated that the legate had not mentioned possessing such authority, the *breve* was presumably a strongly worded admonition to the duke to lay down his arms, on pain of excommunication. Or perhaps Andrea merely referred to his power to excommunicate in such circumstances, even if he did not flourish the instrument itself. The duke at once lost his temper and it was all Lucas could do to calm him down. Charles then said he wanted the restoration of all that Louis had seized from him by force or fraud, an unmistakable reference to Saint-Quentin and Amiens. He had already, he said, renewed his truces for a year (in March 1473) at the request both of his allies and of the king, and he did not intend to prolong them. But if the pope really wanted peace, then there were two methods: either Charles would send ambassadors to Rome to argue his case, or, if the pope wished the duke himself to go before him, then he was willing to do so. The audience ended with some desultory verbal skirmishes about the papal alum agreement and the duke's request for the creation of one or two Burgundian cardinals.

After the legate's return to France, Charles apparently heard nothing further until Andrea issued his bull of excommunication from Cléry in

Orléannais on 13 October. The view later gained credence in Rome that the excommunication was the culmination of a plot hatched between Andrea, Louis XI and Pietro Riario, the pro-Milanese (his brother had recently wed a natural daughter of Galeazzo Maria) cardinal of San Sisto and influential nephew of the pope himself;[59] the plot had been kept secret from the cardinals and even from Sixtus IV. This interpretation of events has been accepted by historians,[60] and it is a fact, as we saw earlier, that Louis was reported to have urged Bessarion in 1472 to force the dukes of Burgundy and Brittany to lay down their arms by the threat of excommunication. But in 1473 the influence of other factors should not be overlooked. Andrea may not have seriously considered using his power to excommunicate when he first arrived at the Burgundian court, but his impression of the duke, whose ambition and pride he felt to be a danger equally to Louis, Galeazzo Maria and Sixtus IV, possibly convinced him that he had to restrain him by extreme measures. Whatever did actually happen at this audience, it is clear that the legate came away feeling both humiliated and angry. Moreover, there was unmistakably some personal friction or rivalry between the two legates. Lucas resented Andrea's clumsy performance because he was the one left with the task of dissuading the duke from a view to which he was then increasingly inclined, namely that Sixtus IV was hostile to him and favourable to his enemies; for Lucas, Andrea's behaviour had destroyed the work of months. Andrea, on the other hand, felt that the resident legate was not only failing to uphold papal interests through being too close to the duke but was also actually encouraging him.[61]

Charles did not rush his counter-attack. He had his appeal against excommunication drawn up in Latin during a three weeks' visit he paid to Dijon in January and February 1474. Dated 8 February, it was read, published and registered in the Parlement of Dijon three days later, in the presence of Lucas de Tolentis and Louis de Bourbon, bishop of Liège.[62] The wording was reasonable yet forceful. As a preamble Charles lamented the spiritual harm the excommunication would cause his subjects and argued that at this time the need for Christian unity should take precedence over Louis XI's vendettas. He then explained why he had not made a long-term peace with the king. His wars in France, he said, were purely defensive in view of Louis' part in the brief deposition of Edward IV and his seizure of the Burgundian towns of Saint-Quentin and Amiens. He had been on the point of making peace, on his own terms, when Louis murdered (this was now a standard accusation by the king's foes) his brother Charles of France and this had forced him to resume hostilities in 1472. Turning to the activities of papal mediators, he complained that Bessarion had visited neither himself nor his ally the duke of Brittany. He claimed he was right to resist the appointment of d'Estouteville as Bessarion's successor, on the grounds of partiality. As for Andrea, the duke felt he had been too eager to pass judgement rather than simply to assist in the peacemaking process. Charles said that in fact he had wanted peace in the summer of 1473 but only if Louis XI, as the original aggressor, made the first move, preferably by restoring the seized Somme towns. He protested that Andrea — to whom he referred disdainfully as *'levissimus homo quidam de Spiritibus'*[63] — had not mentioned the sanction of excommunication in the event of non-compliance. Indeed, he suggested that the whole affair was a conspiracy between the legate and the king. The legate's temerity gave substance to this theory and he was sure the Holy See could neither have had prior knowledge of nor approved the action Andrea took subsequently. In short, his quarrel was with the legate — and, of course, with Louis XI too — and not by any means with Rome.

This appeal was presented in Rome probably during the second week of March 1474 by Philibert Hugonet.[64] Its submissive and respectful tone made a favourable impression. The suspicion that the excommunication was to some extent a plot by Louis in league with an over-zealous and partisan legate aroused sympathy for the duke and scorn for the king, who was held to have resorted to underhand means because he was afraid to meet his opponent in open warfare. Charles took steps to air his own views in the curia through Lucas de Tolentis, who returned to Rome in the spring and who was then commissioned to solicit the opposition of the Mantuan cardinal, Francesco Gonzaga, to the bull's ratification. Above all, the Roman side of the tripartite conspiracy had by now been gravely weakened by the death in January of Pietro Riario, cardinal of San Sisto, by whom some considered the scheme to have been originally conceived. The pope himself was seriously embarrassed by the whole affair. His authority and that of the Holy See as such had been compromised by Andrea's precipitancy, by the fact that the pope had been kept in the dark over his legate's intentions and by the one-sided and obviously politically motivated manner in which Andrea had fulfilled his commission. Sixtus decided that the excommunication would have to be fully discussed before it could be ratified. A consistory held on 16 March 1474 merely appointed a committee of six cardinals to examine the matter more thoroughly. By the beginning of April the committee concluded that it could go no further until it had heard directly from Louis

XI, to whom a courier was dispatched with all urgency. This effectively shelved the matter for at least a month and in the event the excommunication was never officially registered.

Between now and the end of the duke's reign no further attempts were to be made by papal legates to re-establish harmony between Burgundy and France. When exactly Andrea dei Spiriti left France is not clear,[65] but by the time his successor arrived — Niccolò Sandonnino, bishop of Modena — Charles and Louis had already arranged matters to their own satisfaction by the treaty of Soleuvre dated 13 September 1475,[66] which, designed to last for nine years, brought about the long-term settlement so much desired by successive popes and which remained in force for the rest of the duke's lifetime.

Charles, did, however, follow carefully the course of one other legation to France which took place during this period: that of Giuliano della Rovere, cardinal of San Pietro in Vincoli and another nephew of Sixtus IV, to the papal enclave of Avignon in the first half of 1476.[67] Indeed, so close was his connection with the legate — or, at least, the connection of his agents — that at one stage it seemed possible he might be able, with Giuliano's blessing, to raise the Burgundian flag over the walls of Avignon. By the beginning of 1476 relations between Louis XI and Rome had deteriorated greatly. In January Louis began to make arrangements to summon a general council of the Church and in February he virtually repealed the concordat of 1472. Another indication of his attitude was the gradual encroachment of royal authority in Avignon, which Sixtus suspected him of wishing to annex by degrees, aided by the fact that the legate of the city was Charles de Bourbon, archbishop of Lyon and the king's relative and confidant. On 12 February the pope dismissed Charles de Bourbon and replaced him as legate by Giuliano della Rovere. Giuliano left Rome a week later and arrived in Avignon just after the middle of March. Louis's reaction to Giuliano was predictably one of suspicion. He regarded the bulk of his entourage as partisans of his enemies, the duke of Burgundy and the king of Naples (just as he had objected to Bessarion's companions in 1472). He came to fear that the legate was in league with both King René of Anjou and the duke of Burgundy, and that he was negotiating with these princes in order to resist the French crown. Louis even suspected that the legate would go to the lengths of placing Avignon in Burgundian hands, in order to keep it from falling into French hands, and he interpreted the return to the Burgundian court of Lucas de Tolentis, whose fondness for the duke was well known, as a sign that the pope too was thinking along these lines.[68]

His apprehension, however, was not entirely justified. Sixtus certainly told the Milanese ambassador in Rome that he wanted Lucas to win Burgundian help for Giuliano, but he probably envisaged no more than diplomatic pressure, and he had no intention of actually handing Avignon over to Charles, for he feared him even more than Louis. He knew the possession of Avignon would strengthen the duke in relation to Provence and Savoy, thus making it easier for him to lead an army across the Alps into Italy should he wish to do so, as the pope suspected he did.[69] In fact, the major responsibility for these speculations lay with the legate himself, whose comparative youth (he was born in 1445) and inexperience, and perhaps too the difficulties of his mission and the sheer determined hostility of Louis' reaction to his appointment, led him to act rashly on his own initiative. He maintained close contact with Lucas de Tolentis at the Burgundian court. Lucas was given to understand that, while Sixtus was reluctant to allow Avignon to pass from papal control, he preferred that it should be placed under Burgundian protection rather than that it should be taken over by Louis XI. To this end, Lucas claimed, the pope was prepared to go so far as to help Charles financially against the Swiss, thus enabling him to finish that campaign speedily and turn his attention to Avignon, and to make him Gonfalonier of the Church.[70] It was at this time too, towards the end of April 1476, that Lucas was later said (though the report is not very convincing) to have urged the duke to intervene militarily in Avignon.

Charles by no means rejected such proposals out of hand. His Piedmontese confidant Agostino dei Corradi di Lignana, abbot of Casanova, travelled to see Giuliano in March and possibly again in May. Giuliano told him he would try to visit the Burgundian court because the pope wanted to reach an understanding with him, since he placed more trust in Charles than in any other ruler.[71] By the latter part of April the duke was proposing to send another of the Italians in his entourage, the Venetian Francesco Querini, to Rome in order to obtain confirmation from Sixtus of his legate's suggestion about a Burgundian protectorate of Avignon; Querini was to stop in Milan to ensure that Galeazzo Maria used his strong influence in Rome to prepare a suitable reception for him there.[72] Charles's involvement can be deduced from the remarks he made to the Milanese ambassador at the beginning of April. He did not deny French complaints about Burgundian interference in Avignon but merely declared the complaints unjustified, on the grounds that it was Louis who had interfered first and, before that, had meddled in Burgundian affairs; in any case it was incumbent on him as a Christian prince to help the legate.[73] But the degree of importance which he attached to Avignon is another question. If in 1476 his priority was the defeat of the Swiss, he also maintained many irons in the diplomatic fire at the same time. Viewed in this light, Avignon offered a variety of possibilities, both as a useful territorial acquisition in itself and as assistance to his efforts to obtain Provence. It is significant that Francesco Querini, whom he chose as his envoy to Rome to investigate the proposals made by Giuliano, was also the agent to whom he had for some time been entrusting his negotiations with King René.[74] By the same token, however, the attraction of Avignon as a stepping-stone to Provence was lessened at the beginning of April by King René's submission to Louis XI in Lyon, recognising Louis' claim to Provence after René's death. Moreover, Charles did not in the event bother to send Querini to Rome until the middle of May.[75] It is difficult to say whether the delay should be attributed to the duke's indecision, to a basic lack of interest in Avignon, or to the protests at the choice of Querini by his Milanese ally, who had for some years distrusted the Venetian and who was now reluctant to cooperate with the duke by receiving him at his court for consultations. But the absence of haste suggests that by then he gave a much lower priority to helping Giuliano than he had in March. His selection of Querini was taken by the Milanese ambassador at his court to be a pointer in the same direction, for Charles set no great store by him and was seen to indulge and tolerate, rather than esteem, him.[76]

In any case, the initiative by now lay firmly with Louis XI. Like René of Anjou a little earlier, Giuliano was forced to submit to the king's demands in the first half of May. Charles did not appear greatly upset by the news, although what he considered the legate's feebleness in not having resisted more energetically led him to make some sardonic comments about the ingratitude of priests.[77] The only comfort for him was the disgrace of Andrea dei Spiriti. Andrea had accompanied the legate to France and soon after their arrival had been sent to prepare the legate's reception at court. Instead, he had tried to take advantage of past friendships, and of Louis XI's aversion to Giuliano, to the extent of trying to win the king's support for his own appointment as legate and for his promotion to cardinal. The intrigue was quickly discovered and Andrea was repudiated by both the king and the legate. On hearing the news, Charles laughingly remarked to the Milanese ambassador that Andrea had at last received his just deserts.[78]

The last of the legates to be considered is Alessandro Nanni (or Numai),[79] bishop of Forlì. Alessandro differed from his predecessors in three respects. He was concerned with the duke's affairs in the Empire rather than in France; he was the only legate to win the duke's trust; and, largely as a consequence of this, he did succeed in making peace. At the end of July 1474 Charles laid siege to the town of Neuss near Cologne, and in the archbishopric of that name. The siege, which was to last almost a year, was undertaken initially in order to help his ally, Archbishop Ruprecht of Cologne, who had appointed him his protector, against those who had for several years resisted his authority. But the dispute soon widened to include, on the one hand, those in the Empire who supported the party headed by the duke of Burgundy and by Frederick, count palatine of the Rhine and brother of the archbishop of Cologne; and, on the other, the enemies of this group, plus the friends of the town, chapter and Stift of Cologne. Over the months, moves were made to raise a huge army under the leadership of the emperor, who hoped for French help, in order to march to the defence of Neuss, so that much of the Empire seemed about to be plunged into a major war. It was to avert this that the bishop of Forlì was appointed legate *ad partes Germaniae* by Sixtus IV on 15 February 1475.[80] He first arrived in the Burgundian camp in mid-May and straight away urged the duke to make the peace which the growing Turkish menaced rendered imperative. Charles gave the response customary to him on such occasions. His war was defensive and the emperor should make the first move; as for his Christian duties, he was in fact helping to protect the rights of the Church in standing by the archbishop of Cologne.[81] Yet less than a fortnight after this discouraging start, the legate was able to bring about a truce and a provisional peace treaty designed to last for a year. Contemporaries were unanimous in his praise, regarding him as something of a miracle-worker. But although he showed great diligence and finesse in mediating between the duke and the emperor, it is unlikely that he could have achieved so much had either of them opposed his efforts. In contrast with previous occasions, however, both parties in the dispute wanted peace. The emperor felt betrayed by Louis XI, whose promises of military aid had proved valueless, and he was loath to proceed without such assistance. Charles too, despite his earlier uncompromising response to the legate, was prepared to make concessions because he wanted to disengage from Germany so that he could turn once again to France, which his ally the king of England had undertaken to invade in the summer. Both parties had already made tentative efforts to reach a settlement before the legate's mission gathered momentum. Nanni, in other words, did not so much bring forth peace *ex nihilo* as provide a means whereby the two main parties concerned could come to an agreement which both wanted and by which neither lost face. Not only did this peace allow Charles to disengage from Neuss so as to prepare for the English invasion of France and for his own campaign in Lorraine; it gave him more room for manoeuvre in future, as both the duke of Lorraine and the Swiss were excluded from it. Nor did the legate's help end there. He was tireless in ensuring that the provisional truce agreed at Neuss was extended into a formal peace treaty and alliance between Charles and the emperor, which was signed on 17 November 1475 (and published in Lausanne Cathedral on 14 April 1476); he also helped to arrange the submission of Nancy to the duke in December; and he was at his side when Charles entered the city to be recognised by the Estates of Lorraine as their ruler at the end of that month.[82]

At Neuss Nanni had threatened to punish recalcitrance by excommunication but, unlike Andrea dei Spiriti in 1473, he had made this threat impartially to both sides. His only concern was peace. But, insofar as peace with the emperor was then in the duke's interests, his mediation could he interpreted as favouring the Burgundian cause, and indeed the Milanese chancellor accused him of having become Charles's creature,[83] even though by June 1476 the duke was reported to have quarrelled with him. Nonetheless, the legate made one further attempt at mediation between the duke and his enemies. This was at the end of 1476 and involved Charles on the one hand and, on the other, Duke René of Lorraine and his Swiss and Austrian allies. By now René had regained much of the ground lost a year before and Charles was fighting back by laying siege to the capital, Nancy. The legate sought to arrange a ceasefire on the basis of a Burgundian withdrawal from Lorraine, and travelled to Basel and Zürich to put his plan before the Swiss. The opposition he met now, however, was much greater than at Neuss eighteen months previously. The Swiss were agreeable to a Burgundian evacuation of Lorraine but they also wanted Charles to be unequivocally branded as the aggressor; they wanted to ensure that René's title to his duchy was not prejudiced by a ceasefire; and some of them were suspicious of the legate himself, fearing that he was aiming to divide them from René in order to allow Charles to wriggle off the hook on which his own actions had ensnared him.[84] In any case, Charles was not interested in a truce. Despite the inclemency of the season and the weakness of his army, he felt that, with persistence, he could recover Nancy and, with the capital in his hands, largely restore his earlier dominance in Lorraine. The legate's failure at this juncture illuminates the reasons for his earlier success and reminds us of the tribulations of his predecessors: only if he enjoyed the cooperation of all parties concerned could he hope to make progress.

Church and state

During Charles the Bold's reign there were several conflicts between church and state but they did not necessarily impinge on his relations with the papacy itself. For example, although the opposition to the duke's mortmain taxation, imposed in 1474, was perhaps the most serious conflict of this kind,[85] Sixtus IV himself did not intervene nor, apparently, did he take sides or indeed show any interest, despite the appeals of the tax's opponents and despite the fact that the latter received some support from one of his legates, the bishop of Forlì.[86] In another case — the dispute over the pension payable to Lucas de Tolentis from the revenues of the Norbertine abbey of Tongerlo, granted by the displaced commendatory abbot Ferry de Clugny but refused by the elected abbot Jan Kinschot — Charles found himself in the position of defending the papal right to make commendatory appointments against his own clergy. But he did so not to support the principle itself but to uphold the interests of a cherished papal legate and to defend this means of rewarding him. Conversely, while Sixtus IV initially upheld his legate's right to the pension, he later changed his mind and retracted; but he was not abandoning a point of principle so much as a legate whom he no longer trusted.[87]

On a political and diplomatic level, however, more dangerous clashes could occur when the duke and the papacy disagreed about ecclesiastical matters in Burgundian lands. Papal taxation and papal appointments were two of the main areas of potential conflict. The sale of papal indulgences was a form of indirect taxation. During his long legation Lucas de Tolentis sold a wide range of crusading, jubilee and other kinds of indulgences. He was empowered to sell them not only in Charles the Bold's lands but also beyond, first in the sees of Metz, Toul and Verdun and later in any place whither he happened to accompany the duke. The reaction of the duke's subjects was mixed. One who objected was Adrien de But, monk and annalist of the abbey of Ter Duinen at Koksijde in Flanders. He complained bitterly at the flow of such large sums of money to Rome as a result of these transactions. They weighed almost as heavily on the people, he wrote, as the duke's own taxes; he regarded both forms as oppressive and in fact seemed to couple them together. But there was a definite demand for papal indulgences and others welcomed their sale, either as purchasers or, like the municipal authorities of Ghent in 1467 and 1468, as sponsors who stood to benefit economically from the influx of pilgrims attracted by the proclamation of a jubilee indulgence.[88]

As for the duke, he had little objection to the sale of indulgences as such if allowing it helped to ingratiate him with the papacy; moreover, the extension of Lucas de Tolentis's legatine powers to neighbouring areas such as Metz, Toul and Verdun might suggest papal recognition that they belonged within the Burgundian sphere of influence. Direct taxation was another matter; it was something that touched him directly, both financially and politically, and caused him to adopt a firmer attitude. In 1468 he refused to permit Stefano Nardini, legate *ad partes Galliae*, to collect in his lands a crusading tithe imposed by Paul II; always quick to assert his independence of the French crown, he maintained that he was not bound by the fact that Louis XI had agreed to its levy within the kingdom of France.[89] Indeed, like Adrien de But, he may have come to resent the outflow of funds to Rome, since he complained in 1473 that Sixtus IV was trying to extract as much money as he could from Charles's subjects. The papal alum monopoly which lasted from 1468 to 1473 (discussed more fully in the next section) was an indirect form of taxation, insofar as a monopoly was at all necessary to ensure a market for a product from whose sales the bulk of the proceeds went to Rome, albeit for a good cause — the crusade. The arrangement seems to have been unpopular with the duke's subjects from the first but Charles ignored their complaints for five years, and when he ended it in 1473 he did so only for reasons of his own and not to satisfy his subjects.

The fact was that, providing his honour and status were respected, Charles had no fundamental objection to papal taxation as such, especially if he were offered a share of the proceeds (as he was in the case of the alum monopoly). On several occasions he asked for, or the pope offered, a share in a papal levy, although the outcome is often difficult to trace. In 1469 Paul II offered to grant a tithe on ecclesiastical property in the duke's lands, in order to pay for the Burgundian expedition to Italy which he wanted to induce Charles to make.[90] Notably, in April 1475 Charles took it into his own hands to order a levy on his clergy which, he proclaimed, tradition and his and his predecessors' devotion to the crusade justified.[91] Perhaps, though, he did not go ahead with this plan, for in December he sent an archdeacon on a secret mission to Rome to ask the pope to allow him to levy a tithe on his clergy as a reward for what he called the house of Burgundy's renowned attachment to the crusade;

he calculated that it would bring in between 300,000 and 400,000 *écus*, of which he promised to remit a quarter to Rome. This communication may have revived Sixtus IV's hopes that the duke would abandon his campaigns in the west to lead a crusade in the east. At least, in his instructions for Lucas de Tolentis in February 1476, he empowered the returning legate to promise Charles a tithe and a share in the proceeds of the sale of jubilee indulgences if he did undertake to go on crusade.[92] Moreover, two months later there was talk, as we saw earlier, that the pope might be prepared to help finance the duke's campaigns against the Swiss, so as to enable him to be in a position to prevent Louis XI seizing Avignon.

After the battle of Murten, Charles again took the initiative, though apparently with scant success. Needing money urgently for the rebuilding of his army, in July he assembled the Estates of Burgundy at Salins. During the assembly the clergy approached Lucas de Tolentis for a short-term loan of 12,000 francs to help them meet the duke's requests. The legate, who had just attracted large crowds of pilgrims to the Franche-Comté and had collected commensurate sums of money by proclaiming the jubilee, refused on the grounds that he had no mandate for such loans and that, in any case, the money was needed by the pope, destined as it was for the crusading fund. Whether the clergy were put up to making their request by the duke himself we do not know, but immediately after the legate's refusal the duke's financial officers tried to put pressure on him to relent, which seems to have had some success. Unfortunately the precise outcome is not revealed by the Milanese ambassador, our fullest source for the episode, although he did describe the legate as resisting fiercely and threatening to excommunicate anyone, even Charles himself, who dared lay hands on him.[93]

Papal provision to benefices was the other major area of potential conflict between the duke and Rome. Whereas his father Philip, whose friendship was highly valued by successive popes as a pillar of support against the conciliarists and as a would-be crusader, had experienced little difficulty either in obtaining benefices for his friends and relations or in securing the appointment of his nominees to sensitive and strategic sees both inside and outside his own lands, Charles found the going harder. He may have been more bullying and forceful than his predecessors in the lengths to which he would go to support his candidates, or perhaps it was just that circumstances dictated he had to be.[94] The system of papal provisions had faults which tended to be noticed by rulers only when it did not work in their favour. Although Louis XI complained that Paul II was unduly favourable to the duke of Burgundy, Charles did not view matters in the same light. In 1472 he sent Antonio dei Corradi di Lignana to Rome to protest against the grant of a certain provostship in his lands made without his permission, and at the end of that year he voiced the desire to be able to dispose of benefices in his lands as freely as he felt Italian rulers did in theirs.[95] The instalment by the pope in Burgundian benefices of priests sympathetic to Louis XI seems to have been a point at issue between Charles and Sixtus IV at this time particularly, and one on which the king of Naples was asked to mediate.[96]

The duke was especially upset by the conferment of the see of Amiens in July 1473 on the French king's candidate, Jean de Gaucourt, in preference to his own, Ferry de Clugny, not only because of the efforts he had made on Ferry's behalf but also, perhaps, because he felt the appointment in some way ratified Louis's seizure of the town in January 1471 (a seizure which, as we saw in the last section, was one of the main obstacles until 1475 to a Franco–Burgundian settlement). Yet shortly afterwards, in September, Ferry was compensated by promotion to the almost equally important see of Tournai; and in fact Charles had few grounds for serious dissatisfaction with papal appointments to the major benefices, if only because the bulk of them had already been filled by Burgundian nominees during the reign of his father.[97] Certainly no contemporary evidence has yet been discovered to support the view put forward almost a century later (by agents of King Philip II of Spain, whose political reasons were obvious) that Charles had hoped to bring about some fundamental diocesan reorganisation with the aim of establishing a Burgundian 'national' church.[98]

In December 1472 Lucas de Tolentis wrote to Pope Sixtus warning him of the dangers of inflexibility in his relations with the duke, for he feared this would cause Charles to incline towards those in his entourage who spoke forcefully in favour of church reform. These men complained about unsuitable papal appointments to benefices and about papal intrusions which neglected the traditional rights of local patrons; they wanted to restrict ecclesiastical wealth and purge the forms of religion of undue ornamentation and ostentation.[99] Seen in context, however, these criticisms appear to have been something less than disinterested. By the end of 1472 the duke's dissatisfaction with Sixtus IV was so deep that he was prepared to consider drastic remedies. Irritated by the working of the alum monopoly, angered by unacceptable papal appointments, exasperated by the pope's continuing refusal to create a Burgundian cardinal, and enraged by the choice of Guillaume d'Estouteville to succeed Cardinal Bessarion as legate to France and

Burgundy, he talked of convoking a general council of the Church and of summoning the pope to answer before it.[100] No threat could have been better calculated to alarm a pope in the second half of the fifteenth century, when the abasement of the papacy during the Schism and the conciliar epoch was still a vivid memory. On the other hand, the currency of conciliarism could be devalued by a too overtly political usage, and in general Charles was cautious in employing the language of the reformers: far more cautious than, for instance, Louis XI. At other times he was reported to have been associated with conciliar schemes but only in a secondary role: in conjunction, for example, with the electoral princes of the Empire and Edward IV in 1473;[101] with Louis XI in 1468[102] and 1476;[103] and with Frederick III in 1476.[104] But it does seem that he never rendered his obedience to Sixtus IV or, if he did, that he delayed doing so until late in his reign.[105]

It should not be concluded, though, that his criticisms of the papacy, particularly during the pontificate of Sixtus IV, were solely the result of political dissatisfaction or the justification for diplomatic retaliation.[106] Of the deadly sins, Charles might well have been accused of pride and wrath, but he was innocent of lust, gluttony or sloth. Moreover, in his own narrow but sincere fashion he was deeply pious. According to the standards expected of princes of his time, he was a faithful son of the Church, as the legate Tolentis pointed out to Sixtus IV, and he desired keenly to be accepted as such. He claimed his wars were fought only in self-defence and therefore legitimate, and in some, such as those at Liège and Neuss, he cast himself as defender of the Church and of those of her representatives who had themselves asked him to come to their aid. He certainly took steps to propagate this image of righteousness and to convince the world that only the hostility of his enemies prevented him doing what he really wanted, namely to fulfil the vow to go on crusade that he had made as a young man in 1454. It is not easy to decide how far his diplomatic relations with Rome were influenced by moral considerations but he may well have looked askance at some of the more flagrantly worldly aspects of the curia. He appears to have disapproved, for example, of Pietro Riario, cardinal of San Sisto and nephew (or, as some said, natural son) of Sixtus IV, describing him as conceited, illiterate and lascivious, while on another occasion he protested that the funds from the sale of papal alum in his lands had been misappropriated by private individuals instead of being used, as intended, to further the defence of the faith against the infidel. Political attacks on the Church have usually been masked by pious words but these particular utterances have the ring of sincerity.

Despite, or perhaps even because of, this sincerity, Sixtus IV seems to have come to fear and dislike Charles. Already in 1473 he had been alarmed by the possibility that the Burgundian–imperial marriage then in prospect, and the increase in the duke's power that it portended, might tempt him to meddle in ecclesiastical affairs.[107] After the battle of Grandson he expressed the hope that in his next encounter with the Swiss Charles would suffer a greater disaster than in his first. It could well be that Sixtus was apprehensive about the duke's military progress precisely because he viewed him not only as a powerful figure on the diplomatic scene but also as a potential and over-zealous reformer of the Church. After all, the portrayal of Charles as 'the Bridegroom of the Church' by one of his encomiasts — Simon Mulart, dean of Heinsberg, in his *De ortu, victoria et triumpho domini Karoli ducis Burgundie moderni*, composed about 1469–1470 — has been held to foreshadow and prepare the way for the papal candidature of his son-in-law Maximilian of Austria in 1512–1513.[108]

The papal alum monopoly in the Burgundian Low Countries

Alum was a product that during the Middle Ages was put to a wide variety of industrial and domestic uses. The largest quantities and best qualities of alum were produced by the mines in and around the eastern Mediterranean and Black Sea, but by the mid-fifteenth century the advance of the Turks was threatening Christendom's supplies. Even if the Turks did not prohibit the sale of alum, the danger remained that, by buying from them, Christian consumers would in effect be subsidising the infidels' future conquests. A providential solution became possible in 1460, when rich and accessible deposits of good quality alum were discovered at Tolfa in the Papal States. Pius II and then Paul II set up a company to mine and market this alum, which became known as 'crusading alum' because the proceeds from its sale were placed in a special fund in Rome destined to finance a crusade and, in the meantime, to provide relief for refugees fleeing from the Turks. Furthermore, the papacy endeavoured to establish a monopoly for its own product by forbidding believers under pain of excommunication to use or import alum from Turkish-controlled mines and by seeking to restrict the output and consumption of alum from Christendom's own sources.

The papacy was especially eager to extend the monopoly to the

Burgundian Low Countries, because, with their textile industries, they were heavy users of alum. In 1466 Lucas de Tolentis was sent to the Burgundian court empowered to negotiate an agreement. He made little progress with Philip the Good, but Charles the Bold, within six months of his accession in June 1467, committed himself in principle to allowing a papal monopoly. The subsequent treaty, concluded only on 5 May 1468 and confirmed by ducal ordinance on 24 June, stipulated that Tolfa alum would be sold in his lands by the Medici bank, acting as agents for the papacy, at a fixed price of 4½ *livres* (of 240 *gros*) per *carica* (weighing approximately 180 kilograms). The sale and import of all other alum was forbidden, as was the use of substitutes. The duke was given an incentive to uphold the treaty by his entitlement to a fee of 6 *sous* per cargo sold. The papal legate Tolentis too had an inducement to promote sales, since it was out of these that his salary was paid. The treaty was designed to last for twelve years, but, as if in anticipation of trouble ahead, there was an important proviso: the agreement could be suspended by the duke if in neighbouring countries the price of alum, whether from Tolfa or elsewhere, fell below the price fixed for papal alum in his lands.

In fact the agreement was neither implemented immediately nor, once implemented, was it to be completely effective. Shortly before its conclusion in May 1468 Charles had expressly permitted his subjects freely to import alum of any provenance. The presence of these stocks presumably made the immediate enforcement of a papal monopoly difficult, for at the beginning of 1469 the duke successfully asked the pope for an eighteen-months' stay of execution until supplies of non-papal alum could be exhausted, and later he obtained a further delay of six months, during which time Paul II exacted a levy of 4 *sous* on the sale of every cargo of non-papal alum. From the beginning of 1471 more vigorous efforts at enforcement were made. In the spring Paul sent an official of the papal camera, Tommaso dei Vincentii (or de Vincentiis), to assist Lucas de Tolentis, and in the summer an agent of the Medici bank in Rome, Carlo d'Ugolino Martelli, was sent to supervise the efforts of his colleagues in Flanders. For his part, Charles impounded the remaining stocks of non-papal alum, and attempts were made to prevent its further importation. But the monopoly seems never to have been made complete. It was always unpopular with consumers, but more important was the fact that the attitude of the duke himself had changed as a result of his irritation with Paul II's successor, Sixtus IV. As if in anticipation of this, Sixtus sent another alum commissioner, Domenico Albergati, to Flanders in the summer of 1472. Albergati's efforts, however, seem to have been unavailing, and from August 1473 the monopoly was effectively suspended through the issue of ducal letters authorising for a period of two years the import of non-papal alum, provided that it was of Christian provenance.

While the economic aspects of this alum agreement have been studied in depth,[109] its political and diplomatic aspects have received far less attention. It embodied, in effect, a forced levy by Rome on the duke's subjects. In this respect, it comes within the purview of Church–state relations. It was undoubtedly unpopular with the duke's subjects from the first, and they put up strong resistance. Even though the papal monopoly of sales and distribution was far from complete, it nonetheless kept prices higher than they would have been otherwise. Not only the price of the Tolfa alum but also its marketing seems to have aroused resentment, because it was alleged not to have been sold in small enough quantities for average purchasers, who complained further that the middlemen to whom they were thus forced to resort gave short measure and adulterated quality.[110] Moreover, although Tolfa alum was regarded as being of a superior quality to other varieties, top-quality alum was not necessary for all the uses to which alum was put, helping to explain the market for inferior varieties, which continued to be imported illicitly. The duke also received objections from some of the foreign merchants resident in his lands; they complained that restrictions on the import and sale of non-papal alum infringed their traditional commercial privileges, which, they claimed, permitted them to trade in any commodity they wished.[111]

The duke was thus placed in an invidious position between the complaints of his subjects and the demands of Rome. He was certainly aware of, and to some extent sympathetic towards, the objections of his subjects. He managed to delay implementing the treaty for almost three years after its conclusion in May 1468; not even after renewed papal pressure in 1471 was it fully implemented; and the complaints of his subjects undoubtedly provided one reason for his suspension of the treaty in 1473. On the other hand, the fact that Charles waited this long before complying with his subjects' wishes suggests that their views did not constitute the only consideration affecting his decision. He had been content until then to acquiesce in an agreement which, though unpopular, allowed him to share the proceeds. In 1473 he was prepared to forego this share because, by conceding the States General's demand for the suspension of the monopoly, he was now able to obtain in return an even better deal, namely a grant for six years towards the upkeep of his army.[112]

[94]

Nonetheless, his decision to suspend the monopoly cannot be satis-factorily explained by reference to domestic politics alone. Diplomatic considerations played a significant, and perhaps even dominant, role. Indeed, if we retrace our steps, it might be said that such considerations had provided the major reason for his agreeing to the treaty in the first place. On 4 February 1468 Charles had written to Paul II from Lille to express the wish that relations between them might be as close and, on his side, as obedient as those between their respective predecessors, Philip the Good and Pius II.[113] Yet this wording should by no means be interpreted as showing that the duke's devotion was such that he would serve the interests of the Church without thought for his own. The fact that he had already agreed in principle, before the end of 1467, to allow a monopoly for papal alum in his lands, yet did not actually conclude the agreement until May the following year, suggests that he regarded his agreement as a *quid pro quo* for a papal dispensation for his marriage to Margaret of York. Even after the promise of the dispensation (acknowl-edged in the letter mentioned above), he delayed concluding the alum agreement until the scope and wording of the dispensation had been subjected to close scrutiny in England. When this examination gave rise to doubts about the document's validity, if only temporarily, the duke was enraged. It was reported that he could hardly have been more dis-enchanted with the pope and some even said that he threatened to convoke a council of the Church.[114] The conclusion that Pope Paul used the dispensation as an inducement to Charles to allow a monopoly in his lands for papal alum is strengthened by the fact that he employed similar tactics, though unsuccessfully, in England, where his legate, the bishop of Lucca, was empowered not only to issue a dispensation for the Anglo–Burgundian marriage but also to negotiate an alum agreement similar to that reached in the Low Countries.[115]

Once the agreement was made, Charles no doubt expected a reward in the form of favourable treatment in his future dealings with Rome, especially because, among contemporary rulers, he was the only one to have consented to such an arrangement: his father had vacillated, while Edward IV and Louis XI probably refused outright.[116] His subsequent delay in fully implementing the agreement for almost three years served a dual purpose, disarming to some extent the opposition of his subjects and giving him a bargaining counter in his relations with Paul II; one of the concessions he probably hoped to extract from the pope by this means was the creation of one or even two Burgundian cardinals (a subject treated more fully in the next section). In 1471 the duke at last began to enforce the monopoly more strictly. Unfortunately, Paul II was succeeded during the summer by Sixtus IV and the new pope's actions regarding the duke — particularly his choice of legates to France and Burgundy and his refusal to create the Burgundian cardinal promised by his predecessor — were not calculated to improve relations. Already in June 1472 Charles was talking of the possibility of being forced to end the monopoly because of its impracticalities and inequities, against which his subjects were by now protesting vigorously.[117] This veiled threat, however, was probably designed to convey the duke's own sense of grievance against the pope as much as that of his subjects against the Tolfa monopoly. In December 1472 he summoned Lucas de Tolentis to his council chamber, expatiated for over an hour on his grievances against Sixtus (a speech characterised by our source as '*grand exordio e longho parlamento ornato*'), and then declared the alum treaty revoked. This performance was described by another papal agent in Flanders as merely a bluff ('*fictione*');[118] nevertheless, within eight months the treaty was formally suspended.

The usual explanation for that decision — indeed, it was the one offered by the duke himself — is that Charles surrendered the treaty as a concession to his subjects. But this version is not totally satisfactory because it does not fit all the known facts. The attitude of his subjects was only one factor influencing the duke's decision. The suspension of the treaty was also in part a concession to his ally, King Ferrante of Naples, because he hoped to obtain from him a large financial subsidy in return; the subsidy was to come from the proceeds of selling the stocks of Neapolitan alum that had for some time lain immobilised as a result of the papal monopoly.[119] This suggestion is plausible not only for political but also for commercial reasons. We know that, in general, Ferrante was anxious to increase the wealth of his impoverished kingdom by fostering commerce. One of his particular interests, moreover, was to promote the sales of the alum (albeit of a rather poor quality) from the mines he owned at Ischia, despite the brief attempt made by the papacy and the Medici in 1470–1471 to squeeze these supplies out of the market for Christian alum. Thus, in 1467 he made a commercial pact with Edward IV and in the following year there was talk of arranging a sales monopoly in England for Neapolitan alum, similar to that established at the same time for Tolfa alum in Flanders. Ferrante was especially keen to break into the Low Countries market and to combat the papal monopoly there. His treaty with the duke of February 1471 contained a clause designed to prevent restrictions on trade between their respective territories, and subsequently Ferrante and Neapolitan merchants made determined attempts to break the monopoly enjoyed by papal alum in the duke's lands.[120]

A further reason for the duke's decision to suspend the monopoly was that it no longer served the purpose he had originally intended it to serve. The treaty of May 1468 had been designed in part to portray Charles as a better son of the Church than most other contemporary rulers, and therefore to show that he possessed a stronger moral and political claim than they to papal favour in diplomatic or ecclesiastical conflicts where the Holy See was likely to have to declare for one party against another, especially of course in those between the duke and Louis XI. But the force of this claim was weakened by the election in 1471 of Sixtus IV who, at least initially, displayed a preference for the French king over the duke of Burgundy; it was further eroded in 1472 when the concordat negotiated with Louis XI at last ended decades of bitter disagreement over the Pragmatic Sanction of Bourges. By now Charles must have reasoned that the diplomatic advantages of the papal monopoly for his relations with Rome had declined to the point at which they no longer outweighed its domestic disadvantages, not to mention the friction it caused in his relations with his Neapolitan ally.

The exact timing of the suspension of the monopoly presents some problems of explanation. The free import of Christian alum from 28 August 1473 was authorised in letters patent issued by the duke on 7 June. Yet Ferrante had made his offer of money in return for a suspension of the monopoly at least as early as March,[121] and the States General (which, so Charles claimed, had forced him to break the agreement with Rome) broke up on 1 April. Why, then, the delay? The answer may be that in the spring of 1473 Sixtus IV was known to be about to elevate a new batch of cardinals; Charles wanted at least one of them to be Burgundian; and the prior suspension of the monopoly would have adversely affected the chances of that. One of his candidates, Philibert Hugonet, was given the red hat on 7 May and the news arrived at the Burgundian court fifteen days later.[122] With this promotion, probably the last obstacle to the suspension of the monopoly was removed, while the abrasive attitude displayed in July by the papal legate Andrea dei Spiriti on his visit to the Burgundian camp outside Nijmegen[123] can only have confirmed the duke in his decision. Alum from Tolfa continued to be imported thereafter,[124] but the question of re-establishing the papal monopoly does not seem to have been raised again during the remainder of the duke's reign.

The search for friends at the papal court

Charles the Bold well knew the value of having papal support, not least because, unlike his father, he could not count on receiving it automatically; for example, his public attitude to the crusade was influenced to a considerable degree by a desire to ingratiate himself with the papacy. Not that he was ever completely satisfied by the Holy See, for he was quick to accuse Paul II, and even more Sixtus IV, of being biased against him and of favouring his enemies, especially Louis XI. But he was not content to leave to chance the business of getting his own way; this section will illustrate how, and with what success, he took steps to win friends (and place his own agents) at the curia in order to ensure that his case never went unheard there. The need to exert direct pressure on the pope in this way arose not least because the French king attempted to do the same. Chastellain wrote that Charles the Bold's suspicion of Stefano Nardini in 1468 was caused by his fear that Nardini was the legate of a pope who had already been wholly won over to the king's point of view by Louis's own agents at the curia, and in May 1475 Charles complained to the bishop of Forlì that the pope and cardinals seemed to favour Louis against him.[125] Again we find rivalry with France influencing his relations with Italy. But the winning of papal friendship was only a means to an end. Charles wanted positive evidence of Rome's good disposition towards him, such as promoting his nominees to benefices when requested, granting marital dispensations, appointing as legates to Burgundy only those acceptable to him, and, in general, displaying an inclination to do as Charles wished, particularly when his wishes conflicted with those of others.

More than one method of obtaining spokesmen at the curia was employed by the duke. He usually tried to make friends of the papal legates who came to his court, succeeding with some, failing with others. He certainly won over Lucas de Tolentis. In his letters to Pope Sixtus written in 1472 and 1473 we find Lucas expressing admiration for the duke's religious devotion and struggling to persuade the pope not to pursue policies which might alienate him. He particularly warned Sixtus of the danger of losing Burgundian goodwill through an attempt — in any case, not certain of success — to seek a *rapprochement* with Louis XI ('*hic perdere et alibi non capere non est utile*').[126] At Abbeville in August 1472 Charles named him his *maître des requêtes*;[127] in 1474 he empowered him to rally opposition in Rome to his recent excommunication; and, when Lucas returned to the duke's side, in March 1476, the

Mantuan ambassador in Rome noted that he was '*molto accepto e creduto da quello signore*'.[128] Some objected to him precisely for that reason. The duke of Milan worked on the pope to recall him in 1474, and, in 1476, perhaps because it was well known how much Charles trusted Lucas, Louis XI suspected that his return as legate to Burgundy was a sign of papal hostility towards France.[129] Charles seems to have achieved a similar intimacy, eventually, with Pietro Aliprandi and Alessandro Nanni. Aliprandi, intent as we saw earlier on upholding Milanese interests at the Burgundian court, had managed in 1474 to displace Lucas de Tolentis as legate there; but some of his initial hostility to Charles must have been quickly moderated, because when he returned to Rome in September 1474 it was '*per ambasciatore del duca de Borgogna*'.[130] Nanni, as legate to Germany, had won the duke's gratitude in 1475 by helping to convert his relations with the emperor from confrontation to alliance. To some, however, Nanni appeared to have identified papal interests too closely with those of Burgundy and it was for this reason that the Milanese chancellor sought in January 1476 to have him recalled by Sixtus IV.[131]

The duke's Italian allies were expected to uphold his interests in Rome. The fact that Paul II was Venetian helped foster the duke's relations with both the republic and Rome between 1467 and 1471. Similarly, in 1474 Charles asked Cardinal Francesco Gonzaga, son of his friend Marquis Lodovico of Mantua, to oppose both the ratification of the bull of excommunication issued by Andrea dei Spiriti and the persecution, as he termed it, of Tolentis simply because he was considered to be '*nobis et rebus nostris affectatus*'.[132] As for King Ferrante, the extent of his supposed influence in Rome was one of the arguments adduced by Charles in favour of his election to the Order of the Golden Fleece in May 1473.[133] At the end of 1472 Ferrante had urged Sixtus — '*per utilità de le cosse christiane*', as the Venetian ambassador in Naples phrased it — to satisfy the duke's demand for the creation of a Burgundian cardinal, as promised but not actually carried out by his predecessor.[134] Asked by Sixtus shortly afterwards to mediate between Burgundy and Rome in order to avert probable conflict, Ferrante suggested the pope should go a long way towards satisfying Charles. He should withdraw hostile and suspect French priests from benefices in the duke's lands, revoke the appointment of d'Estouteville as legate to France and Burgundy, and promote not one but two Burgundian cardinals;[135] Charles, however, was still dissatisfied because he would have preferred the pope to approach him directly instead of through an intermediary. When, in May

1473, his request for a Burgundian cardinal was at last granted in the person of Philibert Hugonet, the well-informed Milanese ambassador in Rome marked Hugonet down as likely to vote with the Neapolitan bloc in the college of cardinals and against the supporters of the duke of Milan; and in the following year Ferrante exerted his influence at the curia against the ratification of his ally's recent excommunication.[136]

During the early years of Sixtus IV's pontificate, however, the dominant influence at the curia was that of the duke of Milan. As a result of the treaty of Moncalieri in January 1475, therefore, Charles must have hoped to see his new ally's influence in Rome used on his behalf. There is evidence to suggest that these hopes were in some part realised. In May 1475, for example, the Milanese ambassador in Rome was instructed to further Charles's request for the promotion of his confessor, Enguerrand Seignart, bishop of Salubrie (or Salubria), to the vacant see of Auxerre and to assist an envoy of the duke who was on his way to confer with Anthony of Burgundy (then returning up the peninsula from Naples); he was enjoined by his master to foster these matters as if he were acting on behalf of Galeazzo Maria himself.[137]

This aspect of the Milanese alliance must have appealed equally, if not more so, to a number of Burgundian courtiers, and therefore have influenced their preference for Galeazzo Maria over the duke's other allies in Italy. An example is Guy de Brimeu, lord of Humbercourt, count of Megen and one of the duke's most trusted and powerful officials, who was anxious to further the ecclesiastical career of his brother Philippe. In 1473 he and his master had impressed on Lucas de Tolentis their strong desire to see Sixtus IV appoint Philippe administrator of the see of Amiens, and in 1474 the duke had asked Ferrante to write to Rome recommending Philippe for the see of Lausanne;[138] but neither request produced results. In 1475 the duke's Neapolitan secretary Giovanni di Candida was sent to Rome to press again Philippe's claims; Galeazzo Maria assisted by instructing his ambassador in Rome to urge the pope to grant him the first bishopric to fall vacant within the duchy of Milan.[139] In February 1475 Charles de Neuchâtel, bishop of Besançon, asked Galeazzo Maria, through Panigarola, to favour his affairs in Rome and in July, again through Panigarola, Guillaume Hugonet asked Galeazzo Maria to favour his brother Philibert.[140] Another aspirant was Charles the Bold's Neapolitan doctor, Matteo de Clariciis da Troia. He never (as far as one can tell) took holy orders, but he had a claim on Galeazzo Maria's gratitude through his advocacy of the Milanese cause at the Burgundian court. Already in 1475 he had asked his brother Salvatore, Charles the Bold's secretary — who was at this time charged with several missions between Burgundy and Milan in an attempt to persuade Galeazzo Maria to send his ally troops — to ask Sforza on his next visit to Milan to support his request for the bishopric of Autun to be reserved for him after the death or translation of the present incumbent, Jean Rolin.[141] In 1476 Matteo persuaded Galeazzo Maria to write to Charles asking him to reserve the see of Chalon-sur-Saône (then held by Jean de Poupet) at its next vacancy. Charles professed willingness and wrote to the pope to ask for this reservation,[142] and as a mark of earnest also wrote in his own hand to '*mon bon frère le duc de Millan*' asking him to use his influence in Rome to support this request.[143] Delighted though he was, Matteo, as a form of insurance, asked Galeazzo Maria, through Panigarola, to reserve him a bishopric in his own lands, and, in order to increase the force of the request, he wrote himself to the duke of Milan.[144]

The growth of support for the duke of Burgundy within the college of cardinals was in part a reflection of the increase in Burgundian influence in Italy generally. The constant rivalry with the king of France is again easy to detect, and the rise of Charles *vis-à-vis* Louis is reflected in the comments of those at the curia who praised the duke at the expense of the king.[145] Little evidence has come to light to suggest that Charles distributed favours and largesse to clients at the curia, as his father had perhaps done,[146] though this may have happened. Nor is it easy to identify individually more than a few of his partisans among the cardinals. Cardinal Francesco Gonzaga can probably be so described. Iacopo Ammanati-Piccolomini, cardinal-bishop of Pavia, was a friend of the Neapolitan ambassador at the Burgundian court, Francesco Bertini, with whom he had corresponded at least since 1465, and may well have shared Bertini's admiration for Charles. Thus in 1472 he wrote to his friend asking to be commended to the duke, '*cuius animum et gloriosa opera ex tuis litteris cupide legi*', and we know that in the previous year he had urged Sixtus IV not to try to curry favour with Louis XI by appointing d'Estouteville legate to France, arguing that the king was too untrustworthy (a typically Burgundian opinion) for such a gesture to work.[147] In a dispute two years later with the abbot of Liessies in Hainaut, Charles sought the support of Cardinal Teodoro of Monferrato.[148] The powerful Pietro Riario too may have flirted with the duke. In March 1472 he was reported to have promised the Burgundian ambassadors then returning through Rome from Naples that he would give his protection to the affairs of their master and to those of Charles of France. For this he was rebuked by the duke of Milan. Riario hastened to make clear that he had in no way aligned himself with the enemies of Milan and France but had only offered his friendship in general terms and out of politeness.[149] The following month, however, he seems to have helped a Burgundian ambassador (Antonio dei Corradi di Lignana) and his assistants to obtain at a reduced rate some ecclesiastical privileges from the papal camera.[150] In December, though this time *with* the approval of Galeazzo Maria, who was now endeavouring to improve relations with Charles, he extended the hand of friendship to another Burgundian envoy, Johann von Espacht.[151] But Charles does not seem to have been grateful for these overtures by a man he held in contempt, and it may therefore be significant that, as we have seen, Riario was generally considered the man responsible for hatching the plot to have the duke excommunicated in October 1473.

In any case, Charles was not content to rely solely on the influence of allies and friends in Rome; he wanted to have his own agents there, who would be directly accountable to himself alone. What with clerics and lawyers, students and diplomats, not to mention casual visitors such as pilgrims, there must have been many of his subjects in Rome from whom to choose. It is sometimes possible to discover the names of some of them. It is less easy to specify which of them were there on ducal business, but probably those attached to the papal court could be so employed as the need arose. Jean Adournes, for instance, spent some time at the curia after 1471, partly in the service of Philibert Hugonet whom he accompanied on legations to the Papal States and Tuscany.[152] Henri de Berghes (or Hendrik van Bergen) was described by the Milanese ambassador in Turin in May 1476 as having previously spent six years in Italy, of which two were at the curia (the others at Perugia University); he was returning to Rome now in the capacity of ducal proctor.[153]

The office of proctor was an important one. Philip the Good had maintained a *procureur* in Rome,[154] as had at least one of his ecclesiastical relatives,[155] and Charles followed suit. If '*ses gens estans a Romme*' mentioned in the ducal accounts for October 1467 were not specifically described as proctors, Jehan de la Motte *was* so described in August 1468; so too was Henri de Berghes, while in 1474 the duke's ambassador to Ferrante, Pierre (or Pieter) Bogaert, was recorded on his arrival in Rome from Naples as sending one of the duke's proctors there to Milan to ask Galeazzo Maria on his behalf for a safe-conduct.[156] Bogaert, in fact, had himself served both Philip the Good and Charles the Bold as proctor in Rome between at least 1458 and 1472; at the same time he was employed at the curia as a clerk (as both *scriptor* and *abbreviator*) by successive popes from Nicholas V to Paul II.

Though proctors were useful, Charles was convinced that, in order to have a spokesman near the real seat of power at the curia, he needed to obtain the red hat for one or more of his nominees. Most contemporary rulers felt the same but not all could be satisfied, for the number of cardinals was limited by papal electoral capitulations and an increasing number of those promoted were Italian. Moreover, it was always easy for a pope to use the not necessarily disingenuous excuse that he could not satisfy the demands of one ruler because to do so would necessitate acceding to the similar wishes of others. Thus, in 1460, Charles (then count of Charolais) had already met with refusal when he asked Pius II to grant the red hat to Jean Jouffroy, bishop of Arras, because the pope claimed that, if he satisfied this Burgundian request, he could not refuse those of the kings of Aragon and France and of the duke of Savoy;[157] it was clearly implied that, since he was unable to do both, he would have to do neither. This was a dilemma that Charles faced repeatedly in the following years, but he could and did argue that he had a particularly strong case.[158] In 1472 he complained to Lucas de Tolentis that no Burgundian cardinal had been created for twenty years, a reference to Jean Rolin, bishop of Autun and son of Philip the Good's chancellor Nicholas, who had been promoted by Nicholas V in 1448 and who lived until 1483, although, apparently, without making a great impact on his age; Charles obviously disregarded Jean Jouffroy, who, though created cardinal in 1461 after largely Burgundian pressure, thereafter became a devoted servant of Louis XI. By contrast, there were two French cardinals at the time of Charles's accession: Guillaume d'Estouteville, archbishop of Rouen (promoted in 1439), and Alain de Coëtivy, bishop of Avignon (promoted in 1448). Moreover, in the promotions of September 1467 Jean Balue, bishop of Angers, was promoted, followed, in those of 1473, by Philippe Lévis, bishop of Arles, and, in December 1476, by Charles de Bourbon, archbishop of Lyon. Thus, even though Alain de Coëtivy and Philippe Lévis died in 1474 and 1475 respectively and though Jean Balue, having fallen from grace in 1469, was kept prisoner by Louis XI up to and beyond 1477, nonetheless there was at any given time in the duke's reign at least one cardinal who was a partisan of the king, and sometimes there were two or three. Even Charles's ally Edward IV had his own cardinal — Thomas Bourchier, archbishop of Canterbury — promoted in September 1467.

The manner in which Charles eventually succeeded in his quest illustrates both the intricacies of papal diplomacy during the Renaissance and, once again, the duke's rivalry with Louis XI. He pressed for not one but two Burgundian cardinals, his nominees being: first, Ferry de Clugny, the successor in 1473 of Guillaume Fillastre as both bishop of Tournai and chancellor of the Order of the Golden Fleece and brother of Guillaume, protonotary apostolic and ducal councillor; and, secondly, Philibert Hugonet, protonotary apostolic and, from 1472, bishop of Mâcon, whose brother Guillaume, lord of Saillant, was ducal chancellor from May 1471. Aware of the importance the duke attached to his claim, Paul II tried in 1469 to entice him to support his diplomatic schemes in Italy by offering the red hat to Ferry de Clugny.[159] But no action was taken until the very end of his pontificate. Shortly before his death in August 1471, it was being reported that Paul had already chosen the four candidates to be promoted at his next creation of cardinals. They were two Venetians, Giovanbattista Savelli and Pietro Foscari; a Hungarian, the archbishop of Esztergom; and a fourth who was a Burgundian, probably Ferry de Clugny rather than Philibert Hugonet.[160] That this promise of promotion, as it was held to be by those concerned, was accepted as genuine by the duke of Milan[161] speaks in favour of the reliability of these reports. The promotions were said to have been delayed out of respect for Louis XI (who could have been expected to oppose the choice of the Venetians and, still more, that of a Burgundian); but Paul had apparently stipulated, as if anticipating trouble, that they were to be considered valid should his premature death prevent ratification.[162] Unfortunately, it was just at this confused stage that he died.

Charles undoubtedly regarded Paul II's promise, whatever the circumstances attending it, as binding on his successor. Thus in April 1472 his agent Antonio dei Corradi di Lignana was in Rome to complain that it had not been kept by Sixtus IV.[163] During this time the papal legate at the Burgundian court was repeatedly assailed by the lamentations of the duke and his advisors about the lack of a Burgundian cardinal. Shortly before Christmas 1472 a ducal ambassador, allegedly using much rude and aggressive language, threatened in consistory that his master would cease to recognise Sixtus as pope (something, in fact, which apparently he had never done formally in the first place), stop his subjects going to Rome, and appeal to a council of the Church unless the pope created a Burgundian cardinal.[164] Shortly before, Charles had been observed by Pietro Aliprandi to pretend to tear up his alum treaty with Rome as a protest against papal provocations, not the least of which was Sixtus IV's failure to honour the promise made by his predecessor.[165]

In his first creation in December 1471 Sixtus had played safe by limiting the promotions to two, his nephews Pietro Riario and Giuliano della Rovere.[166] He was unwilling to be bound by the acts of his predecessor, not only for reasons of pride but also in order to avoid the likely political complications in view of the known objections of Louis XI and Galeazzo Maria. Moreover, during the summer of 1472 he was being urged by Louis to grant the red hat to the archbishop of Lyon. Sixtus felt he could not agree to this request without at the same time balancing it by promoting a Burgundian, but that would have obliged him to ratify the promotion of the two Venetians provisionally made by Paul II in 1469 and he was most reluctant to have to double the Venetian representation in the consistory.[167] So he evaded the problem by doing nothing. He was certainly anxious not to offend Louis at the same time as trying to negotiate a concordat with him, but it is possible also that he hoped to put pressure on Charles by delaying creating a Burgundian cardinal until the duke showed a more conciliatory attitude towards Rome; Charles himself was reported to have suspected that Sixtus had declared he would not satisfy the duke until he heard that Cardinal Bessarion's peace mission to France and Burgundy had succeeded and until the duke had rendered his obedience to the pope.[168]

On 5 April Sixtus assembled the consistory to create new cardinals, but the members — who did not want their numbers to be increased — persuaded him to delay until Pentecost. They reasoned that the promotion of a Burgundian now would offend Louis XI and possibly also remove the last weapon the pope had with which to induce the duke to take a more cooperative attitude, whereas, if they waited a little, Charles and Louis might soon make peace, so that it would then be possible to satisfy the duke without offending the king.[169] Charles hastened to reassure the cardinals. An emissary of his arrived in Rome in the latter part of April 1473 to apologise for the menaces uttered by his envoy in December and to announce that peace between Burgundy and France was at last imminent.[170] Louis too launched a diplomatic offensive; while again pressing the promotion of the archbishop of Lyon, he urged the pope not to promote without his consent any subject of the duke of Burgundy (or of the duke of Brittany), except Ferry de Clugny, whom he seems to have had hopes of enticing from his Burgundian allegiance.[171]

By now Sixtus seems to have decided that he could no longer resist Burgundian demands, but at the same time he was still reluctant to be obligated to either Louis or the Venetians and to have to satisfy them as well. It is interesting to see how he tackled the dilemma. Instead of Ferry de Clugny, the front-runner since 1469, on 7 May 1473 he gave the red hat to Philibert Hugonet. In this way he satisfied Charles without being bound — as he felt he would have been had he chosen Ferry — to act on the promises made by his predecessor to the two Venetian candidates.[172] He was also said to be optimistic that the choice of Philibert Hugonet would improve relations with Burgundy by gaining the support of Philibert's brother Guillaume, the ducal chancellor.[173] This promotion was thus a great triumph for Charles in view of his many previous rebuffs. It was also a victory over Louis XI, whose bluster failed either to prevent the promotion of the duke's candidate or to secure that of his own, the archbishop of Lyon; nor was he mollified by the choice instead of Philippe Lévis, bishop of Arles, because he regarded him as a client of King René of Anjou, and in fact he was so annoyed that he bitterly accused both the pope and the cardinals of simony. Certainly, all at the Burgundian court rejoiced at Hugonet's elevation, except, perhaps, Ferry de Clugny. In a rare display of tact, Charles disguised his own pleasure for Ferry's sake. Moreover, he declared that he would only rest content when Ferry too obtained the red hat. But this was not to be, at least in the duke's lifetime. After his next creation of cardinals, Sixtus wrote to Tolentis on 28 December 1476 asking him to convey to Charles his regrets that he had still been unable to satisfy Ferry; he had wanted to but could not do so without also satisfying either Foscari and Savelli or, at least, provoking those Venetians, if he refused them, into scandalous scenes of protest in consistory. Yet had Charles lived to receive this letter, he would not have failed to notice the promotion this time of Louis XI's candidate, the archbishop of Lyon. Ferry had to wait for promotion until 1480 and he then lived to enjoy his new rank for just three years.[174]

The Milanese ambassador in Rome described Philibert Hugonet shortly after his promotion in disparaging terms, saying that he was of little account.[175] Nonetheless, he soon began to prove useful. In the summer of 1473 he pressed Charles the Bold's objections to Louis XI's candidate for the see of Amiens, while the duke urged the pope to create Hugonet legate *a latere* for his forthcoming meeting with the emperor; again, it was Hugonet who, in March 1474, presented his master's appeal against excommunication.[176] Later that year, at a time when the dukes of Burgundy and Milan were sounding out the possibility of an alliance through their representatives in Rome, Hugonet was able to establish that Galeazzo Maria really did want an alliance, so that formal negotiations then became possible elsewhere about the conditions.[177] After the conclusion of that alliance in January 1475, Hugonet was able, as we have seen, to strengthen his efforts as his master's spokesman through coordination with his Milanese counterparts in Rome. Hugonet's promotion could not prevent Andrea dei Spiriti from issuing a bull of excommunication against Charles in 1473, but it did probably help to improve relations between the duke and Rome in 1474 and 1475, an improvement that was all the more striking after the tension marking the early years of Sixtus IV's pontificate. Other factors contributed to this *détente*, among them the treaty of Moncalieri, the poor impression made in Rome by the behaviour of Louis XI, and the duke of Burgundy's own propaganda, all of which have been mentioned earlier.

It has often been said that Charles was a ruler more feared than loved, both by his subjects and by his allies. Certainly, in his search for partisans in Rome he was concerned to obtain support rather than affection, and in his relations with the Holy See he wanted not just goodwill but its tangible effects. The main factor in the equation, the person of the pope himself, could not be altered by Burgundian pressure, and Charles suffered a setback when Paul II was succeeded by Sixtus IV. Nonetheless, he continued to build up his own party at the curia, so that his relations with Sixtus IV gradually improved, less through a modification of his own policies than by changing the pope's opinion of him. The process was aided considerably by the elevation to the cardinalate of Philibert Hugonet in May 1473 and by the treaty of Moncalieri with Galeazzo Maria in January 1475, which gave him a powerful ally in Rome. But by the same token the deterioration in relations with Milan from about the end of 1475 harmed his influence at the curia, and, as Sixtus came to share Galeazzo Maria's fears of a Burgundian invasion of Italy, the pope had come by the end of 1476 to be one of his most outspoken critics. No amount of friends at the curia could now prevail against the unfavourable view of Charles the Bold formed by Sixtus as a result of the duke's own actions.

* * *

Relations between Burgundy and the Holy See were far less smooth and amicable under Charles the Bold than they had been in the reign of his father, and it could be argued that Charles forfeited the status of 'most favoured ruler' enjoyed by Philip the Good. This was the result in part of his own actions; he was quick to resent and reject papal admonitions when he felt they ran counter to his interests, while his diplomatic manner in dealing with Rome was more often brusque and assertive than cajoling or submissive. Yet the perceptible change and deterioration in the tenor of relations between Burgundy and the Holy See cannot be explained wholly or even mainly in such personal terms. In fact, at an individual level, Charles displayed a number of qualities that were admirable in the eyes of the Church, and in his personal devotion and piety, however conventional they may have been, he could hardly be regarded as inferior to Philip the Good.

The change should be attributed rather to a modification, during his reign and already in the latter years of his father's, of the objective circumstances helping to determine the character of relations. It was these which shaped the papal attitude towards Burgundy and hence, in turn, influenced the duke's reaction to Rome. Philip the Good had entered into the good graces of successive popes by his firm opposition to the conciliarists, thereby distinguishing himself sharply from King Charles VII of France, who had not scrupled to negotiate the Pragmatic Sanction of Bourges with the Council of Basel in 1438; and he had retained papal favour by his positive attitude towards the crusade. By 1467, however, the conciliarist threat to the papacy had receded and, in the eyes of the Holy See, the contrast between Burgundy and France was no longer so marked. If Charles agreed to a monopoly in his lands for Tolfa alum, Louis XI was prepared to modify or abandon the Pragmatic Sanction. Moreover, if the duke's attitude towards the crusade was neither as indifferent nor as cynical as that of some of his contemporaries, his initiatives in this direction were necessarily cautious in view of the vast united effort required of Christendom simply to stem the infidels' advance, let alone to go on the offensive and recover Constantinople or the Holy Land itself. Finally, it bears repetition that the intimacy of his relations with the various states of Italy added to his relations with Rome a further complication not experienced to anything like the same degree by Philip the Good. The last Valois duke was clearly no less assiduous than his father in airing his point of view at the curia through friends and spokesmen but, because of the factors listed above, the chances of a favourable hearing were much smaller.

Charles, nonetheless, was able to adapt to the new situation both skilfully and, on the whole, with some measure of success. It is true both that he suffered the ignominy of excommunication, however short-lived and dubious, and that he complained about some papal appointments to benefices in his lands; but, on the other hand, the excommunication was not actually ratified and the general record of papal appointments gave him few genuine grounds for serious discontent. On the credit side should be noted the promotion of a Burgundian cardinal, the manner in which Charles allowed legates to help but not hinder his diplomacy, the intimacy he established with some of them, and the grant of marital dispensations which facilitated his diplomatic policies. Above all, as in his relations with the lay rulers of Italy, his concern was not to be outdone by the king of France; it can hardly be denied that he at least held his own against Louis XI, and Charles himself would doubtless have regarded this as success enough.

Notes

1. Vaughan's *Philip the Good* contains a chapter on 'Philip the Good and the Church', but there is no similar chapter in his *Charles*. Of great value is the article by J. Paquet, 'Une ébauche de la nonciature de Flandre au XVe siècle: les missions dans les Pays-Bas de Luc de Tolentis, évêque de Sebenico, 1462–1484', *BIHBR*, 25 (1949), 27–144, while some aspects of the subject are considered in my 'Diplomatic aspects of Charles the Bold's relations with the Holy See', *BMGN*, 95 (1980), 265–78. For Louis XI the main works are still J. Combet, *Louis XI et le Saint-Siège, 1461–1483* (Paris, 1903) and P. Ourliac, 'Le concordat de 1472. Étude sur les rapports de Louis XI et de Sixte IV', *Revue historique de droit français et étranger*, 4th ser., 21 (1942) 174–223, and 22 (1943), 117–54, both of which also deal in passing with Charles the Bold.
2. I have not, for example, investigated the papal archives, except through the works of others, although I have used the correspondence of the Milanese and Mantuan ambassadors in Rome (ASM 62–83 and AG 843–6), together with the papers of Cardinal Podocataro in Venice (ASV), on which see V. Ilardi, 'Fifteenth-century diplomatic documents in western European archives and libraries (1450–1494)', *SR*, 9 (1962), 64–112 (pp. 77, 79) [Italian version 1968 'I documenti diplomatici del secolo XV negli archivi e biblioteche dell'Europa occidentale (1450–1494)' reprinted in his *Studies in Italian Renaissance diplomatic history*, Variorum Reprints Collected Studies (London, 1986), no. VI, 349–402 (pp. 364, 365)].
3. Bittmann, *Ludwig XI. und Karl der Kühne*, I/2, 407–8; II/1, 315–16.
4. ASV, P, 1, no. 26: '. . . *nos enim Dilectissime Fili quod decet desideriis tuis morem gerere parati sumus*'.
5. Giovanni Pietro Arrivabene to the marchioness of Mantua, Rome, 5 May 1470 and 11 April 1471 (AG 844).
6. Sforza Bettini to the duke of Milan, Ham, 11 June 1471 (ASM 538). On the questions of the alum monopoly and the Burgundian cardinal, see below, 'The papal alum monopoly' and 'The search for friends at the papal court'.
7. L. Pastor, *The history of the popes from the close of the Middle Ages*, trans. F.E. Antrobus *et al.*, 40 vols (London–St Louis, 1923–53), IV (1949), 203; F. Catalano, 'Il ducato di Milano nella politica dell'equilibrio', in *Storia di Milano*, 16 vols (Milan, 1953–62), VI (1956), 227–418 (pp. 273–4); E. Lee, *Sixtus IV and men of letters* (Rome, 1978), 21–3, 29–31, 62, 64, 207, 211, 217–18. For the next sentence see the duke of Milan to Nicodemo Tranchedini

da Pontremoli, Cremona, 17 August 1471 (ASM 68); Ourliac, 'Le concordat de 1472', 201; and Arrivabene to the marquis of Mantua, Rome, 18 December 1474 (AG 845).

8. Nicodemo Tranchedini, Rome, 20 November 1471, and Tranchedini and the bishop of Novara (Giovanni Arcimboldi), Rome, 28 November 1471, both to the duke of Milan (ASM 68); Cardinal Francesco Gonzaga to his father, the marquis of Mantua, Rome, 29 November 1471 (AG 844).

9. Paquet, 'Une ébauche', 89; this fundamental article contains thirteen letters written by Lucas de Tolentis to Sixtus IV in 1472–1473 which will be used extensively in following pages.

10. Below, section 'Papal mediation in disputes'.

11. *Carteggi*, I, no. 212.

12. He told the chapter meeting of the Order of the Golden Fleece in May 1473 that he had represented the Holy See '*pardeça*' for fifteen years (AOGV III, 39), which would place his arrival in the Low Countries in 1458 not long before Calixtus III's death. For what follows on his early career see Paquet, 'Une ébauche', 32–4, 62–4, and for some additional material see R.J. Walsh, 'The coming of humanism to the Low Countries: some Italian influences at the court of Charles the Bold', *Humanistica Lovaniensia*, 25 (1976), 146–97 (pp. 151–2).

13. The duke of Milan to Tranchedini and the bishop of Novara, Vigevano, 10 December 1471 (ASM 68) and the bishop to the duke, Rome, 28 July 1472 (ASM 70); J.B. Goetstouwers, 'Notes sur les papiers d'affaires de Pierre de Hagenbach et spécialement une lettre d'indulgence accordée en 1472 par le nonce Lucas de Tolentis', *Analectes pour servir à l'histoire ecclésiastique de la Belgique*, 3rd ser., 7 (1911), 222–7 (p. 227). This recall therefore took place about a year earlier than postulated by Paquet, 'Une ébauche', 34 note 2.

14. *Carteggi*, I, nos 181–2.

15. Cristoforo da Bollate to the duke of Milan, Vendôme, 10 October 1473 (ASM 540).

16. Paquet, 'Une ébauche', 113, 114.

17. Sacramoro to the duke of Milan, Rome, 25 October 1473, and Cicco Simonetta to Sacramoro, Pavia, 27 October 1473 (both ASM 73).

18. AG 2187, f. 1121; AG 845.

19. Simonetta, *Diarii*, 58; Sacramoro to the duke of Milan, Rome, 24 September 1474 (ASM 77); *CSP Milan*, I, no. 300; and *Chronologische lijsten van de geëxtendeerde sententiën en Proces-bundels (dossiers) berustende in het archief van de Grote Raad van Mechelen*, ed. J.T. de Smidt, J. van Rompaey and others, 3 vols (Brussels, 1966–79), I, 73.

20. *Urkundliche Nachträge zur österreichisch-deutschen Geschichte im Zeitalter Friedrich III.*, ed. A. Bachmann (Vienna, 1892) 391–3.

21. ASV, P, 1, no. 261.

22. See, for example, Sacramoro and Agostino dei Rossi to the duke of Milan, Rome, 18 January and 1 February 1476, and Sacramoro to the duke, Rome, 21 February and 1 and 29 March 1476 (all in ASM 80), and same to same from same, 9 and 30 May (ASM 81). A published example of the pope's 'nationalist' language is in Perret, *Histoire*, II, 76.

23. Walsh, 'Charles the Bold and the crusade', 80.
24. J.J.N. Palmer, 'England, France, the papacy and the Flemish succession', *JMH*, 2 (1976), 339–64.
25. They were descended in the fourth and third generations respectively from King Edward III of England. The negotiations for, and the celebration of, the marriage are described in detail by Vaughan, *Charles*, 45–6, 48–53.
26. Calmette and Périnelle, *Louis XI et l'Angleterre*, 97 note 3; and *Codice aragonese*, ed. F. Trinchera, 3 vols (Naples, 1866–74), I, no. 342.
27. C.A.J. Armstrong, 'La politique matrimoniale des ducs de Bourgogne de la maison de Valois', reprinted, from *AB*, 40 (1968), in his *England, France and Burgundy in the fifteenth century* (London, 1983), 237–342 (pp. 279–80); Charles to Paul II, Lille, 4 February 1468 (ASM 515: copy).
28. Below, 'Papal mediation in disputes'.
29. A. de Fouw, *Philips van Kleef* (Groningen, 1937), 13–14; Vaughan, *Philip the Good*, 290–2.
30. Both letters in ASV, P, I, no. 26.
31. *'mercantia'*: Cristoforo da Bollate to the duke of Milan, Senlis, 29 April 1474 (ASM 541).
32. There were doubts about both whether Henry IV really was Juana's father and whether his marriage to her mother Juana of Portugal had been valid, having been celebrated without the grant of the necessary dispensation; and Henry himself alternately declared both Juana and his sister Isabel as his heiress.
33. For this and the next paragraph see Dürr, 'Ludwig XI., die aragonesisch-castilianische Heirat und Karl der Kühne'; H. Stein, *Charles de France* (Paris, 1919/21), 397–409; and Bittmann, *Ludwig XI. und Karl der Kühne*, I/2, 424–9, 514–31, 539–46, 552–3, 566.
34. *Deutsche Reichstagsakten 1468–1470*, 64–5.
35. Paquet, 'Une ébauche', 108; Sacramoro to the duke of Milan, Rome, 2 and 25 August 1473 (ASM 73).
36. Below, Chapter 6, 'Federico d'Aragona'.
37. Wilwolt von Schaumburg, *Die Geschichten und Taten*, ed. A von Keller (Stuttgart, 1859), 26; H. Wiesflecker, *Kaiser Maximilian I.*, 5 volumes so far published (Munich, 1971–86), I, 107; W. Paravicini, 'Bemerkungen zu Richard Vaughan: Charles the Bold', *Francia*, 4 (1976), 757–73 (p. 769). For what follows on the truce and the peace treaty of November 1475 see Wiesflecker, *Kaiser Maximilan I.*, I, 108–9, and Vaughan, *Charles*, 381–2, 420–1.
38. *Urkundliche Nachträge zur österreichisch-deutschen Geschichte im Zeitalter Friedrich III.*, 391–3.
39. As was suggested by Combet, *Louis XI et le Saint-Siège*, 134, and, to a lesser extent, by Ourliac, 'Le concordat', 202; for the next sentence see J. Schlecht, *Andrea Zamometić und der Basler Konzilsversuch vom Jahre 1482* (Paderborn, 1903), 40*.
40. The only first-hand source for his visit to the Burgundian court is the chronicle of Chastellain in his *Oeuvres*, V, 349–55; see also Vaughan, *Charles*, 16, and Paravicini, *Guy de Brimeu*, 139 and note 176. His mission to France is described in *Lettres de Louis XI*, III, 193–4, 214–17, 260; in P. Richard,

'Origines de la nonciature de France', *Revue des questions historiques*, 88 (1905), 103–47 (pp. 110–11); and in Bittmann, *Ludwig XI. und Karl de Kühne*, I/1, 307.

41. C. Marcora, 'Stefano Nardini, arcivescovo di Milano (1461–1484)', *Memorie storiche della diocesi di Milano*, 3 (1956), 257–438 (p. 285); *Extrait d'une ancienne chronique*, in Commynes, *Mémoires*, ed. Godefroy and Lenglet du Fresnoy, II, 173–221 (p. 191).

42. The description of events in Liège which follows is based on Vaughan, *John the Fearless*, 49–66, *Philip the Good*, 58–62, 220–4, 391–7, and *Charles*, 11–31, and on Bittmann, *Ludwig XI. und Karl der Kühne*, I/1, 193–367.

43. *Mémoire du légat Onufrius sur les affaires de Liège*, ed. S. Bormans (Brussels, 1885); see also the broadly similar poetical version by Angelo de Curibus Sabinis, *De excidio civitatis Leodiensis*, in *Veterum scriptorum . . . collectio*, ed. E. Martène and U. Durand, 9 vols (Paris, 1729–33), IV (1729), cols 1379–1500.

44. Commynes, *Mémoires*, I, 147–8; compare G. Kurth, *La cité de Liège au moyen-âge*, 3 vols (Brussels-Liège, 1909–10), III, 370–1.

45. Published in *Cent-dix lettres grecques de François Filelfe*, ed. and trans. E. Legrand (Paris, 1892), 240.

46. For example see his *Mémoire*, 3, 36, 43–4, 49, 61, 71, 74–5, 86–7, 92–3, 96–8, 102–3, 116, 123, 141, 145–6, 151–2, 154, 166, and Curibus Sabinis, *De excidio*, cols 1381, 1400–1, 1403, 1413, 1433, 1439–41, 1443–8, 1452, 1466.

47. Vaughan, *Charles*, 28–9.

48. Willem van Berchen, *Gelderse Kroniek*, ed. A.J. de Mooy (Arnhem, 1950), 121, 123; Vaughan, *Charles*, 115–18.

49. S.B.J. Zilverberg, *David van Bourgondië* (Groningen-Jakarta, 1951), 37.

50. For what follows see especially P. Ourliac, 'Louis XI et le cardinal Bessarion', *Bulletin de la Société archéologique du Midi de la France*, 3rd ser., 5 (1942), 33–52, and L. Mohler, *Kardinal Bessarion*, 3 vols (Paderborn, 1923–42), III, 566–9 (Bessarion's letters from Saumur, 15 August 1472, to Louis XI and the duke of Brittany).

51. Copy in ADN B 18842.

52. Bittmann, *Ludwig XI. und Karl der Kühne*, I/2, 532–628.

53. For this and the rest of the paragraph see Paquet, 'Une ébauche', 78–9, 82–3, 91, 93, 96–7, 100–3.

54. Louis' request is reported in the letter of the bishop of Novara to the duke of Milan, Rome, 23 November 1472 (ASM 71).

55. Vespasiano da Bisticci, *Le vite*, ed. A. Greco, 2 vols (Florence, 1970–6), I, 170, 174.

56. For this paragraph see the bishop of Novara and G.A. Cagnola to the duke of Milan, Rome, 29 October 1472 (ASM 71); *Carteggi*, I, no. 183; Francesco Maletta to the duke of Milan, Naples, 30 March 1473 (ASM 223, summarising the lost letter of Francesco Bertini to the king of Naples from Brussels, 26 February 1473); and Paquet, 'Une ébauche', 97–9, 103.

57. The main accounts of his mission are Combet, *Louis XI et le Saint-Siège*, 125–6; Richard, 'Origines de la nonciature de France', 115–16; Ourliac, 'Le concordat', 199–201; Paquet, 'Une ébauche', 109–11, 114; and Bittmann, *Ludwig XI. und Karl der Kühne*, II/1, 159–62.

58. See, for example, the duke of Milan's letter to Andrea from Pavia, 19 June 1475 (ASM 79), in which he describes him as a great friend of long standing.

59. Not the cardinal of Rouen, Guillaume d'Estouteville, as stated by Ourliac, 'Le concordat', 200.

60. Based on the letter of Sacramoro to the duke of Milan, Rome, 3 April 1474 (ASM 75), printed in *Dépêches . . . Charles-le-Hardi*, I, no. 2, and in J. Chmel, 'Briefe und Aktenstücke zur Geschichte der Herzöge von Mailand', *Notizenblatt*, 6 (1856), *passim* (p. 78). It is not perhaps unreasonable to speculate that the timing of Louis XI's ratification of the concordat — though this had been promulgated by papal bull over two months earlier — less than three weeks after the issue of Andrea's bull of excommunication was something more than coincidence. Hans Knebel explained the excommunication as Sixtus IV's method of forcing Charles to stop undermining the peace of Christendom and thereby preventing a crusade: *Diarium*, I, 98.

61. Cristoforo da Bollate to the duke of Milan, Vendôme, 10 October 1473 (ASM 540).

62. Published in Commynes, *Mémoires*, ed. Godefroy and Lenglet du Fresnoy, III, 261–70. A copy, with Italian translation, is in ASM 515. The Milanese ambassador in Rome obtained a copy from Philibert Hugonet himself in March 1474 and, in his haste to pass it on to his master, he sent off each section by a different courier as he transcribed it: Sacramoro to the duke of Milan, 16 March 1474 (ASM 75).

63. In his letters of credence for Lucas de Tolentis addressed to Cardinal Gonzaga, 23 March 1474 (AG 2187, f. 1121).

64. For this paragraph see Sacramoro to the duke of Milan, Rome, 12 and 16 March 1474 (ASM 75); and Ourliac, 'Le concordat', 200–1.

65. His return to Rome was still being awaited in June 1475: the duke of Milan to Sacramoro, Pavia, 19 June 1475 (ASM 79). He went back to France with Giuliano della Rovere in March 1476, as we shall see shortly.

66. The bishop of Modena's instructions, including a commission to make peace between Louis XI and the dukes of Burgundy and Brittany, are dated on different days in August: Richard, 'Origines', 116–17. It is unlikely, therefore, that he reached France before the treaty of Soleuvre was concluded, still less that he influenced it in any way.

67. The main accounts are Combet, *Louis XI et le Saint-Siège*, 140–51; L.H. Labande, *Avignon au XVe siècle* (Monaco–Paris, 1920), 188–234; and Ourliac, 'Le concordat', 202–12.

68. Having left Rome probably towards the end of February 1476, Lucas arrived in the Burgundian camp outside Lausanne before the end of March: *Carteggi*, II, no. 485.

69. Sacramoro to the duke of Milan from Rome, 16 March 1476 (ASM 80) and 9 May 1476 (ASM 81).

70. *Carteggi*, II, nos. 532–3. For the next sentence see Labande, *Avignon au XVe siècle*, 219 note 3.

71. *Carteggi*, II, nos. 487, 573.

72. *Carteggi*, II, no. 532.

73. *Carteggi*, II, no. 493.

74. The activities of Querini (and of a brother whose Christian name is not recorded) as an intermediary between King René, Count Charles of Maine (René's nephew and heir in Anjou and Provence) and Charles the Bold are described by Panigarola: *Carteggi*, II, nos. 416, 418, 488, 522.

75. He arrived in Turin on 18 May: Francesco Pietrasanta to the duke of Milan, Turin, 18 May 1476 (ASM 495).

76. *Carteggi*, II, nos. 468, 478.

77. *Carteggi*, II, nos. 554, 541.

78. *Carteggi*, II, no. 493.

79. The form Nanni is preferable if only because the form Numai, used by some contemporaries, casts doubt on his mother's husband being his father: P. Ughelli, *Italia sacra*, 10 vols, 2nd edtn (Venice, 1717–22), II (1717), 584.

80. Pastor, *The history of the popes*, IV, 284.

81. *Carteggi*, I, no. 297.

82. For Nancy see *Lorraine et Bourgogne (1475–1478). Choix de documents*, ed. J. Schneider (Nancy, 1982), 116.

83. Walsh, 'Diplomatic aspects', 268 and note 8. For the rest of the sentence see J. Schneider, 'Un conseiller des ducs de Bourgogne: Georges de Bade, évêque de Metz (1459–1484)', in *Cinq-centième anniversaire de la bataille de Nancy (1477). Actes du Colloque . . .* (Nancy, 1979), 305–38 (pp. 323–4) and *Lorraine et Bourgogne*, 191.

84. Combet, *Louis XI et le Saint-Siège*, 139–40; *Die Eidgenössischen Abschiede aus dem Zeitraum von 1421 bis 1477*, ed. A.P. Segesser (Luzern, 1863), 625–8, 636–7, 648; *Chronique de Lorraine*, ed. L. Marchal (Nancy, 1859), 257–8; Knebel, *Diarium*, II, 40, 55, 70, 72–3, 82; *Lorraine et Bourgogne*, 176–82, 187–93.

85. A.G. Jongkees, 'État et Église dans les Pays-Bas bourguignons: avant et après 1477', in *Cinq-centième anniversaire de la bataille de Nancy (1477). Actes du Colloque . . .*, 237–47 (pp. 237–40).

86. J. Bartier, 'Quelques réflexions à propos d'un mémoire de Raymond de Marliano et de la fiscalité à l'époque de Charles le Téméraire', *BMGN*, 95 (1980), 349–62 (p. 359).

87. U. Berlière, 'La commende aux Pays-Bas', in *Mélanges Godefroid Kurth*, 2 vols (Paris, 1908), I, 185–201 (pp. 192–3, 196–201); A. Erens, 'Thierry van Tuldel et la commende en Brabant, 1470–1490', *Analecta Praemonstratensia*, 1 (1925), 321–56 (pp. 322–47); R. van Uytven, 'Wereldlijke overheid en reguliere geestelijkheid in Brabant tijdens de late Middeleeuwen' in *Sources de l'histoire religieuse de la Belgique . . . Actes . . .* (Louvain, 1968), 48–134 (pp. 128–32).

88. Paquet, 'Une ébauche', 62–6, 69–74, 128–34, 136–7; A. de But, *Chronique*, in *Chroniques relatives à l'histoire de la Belgique sous la domination des ducs de Bourgogne (textes latines)*, ed. J.B.M.C. Kervyn de Lettenhove, 3 vols (Brussels, 1870–6), I, 21–717 (p. 506); F. Rémy, *Les grandes indulgences pontificales aux Pays-Bas à la fin du moyen âge 1300–1531* (Louvain, 1928), 91–7.

89. J.M. Pesez, 'Chevaucheurs et courriers du duc de Bourgogne Charles le Téméraire' (unpublished thesis — Thèse de Diplôme d'Études Supérieures soutenue devant la Faculté des Lettres — University of Lille, 1954), 118. For

the next sentence see Barbaro to the doge, Naples, 29 March 1473 (BNMV 8170/V, 22), summarising the lost letter of Francesco Bertini to King Ferrante from Brussels, 26 February 1473.

90. Bittmann, *Ludwig XI. und Karl der Kühne*, I/2, 407–8.
91. L.P. Gachard, 'Analectes historiques. Septième série', *BCRH*, 2nd ser., 12 (1859), 359–516 (pp. 391–4); R.E. de Moreau, *Histoire de l'Église en Belgique*, 5 vols (Brussels, 1940–52), IV (1949), 112; and *CSP Milan*, I, no. 279.
92. Walsh, 'Charles the Bold and the crusade', 74.
93. *Carteggi*, II, no. 643. On Lucas's activities as a seller of indulgences at this time see J. Rott, 'Note sur quelques comptes de collecteurs pontificaux du XVᵉ siècle concernant la France', *MAHEFR*, 51 (1934), 293–327 (pp. 304–5, 316–17, 324–7), who does not, however, mention this particular incident, although it is referred to, somewhat imprecisely, in *Lorraine et Bourgogne*, 191. On the importance of the proceeds of the sales of indulgences to the finances of both the papacy and the rulers in whose lands they were collected at this time, and on the shortages of certain types of local currency thus revealed, see J.A.F. Thomson, *Popes and princes, 1417–1517. Politics and polity in the late medieval Church* (London, 1980), 87–8, 175, and J. Favier, 'Circulation et conjoncture monétaires au temps de Marie de Bourgogne', *Revue historique*, 272 (1984), 3–27.
94. Vaughan, *Philip the Good*, 215–37; *Charles*, 183.
95. Letter to the duke of Milan from Rome with signature missing, 10 April 1472 (ASM 69); Walsh, 'Relations', 391 and note 72.
96. For his pleas to Ferrante and, later, Galeazzo Maria to intercede on his behalf in Rome see below, 'The search for friends at the papal court'.
97. Walsh, 'Diplomatic aspects', 269–70.
98. Jongkees, 'État et Église', 244–5, and 'Charles le Téméraire et la souveraineté', *BMGN*, 95 (1980), 315–34 (pp. 333–4), and the references cited there, to which should be added *Documents inédits sur l'érection des nouveaux diocèses aux Pays-Bas (1521–1570)*, ed. M. Dierickx, 3 vols (Brussels, 1960–2), I, 59–75, and III, 237.
99. Paquet, 'Une ébauche', 99; Bartier, 'Quelques réflexions', 353.
100. *Carteggi*, I, nos. 183, 193.
101. Bittmann, *Ludwig XI. und Karl der Kühne*, II/1, 94.
102. Pastor, *The history of the popes*, IV, 105 (unnumbered footnote).
103. Perret, *Histoire*, II, 74–5; Ourliac, 'Le concordat', 204.
104. *Carteggi*, II, no. 502.
105. Soon after Sixtus IV's election he wrote to Ferrante urging him to withhold obedience, but his letter arrived too late: Ferrante to Charles, Vairano, 23 February 1472 (ADN B 18842). He himself was reported still not to have done so by October 1472 when Edward IV took this step, nor yet by December 1474 when another ally, the duke of Brittany, at last relented, despite Charles the Bold's dissuasion: the bishop of Novara to the duke of Milan, Rome, 4 October 1472 (ASM 71); Paquet, 'Une ébauche', 127; and Sacramoro to the duke of Milan, Rome, 15 December 1474 (ASM 78).
106. For what follows see Vaughan, *Charles*, 161, and my 'Charles the Bold and the crusade', 76–7, and 'The coming of humanism', 181 and note 148.

107. For this and the next sentence see Sacramoro to the duke of Milan, Rome, 17 August 1473 (ASM 73: '. . . *crede che facendo loro questa parentela lo doverà instigare sempre a novità, spirituale e temporale . . .*') and Rome, 29 March 1476 (ASM 80).

108. P.C. Boeren, *Twee Maaslandse dichters in dienst van Karel de Stoute* (The Hague, 1968), 9.

109. See especially L. Liagre, 'Le commerce de l'alun en Flandre', *MA*, 61 (1954–5), 177–206; R. de Roover, *The rise and decline of the Medici bank 1397–1494* (Cambridge, Mass., 1963), 152–64, 438–41; J. Delumeau, *L'alun de Rome, XVᵉ–XIXᵉ siècle* (Paris, 1962), 7–22, 32–6; and W.P. Blockmans, *De volksvertegenwoordiging in Vlaanderen in de overgang van Middeleeuwen naar nieuwe tijden (1384–1506)* (Brussels, 1978), 406–9. The text of the treaty is printed in *Codex diplomaticus dominii temporalis S. Sedis*, ed. A. Theiner, 3 vols (Rome, 1861–2), III, 451–5. Some of the arguments in this section were anticipated, though more briefly, in my 'Diplomatic aspects', 273–6.

110. Paquet, 'Une ébauche', 87.

111. Paquet, 'Une ébauche', 87. These objectors probably included the Genoese, who resented being squeezed out of the alum trade, which they had once dominated, by their Florentine rivals. See J. Finot, *Étude historique sur les relations commerciales entre la Flandre et la république de Gênes au moyen âge* (Paris, 1906), 191–2; M.L. Heers, 'Les Génois et le commerce de l'alun à la fin du moyen âge', *Revue d'histoire économique et sociale*, 32 (1954), 31–53; Liagre, 'Le commerce de l'alun en Flandre', 203; and Delumeau, *L'alun de Rome*, 92–5.

112. Charles himself claimed that, in return for this grant, he had been forced ('*coactus*') to sacrifice the papal monopoly: Paquet, 'Une ébauche', 107; and this claim has been accepted by the majority of historians, e.g. Liagre, 'Le commerce', 203, though not, more recently, by Blockmans, *De volksvertegenwoordiging*, 408–9, who recognised the part played by political and diplomatic considerations.

113. Copy in ASM 515.

114. *Carteggi*, I, no. 150; Pastor, *The history of the popes*, IV, 105 (unnumbered footnote).

115. G. Zippel, *Storia e cultura del Rinascimento italiano* (Padua, 1979), 332–4; see also, on the diplomatic horse-trading over the alum treaty, M. Ballard, 'An expedition of English archers to Liège in 1467, and the Anglo–Burgundian marriage alliance', *Nottingham Medieval Studies*, 34 (1990), 152–74 (pp. 161–2).

116. Louis XI sought to obtain supplies from other sources, while encouraging prospecting for alum within his kingdom: Gandilhon, *Politique économique de Louis XI*, 186–7.

117. Paquet, 'Une ébauche', 87.

118. *Carteggi*, I, no. 183.

119. For the context see above, Chapter 1, 'The material value of the Italian alliances: fulfilment'. For the next four sentences see P. Sposato, 'Attività commerciali degli Aragonesi nella seconda metà del Quattrocento', in *Studi in onore di Riccardo Filangieri*, 2 vols (Naples, 1959), II, 213–31; de Roover, *The rise and decline of the Medici bank*, 154–6; and C.L. Scofield, *The life and reign of Edward the Fourth*, 2 vols (London, 1923), I, 402, 484.

120. Bartier, *Légistes et gens de finances*, 447; C. Desimoni and L.T. Belgrano, 'Documenti ed estratti inediti o poco noti riguardanti la storia del commercio e della marina ligure. I. Brabante, Fiandra e Borgogna', *Atti della Società ligure di storia patria*, 5/III (1871), 355–547 (p. 446, no. 129); ASV, SS, XXV, 128ᵛ–9; *Carteggi*, I, no. 193; Paquet, 'Une ébauche', 113.

121. Charles had then refused it: Barbaro to the doge, Naples, 21 March 1473 (BNMV 8170/V, 19).

122. Paquet, 'Une ébauche', 105.

123. Above, 'Papal mediation in disputes'.

124. Finot, *Étude*, 243–4; Paquet, 'Une ébauche', 129; and Blockmans, *De volksvertegenwoordiging*, 408.

125. Chastellain, *Oeuvres*, V, 351; *Carteggi*, I, no. 297.

126. Paquet, 'Une ébauche', 90 (Antwerp, 21 September 1472).

127. *Extrait d'une ancienne chronique*, in Commynes, *Mémoires*, ed. Godefroy and Lenglet du Fresnoy, II, 199 note 61. Lucas was later to serve Mary and Maximilian in the same capacity, and earlier, in 1465, he had also been appointed councillor by Philip the Good: Paquet, 'Une ébauche', 33, 35–6.

128. Arrivabene to the marquis of Mantua, 9 March 1476 (AG 845).

129. Sacramoro to the duke of Milan, Rome, 17 June 1476 (ASM 81).

130. Sacramoro to the duke of Milan, Rome, 29 April 1474 (ASM 77).

131. Walsh, 'Diplomatic aspects', 268 and note 8.

132. The phrase is from his letters of credence on behalf of Lucas addressed to Cardinal Gonzaga, dated Vesoul, 23 March 1474 (AG 2187/1121). Lucas had been equipped with similar letters of credence when he returned to Rome in the winter of 1471–1472: the duke of Milan to Nicodemo Tranchedini and the bishop of Novara in Rome, Vigevano, 10 December 1471 (ASM 68).

133. AOGV III, 33ᵛ (de Reiffenberg, *Histoire de l'Ordre*, 73).

134. Barbaro to the doge, Naples, 20 November 1472 (BNMV 8170/IV, 34).

135. Walsh, 'Diplomatic aspects', 271 note 15; for the next sentence see the summaries of the lost letter of Bertini to Ferrante from Brussels, 26 February 1473, by Barbaro to the doge, Naples, 29 March 1473 (BNMV 8170/V, 22) and by Francesco Maletta to the duke of Milan, Naples, 30 March 1473 (ASM 223).

136. Sacramoro to the duke of Milan from Rome, 12 July 1473 (ASM 73); Ferrante to Antonio Cincinello, his ambassador in Milan, from Aversa, 25 March 1474 (ASM 225).

137. Galeazzo Maria to Sacramoro, Pavia, 12 and 23 May (ASM 79). Whether as a result of these endeavours or not, Seignart was appointed bishop of Auxerre in March 1476: C. Eubel, *Hierarchia catholica Medii Aevi*, 2 vols (Münster, 1913–14), II, 99.

138. Paquet, 'Une ébauche', 117; *Carteggi*, I, no. 219.

139. The duke of Milan to Sacramoro, San Giorgio, 14 September 1475 (ASM 79). Candida was empowered by Charles to go to Naples also, for reasons unspecified: V. Tourneur, 'Jehan de Candida', *Revue belge de numismatique*, 70 (1914), 381–411, and 71 (1919), 7–48, 251–300 (p. 9) comments 'Jusqu'à présent, aucune pièce relative à cette double ambassade n'a été découverte'. But Philippe de Brimeu never did obtain a bishopric, though he did receive many lesser benefices: Paravicini, *Guy de Brimeu*, 446–8, 505–6, 508.

140. *Carteggi*, I, nos. 25, 327.
141. *Carteggi*, II, no. 343.
142. From the camp at Lausanne, 11 April 1476 (ASM 519).
143. From the camp at Lausanne, 11 April 1476 (ASM 516 — misfiled [when I consulted it], this being the *carteggio* for the first six months of 1475).
144. *Carteggi*, II, nos. 516–17. In 1476 Charles also tried to have the recently vacant abbey of Cherlieu in Burgundy reserved for Matteo, though unsuccessfully, and in any case Matteo was to die, in July 1476, before the vacancy was filled the following year: L. Besson, *Mémoire historique sur l'abbaye de Cherlieu* (Besançon, 1847), 78.
145. For example, Battista di Giovanni ('batista de giovane') to the duke of Milan, Rome, 11 October 1474 (ASM 77); Zaccaria Saggio to the marquis of Mantua, Milan, 8 April 1476 (AG 1625); and R.J. Walsh, 'Vespasiano da Bisticci, Francesco Bertini and Charles the Bold: an examination of Charles the Bold's relations with Italy', *European Studies Review*, 10 (1980), 401–27 (p. 413).
146. Vaughan, *Philip the Good*, 205–6.
147. I. Ammanati-Piccolomini, *Epistolae et commentarii* (Milan, 1506), 262; Combet, *Louis XI et le Saint-Siège*, 120–1. Another friend and patron of Bertini was Bartolomeo Roverella, cardinal-archbishop of Ravenna: Walsh, 'The coming of humanism', 149.
148. J. Peter, *L'abbaye de Liessies en Hainaut* (Lille, 1912), 107 note 3.
149. The bishop of Novara to the duke of Milan, Rome, 10 and 22 March 1472 (ASM 69).
150. '*una bola de pleno dominio absque exceptione*': Assalito Maletta to the duke of Milan, Rome, 25 April 1472 (ASM 69).
151. Riario to the duke of Milan, Rome, 28 February 1473 (ASM 72).
152. M.E. de la Coste, *Anselme Adorne* (Brussels, 1855), 303–4; É. Hautcoeur, *Histoire de l'église collégiale et du chapitre de Saint-Pierre de Lille*, 3 vols (Lille–Paris, 1896–9), II (1897), 168–9; P. Glorieux, 'Un chanoine de Saint Pierre de Lille, Jean Adourne', *Bulletin du Comité flamand de France*, 18 (1971), 295–324 (pp. 320–1).
153. Francesco Pietrasanta to the duke of Milan, 20 May 1476 (ASM 495); *Carteggi*, II, no. 561.
154. Vaughan, *Philip the Good*, 205. Of those who held the post, we know the names of Jean Vivien and Jean Tronchon (Bartier, *Légistes*, 127 and note 3, 407, 408) and of Ferry de Beauvoir, later bishop of Amiens (Bartier, *Légistes*, 126 and note 1; C. Thelliez, 'A propos du testament de Jean de Bourgogne', *Anciens pays et assemblées d'états*, 62 (1973), 31–91 (pp. 38, 39)).
155. Jean de Bourgogne, natural son of John the Fearless, kept a Jean Nilis in Rome as his proctor and solicitor during the time he was bishop of Cambrai (1439–1480): Thelliez, 'A propos du testament de Jean de Bourgogne', 78, 79.
156. Sacramoro to the duke of Milan, 15 August 1474 (ASM 77). For the others mentioned in this paragraph see Walsh, 'The coming of humanism', 188, 192, and 'Diplomatic aspects', 72 and note 21.
157. Bartier, *Légistes*, 127 note 7 (on 128).
158. For the rest of this paragraph see Paquet, 'Une ébauche', 98, and Eubel, *Hierarchia catholica Medii Aevi*, II, 8, 11, 13–17.

159. Bittmann, *Ludwig XI. und Karl der Kühne*, I/2, 407–8; Lucas de Tolentis's letter to the pope from Lille, 6 February 1469 (copies in ASM 515 and 536) seems also to refer to this offer.

160. Eubel, *Hierarchia*, II, 15 note 6 stated that the fourth candidate was Ferry de Clugny. That the promise was made to Ferry, as it had been in 1469, is suggested also by events in 1473 (as we shall see shortly), although Giovanni Bianchi, writing to the duke of Milan from Rome, 1 August 1471 (ASM 68), named the fourth candidate as 'the Burgundian protonotary', which would suggest Philibert Hugonet. The fourth candidate named by Pastor (*The history of the popes*, IV, 123) was neither Hugonet nor Ferry de Clugny but the bishop of Tarragona.

161. The duke to Tranchedini in Rome, Galiate, 23 September 1471 (ASM 68).

162. Pastor, *The history of the popes*, IV, 123.

163. Letter to the duke of Milan from Rome, 18 April 1472, with signature missing (ASM 69). For the next sentence see Paquet, 'Une ébauche', 98.

164. The bishop of Novara and G.A. Cagnola to the duke of Milan, Rome, 19 December 1472 (ASM 71). The ambassador is not here named, although he was later described as a bishop (the bishop of Novara to the duke of Milan, Rome, 5 February 1473, ASM 72), which would seem to rule out Dr Johann von Espacht, who was also in Rome on Charles the Bold's behalf in December 1472 (Pietro Riario to the duke of Milan, Rome, 12 December 1472, ASM 71).

165. *Carteggi*, I, nos. 182–4.

166. Eubel, *Hierarchia*, II, 16.

167. The bishop of Novara to the duke of Milan, Rome, 28 July 1472 (ASM 70).

168. Paquet, 'Une ébauche', 83.

169. Sacramoro to the duke of Milan, Rome, 8 April 1473 (ASM 72).

170. Same to same from same, 21 April 1473 (ASM 72).

171. J. Lesellier, 'Une curieuse correspondance inédite entre Louis XI et Sixte IV', *MAHEFR*, 45 (1928), 21–37 (pp. 21–4). Louis had even greater hopes of seducing Ferry in the second half of 1473 when he was able to play on Ferry's chagrin at failing to be given the red hat: Bittmann, *Ludwig XI. und Karl der Kühne*, II/1, 171–2, 186–7.

172. Giovanni Andrea Ferrofini to the duke of Milan, Rome, 9 May 1473 (ASM 72); Ammanati-Piccolomini, *Epistolae et commentarii*, ff. 260^v–1 (Ammanati-Piccolomini to Francesco Bertini, Rome, 7 July 1473).

173. Ferrofini to the duke of Milan, Rome, 9 May 1473 (ASM 72).

174. For this paragraph see Lesellier, 'Une curieuse correspondance', 24–37; Paquet, 'Une ébauche', 105–6; ASV, P, 1, no. 261; and Eubel, *Hierarchia*, II, 16, 17, 19. Foscari and Savelli had to wait for their promotions until 1477 and 1480 respectively: Eubel, *Hierarchia*, II, 18, 19.

175. Sacramoro to the duke of Milan, 8 May 1473 (ASM 72); see also S. Infessura, *Diario della città di Roma*, ed. O. Tommasini (Rome, 1890), 77.

176. Sacramoro to the duke of Milan, Rome, 5 July and 2 August 1473 (ASM 73) and 12 March 1474 (ASM 75).

177. Sacramoro to the duke of Milan, Rome, 5 and 23 November 1474, and the duke to Sacramoro, Milan, 13 November 1474 (all in ASM 77).

CHAPTER THREE

Relations with Florence and the Activities of Tommaso Portinari

Charles the Bold's relations with the republic of Florence — and with the successive heads of the city's *de facto* ruling family, the Medici, Piero (1464–1469) and his son Lorenzo (1469–1492) — were rather different in kind from those he maintained with the other major secular powers of Italy, and this accounts for their treatment here in a separate chapter. Diplomatically, these relations were always distant. Both the republic and the Medici family itself had long enjoyed close, almost dependent, links with the French crown, and it was mainly for this reason that Florence, alone of the four major secular states in the peninsula, never made an alliance with Charles. Economically, however, the ties between Florence and Valois Burgundy were much closer. Moreover, the Medici had a financial link with Burgundy on their own account, through the establishment in 1439 of a subsidiary branch of their bank in Bruges. The significance of these economic ties was increased by the fact that they inevitably took on a political dimension. For example, the Medici bank had subsidiary branches not only in Bruges but also in Lyon and London, and economic considerations played a large part in deciding the attitude adopted by both the Medici and the Florentine republic towards Burgundy and France. Again, Tommaso Portinari, the manager of the Bruges bank during the reign of Charles the Bold, was one of the most prominent of the many Italians who frequented his court, and, because Florence accredited no ambassador to Burgundy, Portinari was occasionally called upon to act in a quasi-diplomatic capacity on behalf of the republic or of the Medici.

The importance of the career of Tommaso Portinari justifies the emphasis implied in the title of this chapter. The concentration on one man is explained also by the fact that Portinari's political and economic activities during Charles the Bold's reign have never been fully studied together, so that some aspects still remain controversial: for example, the extent and wisdom of his financial links with the duke himself. At the same time, it should be remembered that he served not one but two masters: the Medici, as manager of the Bruges bank, and the duke, as councillor. Consequently, his attitude towards the duke must sometimes be differentiated from that of both the Medici and the Florentine republic; the former was not always simply a reflection of the latter.

Tommaso Portinari's career before the accession of Charles the Bold

Tommaso Portinari (1428–1501) came from a Florentine family which had become prominent since the thirteenth century in Florentine trade and, since the fourteenth, in the service of the Medici; for example, the first manager of the Medici bank in Bruges was his cousin Bernardo. It was probably in the early 1440s, while he was still in his teens, that Tommaso himself travelled to Bruges to learn banking. He quickly displayed great self-confidence and ambition, but it was not until April 1465, after much insistence on his part, that he was appointed manager of the Bruges bank in succession to the dour Angelo Tani.[1] By this time he had already established a connection with the Burgundian court; indeed, a year before his appointment he had been accused, presumably by colleagues, of neglecting the interests of the bank by spending too much time at court.[2]

This flamboyance, which distinguished him so sharply from the bulk of his more cautious colleagues, was to be one of his enduring characteristics. The Medici bank engaged not only in banking but also in trade; for example, its branches served as outlets for Florentine silk and other commodities. But both Cosimo de' Medici (1434–1464) and his son Piero had enjoined caution in the dealings of the Bruges bank with the Burgundian court.[3] Under Portinari's guidance, however, this policy came to be considerably modified. One of his colleagues, Carlo Cavalcanti, was empowered to specialise in the sale of silk fabrics and brocades at court, and we can trace purchases of silk and other luxury articles made by the court through payments to Portinari recorded in the Burgundian accounts at the close of Philip the Good's reign.[4] The facilities for safe and speedy communications and for the transfer of funds which Portinari commanded also proved most useful to Philip. For example, in 1463 he was entrusted with carrying letters from Philip to Francesco Sforza, and in April 1467 the duke's officials repaid him a sum of 35 *livres* which, at Philip's request, he had instructed the Medici bank in Rome to pay to the papal camera for '*une bulle confessionale*'. A most important transaction took place just a month after he became manager of the Bruges bank. In May 1465 he secured the farm of the ducal toll levied at Gravelines on English wool imported into the Low Countries from the English staple at Calais, and on other merchandise passing through Gravelines on its way to and from Calais. In the charter which granted this farm to him and to the Medici company in Bruges he was described for the first time as a ducal councillor.[5] From this time onwards the finances of the Bruges bank were to become increasingly entwined with those of the court, for the court was probably now the bank's largest single customer.

Portinari was on good terms also with the future Charles the Bold, then count of Charolais, and managed to remain so despite the bitter quarrel which erupted between Charles and his father in 1464–1465. In 1463 and 1465 he acted as a messenger between Charles and Francesco Sforza,[6] and in the spring of 1466 he was sent by Charles to Saint-Omer to meet the earl of Warwick and help prepare the way for negotiations concerning the projected marriage between Charles and Margaret of York. By now he can perhaps be said to have belonged to that close circle of friends and advisers which formed around Charles in the latter years of Philip's reign and which provided the nucleus of a new administrative personnel after his accession in 1467.[7]

Portinari's position at the court

At least as early as May 1465 Portinari had been designated a councillor by Philip the Good and he served his successor in a similar capacity. The first occasion on which he appears to have been described as Charles the Bold's councillor was in a ducal mandate issued at Brussels on 1 October 1467 by which he was granted a reduction in the farm of the Gravelines toll.[8] Apart from that of councillor, however, he held no official post in the government. His importance to the duke lay in the services he rendered and was not derived from any particular rank held in the Burgundian administration. This point is worth emphasising. In later chapters we shall see that Charles employed several Italians as diplomats and councillors; that his household contained a significant number of Italian squires, secretaries and doctors; and that the Italians in his army could be counted by the thousand. But there are no signs that Italians made a similar impact on the civil service and financial administration proper, the backbone of the Burgundian state.[9]

Unlike many of the other Italians in the ducal service, Portinari did not in general follow the court; his duties as manager of the Medici bank in Bruges dictated that he spend the bulk of his time there. On the other hand, as a ducal councillor, he could be summoned to court whenever required. For example, in the first week of February 1468 and in the last week of March the same year messengers were sent to him with instructions to join the duke,[10] who was then at Brussels and Mons respectively. Similarly, when Charles met Frederick III outside Trier on 30 September 1473, Portinari was one of those in attendance. He was dressed at the duke's expense in a colourful outfit of crimson-violet figured satin and a pourpoint of crimson satin; it is interesting to find that the nine men arrayed in this particular sartorial combination included some of the duke's most influential officials, such as Jean Carondelet, Thomas de Plaine, Vasco de Lucena, Nicolas de Gondeval and Jean le Gros.[11] At other times he kept, or was kept, in close touch with Charles the Bold's business by the various ducal officials. For example, on 9 August 1475 the president and officers of the *Chambre des comptes* at Malines wrote to thank him profusely for a letter just received from him containing certain unspecified but valuable information about matters which they declared to be of great importance.[12] In October that year the officials at Malines sent a messenger with all haste to Portinari bearing letters close concerning certain unspecified ducal affairs.

One reason for such consultation was that Portinari was deeply involved with the administration and collection of some of the Burgundian state revenues. He farmed the Gravelines toll throughout Charles the Bold's reign.[13] In 1471 he was described as one of the three ducal commissioners empowered to levy the duty which Charles imposed on papal alum imported into his lands, and when the duke suspended the papal alum monopoly in 1473, it was Portinari who was charged with raising the same levy on imports of non-papal alum.[14] He seems also to have been concerned with helping the duke find the money necessary for paying his troops. Moreover, as manager of the Bruges bank, he was in a position to place the facilities of the Medici network as a whole at the duke's disposal. The Medici, for example, had branches of their bank in Rome and London, and between October 1467 and August 1468 we find Portinari arranging for the payment of messengers sent to Charles by his proctors in Rome, for the payment of an envoy sent to Rome by the duke in order to obtain a dispensation from the pope for his marriage with Margaret of York, and for the transmission of letters from the duke to his agent in England.[15] Again, when on 24 March 1468 a truce between England and Burgundy was arranged by the proctors of Edward IV and Charles the Bold at Brussels, it was agreed that their masters' confirmation of the truce should be exchanged in Portinari's headquarters, the Hôtel Bladelin in Bruges. Portinari was also concerned, in a manner unspecified by the Burgundian accounts, with the making of the ducal seal at the beginning of the reign;[16] and when, at Easter 1475, the brother of the queen of England, Anthony Woodville, Earl Rivers, asked Charles for an advance on his Burgundian annual pension of 1,200 *livres*, the duke ordered his officials to pay Woodville through Portinari.

In 1475 the Milanese ambassador Panigarola described Portinari as extremely well-informed on Burgundian affairs.[17] Such a judgement is quite understandable in view of the numerous contacts which he maintained with members of the court, both Burgundian and Italian. Two examples from the reign of Philip the Good are Antoine de Croy and Guillaume Bische;[18] in fact, Bische had a deposit account with the Medici bank in Bruges, as did Louis de Bruges, lord of the Gruuthuse, and Olivier de la Marche, master of the ducal household, while Guy de Brimeu was one of perhaps several leading courtiers who borrowed from Portinari. He was described by a Milanese agent in Bruges in 1471 as being on good terms too with Pierre or Pieter Bladelin, whose house he had bought for the Medici bank in 1466.[19] We know also of his dealings with some of the Italians at court. To Rodolfo Gonzaga he lent money during the Mantuan prince's short but unexpectedly expensive visit to the Burgundian court in 1469–1470.[20] The Venetian ambassador Bernardo Bembo too seems to have turned to him for money to tide him over while awaiting remittances from home.[21] Portinari was designated to handle some of the money bequeathed in 1475 by Raimondo Marliani, the eminent Milanese legist and councillor of Charles the Bold, for the foundation in Pavia of a college bearing his family's name.[22] Antonello da Campobasso, one of the companions of Don Federico on his visit to the Burgundian court in 1475–1476, deposited a sum of 100 ducats given him by the Neapolitan prince during that visit with the Medici bank, presumably at the Bruges branch.

Portinari was particularly useful to the Milanese because letters and money could be easily and safely transmitted between Bruges and Milan;

after all, the Medici bank had branches in both cities, their managers were the two Portinari brothers, respectively Tommaso and Accerito (who had succeeded the eldest brother Pigello in October 1468), and relations between Milan and Florence were close. For example, when Galeazzo Maria dispatched his Flemish choirmaster Gaspar van Weerbeke to Flanders in 1472 to recruit some of his compatriots for the ducal chapel, the requisite money was sent to him via the Milan and Bruges branches of the Medici bank.[23] Those who perhaps made most use of this link were the Milanese agents and diplomats north of the Alps. The Sforzaphile papal nuncio Prospero Schiaffino da Camogli borrowed money from Portinari while he was in France in 1461 and it was through Portinari that he sent letters to Francesco Sforza.[24] In 1464 the Milanese ambassador in France, Alberico Maletta, entrusted his letters to Portinari for safe transmission.[25] In the winter of 1472–1473 the papal nuncio Pietro Aliprandi received letters from Galeazzo Maria by way of Portinari; he also expected remittances from Milan to be sent through the Medici bank in Bruges; and it was there that he gathered some of his information.[26] Similarly, Galeazzo Maria used him in 1473 as an intermediary to pass on his letters to Carlo Visconti, his ambassador at the imperial court. The duke of Milan, however, was not as quick in sending money to his agents, so that they were often forced to borrow from Portinari. Thus in December 1475 Panigarola complained that his master's remittances were irregular, late and inadequate and that, if the Florentine had not lent him 150 *écus* the previous month, he would already have died of hunger![27] In fact, Portinari seems to have been one of several of Charles the Bold's councillors and courtiers who advocated better relations with Milan even before the conclusion of the treaty of Moncalieri in January 1475.

Like a handful of the Italians at court, we know what he looked like; in fact, from the number and quality of his portraits we are probably better informed about his appearance than about that of any of the others, and this is testimony both to his self-assurance and to his prominence in court circles. He was painted twice by Hans Memling, probably in 1470 (now in the Galleria Sabauda, Turin) and again about a year later (now in the Metropolitan Museum of Art, New York).[28] Between about 1473 and 1478 he was painted also by another Flemish master, Hugo van der Goes (now in the Uffizi, Florence). These pictures emphasise the same characteristic features: a certain gauntness, short dark hair and tightly pressed lips, and, perhaps most striking, an almost visionary expression in his eyes, which stare fixedly into the distance.

There is no doubt that Charles and Portinari were very close. After all, the difference in their ages was only five years, Portinari being the elder. They may also have felt some affinity of temperament. Charles clearly trusted the Florentine greatly and had been confiding in him at least since the early 1460s. In the contract with Portinari of March 1471 Lorenzo de' Medici specifically allowed him to continue doing business with Charles on the grounds of his intimacy with the duke.[29] For his part, Portinari did not hide his admiration of the duke. In 1471 he was described by one of the duke of Milan's agents as '*borgonione*',[30] and four years later, in a letter to the duke of Milan, he himself referred to Charles as '*glorioso*', '*invicto*' and '*magnifico*'.[31] Such admiration was far from unusual among the Italians in the duke of Burgundy's entourage or, indeed, in the peninsula itself. But Portinari went further than others by showing his faith in terms of hard cash: in 1471 he was the only taker for a block of annuities issued by the city of Bruges as a means of financing a loan to Charles.[32] By the following year his feeling of security and confidence in the future were such as to allow him to promise to the church of Santa Maria Nuova in Florence an annual sum of 700 *livres* for the rest of his life.

However, on the basis of the Memling portrait now in New York the art historian Aby Warburg described Portinari disapprovingly as a 'financial condottiere' whose reckless temperament led him naturally but foolishly into allying his fortunes with those of the equally unstable Charles the Bold.[33] Certainly, both Cosimo and Piero de' Medici had grave doubts, because of his ambition and wilfulness (qualities which recall the standard accusations made by historians against the duke), about Portinari's suitability for the post of manager of the Bruges bank and for this reason long hesitated to appoint him.[34] In support of Warburg, though using more tangible forms of historical evidence, both Armand Grunzweig and Raymond de Roover wrote slightingly of Portinari's egotism and, in particular, deplored what they considered to have been his abysmal judgement in thinking so highly of Charles; they contended that this miscalculation was largely responsible for the eventual failure of the Bruges branch of the Medici bank, a failure which in turn they held to have contributed appreciably to the decline of the Medici bank as a whole. The validity of these views will be assessed in the next three sections.

Portinari's business connection with the court

As de Roover emphasised, the economic context in which fifteenth-century banking operated was not unduly favourable, especially compared with the great days of the thirteenth century.[35] Consequently, Cosimo and Piero de' Medici concerned themselves more with stability than with expansion; they eschewed risks and particularly deprecated business with princes. Portinari, on the other hand, was prepared to take such risks. He may have been influenced by friendship with the dukes of Burgundy and by the appeal of the courtly life. But clearly there was also some basis of rationality in his calculation that the dangers of doing business with rulers were being over-estimated by his superiors. Though criticised by some historians for his comparatively bold attitude, the record shows that he was far from entirely foolhardy. It should be remembered that a certain spirit of enterprise was necessary in view of the fact that the Florentines were by no means the largest of the Italian mercantile communities in the Burgundian Low Countries. For example (to use, for want of something better, somewhat impressionistic evidence): in the procession of Italian merchants which welcomed Margaret of York into Bruges following her marriage to Charles on 3 July 1468, the Florentines, according to most accounts, were preceded and outnumbered by the Venetians and Genoese.[36] Yet it was Tommaso Portinari who, as 'the Maister of the Flarentynes' leading the whole procession, was singled out for special mention in the account of an anonymous English eyewitness, while Olivier de la Marche, that most aristocratic of chroniclers, also referred, in describing the event, to the bourgeois Portinari (but to none of the other merchants) by name.

Thus, in terms of prestige, the links with the court which Portinari had largely been responsible for bringing about could be said to be already paying dividends, not only for himself but also for the Florentine 'nation' in Bruges, which, perhaps significantly, elected him several times as its consul.[37] Portinari himself might well have contended that these links were also paying dividends of a commercial nature. Not the least of the advantages, in his opinion, to be derived from the farm of the Gravelines toll (about which Piero de' Medici had been typically cautious) was the fact that, by taking it on, he was putting an end to the monopoly enjoyed by his Lucchese rival Giovanni Arnolfini, who had farmed it since 1450; also, he argued, it opened up the prospect of selling much larger quantities of Florentine silk and other commodities at court, a market previously dominated by the silk of Lucca, the main rival of the Florentine industry.[38] By 1470 another Florentine merchant, Benedetto Dei, was able to boast that the Florentines ruled the Low Countries through their dominance of the wool and alum trades and because of the leases of state revenues which they held.[39] In the following year Lorenzo de' Medici himself reluctantly conceded the value of Portinari's links with the court, allowing him to continue doing business with Charles on the grounds of his intimacy with the duke.

An idea of the quantity of business which Portinari did with the court can be gauged from the Burgundian accounts. Some of the payments there recorded are comparatively small. For example, he received 134 *livres* 8 *sous* for eight ells of cloth of gold which the duke bought from him as a gift to be presented to the church of Saint Donatian in Bruges when he made his *joyeuse entrée* into the city in April 1468.[40] A larger sum was the 1,957 *livres* 8 *sous* which he was paid for the sale and delivery of silk and cloth of gold for the funeral of Philip the Good in June 1467. But he seems to have cornered the market in supplying the court for the festivities occasioned by Charles the Bold's marriage in July 1468. In October that year he was paid the colossal sum of 53,773 *livres*, 17 *sous* and 10 *deniers* for the sale and delivery of the silk, wool and cloth of gold required to clothe the duke, his wife and mother, his guests and his household at the wedding; this sum also included the costs arising from the chapter meeting of the Order of the Golden Fleece held at Bruges in May 1468.[41] Such a huge sum is strikingly similar to the 57,000 *livres* which Charles owed the Medici bank at the time of his death. That debt is usually assumed to have consisted simply of loans, but it could equally well have been incurred for such services rendered and goods delivered as those just outlined.[42] Other examples illustrate Portinari's role as supplier — one might almost say chief supplier — to the court. The duke's meeting with Frederick III in 1473 was every bit as splendid an occasion as his wedding in 1468 had been, and Portinari again made a killing; he supplied the duke and his household with silk and cloth of gold costing 27,300 *livres*, although he was not, it appears, paid in full until early in 1475.[43] But he did not despise lesser items and in August 1476 he sold the duke 850 quarters of '*bois vif de Romanie*' costing 142 *livres* 16 *sous* which were to be taken to Lille for the furnishing of the ducal artillery.[44] Finally, we know that pieces of Florentine brocade were captured by the Swiss in their three battles with Charles in 1476–1477, and it may not be idle to speculate that at least some of them had been supplied by Portinari.

The Medici bank, which for most of the duke's reign acted as depository for the papacy, had branches in Rome, Bruges and London, and this network matched and reinforced the political and economic nexus which linked Florence and Rome with England on the one hand, and Burgundy on the other. During this period, the Medici had an agreement with the papacy whereby they extracted and marketed the alum from the papal mines at Tolfa and remitted the proceeds to the papal camera. As a result, it was Portinari to whom, as the Medici's representative in Flanders, the task fell of transferring the profits, through the bank's internal channels, to Rome.[45] He was closely concerned with the alum trade for another reason, since he served for a time as one of the officials empowered by Charles to levy the ducal commission imposed on imported alum, both papal and non-papal. This north–south axis can be illustrated in other ways. For instance, the proceeds from the indulgences sold in Ghent by the papal legate Lucas de Tolentis in 1467 were handed over to Portinari through a proctor, to be delivered by him to Rome.[46] In 1474 he again transferred to Rome a sum obtained by the sale of indulgences, but this time from the hands of the bishop of Lincoln in England.[47] It is not irrelevant to note that by this time Tolentis's powers had been extended to England, while the London branch of the Medici bank had been amalgamated with that in Bruges.

Portinari's loans to Charles the Bold

At his death Charles owed the Medici bank in Bruges 57,000 *livres* (of 40 *gros*). Undeniably this was a large sum; in fact, it represented over three times the total capital invested by the Medici and their partners in the Bruges bank itself in the period from 1470 until the end of the duke's reign.[48] But what proportion consisted of loans in the strict sense? Since historians, almost without exception, have condemned Portinari for lending to Charles, the answer to that question is crucial if we are to arrive at a true assessment of his commercial acumen. But the answer is not easy to obtain. Loans to the duke, and repayments by him, are difficult to trace in the Burgundian records[49] while, conversely, it is easier to find evidence of payments for the goods and services which must not be confused with loans as such.

The best documented example of Portinari's financial role is the part he played in the payment of the dowry of Margaret of York.[50] By the treaty of marriage concluded on 16 February 1468, Edward IV and Charles the Bold agreed that the money which the king of England stipulated he would pay to the duke of Burgundy as Margaret's dowry of

200,000 *livres* (of 50 *gros*) should be transferred through the hands of Portinari. As a ducal councillor and manager of the Medici bank in Bruges, Portinari was a natural choice for Charles. He was an equally intelligible choice for the king of England, given that the Bruges branch of the Medici bank had close links with the London branch, reflecting the interdependence of the Flemish and English economies. Edward paid the first instalment of 50,000 *écus* to Charles through Portinari only just before the duke married Margaret on 3 July 1468, and it was on the wedding day itself that Portinari handed the money over to the duke's receiver-general. Tardiness was to be typical of Edward's record in paying off the dowry. During 1472, again through Portinari, he paid Charles a further 53,625 *livres* in three instalments. By 29 July 1474, when he promised to pay off the remainder in annual instalments of 10,000 *écus*, the outstanding debt had fallen to 85,000 *écus*. Before the end of 1476 Portinari was able to pass on to the ducal treasurers another 13,000 *livres*. But at the time of the duke's death in January 1477 Edward still owed over 40 per cent of the sum which he had originally agreed, almost nine years previously, to pay. Subsequently, this balance seems to have been tacitly annulled by Mary and Maximilian in their anxiety to win Edward IV's alliance against France, although the unfortunate Margaret herself never abandoned her claims.

The help given to both Edward and Charles by Portinari undoubtedly made a great contribution to the accomplishment of the marriage even if he could not extract from Edward the full amount promised. It is unclear whether or not he sometimes paid instalments on the dowry before he himself had actually received the money from England. But if he did, then he was surely making in effect a loan not to Charles but to Edward. In other words, his recorded loans to the duke, if we ignore these particular figures, would appear to have totalled far less than the amount indicated by Maeght.[51]

Other specific instances of his lending are less easy to find. One tantalising but imprecise instance comes from 1470. On 10 July Rodolfo Gonzaga wrote to his mother from Saint-Omer complaining that he was short of money and that, worse still, he could for the time being borrow nothing from Portinari, as he had done earlier in his stay at the Burgundian court, because the Florentine's resources were severely stretched owing to his involvement with the duke's current military and diplomatic expenses.[52] Portinari's loans to the duke might have been expected to have increased considerably after 1471, and especially after 1473. The contract he made as manager of the Bruges bank with Piero de' Medici in October 1469 had strictly enjoined him to avoid dealings with Charles and with other princes, particularly the extension of credit, on the grounds that more risk than profit was likely to ensue. In the next contract, this time with Lorenzo de' Medici, which took effect from March 1471, that advice was repeated, but Portinari was now specifically allowed to lend the duke up to 36,000 *livres* of 40 *gros*. The contract of March 1473, however, made no mention of any such restriction on loans to the duke, and it was this contract that lasted up to and beyond the end of his reign.[53]

Tommaso Portinari's name certainly appears several times in the Burgundian accounts for the years 1473–1476, but mostly the records refer not to loans but to book transfers of money which he effected in order to enable the duke to pay his soldiers. Already in 1467 we find Portinari paying small sums of money to certain English soldiers in the Burgundian army at the command of the duke and his captain Sir John Middleton.[54] Similarly, in 1473 it was through Portinari that some of the duke's Italian captains received the funds necessary for them to recruit their compatriots into the Burgundian army. Towards the end of that year he provided the duke's officials with a letter of exchange for 4,000 gold marks payable at Geneva. The Medici bank itself no longer had a branch there, so Portinari's help was all the more valuable, especially as the Italian troops recruited by Charles often passed through the duchy of Savoy on their way to join his army.[55] In mid-1474 Yolande, regent of Savoy, asked Charles to send her a hundred of his lances in order to guarantee her safety against the intrigues of Louis XI. In December the duke instructed Guillaume de Rochefort, his representative in Savoy, to recruit a hundred lances for Yolande's protection — he was to do this in northern Italy, since she was then holding court at Turin — and ordered that 3,000 *écus* should be sent to Guillaume through Portinari, who would provide him with a letter of exchange for that amount payable at Geneva.[56] As a final example, Portinari in August and September 1476 transferred at the duke's command the sum of 51,000 *livres* in ready cash from the Low Countries to the duchy of Burgundy. It should be stressed that this was actually the duke's own money, raised from taxation; Portinari merely undertook, at his own risk but in return for a fee of 2,000 *livres* payable on delivery, to ensure its safe arrival.[57] There is no evidence that he took the money physically all the way from Bruges to Burgundy. What he seems to have done is to have banked it in Bruges and then to have arranged for a similar sum to be paid out in Lyon and to be transferred to Charles from there. This expedient did reduce both the distance and the risk, although there was, of course, the danger of incurring the wrath of Louis XI should he find out. Portinari eventually received his fee of 2,000 *livres* about six months after the battle of Nancy.

Some historians have argued that the duke's finances were in a state of collapse by January 1477 and that they had been in such a condition for several months or even years previously. Figures which are claimed to support this judgement have been produced by Michel Mollat. An almost entirely opposite view, however, was taken by Richard Vaughan, who not only questioned the value of Mollat's figures but also argued, with the aid of numerous examples, that the pessimistic assessment of the duke's finances, even in the latter part of his reign, is unrealistic and cannot be upheld on the basis of the evidence so far produced by its proponents.[58] For present purposes it is sufficient to point out that, as far as Portinari was concerned, the duke was able to obtain from him substantial financial assistance right up to the end of his reign. Whether or not Portinari was by then ignoring instructions from Lorenzo de' Medici to curtail his financial involvement with the duke is a question for which direct evidence is hard to come by. Nonetheless, as late as September 1476 Louis XI told the Milanese ambassador at his court that Charles the Bold's past successes had had three main causes: chance; the desire of others to see him succeed; and, significantly, the power of money (*'forza de denari'*).[59] As for Portinari himself, Philippe de Commynes was greatly impressed by the apparent ease with which he was able to make large sums of money available to Charles; he praised the duke's wisdom in maintaining his credit with Portinari, although he confessed to reservations about the Florentine's judgement in lending to princes.

In a work such as this on the duke's relations with Italy, it is fitting that we can cite two pieces of Italian evidence germane to the discussion. In the early months of 1476 the duke's mercurial Venetian confidant Francesco Querini conceived a scheme whereby Charles, who was by that time the virtual ruler of Savoy, should place Vercelli — a town subject to the dukes of Savoy but, for geographical reasons, coveted by Galeazzo Maria — into the duke of Milan's hands as security for a loan which Galeazzo Maria would then make to his Burgundian ally as his part of the bargain. Charles refused to have anything to do with it. He may have been suspicious of the plan simply because of the person of its proposer. But for the purposes of our argument it may be noted also that the duke, whose finances some have said were by now in ruins, told Querini bluntly that he had at that time no need of money.[60] Finally, two or three months later, Charles was offered by Don Federico the sum of

200,000 *écus* for the hand of his daughter Mary in marriage, but he refused for the same reason as he had given to Querini: he had enough money at present and, with God's grace, did not need any.

The economic consequences for the Medici bank

The debt which Charles owed to the Medici bank in Bruges at the time of his death amounted, as mentioned earlier, to some 57,000 *livres* of 40 *gros*. However, the bare fact that he died in debt is open to more than one interpretation. It should by no means be taken automatically as proving either that he was bankrupt in January 1477 or that he would have been incapable of paying his debts had he lived longer. After all, his great-grandfather Philip the Bold had also died heavily in debt, but this, it has been argued, could be taken to show that his credit had remained good until the end of his life rather than that he left the ducal finances in ruins. It is true that, in contrast, Philip the Good is said by Philippe de Commynes and Olivier de la Marche to have left to Charles in 1467 a treasure of 300,000 or even 400,000 gold crowns in the castle of Lille, not to mention other articles of great value, but such assertions are treated with some scepticism by Vaughan.[61] Problems arise also in determining the composition of the debt owed by Charles in 1477. The evidence presented in preceding pages suggests that the proportion of the debt consisting of loans has been over-estimated, that these supposedly predominating loans are hard to trace and that the element of the debt which represented payments due for goods and services supplied by Portinari has been too often overlooked.

It must be stressed that the opportunities for selling goods and services to the court had been seized only because Portinari had displayed the necessary enterprise. He rightly saw the court as a vast market to be tapped. He was not afraid of doing business with the dukes of Burgundy, even though his superiors consistently deprecated dealings with princes. But he was prepared to do more than just supply the court. As manager of the Medici bank in Bruges, rather than simply on his own account, he was frequently employed by both Philip the Good and, in particular, by Charles the Bold to handle, collect and distribute state revenues. In doing so, he revealed an eye for business on a scale which was perhaps more typical of the sixteenth century, when Italian bankers, especially the Genoese, came almost to control the finances of the last Valois duke's descendants, Emperor Charles V and his son King Philip II of Spain.

The advantages stemming from this connection with the Burgundian court have been outlined above: Portinari not only enabled Florentine products to win a much larger share than before of the rich market for luxury textiles which the court offered, but he also farmed the Gravelines toll, he levied ducal imposts on imported alum, and he was paid for placing the financial facilities of the Medici bank as a whole at the disposal of the dukes. At the same time there was, of course, a danger that he might become too involved with state finances. This fate befell the London branch of the Medici bank after the upheavals of 1470–1471. But the collapse of the London bank would have served as a constant reminder of the dangers of over-commitment. Moreover, it should be borne in mind that Portinari was not simply being recklessly generous with his superiors' money, as sometimes supposed. On the contrary, he had a personal interest in protecting his investments because he was risking his own money. The local branches of the Medici bank were legal entities run not by salaried managers on behalf of a centralised organisation but by business partners who, like the Medici themselves, had a capital stake in the success of the enterprise.[62]

In 1478 Lorenzo de' Medici complained that Portinari had won Charles the Bold's favour at the financial expense of Lorenzo himself. The accusation was unjust. But it can be said that in certain of his dealings Portinari did manage to enrich himself while impoverishing Lorenzo. In 1474 or 1475, for instance, he borrowed at interest in order to invest in a risky and subsequently profitless Portuguese expedition to the coast of West Africa; he set up a separate company to handle the wool trade, which was still yielding handsome profits, so that the lion's share of these was pocketed thereafter by Portinari himself, while the Bruges bank was saddled with the costs of other, loss-making ventures; and in his contract with Lorenzo in 1473 he contrived to be allotted some 27½ per cent of the profits from the business of the Bruges bank (assuming that any were to be made), even though his share in the capital invested represented only 12½ per cent of the total. But none of these deficiencies was due to his dealings with the duke. In fact, the losses incurred by the London branch, which were taken over by the Bruges bank in 1473 and which were largely the result of the indebtedness of Edward IV, amounted — at 108,000 *livres* of 40 *gros* — to very nearly double the sum owed in 1477 by Charles the Bold.[63] In other words, Portinari was not unsuccessful in avoiding the dangers which could have arisen from too close an involvement with Charles. On the other hand, what did have a serious effect on the fortunes of the Bruges bank was the duke's death in

1477 and its aftermath, when to internal upheavals were added the perils and costs of war with France. It was at this time that Portinari lost the farm of the Gravelines toll, which was temporarily abolished, and, in order to induce Mary and Maximilian not to renege on their predecessor's debts, he was forced to lend them a further 20,000 *livres*;[64] but in the circumstances Mary and Maximilian were far less likely than Charles the Bold had been to be able to repay him.

The troubles in the Low Countries were serious but they were not the major cause of the difficulties experienced in the latter part of the 1470s by the Medici bank as a whole. The major problem arose from the loss of the papal alum contract in 1473 and the replacement of the Medici by the Pazzi as the papacy's bankers in the following year. These events seriously weakened the bank's financial base. Moreover, from 1478 until 1480 the strained relations between the Medici and the papacy deteriorated to the point where Florence found herself involved in an exhausting war with Sixtus IV and King Ferrante. As a result, Lorenzo was pushed in the direction of retrenchment, so that in Bruges, where losses (excluding those taken over from the London branch) amounted — according to the most conservative estimates — to at least 17,500 *livres* of 40 *gros*, he extricated himself from his association with Portinari between August 1480 and February 1481. His dissatisfaction extended to Tommaso's brother Accerito, manager of the Milan branch, with whom Lorenzo had severed his business ties shortly before.[65] Despite the size of the losses incurred in Bruges, it is possible that Lorenzo's motives were not purely financial. It has been suggested that Louis XI, in his eagerness to cut off Mary and Maximilian from their sources of credit, put pressure on Lorenzo by making an offer of diplomatic support against his enemies in Italy conditional on the closure of the bank in Bruges.[66] This suggestion, though lacking direct evidence to support it, is not implausible. Louis XI had complained on previous occasions about the financial help given to his enemies by the various branches of the Medici bank.[67] As for Lorenzo, we know that in his stewardship of the bank he was notoriously swayed to a greater extent by political, as opposed to purely financial, considerations than his father and grandfather had been.

If the Bruges bank was closed partly as a result of political considerations, then this suggests that its financial plight was less desperate than Lorenzo believed or professed to believe. Certainly, Portinari himself made out a cogent, if obviously not disinterested, case for its reprieve, and his arguments seem to have convinced the agent sent from Florence in 1480 specifically to wind up its affairs.[68] It cannot, of course, be denied that by this time the Bruges bank under Portinari's guidance had made large losses rather than profits for Lorenzo (if not necessarily for its manager). On the other hand, the extent to which these losses were the result of his connection with Charles the Bold is disputable. Most historians have concluded that they did result from that connection. They doubt Portinari's wisdom in admiring the duke, condemn his close involvement with the court and, in particular, judge his lending to Charles to have been nothing short of reckless. These assumptions need to be re-examined. Portinari was not unusual in regarding the duke as a magnificent prince. On balance, there seems to be little justification for regarding his business connection with the court as generally harmful to the Medici; one might almost argue the opposite. In any case, his major difficulties did not begin until after 1477. Finally, while exact figures are hard to come by, there can be no doubt that the extent of his lending to Charles has been greatly over-estimated. It is true that both the Bruges bank and Tommaso Portinari ended their days in a state of sad impoverishment; but, by the same token, this consideration serves only to remind us that for both of them the years of prosperity were those of the reign of Charles the Bold.

Diplomatic relations with the republic of Florence

Not a great deal has been written about the duke's relations with the Florentine republic; certainly, far less attention has been paid to his links with Florence than to those with, for example, Milan or Venice; and, when historians have dealt with these relations, they have tended to concentrate on the economic aspects. In fact, it has not previously been noticed in this context that Charles had himself a personal interest in the health of the Florentine economy, since he held shares in, or a pension payable from, the Monte Comune (the Florentine public debt). Shortly after his accession the duke, together with his mother Isabel of Portugal, wrote to the republic complaining about delays in receiving what was due to them. After investigating, the prefects of the Monte Comune reported that delays had indeed occurred, mainly as a result of the tightness of funds caused by recent military expenses, but they promised to make the claims of Charles and his mother a priority (*'daturos se pro viribus operam ut vestrarum pensionum in primis habeatur ratio'*). On 23 December 1467 the republic — or Piero de' Medici himself? — wrote to

Charles and Isabel to pass on this promise, assuring them of Florentine goodwill towards their 'regal' persons.[69]

A concentration on ties between Burgundy and Florence of an economic character is prompted also by the relative scarcity of evidence — compared with the records for the other major Italian states — concerning contacts of a diplomatic kind. A Florentine envoy, according to reports received by the Venetian senate, accompanied the Milanese ambassadors who visited the Burgundian court in the summer of 1469,[70] but no other examples of Florentine representatives at Charles the Bold's court have come to light,[71] while the duke never sent a major embassy to Florence. The contrast between these tenuous links and Charles's much closer and more amply documented ties with Naples, Venice, Milan and Rome is striking. The comparative lack of diplomatic activity, however, brings us back to the fact that Florence was a commercial republic. According to the much-travelled Benedetto Dei, Florence maintained a large network of spies and reporters in most cities and at most courts of Europe and beyond[72] (presumably the majority were merchants), and perhaps this informal system delayed the accrediting of Florentine resident ambassadors to ultramontane courts. The republic's consuls in Bruges, for instance, may themselves have exercised some of the functions of a resident ambassador. Compared with those of other Italian 'nations' in the Burgundian Low Countries, the Florentine consuls were more closely supervised from home but, on the other hand, they were also invested with greater powers over those they represented; we shall see that in 1473 Tommaso Portinari, himself several times Florentine consul, represented Lorenzo de' Medici at the Burgundian court in what can only be described as a quasi-diplomatic capacity.

Because of the comparative scarcity of evidence for diplomatic ties, it is tempting to use the evidence stemming from the economic links as a guide to the duke's political relationship with the republic. Such an approach, however, would be misleading. The dangers of reading too much into the economic evidence can be illustrated by reference to the attitudes of Piero and Lorenzo de' Medici respectively towards loans to Charles. While the cautious Piero forbade, in the contract with Portinari of 14 October 1469, any extension of credit to the duke, Lorenzo gradually withdrew and eventually ended these restrictions. By this standard, it would seem that Lorenzo was the more sympathetic to Charles; yet we shall see that, if anything, Lorenzo was less favourable than Piero to the duke.

In any case, the attitude towards certain rulers shown by the heads of the Medici bank was not always identical to that of their local managers, who, as business partners of the Medici rather than as simply employees, had a significant measure of independence; consequently, for reasons of convenience, commercial advantage or political preference, they often acted on their own initiative in leaning towards the interests of the local rulers. The activities of Piero de' Medici's managers caused Louis XI in 1468 to ask him to remove Tommaso Portinari and Gerardo Canigiani from Bruges and London respectively, and it was at this time also that the king expelled the manager of the Lyon branch (Franceschino Nori) from France for lending money to his enemies, notably Philip of Savoy who had recently taken up residence at the court of Charles the Bold.[73] In February 1473 he again complained that the Medici bank was acting in a hostile manner by subsidising his two main enemies, the king of England and the duke of Burgundy. But against the Burgundophile Portinari should be set the manager of the Lyon branch after Franceschino Nori's departure, Lionetto Rossi, who on several occasions helped Louis XI, notably over the king's relations with Milan at times when doing so hindered Burgundian diplomacy. It was in his house in Lyon that the proctors of Galeazzo Maria and Louis renewed their alliance in January 1473. Similarly, in the spring of 1476 Rossi endeavoured to mediate between Louis and Galeazzo Maria, then still allied to Charles, and provided lodgings in his house for the agent whom the duke of Milan sent to Lyon at that time with instructions to sound out the possibility of a reconciliation with the king.[74] In addition, Rossi lent money to Louis and provided the kind of financial facilities which Portinari made available to Charles in Bruges.

If we must avoid identifying the political preferences of local managers with those of the heads of the Medici bank, so also we should beware of using them as a guide to the attitudes of Florence herself. As the republic wrote to Louis on 28 January 1475 in a letter asking for his benevolence towards her merchants in France, '*omnes nostra spes semper fuit in regibus Francorum*'.[75] This traditional connection goes a long way towards explaining why several Florentine ambassadors were sent to his court but almost none to that of Charles the Bold.[76] In fact, Florence was the only one of the four major Italian secular powers never to make, at some time or other, a treaty or alliance with Charles. For both political and commercial reasons the republic was anxious to avoid becoming involved in conflicts north of the Alps. In Italy also it served her interests to steer clear of binding commitments. Lorenzo de' Medici, for example, tried hard to balance between, and to reconcile, the duke of Milan, allied to Louis, and the king of Naples, allied to Charles.[77] But such an attitude, as we shall see, can hardly be classed as one of neutrality, for during Charles the Bold's reign the Florentines showed the king of France an almost unswerving benevolence which, in the circumstances, ruled out an equal friendship with the duke of Burgundy.

For the first two years of his reign the evidence for Florentine relations with Burgundy is sketchy. For more direct contacts we have to wait until the summer of 1469. It is possible that a Florentine ambassador then arrived at the Burgundian court but unfortunately our only source tells us neither his name nor his business.[78] We do know, however, that in June the Burgundian herald Gorinchem was received in Florence. He said he had no specific business to conduct there but had come merely as part of a circular tour of Italy (*'sed tantum visendi gratia circumire Italiam'*). He was sent on his way with kind words and a letter dated 18 June in which the republic proffered her wishes for the duke's prosperity. The republic's attitude seems to have altered to some extent over the next couple of years. The death of Piero in December 1469 left as head of the Medici dynasty the youthful Lorenzo, who, in his inexperience, tended to cleave ever more closely to his major allies, Milan and France. In December 1471 a Burgundian embassy led by Philippe de Croy, lord of Quiévrain, passed through Florence on its way to Naples, but the ambassadors did not wait to pay a courtesy visit to Lorenzo because he was then entertaining envoys from Louis XI.[79] On their return through Florence in March 1472 they were deliberately shunned by Lorenzo and departed extremely displeased. In fact, in Lorenzo's early years Florence seems to have been regarded at the Burgundian court as little more than a satellite of Milan.[80]

The following year witnessed a marked deterioration in relations between Charles and Lorenzo. Like Galeazzo Maria, Lorenzo found himself endangered by the confrontation between Burgundy and France. He did not want to be forced to takes sides but, clinging to his alliance with France, he ran the risk of incurring the hostility of Burgundy. The prospect of a conflict between Charles and Lorenzo would have pleased those whose opposition to the Medici regime had led to their exile from Florence. In the winter of 1472–1473 a horde of Italian exiles — encouraged by, and encouraging, the rumours of a Burgundian expedition across the Alps — made their way to the duke's court. There was certainly a Florentine contingent among them and it was presumably they who talked of the possibility of the duke launching an attack on Florence. One of them was Neri Acciaiuoli who, along with his father Agnolo, had been banished in 1466 after trying unsuccessfully to overthrow Piero de'

Medici. Although Agnolo died in 1470, Neri continued to nurse his grievances and in December 1472 he was reported as leaving Italy for the Burgundian court.[81] His presence there undoubtedly perturbed Lorenzo, who wrote to Tommaso Portinari about his worries. Portinari, however, replied that Charles would offer Neri soothing words in order to get rid of him (*'per quitarse de lui'*) but would otherwise give him no encouragement. Lorenzo's ending of restrictions on Portinari's lending to Charles in March 1473 may have been an attempt to placate the duke; certainly, if, as some historians maintain, Lorenzo distrusted Portinari's willingness to extend credit to the duke, it is difficult to provide another, more convincing explanation for this action.[82]

Another reason for the decline in relations in 1473 was Lorenzo's involvement with Louis XI's intrigues to entice the king of Naples from the Burgundian to the French side.[83] On 19 June 1473 Louis wrote to Lorenzo asking him to pass on to Ferrante his proposals for a marriage alliance. The dauphin Charles would marry Ferrante's eldest daughter Beatrice; for his part, Louis would promise never to uphold the claims of the house of Anjou to the throne of Naples and, in return, he expected Ferrante to help him against his enemies, especially the king of Aragon. In view of Louis' recent complaints about the support given by the Medici bank to Edward IV and Charles the Bold, Lorenzo could hardly refuse to cooperate, and the French king's letter was handed to Ferrante by the manager of the Medici bank in Naples. Ferrante was not tempted in the least and wrote to Louis on 9 August rejecting his proposal. But Charles let it be known that he was furious with Lorenzo for having so much as assisted a scheme so prejudicial to him. Lorenzo hastened to write him a letter excusing his actions; it was handed to Charles by Portinari who amplified the apology and sought to explain away his master's conduct. Only partly mollified, Charles still thought it necessary to write Lorenzo a letter from Thionville on 7 December rebuking him for his folly but condescending on this occasion to forgive him, provided he gave no cause for complaint in future and endeavoured to maintain the amity which, he said, had always prevailed between the dukes of Burgundy and the Medici.

Mina Martens has argued that the duke's suspension of his alum agreement with the papacy in 1473 and his decision to levy mortmain taxation from 1474 were designed to put pressure on Pope Sixtus to modify his growing hostility towards Florence and that these policies, therefore, were the outcome of his amity with the republic. Since, however, she adduces no detailed supporting evidence, the argument appears to be based on little more than the principle of *post hoc, propter hoc*.[84] In fact, as we saw in the previous chapter, Charles had many other compelling reasons for suspending the alum treaty, while, as far as can be ascertained, he and the pope considered the mortmain legislation a purely internal matter. Moreover, in the light of what has just been said about Burgundian relations with Florence, it can hardly be maintained that Charles regarded Florence by this time as a firm ally. As for Florence, she showed herself in 1474 to be most anxious to conciliate the king of France, lest he should be provoked by any traces of an inclination towards Burgundy into taking reprisals against her commerce.[85]

By 1475 the intensification of the hostility between France and Burgundy, and the danger that Italian powers might be forced to take sides in the conflict, brought home to the republic the need for an attitude of vigilant caution, perhaps even of neutrality. Following the formation of a triple alliance between Florence, Milan and Venice in November 1474 and the conclusion of the treaty of Moncalieri between Burgundy and Milan in January 1475, the republic found herself in an embarrassing position because, while still herself allied to France, her two principal Italian partners, Milan and Venice, were both now committed to Burgundy. It was about this time that Charles tried to complete his circle of alliances in Italy by coming to some understanding with Florence. Hoping only to ensure that Florence gave no assistance to Louis, he did not want a bipartite alliance as such. Instead he asked to be included in the republic's alliance with Milan and Venice; or, if that proved unacceptable, he said he was prepared to settle for a declaration by Florence that she would at least stay neutral in the event of war between Burgundy and France. These proposals gravely embarrassed Florence. She resented the growing encroachment of ultramontane powers on Italian affairs. This resentment applied not only to Charles but also to Louis, whose attempts to revive the plan for an alliance with Naples brought forth protests from Lorenzo. But the Florentines still attached the greatest importance to maintaining unhindered their commercial links with France. They therefore opposed Charles the Bold's proposal that he be included in their alliance with Milan and Venice, even though these two states, especially Milan, were prepared to accept it; but they *were* willing to accept his second suggestion and, with Venice acting as intermediary, told Charles in February 1475 that they were prepared to adopt an attitude of neutrality as between him and Louis.[86]

In October 1475 Charles asked Galeazzo Maria to mediate a Burgundian alliance with Florence,[87] but nothing seems to have come of this, and the prospects of a closer understanding with the republic were by now becoming ever more remote. Not only was Florence showing herself increasingly independent of Milan but also, in the first half of 1476, Lorenzo came to share the apprehension felt by other Italian rulers at the duke of Burgundy's apparently insatiable ambition and at the persistent rumours of a Burgundian descent on Italy. Far from wanting to take sides between Charles and Louis, Lorenzo advocated Italian unity and preparedness in order to repulse the dreaded ultramontane attack, whether it was led by Charles or even by Louis.[88] His opinion of Charles can be deduced from a remark he made to the Milanese ambassador just before the battle of Grandson: he said that the duke was labouring under the delusion that he was a second Alexander the Great. After the battle of Murten, Lorenzo was glad to help Galeazzo Maria defect from his Burgundian alliance and achieve a reconciliation with Louis XI.[89] Unlike Venice and Naples, the Florentines were unmistakably pleased by Charles the Bold's defeat and death at the battle of Nancy; in May 1477 they wrote to Louis XI telling him of the extreme joy they had felt on hearing the news.

The Florence of Lorenzo de' Medici certainly welcomed the duke's downfall, but some historians have gone further and maintained that Lorenzo himself contributed in some degree to bringing it about, by refusing to lend him money towards the end of his reign. This is an important problem that deserves to be treated in some detail. It has been argued by historians of this persuasion that Lorenzo, whether because of personal hostility, pressure from Louis XI or simple financial instinct, cut off Charles the Bold's credit with his bank at some time in 1475 or 1476. This action, the argument runs, helped increase the duke's insolvency in the final crucial months of his reign; forced to find alternative sources of income, he had to resort to heavy taxation which not only did not provide the funds necessary to equip an army capable of giving him an even chance against his enemies, but also served merely to cause further difficulties for him by provoking his subjects to the verge of rebellion.[90] Although this theory has gained some currency, certain objections can be made to it. The proposition that Charles really was insolvent in the last phase of his reign is, as we saw earlier, open to doubt. As for Lorenzo, the historian of the Medici bank — while accepting the view that the duke's finances were in ruins by the middle of 1476 and suggesting that Lorenzo was by now worried that the duke was in danger of a disaster which, through his financial links with Portinari in Bruges, could have serious repercussions for the Medici bank as a whole — did not himself argue that Lorenzo was alarmed to the extent of refusing Charles any more money.[91] Moreover, the only direct evidence we have for Lorenzo's attitude towards lending to the duke at this time is the contract with Portinari of March 1473, and yet it was by this contract, as we have seen, that he released Portinari from all previous restrictions on extending credit to Charles.

Such other evidence as has been offered is only indirect and, indeed, ambiguous. The fact that Antoine de Montjeu went to Italy at the beginning of 1473 apparently in order to raise money for his master there hardly proves, as Gandilhon asserted, that Charles could no longer obtain loans from the Italian bankers in his own lands.[92] Two years later Anthony of Burgundy was sent by Charles on an embassy to Italy, taking with him — according to reports transmitted by the Milanese ambassador at the French court — all the ducal treasure and jewels so that they could be pledged as security in the peninsula in order to enable him to obtain men and money there.[93] Patently this source is only an indirect one. Moreover, against it one should mention the fact that Italian ambassadors at the major courts of Italy visited by Anthony were unanimous in saying absolutely nothing about any attempt by him to raise loans. Of course, such an argument from silence is unconvincing by itself, until one takes into account the consideration that, even if Anthony's business had been conducted in secret, the record of these ambassadors suggests they would still have uncovered something of its nature. But, allowing that Anthony did take ducal treasure with him, what conclusion should be drawn? Treasure and jewels were a realisable asset; clearly Charles was still not without resources. If he entrusted them to Anthony to take to Italy, that does not necessarily mean he could not raise cash in his own lands. His reason was more likely to have been that of convenience. If Anthony was empowered to hire troops in Italy — and he does, in fact, appear to have hired some[94] — then it would have been both safer and easier for him to take treasure rather than a large amount of coin. It seems to be bending the evidence to interpret the reports mentioned above as showing that Lorenzo had by now instructed Portinari to stop lending money to Charles.[95]

As it happens, there is a piece of evidence which has been overlooked by proponents of this view, even though it might seem to help their case.[96] On 9 September 1476 Giovanni Pietro Panigarola, recalled from his post as Milanese ambassador at the Burgundian court, reported back to Galeazzo Maria. He brought a letter from the duke of Burgundy containing several lines written by Charles himself and three specific proposals:

that Galeazzo Maria should mediate an honourable peace between the duke of Burgundy and the Swiss; that he should help Charles establish a Burgundian–Milanese condominium in Savoy–Piedmont; and that he should help him also with money, secretly at a certain time, through the Medici bank (*'lo adiuti de dinari per la via del bancho di Medici secretamente ad certo tempo'*), so as to enable Charles either to defend himself, if required, against Louis XI or to restore Yolande, the regent of Savoy who was then held a Burgundian prisoner, as nominal ruler of Savoy.

The request for money through the Medici bank could be interpreted as meaning that he felt he would be unable to secure it without the help of Galeazzo Maria, who was widely reputed to enjoy great influence over Lorenzo, and this in turn could imply that Portinari in Bruges, or Lorenzo through Portinari, had refused him any more loans. Nonetheless, the grounds for this interpretation are rather insubstantial. To start with, Charles was not asking for money immediately but only at a certain time in the future. Moreover, the request for Galeazzo Maria's assistance could be taken as meaning not that Charles could get no help in Bruges but simply that it was more convenient — especially with regard to operations from the duchy of Burgundy itself, where he then was — for him to be supplied from the Medici bank in Milan which, managed by Tommaso Portinari's brother Accerito, was even more linked to the Sforza dukes than the Bruges branch was to the dukes of Burgundy. After all, in a similar case not long before, Galeazzo Maria had offered to stand surety for Yolande of Savoy should she wish to borrow from the Medici bank in Milan.[97] But, above all, the circumstances in which Charles made his request should be taken into account. By September 1476 Galeazzo Maria had renewed his former alliance with France, thereby abandoning, as symbolised by the return of Panigarola, that with Burgundy. In other words, Charles could by this time have had little hope that the duke of Milan would meet his requests. His intention, therefore, must have been the more limited one of discovering how far Galeazzo Maria was now committed to Louis XI; for example, the proposal that the duke of Milan should take over control of Piedmont, to which he had long aspired, while Charles did the same in Savoy, was clearly designed to make Sforza think twice before renouncing his alliance with Burgundy. Significantly, it was in this light that Galeazzo Maria himself interpreted the letter. He sent it to his ambassador in France to pass on to Louis XI as evidence both of Charles the Bold's continuing duplicity and of his own determination to place his trust henceforth in the king of France.[98] It is possible, of course, that

Lorenzo did at some time forbid Portinari to lend money to Charles (though, as we have seen, there is no evidence for such a prohibition) and that Portinari continued to lend, but from resources of his own rather than from those of the Medici bank. But this was not how it seemed to the duke's enemies. For example, the Swiss, who, like Louis XI, seem to have resented his '*forza de denari*', did not hide their feeling that, in supplying loans to Charles, Portinari was simply acting on the instructions of his superiors; in September 1476 their ambassadors complained to Louis that the Florentines had shown themselves to be traitors by lending him money through Portinari.[99] Yet even if Lorenzo had banned loans from the Medici bank to Charles, and Portinari had obeyed his instructions, how much difference would this have made to the duke's finances? It is true that, whereas Philip the Good had relied for credit on a variety of Italian bankers, Charles the Bold's borrowing from such sources was confined almost exclusively to the Bruges branch of the Medici banks;[100] the extortion, for example, of substantial loans or fines from the Lombard moneylenders in Flanders through the temporary closure of their pawnshops, as in 1473, could, by its very nature, be only an occasional expedient. But Charles was by no means dependent on the Medici for loans. He could obtain them also from, for instance, the towns of his lands, and on occasions he extracted what was virtually a forced loan from his civil servants by withholding or reducing their salaries.[101] Yet the main source of funds was not loans at all but taxation, and, as Vaughan argues, in terms of *aides* granted and levied, Duke Charles was astonishingly successful. It is easy but wrong to overestimate the fiscal importance of Italian bankers at this period. French kings of early modern times, for example, seem to have resorted little to foreign merchants for loans because, owing to the 'fiscal absolutism' achieved by Charles VII and Louis XI, their ability to tap the resources of their subjects through taxation was so great.[102] The same argument, however, could equally be applied to the last Valois duke of Burgundy.

*   *   *

Charles the Bold's relations with the republic of Florence were usually tenuous and often cool. Although he succeeded briefly, between the beginning of 1475 and the middle of 1476, in seducing the duke of Milan from his alliance with Louis XI, the ties between Florence and the French king were too strong for him to break. His links with the Medici themselves were rather more complex. Lorenzo first reduced and then ended the restraints which had been imposed by his father Piero on Tommaso Portinari's lending to the duke, and, contrary to what some historians have asserted, it seems that Portinari was able to continue giving Charles financial assistance right up to the end of his reign. This should not, however, be regarded as showing that Lorenzo himself was, in general, favourably inclined toward the duke, either personally or politically. In fact, the contrary is probably nearer the truth, and Lorenzo's suspicion of Charles seems to have influenced also his estimation of Portinari, for he thought that his manager in Bruges was misled by admiration for Charles into devoting himself more to the interests of Burgundy than to those of the Medici bank.

As for Portinari, it should be remembered how difficult his position was. As manager of the Bruges branch of the Medici bank, he was bound to foster that institution's commercial interests, but at the same time his duties as ducal councillor forced him to take into consideration those of Charles too, and when the two conflicted he may have preferred to antagonise the master who was further away, Lorenzo, rather than the duke. Moreover, as a partner with a capital stake in the Bruges bank, he had his own interests to serve, independent to some extent of those of either Lorenzo or Charles. There can be no doubt that he was an enterprising and self-willed man, but whether it is reasonable to call him reckless, as Lorenzo did and as historians have since, is another matter. His loans to Charles the Bold, it has been argued above, were largely balanced by the additional business at the Burgundian court which he was enabled to secure by means of them; his major difficulties stemmed from the insolvency not of Charles but of his successors; and in any case his dealings with the court constituted only one of several — the others being more important — developments which combined in the 1470s and 1480s to push the Medici bank as a whole towards decline.

In the course of his long life Tommaso Portinari served several masters: the Medici, the Valois dukes of Burgundy and their Habsburg successors. His eventful career scaled the heights of fame and prosperity and plumbed equally the depths of misfortune.[103] He himself would no doubt have looked back with fondest memories on the decade or so of his association with the last Valois duke of Burgundy, when he reached the pinnacle of success. But Portinari was only one of the many Italians who swelled the entourage of Charles the Bold, and it is with these men that the next four chapters will be concerned.

Notes

1. The best account of his banking career is by de Roover, *The rise and decline of the Medici bank,* 92–4, 157–64, 350–7 (notes on pp. 426–7, 439–41, 473–8). Some of his business correspondence with Cosimo, Giovanni and Piero de' Medici was published in *Correspondance de la filiale de Bruges des Medicis,* ed. A. Grunzweig, one volume only published (Brussels, 1931); in the introductory pages Grunzweig utilised other documents which he had intended to publish in the second volume. More recently, J. Hook, *Lorenzo de' Medici: an historical autobiography* (London, 1984), 29, 30, 64, 108, 151, shares the unfavourable view of Portinari.
2. De Roover, *The rise,* 339, 340.
3. *Correspondance,* I, 73, and H. Sieveking, *Die Handlungsbücher der Medici* (Vienna, 1906), 50.
4. De Roover, *The rise,* 93; ADN B 2064, ff. 127, 128, 146, 208ᵛ–9. For the next two sentences see M. Martens, 'La correspondance de caractère économique échangée par Francesco Sforza, duc de Milan, et Philippe le Bon, duc de Bourgogne (1450–1466)', *BIHBR,* 27 (1952), 221–34 (p. 233 note 9), and ADN B 2064, ff. 129v–30.
5. De Roover, *The rise,* 340–1, 475 note 109.
6. *Carteggi,* I, no. 96; *Correspondance,* I, xix; B. Buser, *Die Beziehungen der Mediceer zu Frankreich während der Jahre 1434–94* (Leipzig, 1879), 130. For the rest of the sentence see *Correspondance,* I, xix, 140, and de Roover, *The rise,* 340, 476 note 121.
7. Vaughan, *Charles,* 4–5.
8. ADN B 2065/64,735.
9. On this point see also below, Chapter 4, 'The position and functions of the Italians at court'.
10. ADN B 2068, ff. 41ᵛ, 50–50ᵛ.
11. ADN B 2098/67,326. See also A. de Schryver, 'Notes pour servir à l'histoire du costume au XVᵉ s. dans les anciens Pays-Bas et en Bourgogne', *AB,* 29 (1957), 29–42 (pp. 34–5) and Vaughan, *Charles,* 141–4.
12. ADN B 17717 (dossier entitled 'Portinari (Thomas) conseiller du duc'), edited by X. Maeght, 'Les emprunts de Charles le Téméraire' (unpublished thesis, 'Mémoire principal pour le Diplôme d'Études Supérieures', University of Lille, 1956), 113. For the next sentence see ADN B 3377/113,553.
13. De Roover, *The rise,* 340–1.
14. ADN B 2084, f. 49ᵛ, and B 2107/67,346. For his interest in the alum trade see also below, 'The economic consequences for the Medici bank'.
15. ADN B 2064, f. 334ᵛ, B 2067, f. 422, and B 2068, f. 193. For the next sentence see P. Bonenfant, 'Actes concernant les rapports entre les Pays-Bas et la Grande-Bretagne de 1293 à 1468', *BCRH,* 109 (1944), 53–125 (p. 119).
16. ADN B 2064, f.233. Portinari's part in the making of the ducal seal may, however, have consisted of a responsibility for its manufacture and for choosing its designers, because its engraver was possibly his Florentine compatriot Niccolò di Forzore Spinelli: G.F. Hill, *A corpus of Italian medals of the Renaissance before Cellini,* 2 vols (London, 1930), I, 243–4. For the next sentence see Charles

to his *'trésoriers sur le fait du demaine'* from the camp at Neuss, 2 April 1475 (ADN B 17717: dossier entitled 'De Rivières et d'Escales (le sgr.) pension').

17. *Carteggi*, II, no. 336.

18. De Roover, *The rise*, 341, 476 notes 123, 132, and *Correspondance*, I, xviii, 140 (no. 46). For the next sentence see de Roover, *The rise*, 106, 352; H. Stein, *Olivier de la Marche* (Brussels, 1888), 199–200; and Paravicini, *Guy de Brimeu*, 401, 581.

19. Calmette and Périnelle, *Louis XI et l'Angleterre*, 327.

20. Rodolfo to his mother from Ghent, 23 January 1470, and from Saint-Omer, 10 July 1470 (AG 2100).

21. Bembo to Doge Niccolò Marcello, Dijon, 16 February 1474, asking him to pay to the Medici bank in Venice the value of a letter of exchange for 1,000 ducats of 58 groats obtained by Bembo from the Medici bank in Bruges (Florence, Biblioteca Nazionale Centrale, Fondo Principale/Fondo Nazionale, II V 13, ff. 152–2ᵛ), brought to light by P.O. Kristeller, *Iter Italicum. A finding list of uncatalogued or incompletely catalogued humanistic manuscripts of the Renaissance in Italian and other libraries*, 6 vols (London–Leiden, 1963–92), I, 115, who, however, wrongly describes it as a letter from Bembo to Charles the Bold.

22. Walsh, 'The coming of humanism', 172. For the next sentence see B. Croce, 'Rettificazione di dati biografici intorno a Cola di Monforte' in his *Aneddoti di varia letteratura*, I (Bari, 1953), 220–55 (p. 251 note 2).

23. E. Motta, 'Musici alla corte degli Sforza', *ASL*, 2nd ser., 4 (1887), 29–64, 278–340, 515–61 (p. 304 note 1).

24. *Dispatches of Milanese ambassadors*, II, 375; *Dépêches des ambassadeurs milanais en France sous Louis XI et François Sforza*, ed. B de Mandrot and C. Samaran, 4 vols (Paris, 1916–23), I, 3, 29.

25. *Dépêches . . . Louis XI*, II, 15 and (partly translated in *CSP Milan*, I, 113) 252.

26. *Carteggi*, I, nos. 183 (partly translated in *CSP Milan*, I, 172), 191, 193. For the next sentence see the duke of Milan to Carlo Visconti, Pavia, 22 October 1473 (ASM 515).

27. *Carteggi*, II, no. 386.

28. K.B. McFarlane, *Hans Memling*, 13, 19–20, 40 note 50, plates 75, 133. For the next sentence see S.N. Blum, *Early Netherlandish triptychs* (Berkeley–Los Angeles, 1969), 77–86; B. Hatfield Strens, 'L'arrivo del trittico Portinari a Firenze', *Commentari*, n.s. 19 (1968), 315–19; and C. Thompson and L. Campbell, *Hugo van der Goes and the Trinity panels in Edinburgh* (Edinburgh, 1974), 105.

29. Sieveking, *Die Handlungsbücher der Medici*, 52.

30. Calmette and Périnelle, *Louis XI et l'Angleterre*, 327.

31. *Carteggi*, I, no. 271.

32. Maeght, 'Les emprunts de Charles le Téméraire', 53. For the next sentence see *Correspondance*, I, xl.

33. A.M. Warburg, 'Flandrische Kunst und florentinische Frührenaissance' (1902), reprinted in his *Gesammelte Schriften*, 2 vols (Leipzig–Berlin, 1932), I, 187–206 (p. 199 for the phrase cited) and in his *Ausgewählte Schriften* (Baden-Baden, 1980), 103–24 (p. 116).

34. De Roover, *The rise*, 338–9. For what follows see *Correspondance*, I, xx, xxiv,

and de Roover, *The rise*, 338–9, and *Money, banking and credit in medieval Europe* (Cambridge, Mass., 1948), 38, 86–7.

35. De Roover, *The rise*, 358–75.

36. Vaughan, *Charles*, 49–52; similarly in 1440 on the occasion of Philip the Good's ceremonial entry into Bruges (Vaughan, *Philip the Good*, 245). For what follows see T. Phillipps, 'Account of the marriage of Margaret, sister of King Edward IV, to Charles, duke of Burgundy, in 1468', *Archaeologica*, 31 (1846), 326–38 (p. 331) and de la Marche, *Mémoires*, III, 113–14.

37. *Correspondance*, xxxix.

38. De Roover, *The rise*, 340.

39. R. Ehrenburg, *Capital and finance in the age of the Renaissance* (London, 1928), 196. Among Dei's friends was Tommaso Portinari with whom he stayed in Bruges in 1476 and 1477: M. Pisani, *Un avventuriero del Quattrocento. La vita e le opere di Benedetto Dei* (Genoa etc, 1923), 68, 100, 116. For the next sentence see Sieveking, *Die Handlungsbücher der Medici*, 52.

40. ADN B 2070/65, 156. For the next sentence see ADN B 2064, ff. 224^v, 225.

41. ADN B 2068, ff. 374^v–85; see also de Schryver, 'Notes', 34 note 5.

42. A point conceded by Maeght, 'Les emprunts', 87 note 1, and made also by Vaughan, *Charles*, 258–9, though without producing much substantiating evidence.

43. ADN B 2104, f. 68^v; see also de Schryver, 'Notes', 34 and note 4.

44. ADN B 2111/68,006. For the next sentence see the exhibition catalogue *Die Burgunderbeute*, 2nd edtn (Bern, 1969), 258–9.

45. For his activity in the alum trade see especially de Roover, *The rise*, 153–8.

46. W.E. Lunt, *Papal revenues in the Middle Ages*, 2 vols (New York, 1934), II, 469–74, and de Roover, *The rise*, 448 note 26.

47. W.E. Lunt, *Financial relations of the papacy with England 1327–1534* (Cambridge, Mass., 1962), 517. For the next sentence see Paquet, 'Une ébauche', 48, and de Roover, *The rise*, 334.

48. De Roover, *The rise*, 344, 348, 478 note 170. For this section in general I am much indebted to the thesis of Maeght, 'Les emprunts', although it will be seen that I disagree with some of his conclusions; the importance of Maeght's thesis for this discussion is increased by the fact that it is central to the arguments of Mollat (see next note).

49. A point made for the loans in general, and not just for those of Portinari, by M. Mollat, 'Recherches sur les finances des ducs Valois de Bourgogne', *Revue historique*, 219 (1958), 285–321 (p. 319).

50. What follows is based on the figures — derived from both Burgundian and English sources — given by Maeght, 'Les emprunts', 82–4, and by Armstrong, *England, France and Burgundy in the fifteenth century*, 281–2, 314–17, 321–3, who does not, however, appear to have used Maeght's findings.

51. Maeght, 'Les emprunts', table between pp. 83 and 84 listing Portinari's loans; payments towards Margaret's dowry here account for over 120,000 out of a total of 129,425 *livres*.

52. In AG 2100: '. . . *queste spese grandissime ale quale questo Signor conferisce, e di l'armata e d'il re de Ingelterra e d'il duca de Bertagna, è cagione di farci stare tre e quattro mesi sanza denari, e quello che pegio mi fà è che Tomaso Portinari, il quale*

era mio subsidio, è così forte avolupato in far queste grosse provisione che per mia fede non credo potere havere socorso da lui'.

53. The contracts are analysed by de Roover, *The rise*, 343–6.

54. ADN B 2064, f. 334ᵛ. For the next two sentences see *Correspondance*, I, xxiii, and Maeght, 'Les emprunts', 83.

55. An incident that occurred early in 1474 may have been connected with this or with a similar transfer of funds. The turbulent Jean-Louis of Savoy, bishop of Geneva and brother-in-law of Yolande, seized from a banker of Geneva some 6,000 *écus* which had been sent there by Charles for the payment of his Italian troops. Jean-Louis's action stemmed from his annoyance with the duke for having failed, so he claimed, to keep a promise made to him regarding the bestowal of a certain bishopric. Charles was understandably furious and vowed vengeance. See Cristoforo da Bollate to the duke of Milan, Senlis, 29 March 1474 (ASM 541).

56. There seems, however, to have been some delay on Guillaume's part; he returned briefly to the Burgundian court from Italy early in 1475 and did not set off back until March that year. See *Carteggi*, I, no. 219; Mangin, 'Guillaume de Rochefort', 30; and *Carteggi*, I, no. 262 (Panigarola, reporting that the sum transferred was said to be sufficient to cover four months' expenses).

57. AGR CC 25543, ff. 190–1, translated by Vaughan, *Charles*, 259–60. For what follows see *Carteggi*, II, no. 648.

58. Mollat, 'Recherches', 305–7, 310, 314, 317–19, and 'Une enquête à poursuivre: la situation financière de Charles le Téméraire dans les derniers temps de son règne', in *Cinq-centième anniversaire de la bataille de Nancy (1477). Actes . . .* (Nancy, 1979), 175–85; Vaughan, *Charles*, 407–15. See also W. Prevenier, 'Financiën en boekhouding in de Bourgondische periode', *TG*, 82 (1969), 469–81 (pp. 473–5: criticisms of Mollat).

59. Francesco Pietrasanta to the duke of Milan, 2 September 1476 (ASM 542; printed by Chmel, 'Briefe und Aktenstücke', 196–9 (p. 197), translated by P.M. Kendall, *Louis XI* (London–New York, 1971), 310). For what follows see Commynes, *Mémoires*, ed. Calmette and Durville, III, 42.

60. *Carteggi*, II, no. 509. For the next sentence, see *Carteggi*, II, no. 637.

61. Vaughan, *John the Fearless*, 103–4, and *Charles*, 407; cf Commynes, *Mémoires*, ed. Calmette and Durville, II, 93; de la Marche, *Mémoires*, III, 56.

62. De Roover, *The rise*, 77–95 and, for the next sentence, 478 note 172.

63. De Roover, *The rise*, 344, 346–7, 349. On Portinari's dispute with the Hanse following the seizure in 1473 by a Danzig captain of the galley the San Matteo — owned by the Medici bank, perhaps with Charles holding some joint share — see my 'The coming of humanism', 173, and 'Charles the Bold and the crusade', 71, and the further references cited there. The claimed losses for vessel and cargo (of which the main constituent was alum) together were 80,000 gold florins. Perhaps a fraction of this was covered by insurance, while Portinari's nephews were awarded a judicial settlement of 12,000 or 16,000 florins, but only more than thirty years later.

64. De Roover, *The rise*, 348; Maeght, 'Les emprunts', 87–8.

65. De Roover, *The rise*, 274–5, 350–4.

66. *Correspondance*, I, xxxi–xxxii; Gandilhon, *Politique économique de Louis XI*, 364; and Simonetta, *Diarii*, 246–7.

67. *Lettres de Louis XI*, III, 251–2, 258–61; Gandilhon, *Politique économique*, 361–2. For the next sentence see A. von Reumont, *Lorenzo de' Medici*, 2 vols (Leipzig, 1874), I, 306–8; A. Rochon, *La jeunesse de Laurent de Médicis* (Paris, 1963), 236 note 192; and de Roover, *The rise*, 257, 273, 316.

68. De Roover, *The rise*, 353.

69. 'regal': the letter (ASF, Signori — Missive — Prima Cancelleria, reg. 45, f. 179) refers to Florentine gratitude for favours received '*ab regia magnitudine vestra*'. Another — or possibly, by inheritance, the same? — investment in the Monte Comune was that held by Isabel's brother Dom Pedro (and by his children after his death in 1449), about which, because of the delays in interest payments, Isabel had complained to the republic on previous occasions. See *Correspondance*, I, 74; F.M. Rogers, *The travels of the Infante Dom Pedro of Portugal* (Cambridge, Mass., 1961), 25, 27–9; and R. Nagel, 'Eine portugiesisch–klevische Heirat im Jahre 1453', *Aufsätze zur portugiesischen Kulturgeschichte*, 13 (1974–5), 320–7 (p. 324).

70. ASV, SS, XXIV, 27ᵛ; the name of the envoy is not given.

71. I searched fruitlessly in the following series of diplomatic records from this period in ASF:– Copiari de Lettere Responsive, regs 1, 2; Registri di Lettere Esterne alla Repubblica, 8; Signori — Legazioni e Commissarie — Risposti Verbali di Oratori, reg. 2; Carte di Corredo — Legazioni e Commissarie, reg. 61; and Consulte e Pratiche, reg. 60. But this does not rule out the possibility of other researchers finding more.

72. Pisani, *Un avventuriero . . . Dei*, 8. For what follows see de Roover, *Money, banking and credit in medieval Bruges*, 19.

73. *Lettres de Louis XI*, III, 251–2, 258–61, and Gandilhon, *Politique économique*, 361–2. For the next sentence see Cristoforo da Bollate to the duke of Milan 'ex Avantdomo' (Vendôme?), 18 February 1473 (ASM 540).

74. Cristoforo da Bollate to the duke of Milan, Lyon, 16 January 1473 (ASM 540); Giovanni Bianchi to the same from the same, 22 and 25 March 1476 (ASM 495). For the next sentence see Gandilhon, *Politique économique*, 356–64, and Pasquier, *Un favori de Louis XI. Boffille de Juge*, 111, 150–1, 157–8, 180–1.

75. ASF, Signori — Missive — Prima Cancelleria, reg. 46, f. 146. For some examples see D. Weinstein, *Savonarola and Florence* (Princeton, N.J., 1970), chaps. 1, 3. Louis XI in particular endeavoured to uphold the prestige of the Medici and to attach them more closely to the French crown, permitting Piero in May 1465, for example, to quarter the *fleur de lys* with the Medici arms and nominating Lorenzo in August 1470 as his councillor-chamberlain: Rochon, *La jeunesse de Laurent de Médicis*, 203.

76. For Florentine ambassadors to the court of Louis XI see *Négociations diplomatiques de la France avec la Toscane*, ed. G. Canestrini and A. Desjardins, 5 vols (Paris, 1859–86), I, 100–4.

77. C. Bonello Uricchio, 'I rapporti fra Lorenzo il Magnifico e Galeazzo Maria Sforza negli anni 1471–1473', *ASL*, 9th ser., 4 (1964–5), 33–49.

78. ASV, SS, XXIV, 27ᵛ. For what follows see ASF, Signori — Missive — Prima Cancelleria, reg. 46, ff. 16–16ᵛ.

79. Barbaro to Doge Niccolò Tron, Naples, 24 December 1471 (BNMV 8170/1, 32). For the next sentence see Buser, *Die Beziehungen der Mediceer zur Frankreich*, 158.

80. For example, when the count of Campobasso arrived in Piedmont to recruit Italian soldiers for Charles at the end of 1472, he told the Milanese ambassador at the Savoyard court of his hopes for an alliance between their respective masters, adding that, if Charles were allied to Galeazzo Maria, he would be, through Milan, the ally of Florence also: Antonio d'Appiano to the duke of Milan, Vercelli, 31 December 1472 (ASM 489); clearly the foreign relations of Florence were seen by Campobasso as being decided in Milan.

81. For what follows see Iohanne Antonio Marianis to the duke of Milan, Carpi, 26 December 1472 (ASM 539) and Portinari to Lorenzo, Bruges, 8 August 1473 (ASF, MAP, XXI, f. 408).

82. E.B. Fryde, 'Lorenzo de Medici's finances and their influence on his patronage of art', in *Studi in memoria di Federigo Melis*, 5 vols (Naples, 1979), III, 453–67 (p. 459) has indeed given another explanation, namely that the importance to the Medici bank of the papal alum contract made it excessively dependent on the goodwill of Charles the Bold, who demanded huge loans which Portinari was eager to advance. However, although this argument is not implausible, Fryde produces no evidence in support, while against it is the fact that the treaty setting up the papal alum monopoly in the Low Countries had been agreed almost five years previously, yet for most of this period, as we have seen, Portinari's lending to the duke had been forbidden altogether by Piero and then, from 1471, restricted by Lorenzo to 36,000 *livres* of 40 *gros*. If the alum monopoly had had the effects Fryde postulates, then one would have expected the restrictions on Portinari's lending to have been removed long before March 1473.

83. For what follows see *Négociations diplomatiques de la France avec la Toscane*, I, 161–5 (letters of Louis XI and Ferrante) and Buser, *Die Beziehungen*, 448–9 (letter of Charles).

84. M. Martens, 'Les maisons de Médici et de Bourgogne au XVe siècle', *MA*, 56 (1950), 115–29 (p. 125).

85. Buser, *Die Beziehungen*, 165–6, 172, 451–2, and *Négociations diplomatiques de la France avec la Toscane*, I, 166–7.

86. Buser, *Die Beziehungen*, 168–72; ASV, SS, XXVI, 176^v–7, and XXVII, 4^v; Leonardo Botta to the duke of Milan, Venice, 16 February 1475 (ASM 361) and 1 and 10 March 1475 (ASM 362). The jaundiced Hans Knebel (*Diarium*, I, 200) described Florence as one of those Italian powers actually allied to Charles in April 1475.

87. *Carteggi*, II, no. 363.

88. Buser, *Die Beziehungen*, 177–81, 453–8. For the next sentence see Catalano, 'Il ducato di Milano nella politica dell'equilibrio', 301, and, more fully, L. de' Medici, *Lettere*, II, 514.

89. Buser, *Die Beziehungen*, 183–4. For the next sentence see *Négociations diplomatiques de la France avec la Toscane*, I, 167–8.

90. Gandilhon, *Politique économique*, 363–4; Mollat, 'Recherches', 319, and 'Une enquête à poursuivre' 183–5; Kendall, *Louis XI*, 296.

91. De Roover, *The rise*, 348 and 478 note 169.

92. Gandilhon, *Politique économique*, 383. One might add that, on examination, the authorities cited by Gandilhon in his footnotes do not even show that the purpose of Antoine de Montjeu's visit *was* to try to raise money in Italy.

93. *Dépêches* . . . *Charles-le-Hardi*, I, 28–9 (Cristoforo da Bollate to the duke of Milan, Paris, 3 February 1475).
94. Below, Chapter 7, 'Chronology of recruitment'.
95. This is the interpretation, however, of Maeght, 'Les emprunts', 84–6, and of Gandilhon, *Politique économique*, 384, followed by Mollat, 'Recherches', 319, and (from 1476) 'Une enquête', 183. By comparison, Philippe de Croy set out in September 1471 for an embassy to Rome and Naples '*merveilleuzement pourveu et atinté de riches juiaus, abis et vasselles et de toute autre chose alavenant*' (Jean de Haynin, *Mémoires*, ed. D.D. Brouwers, 2 vols (Liège, 1905–6), II, 131); but there has been no suggestion that Philippe's purpose in taking such valuable luggage was to enable him to raise in Italy a loan which his master could not obtain in his own lands.
96. For what follows see Galeazzo Maria to Francesco Pietrasanta, Galiate, 10 September 1476 (ASM 542).
97. Yolande had not hesitated to accept the offer: see her letter to Galeazzo Maria from Rivoli, 19 January 1476 (ASM 494).
98. In November Charles was still making overtures to Galeazzo Maria: see his letter of credence for his secretary Giovanni di Candida dated 8 November, presented to the duke of Milan by Candida on 16 December, printed in Simonetta, *Diarii*, 228–9.
99. Pietrasanta to the duke of Milan 'ex Avantdomo' (Vendôme?), 15 September 1476 (ASM 542). For the phrase '*forza de denari*' see the same to the same from the same, 2 September 1476 (ASM 542), printed by Chmel, 'Briefe und Aktenstücke', 197, translated by Kendall, *Louis XI*, 310.
100. Mollat, 'Recherches', 318–19. It seems that, as count of Charolais, Charles had also borrowed from the Lyon branch: Bartier, *Légistes et gens de finances*, 167 note 1 (1466). For the next sentence see P. Morel, *Les Lombards dans la Flandre française et le Hainaut* (Lille, 1908), 26–7, 230–42.
101. Vaughan, *Charles*, 408–9 and, for the next sentence, 414.
102. M. Wolfe, *The fiscal system of Renaissance France* (New Haven–London, 1972), 63–6.
103. For his career after 1477 — he returned to Florence in 1497 and died there in 1501 — see *Correspondance*, I, xxxii–xl, and de Roover, *The rise*, 348–57, and, for what is of particular interest to English historians, the careers of one of his sons and of other relatives in this country, see *Correspondance*, xl–xli. The military engineer Giovanni Portinari who worked on fortifications at, among other localities, Sandown and Berwick-upon-Tweed for Henry VIII and Elizabeth I mentioned by C. Platt, *The castle in medieval England and Wales* (London, 1982), 195, and by J.R. Hale, 'Tudor fortifications: the defence of the realm, 1485–1558', in his *Renaissance war studies* (London, 1983), 63–97 (pp. 90, 96), both of whom give further references, is presumably the same as the 'Sir John Portinary' recorded as living in London in 1572: G. Anstruther, 'The last days of the London Blackfriars', *Archivum Fratrum Praedicatorum*, 45 (1975), 213–36 (pp. 218, 219, 234).

CHAPTER FOUR

The Italian Milieu at Court

From politics we turn now to personnel. In the first three chapters we examined Charles the Bold's diplomatic relations with the major states of Italy. This chapter and the next three will concentrate on the Italians who came to his court, mainly, it would seem, as a result of those diplomatic relations. Some of them — the diplomats, princes and soldiers — form sufficiently distinct and important groups to justify the devotion to them of separate chapters, but they will also be mentioned here in the context of what may reasonably be called the Italian milieu at the court of the last Valois duke of Burgundy. The composition of the Burgundian court in terms of personnel had always been to some extent multinational, comprising many who came from lands which were not subject to the dukes themselves. But it was under Charles the Bold that the Italian element increased so dramatically, and it can be argued that in his reign it was the Italians who provided the largest of the foreign contingents. The size of this Italian element has been often suspected but never fully appreciated. This is probably due mainly to the nature of the sources. The chroniclers provide only a limited amount of information; the major source — the Italian diplomatic material which gives many details not only about the Italians' activities at court but also about their Italian background — has previously been only partly utilised in this connection. The same can be said of the invaluable series of financial accounts preserved at Lille which supplement as well as corroborate Italian sources, once one has learned to recognise Italian names in their Gallicised or Burgundicised forms. This chapter will attempt to explain who these Italians were, both to give an idea of what they were like, as individuals and as functionaries in a social and political context, and particularly to illuminate their activities at court. The material presented will provide a background to make more intelligible what follows in the next three chapters. It is also relevant to the vexed question of the extent to which Charles — especially when compared with his three predecessors — exhibited characteristics which might be termed Italianate, for it is largely the number of Italians with whom he loved to surround himself which causes the question to be raised in the first place.

The position and functions of the Italians at court

Charles the Bold's confidence in and liking for Italians are well illustrated by their prominence in his service. Among those closely attached to his person in the ducal household we might mention particularly the squires, doctors and secretaries. At least half a dozen of his menservants were Italian. Usually we know little about them other than their names, except in instances where some were later given higher office, such as a command in the army. The only one recorded by a chronicler was Gianbattista Colonna from Rome (*'Jehan Baptiste natif de Romme du lignaige de ceulx de Coulombe'*), who was credited by Jean Molinet with locating his former master's body after the battle of Nancy.[1] For further examples we have to look to other sources. Few seem to have been of great individual significance but their geographical origins are noteworthy, because most areas of the Italian peninsula were represented among the duke's personal attendants. Thus 'Jehan Baptiste dit Coghe', who was paid at a rate of six *sous* daily for attendance on Charles from February to December 1471, was described in the Burgundian accounts as a native of Ferrara.[2] The Piedmontese Ameo or Amedeo di Valperga seems to have entered the ducal service, some time before May 1474, as an *escuyer d'escuyerie*,[3] but before the end of the year he had graduated to the command of a hundred-lance company in the ducal army. One of perhaps several Genoese was Francesco Spinola, whom Charles described in 1476 as *'noster domesticus servitor'*.[4] Naples was represented by Rainieri Mancella, who as well as holding the important post of governor of Nijmegen also served the duke as an *escuyer de chambre* (*'scaderi de camara'*).[5] The provenance of others is uncertain. For example, 'Francisque dela Baye' merely described himself as an *'escuier ytalien'* when giving a receipt on 27 March 1473 for a ducal gift of ten *livres*, while 'Jean Signies', signing on 3 April 1475 a receipt for payment of the costs of a journey to Provence, termed himself the duke's *'escuier ytalien et varlet de chambre'*.[6] Italian also, possibly, was the 'Bernard de Paze, *escuier pannetier*' who received a ducal gift of 48 *livres* on 30 November 1471,[7] the name being reminiscent of the Roman line of the dei Pazzi. The form 'Pierro Darento', the name of an *escuier* who received a ducal gift of thirty *livres* on 26 August 1471,[8] likewise suggests an Italian origin. Of course, as a proportion of the fifty squires each of the *paneterie* and of the *écurie* which the ducal household contained in 1474, according to Olivier de la Marche's description, these nine names — assuming that they are all Italian — do not represent an outstandingly large proportion, but, on the other hand, they are not negligible and there may yet be more to be discovered.

Charles, influenced perhaps by the success of the doctor of the Milanese ambassador in France in treating his father in 1462 when Philip had been considered unlikely to recover from an illness then afflicting him,[9] was quite happy, as far as his health was concerned, to place his greatest confidence in an Italian doctor, Master Matteo de Clariciis (died 1476), from Troia in the kingdom of Naples. Matteo, though his career at the Burgundian court is known to us only from Italian sources, was an important figure because he had access to the duke night and day, and, for this reason and because Charles so clearly valued him for his counsel as well as for his medical knowledge, his friendship was sought by many of the leading Burgundian courtiers.[10] For a time the duke retained another Italian doctor or surgeon (our source has '*chirurgico*'), a Master Agostino de' Cani da Voghera, of whom we know only that he left Charles after the battle of Murten and sought service with the duke of Milan.[11] Other Italian physicians were probably called in from time to time. The Milanese ambassador noted that Angelo Cato (died 1496), doctor to the Neapolitan prince Don Federico, treated the duke during his illness at Lausanne in April and May 1476,[12] while, according to the Milanese ambassador in Savoy, Charles was helped towards recovery from that same illness by the regent Yolande's doctor, Master Bartolomeo.

Whether for their calligraphy or for their knowledge of Latin, Charles employed several Italian secretaries. The most famous was Giovanni di Candida (died 1495?); during his time at the Burgundian court Giovanni managed to find the leisure in the midst of his official duties to produce a (disputed) number of exquisite portrait medals both of the duke and of other prominent persons, Italian as well as Burgundian, at the court (see Plate 2).[13] More obscure — like his brother Matteo, the duke's doctor just mentioned — was Salvatore de Clariciis da Troia (died post-1476). The first we hear of him in the Burgundian service is a letter of credence addressed by Charles from Malines on 10 July 1474 to the duke of Milan in recommendation of *'dilectus secretarius noster Salvator Claritius'*.[14] The Anselmino da Prato who went to Milan to buy arms for Charles in the spring of 1476 was another Italian secretary.[15]

Of the duke's councillors, Dr Raimondo Marliani or de Marliano (died 1475) was a Milanese legist renowned for his erudition who, in the reign of Philip the Good, had taught at the Burgundian universities of Dôle and Louvain.[16] Another Italian councillor was Master Stefano dei Corradi di Lignana or 'Maistre Estienne de Conradis de Lignana', doctor of laws from the diocese of Vercelli, who was appointed on 5 February 1474 to join the twenty other lay councillors of the new parlement set up by Charles at Malines in December 1473.[17] The designation of councillor was often accorded by the duke to Italians whom he dispatched on diplomatic business. For instance, in letters of credence written at Jougne on 13 February 1476 and addressed to the duke of Milan on behalf of Francesco Querini, who was to consult with Galeazzo Maria on Burgundian projects regarding Provence, Charles described his envoy as *'dilectus ac fidelis noster consiliarius et camellanus'*.[18]

Querini was one of several Italians who appeared only intermittently at court because they were attached to the duke more by ties of interest and affection and, perhaps, by the occasional gratuity, than by formal enrolment in his service. Such men were often sent on diplomatic errands. Another example is Agostino Fregoso or de Campofregoso (ca. 1453–1486), a young Genoese who first received payment for attendance at court on 8 October 1474 and who, at the end of the following year, was sent by Charles to accompany the imperial ambassador Hessler to Rome.[19] Missions so entrusted were not all to Italy. For instance, Agostino dei Corradi di Lignana, abbot of the Cistercian house of Casanova in the diocese of Turin, was sent to placate the Swiss in the summer of 1473.[20] The duke's Italian secretaries too were occasionally employed in a diplomatic capacity. Salvatore de Clariciis, who, as we saw earlier, was sent to Milan in 1474, returned there in 1475.[21] Giovanni di Candida in fact undertook during his eight years in Burgundian service (1472–1480) no fewer than six missions, two to Germany and four to Italy. Charles used others of his Italian servants in this way. Thus Antonio dei Corradi di Lignana, brother of Agostino and later better known as a commander in the Burgundian army, went to Venice in 1471, accompanying Guillaume de Rochefort,[22] and he was again in Italy on the duke's behalf in the first half of 1472;[23] Ameo di Valperga was sent to Savoy in the spring of 1474; and Francesco d'Este (1429–post-1486) was one of the most prominent members of the embassy to Naples led by Anthony of Burgundy in 1475.

In view of the pre-eminence enjoyed, or at least claimed, by Italians at this period in the field of diplomacy, Charles must certainly have found it beneficial to entrust such missions to the Italians in his service. With regard to Italy in particular, he cannot have failed to become extremely well-informed.[24] Moreover, there were unique advantages in employing Italians on diplomatic tasks in their homeland. In 1475, for example, Galeazzo Maria asked Charles to use Salvatore de Clariciis in preference to any others for all future Burgundian embassies to Milan, especially those of a confidential nature, because, he wrote, an Italian could best understand one of his compatriots; the understanding implied seems to have been as much psychological and political as merely linguistic.[25]

The largest group of Italians in the duke's service, the soldiers, did not by definition pass the bulk of their time at court. On the other hand, with a ruler such as Charles, who spent so much of his reign actively campaigning and who did not possess a fixed capital, the distinction between court and camp was often not a very sharp one. Moreover, his foremost generals would be summoned before the duke for consultations from time to time, while some of their sons had to perform their duty by occasional attendance at court; for example, Angelo and Giovanni di Monforte, sons of the count of Campobasso, received respectively 36 and 30 *sous* per day for being at court from July to December 1473. Just as there was a high proportion of Italians in the duke's army, so also his personal bodyguard included Italians, at least from 1474.[26]

Other Italians who appeared at court occasionally were the merchants based in the Valois Low Countries, particularly in Flanders. Tommaso Portinari was by no means unique in this respect, although he was exceptional in his eminence, but partly, perhaps, because about the others we know far less. One of his colleagues was Carlo Cavalcanti whose personality fitted him admirably to sell silk fabrics and brocades at court.[27] We might mention also the Genoese Giovanni Doria and the Florentine Carlo Martelli, who were authorised by Charles in 1475 to farm the ducal tolls levied on imported papal alum,[28] and the Flemish-Genoese Anselme Adournes (1424–1483), mayor of Bruges, ducal councillor and a man of some refinement, who was sent by Charles on a mission to the Polish court in 1474 in connection with the crusade.[29] Those to whom the duke resorted most frequently were probably the arms suppliers such as, among the Milanese and Lombards, 'Martin Ronde(e)l', Ambrogio Ruffino, Baldassare Corneto and others of his family, mostly at Bruges, the Merate brothers at Arbois, and 'Alexandre du Pol' at Dôle.[30] A Venetian merchant resident in Bruges, Lodovico Moro ('Loys Moro'), was paid 2,390 *livres* by the ducal *receveur d'artillerie* in October 1469 for 11,950 *quartiers* of '*bois vifz de Romenye*'; the consul of the Venetian merchants in Bruges, Alberto Contarini, was paid 1,065 *livres* 12 *sous* (of 40 *gros*) for 3,700 *quartiers* of the same material in August 1476.[31] Italian merchants also figured in a number of commercial disputes which came before the ducal courts. It was probably with this in mind that Felice Orsini wrote to the duke of Milan from Alessandria on 20 April 1475 that the treaty of Moncalieri made with the duke of Burgundy three months earlier was good news for all Galeazzo Maria's subjects.[32] Indeed, as a result of the treaty Charles rescinded on 31 March 1475 all sanctions formerly imposed on Milanese merchants trading in his lands as a reprisal for their master's alliance with Louis XI; and on 28 April the bishop of Como (the Sforzaphile Branda da Castiglione) wrote to the duke of Burgundy from Pavia asking him to intervene in a case involving three Genoese merchants, Lazzaro Lomellini and Luciano and Bartolomeo Centurioni.[33] Similarly, a section of the instructions drafted in November 1468 for Antonio Dandolo, Venetian ambassador-designate to Burgundy, concerned the action he was to take regarding a couple of cases then pending which involved Venetian merchants in Flanders.[34]

As a group, perhaps the most imposing of the Italians at court were the diplomats. Naples, Venice and Rome were represented there almost continuously throughout the reign of Charles the Bold and in 1475 their representatives were joined by an ambassador from Milan, Giovanni Pietro Panigarola; incidentally, when trying to compute the size of the Italian *corps diplomatique*, it should be remembered that, for every ambassador, there were probably between half a dozen and a score or more of attendants, such as secretaries and notaries. It was a vital part of the ambassadors' job to be at court as often as possible in order to catch the duke's ear and to gather information. This task was made easier by the duke's fondness for them. He frequently gave them gifts or arranged a prominent place for them on ceremonial occasions and, in some cases, entrusted them with discharging ducal business.[35] The Italian princes too spent much of their time at court. For example, among those included in the ducal *estat* on 31 July 1470 we find both Rodolfo Gonzaga (ca. 1451–1495) and Francesco d'Este; during his time at the Burgundian court in 1469–1470, Rodolfo frequently served the duke at table and even helped him undress before Charles retired at night.[36]

The evidence suggests that Charles had a marked predilection for Italians. Nonetheless, it is noticeable that the offices he bestowed on them were mainly those attached to his person and in his household. The Italians, in other words, were not given the major jobs in the Burgundian bureaucracy proper, such as the chancellorship or any of the main financial posts like the receivership-general. Though one may speculate about the reasons for this, it might be remarked that no particular discredit was reflected on the Italians by the rather informal and peripheral position they occupied in the service of Charles the Bold, for under all four Valois dukes the administrators employed in the central institutions of state were recruited mainly from the French-speaking territories.[37] That is to say, the Italians, who as outsiders could lay no special claims to Charles the Bold's beneficence, suffered only the same degree of discrimination as those of his own subjects who happened to come from the non-Francophone areas. Still, the failure of the Italians to break the Francophone monopoly in the Burgundian bureaucracy is worth bearing in mind when one attempts to assess their possible influence on Charles in the fields of governmental practice and political theory; for example, the household reforms instituted by his ordinances of 1469 and especially of 1474 have been described as stemming completely from within the Burgundian courtly tradition itself, with no perceptible trace of Italian influence.[38]

Some personal characteristics

In Chapter 7 we shall see that the bulk of the duke's Italian soldiers were recruited between the latter months of 1472 and the middle of 1473. In the case of the Italians at court, however, there would seem to have been a wider chronological spread. Thus, the careers of, for example, Tommaso Portinari and Francesco d'Este began in the reign of Philip the Good; we saw earlier that Charles could already count a number of Italians among his squires in 1471; and, as for the diplomats, Naples and Venice were both maintaining residents at his court by the second half of that year (respectively Francesco Bertini and Bernardo Bembo). Others came later. Agostino dei Corradi di Lignana, abbot of Casanova, was acting on the duke's behalf in Italy in the spring of 1472; Giovanni di Candida's employment by Charles began on 15 October 1472; and Francesco Querini had established a connection with the court at least as early as January 1473.[39]

The duke's recruitment of Italian mercenaries in 1472–1473, however, did probably stimulate other Italians thereafter to seek employment at his court, for Charles appeared to be not only a rich and generous patron but also a powerful ruler whose support might be enlisted by malcontents for the furtherance of their own private or political feuds in the homeland. Perhaps Matteo de Clariciis was one of these; his antecedents are obscure but he may be identifiable with the 'Messer Matheo medico' who, on the advice of Giacomo Galeota, was called in to treat two envoys of the marquis of Mantua when they fell ill at Besançon on their way to Brittany in 1473.[40] Equally, however, it should be noted that several of those who arrived at this time did not come directly from the peninsula; some, the Neapolitans especially, had already left Italy in the 1460s and taken service with the house of Anjou in Provence and Catalonia before transferring to the Burgundian service. This was the case with certain of the captains, such as the count of Campobasso and Giacomo Galeota; it was true too, among those in the household, of Matteo de Clariciis, Giovanni di Candida and Rainieri Mancella and probably also of the Venetian Francesco Querini, who after leaving Italy in 1468 had found service with Duke John of Anjou.[41]

Following this influx in 1472–1473, other Italians probably arrived steadily, if more gradually, throughout the latter years of Charles the Bold's reign. Agostino Fregoso, for instance, had been at court before May 1474, when he returned briefly to Italy, although he does not appear to have begun to receive regular payments for attendance on the duke until 8 October that year.[42] Similarly, in March 1475 and September 1475 respectively two eminent Italians arrived for the first time: the Milanese ambassador Panigarola and the Neapolitan prince Don Federico (ca. 1450–1504).

Taking these various groups together, it appears that all the main regions of the peninsula were represented at court, notably the kingdom of Naples, Piedmont, Liguria and Lombardy, but also Ferrara, Venice and Tuscany. With such a large catchment area and given the divided state of Italy in the 1460s and 1470s, the court inevitably witnessed the formation of Italian factions; these will be considered in more detail in the next section of this chapter.

There were two main and complementary reasons why Italians chose to flock in such numbers to the Burgundian court under the last Valois duke: the attractions of his service, and the lack of prospects offered by staying in the peninsula. In this context a distinction can to some extent be drawn between exiles and expatriates; exiles were those who were more or less forced to look outside Italy for employment because their political preferences made it virtually impossible to stay in their homeland, while the expatriates can be classified as those for whom the decision to leave Italy was made more freely, since, although nothing prevented them from remaining in the peninsula, they thought they could more easily better themselves north of the Alps. The Neapolitans usually fell into the category of exiles. For example, Cola di Monforte, Giacomo Galeota and Giovanni di Candida are all known to have picked the losing side in the succession dispute between Angevins and Aragonese in the early years of the reign of King Ferrante; another Angevin was Rainieri Mancella, who was in fact the godson of King René himself.[43] Similar considerations apply to the Genoese. Agostino Fregoso was an exile from Genoa; his father Lodovico, who had been doge of Genoa three times,[44] was the leader of those who objected to the government of their city by the Sforza dukes of Milan which had begun in 1464. Another Genoese exile at the Burgundian court was Gian Luigi Fieschi (1441?–1508), who arrived early in 1473. The political implications of Gian Luigi's presence there were such that his elder brother Obietto, who himself was later associated with opposition to Sforza rule in Genoa but who at this time was trying to be conciliatory, felt it necessary to apologise to Galeazzo Maria through the Milanese ambassador in Rome, saying that Gian Luigi had acted against his advice.[45]

In some cases the line between exile and expatriate is less easy to draw. Francesco d'Este, who seems to have been sent to Burgundy by his father, Marquis Leonello, in 1444 because there were few prospects for him in Ferrara, became a proscribed exile in 1471, when he intervened unsuccessfully in the *coup d'état* staged against the succession of Ercole d'Este by Francesco's cousin Niccolò.[46] Ameo di Valperga was not exactly an exile from Savoy-Piedmont but he may well have felt uncomfortable there before he joined the Burgundian service. In 1462 his father Giacomo, then chancellor of Savoy and a close friend of Louis XI, had been murdered in a *putsch* designed to curtail the growing influence of the king of France, and after his death certain of the family estates around Masino were confiscated and sold. In 1472 the regent Yolande was reported to be suspicious of Ameo and his brothers because of their complaints about her treatment of them, and in 1475 Charles had to intercede with her on their behalf for the restoration of the disputed lands, although it is unclear whether or not he was successful. Similarly, Francesco Querini had fled from Venice in March 1468 in order to avoid paying a fine imposed by the republic for a commercial offence, although the fact that he was afterwards taken into the service of Duke John of Anjou and then of Charles the Bold may have given him some protection, for he was later able to return to Venice as emissary of both those rulers.

Among the expatriates might be mentioned Raimondo Marliani, Agostino dei Corradi di Lignana and a son (whose name we do not know) of Carlo Fortebracci, count of Montone. Fortebracci successfully sent an envoy to Charles, then meeting Frederick III at Trier, in the autumn of 1473 to negotiate a position in the ducal service for one of his sons.[47] Marliani certainly furthered his career by taking up Philip the Good's invitation to teach law at Dôle University in the 1440s; he would not have been approached if his academic reputation had not already warranted it, but it was only after leaving Italy that he really made his mark in the world of scholarship. Agostino dei Corradi di Lignana must have found it comparatively easy to pass from the service of the dukes of Savoy, under whom he had gained renown — even notoriety — as a diplomat, to that of Charles the Bold; relations between Burgundy and Savoy had long been very close and, in particular, the alliance existing between Savoy and Venice from about 1467 until the middle of 1471, which helped bring Charles into an informal tripartite league with these two powers in the early years of his reign, had been negotiated and promoted by Agostino.

The talents of men such as these would have made them quite capable of securing employment in the service of one or other of the major Italian rulers without having to consider emigration. But others, largely for political reasons, were not so fortunate; their incessant peregrinations and pleas for patronage rendered them something of an embarrassment in Italy and, eventually realising this themselves, they looked elsewhere. Not untypical perhaps was Agostino Fregoso, who was described in 1471 by the Milanese ambassador in Rome — disdainfully rather than sympathetically — as a wandering squire.[48] It was the presence of men like this at the Burgundian court that so exasperated the Italian ambassadors there and led them to call Charles the Bold's judgment into question; at Trier in 1473 the Neapolitan Bertini bemoaned the duke's apparent trust in frivolous adventurers who, without a penny to their name, tried to convert him to the most hare-brained schemes, while in 1476 the Milanese Panigarola, referring to Francesco Querini, resignedly told his master that Charles never turned anyone away ('. . . è di natura che ad tuti chi veneno dà pasto . . .').[49]

It is justifiable to talk of an 'Italian milieu' at court not only because of the Italians' numbers but also because they formed a distinct and self-conscious group, many of whom, sometimes before and sometimes after they came to Burgundy, knew each other and were linked together socially, politically or by ties of blood. Matteo and Salvatore de Clariciis, for instance, were brothers. Antonio and Pietro dei Corradi di Lignana, captains in the duke's army, were brothers of Agostino, abbot of Casanova, and in 1473 Agostino referred to '*uno suo nepote doctore chi è rimasto presso el Duca*' who may have been the Stefano dei Corradi di Lignana mentioned above as a councillor in the Parlement of Malines.[50] Agostino Fregoso was a cousin of the Giangaleazzo Fregoso appointed admiral by Charles in 1473; they were respectively great-grandson and grandson of Pietro Fregoso (died 1404).[51] Rainieri Mancella was married to a daughter of Giacomo Galeota,[52] while some of Giovanni di Candida's more distant relations were related to Giacomo Galeota and Cola di Monforte.[53] Francesco d'Este and Rodolfo Gonzaga were related by marriage: the first wife of Francesco's father Leonello (though she was not the mother of Francesco himself, who was illegitimate) was Margherita Gonzaga, sister of Rodolfo's father, Marquis Lodovico. Francesco guided Rodolfo's first faltering steps at the Burgundian court in 1469, coaching his deportment and giving useful counsel, gleaned from experience, on the number and type of gifts he would be expected to present to the courtiers, as well as recommending a translator who knew French.[54] Francesco was likewise related by marriage to the other Italian prince at court, Don Federico: in 1473 Don Federico's sister Leonora married Duke Ercole d'Este of Ferrara and Modena, the half-brother of Francesco's father Leonello. The interconnections of Italian princely families such as the Este were tentacular, so it is not surprising to find that Francesco was also related, if distantly, to one of Charles the Bold's Italian captains, Giberto da Correggio: the wife of Giberto's paternal uncle Niccolò was Beatrice d'Este, the illegitimate half-sister of Francesco's father.[55]

If the nobles and princes were a close-knit group, so too were the merchants. When Anselme Adournes was sent by Charles on a mission to the Polish court in 1474, he was empowered by his colleague Tommaso Portinari to intercede with another Italian there, Filippo Buonaccorsi, chief minister to King Casimir IV, for help over the commercial dispute with the city of Gdańsk in which Portinari had been involved since the summer of 1473.[56] It is noteworthy that one of the duke's numerous illegitimate half-brothers was half-Italian and had links with the Italian merchant community. This was Raphael de Marcatellis (1437–1508), abbot of St. Bavo in Ghent from 1478 until his death and a renowned bibliophile; the family of his mother (of whom we know only that her first name was Barbara) belonged to the Italian colony in Bruges, while her husband, Bernardo de Marcatellis, from whom Raphael derived his surname, was the representative there of a Venetian trading association.[57] Moreover, the merchants, with their wealth of local knowledge, were probably one of the main quarters to which Italian ambassadors turned for help and information not only on arrival at court but also throughout their stay. One such, as we saw in the last chapter, was Portinari, but other examples can be cited. Around Christmas 1472 the papal nuncio Pietro Aliprandi gave a small dinner party; among his guests were another papal envoy, the alum commissioner Domenico Albergati, and two Italian merchants, the Milanese Giorgio Ruffino and the Genoese Lazzaro Lomellini.[58] Again, when a Milanese agent, Francesco Salvatico, was arrested by Burgundian officials early in 1471 — he was trying to cross to England, having been sent by Galeazzo Maria to congratulate Henry VI on his restoration — it was to Italian merchants in Bruges that he turned for intercession with the duke for his release, namely Portinari, Biagio da Birago, Ambrogio Ruffino and Luchino della Chiesa.[59]

To Burgundian chroniclers and officials, many of these Italians were little more than names — names, moreover, which in some cases they 'naturalised' almost beyond recognition. Among their compatriots at court, however, the Italians were people who usually knew each other, at least by reputation and sometimes personally, and hence were familiar with each other's peninsular background and pre-Burgundian careers. This was particularly true of the diplomats, whose business it was, of course, to know such things. Thus Giovanni Palombaro or Palomar, the Neapolitan ambassador who arrived at court for a second time in March 1476, would have been known already to his Milanese counterpart Panigarola, because both men had been accredited to the court of Louis XI in the 1460s: Panigarola from April 1465 until about October 1468,[60] Palombaro around the turn of 1467–8.[61] Antonio d'Appiano, Milanese ambassador at the court of Savoy from 1470 or 1471 to 1476, had been a domestic servant of the count of Campobasso until the war of the Neapolitan succession, when their paths had separated, so he was embarrassed when his former master, now in Charles the Bold's service, arrived at the Savoyard court in December 1472, although the count most affably showed himself willing to let bygones be bygones.[62] It was at the insistence of the papal legate Lucas de Tolentis that Charles in 1476 considered giving a military command to one Pietro Cermeson. Typical of the value of these contacts between Italians, and of what they themselves wrote about the contacts, is the fact that without Italian sources, particularly the dispatches of Panigarola, we should know next to nothing concerning two such interesting and important people as Matteo and Salvatore de Clariciis.

Finally, it should be noted that these Italians formed an important link between Burgundy and Renaissance Italy. Some of them — notably, but not only, the diplomats — were men of learning and refinement who maintained contacts with the major humanist circles of the peninsula. Moreover, they found at the Burgundian court an atmosphere that can reasonably be described as receptive. The duke himself could certainly speak Italian and some of his advisers had even studied in Italy, while others went there on diplomatic business. The exact degree of the Italians' cultural influence is difficult to assess, and such research as has been done suggests that it was not especially deep or long-lasting. Nonetheless, when considering the spread of Italian values and literature to the lands of Valois Burgundy, the presence of these Italians at the court of Charles the Bold should not be overlooked.[63]

Factions

Although, compared with earlier and later periods, Italy was relatively free during the ten years of Charles the Bold's reign from internal upheaval and external invasion, it remained a divided and troubled land. Italian rulers sought to present an image of unity to the outside world but this was mainly because they were well aware — and especially those like Galeazzo Maria of Milan and King Ferrante of Naples whose regimes rested on uncertain juridical and political foundations — of the temptations which such divisions could offer to would-be invaders from across the Alps. Equally aware of this situation were the Italian malcontents who travelled over the mountains to the court of Charles the Bold. Italians both inside and outside the peninsula were impressed by his power and riches,[64] and there can be little doubt that many of the Italians at court hoped to use the might of Burgundy to further their own ends in the peninsula.

Their intrigues faithfully reflected in microcosm the feuds and rivalries obtaining in the peninsula itself. All shades of opinion were represented at court. In essence, however, there were only two main factions, the anti-Milanese and the anti-Neapolitans. The most bitter of the anti-Milanese were the Genoese, who yearned to restore the independence of their city or, at least, their personal pre-eminence within it. They were especially prominent among those who urged Charles to take an army into the peninsula in the early months of 1473, and it was then that Giangaleazzo Fregoso and Gian Luigi Fieschi arrived at the Burgundian court. Agostino Fregoso, another Genoese exile, probably did not arrive until 1474 but in the following year he was at the centre of a plot hatched by the king of Naples in conjunction with Agostino's father Lodovico to expel the Sforza from Genoa, becoming engaged to Gentile, the daughter of Ferrante's close friend Federigo da Montefeltro, duke of Urbino. The Fregoso were doubtless glad of a powerful ally in Italy such as the king of Naples, while Ferrante was keen not only to strike a blow at the duke of Milan and gain control of a city which, he claimed, had been promised to his father by the last Visconti duke of Milan, but also, it seems, to gain in Genoa a stepping-stone to Provence, which he had come increasingly to covet. Agostino and his fellow Genoese were suspected of trying to turn Charles against Milan, and before he left court on 24 November 1475 he certainly attempted to persuade at least one of the duke's Italian soldiers, Francesco Spinola, and perhaps others, to go with him.[65] In June 1476, six months after his return to Italy, a rebellion against Milanese rule did break out in Genoa; it was swiftly put down, though not without difficulty, but at least the rumoured outside help for the conspirators did not materialise.

The hostility to Milan of the Piedmontese Corradi di Lignana brothers, particularly that of Agostino, abbot of Casanova, arose from a mixture of political and personal reasons. Before joining Charles the Bold, Agostino had been the main instigator of Savoy's anti-Milanese alliance with Venice. But Galeazzo Maria also tended to regard him as a personal enemy, for in March 1466 Agostino and some companions had briefly kidnapped Galeazzo Maria in the Novalesa as he was hurrying back to Milan from France to succeed his recently deceased father Francesco on the ducal throne.[66] Galeazzo Maria professed to Louis XI shortly after his release that he was sure Agostino had acted less as a malicious freelance in attempting to destabilise the Sforza regime than as the agent of the duke or duchess of Savoy, but this did not mitigate his aversion to a man of whom, as he told Panigarola, he was perfectly entitled to say that there was no-one towards whom he had more reason to be hostile; indeed, according to Agostino himself in 1473, Galeazzo Maria had hanged one of his nephews. The duke of Milan's ill-will extended also, as we shall see, to Agostino's brothers, Antonio and Pietro, who certainly reciprocated; in January 1473, for example,

Antonio and Agostino were reported (if only by the unreliable Francesco Querini) to have promised Charles that, with the help of Bartolomeo Colleoni, they would overthrow Sforza rule in Milan, Genoa and Pavia.

There were few Venetians in Charles the Bold's service, either at court or in the army, but to Galeazzo Maria all Venetians were suspect, at least in the period before 2 November 1474 (the date of his alliance with the republic) during which he regarded Venice as his main enemy in Italy. It was this attitude which caused him to regard Francesco Querini with a distrust bordering on hostility. In fact, Querini was quite eager to win the duke's favour, but his own actions and character made success difficult. Early in 1473 he had been sent by Charles to Venice to sound out the possibility of the republic releasing their captain-general Bartolomeo Colleoni so that he could join the Burgundian army. Since it was widely rumoured that Charles wanted Colleoni's expertise for use either against Galeazzo Maria himself or against Galeazzo Maria's ally Louis XI, Querini was tainted in the duke of Milan's eyes by association. More than this, however, Querini not only assured Charles incorrectly that Venice *would* release Colleoni but also, still more improbably, that the duke of Milan would allow him passage across his lands on the journey to Burgundy, a report that annoyed Galeazzo Maria because it was bound to compromise him with Louis XI. As for Charles, such frivolous raising of false hopes was too much even for one as tolerant of Italians as he was, and he placed Querini under detention on his return.[67] Querini, plausible but superficial, was perhaps not untypical of many of the Italian expatriates forced to live by their wits. The Milanese ambassador at the imperial court in 1473 called him a charlatan, while in 1476 Panigarola considered him an intriguer ('*brogliatore*') and lamented the fact that north of the Alps there were people who, under the cover of letters of credence, traded in diplomatic fantasies.[68] Nonetheless, it is worth remarking that, although he was not exactly *persona grata* in his native Venice, Querini does not appear to have sought to turn Charles against her.

The anti-Neapolitan faction was composed largely of true exiles, in the sense given above, from the kingdom of Naples itself, they having been compelled to leave their homeland by their support of the Angevins' claim to the throne. Through men such as Giovanni di Candida, Rainieri Mancella and the de Clariciis brothers, this group was well represented in the ducal household, and even better represented in the army, where several of the top commands were held by Neapolitan exiles such as the count of Campobasso and Giacomo Galeota, who in turn were outnumbered by their compatriots among the rank-and-file.

For much of his reign, it was easier for the opponents of Milan to prevail on Charles than for the opponents of Naples. The reason is patent. Before 1475 Galeazzo Maria was regarded as an enemy because of his alliance with Louis XI. Conversely, King Ferrante was an ally of Burgundy, and, as Charles said in 1473 in order to calm Ferrante's unease at the presence of so many of his exiled subjects in the ducal service, it was more likely that he would win over the exiles to love Ferrante than that he would be persuaded by them to share their hostility to the king of Naples.[69] This situation, however, changed sharply in 1475. In November 1474 Galeazzo Maria had made an alliance with Venice, previously his worst enemy in Italy, while his relations with the king of Naples, whose ally the Venetians had once been and who himself had at one time been regarded by Galeazzo Maria as a friend, continued to deteriorate but now even more severely than before. The resulting confrontation encouraged the enemies of Milan, such as the Genoese, to establish close contacts with Ferrante, while the Neapolitan exiles courted Galeazzo Maria. But the contest between the two factions was uneven. After the treaty of Moncalieri in January 1475, Galeazzo Maria now stood on an equal footing with Ferrante as a Burgundian ally. Moreover, in the first few months of the alliance at least, Charles showed a marked preference for Milan over Naples whenever the two came into conflict.

Of course, long before this Galeazzo Maria had had partisans at the Burgundian court. One such was the Piedmontese Giacomo dei Vischi of the counts of San Martino, who had served as a link between Burgundy and Milan since the time of Philip the Good.[70] During the reign of Filippo Maria Visconti he had studied in Milan.[71] He was mentioned by Olivier de la Marche in connection with a tournament held at Ghent in December 1445.[72] In 1452 he was one of Philip's councillor-chamberlains and served in the ducal bodyguard at the battle of Rupplemonde on 16 June that year.[73] In 1456 and 1461 he was sent to the Burgundian court from Milan to convey messages from Francesco Sforza, and he was in Milan in 1459 to greet the embassy sent by Philip to the Congress of Mantua.[74] His son Filippo was at court on 31 July 1470 when he received 15 *sous* for attendance on Charles the Bold. By the following year Giacomo himself, as we shall see in Chapter 7, was holding a command in the Burgundian army. One might also mention in this context Tommaso Portinari. As a Florentine, Portinari would tend to look on Galeazzo Maria as a friend. In addition he had a personal, commercial interest in fostering good relations with Milan because his elder brother Accerito was manager of the Medici bank there. On 11 April he wrote to Galeazzo Maria from Bruges expressing great joy at the new Burgundian alliance with Milan, which, he claimed, he himself had been advocating for years.[75]

However, certainly the treaty of Moncalieri encouraged such Milanese partisans to come more into the open. For example, within days of his arrival at the Burgundian court on 13 March 1475, the Milanese ambassador Panigarola was approached by Matteo de Clariciis, who was anxious to recommend himself to Galeazzo Maria as an old Sforza partisan ('Sforzescho vechio'), while on 17 March Giacomo Galeota contacted the duke of Milan personally in a letter expressing similar sentiments.[76] A quick perusal of the Burgundy carteggi of the Potenze Estere series in the Sforza archives shows that the duke of Milan had a number of Italian correspondents both at court and in the army, such as Giacomo dei Vischi, Salvatore and Matteo de Clariciis and, another Neapolitan, Troilo da Rossano. It must have been reassuring to him to know he had so many supporters in the ducal entourage. It must also, in some instances, have been useful. Matteo de Clariciis, for example, worked hard, as an Angevin of old, to blight the prospects of the match between Don Federico and Mary of Burgundy which both he and the duke of Milan feared so much, and when Guillaume de Rochefort cast aspersions on the duke of Milan's good faith because he had not sent help to Charles against the Swiss, it was Matteo who sprang to Galeazzo Maria's defence.[77] The partisans of Milan were not, of course, totally disinterested. Galeazzo Maria was a rich and influential ruler whose patronage could be useful, especially in the event of the Sforzaphiles returning to Italy. Certainly Matteo de Clariciis asked for Galeazzo Maria's help in obtaining ecclesiastical preferment, as we saw in Chapter 2, while Cola di Monforte and Giacomo Galeota seem to have hoped at one time to be given commands in the Milanese army once their contracts with Charles the Bold had expired.[78]

Charles was, in general, a ruler hospitable to strangers and he seems to have been prepared to tolerate the presence of Italian factions at his court. This was partly because they could be useful to him. Before 1475 he could show Galeazzo Maria, by accepting such as the Genoese exiles into his service, that the duke of Milan would be well advised not to align himself too closely with France or else Charles might retaliate by lending his powerful support to Galeazzo Maria's enemies. In the early months of 1473 Charles was able to use the appearance of countenancing the exiles' schemes of an expedition to Italy to divert attention away from his plans for the conquest of the duchy of Guelders, while at the same time he frightened Galeazzo Maria into worrying about his own security so that he was reluctant to send help to France against Burgundy. In the summer of that year Charles sent an envoy to the Swiss to offer friendship and to urge them to join forces against the duke of Milan, whom he described as their common enemy. The choice of this envoy, Agostino dei Corradi di Lignana, a man long renowned for hostility to the Sforza, was carefully calculated to overcome the suspicion of Charles felt by the Swiss and to assure them of his sincerity.[79]

On the other hand, there were instances when harbouring exiles could prove embarrassing, for, though Charles did not intend to be swayed by them, the appearance or just the possibility of being under their influence could be enough to damage relations with his Italian partners. In 1473, for example, the republic of Venice and the king of Naples made abundantly clear their opposition to the prospect of the Burgundian descent on Italy rumoured to be imminent and which the exiles were known to be urging, since they objected to any outside interference in the affairs of the peninsula, even if the invader were their ally, and Charles's likely victim, the duke of Milan, their enemy. Sometimes Charles's allies had more particular cause for concern. From the end of 1472 onwards Ferrante repeatedly complained to him about accepting Neapolitan exiles into his service. He was especially afraid of the count of Campobasso, and, when he sent his son Don Federico to Burgundy in 1474, his main purpose, apart from the possibility of his son's marriage to the duke's heiress Mary, was said to be his eagerness to counteract the count's influence on Charles; he wanted Federico to be installed in all the offices which Campobasso then held.[80] Similarly, the Venetian senate instructed Bernardo Bembo in 1473 to convey to the duke its objections to Francesco Querini, who, as an exile, was displaying the same reprehensible characteristics which, it said, had led to his exile in the first place.[81] Querini later proved to be a hindrance to good relations with Milan as well. In the spring of 1476 Charles wanted to send him to Galeazzo Maria to confer on affairs in Provence, but Galeazzo Maria, remembering the complications caused by Querini's precipitance over Colleoni three years earlier, instructed Panigarola to impress on Charles, politely but firmly, that he would not accept Querini as his representative. Charles did eventually send him anyway but his ally's objections had by this time caused an irritating delay.[82]

Again, his patronage of the Corradi di Lignana brothers, which had been useful when he had been at loggerheads with Galeazzo Maria, proved to be something of an obstacle when he wanted to mend relations.

For almost eighteen months before the conclusion of the treaty of Moncalieri, Charles was in dispute with Galeazzo Maria over some military equipment seized in Milan by Sforza's officials in the summer of 1473, having been bought by Antonio and Pietro when recruiting Italian mercenaries for the Burgundian army.[83] Galeazzo Maria's justification was that they were rebels guilty of (unspecified) crimes against him, but that this action was in no way directed against Charles himself; Charles, however, insisted that the confiscation certainly did constitute a hostile act and one worthy of reprisals, since the equipment seized was ultimately his, having been paid for with his money, and that in any case the brothers could not be punished by Galeazzo Maria as rebels because they had never been his subjects. Clearly feeling the issue to concern his prestige as well as his pocket, he sent his king of arms twice to Milan to remonstrate.[84] Galeazzo Maria offered to relent, but despite two more letters to him from Charles,[85] the seized goods had still not been returned by November 1474 when the negotiations which were to lead to the treaty of Moncalieri began. In fact, that treaty was for a time put in jeopardy by Charles's insistence on the restoration of the goods as a precondition of negotiations, but he eventually gave way in response to the pleas of the treaty's mediator, Yolande of Savoy, who argued that once the main issue was settled, namely the alliance itself, then other, minor matters could easily be dealt with subsequently.[86]

Italian rulers sometimes feared that Charles would be seduced by the schemes proposed by the exiles, and on occasions he himself was not averse to giving this impression, but how far was he really influenced by them? The fact is, of course, that he never did undertake an expedition to the peninsula and, even though he must sometimes have been sorely tempted, he could not have failed to be aware of the tremendous logistical and diplomatic problems involved. Moreover, territorial expansion in Italy seems not to have figured among his major long-term priorities. In any case it could be argued that the main factions, the anti-Milanese and the anti-Neapolitan, though not always evenly matched, did nonetheless tend overall to cancel each other out. Nor should it be overlooked that the exiles' motives were themselves mixed, for, if they wished to gain revenge on their enemies by persuading the duke of Burgundy to adopt a hostile posture towards them, their purposes could be served equally well by reconciliation. When the embassy to Naples led by Anthony of Burgundy which took place in 1475 began to be mooted in 1474, it was suggested that Anthony should try to engender a reconciliation between Ferrante and the Neapolitan exiles and even that he should take some of them with him. As a result, the Neapolitan ambassador predicted, few of the Neapolitans would in these circumstances remain if only Charles would give them permission to leave; he singled out Rainieri Mancella as one who was particularly keen to return if forgiven by Ferrante.[87]

Similar considerations apply to the Corradi di Lignana brothers. We find Agostino making overtures to Galeazzo Maria already in 1473; owing to Milanese hostility, he felt it unsafe to return to his abbey of Casanova in Piedmont, but he very much wanted to go back to Italy because the expense of maintaining the appearances demanded at the Burgundian court was crippling and because, old and ill, he no longer had anything to expect in life.[88] In November 1475 Charles wrote to Galeazzo Maria asking for a safe-conduct through Milan on the abbot's behalf since he wanted to send him on a mission to Rome; the request specifically refers to his needing a safe-conduct because Sforza's ill-will towards him made it risky to travel without one. The duke of Milan, however, was embarrassed by the request because, while he wished to avoid offending his ally, he had always vowed that if he ever laid hands on Agostino he would treat him as he himself had been treated by Agostino ten years before in the Novalesa. Two months later, though, he did grant a safe-conduct, if only on condition that Agostino gave no more cause for complaint, and Charles himself warned the abbot of dire punishment at his hands if he ever did. Agostino's brothers appear to have had to wait longer for a reconciliation and, it seems, in the end in vain. A month after his arrival at court the Milanese ambassador Panigarola was asked by Charles to write to his master to forgive Antonio and Pietro for any offence (always unspecified) which they might have committed against him and, further, to restore the goods seized in 1473, arguing that they should not be made to suffer for what their brother had done.[89] The next day, 11 April 1475, Antonio himself wrote to Galeazzo Maria in the most humble terms, begging his favour and declaring himself to be his *'fidelissimo servitore'*, as, he insisted, he always had been and always would be. But these pleas do not seem to have had the desired effect, for when Anselmino da Prato was sent to Milan in April the following year to buy munitions he was also empowered by Charles once again to ask Galeazzo Maria to pardon Antonio, seeing that he had now pardoned Antonio's brother Agostino, and also to grant his favour to the wife and sons of the late Pietro, who had been killed at the battle of Grandson. The duke of Milan gave Anselmino an amiable reply but no more and in June Antonio too died in battle, at Murten.

The Italian ambassadors were another group who took part in these factional struggles and, in view of the volatility of the Italian political scene, the surveillance of exiles came to be a vital part of their duties, not only in Burgundy but also at other ultramontane courts. Thus at the time of Charles the Bold's meeting with Frederick III at Trier the Milanese ambassador at the imperial court, Carlo Visconti, promised to keep an eye on the abbot of Casanova because, he wrote, sometimes a small spark can cause a big fire and such people had to be made to realise that lords had long arms.[90] Similarly Bernardo Bembo was told by the Venetian senate to warn Charles against Francesco Querini; Francesco Bertini repeatedly urged the duke to dismiss the Neapolitan exiles he had taken into his service; and Panigarola endeavoured to counter the intrigues of the Genoese. This was not a pleasant part of their job because they could not avoid some personal contact with those whose credit they were striving to undermine and, in Bertini's case, distaste becomes obvious at once in his disdainful references to the mutual rivalry of the Neapolitans in the ducal service.[91] Panigarola resorted to intrigue in order to discover what schemes the Genoese were hatching and in September 1475 he derived much satisfaction from contriving to intercept and pass on to his master a letter written in cipher by Lodovico Fregoso in Italy to his son Agostino.[92]

The ambassadors also struggled against each other in order to win the favour of the duke towards their respective masters. For much of Charles the Bold's reign Galeazzo Maria was apprehensive about the hostile influence over him which he felt the Venetians were exercising. So worried was he in 1469 that he sent ambassadors to assure the duke of his goodwill and, more specifically, to turn him against the Venetians. Even if the subject of relations with the republic did not come up at their audience, they were instructed to guide the discussion in that direction so that they could use the by now conventional argument that since the Venetians, as republicans, were the sworn enemies of monarchy, then neither Charles nor indeed any other prince could put his trust in them.[93] This embassy, however, had little effect for the simple reason that Charles the Bold's hostility to Milan stemmed from his own political convictions and was not just the result of Venetian influence. The Milanese found this hard to credit and in 1473 one of Galeazzo Maria's partisans attributed the duke's enmity towards Milan and France, together with his desire for the royal crown which he hoped to obtain from Frederick III and which, it was felt, would be a threat to Galeazzo Maria, to the instigation of the Venetian ambassador Bembo.[94] Such fears were only increased by the fact that Galeazzo Maria did not maintain a permanent representative of his own at the Burgundian court until 1475; before then he had to rely on the advocacy of his supporters in the ducal entourage and on the efforts of Sforzaphile papal nuncios such as Stefano Nardini, Pietro Aliprandi and Andrea dei Spiriti, and it was the last two who, as we saw in Chapter 2, helped to secure the recall of the legate Lucas de Tolentis in 1474 on the grounds that he was devoting himself more to the interests of Venice than to those of the pope. By the time Giovanni Pietro Panigarola arrived at court in March 1475, his master had been reconciled with Venice, so that the main enemy Panigarola had to face was the Neapolitan ambassador Francesco Bertini, an expert operator (*'un gran pratico'*) as Guillaume de Rochefort described him.[95] Bertini, the longest-serving of all the Italian ambassadors at court, was a worthy rival. Panigarola had to counter not only the great intimacy which Bertini had built up with Charles but also his intrigues with the enemies of Milan in Burgundy, notably the Genoese. Panigarola retaliated by forging links with the Neapolitan exiles and it was clearly with great relief and some malice that he told his master about Bertini's death in November 1475.[96] Bertini's successor, Giovanni Palombaro, was by comparison something of a lightweight and he posed the Milanese ambassador far fewer problems.

Several of the Burgundian courtiers themselves seem to have taken sides in these factional struggles or, at least, to have shown some preference for one or other of the three main secular powers represented at court, Venice, Naples and Milan. Certainly, we know that Panigarola felt it advisable for his master to send gifts and friendly letters to those leading courtiers whom he designated as potentially useful, and presumably other ambassadors did likewise. This is interesting because, although we know in detail the course of Charles the Bold's policies in relation to Italy, we know very little about their formulation. Some examples will help. Guillaume Fillastre, bishop of Tournai and chancellor of the Order of the Golden Fleece, appears to have been an advocate of an alliance with Venice. In August 1467, only two months after Charles the Bold's accession, he urged the Venetian senate (he was then in Venice on his way to Rome) to send an ambassador to Burgundy to discuss an alliance, assuring it that his master would be favourable.[97] When Antonio Dandolo was at the Burgundian court in the summer of 1469, he wrote home that Fillastre was again recommending an alliance and that Anthony of Burgundy also supported the idea. Shortly after the alliance had been concluded in the summer of 1472, Guillame de Rochefort was described as an *'amico veneto'* and Philippe de Croy, lord of Quiévrain, as a *'gran partesano veneto'*.

By contrast, King Ferrante of Naples appears to have had few supporters among the Burgundian courtiers and seems to have been regarded as something of an interloper who had seized by force a throne which by rights belonged to the house of Anjou, while on a personal level the rumours of his perfidy which had already spread outside Italy damaged his reputation. Thus at the chapter meeting of the Order of the Golden Fleece held at Valenciennes in May 1473, Ferrante's election aroused scant enthusiasm among the members. Even though only Philippe Pot objected outright, the others acquiesced simply out of deference to the duke himself, who had proposed this candidature. They had reservations about Ferrante's eligibility not only on technical grounds — he was already a member of the Order of the Garter and this same objection based on a requirement of exclusivity had ruled out the king of Portugal when proposed for election in 1468 — but also for moral or chivalric reasons: he was not a knight *sans reproche* because he was widely thought to have arranged the murder of the troublesome condottiere Giacomo Piccinnino ('*conte Jacquemeno*', as the recorder of the proceedings referred to him), who had died in mysterious circumstances in 1465. To the technical objections, Charles, whose personal choice Ferrante obviously was, replied with some intricate special pleading. As for the death of Piccinnino, he argued that if anyone was to blame it was the late duke of Milan, Francesco Sforza. He advocated his ally's membership mainly for diplomatic reasons; Ferrante was a bulwark against Milan and a link between Burgundy and the king of Aragon, the pope, Venice and Savoy. But he also clearly admired Ferrante's personal qualities. To the members he praised his ally's wisdom, courage and experience. He particularly admired his resilience in the face of adversity, for the king of Naples had had to overcome early disasters to win his throne against the Angevins. When announcing his Neapolitan alliance in 1471 Charles had, through his spokesman Guillaume Hugonet, praised Ferrante because he had not despaired in the face of setbacks but by '*grande magnanimité et haulteur de couraige*' had overcome his enemies. Similarly, he was to promise the Estates of Burgundy in July 1476 that he would recover from the recent reverses suffered at the hands of the Swiss just as certain heroes of antiquity had done before him, not to mention more modern examples like Ferrante; to compare someone with the ancients was the highest compliment Charles could have offered.[98]

Inevitably, because the bulk of the Italian source material is Milanese, we know most about the partisans of Galeazzo Maria. Their motives were multiple. Obviously many would have advocated an alliance with

Milan even before 1475 because Galeazzo Maria, with his power and influence, would have been a valuable friend for their master to win. Thus on returning to Italy after his embassy to Burgundy in 1469 and advising Galeazzo Maria to ally with Charles, the Milanese ambassador Marquis Gian Lodovico Pallavicino mentioned Guillaume Bische as one of those who would try to help bring this about; similarly, Philippe Pot, who had been to Italy in 1468, later expressed great admiration for Galeazzo Maria's army.[99] The attachment of others to Milan reached back to the time of Francesco Sforza, who had cultivated good relations with Philip the Good and who had impressed many of Philip's advisers by his splendid treatment, on its passage through Milan, of the Burgundian embassy sent to the Congress of Mantua. This was true of Philippe de Croy, lord of Quiévrain, who, after leading an embassy to Naples in 1472, wanted to return via Milan in order to pay his respects to the duke and thus to repay the kindness shown by the duke's father to Philippe's father Jean, count of Chimay, who had been one of the leaders of the embassy to the Congress of Mantua; he also expressed the wish that when he returned home he would at last find the dukes of Burgundy and Milan united (*'una cosa medesma'*). Galeazzo Maria, however, refused to grant him a safe-conduct through his lands lest he should compromise himself in the eyes of Louis XI.[100] Nonetheless, Philippe or one of his companions had aired the view that Galeazzo Maria was far inferior to his father, being prouder than was justified and too close to the king of France. Even so, the duke of Milan was still a potentially useful patron and for this reason Burgundians in Italy tended to try to ingratiate themselves with him; thus in 1473 Jean de Luxembourg, nephew of the count of Saint-Pol, asked Francesco d'Este, who was then in Italy, to obtain for him a safe-conduct through Milan because he was very eager to visit Galeazzo Maria.[101]

When the alliance between Milan and Burgundy finally came about in January 1475, Panigarola found the whole court in rejoicing, such was the importance attributed to it.[102] According to Guillaume de Rochefort, the decision on the Burgundian side to conclude the alliance was largely due to Guy de Brimeu.[103] Diplomatic considerations were doubtless uppermost in Guy's mind but, in addition, he hoped to ingratiate himself personally with Galeazzo Maria,[104] and in so doing, to gain the duke of Milan's patronage for his brother Philippe. Another who was pleased at the alliance was Anthony of Burgundy, who, on hearing the news — he was then in Piedmont on his way to Naples — leapt with joy (*'fece un salto de alegreza'*).[105] Later that year Ferrante sought to arrange a marriage with a Neapolitan princess for either Anthony or his son, and when Anthony returned to the Burgundian court Ferrante's son Federico endeavoured to win his favour, but, as Anthony told Panigarola, all this counted as nothing against the good graces of the duke of Milan, which he preferred to those of Ferrante and which he risked losing if he became a friend of Naples.[106] Shortly after the treaty of Moncalieri was concluded, Guillaume de Rochefort wrote to the duke of Milan to express his pleasure; in thanking him, Galeazzo wrote that he had instructed Panigarola to confer with Guillaume as much as with Charles himself.[107] At the beginning of May 1476 Panigarola opined that Guillaume was the most influential of all the duke's advisers, but by this time Guillaume himself had begun to entertain reservations about Galeazzo Maria's value as an ally. He told Charles that the duke of Milan was engaged in negotiations with Louis XI and that he was being deceitful in not sending help against the Swiss, and his intimacy with Yolande of Savoy also helped create a rift between him and the duke of Milan, because he suspected Galeazzo Maria of harbouring designs on some of Yolande's dominions in Piedmont and of wanting to discredit her with Charles. For a time, after the failure of Burgundian agents to seize young Duke Philibert of Savoy at the end of June 1476 when Philibert's mother and younger brother had been kidnapped, Guillaume fled from court because Charles blamed the fiasco on him, accused him of having had treasonable dealings with the inconstant Yolande and said he never wanted to see him again.

The dispersal of the Italians from the court

The Italians around Charles the Bold had already begun to dwindle in numbers before his death, and this decline continued, but more rapidly, thereafter. The process can be illustrated by reference to some of the major figures, although often dates cannot be supplied for the departure of the more obscure. Raimondo Marliani died at Louvain on 20 August 1475. The Neapolitan ambassador Bertini, who died at Besançon on 22 November 1475,[108] was never formally replaced, although Giovanni Palombaro, Neapolitan ambassador in Savoy, doubled as ambassador at both the Savoyard and Burgundian courts during the spring and early summer of 1476. Salvatore de Clariciis left in February 1476 to return to Naples, where he hoped to be able to protect his brothers remaining there against the molestations of the king;[109] his other brother Matteo died at Salins on 22 July that year. Don Federico had departed precipitately in the previous month just before the battle of Murten. The last Italian ambassador to leave was Panigarola, who did so either at the end of August or at the beginning of September 1476. We do not know if Francesco d'Este departed before or after the battle of Nancy but he had certainly done so by 7 July 1477 when Louis XI appointed him governor of Montpellier.[110] Francesco Querini too had by then already left, if we dare assume that it is safe to identify him with the Venetian official of the same name who in April 1477 was handling negotiations between the count of Campobasso and the republic over the count's application for a command in the army. Rainieri Mancella was for a time retained by Maximilian as a squire,[111] but it is possible that he followed his father-in-law Giacomo Galeota to France where Giacomo went in July 1480. For Agostino dei Corradi di Lignana it was comparatively easy to return to his former allegiance to Savoy, and in October 1477 we find him in Naples entrusted with promoting a marriage between Don Federico and Anne of Savoy.[112] Giovanni di Candida was in Italy on ducal business when the disastrous battle of Nancy was fought; nonetheless, he returned to the Burgundian court and must have been one of the last, if not the very last, of the Italians to leave, which he did in July 1480, taking service shortly afterwards with Louis XI, although the licence to leave which he received from Maximilian dated 12 July 1480 stated that he intended to return to his native Naples so that he could end his days there.[113] The chronology of this dispersal is similar to that for the soldiers. Their ranks had already been thinned before January 1477 by death and desertion, and of the survivors few seem to have stayed long in the service of Charles the Bold's successors, preferring either to join the French army or, more often, just to return to Italy without necessarily even negotiating posts there beforehand.[114]

The timing of these various Italian departures is important for its relevance to the question of the Italians' influence on Valois Burgundy, especially under Charles the Bold but also after 1477. Their motives for going are equally pertinent to that problem: why was it that so many preferred to leave rather than stay, not only in the years immediately after January 1477 but also during the months leading up to the battle of Nancy? Obviously we must omit from the discussion those removed by death, like Raimondo Marliani and Matteo de Clariciis, as well as the princes and ambassadors, such as Don Federico and Panigarola, who were ordered to depart by their masters and who therefore had no choice in the matter. Conversely, the merchants who stayed in the Low Countries, such as

Tommaso Portinari, are also peripheral to the problem, for they chose to reside in the lands of the dukes of Burgundy regardless of contacts with the court, and commercial considerations kept them there after Charles the Bold's demise. But what of those Italians taken directly into his service? Undoubtedly the death of the duke himself was a major consideration in their decision to leave, since it was Charles himself whose service had seemed so attractive and who had especially welcomed Italians to his court. Of course, some may have prospered under his successors. It was not until July 1477, for example, that Stefano dei Corradi di Lignana became ordinary professor of civil law at the University of Louvain, and in January the following year another Italian academic began to teach there, Lodovico Bruni, lecturer in poetry.[115] Appointments such as these do not have a major bearing on the question of specifically court attitudes towards Italians but it is interesting to note that in the early years of his rule in the Low Countries Maximilian did employ at least one Italian as a diplomat (apart from Giovanni di Candida), namely Messer Giusto Baldino of Padua, doctor of laws, who was sent to Rome in 1478 and who, moreover, is not known to have served Charles earlier.[116] On the whole, however, there is little evidence that either Mary of Burgundy or, initially, Maximilian shared their predecessor's fondness for Italians, and this change in the intellectual atmosphere of the court must have reduced the willingness of the Italians to remain in the Burgundian service.

The circumstances of Charles's death, almost as much as his death itself, weakened their position. The suddenness of the demise of a ruler who had kept his affairs under such tight control contributed greatly to the upheavals which marked his daughter's accession, and the ensuing wars with France, together with the growing self-assertion of her subjects, severely limited Mary's room for manoeuvre in financial matters such as courtiers' wages. Certainly, the difficulties experienced by Giovanni di Candida in extracting from the Burgundian treasury the various sums of money owed to him seem to have been a factor in his decision to leave, and his brief imprisonment by Maximilian in 1478 appears to have been the punishment incurred for derogatory comments made by him about Maximilian's parsimony as a result of these difficulties.[117]

The political results of the disaster at Nancy were also significant in this context. After 1477 a reaction set in against the methods of government employed by Charles and against the men associated with them. Thus the Flemish-Genoese Anselme Adournes, formerly a ducal councillor, was put on trial by the people of Bruges, and although lack of evidence prevented his conviction he felt it advisable some time afterwards to flee to Scotland, where he enjoyed the protection of James III.[118] It could be argued also, as we shall see in Chapter 7, that Charles the Bold's use of Italian mercenaries for garrison duty was unpopular with his subjects. Similarly, two commercial disputes which occurred in 1473 suggested that Italian merchants in Flanders were not always well loved by the local population. In the first, a Florentine galley carrying a cargo of papal alum destined for Tommaso Portinari was seized off Gravelines by privateers from Gdańsk acting in league with or on behalf of the Hanse. Since it had been flying the Burgundian flag, Portinari was able to obtain ducal authorisation for reprisals against Hanseatic merchants in Bruges, but the Flemish cities prevented their enforcement because, as de Roover has put it, they were very much opposed to a breach with the Hanse for the sake of an alum cargo belonging to Italians.[119] In the other dispute, Lazzaro Lomellini, the Genoese merchant resident in Bruges mentioned earlier, sought to export quantities of corn to Italy but, despite ducal permission, was prevented by the opposition of Bruges and Ghent, who feared shortages and high prices, and also, significantly, by that of the *chambre des comptes* at Lille, whose officials dreaded the upheavals which scarcity could bring.[120] Of course, Lomellini was defeated because too many powerful forces were opposed to corn exports, not simply because he was Italian. Similarly, Anselme Adournes was joined by several Burgundian officials in falling foul of the popular reaction in 1477, while, in relation to garrisons composed of Italian mercenaries, it could be argued that any troops stationed in populated areas would have been resented, regardless of nationality. Taken together, however, these instances suggest that the Italians were tainted by association with the policies of their ducal master, sufficiently, perhaps, to render most Italians unpopular in the eyes of his subjects; and in Giovanni di Candida's case there seems to have been evident a dislike of all the duke's foreign servants.[121]

Yet even before the Italians lost the protection of Charles the Bold in 1477 many of them were showing signs of wanting to return to Italy at some stage. We saw that a number of the Neapolitans hoped for a reconciliation with Ferrante which would allow them to go back to Naples, and others, by their correspondence with rulers such as the duke of Milan especially and also with the marquis of Mantua and Lorenzo the Magnificent, were clearly trying to ingratiate themselves with those whom they might one day need as patrons. Conversely, very few put down any kind of roots in the lands of their adopted master. Raimondo Marliani, probably while he was teaching at the University of Dôle, married a local girl, Jeanne, daughter of the lord of Saint-Hilaire, and he remained in Valois Burgundy even after her death, but he never forgot his homeland, and in his will he provided for a sum of money to be paid annually to the Scuola della Malastella, a body devoted to succouring the inmates of the Malastella prison in Milan.[122] Agostino dei Corradi di Lignana from 1474 until at least 1476 was titled abbot of Saint-Claude in Burgundy, but he did not hold the abbey in his own right. Instead he seems briefly, presumably for reasons of convenience, to have exchanged with Jean-Louis of Savoy, bishop of Geneva, his abbey of Casanova against that of Saint-Claude, held by the bishop of Geneva *in commendam* from 1472 until about 1484; in 1478 the exchange led to hostilities because Jean-Louis wanted to keep Casanova. Perhaps the enmity of the duke of Milan was a reason for Agostino's willingness to exchange Casanova for Saint-Claude temporarily, but even so he had no wish to remain an expatriate.[123]

The next question is why the Italians were so reluctant to settle. Two reasons suggest themselves. The first is that Charles may have been ungenerous. He gave gifts of money to the Italians on numerous occasions but not, as far as one can tell, estates or lordships. By contrast Louis XI seems to have bestowed all kinds of favours — lands, titles and offices — on those Italians whom he retained in his service, such as the Neapolitan Boffillo del Giudice. As for Charles, he was described by Rodolfo Gonzaga as not a lavish spender by nature ('*non essendo molto largo nel spendere di sua natura*'); this view is reminiscent of the passage in the memoirs of Commynes where, in an implicit comparison with the French king, the duke's gifts are described as not lavish because, wishing everyone to enjoy his liberality, he spread his largesse too widely and therefore too thinly.[124] It is possible also that some of the Italians may have become disillusioned with him in time. For example, many disliked what they regarded as his cold-blooded cruelty and intemperate vanity and ambition.[125] Perhaps by this time some of them were beginning to have forebodings of disaster. Even so, however generous or congenial, Charles could not have made them forget their native land. When Rainieri Mancella married, he chose as his wife the daughter of his fellow Neapolitan Giacomo Galeota. Such marriages were the result of a reluctance to intermarry, less on the part of the duke's subjects than of his Italian friends. For example, when Tommaso Portinari married in 1469 it was to a Florentine lady, Maria Bandini-Baroncelli, whom he travelled all the way from Bruges to Florence to collect because, he said, his friends had threatened to make him take a local girl to wife if he remained a bachelor any longer.[126] Attachment to the homeland showed itself in other ways. Even a man like the Flemish-Genoese Anselme Adournes, whose family had been settled in Flanders for generations, preferred to choose an Italian university, Pavia, for the bulk of his son Jean's studies rather than a 'local' one, such as Louvain or Cologne.[127]

The inescapable conclusion seems to be that at the bottom of their hearts the Italians just did not want or intend to spend the remainder of their lives north of the Alps, even in the service of a ruler as sympathetic as Charles the Bold. They had come to Burgundy — some before about 1472, but most probably after — because the duke's court offered opportunities which could not be bettered, or were simply not available at all, in the peninsula. Nevertheless, they always kept open the option of returning and their eventual decision to leave was merely precipitated by the death of Charles, for this calamitous event robbed them of a patron and protector, while it exposed them at the same time to the unpleasantness of financial retrenchment and local hostility. In some respects a comparison can be made between them and the so-called Burgundian 'traitors'. Thus we find that members of both groups not only left the Burgundian service at about the same time, during the crisis years 1476 to 1480, but also that one or two of the Italians, like rather more of their Burgundian counterparts, ended up, if somewhat reluctantly, in the service of Louis XI. But there was one important difference between them. The Italians had not been born subjects of the dukes of Burgundy; whether from choice or circumstance, they remained unencumbered by landed possessions in the dukes' territories; and as a result they did not feel the need to choose between France and Burgundy in the wars which followed the death of Charles the Bold. They could, at least, return to some part or other of the Italian peninsula. By contrast, the Burgundian refugees from the shipwreck of the Valois state had no such option; service with Louis XI was their only chance of survival.[128]

Notes

1. Molinet, *Chroniques*, I, 167.
2. ADN B 2079.
3. Letter of Charles the Bold to Yolande, regent of Savoy, from Luxembourg, 2

May 1474, in Guichenon, *Histoire . . . Savoie*, IV/1, 399. Ameo had just returned from Savoy, bringing confirmation that Yolande wished to be included in the duke's truce with Louis XI. On his career in the duke's army see below, Chapter 7. He was still alive in 1491, when he was at the French court: H.F. Delaborde, *L'Expédition de Charles VIII en Italie* (Paris, 1888), 220–2.

4. In a letter to the duke of Milan (*Carteggi*, II, no. 484); Spinola (who was described in the previous year as one of Charles the Bold's soldiers: *Carteggi*, II, no. 378) had asked Charles to request Galeazzo Maria to give a certain office in Genoa to his father Baldus.

5. He was referred to in both capacities as early as November 1473: *Lorraine et Bourgogne*, 28; see also Paravicini, *Guy de Brimeu*, 336 (governor of Nijmegen, December 1473) and *Carteggi*, I, no. 248 (governor of Nijmegen and *escuyer de chambre*).

6. ADN B 2086/66,378; ADN B 2106/67,764.

7. ADN B 2087/66,468. A 'Bernard de Paze' was one of Maximilian's 51 *pannetiers* in September 1477: L.P. Gachard, 'Analectes historiques. Cinquième série', *BCRH*, 2nd ser., 9 (1857), 103–256 (p. 119).

8. ADN B 2087/66,436. A 'Perrot d'Arento' had been a page of Philip the Good in 1450; Charles the Bold had bought a horse from 'Piero darrento' to give as a gift to Jean de Poitiers, lord of Crécy, in 1468; and a 'Piero d'Arento' received a ducal gift of 80 *livres* on 10 September 1473 after the fall of Venlo. See W. Paravicini, 'Soziale Schichtungen und soziale Mobilität am Hof der Herzöge von Burgund', *Francia*, 5 (1977), 127–82 (p. 158); AGR CC 1923, ff. 90, 90ᵛ; and L.P. Gachard, 'Analectes historiques. Troisième série', *BCRH*, 2nd ser., 7 (1855), 25–220 (p. 54).

9. *Dépêches . . . Louis XI*, I, 189–93 (the ambassador was Tommaso da Rieti). I see no evidence for Vaughan's assertion (*Philip the Good*, 131–2) that the doctor in question was the duke of Milan's own physician Luca d'Alessandria (although I accepted it in my 'The coming of humanism', 175). However, another of Francesco Sforza's physicians, Guidone da Crema, did treat Jean de Croy in 1459 when he fell ill at the Congress of Mantua, and successfully too, much to the lasting gratitude of Philip the Good and the Croys: *Dispatches*, I, 342 n. 2, and II, 230–1; *Carteggi*, I, no. 31.

10. *Carteggi*, II, no. 386.

11. Giovanni Bianchi to the duke of Milan, Turin, 6 July 1476 (ASM 496).

12. *Carteggi*, II, no. 536, which corroborates Philippe de Commynes' assertion that Cato treated Charles (*Mémoires*, II, 129); see also my 'The coming of humanism', 175 note 118. For the next sentence see *Dépêches . . . Charles-le-Hardi*, II, no. 185.

13. For his career at the Burgundian court and on the portrait medals see Tourneur, 'Jehan de Candida', and Hill, *A corpus of Italian medals*, I, 211–18, and for his later career in France, when he turned his hand to writing history, see my 'The coming of humanism', 163 and note 67, and the further references cited there; also the entry by R. Scheurer in *DBI*, XVII (1974), 774–6.

14. *Carteggi*, I, no. 220 (the letter was written by Giovanni di Candida); Salvatore's task was to ask Galeazzo Maria to ensure the return to the Burgundian camp of Italian troops who had fled after receiving advance payments.

15. *Carteggi*, II, no. 486. Anselmino was certainly already in Charles the Bold's service by April 1475 (Gachard, 'Analectes historiques. Septième série', 394); he may have come to the duke via Savoy if he can be identified with the 'Ansermin du Prat' employed by Yolande as her envoy to Charles in 1472 (Daviso, *Iolanda*, 116).

16. An inscription dated 1596 on the door of the Collegio Marliani which he founded in Pavia — reproduced by Z. Volta, 'Del Collegio Universitario Marliani in Pavia', *ASL*, 2nd ser, 9 (1892), 590–628 (p. 596) — describes him as having been Charles the Bold's councillor. For further information see my 'The coming of humanism', 164–7, and 'Relations', 397 note 59.

17. L.T. Maes and G. Dogaer, 'A propos de l'ordonnance de Thionville promulguée par Charles le Téméraire en 1473', *AB*, 45 (1973), 45–9 (p. 49 n. 4); see also my 'The coming of humanism', 163–4, and Paravicini, *Guy de Brimeu*, 396 note 612, and 720.

18. *Carteggi*, II, no. 415.

19. ADN B 3438/119,105; *Carteggi*, II, no. 376.

20. Bittmann, *Ludwig XI. und Karl der Kühne*, II/1, 477–84. The exact date of his death is uncertain and we know only that he was dead by 1500, when his successor as abbot of Casanova was appointed: F.A. Della Chiesa, *S.R.E. cardinalium, archiepiscoporum, episcoporum et abbatum pedemontane regionis chronologica historia* (Turin, 1645), 285.

21. He left Milan on 5 February with the Milanese ambassador-designate to Burgundy, Panigarola, was with the duke of Milan at Pavia just after the middle of May and was sent back again towards the end of July, but this time Galeazzo Maria invoked his plague regulations as an excuse not to see him: Simonetta, *Diarii*, 153, 166; *Carteggi*, II, no. 332. His mission was to persuade the duke of Milan to send help to Charles according to the latter's interpretation of the terms of the treaty of Moncalieri.

22. Perret, *Histoire*, I, 581–3.

23. He arrived in Rome towards the end of April, intending to return thence to Burgundy through Venice: Assalito Maletta to the duke of Milan, Rome, 25 April 1472 (ASM 69). On Ameo di Valperga see Guichenon, *Histoire . . . Savoie*, IV/1, 399, and on Francesco d'Este, see below, Chapter 6.

24. The deficiencies of his courier system in comparison with those of Louis XI and Galeazzo Maria have been castigated by Pesez, 'Chevaucheurs et courriers du duc de Bourgogne Charles le Téméraire', 153–8, who argued that acting on insufficient information was a symptom of his 'rashness', although a less bleak picture has been drawn by J.M. Cauchies, 'Messageries et messagers en Hainaut au XVᵉ siècle', *MA*, 82 (1976), 89–123, 301–41. It should, however, be remembered that, at least with regard to Italy, the courier system was by no means his only means of collecting information, because he had his own contacts in the peninsula and so did the Italians at court. For example, in 1475 we find Panigarola reading out aloud to him copies of letters written to Galeazzo Maria by the Milanese ambassador in Naples (*Carteggi*, II, no. 363), while at other times Charles could form his own opinion of events in Italy by comparing the conflicting accounts of them provided by the Italian ambassadors at his court.

25. *Carteggi*, I, no. 300.
26. ADN B 3437 (the Monforte brothers) and ADN B 3438/119,098 (body-guard).
27. De Roover, *The rise*, 93.
28. Finot, *Étude*, 243–7.
29. For this mission and his library see my 'Charles the Bold and the crusade', 70–2, and 'The coming of humanism', 171–2. His two van Eycks are discussed by C. Aru and E. de Geradon, *La Galerie Sabauda de Turin*, Les Primitifs Flamands, I: Corpus de la peinture des anciens Pays-Bas méridionaux au quinzième siècle, 5 (Antwerp, 1962), 5–13. On his connection with Scotland see now also N. Macdougall, *James III* (Edinburgh, 1982), 88–9, 190–1; Macquarrie, 'Anselm Adornes', 20–1. The first of his ancestors to settle in the Low Countries was his great-great-great-grandfather Obizzo I, who fought alongside Guy de Dampierre, count of Flanders, in Syria and North Africa, settled in Flanders in 1269 and was buried at Ghent in 1309.
30. C. Gaier, *L'industrie et le commerce des armes dans les anciennes principautés belges du XIIIme à la fin du XVe siècle* (Paris, 1973), 123–4; de Schryver, 'Notes', 38–40.
31. ADN B 2074/65,325 and B 2111/68,010. To these Venetian merchants we might add Girolamo Morosini, 'patron' of one of the galleys commissioned by Philip the Good for his abortive crusade in 1464, who was still claiming payment in 1468: see the letter of the officials of the *Chambre des comptes* at Lille, 19 February 1468, to Charles the Bold's chancellor Pierre de Goux, in ADN B 17702 (dossier entitled 'Maurezin (Jérome)').
32. *Carteggi*, I, no. 281. For the next sentence see P.M. Perret, 'Le manuscrit de Cicco Simonetta (Manuscrit Latin 10133 de la Bibliothèque Nationale)', *Notices et extraits des manuscrits de la Bibliothèque Nationale et autres bibliothèques*, 34 (1891), 323–63 (p. 357: ff. 398^v–400); I have been unable to trace the exact form or date of the imposition of these reprisals.
33. On the same day he also wrote to Panigarola to secure his help; both letters are in ASM 516.
34. ASV, SS, XXIII, 147.
35. On the ambassadors in general see below, Chapter 5.
36. J. Brun–Lavaine, 'Analyse d'un compte de dépense de la maison du duc Charles de Bourgogne', *Bulletin de la Commisssion historique du département du Nord*, 8 (1865), 189–232 (pp. 202, 209); letter to Marchioness Barbara of Mantua by Rodolfo's guardian Enrico Suardi, The Hague, 5 October 1469 (AG 567; translated by Vaughan, *Charles*, 192).
37. Bartier, *Légistes et gens de finances*, 44–56.
38. Schwarzkopf, 'La cour de Bourgogne et la Toison d'Or', *PCEEB*, 5 (1963), 91–104 (pp. 97, 99–100, 102–3).
39. The duke of Milan to Francesco Todeschini-Piccolomini, cardinal of Siena, Milan, 28 March 1472, and the bishop of Novara to the duke of Milan, Rome, 13 April 1472 (ASM 69); Tourneur, 'Jehan de Candida', 287, 283. On Querini, see Antonio d'Appiano to the duke of Milan from Vercelli, 10 January 1473 (ASM 490).

40. Galeota to Lodovico Gonzaga, Jussey, 29 September 1473 (AG 629, no. 65); see also P.M. Perret, 'Jacques Galéot et la république de Venise', *BEC*, 52 (1891), 590–614 (p. 593).

41. F. Solsona Climent, 'Aspectos de la dominación angevina en Cataluña (1466–1472). La participación italiana y francesa en la revolución contra Juan II de Aragón', *Cuadernos de Historia J. Zurita*, 14–15 (1963), 31–54 (pp. 34–6, 40–2); *Carteggi*, I, no. 183; and (Querini) Perret, *Histoire*, I, 495–6.

42. Sacramoro to the duke of Milan, Rome, 2 May 1474 (ASM 76); ADN B 3438/119,105.

43. *Les comptes du roi René*, ed. G. Arnaud d'Agnel, 3 vols (Paris, 1908–10), I, 39 (no. 1520): payment to 'René Mansel, filleul du roy et homme d'armes de la compaignie du conte de Campobas', 7 May 1477.

44. 16 December 1447–4 September 1450, 25 July 1461–14 May 1462 and 8 June 1462–7 January 1463: L.M. Levati, *Dogi perpetui di Genova an. 1339–1528. Studio biografico* (Genoa, 1930), 334–53.

45. The bishop of Novara to the duke of Milan, 25 February 1473 (ASM 72).

46. Below, Chapter 7, 'Chronology of recruitment'. For what follows see Antonio d'Appiano to the duke of Milan, Vercelli, 22 September 1472 (ASM 489); *Carteggi*, I, no. 267; Perret, *Histoire*, I, 496 note 3.

47. Cusin, 'Impero, Borgogna', 39.

48. '. . . *uno de li più pelegrini scudieri vedessi mai . . .*': Nicodemo Tranchedini to the duke of Milan, 20 August 1471 (ASM 68). Agostino had apparently come to Rome in the hope of winning Sixtus IV's support for his schemes regarding Genoa.

49. Cusin, 'Impero, Borgogna', 41; *Carteggi*, II, no. 508. A similar complaint was made in 1473 by the papal envoy Andrei dei Spiriti: '. . . *dice non conosce alcuno principe più inebriato et perduto da fumi et ambitione che lo dicto duca né che più facilmente creda ad persuasori et assentatori de lui*'. See Cristoforo da Bollate to the duke of Milan, Vendôme, 10 October 1473 (ASM 540), summarised by Bittmann, *Ludwig XI. und Karl der Kühne*, II/1, 161.

50. Cusin, 'Impero, Borgogna', 40.

51. P. Litta, *Famiglie celebri italiane*, 11 vols (Milan, 1819–85), II (1825), 'Fregoso di Genova', tables 2, 4, 5, 6.

52. He was already referred to as Galeota's '*hijo*' when the two were in Catalonia in 1471: Solsona Climent, 'Aspectos de la dominación angevina en Cataluña', 36. Perhaps this may be connected with Galeota's application to King Ferrante early in 1470 for a safe-conduct to cover an envoy he wished to send to Naples concerning the marriage of his daughter: *Fonti aragonesi*, III/2, 89 (no. 454). But in 1475 Salvatore de Clariciis implied that the marriage was of only recent date: *Carteggi*, I, no. 248.

53. B. Candida Gonzaga, *Antico manoscritto di Carlo de Lellis sulla famiglia Filangieri* (Naples, 1887), 93–5, 145–6.

54. Rodolfo to Marchioness Barbara, The Hague, 16 September and 20 October 1469 (AG 2100) and Enrico Suardi to the same, Ghent, 21 January 1470 (AG 567). The translator was an Italian who had once been a tapestry maker in Mantua and, at the Burgundian court, a servant recently of Francesco d'Este. L. Campbell, 'Cosmè Tura and Netherlandish art', in *Cosmè Tura.*

Painting and design in Renaissance Ferrara, ed. A. Chong (Boston, 2002), pp. 71–105 (p. 82), suggests that 'ziacheto' could have been the famous Jacquet of Arras or possibly Jacques/Jacquet Dours. This article provides ample illustration of contacts between Burgundy and Italy through art.

55. See the genealogical table in A. Arata, *Niccolò da Correggio* (Bologna, 1934) between pages 204 and 205.

56. Buonaccorsi (Callimachus) to Portinari from Toruń, 4 June 1474(?), in his *Epistolae selectae*, ed. I. Lichońska, G. Pianko and T. Kowalewski (Wratislava–Warsaw–Cracow, 1967), 64, 66, 68.

57. G. Meersseman, 'La raccolta dell'umanista fiammingo Giovanni de Veris "De arte epistolandi"', *IMU*, 15 (1972), 215–81 (pp. 252–5).

58. *Carteggi*, I, no. 183.

59. Calmette and Périnelle, *Louis XI et l'Angleterre*, 325, 327. The unfortunate thing for Salvatico was that by the time he arrived in the Low Countries and prepared to cross the Channel Henry VI had again been deposed by the returning Edward IV!

60. *Dépêches . . . Louis XI*, III, 83, 285–6; *Dispatches*, III, l–liii.

61. *Codice aragonese*, I, nos. 3, 48, 102, 231, 314, 342, 373; Perret, *Histoire*, I, 482; Ferrante to the duke of Milan, 9 July 1467 (ASM 216: letters of credence for '*lo magnifico et amato camarerj nostro Joan palomar*'). He returned briefly to France in March 1469: Perret, *Histoire*, I, 562; Sforza Bettini to the duke of Milan, Amboise, 21 March 1469 (ASM 536).

62. D'Appiano to the duke of Milan, Vercelli, 31 December 1472 (ASM 489). For the next sentence see *Carteggi*, II, no. 604.

63. I have discussed the question more fully in my 'The coming of humanism to the Low Countries'.

64. Walsh, 'Vespasiano da Bisticci', 410–12.

65. *Carteggi*, II, no. 376. For the rest of the paragraph see M. Rosi, 'La congiura di Gerolamo Gentile', *ASL*, 5th ser., 16 (1895), 176–205.

66. P. Magistretti, 'Galeazzo Maria Sforza prigionere nella Novalesa', ASL, 2nd ser., 6 (1889), 777–807. For what follows see G. Filippi, *Il matrimonio di Bona di Savoia con Galeazzo Maria Sforza* (Turin, 1890), 25–7; *Dispatches*, III, xliii–iv; *Carteggi*, II, no. 436; Cusin, 'Impero, Borgogna', 40; Antonio d'Appiano to the duke of Milan, Vercelli, 10 January 1473 (ASM 490).

67. Francesco Maletta to the duke of Milan, Naples, 23 August 1473 (ASM 224), summarising letters, now lost, of Francesco Bertini from the Burgundian court to Ferrante; Cusin, 'Impero, Borgogna', 40, 49; the bishop of Como, Giovanni Pallavicino di Scipione and Antonio d'Appiano to the duke of Milan, Geneva, 15 March 1476 (ASM 494: '. . . alias fu destenuto bon tempo da monsignore de Borgogna . . .').

68. Cusin, 'Impero, Borgogna', 42; *Carteggi*, II, no. 468.

69. Zaccaria Barbaro to the doge, Naples, 25 April 1473 (BNMV 8170/VI, 31). Similarly he maintained his alliance with Edward IV despite harbouring a number of Lancastrian exiles: Commynes, *Mémoires*, ed. Calmette and Durville, I, 206–7; Vaughan, *Charles*, 61; Ballard, 'An expedition', 166–70.

70. As with other Italians, there is a problem of nomenclature. In a letter to the duke of Milan from Dijon on 11 June 1475 (ASM 542) Giacomo signed himself

'Jacobus vasch'. In a letter to the Milanese chancellor Simonetta written '*ex Vischis*' on 26 November 1476 he signed himself 'Iacobinus de Vischis' (A. Tallone, *Parlamento sabaudo*, V/1 (Bologna, 1932), 187). In letters of credence addressed to the duke of Milan written at Lausanne on 25 May 1476, Charles the Bold referred to '*Jacobus de vischis ex comitibus Sancti Martini*' (*Carteggi*, II, no. 581). In an affidavit for Charles the Bold's financial officials he signed himself on 12 August 1471 as 'Jaques de Visque, comte de Saintmartin' (Taparel, 'Le duché Valois de Bourgogne et l'Orient ottoman', 278). The first two documents are in Italian, the third in Latin, the fourth in French.

71. For this and his connection with the humanist Francesco Filelfo see my 'The coming of humanism', 178–9.

72. De la Marche, *Mémoires*, II, 104. Olivier mentioned Giacomo as one of the 300 crack lances maintained by Filippo Maria Visconti at this time. It is not clear whether de la Marche meant that Giacomo actually took part in this tournament, but he seems to have been at the Burgundian court in this period, for, together with Jean Jouffroy, he was sent by Philip the Good to Rome in October 1446 to ask Pope Eugenius IV to lift the excommunication which he had placed on the duchy of Luxembourg: *Inventaire des chartes et cartulaires du Luxembourg*, ed. A. Verkooren, 5 vols (Brussels, 1914–31), IV (1917), 293 (no. 1726); Taparel, 'Le duché Valois de Bourgogne et l'Orient ottoman', 278.

73. *Mémoires pour servir à l'histoire de France et de Bourgogne*, ed. L.F.J. de la Barre, 2 vols (Paris, 1729), II, 190, 217; Martens, 'Correspondance', 228 n. 1; Chastellain, *Oeuvres*, II, 305.

74. Martens, 'Correspondance', 223; M. d'Escouchy, *Chronique*, ed. G. du Fresne de Beaucourt, 3 vols (1863–4), II (1863), 385; London, British Library, Additional MS 54156, f. 380. For the next sentence see Brun-Lavainne, 'Analyse', 217.

75. *Carteggi*, I, no. 271. As early as 8 April 1468 Portinari had expressed a wish to see friendship between Charles the Bold and Galeazzo Maria: *Carteggi*, I, no. 151.

76. *Carteggi*, I, nos. 256–7.

77. *Carteggi*, II, nos. 496, 572.

78. *Carteggi*, I, no. 304.

79. Bittmann, *Ludwig XI. und Karl der Kühne*, II/1, 477–84.

80. Maletta to the duke of Milan, Naples, 28 October 1474 (ASM 226).

81. '. . . *et nominam et mores Francisci Querino Cel. Sue declarate qui per illius demerita multiplicia exul a patria vivendi modum queritat illis eisdem modis et mendacibus artibus quibus nostram meruit indignationem . . .*' (ASV, SS, XXVI, 5ᵛ: 19 March 1473).

82. *Carteggi*, II, no. 497.

83. D'Appiano to the duke of Milan, Turin, 16 August 1473 (ASM 490).

84. *Carteggi*, I, nos. 207, 209.

85. *Carteggi*, I, nos. 215, 222 (2 May and 2 August 1474).

86. The duke of Milan to d'Appiano, Villanova, 24 November 1474, and Yolande to Charles, Moncalieri, 24 November 1474 (both in ASM 491).

87. *Carteggi*, I, no. 219.

88. Cusin, 'Impero, Borgogna', 40. For what follows see *Carteggi*, II, nos. 379, 387, 435–6, 470, 506.
89. *Carteggi*, I, no. 272. For what follows see *Dépêches . . . Charles-le-Hardi*, I, no. 30, and Simonetta, *Diarii*, 199–200.
90. Cusin, 'Impero, Borgogna', 40.
91. *Carteggi*, I, no. 203.
92. *Carteggi*, II, no. 357.
93. *Carteggi*, I, no. 157 ('instructio particularis' for Marquis Gian Lodovico Pallavicino and Tommaso Tebaldi).
94. Cristoforo da Bollate to the duke of Milan, Vendôme, 10 October 1473, reporting the accusations of Andrea dei Spiriti (ASM 540).
95. *Carteggi*, I, no. 305.
96. *Carteggi*, II, no. 376.
97. *Calendar of state papers and manuscripts, relating to English affairs, existing in the archives and collections of Venice and in other libraries of northern Italy*, 38 vols (London, 1864–1947), I, ed. R. Brown (= 1202–1509), no. 407, from ASV, SS, XXIII, 60ᵛ. For what follows see ASV, SS, XXIV, 27–27ᵛ, and *Carteggi*, I, no. 183.
98. De But, *Chronique*, 269, 367, 422, 476; T. Basin, *Histoire de Louis XI*, ed. C. Samaran and M.-C. Garand, 3 vols (Paris, 1963–72), I, 132, 134; AOGV, III, 31–2ᵛ, summarised by de Reiffenberg, *Histoire*, 72–3; Bartier, *Légistes*, 444; *Carteggi*, II, no. 634. For Charles the Bold's view of Francesco Sforza's part in Piccinino's death as early as 1465 and for the views of the members of the Order of the Toison d'Or about the election of foreign rulers expressed at the 1473 meeting see also *Dépêches . . . Louis XI*, III, 351; C.A.J. Armstrong, 'Had the Burgundian government a policy for the nobility?' [1964], reprinted in his *England, France and Burgundy*, 213–36 (p. 231).
99. *Carteggi*, I, nos. 153, 164; *Dépêches . . . Charles-le-Hardi*, II, no. 220.
100. Maletta to the duke of Milan, Naples, 17 February 1472, and the duke to Maletta, Vigevano, 6 March 1472 (ASM 221). For the next sentence see Barbaro to the doge, Naples, 6 February 1472 (BNMV 8170/II, 3); Walsh, 'Relations', 389–90.
101. Francesco to the duke 'ex Ipporigia', 6 October 1473 (ASM 490).
102. *Carteggi*, I, no. 255.
103. *Carteggi*, I, no. 229.
104. *Carteggi*, I, nos. 263, 315; Paravicini, *Guy de Brimeu*, 470 n. 79. For the rest of the sentence see Galeazzo Maria to Sacramoro in Rome, San Giorgio, 14 September 1475 (ASM 79).
105. Gerardo to the duke of Milan 'ex Nucea'(?), 14 February 1475 (ASM 492).
106. *Carteggi*, I, no. 382. In 1463 a visit by Anthony to Milan had encouraged him to think that either he or his son would marry a daughter of Francesco Sforza but nothing came of it: Walsh, 'Relations', 382.
107. *Carteggi*, I, no. 244. For what follows see *Carteggi*, II, nos. 525, 545, 565, 573, 623, 626.
108. *Carteggi*, II, no. 376; this is the only source for the precise date of his death.
109. Ferrante was allegedly molesting the brothers in reprisal for the partisanship

shown by Salvatore and Matteo towards the duke of Milan and against himself; see *Carteggi*, II, nos. 409 and (for the next sentence), 641.

110. G. Dupont-Ferrier, *Gallia Regia*, 6 vols (Paris, 1942–61), IV (1954), 207. For the next sentence see Croce, 'Il conte di Campobasso', 154.

111. For payments to him in September and October 1477 see Gachard, 'Analectes historiques. Cinquième série', 121; ADN B 2112/68,071. The payment made to him in May 1477 by King René (*Les comptes du roi René*, I, 39, no. 1520) may suggest that, having gone to Provence with the count of Campobasso, Rainieri was then unable, or decided not, to return to Italy as Campobasso did.

112. G.G. Pontano, *Lettere inedite in nome de' reali di Napoli*, ed. F. Gabotto (Bologna, 1893), no. 30.

113. Simonetta, *Diarii*, 228–9; Tourneur, 'Jehan de Candida', 45–6, 297–8.

114. See below, Chapter 7, 'Chronology of recruitment'.

115. H. de Vocht, *History of the foundation and rise of the Collegium Trilingue Lovaniense 1517–1550*, 4 vols (Louvain, 1951–5), I, 217 note 1, 164–5.

116. Simonetta, *Diarii*, 261. Some details of his diplomatic career are given by A.M. Fobe, 'De diplomaten van het Boergondische hof (1477–1506)', 3 vols (unpublished thesis, Proefschrift ter verkrijging van een graad van Licenciaat in de Letteren en Wijsbegeerte, Rijksuniversiteit Gent, 1970), III, C/7; and by L. Cerioni, *La diplomazia sforzesca*, 2 vols (Rome, 1970), I, 134. For Italian diplomats in Maximilian's service in the 1490s see W. Höflechner, *Die Gesandten der europäischen Mächte, vornehmlich des Kaisers und des Reiches, 1490–1500* (Vienna, 1972), 27–8, 31, 35–7, 38–9, 43, 46, 58, 69–71, 87–8, 262–3, 283.

117. Tourneur, 'Jehan de Candida', 28–9, 45–6, 283–93.

118. De la Coste, *Anselme Adorne*, 337–68; MacDougall, *James III*, 190–1.

119. De Roover, *The rise*, 347.

120. For what follows see J. Godard, 'Dans les Pays-Bas bourguignons: un conflit de politique commerciale', *Annales d'histoire sociale*, 1 (1939), 417–20; Blockmans, *De volksvertegenwoordiging*, 468–9; M.J. Tits-Dieuaide, *La formation des prix céréaliers en Brabant et en Flandre au XVe siècle* (Brussels, 1975), 348.

121. This was the view of Tourneur, 'Jehan de Candida', 45. Of course, the employment of foreigners in the Flemish administration by the counts of Flanders and by the dukes of Burgundy had been unpopular with the local inhabitants throughout the fourteenth and fifteenth centuries: W. Prevenier, 'Officials in town and countryside in the Low Countries. Social and professional developments from the fourteenth to the sixteenth century', *Acta Historica Neerlandica*, 7 (1974), 1–17 (pp. 12–15).

122. J.N. Paquot, *Mémoires pour servir à l'histoire littéraire des dix-sept provinces des Pays-Bas . . .*, 18 vols (Louvain, 1763–70), VIII (1766), col. 428; A. Noto, *Gli amici dei poveri di Milano* (Milan, 1953), 97.

123. D.P. Benoît, *Histoire de l'abbaye et de la terre de Saint-Claude*, 2 vols (Montreuil-sur-Mer, 1890–2), II, 224–5; Colombo, *Iolanda*, 209–11.

124. Rodolfo to his mother, the marchioness of Mantua, Ghent, 23 January 1470 (AG 2100); Commynes, *Mémoires*, ed. Calmette and Durville, II, 154.

125. See my 'Charles the Bold and the crusade', 79–80, 83, and 'Vespasiano', 413–15.
126. See Portinari's letter to Piero de' Medici from Bruges, 7 December 1469, in Warburg, *Gesammelte Schriften*, I, 377–8, and L. de' Medici, *Lettere*, I, 184–6, 281, 290.
127. Glorieux, 'Un chanoine de Lille, Jean Adourne', 298–300. Jean studied law at Pavia from mid-1465 until early in 1470, before which he had spent about a year at Paris University. When he and his father passed through Italy in 1470 on their way to the Holy Land, they received a warm reception in both Genoa and Milan because of their family connections with the Adorno: *Itinéraire d'Anselme Adorno*, 434–6.
128. R. Vaughan, *Valois Burgundy* (London, 1975), 84; see also his *Charles*, 231–4.

CHAPTER FIVE

Diplomats and Diplomacy

This chapter will focus on the activities of the Italian diplomats at the court of Charles the Bold. The historical background was provided in the first three chapters, where the closeness of the duke's relations with Italy was demonstrated. In fact, his alliances with Naples, Venice and Milan constituted the main reason for the presence at his court of a sizeable group of Italian diplomats. This was true particularly of the resident ambassadors, for in the early stages of the development of the institutions of permanent diplomacy Italian rulers did not, as a rule, send resident ambassadors to the courts of ultramontane rulers unless their relations with those princes were already friendly.

The Italian diplomats at Charles the Bold's court formed a distinct group. They were bound together by their mutual friendships or rivalries, and they were distinguished from the other Italians by the special honour with which they were treated by the duke and his courtiers and by the precedence accorded them on ceremonial occasions. They are interesting for a number of reasons. The duke's attitude towards them provides a yardstick by which to measure not only his fondness for Italians but also the extent to which he was influenced in one specific area by Italian modes of thought. For the historian of diplomacy the activities of these particular diplomats form a case study illustrating the transition from the medieval to the Renaissance or early modern period. This transition took place first in Italy and was accelerated north of the Alps by the influence and example of Italian diplomats sent to ultramontane courts. Charles the Bold's was not, of course, the only ultramontane court where Italian diplomats could be found in significant numbers during the third quarter of the fifteenth century; one thinks also of the courts of Charles VII and Louis XI of France, of Emperor

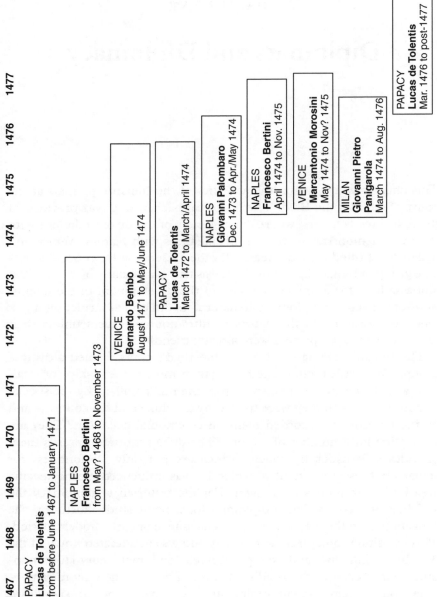

Figure 1 Italian diplomats at the court of Charles the Bold.

Frederick III and of Matthias Corvinus of Hungary. Nonetheless, there is sufficient material surviving from Charles the Bold's reign to enable us to analyse, in some detail, the techniques of Italian Renaissance diplomacy and the minutiae of the diplomat's daily routine and conditions of life. Moreover, as will be argued below, some of the Italian diplomats at his court can legitimately be defined as resident ambassadors, and this is particularly significant in view of the fact that the office of resident is considered to be the herald and then the hallmark of a new era in diplomacy. Yet developments at the duke's court have hitherto been but scantily treated by historians of diplomacy. Finally, the presence of these ambassadors at his court tells us something about the political condition of Italy at that time. Whether they liked it or not, Italian rulers could not insulate the peninsula from events north of the Alps. Consequently, they had to send representatives to ultramontane courts such as that of Charles the Bold in order to gather information on the activities of their enemies, both existing and potential, to foster relations with friendly northern rulers, to maintain surveillance of discontented exiles and to counter the intrigues of hostile Italian neighbours who might try to improve their position in Italy through intrigues with interested parties beyond the mountains.

The Italian ambassadors: Naples

The kingdom of Naples under the Aragonese dynasty has been largely ignored by historians of Renaissance diplomacy in favour of the great republics of Florence and Venice and the duchy of Milan under the Sforza dukes. This neglect can be explained mainly by reference to the paucity of the surviving Neapolitan archives compared with the wealth of material surviving in Florence, Venice and Milan; even so, the sheer scale of King Ferrante's diplomatic activities can be readily grasped.[1] Indeed, his assiduity in dispatching ambassadors to all quarters of Europe alarmed even a ruler as active and as abreast of the diplomatic developments of his time as Galeazzo Maria.[2] Moreover, as far as the story of Charles the Bold's diplomatic relations with the rulers of Italy is concerned, the king of Naples and his ambassadors can be said to have held pride of place. Ferrante was a ruler much admired by Charles, as he was also by Louis XI.[3] The alliance with Naples of 1471 was the first that Charles concluded with any Italian ruler. Ferrante was represented at the Burgundian court, in the persons of Francesco Bertini and

Giovanni Palombaro, longer and more continuously — from probably some time in 1468, and certainly from the summer of 1470, until just after the middle of 1476 — than any other secular Italian ruler, and it was one of his ambassadors, Bertini, who, with the single exception of the papal legate Lucas de Tolentis, was the longest serving of all the Italian ambassadors at Charles's court. Francesco Bertini (died 22 November 1475)[4] was a citizen and possibly also a native of Lucca[5] who had served the papacy in a minor diplomatic capacity during the 1450s and 1460s before entering the service of King Ferrante in the latter months of 1465; it was with the help of Ferrante's recommendation that he was promoted bishop of Andria on 20 October 1465 and bishop of Capaccio on 18 September 1471, both sees being situated within the kingdom of Naples.[6]

The embassy to the Burgundian court was to be the major event of his life. Unfortunately it is impossible to state with certainty either when he left Naples or when he arrived in Burgundy. The first description of him specifically as ambassador at the court of Charles the Bold occurs in the procuration dated 4 August 1470 empowering him to conclude an alliance with the duke.[7] It cannot be ruled out, however, that he had already been in Burgundy for some time, because there are several references to the presence of a Neapolitan ambassador at the Burgundian court before August 1470. Thus one of the Milanese ambassadors who visited Charles in the summer of 1469 mentioned a Neapolitan ambassador in his subsequent report; a Neapolitan ambassador was among the dignitaries present at the formal submission to the duke of the delegates of the city of Ghent at Brussels on 15 January 1469; and the chronicler Jean Molinet, citing a now lost passage of his predecessor Chastellain, wrote that a Neapolitan ambassador participated in the chapter meeting of the Order of the Golden Fleece held at Bruges in May 1468.[8] We cannot, however, be absolutely certain that Bertini was the man in question, since none of these sources gives the name of the ambassador concerned. What complicates matters is the fact that, as we shall see shortly, another Neapolitan ambassador, Garzia or Garcia Betes, was in England before February or March 1470, and since it is likely, for reasons both of etiquette and of diplomacy, that Betes spent some time at the Burgundian court before crossing the Channel to England on his outward journey, then it could have been he who was the Neapolitan ambassador in question. A further complication arises from the fact that, according to his biographer, Bertini stayed for a while at the English court before going to Burgundy, and the arrival of a Neapolitan ambassador in London was recorded in April 1469, together with his stated intention to stay for several months.[9] Thus, even if Betes was the ambassador who arrived in London in April 1469, that would not automatically preclude him from having been the same person as the Neapolitan ambassador who was with Charles the Bold in May 1468 and January 1469. Equally, Bertini could not have been at the Burgundian court before 1469 if it was only in April that year that he arrived in London, from where he went on subsequently to the Low Countries.

Yet it remains possible that it was Bertini who was with Charles in May 1468 and January 1469, that the Neapolitan ambassador who arrived in London in April 1469 was Betes, and, finally, that Betes, on this occasion, went directly to England without visiting the duke of Burgundy first. There is one piece of evidence which tilts the balance in favour of Bertini. In November 1473 he was described by both the Milanese ambassador at the imperial court and by the Milanese chancellor as having by that time spent no less than five years at the Burgundian court.[10] This would place his arrival there in the latter part of 1468.

We know nothing of his original instructions; indeed, if we did, there would be little difficulty in dating either his departure from Naples or his arrival in Burgundy. But their essence was probably an injunction simply to convey home, as speedily and as accurately as possible, full information of events in Burgundy and France and to seize every opportunity to foster relations between his master and the duke. It is unlikely, by contrast, that he set out with powers to conclude an alliance; those only came later. Nonetheless, the good impression which he seems to have made on Charles contributed substantially towards facilitating the Burgundian–Neapolitan alliance of 1471, and over the next four years his influence helped prevent the complete collapse of that alliance which subsequent disagreements between Charles and Ferrante seemed likely at times to bring about. Bertini had only one break from his embassy in Burgundy and it was comparatively brief. Towards the end of 1473 he was recalled to Naples to receive updated instructions, the need for which arose from the possibility of a marriage between Ferrante's younger son Federico and Charles's heiress Mary. He must have left the Burgundian court about the middle of November, because on the last day of that month he was in Vigevano in the duchy of Milan, where he met the duke.[11] He arrived back in Naples about mid-January 1474 and left on 16 March, returning to the Burgundian court towards the end of April. For the next year and a half, until his death on 22 November 1475, he assiduously followed the court without interruption. The originals of his letters home have, most regrettably, been lost, but fortunately a handful of copies and summaries survives.[12]

The ambassador who looked after Ferrante's interests at the Burgundian court during Bertini's return to Naples in the winter of 1473–1474 and also, following Bertini's death, for a few months in 1476, was a man whose surname presents some difficulty: Giovanni Palombaro or Palomar (or Pallomaro).[13] The presence or absence in our sources of the 'b' may be the result simply of variations in the phonetic sensitivity of contemporaries who were less rigorous over orthographical uniformity than we are today. But it could provide a clue to his geographical and national origins. If Palombaro were in some way toponymic, then that would suggest an Italian and probably a Neapolitan origin (either from the city or from the kingdom of Naples); locations such as Palombai, the grottoes of Palombe, Palombaro, Palombara and Palombara Sabina suggest themselves. The form Palomar, on the other hand, suggests an Iberian origin, in which case our ambassador might have been one of the Aragonese whom Alfonso V brought to Naples in the 1430s and 1440s.[14] His own signatures serve only to increase the confusion.[15] Suffice it to say that in the following pages the more Italianate form will be used. Palombaro must have been chosen to substitute for Bertini in the late summer of 1473, because he arrived at Pavia on 26 September, but he did not leave until 24 October, the reason given for the delay being that he wanted to avoid any suspicion of collusion falling on his master if, while he was travelling to Burgundy, Charles the Bold attempted some enterprise in Italy. By 8 November he had advanced only as far as the Savoyard court, then at Ivrea, and it was probably not until the first week of December that he reached his destination.[16] He remained at the Burgundian court for about five months, until the end of April or perhaps the beginning of May the following year.

After Bertini's death in November 1475 Palombaro was a natural choice as temporary replacement. He had been ambassador to Savoy since June 1475, but, when the Savoyard court moved to Lausanne in March 1476, he was able for the next few months, because Charles the Bold was then campaigning in the vicinity against the Swiss, to serve as ambassador to the Burgundian court as well.[17] He seems to have remained with Charles for some time after the battle of Murten, for he was at Salins, where the duke had assembled the Estates of Burgundy, in the second week of July, but this is the last trace of him in Charles's reign. However, he was now qualified as something of an expert on Burgundian affairs, for two years later Ferrante utilised his experience by sending him to the court of Mary and Maximilian; he attended the chapter meeting of the Order of the Golden Fleece held at Bruges in November 1478.

Bertini and Palombaro were the main Neapolitan ambassadors at the court of Charles the Bold, but four other, lesser envoys should be mentioned. A 'Messire Jehan Durmont, *chevalier*' was at court in the late summer of 1469.[18] An Antonello da Campagna arrived in the following summer, leaving in the first half of July. His ostensible purpose was simply to bring a gift of some horses from Ferrante to the duke, but, in addition, he was probably instructed to use this opportunity to further the general progress of Burgundian–Neapolitan relations, which were then reaching the stage where negotiations for an alliance would shortly begin.[19] Garzia (or Garcia) Betes[20] visited the Burgundian court at least three times on his way to and from England. He stayed briefly at the Burgundian court early in 1470 when returning from England to Naples.[21] In the following summer Ferrante decided to send him back to England to take gifts of horses to Edward IV and Charles the Bold, although Galeazzo Maria suspected that the real reason was to congratulate the two rulers on their victory over Louis XI represented by Edward's recent defeat and deposition of Henry VI. Betes was still in Naples in the second half of 1471 but had arrived at the Burgundian court by about February the following year.[22] He stayed in England for almost four years, visiting the Burgundian court, then in Lorraine, in January 1476 on his return. The Milanese ambassador in Venice learned that Betes, who by this time had reached Ferrara, had actually been expelled from England as a form of reprisal by Edward for Ferrante's dealings with the king of France; shortly before this expulsion Edward had read aloud to his barons a letter written by the king of Naples to Louis in which Ferrante had calumniated his erstwhile English ally. Giovanni (following Italian sources) or Joan Olzina, who came from a Valencian family which had long served the Aragonese crown and who had himself become secretary to Alfonso V as early as 1425,[23] went to the Burgundian court in 1475. He was among the most senior of those deputed by Ferrante in October 1474 to accompany his son Federico to Burgundy, where it was hoped he might be able to win the hand of the heiress Mary; a list compiled by one of Federico's attendants termed him the prince's treasurer.[24] But whereas Federico and the bulk of his party were held up in the Franche-Comté for some time because hostilities with the duke of Lorraine and the Swiss rendered further progress unsafe, Olzina was able to slip through, for he was in Bruges by the second half of April 1475 and at the end of August he was in Namur. His specific task seems to have been to foster, from the vantage-point of the Burgundian court, his master's relations with the king of Aragon.[25]

The Italian ambassadors: Venice

The Venetian republic maintained a series of ambassadors at the court of Charles the Bold: Antonio Dandolo, around Christmas and New Year 1467–1468 and again from about May 1469 until mid-1470; Bernardo Bembo, from August 1471 until May or June 1474; and Marcantonio Morosini, from May 1474 until about November 1475. The Venetian senate also decided early in 1476 to send a replacement for Morosini but nothing came of it. Venetian interests were further represented by the consul of the Venetian merchants in Bruges, Alberto Contarini.

Antonio Dandolo was chosen as ambassador to Burgundy on 12 August 1467. The Venetians had for some time been suspicious of Louis XI but the immediate cause of their decision to establish closer links with Charles the Bold seems to have been a visit from Guillaume Fillastre, bishop of Tournai; travelling to Rome on ducal business, Fillastre stopped in Venice in August 1467 to suggest — apparently on his own initiative, though he could have been acting on instructions — that the Venetians should follow the example of many other rulers by seeking an alliance with his master, assuring them that their overtures would be well received. In fact, Dandolo's instructions, dated 23 October, did not mention the possibility of an alliance. Instead he was instructed simply to offer Charles condolences on his father's death and congratulations on his own accession, to commend to him the Venetian merchants in his lands, and to stay a maximum of two weeks, returning sooner if possible. By early December at the latest he had reached Worms, whence he wrote to the senate recounting Charles's recent successes against Liège, news which delighted the Venetians; as the Milanese ambassador in Venice wrote, '*tanto comendano dicto ducha quanto s'el fusse Dio in terra*'. A week or so later, Dandolo was ceremonially escorted into Maastricht by, according to an anonymous Italian source, 'Aloso'(?) of Cleves and Baudouin, bastard of Burgundy. On 28 December he and his party were formally received by the duke at Brussels.[26] How long he stayed we do not know, but if he followed his instructions he must have left in January 1468.

In 1469 he was to undertake a second and longer embassy. On 22 November 1468 the senate had given instructions that he should leave the court of Savoy for that of Burgundy. He was then dealing with the ratification of a treaty between Savoy and Venice and, when that had still not been completed a month later, he was instructed on 30 December to set out anyway. When he left is not clear but it seems that he did not reach the Burgundian court, then at Saint-Omer, until the first or second week of May 1469. His main task was to intercede with the duke on behalf of a number of Venetian merchants involved in legal cases then pending and to secure the renewal of the privileges of the Venetian 'nation' in the Low Countries. But although questions of commerce were the initial cause of his dispatch to Burgundy, it was the prospect of an alliance between Charles and the republic, for which the duke seemed the more eager, which kept him there for over a year. No alliance was concluded, however, and on 8 June 1470 the senate wrote to Dandolo giving him permission to return home and naming as his successor Bernardo Bembo. Dandolo was still with Charles at Saint-Omer on 5 July 1470 but he probably took his leave shortly after. From the letter which the senate wrote to the duke on 8 October thanking him for his treatment of Dandolo and informing him that his replacement would be Bembo, it appears that Dandolo had by then already been in Venice for some time.[27]

Bernardo Bembo (1433–1519),[28] the second and longest-serving of the three Venetian ambassadors at the court of Charles the Bold, had already been designated to succeed Dandolo when the latter was recalled in June 1470, but the republic's preoccupation with the war against the Turks delayed his departure for a year. On 26 April 1471 Charles wrote to the republic requesting the services of her captain-general Bartolomeo Colleoni for the period after his recently concluded truce with Louis XI expired. The senate replied on 3 June that for the present Colleoni could not be spared, but that Bembo would leave within ten days to explain to the duke the reasons why.[29] But, as Bembo himself tells us in his commonplace book, he did not leave until 12 July.[30] His instructions, dated 16 July 1471 (and, therefore, sent to him after he had left Venice), listed several specific tasks which he was to carry out immediately on arrival. He was to excuse to Charles the delay between Dandolo's departure and his own arrival; to explain the dangers now posed by the advance of the Turks; to inform the duke of the conclusion of an alliance between Venice and Naples; to congratulate him on the victory represented by Edward IV's restoration; and to secure his protection for Venetian merchants not only in Flanders but also in England. His longer-term task was simply to stay at the Burgundian court until further notice, fostering Venetian relations with the duke and writing home daily on events in the region.[31]

He reached the Burgundian court, then at Abbeville, in August.[32] At this stage the Venetians, though eager for good relations, were reluctant, in view of the Turkish war, to commit themselves to a firm alliance which might require them to send help to Charles. Preliminary negotiations started soon after Bembo's arrival, but it was not until 16 March 1472 that the senate empowered him to conclude an alliance. The treaty was signed in June and ratified by both parties and by their respective allies before the end of the year. Thereafter Bembo stayed on at court, and his growing intimacy with the duke, together with his supposed malevolent influence over him, aroused great apprehension among the enemies of both Burgundy and Venice. Even so, a rift began to grow up between the allies. Whereas Charles wanted the republic to help him in his campaigns north of the Alps, on the grounds of mutual interest as well as obligation, the Venetians urged him to help *them* against the Turks. By the beginning of 1474, having been on duty for two and a half years, Bembo was anxious for recall, especially as his successor, Marcantonio Morosini, had been chosen on 23 September 1473.[33] But the senate hesitated, in view both of the complications arising from the duke's continuing requests for permission to hire Colleoni and of Bembo's accumulated experience in dealing with him; it did, however, write to Bembo on 23 March 1474 agreeing to his departure once his successor, who was due to set out three days hence, had arrived and been briefed. Bembo did not have to wait long and he must have left the Burgundian court, then at Luxembourg, in late May or early June, judging by the fact that on his return journey he passed through Pavia on 2 July.

Although Marcantonio Morosini (ca. 1417–post-1501) had been chosen as Bembo's successor on 23 September 1473 and his departure fixed for 26 March 1474, his departure was delayed by the arrival in Venice at the end of March 1474 of two Burgundian envoys, Antoine de Montjeu and Lupo de Garda, who wanted to discuss further the possibility of recruiting Colleoni. As a result, Morosini's instructions were not drawn up until 2 April.[34] He was given only two specific tasks to carry out immediately on his arrival at the Burgundian court: to confer with Bembo on the current state of the Colleoni negotiations, and to justify to Charles the republic's recent actions in Cyprus, which had amounted to a virtual annexation of the island at the expense of the claims of Savoy, another of the duke's allies. Apart from this, he was instructed merely to ensure that the republic was included as a Burgundian ally in any treaty which the duke might make with Louis XI, and to keep the senate fully informed about events in the region. After receiving his instructions, he seems to have delayed further for several days, as he did not reach Milan until 15 April,[35] but he had probably arrived at the Burgundian court by the end of May or the beginning of June, thus allowing Bembo to leave. He appears to have performed competently enough but he was given little scope for improving relations between Venice and Burgundy because of the conflict in interpreting the terms of the treaty; each party wanted the other to provide assistance against their respective enemies and neither would give way. Morosini suffered some illness during his embassy and this caused him to increase his efforts to secure a recall by the time he had been in post for over a year. The senate granted his request on 25 July 1475 and Morosini received notification of this the following month but he seems to have stayed on until the latter part of November. His journey home, however, was relatively swift, since on his return he had reached Novara by 7 December.

It is a tragedy that none of the original dispatches which these three Venetian ambassadors sent home is extant. Along with many other documents of the period they were presumably lost in the two fires of 1575 and 1577 which destroyed much of the Doge's Palace, where the republic's main archives were then housed.[36] Moreover, we have even fewer copies for the Venetians than we do for the Neapolitan ambassadors (whose original dispatches have likewise failed to survive): one Milanese copy for Bembo,[37] another for Morosini,[38] and nothing at all for Dandolo.

Some mention, finally, should be made of Alberto Contarini, consul of the Venetian 'nation' in Bruges and a merchant who had a commercial connection with the court. Because the Venetians had made no provision for replacing Morosini following his departure in November 1475, they were caught short by developments in French–Burgundian relations and had to call on Contarini to act in a quasi-diplomatic capacity. In the truce of Soleuvre of 13 September 1475 Charles had included Venice as his ally, and by the terms of the truce she was given until 1 January 1476 to ratify this inclusion. Unfortunately it must have taken anything up to two months for the necessary notifications and communications to pass between Venice and the Burgundian court, and by the time all this had taken place Morosini had either left or, if he had not, did not have the time to deal with the matter before he did. In any case it was Contarini who was given the task of securing the inclusion of Venice in the truce. He, however, missed the deadline, partly because of the delay both in receiving instructions from Italy and in arranging a meeting with Louis XI (he did not arrive in Paris until 29 December), and partly because of the latter's deliberate procrastination; Louis hoped that exclusion would place the Venetians in an isolated position where he could prise them away from Burgundy by the threat of attacking their shipping and by the enticement of an alliance against their former enemy Galeazzo Maria (whom he was equally eager to entice from the Burgundian camp). Following his rather dejected return from France, Contarini was granted an audience by Charles at Besançon on 26 January 1476. After describing and denouncing Louis XI's duplicity, he asked the duke to regard the republic's acceptance of her inclusion in the truce as binding, even though the deadline had passed, and thereby to accept responsibility for preventing French attacks on her shipping. Charles replied characteristically that the keeping of the truce depended not on legal formalities but on the political fact of his own power and consequent ability to scare Louis into ceasing his machinations against himself and his allies.[39]

Immediately on receipt of the consul's letter of 29 January recounting these events, the senate wrote to the duke on 22 February urging him to adopt the course of action proposed by Contarini. It also voted to send an ambassador to Burgundy to deal with the matter; the mission was regarded as being of such importance that the senate decreed a fine of 1,000 ducats if the candidate to be selected refused.[40] The man chosen was reported to have been Giacomo da Ca' da Mezzo, about whom little is otherwise known.[41] In the event, however, no ambassador was sent, even though the decision to send one was reaffirmed early in June. Instead the gravity of the situation which resulted from the Burgundian defeat by the Swiss at Murten later the same month prompted the republic to tackle the problem of relations with France more directly by sending Francesco Donato as ambassador to France in August; although anxious to avoid giving the impression of abandoning their Burgundian alliance, the Venetians felt it advisable to write to Contarini at the beginning of that month instructing him to explain and justify their actions to the duke.[42]

The Italian ambassadors: Milan

The Milanese diplomatic presence at Charles the Bold's court was much more sparse than that of either Naples or Venice, for one obvious reason: at this period it was not yet the custom of Italian rulers to maintain ambassadors on a long-term basis at the courts of ultramontane rulers with whom they were not on close terms, and until the treaty of Moncalieri in January 1475 Charles and Galeazzo Maria regarded each other as enemies. But following that treaty, the duke of Milan sent Giovanni Pietro Panigarola to stay at the Burgundian court until further notice, and for almost a year and a half Panigarola stuck to the duke like a leech.[43] During this time another Milanese embassy briefly visited Charles, at the beginning of 1476. Before 1475 only one other Milanese embassy took place; this was in the summer of 1469.

The 1469 embassy was led by Marquis Gian Lodovico Pallavicino (1425–1481)[44] and Tommaso Tebaldi da Bologna (ca. 1415–1475).[45] Their official instructions, dated Abbiategrasso, 7 May 1469, were those of a purely ceremonial embassy. The ambassadors were to say, first, that they had come out of respect for Charles's great fame and virtue and as a sign that Galeazzo Maria wished to continue the friendship enjoyed by their respective predecessors, Francesco Sforza and Philip; further, they were to explain why their master had not been able to send them to '*nostro magiore fratello e patre*' any earlier. Next, with regard to ultramontane affairs, they were to congratulate the duke on his recent peace with Louis XI (presumably a reference to the articles of Péronne) and to stress Galeazzo Maria's goodwill towards Charles's ally the duke of Savoy; finally, they were to find out what would be a pleasing gift to send to the duke, and were to pay their respects to Margaret of York, Isabel of Portugal, Anthony of Burgundy (the duke's wife, mother and half-brother), Philip of Savoy and Duke John of Cleves. However, the ambassadors' *instructio particularis* (dated 5 May 1469) shows that their master had more practical objectives in mind. Having heard that the Venetians, with the support of the pope, were trying to turn Charles against him and his ally Louis XI, the duke of Milan instructed the ambassadors to impress on Charles and his courtiers that the Venetians could not be trusted because they were both perfidious and anti-monarchical.[46]

On 13 June, Pallavicino and Tebaldi arrived at Ghent, where they were received by the duke with much ceremony.[47] For the exchanges which took place at their formal audience we have the ambassadors' own testimony. After they had delivered the messages mentioned and after the chancellor Pierre de Goux had made the conventional reply on his master's behalf, Charles himself intervened to say that he was not convinced by their justification of Galeazzo Maria's recent actions against Savoy. Naturally the ambassadors disputed this. Then, in accordance with their instructions, they warned Charles against an alliance with the Venetians, whom they described as both unreliable and weak. By contrast they extolled the virtues of their master as an ally: he was rich, powerful, influential and trustworthy. Charles accepted these general protestations of friendship but asked for more details. The ambassadors replied that they had no instructions to discuss particularities, although they stressed that their master could not make an alliance with Burgundy which in any way infringed the one he already had with France. The audience ended after Charles had urged them to refer back to their master, saying that he would answer more precisely only when he had been given more details of Galeazzo Maria's intentions. The ambassadors probably set out for home soon after.

Giovanni (or Giovan) Pietro Panigarola, [48] eldest son of the merchant Arrighino, was sent to the Burgundian court to represent Galeazzo Maria as a result of the treaty of Moncalieri. His instructions, dated Milan, 2 February 1475,[49] did not set a time limit on his stay. He was told to say on his arrival that his master had made the treaty in order to renew the good relations between Milan and Burgundy which had existed in the time of their fathers; that Galeazzo Maria had been prevented from doing so earlier by the French alliance inherited from his father; but that, now he had made the alliance with Charles, he wished to maintain it 'perpetuis temporibus'. Panigarola was to announce his master's intention to send one of his brothers to visit the duke of Burgundy,[50] but he was to insist that Charles reciprocate by sending a worthy embassy to Milan (Charles's indifference to this request was later to sour relations with Galeazzo Maria). For the rest, Panigarola's instructions were confined to generalities, such as how to behave towards the other Italian ambassadors and what particular subjects he was to report most fully on to his master. He left Milan on 5 February 1475 and arrived at the Burgundian court, then encamped around Neuss on the Rhine, on 13 March.[51] For the next seventeen months he was almost inseparable from Charles, following him at court, in camp and council chamber, and even on the battlefield. Exactly when he left is not clear. His last dispatch from the Burgundian court, then at La Rivière in the Franche-Comté, was dated 7 August 1476, but he must still have been with the duke a week later when Charles wrote to Galeazzo Maria urging him to reconsider his decision to recall the ambassador. But Panigarola left anyway shortly afterwards; he passed through Turin on 7 September and reported to his master at Galliate two days later.[52]

Panigarola has won a certain amount of posthumous fame through the simple historical fact that, unlike the other Italian ambassadors at Charles the Bold's court, the bulk of his correspondence has survived, providing as a result an invaluable contemporary source for events not only in Burgundy, France and Savoy but also in Germany and England. These dispatches have now been published in full by Ernesto Sestan.[53] The impression they give is of a man personally modest but lion-hearted in defending the interests of his master, unhesitating in refuting the not uncommon slurs made against Galeazzo Maria's reputation, indefatigable in gathering any information which might be useful to the duke of Milan, and shrewd in checking the truth of rumours which could portend danger to him. Nor, it appears, did he shrink from giving his own advice to both Charles and his own master.

Panigarola had been instructed on arrival to ask Charles to send an embassy to Milan in order to impress on the world the solidity of the new alliance. Over the next twelve months, on a number of occasions, Galeazzo Maria repeated the request through Panigarola. But, as Charles gave only promises, while at the same time sending a variety of requests of his own to his ally for military and financial aid, the duke of Milan eventually decided to take the initiative himself. He had made up his mind by the latter part of November to send an embassy to Burgundy,[54] but it was not until February 1476 that any significant progress was made; by then a sense of urgency had been forced on him by the prospect of a meeting between Charles and Louis XI at which he suspected his interests might be sacrificed. The ambassadors finally chosen were Giovanni di Pietro Pallavicino di Scipiono (died 1478), a relative of the Marquis Gian Lodovico Pallavicino who had led the 1469 embassy, Pietro Francesco Visconti (died 1484) and Luca Grimaldi; also attached to the embassy as the duke's personal envoy was Giacomo Alfieri (died 1499).[55] Their master's frame of mind at this time can be deduced from their instructions, dated Milan, 5 February 1476.[56] In all things they were to reply only as specified and were not to exceed their instructions in the slightest. They were to accompany Charles to his meeting with Louis XI, if it took place, and attempt to fathom the king's attitude towards Milan. As for Charles, they were to impress on him and his courtiers that their master's devotion to Burgundian interests could not be doubted, but, if they were asked about the possibility of his helping Charles against the Swiss, they were to reply only that he would not fail in any of his obligations and that their instructions did not empower them to say more. Finally, they were to emphasise that Galeazzo Maria's position at home was strong and that he was on the best of terms with all his neighbours. That the duke of Milan was motivated largely by fear emerges even more clearly from the letter he wrote to Pallavicino and Visconti from Pavia on 23 February 1476.[57] He stressed the importance, if he was not to be caught by surprise by events beyond the Alps, of ascertaining the precise intentions of both Charles and Louis, and he concluded by saying that the one he really feared was not the king but his own Burgundian ally, because he suspected him of wanting to settle his affairs north of the mountains so that he could be free to lead an expedition to Italy, perhaps even against Milan, however much he might pretend otherwise.

Despite such long and minute preparation, the embassy was a fiasco. The ambassadors arrived at Orbe on 25 February but almost a week passed before they were granted a preliminary audience by Charles on 1 March. Early the following day, however, they received from Galeazzo Maria a letter (no longer extant) which instructed them to leave as quickly as was compatible with discharging their business. The ambassadors felt that the preliminary audience already granted had just about given them sufficient opportunity to carry out their instructions, and the receipt of this letter, together with the onset of the battle of Grandson only hours afterwards, made them decide to leave with all haste on the same day. Not surprisingly, their precipitate departure created the worst possible impression in the Burgundian camp, but despite the frantic appeals of Panigarola, who had to bear the brunt of the criticisms which their behaviour provoked, they did not come back, preferring to continue their homeward journey to Italy.[58]

Carlo Visconti and Antonio d'Appiano are two other Milanese ambassadors who should be mentioned because, although not accredited to the Burgundian court as such, they did on occasions have the opportunity to report on events there. Carlo Visconti (died 1497?)[59] was sent to Germany in the summer of 1473 to negotiate with Frederick III for a formal imperial recognition of his master as duke of Milan, remaining in this post until at least August the following year. In November 1473 he was with the emperor at Trier to witness the meeting with Charles the Bold, and his dispatches describing the event are a useful, if not always reliable, source of information. Antonio d'Appiano (died post-1493) was the resident Milanese ambassador at the court of Savoy from 1470 or 1471 until 1476. Since relations between Savoy and Burgundy were so close throughout these years, the deeds of Charles the Bold are mentioned frequently in his correspondence. Of particular interest are the dispatches he wrote during the spring and early summer of 1476 when the Burgundian and Savoyard courts were in close proximity at Lausanne; they complement those of Panigarola.[60]

The Italian ambassadors: Rome

A succession of papal envoys visited the court of Charles the Bold. However, as their activities have been discussed in detail above (Chapter 2), little more needs to be said about them here. The main representative of the Holy See was the Dalmatian Lucas de Tolentis (1428–1491), who represented papal interests in the lands of Burgundy on and off for an unprecedentedly long period of about a quarter of a century, from 1458 until 1484. During Charles the Bold's reign he was in the duke's lands from his accession until his death, apart from two breaks, in the winter of 1471–1472 and from the spring of 1474 until March 1476. The bulk of his correspondence with Paul II and especially with Sixtus IV that survives from these missions has been published by Jacques Paquet.[61] In due course his powers were extended to cover not only the territories of the duke of Burgundy but also certain parts of the Empire and even England and Scotland. In fact, he was to remain in the Low Countries until 1488, although in 1484 he was stripped of his legatine authority by Sixtus IV.

Lucas was entrusted with a variety of tasks: collecting papal taxes and selling indulgences; urging Charles to make peace with his enemies and turn his arms instead against the Turks; supervising the alum agreement concluded between the duke and Paul II in 1468; and generally defending the interests of the Holy See. But this range of duties placed too great a burden on the shoulders of one man, so his efforts were from time to time complemented by those of special envoys. To deal with the alum business, Paul II in the spring or summer of 1471 sent Tommaso dei Vincentii to the Low Countries, where he arrived in or before October; he cannot, however, have stayed long, for by the end of January 1472 he was back in Rome acting as treasurer-general to Paul's successor Sixtus IV.[62] His own successor as special alum commissioner was Domenico Albergati, who was sent from Rome by Sixtus in June 1472; he remained in Flanders longer than his predecessor, because he was still in Bruges, presumably continuing to act as papal representative, in October 1475.[63] Other papal envoys specifically accredited to the Burgundian court were Pietro Aliprandi and Onofrio di Santa Croce, bishop of Tricarico. Aliprandi, designated as papal nuncio to England, had arrived in the

Low Countries towards the end of 1472, having been unable to cross the Channel; from then until about the middle of 1475 he followed the Burgundian court intermittently and seems for a time to have replaced Tolentis as the resident legate, especially after Tolentis's return to Rome in 1474. Onofrio had been sent to Liège in 1468 to settle the dispute between the bishop and his opponents, a matter the duke had considered of close concern to himself. Other legates, though not specifically accredited to Burgundy, visited the duke in the course of missions designed to settle conflicts in which he was involved. Thus Charles was visited by Stefano Nardini, archbishop of Milan and legate to France (died 1484), in October 1467; by Andrea dei Spiriti (died 1504), legate to France, in July 1473; by Alessandro Nanni, bishop of Forlì and legate in the Empire (died 1483), on several occasions in 1475 and 1476; and by Niccolò San Donnino, bishop of Modena and legate to France (died 1499), in March 1476. Two other legates to France, Cardinal Basil Bessarion and Cardinal Giuliano della Rovere, talked in 1472 and 1476 respectively of visiting the duke but never actually did so.[64]

Some general characteristics, personal and professional

When treatises on the functions and qualifications of ambassadors began to proliferate in the fifteenth century as a response to the increasing regularity of diplomatic intercourse, their authors tried hard, though sometimes in an unrealistically academic fashion, to arrive at an exact formula for the ideal ambassador. Qualities such as dignity, learning, experience, affability, diligence, stamina and maturity were all stressed and the correct balance of qualities recommended.[65] But such treatises were more prescriptive than descriptive and theory needs to be compared with practice. The presence of an Italian *corps diplomatique* at the court of Charles the Bold therefore provides a useful opportunity to make a case study of one distinct group of ambassadors and to paint a more realistic picture of the personal and professional qualifications required of diplomats by Italian rulers at this formative stage in the development of Renaissance diplomacy.

Some of the ambassadors were clerics, but in contrast to earlier periods the majority were laymen. As one would expect, all the representatives of the papacy were clerics, including two cardinals (Bessarion and della Rovere), an archbishop (Nardini) and several bishops; Lucas de Tolentis was promoted bishop (of Šibenik) in 1469 and the alum commissioner Tommaso dei Vincentii was similarly promoted (to Terni and later to Pesaro) after his return to Italy, so that the lowest-ranking were the two protonotaries apostolic, Domenico Albergati and Andrea dei Spiriti. As for the other Italian rulers, only the king of Naples was represented by clerics. Francesco Bertini was bishop of Andria when he first went to the Burgundian court, and in 1471 he was promoted to the see of Capaccio, while Giovanni Olzina was described by the Milanese chancellor in 1473 as '*cavaliere de ordine de Sancto Jacomo della Spata et general d'esso ordino de questa provincia de Lombardia*'.[66]

Social status, though insufficient by itself, was often a necessary attribute simply because a ruler might be insulted by the accrediting to him of an ambassador of lowly rank. This was especially true in the case of leaders of *ad hoc* or ceremonial embassies, where, since these missions were of short duration, first impressions were so important. Certainly, Charles himself appears to have been sensitive to such nuances.[67] Of the Milanese, for example, the Pallavicini and Visconti were all of distinguished noble ancestry. On the other hand, an ambassador who possessed sufficient personal standing to render him to some extent independent of his master's favour might be liable to act too much on his own initiative. This was a danger likely to arise most often with long-term embassies, where political contingencies and the hazards of communications made it difficult for all the envoy's actions to be strictly regulated by instructions from home. Thus the only Milanese resident ambassador, Panigarola, was a merchant — a fact upon which Charles himself once commented, albeit good-naturedly[68] — and, consequently, a man whose fortune was all but dependent on the retention of his master's favour. Such dilemmas, however, did not trouble the Venetian republic, because her ambassadors were closely controlled by the senate and because, in any case, embassies could by law be discharged only by members of the traditional senatorial families. It was to this aristocracy that Dandolo, Bembo and Morosini belonged. All three seem to have been reasonably prosperous and socially prominent. For example, before their departure from Venice, Bembo was described by the Milanese ambassador there as '*homo da bene*' and Morosini as '*homo richo*' and '*homo pomposissimo*'.[69] In fact, the description of Morosini as rich points to one important qualification which usually went with social status, namely private wealth. This was important because, whichever ruler they represented, almost all the ambassadors, as we shall see, seem to have found it necessary at one time or another to dip into their own pockets in order to pay not only living costs but also professional expenses when remittances from home were either late arriving or insufficient when they did arrive.

A high level of education was expected. Many of the ambassadors seem to have studied at university. Probably all the Holy See's representatives had studied canon law. We know that Albergati was a doctor of canon law and that Spiriti too was a doctor, presumably also of canon law.[70] Among the others, Tolentis had studied in Italy, probably at Padua; Onofrio was capable of writing (or dictating) a forceful account in Latin of his mission to Liège;[71] Nanni was described by his contemporary Giannantonio Campano, bishop of Teramo, as being famed for *virtus* and *humanitas*;[72] and Nardini was a reformer who sought to improve the educational standards of the clergy.[73] Of the Venetians, Bembo had studied at Padua and was not only a licentiate in arts but also a doctor of both laws. Among the Neapolitans, Bertini had studied at Padua (although the subject studied is not known) and his abilities as a writer won praise,[74] while Olzina had been one of the leading lights in the humanist circle which had formed in Naples at the court of King Alfonso.[75] As for the representatives of Milan, Grimaldi was a doctor, presumably of laws,[76] and Tebaldi was a notary who had studied at Bologna. Educational qualifications were important for a variety of purposes. A legal training was useful in matters relating both to the concession of mercantile privileges and to the negotiation of treaties, whether those treaties were made with Charles himself or concluded between Charles and third parties where the inclusion of the ambassador's master as a Burgundian ally was essential. Thus, all three Venetian ambassadors received instructions to further the republic's commercial interests either by securing trading privileges or by obtaining ducal favour in cases involving Venetian merchants. Treaties of alliance were negotiated by Bertini, on behalf of the king of Naples in 1471, and by Bembo, for Venice, in 1472. In practice, though, treaty-making was an infrequent task and one in any case strictly covered by instructions, so that, for these Italian ambassadors, a legal training was less vital than one would judge it to have been from a comparison with the importance assigned to it at this period by the republic of Florence, where the procedures of diplomacy were particularly bureaucratic and formalised.[77]

A literary background was advantageous in two ways. First, it was a means of establishing a *rapport* with Charles himself, a ruler who welcomed opportunities to discuss the great episodes of ancient history to which he loved to turn in his leisure hours both for instruction and for entertainment. Secondly, literary anecdotes or citations were a standard method used by humanist orators to impress and cajole their audiences, and Italian orators often surpassed their n~rthern counterparts. Grimaldi delivered the formal oration on behalf of his colleagues Pallavicino and Visconti in March 1476, while three years earlier Bembo, Bertini and Tolentis had all made speeches to the chapter meeting of the Order of the Golden Fleece held at Valenciennes.[78] It was partly by this means that the values and style of Italian humanists became more widely known at the Burgundian court. On the other hand, there were few opportunities for the rhetorical set-piece mode of oratory beloved of the Florentines, which, so humanists flattered themselves, was capable of deflecting the course of history and could be of a value in a ruler's strategic armoury equivalent to several troops of cavalry.[79] More often, the Italian ambassador at the Burgundian court might be called upon to extemporise, turning a *bon mot* in response to some observation by Charles, justifying his master against charges of bad faith or producing a non-committal reply to importunate requests made by the duke or by his advisers. Panigarola, with his quick wits and shrewdness plus the great advantage of a fluent command of French, was one who seems to have excelled in this task, despite his misgivings about his admitted lack of formal education.[80]

Experience of office and of public affairs was perhaps the single most important qualification required. Obviously it was important for the ruler who sent the ambassador that the latter should have sufficient experience to enable him to meet the demands of his office. But it was important for Charles too, because this would show him that the ambassador not only enjoyed his master's confidence but was also a man with whom he could effectively do business. The three main types of experience were military, administrative and diplomatic. Military experience alone did not equip a man to be a diplomat, but it could be a useful additional qualification that would enable him to send home informed accounts of military matters, such as the military abilities and policies of the various ultramontane rulers and the sizes and capabilities of their armies. For instance, Giovanni Pallavicino di Scipiono and Pietro Francesco Visconti, the two leaders of the Milanese embassy of 1476, had both served in France in 1465–1466 as captains of the force sent by Francesco Sforza to help Louis XI, while Olzina had in 1446 been captain of six galleys sent by Alfonso the Magnanimous to Genoa, and in March 1473 had acted as Ferrante's military commissioner in Romagna.[81] Administration and diplomacy tended at this time to be complementary rather than separate careers, and most of the ambassadors had previous administrative experience in the bureaucracies of their respective states. Outstanding in this context was Olzina, who had been among the most trusted royal officials in Naples since the early 1430s. The Milanese had usually served an apprenticeship in the lower echelons of the Sforza bureaucracy before being appointed to the duchy's highest decision-making body, the Consiglio Segreto. Tebaldi and Marquis Pallavicino were appointed to it in 1466, Giovanni Pallavicino in 1468, P.F. Visconti in 1472, and Grimaldi and Alfieri in 1475; Panigarola, however, was not appointed until 1477, that is to say after his embassies to France and Burgundy.[82]

But it was diplomatic experience as such which most fitted the ambassador for his task. Bertini, before joining the service of King Ferrante, had been sent by Pope Pius II on a mission to Naples; Palombaro had been sent by Ferrante to Rome in 1458 and to Milan in 1461;[83] and Tebaldi had represented the Sforza dukes of Milan on numerous occasions in Venice, Florence, Rome and Naples in the 1450s and 1460s. But for missions north of the Alps, experience of ultramontane courts was particularly valuable. Of the Milanese, Panigarola and Tebaldi were the best qualified in this respect. Before being sent to Burgundy in 1469, Tebaldi had completed two missions to France (1446–1447, 1456–1457) and two to Savoy (1458, 1464), and was to have been sent to Burgundy in 1466.[84] Panigarola had served as ambassador to Louis XI from about April 1465 until the autumn of 1468, and between his return to Milan early in 1469 and his departure for Burgundy six years later he also went to Genoa in 1469 and 1474, to Savoy in 1469, 1471 and 1473, and to King René of Anjou in 1472.[85] Of the Neapolitans, Bertini had participated in a papal mission to France in 1451, as had Betes in 1466,[86] while Palombaro had carried out three brief embassies to Louis XI between 1467 and 1469. The Venetians, by comparison, seem to have been almost callow. When Dandolo was instructed to proceed to Burgundy at the end of 1467, he was then ambassador to Savoy and this appears to have been his first mission of any sort. Bembo had been entrusted with only one embassy before he was sent to Burgundy, but at least that mission had been outside Italy, namely to the court of King Henry IV of Castile in 1468–1469;[87] after his return from Burgundy he fulfilled two important missions to Florence, but he never again left Italy. As for Morosini, his embassy to Burgundy in 1474–1475 appears to have been his first. Not all the papal envoys by any means were more experienced than this, which may account for some of their difficulties with Charles, although the failure of some could not be attributed solely to inexperience. Nardini had been in France in 1452 and perhaps again on later occasions.[88]

Onofrio had been to Mainz and Liège in 1463–1464 as an assistant to the legate Pedro Ferriz. The diplomatic career of Andrea dei Spiriti was celebrated by a chronicler of his native city of Viterbo; before 1471 he had represented the papacy in Venice, Milan and Ferrara and, outside Italy, in Germany and Hungary.

These examples serve to remind us that, if a diplomat were to be successful at the Burgundian court, experience had to be combined with certain personal qualities, such as affability, humility and patience, since Charles did not take kindly to those whom he regarded as arrogant, devious or frivolous. Bembo, Panigarola and Bertini seem to have been those in whom the necessary qualities were most pronounced. On his departure from Venice in 1471 Bembo was described by the Milanese ambassador there as '*homo da molta domesticheza*', and the Burgundian ambassadors who had left the court for Italy shortly after Bembo's arrival spoke highly of him before the Venetian senate in December 1471.[89] Panigarola too immediately made a favourable impression, being described by both his Neapolitan counterpart Bertini and the leading courtier Guy de Brimeu as bringing credit to himself and to his master alike by the discretion, prudence and businesslike manner of his conduct.[90] Although an ambassador's initiative was limited by his instructions, he could make a certain impact on his master's relations with the duke — for good or ill — through his own personal standing. Thus Bertini was held in universal respect, but his successor Palombaro was regarded by the influential Guillaume de Rochefort — so he told the bishop of Turin in 1476 — as '*un follo*'.[91]

The ages of these ambassadors seem to have varied from the comparatively youthful to the relatively elderly. Of those whose age we know, Tolentis was 34 when he first arrived at the Burgundian court in the winter of 1462–1463; Bembo 37 in 1471; G.L. Pallavicino 44 in 1469; and Onofrio di Santa Croce 49 in 1468.[92] Of the others, Panigarola was the youngest. In fact, after his first public audience he was actually described by the Venetian ambassador as '*homo zovene*', but what he lacked in years he made up for in skill and experience, since, as the ducal doctor Salvatore de Clariciis wrote to Galeazzo Maria shortly after that audience, he performed with such ability as would have done credit to one much older. Yet he could not then have been less than 30 considering that he had already served in France a decade previously. Bertini could hardly have been less than 45 when he died in November 1475, although his biographer judged that he was then still '*molto giovane*'. Tebaldi was at least 54 in 1469, possibly even older. The most senior was Olzina, who was almost certainly over 60 when he arrived in 1475.

When estimating the size of the Italian *corps diplomatique*, it should be remembered that for each ambassador there were a number of attendants. The amount varied considerably depending on the type and provenance of the embassy, and precise figures are seldom available, so the following information is offered only as a rough guide. The 1469 Milanese embassy comprised ten ambassadors, led by G.L. Pallavicino and Tebaldi, and 36 attendants, but this was an *ad hoc* embassy and such expense could not have been borne for the longer period of a resident embassy, even by the wealthy duke of Milan. Panigarola had a number of attendants with him, but they could probably be counted in single figures, which would explain why the loss of one of them at the battle of Grandson and of two more at Murten was such a grievous blow, professionally as well as personally.[93] Whether any of his attendants can be classed as secretaries is hard to say; he wrote the vast majority of his dispatches himself (although some are preserved as copies made by the Milanese chancellery), and this was more the result of obligation than a labour of love since he had a large and complex cipher consisting of 196 symbols to contend with.[94] Of the Venetians, however, Bembo had a secretary, who signed himself Petrus Blanchus.[95] When the senate decided in February 1476 to send Giacomo da Ca' da Mezzo to Burgundy, it stipulated that his retinue would be exactly the same size as that of his predecessors. What that was, was not stated, although some indication is provided by the fact that when Morosini arrived back in the duchy of Milan in December 1475 he had sixteen horse with him, while from other sources it emerges that a Venetian ambassador's retinue generally numbered between ten and twenty, including usually a secretary, perhaps a chaplain and a notary, and menials such as a cook, as well as a trumpeter.[96] The senate had to balance its desire to be showing sufficient honour both to the republic and to the ruler concerned against the costs of so doing. It was probably eager also to restrict a self-important ambassador's opportunities for ostentation: the Milanese ambassador in Venice reported of the patrician Morosini that '*se ha posto pomposamente in ordine*' before leaving for Burgundy. As for papal envoys, Tolentis returned to the Burgundian court in 1476 with letters of safe-conduct from Sixtus IV valid for up to thirty persons. For the Neapolitan retinues, no information is available.

Some clarification should be offered at this stage of the description of these ambassadors as *ad hoc*, temporary, permanent or resident.[97] As the tempo of diplomatic intercourse among rulers increased towards the end of the Middle Ages, so also there developed, imperceptibly at first, a type of embassy which was not limited in duration and whose principal task was more the conveyance of information to its sender and the fostering of relations with the ruler to which it was accredited than the conduct of a specific negotiation. Although the attention directed by some historians towards the evolution of the resident embassy rather than to the growing sophistication of diplomatic technique as a whole has been criticised as excessive and misleading,[98] nonetheless the emergence of permanent diplomacy has generally been taken to signify in international relations the transition from medieval to modern times. The main area of disagreement has been the chronology rather than the significance of this development. The first appearance of resident embassies on a permanent basis took place, it is agreed, in Italy about the middle of the fifteenth century as a result of several interrelated developments: the formation of the Italian League in 1453–1454 and the consequent exchange of diplomatic representatives by most of the leading rulers of the peninsula; the emergence of opposing and frequently shifting alliances among the Italian states; and, arising from this unstable situation, the pressing need for accurate and up-to-date information about the actions and intentions of neighbours. Gradually, Italian residents were sent to stay at courts beyond the Alps, and the system might finally be said to have reached maturity around the end of the fifteenth century when, after these haphazard beginnings, ultramontane rulers reciprocated by maintaining residents in Italy as well as at the courts of their neighbours north of the Alps. Eventually, the office of resident at a given court could be regarded as being in existence even when there was no incumbent and when the office itself was temporarily vacant. A significant part in the spread of this originally Italian institution throughout western Europe was played by the court of Louis XI of France, where a series of Milanese, Florentine and Venetian diplomats could be found. Of these, the Milanese must certainly be regarded as residents,[99] although the case for the Florentines and Venetians is weaker. Yet, by contrast, the Italian residents at the court of Charles the Bold have been almost completely overlooked.[100] It will be argued in the following pages that this collection of Italian ambassadors at his court represents a hitherto neglected stage in the development of permanent diplomacy, a stage every bit as important as the appearance of Italian residents in France under Louis XI: perhaps, even, more important, insofar as Naples and Venice, as well as Milan, were represented there by permanent ambassadors.

The criteria for deciding whether or not an ambassador should be classed as a resident are derived from the nature of their functions, from the length of their embassy and from the degree of awareness shown by contemporaries of a concept of residence. Naturally, not all the Italian ambassadors at Charles the Bold's court met these criteria, but some did and to these the title of resident should not be denied, namely Bertini, Panigarola and the three Venetians, Dandolo, Bembo and Morosini. As regards functions, it is clear that the tasks entrusted to these ambassadors sometimes included those which could have been carried out by temporary envoys, such as the negotiation of trade privileges. Their instructions, however, specified also a wider range of duties which could only be carried out by residents, in particular the conveyance of up-to-date information on political events and the general fostering of relations between their master and the duke of Burgundy.[101] Such ambassadors were not sent simply for the purpose of concluding alliances. For example, Bertini and Bembo, on their departures from Naples and Venice respectively, were not equipped with powers to make an alliance with Charles the Bold; those did not arrive until they had already been at his court for some time. As for Panigarola, he was sent to Burgundy only after the conclusion of an alliance between the duke and his master. The length of the resident ambassador's stay was closely related to, and in part defined by, the nature of his functions. Thus, Dandolo's second embassy lasted over a year; those of Morosini and Panigarola about eighteen months; Bembo's just under three years; and that of Bertini over six. The duration of these embassies justifies as much as any other criterion the use of the term 'resident'.

Another criterion is that of ambassadorial succession. This notion applies especially to the Venetians. Bembo was specifically nominated to succeed Dandolo in 1470, even though he did not set out until a year later. In 1474 he was instructed to remain at the Burgundian court until his successor, Morosini, had arrived, so that he could brief him before leaving. Similarly, Giacomo da Ca' da Mezzo, the ambassador chosen to go to Burgundy in 1476 (though he was never sent), was viewed as Morosini's successor, despite the fact that his mission, which was to deal with the question of the republic's inclusion in the treaty of Soleuvre as Charles the Bold's ally, was by its nature of strictly limited scope and duration. The idea of succession applies also to the Neapolitans, with Palombaro acting as temporary replacement when Bertini returned to Naples in the winter of 1473–1474. This idea was important for the development of the concept of resident embassies, because it led to them being considered impersonally; that is to say, the office itself could be regarded as existing even when there was temporarily no incumbent. For example, shortly after Bertini's death in November 1475 the Milanese ambassador Panigarola noted, somewhat maliciously, that the Neapolitan prince Federico was most upset by it, partly because he had lost a friend and mentor, but also because he found himself forced to act as his own ambassador until his father sent a replacement; he complained that it was not his '*offitio*' to carry out such burdensome duties.[102] As for the concept of residence itself, it is interesting to note that the term '*ressidenzia*' was actually used by one contemporary Venetian chronicler to describe Bembo's embassy to Burgundy.

On the other hand, it remains true that both the office and the concept of the resident ambassador were still rudimentary in Charles the Bold's day. There were several reasons for this. To begin with, because Charles had no fixed capital, and it was the ambassador's duty to follow the court, there was no incentive to construct embassy buildings as such. More important was the fact that it was the general practice of Italian rulers to send resident ambassadors to the courts only of those ultramontane princes with whom they were already friendly, if not allied. Thus, the recall of Panigarola from the Burgundian court in August 1476 was both symbol and result of Galeazzo Maria's recent repudiation of his alliance with Charles. Another reason was that the system depended on reciprocity, and ultramontane rulers, Charles included, had not yet begun to imitate Italian practice by sending their own representatives to stay at Italian courts. It is true that Charles sent a number of envoys to Italy and that some of them stayed for prolonged periods: Antoine de Montjeu, for instance, spent several months on separate occasions in Venice and Malpaga between 1473 and 1475 while engaged in negotiations over his master's attempts to recruit Colleoni. But such envoys cannot be called residents. Equally common, in fact, was the embassy which visited several rulers while in Italy; thus Philippe de Croy and Anthony of Burgundy in, respectively, 1472 and 1475 passed through Venice, Ferrara and Rome on their way either to or from Naples, which was their main destination. In fact, resident embassies were one important area where Charles did not imitate Italian practice, and the rulers of the Burgundian Netherlands did not begin to send them until the early years of the sixteenth century.[103] It might be argued, finally, that the presence of Italian resident ambassadors at the court of Charles the Bold represented something of a false start as regards the subsequent development of Renaissance diplomacy, in that it did not generate the spark of continuity. Italian residents had been accredited to Charles as the result of a particular historical situation, namely the need felt by some Italian rulers to side with him as a means of resisting the growing influence of France. This was already changing before 1477. By 1476 some Italian rulers had come to regard Charles as a greater threat than Louis XI to their independence, while the duke's defeats by the Swiss, especially the one at Murten, inclined them to seek a reconciliation with France. Consequently, all the Italian ambassadors who had been at the Burgundian court in 1475 had left before the end of the following year without having been replaced. Italian ambassadors again appeared at the Burgundian court under his successors, but it would be several years before they could truly be described as resident.

The ambassador and the ruler

Before examining in detail the activities of the Italian ambassadors at court, it is convenient to discuss first their relations with the ruler himself, for winning the trust and respect of the duke was both an important task in itself and one which could in turn facilitate the discharge of others. In establishing a cordial relationship with the ruler, Italian diplomats had a much easier task at the Burgundian than at the French court. Louis XI had a deep-seated suspicion of resident ambassadors and more often than not regarded them simply as spies.[104] Charles, on the other hand, customarily gave the warmest possible welcome to foreigners in general, and to ambassadors in particular. For example, he liked to give the *corps diplomatique* a prominent place on important public and ceremonial occasions. The master of his household recommended that ambassadors be grouped at the *audience* and at the chapter meetings of the Order of the Golden Fleece with princes of the blood, knights of the Order, grand pensionaries and new princes and bishops; that is to say, they were placed in a group which ranked second only to the duke himself.[105]

Examples abound of the prominence accorded to our Italian ambassadors on such occasions. At the chapter meeting of the Order of the Golden Fleece held at Bruges in May 1468, the seat of honour was given to a papal legate; also present, it seems, was a Neapolitan ambassador.[106] It was a papal legate who led the clerical contingent in the procession which greeted the new duchess of Burgundy, Margaret of York, on her entrance into Bruges on 3 July 1468 after her marriage to Charles, and, at the banquet following, the legate was placed on the duke's right hand, at the head of the table at which several bishops and the leading ladies of the court were seated.[107] In May 1473 Tolentis, Bembo and Bertini, together with '*autres estrangiers*', who included an ambassador of the Venetian general Colleoni, were allowed to take part in the festivities and in some of the proceedings of the chapter meeting of the Order of the Golden Fleece held at Valenciennes. For the mass which opened the session on 1 May, the ambassadors sat in a pew on the right-hand side of the Church of St. Paul. At the subsequent banquet they again sat separately from the members of the Order, although their table was cunningly placed on the same level as that of the Order's officers; they were served first — immediately after the duke himself — by four of these officers. Later, they were admitted to the actual chapter meeting to speak on behalf of their masters and particularly on behalf of the crusade.[108]

Bertini and Morosini were both present at the formal reception of their new Milanese colleague Panigarola by Charles in the camp outside Neuss on 15 March 1475.[109] Panigarola and Bertini attended the ceremonial publication of the treaty of Moncalieri just over a fortnight later (when Morosini was absent through illness), the reception of the papal legate Nanni in mid-May, and the reception of the king of Hungary's ambassador at the beginning of June (Morosini being again absent through illness).[110] At Ghent in July, Charles personally introduced Panigarola to his daughter Mary; the ambassador considered her '*zentile*' and '*maynerosa*' but, like her father, small in stature. A few days later at Calais, Charles introduced Edward IV to the ambassador as, he said, his best friend next to the duke of Milan; Panigarola considered the king '*uno belissimo principe*'. Later in the month the duke sent him to visit his wife Margaret at Saint-Omer; he was impressed by her good sense.[111] As a mark of respect for his master, Panigarola was specially honoured on 18 December 1475 when Charles, in the presence of his court and of the assembled Estates of Lorraine, took formal possession of that duchy. The Milanese ambassador was placed near the French ambassador and the papal legate Nanni, to the right of and below the ducal throne. The scale of the honour was emphasised by the fact that the other Italian ambassadors were absent (Bertini was dead and Morosini had left), while the Neapolitan prince Federico was placed on the duke's left.[112] On 14 April 1476 Tolentis, Palombaro and Panigarola sat on the dais in the middle of the Burgundian camp outside Lausanne from which Guillaume de Rochefort announced the conclusion of a peace treaty between the duke and the emperor.

Charles, of course, had his own reasons for honouring ambassadors. While he shared something of Louis XI's suspicious nature, he perhaps felt more confident about his ability to keep state secrets.[113] In any case, he clearly believed that the advantages stemming from the presence of foreign ambassadors outweighed the risks from espionage, for the size of the ambassadorial contingent at court provided a conventional yardstick by which to measure a ruler's influence and prestige, as the duke's ally Ferrante of Naples also realised.[114]

As well as showing the Italian ambassadors formal honour on public occasions, Charles also liked to enjoy their company in the privacy of his quarters, where he engaged in lengthy conversations with them.[115] Such conversations were a necessity for both parties because, since the duke did not maintain residents in Italy, the Italian diplomats at his court were the regular and basic means of communication between himself and their masters. Yet it is clear also that Charles at times took a positive delight in explaining and justifying his actions and plans in detail, as can be seen from, for example, one of the few surviving dispatches of the Neapolitan ambassador Bertini.[116] In such discussions he would make known to his allies the actions he wanted them to take which would benefit him. In return, he expected the ambassadors to provide him with reliable information concerning the state of affairs in the peninsula.[117] From such information, and also by comparing the conflicting accounts given him by ambassadors of rival rulers, such as the duke of Milan and the king of Naples were in 1475–1476, he could form his own opinion as to the true situation in Italy. Sometimes these long conversations arose from his deep, almost obsessive love for his army. As soon as Panigarola arrived at court, he perceived that the duke was at his happiest when either with his troops or talking about them. Charles himself told the ambassador that he could never be in ill humour when dealing with anything which concerned his army.[118] Five hours after sunset on 17 March 1475 he summoned Panigarola to his tent to see his bodyguard take up their positions for the night watch. The manoeuvre took some time and the ambassador remarked that the troops were indeed a sight to see; he was rewarded for his patience (perhaps also for his tact) by an invitation to sup with the duke.

Discursive as he often was on such occasions, it seems he was not always completely frank. He could dissimulate when need be, although more often he was simply secretive. Naturally he wished to disseminate his own propaganda in the peninsula (as Louis XI did); in addition, he wanted to keep secret those of his plans which his allies, rightly or

Plate 2. Medallion in silver-gilt attributed to Giovanni di Candida (before c. 1450–after 1495), assigned to 1474 and the siege of Neuss. (a) Obverse: portrait head, laureated, of Charles, duke of Burgundy. (b) Reverse: a ram (the fleece) between two briquets, inscribed VELLUS AUREUS, with a flint darting sparks on either side. Size of original: 39 mm diameter. Collection of Cecil H. Clough, who retains the copyright.

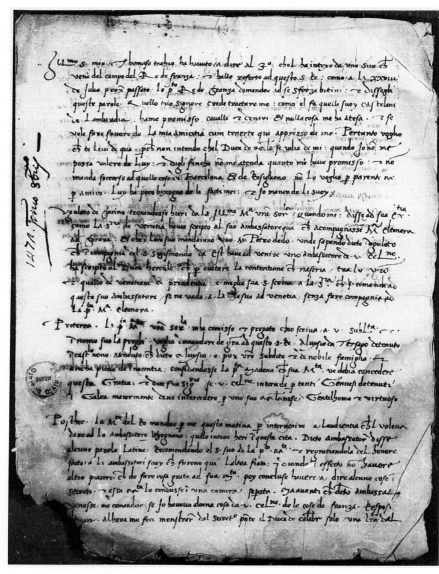

Plate 3. Letter of Francesco Maletta, Milanese ambassador in Naples, to Duke Galeazzo Maria, 1 October 1472, reporting that Charles the Bold has told King Ferrante that a close confidant of his has fled to King Louis XI (did Charles mean Philippe de Commynes?). Archivio di Stato, Milan, *cartella* 223: Sforzesco – Potenze Estere – Napoli. By permission of the Archivio di Stato, Milan, and the Ministero per i Beni e le Attività Culturali.

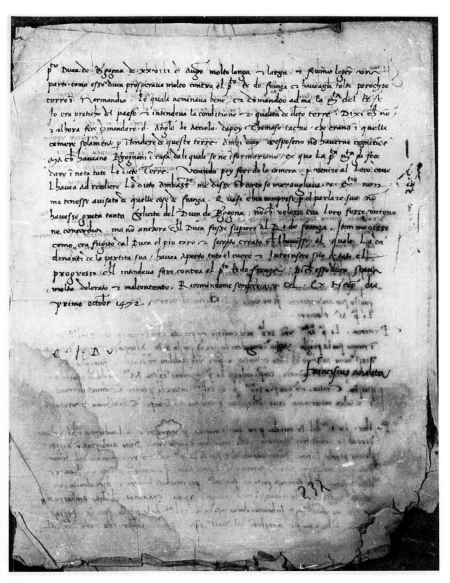

Plate 3. (*continued*)

Plate 4. Charles the Bold, duke of Burgundy, allotting commands to his captains at Nancy, December 1475(?). Copy of Charles the Bold's military ordinances, in British Library, Additional MS 36, 619, f. 5. Illumination attributed to Philippe de Mazeroles. By permission of the British Library.

wrongly, might interpret as inimical to their own interests. It seems, for example, that he did not tell Panigarola of the treaty of engagement of his daughter Mary to Maximilian of Austria which he concluded with the emperor on 6 May 1476; indeed, the duke of Milan had already complained to Panigarola that Charles did not inform him of his plans in advance but only when they were *faits accomplis*.[119]

The fact that so many of Panigarola's dispatches have survived — but so few of those written by the other Italian ambassadors — encourages the impression that Charles was especially intimate with him. Nonetheless, the Milanese ambassador's correspondence does provide a detailed description of the sort of subject which the duke liked to discuss with the Italian residents at his court. Of course, many of his conversations with Panigarola were confined to specialised topics arising from his treaty with Milan, but there is much of more general interest in the ambassador's dispatches. They form, in fact, a major source, not only vivid but also contemporary, for the seventeen months of the duke's reign which Panigarola spent with Charles, including: the last stages of the siege of Neuss; the abortive English invasion of France in the summer of 1475; Charles's conquest of Lorraine in the second half of that year; his campaigns against the Swiss; and his growing *entente* with the emperor.

As Charles was such a hard-working ruler, Panigarola often had to wait until the evening — around supper time, when the duke liked to relax — before he was granted an audience; on occasions, though, the duke might specially send for him to relay an urgent message.[120] Once closeted with him, however, Panigarola received the duke's full atttention. Charles would talk of his affairs or of his income and expenditure for up to three hours at a time.[121] Sometimes he cleared everyone from his chamber so that he could be alone with Panigarola, who, mindful of Louis XI's elusive and suspicious ways, noted this behaviour almost with surprise. Charles liked to think aloud in his presence, to bounce ideas off him in order to find out how the ambassador and his master would respond, and to obtain a second opinion rendered more palatable by its having been apparently unsolicited. This was how the duke's mind worked, Panigarola wrote in his own defence to Galeazzo Maria, who, complaining of the number and variety of the requests for assistance relayed to him from Charles through Panigarola, had concluded that this confusion was attributable to the ambassador's negligence or obtuseness.[122] Charles was not angered by the solicitous if diffident advice which Panigarola occasionally offered him; far from disdaining it, he considered it thoughtfully and on its merits — as, for example, when

Panigarola urged him to advance against the Swiss with great caution and not to risk his own person in battle.[123] Indeed, on 21 June 1476, the eve of the battle of Murten, Charles specifically asked for his opinion as to the imminence of a Swiss attack and the measures necessary to be taken; Panigarola was pleased both on his own account and on that of his master by this honour, and gratified by the favourable reception his views were given by the duke's military advisers.

Panigarola and Charles were at one in their deep suspicion of the king of France. Not only did Panigarola readily assent to the duke's regular tirades against Louis XI's perfidy, but he also spontaneously warned Charles to beware of him.[124] Early in 1476, not for the first time, the king tried to interest Charles in a personal meeting at which their outstanding differences could be settled. The duke was instinctively mistrustful of the proposal, feeling that Louis's real intention was, by delaying him, to prevent a crushing Burgundian victory over the Swiss, whom Charles considered to be Louis' last bulwark against his growing power. Panigarola urged him not to place himself in the king's hands, even if the interview were staged in Rome itself. After the battle of Murten, when the duke's position was much weaker, he provisionally agreed to meet the king on 20 August on a bridge over the River Yonne at Auxerre. He told the Milanese ambassador that if he went to this interview he would go fully alert to the possibility of treachery; Panigarola replied grimly that he did not need to remind him that his grandfather John the Fearless had been murdered in similar circumstances. Of course, he was acting in part on instructions in fanning the flames of the duke's suspicions; his master was understandably afraid of a reconciliation between Charles and Louis in which his own interests might be sacrificed. There are, indeed, difficulties in assessing Panigarola's personal opinions of the comparative merits of Louis and Charles. In fact, when he had first been accredited as Milanese ambassador to the French court in 1465, his praise of Louis was fulsome, and the reader is struck by the fact that the terms in which he described him so flatteringly were very similar to those he employed later to describe the duke of Burgundy. Thus, he wrote that in the campaigns of the War of the Public Weal Louis showed himself brave and indefatigable, taking immense pains in the supervision of his army, displaying a better understanding of military science than his own captains, always exhibiting great willingness to learn about Italian military practice and, in short, conducting himself as courageously as Alexander the Great or Julius Caesar.[125]

Other than as ambassadorial clichés, the similarity in these descriptions of Louis and Charles might be explained in terms of characteristics displayed by the two princes in common as northern rulers, characteristics which were novel and worthy of remark to an Italian, especially to one such as Panigarola, who was then both young and, at least in 1465, inexperienced. Still, however conditioned Panigarola's reaction to the duke was — his master having made an alliance with him because of his disillusionment with Louis — it would seem that the praise of Charles and the vilification of Louis contained in his dispatches from the Burgundian court did largely reflect his own preferences. On the other hand, his later, jaundiced view of Louis was not simply the result of the fact that, in comparison, he admired Charles, nor was it due solely to a desire to please his master, who naturally sought reassurance that he had been wise to change sides. His assessment of Louis seems to have been influenced also by his experiences at the French court. In the autumn of 1468, after serving as ambassador for three and a half years, he was virtually expelled from France. This summary dismissal was caused in part by Louis' dissatisfaction with Panigarola's master and by his deep-rooted suspicion of ambassadors in general; but Panigarola's independence of mind and his habit of offering unsolicited advice, even if unpalatable, perhaps contributed to the king's alienation; and it may be symptomatic that his account of the Péronne interview in 1468 — at which he was not actually present, having been banished to Paris — was (in contrast to that of Philippe de Commynes) favourable to Charles at the expense of Louis. Panigarola, for his part, claimed that his expulsion was the result of the jealous intrigues of Alberto Magalotti, another of the Milanese agents at the French court and one greatly trusted by the king.[126] As for Louis, his distrust of the ambassador did not diminish subsequently, and on more than one occasion after 1468 he described him as his enemy.

If Charles showed a liking for Italian ambassadors in general, he also displayed a particular preference for some of them, while expressing a marked dislike for a few. Bertini, for example, was held in such esteem that, his biographer wrote, Charles did not take it amiss when chided by him for cruelty, and in fact allowed him to conduct some items of ducal business on his behalf.[127] The return of Lucas de Tolentis to his court after two years' absence was unmistakably welcome to him. Other Italian ambassadors enjoyed his good graces. When he stopped at Malines in July 1475 on his way from Neuss to meet Edward IV at Calais, he was met in church by the Venetian ambassador Morosini, who had for some time been absent from court, having been laid low by illness in Bruges. In the presence of the other Italian ambassadors, the duke thanked him for his services in peace and war and, as both a sign of his love for Venice and, in Panigarola's opinion, a recognition for Morosini's '*virtù e facultà*', bestowed upon him the honour of knighthood which, after some hesitation, Morosini accepted. When he took his leave of the duke at Soleuvre in September, Charles wrote to his financial officers commanding them to make Morosini a gift of fifty silver marks; the sum itself, he lamented, could not express his true esteem, since his war expenses prevented him doing all he would have liked financially.[128] Nor is it hard to detect that he had a soft spot for Panigarola, of whom he wrote in August 1476, in a vain attempt to persuade Galeazzo Maria to change his mind about recalling him, that he had perfect confidence in him; he considered the matter of such importance that he took the trouble to add a few lines in his own handwriting at the bottom of the letter to reinforce his plea.[129]

Charles was not the easiest man to get on with: he was egotistical, vain and, on occasions, prone to towering rages rendered more terrifying by their suddenness. Affability and discretion were, therefore, as important as technical expertise if an ambassador was to win and retain his confidence. Among those possessing these personal qualities was, for instance, Bernardo Bembo, who was greatly praised by representatives of Charles the Bold for his qualities of intellect and, above all, of character. It may be too that the diplomat had at times to resort to flattery (as was alleged of Bembo by Andrea dei Spiriti); on the other hand, the accusation that rivals stooped to the sycophancy which he himself disdained was often the excuse of the unsuccessful ambassador.

Yet those who were too haughty, importunate and truculent — or plainly disrespectful, as the duke himself would have it — were bound to fail. Charles, for example, had already become weary of Giovanni Palombaro's incessant requests for support for King Ferrante's attempt to acquire Provence (which in any case he wanted for himself) when he was further angered by learning the contents of Palombaro's dispatch of 16 March 1476, in which the Neapolitan ambassador had attributed the defeat at Grandson entirely to the duke's own shortcomings as man and ruler, and had predicted that the defeat would only be repeated if Charles again ventured forth against the Swiss.[130] Another example is provided by Andrea dei Spiriti. Apart from the actual contents of the message which Andrea brought him on the pope's behalf in July 1473, Charles, as we saw in Chapter 2, was incensed by the admonitory manner in which it was delivered.

The duke's reaction to individual ambassadors was, of course, conditioned to a great extent by the state of his relations with their masters.

This was particularly true of the papal envoys at his court, many of whom suffered in their own person for the duke's displeasure at the supposed favour shown by Rome to his enemy, the king of France, although on one occasion the conciliatory manner of Onofrio di Santa Croce was able to mollify Charles after he had exploded in a blazing temper provoked by the tergiversations of the bishop of Liège, whom the duke had hoped to use as a tool for his expansionist policies.[131] Similarly, the note of politeness with which the Milanese ambassadors' audience began at Ghent in 1469 soon degenerated into one of recrimination, with Charles personally voicing his grievances at Galeazzo Maria's intimidatory attitude towards his allies in Savoy, while the ambassadors tried to justify their master's actions. On the other hand, Charles was capable of displaying great warmth towards the ambassador of a given ruler while retaining his reservations about that ruler's conduct. In spite of his disillusionment by 1475 with both the king of Naples and the Venetian republic and, by 1476, with the duke of Milan as well, he still took their ambassadors, respectively Bertini, Morosini and Panigarola, into his confidence. Indeed, he placed such trust in some of the Italian ambassadors that he employed them occasionally on his own business. The Antonello da Campagna who came to him from Naples in 1470 was commissioned by Charles to return by way of Milan, so that he could offer Galeazzo Maria the prospect of a defensive alliance with Burgundy, membership of the Order of the Golden Fleece and reconciliation with Savoy; a Burgundian courier accompanied him in order to relay back to Charles post-haste the duke of Milan's reply.[132] Another Neapolitan, Francesco Bertini, acted as one of three ducal witnesses to the notarial sealing of the Burgundian alliance with Venice in 1472, and in 1475 he helped mediate between Charles and the emperor. Of the papal agents at his court, Charles employed on his own business Tolentis, Aliprandi and, the Milanese chancellor grumbled, Nanni.[133]

What, conversely, were the ambassadors' views of the duke? They were, in fact, generally favourable, though they cannot be accepted as totally objective. Apart from the exceptional case of the papacy, only friendly Italian rulers were represented for any length of time at the Burgundian court. The ambassador's natural tendency, therefore, was to extol the duke's power and emphasise his good disposition; to do otherwise would have been to cast doubt on his master's wisdom in aligning himself with Charles. We find, for instance, that in a letter written from the Burgundian court in 1472 Bembo heaped praise on the duke and obloquy on Louis XI.[134] Similarly, when Bertini passed through the duchy of Milan on his return to Naples in 1473 and met Galeazzo Maria, he praised Charles for his power, daring and (a virtue not often attributed to him by historians) prudence, as if he had no equal in the world. But — as the duke of Milan wrote dryly to Sforza Bettini, his ambassador in France, on 3 December — this was only to be expected in view of the alliance between Naples and Burgundy; Bertini had spoken as befitted this friendship rather than in accordance with the truth.[135] Conversely, Carlo Visconti (the Milanese ambassador at the imperial court during the emperor's talks with Charles at Trier in 1473), fearful of the duke's supposed designs on Milan but anxious also to reassure his master that there was really nothing to fear, informed Galeazzo Maria that Charles was much given to improbable schemes. The reports sent by Francesco Pietrasanta from Turin in the spring of 1476 were no more impartial. Pietrasanta reflected, in his reports of the parlous state of Charles the Bold's army in Savoy and of the continuous desertions from it, both the fears of those in the Savoyard council of Piedmont (on which Pietrasanta himself occasionally sat) that Charles was intent on annexing the Italian territories of the duke of Savoy, and their hopes that defeat by the Swiss would prevent the realisation of such plans.[136]

When these qualifications have been made, however, there is no lack of evidence to show that the bulk of our Italian ambassadors were very favourably impressed by Charles. Bertini praised him in his correspondence with the cardinal of Pavia; Panigarola's unmistakable admiration and affection may be instanced by his description of Charles at the siege of Neuss as being small of stature but Caesarean in spirit; and the harassed Tolentis, torn between his esteem for the duke and his duties as papal legate, advised Sixtus IV in 1472 to seek an accommodation with Charles, for not only was he a good son of the Church but also a most successful ruler.[137] After his return from Burgundy, Bembo hardly ceased singing the duke's praises and he seems to have been saddened by his sudden death in 1477. Against these eulogistic examples can, of course, be set the denunciations of Carlo Visconti, Andrea dei Spiriti and Giovanni Palombaro already mentioned. We are not, after all, looking in this context simply for truth in the Italian ambassadors' views of Charles but more for the expression of genuine personal opinion as evidence of the impression he made on them. Perhaps the least contentious conclusion would be that the more the ambassadors feared the power and intentions of the duke, the more they tended to belittle or decry him; conversely, if they made an initial attempt to appreciate him and if they saw the might of his army as advantageous to their masters, the more they would be trusted by Charles and the more they would reflect this trust in approbatory descriptions of him. Even so, we can observe several instances of Italian ambassadors displaying a genuine approbation of the duke which arose quite separately from any political conditioning produced by the state of their masters' relations with him.

Finally, it is worth pointing out that the reports sent from the Burgundian court by Italian ambassadors provided one of the main and most influential sources of information from which Italians in the peninsula itself formed their own assessment of Charles. Two features in particular of his reputation in Italy would bear further elaboration: the qualities and defects which most impressed Italians, and the chronological vicissitudes of his reputation. As a ruler, his power and magnificence were lauded, while, as a man, it was his abstemiousness and piety which won him praise. Initially Italians hardly distinguished him from the other fractious French princes who resented the growing power of the monarchy, but he thrust himself into prominence by his successful campaigns in France in 1465, 1471 and 1472 and by those against Dinant and Liège between 1465 and 1468. By the time of the siege of Neuss the Italians were watching his progress with the same avid interest as observers in other parts of Europe. It was at this time that his reputation reached its zenith, and many Italians became convinced that, should a fight to the finish ensue between Burgundy and France, the victor would be Charles. Such a prospect pleased those who had cause to fear Louis XI. Equally, however, some aspects of the duke's character aroused misgivings, notably his ruthlessness towards his enemies, which was denounced as cruelty, and his great ambition, which was felt to be excessive and thus to be tempting fate. By 1476 many were fearful that Italy was included in the scope of his ambition and were apprehensive about his conduct, should he succeed. Such people were relieved and pleased by his defeats at the hands of the Swiss. After his death, his reputation naturally declined. His downfall was seen as the inevitable result of his own vices and follies and as an object lesson in the workings of providence. His fate provoked reflections on divine intervention, and it was his disastrous end that was remembered rather than his earlier triumphs.[138]

Functions at court

Diplomatic technique in the early days of resident embassies has often been studied from the standpoint of status, immunities or ceremonial, and historians have placed great reliance on the evidence of diplomatic instructions, academic treatises and ambassadorial handbooks.[139] The day-to-day functions of the ambassador, the details of the negotiations and intrigues involved in his task after his arrival, though every bit as important as the legal and theoretical framework in which he operated, have received less attention.[140] In the following pages, therefore, the daily functions of the ambassadors' job at the Burgundian court will be described with this in mind, using the wealth of detail, sometimes superficially dull or insignificant, that can be gleaned from the surviving Italian documents. Inevitably there are large gaps. For Milan there are the 150-odd dispatches of Panigarola for the period from March 1475 to August 1476, though very little for the rest of Charles the Bold's reign. Apart from a few copies in the Sforza archives, no dispatches survive from the Venetian and Neapolitan ambassadors, though for Venice the registers of the senate provide glimpses of the instructions given to ambassadors and of the contents of the letters received from them.[141] Most of the evidence, then, relates to Milan, so we must be aware of the danger of incautious generalisation.

Having received both his initial instructions and probably also a cipher to maintain the secrecy of his correspondence with his master,[142] the ambassador faced the long and (especially in winter) hazardous journey across the Alps to the Burgundian court. As he approached, an escort would arrive to greet him and to guide him over the last stages. Panigarola's reception was particularly attentive, in keeping with the duke's joy at having at last achieved an alliance with Milan. Having been provided with an armed escort across Lorraine by an old friend of the Sforza — Georg von Baden, bishop of Metz — Panigarola was met at Maastricht on 12 March 1475 by a small troop of cavalry led by a son of Giacomo dei Vischi. The escort was augmented towards evening by the arrival of the captain of the ducal bodyguard with sixty horsemen. The next morning a son of the count of Campobasso accompanied the ambassador over the final league to the Burgundian camp outside Neuss. On its outskirts Panigarola was greeted by Louis de Bruges, lord of the Gruuthuse, who led him to his lodgings, where Philippe de Croy, lord of Quiévrain, apologised for their inadequacy and promised him an audience with the duke the following day.[143]

Charles seems to have kept the Italian ambassadors waiting longer than they expected for their first formal audience. Thus, when he received Galeazzo Maria's ambassadors in 1469, he felt it necessary to apologise to them through his chancellor for the delay.[144] Panigarola's experience was not dissimilar. After lunch on 14 March 1475, his second day at court, he was led by Philippe de Croy to the duke. Charles doffed his hat, uttered expressions of great joy at seeing him and swore by St George that he would be given a formal audience but added that it would have to wait until the next day because he himself was then busy supervising the siege of Neuss. Panigarola hastened to explain to his master that no disrespect was implied by such behaviour; the procedure at court was very deliberate, even seeming to be more Italian than ultramontane.[145] Such delays were due mainly to the demands of the duke's self-imposed routine of administrative and military commitments which allowed him little flexibility; when the duke was busy with the siege of Nijmegen in July 1473, the papal envoy Spiriti claimed he was kept waiting for several days before being granted an audience and he interpreted this treatment as a personal insult.[146] Another reason was the duke's desire to have a suitably impressive reception prepared. The Milanese ambassadors sent to him in 1476 had to wait a week at Orbe before they were called to camp to be received on 1 March; even then they had to wait until late in the evening before they obtained an audience, because Charles and his army had been on full alert in expectation of an attack by the Swiss. Panigarola later wrote to his master to explain that the delay had implied no dishonour nor had it been due to any negligence on his part. Rather, the duke's tardiness had been caused by his eagerness to meet the ambassadors with full ceremony; unfortunately, however, he had been unable for some time to assemble the necessary pavilions and other requisites. Charles, he added, was a stickler for such formality and in similar circumstances would have kept even Christ waiting.[147]

The first formal audience traditionally provided an opportunity for displays of eloquence. Thus, when, after a dinner at which they were accompanied by three members of the Order of the Golden Fleece, the 1476 Milanese ambassadors were led before the duke, Luca Grimaldi, the lowest-ranking but presumably the most learned of them, delivered a formal oration on their behalf (whether in Latin or French is not stated); Guillaume de Rochefort replied for his master, after which the duke himself added a few courteous and friendly words.[148] Panigarola's first public audience took place '*in una cameretta bene parata*'. The newly arrived ambassador made a very favourable impression, as his Neapolitan counterpart Bertini noticed, partly because of the brisk and businesslike manner in which he made his oration, and partly because he delivered his speech in fluent French. These ceremonies were usually followed by some special festivity to honour the newcomer, such as tournaments and banquets.

Thereafter the ambassador's mission began in earnest. The public audience would be followed by a private one with the duke in which credences would be passed over and more detailed discussion of the ambassador's proposals would begin. Especially for the resident ambassador, the real task commenced only after the first private audience. Although at the start of his mission he would be charged with the delivery of certain specific messages, other tasks would arise in due course which he would have to carry out in accordance with his general obligation to protect his master's interests and with the dictates of his own common sense. These Italian ambassadors at the Burgundian court had to devote much of their time to matters arising from the provisions of their masters' treaties of alliance with the duke. Bertini had to deal from 1471 onwards with the duke's requests for military and financial assistance from the king of Naples against Louis XI and with another matter which, at first separate, gradually became entwined with the question of Ferrante's treaty obligations, namely the projected marriage of Don Federico to Mary of Burgundy. Palombaro's second mission, which arose from his business at the Savoyard court, revolved around the complicated task of arranging, on the one hand, the marriage of Don Federico's younger brother Francesco to a sister of the duke of Savoy and, on the other, persuading Charles to intercede with King René of Anjou to cede Provence as a dowry for Francesco's bride. Of the Venetians, Bembo and Morosini found much of their time occupied by the question of the duke's wish to recruit Colleoni and the republic's refusal to part with him. Panigarola had two main tasks: to relay to his master the duke's persistent requests for some form of Milanese military gesture against the Swiss and the king of France (in return for which Charles hinted he would allow Galeazzo Maria a free hand to extend his power in Piedmont), and to obtain the duke's intercession with the emperor for the imperial investment of Galeazzo Maria with the duchy of Milan which would legitimise his *de facto* rule over this imperial fief. Lucas de Tolentis's laudably persistent attempts to persuade the duke to enforce the monopoly for the sale of papal alum in his lands form the basis of his surviving correspondence with Popes Paul II and Sixtus IV.

Protection of his master's interests in treaties made by the duke with third parties was another major duty. King Ferrante's interest in the growing *entente* between his Burgundian and Venetian allies in 1471 and 1472 can be seen not only in his correspondence with the Venetian senate at this time, but also in the presence of his ambassador Bertini as witness to the notarial signing of the treaty between Burgundy and

Venice in June 1472.[149] The conclusion of the treaty of Moncalieri with Milan in January 1475 much exercised the Neapolitan and Venetian ambassadors. Charles was extremely pleased by the alliance because the help he hoped to obtain from Galeazzo Maria was magnified in his imagination by his disillusionment with his existing Italian allies, Venice and Naples. Ferrante, however, having been for some time on bad terms with Milan, feared that the treaty of Moncalieri might contain some clause directed against himself. These suspicions were fortified by the fact both that Charles did not inform him (although he so informed Florence and the pope) of the conclusion of the treaty, and that Bertini was unable to obtain from the duke, his courtiers or Panigarola precise information as to the alliance's provisions until the treaty itself was proclaimed publicly at the beginning of April.[150] Similarly with Venice. Charles had been irritated by the conclusion of the Venetian alliance with Milan at the beginning of November 1474, not only because the treaty at that time seemed to presage the defection of the Venetians to the French camp, but also because the republic gave him no prior notice of its intentions. He upbraided Morosini for this, responded in kind by not informing Venice of his negotiations with Milan and let it be known that he set little store by the Venetians. In return the Venetian senate neglected the formal courtesy of sending Morosini instructions to congratulate Charles on the conclusion of his alliance with Milan.

The truce of Soleuvre between Charles and Louis XI in September 1475 gave sleepless nights not only to the Venetian consul Contarini, as we saw earlier, but also to the Milanese Panigarola.[151] A month after the conclusion of the truce Panigarola heard that the French king had agreed to include Galeazzo Maria in it as Charles the Bold's ally, but only in the capacity of duke of Milan and not as lord of Genoa; this implied that Louis had withdrawn his recognition from Sforza rule in Genoa, held as a fief of the French crown, and also that Louis might be trying to provide himself with legal justification should he wish in future to attack his former ally during the period of truce with Burgundy. Happily, the rumour turned out to be false, but before Panigarola obtained this reassurance he spent a night of terrible mental torment, so great, he later wrote, was his sense of duty towards his master. Charles was himself grieved by his distress and, in an effort to comfort him, swore by St George that he would rather forego the truce than agree to his ally's partial exclusion from it.

Panigarola's greatest headache, however, came from the duke's successive truces and eventual peace treaty with the emperor after the raising of the siege of Neuss.[152] The disengagement of the Burgundian and German forces at the end of May 1475 had been more of an oral agreement than a formal truce drawn up in documentary form. Consequently neither party took the customary step of including his allies in the settlement. Galeazzo Maria was gravely perturbed by this. Because of the absence of imperial recognition of his title to the duchy of Milan, he began to suspect that Charles and the emperor were in league against him, especially when the negotiations for his imperial investiture proceeded so slowly. He talked as if Charles had betrayed him and urged Panigarola to rectify the situation. After concluding a formal truce with the emperor on 17 November 1475, Charles gave Panigarola a copy but advised him not to send it to Milan until the subsequent alliance itself had been arranged. Many of the relevant papers were for a time feared lost in the battle of Grandson, and Panigarola was still asking for a copy of the imperial–Burgundian peace treaty, proclaimed at Lausanne on 14 April 1476, in the second half of May. Suspicious as he now was of the duke's intentions, Galeazzo Maria wanted an exact copy of the pertinent part of the treaty in which he was included as his ally. The Sforza archives holds a copy in Latin of a declaration made by the duke at Lausanne on 26 May 1476 that he had included Galeazzo Maria in the treaty and that Sforza held 'locum non postremum' in the ranks of his allies thus included.[153] Yet it may be that Galeazzo Maria never received his copy of the treaty itself. Already in the summer of 1475 he had said that the duke's omission of him from the ceasefire ending the siege of Neuss was enough to make him want to return to his alliance with Louis XI and, when he did in fact take this step after the battle of Murten, he justified his actions to the Venetians by referring to the duke's failure to include him in his treaties with the emperor between May 1475 and April 1476.

Although weighty affairs of state such as these occupied much of the ambassador's time, it was his duty also to deal with more mundane matters of trade and commerce. As a consequence of the treaty of Moncalieri, Charles on 31 March 1475 lifted the restrictions and penalties then in force against merchants who were subjects of the duke of Milan. However, the efforts of Panigarola, originally a businessman himself, resulted further in the grant of a separate privilege allowing Milanese merchants who died in the lands of Burgundy freely to bequeath their goods — which had previously been liable, after the merchants' deaths, to confiscation by the duke — and, because Panigarola had friends among Burgundian officials, he obtained the relevant charter for half the price![154] Similarly, the Venetian ambassadors were instructed to foster the interests of Venetian merchants in the Low Countries and England, and the Neapolitan Bertini seems to have exerted his influence to prevent the papal alum monopoly becoming effective in the duke's lands to the detriment of alum from the mines in the kingdom of Naples.

The ambassador could not expect to succeed by his own efforts alone, and on his arrival at the Burgundian court one of his first steps would have been to direct himself towards those whom he knew to be favourable to his master. In return for their help, the duke's advisers expected gifts. The evidence of Panigarola's dispatches suggests that such gifts were not large. He noticed that there were three things particularly pleasing to Burgundian courtiers: gifts of Italian (probably Florentine or Lombard) cloth of gold brocade and velvet from which they could order to be made the splendid robes regarded as *de rigueur* at court (and not crude gifts, or bribes, simply of money); a personal letter from the duke of Milan to flatter their sense of self-importance; and the exercise of Milanese influence in Rome on behalf of themselves or their relatives for the grant of benefices. But if the ambassador were to derive the maximum benefit from his efforts to win friends, it was essential to know who the men of influence really were. Appearances could be misleading. For example, Don Federico and his companions, as we shall see in the next chapter, made strenuous (though in the event unsuccessful) efforts in 1475–1476 to gain the friendship of Anthony of Burgundy, without realising that, despite being the duke's half-brother, his influence was quite small. Conversely, Panigarola was given a head-start by Guillaume de Rochefort and Anthony of Burgundy even before arriving at court.[155] Shortly after leaving Milan in February 1475 he met Rochefort in Turin, and was told the names of those to whom he should address himself at the Burgundian court. When he arrived in Geneva, he met Anthony, who gave him letters and instructions designed both to secure a safe journey and then to direct him to those in authority at court; he did this, he said, because of his great love for the duke of Milan. Probably Rochefort and Anthony would have advised the ambassador to win over Guy de Brimeu before all others, because, as Rochefort told the Milanese ambassador at the Savoyard court, '*è il primo homo a governare appresso el prefato suo S[igno]re et chi ha lui ha tutto*'; moreover, according to the same source, Brimeu had been the prime mover behind the decision to negotiate the treaty of Moncalieri.

Once arrived, there were two main groups among whom Panigarola sought friends: the great Burgundian dignitaries such as Brimeu,

Rochefort, Ferry de Clugny and Guillaume Hugonet; and the Italians in
the army or ducal entourage, especially the Neapolitan exiles, who
tended to favour the duke of Milan, and those who had had some connection in the past with Galeazzo Maria's father Francesco Sforza and
hence described themselves as *Sforzeschi*. It is interesting that Panigarola,
perhaps from his experience of the insinuating ways of the Milanese (and
also French) court, sought out those who had the duke's ear, whether or
not they possessed great official status.[156] One of his best contacts was
the duke's Neapolitan doctor Matteo de Clariciis, whom he described as
most influential. When Matteo died in July 1476, Panigarola was forced
to look for new friends of equal influence. He wrote to his master that he
would cultivate Lupo de Garda, the duke's Portuguese doctor, and Jean
Coulon, the duke's secretary. Another of his intimates who was obviously
of some importance because of his position in the ducal household but
about whom little otherwise is known was Simon Ducaret. Simon was
the duke's first secretary (in which position he had also served Philip the
Good); he knew of the duke's most secret affairs, dealing, in the absence
of Brimeu, with matters of the highest importance; and, according to
Panigarola, he had a personal fortune of 50,000 *scudi*.

The ways in which such friendships could assist the ambassador are
inevitably best illustrated in the dispatches of Panigarola.[157] Rochefort
showed great willingness to help Galeazzo Maria in the negotiations for
his imperial investiture. Salvatore de Clariciis seems to have assisted
Panigarola in obtaining the grant of commercial privileges just mentioned. His brother Matteo helped protect Galeazzo Maria's good name.
In May 1476 a Genoese, Gregorio di Lagneto, who was attached to
Hugues de Chalon in Piedmont (where Hugues was recruiting Italian
troops for Charles) as interpreter, wrote to Matteo to inform him of the
duke of Milan's secret overtures to Louis XI. Such a charge could have
proved embarrassing, especially as it was not altogether without foundation, so Matteo felt it advisable to suppress the information by giving the
letters to Panigarola, who in turn passed them on to his master. As a
former Angevin, Matteo added his efforts to those of the ambassador in
poisoning Charles the Bold's opinion of the Neapolitan prince Federico.
He was probably also Panigarola's most reliable informant.[158] He was
the regular means of communication between the duke and the ambassador and he often passed on to Panigarola confidential information
before Charles himself did, as, for example, at the end of January 1476
when he told him of the offers of French help for a Burgundian attack
on Milan made by Louis XI's ambassador, or, again, at the end of May

1476 when he relayed to him the secret instructions given by Charles to Olivier de la Marche, who was due to leave shortly on an embassy to Milan. On very delicate matters Panigarola turned to Matteo to enlighten him as to the duke's intentions, in the case, for instance, of his attitude towards the imperial investiture for Galeazzo Maria or of his promises to place the passes over the Alps from Savoy into Piedmont into the hands of the duke of Milan. It was Matteo who told him the exact figure (100,000 ducats) which the emperor would accept as the minimum price for the Milanese investiture, information which Charles himself, Rochefort and indeed Panigarola had been unable to elicit. When he died at La Rivière on 22 July 1476, Panigarola wrote to his master straight away to inform him that the duke of Milan had lost the best servant he had in the whole world.

The manner in which the Italian ambassador was to conduct himself towards his colleagues was regarded as a task of some importance and one on which he would be given detailed instructions. For example, the legate Tolentis passed through Vigevano on 13 March 1476 on his way to the Burgundian court and stopped to pay his respects to the duke of Milan. On the same day Galeazzo Maria wrote Panigarola a letter, which he presumably showed to Tolentis first, instructing him to give the legate all possible assistance on his arrival. Immediately after he had left, however, the duke again wrote to his ambassador to say that the previous letter had been written to flatter Tolentis and that he actually wished Panigarola to be far more circumspect with him than that letter had implied.[159] But it was a different case when the ambassadors' respective masters were on good terms. Between 1471 and 1473 Bembo and Bertini received specific instructions that they were to work together and put on a common front in order to demonstrate to the world the amity obtaining between Naples and Venice.[160] Panigarola and Morosini were similarly told to concert their actions in 1475. When Panigarola arrived at court, one of his first visitors was Morosini, who congratulated him on the treaty of Moncalieri. They gradually became accustomed to seeking audience with the duke together.

The difficulties arose when mutually hostile states were represented at the Burgundian court, with the result that the rivalries of their ambassadors reflected in microcosm the political divisions existing in the peninsula. When that happened, the ambassadors were required by fair means or foul to win the duke's ear and turn him against their rivals. Thus it was Venice and Milan who struggled for influence before 1475, and Milan and Naples in 1475 and 1476. The duke of Milan's ability to conciliate

Charles before 1475 was considerably reduced by the fact of his alliance with France. Consequently, his fear of the Venetians, whom he persistently accused of aspiring to the hegemony of Italy, became all the more intense, especially in those periods when the republic maintained an ambassador at the Burgundian court. One of the basic aims of the dispatch of embassies to Charles in 1469 and to the emperor in 1473 was to counter the supposed malevolent influence exercised over the duke of Burgundy by Dandolo and Bembo. Such fears were reflected by his agents north of the Alps. One reported nervously in 1469 that '*i Veniziani sono de continuo al'orechia de questo S[ignore] tuto per aviso*', while in 1473 Andrea dei Spiriti accused Bembo of encouraging the duke's wide-ranging schemes of expansion in general, and his alleged ambition to conquer Milan in particular. Since Galeazzo Maria could do little to counterbalance directly the Venetians' influence at the Burgundian court, his line of attack became more oblique, and, supported by the papal nuncio Aliprandi for reasons of both political sympathy and personal ambition, aimed at discrediting the legate Tolentis, who was a Venetian subject and suspect to Sforza for precisely that reason.[161]

Even more intense was the struggle between the Milanese and Neapolitan ambassadors in 1475–1476. It was undoubtedly taken very seriously by Panigarola, whose dispatches and instructions are the main source for it. According to his own account, he and his master had the best of the contest, although we would hardly expect otherwise from such a source, while Charles doubtless enjoyed giving each party in turn the impression that it was gaining the upper hand. Still, Panigarola must have struck a sympathetic chord when he dilated on the ingratitude shown by Ferrante for the support lent him at the beginning of his reign by Galeazzo Maria's father, for these were exactly the terms in which Charles couched his own complaints against Louis XI.[162] With the active assistance of the Neapolitan exiles in the ducal entourage, Panigarola curried favour with the duke by placing the worst possible interpretation on Ferrante's continuing negotiations with Louis XI and by deprecating the marriage of Princess Mary to Don Federico. When Bertini died both suddenly and unshriven on 22 November 1475, he relayed the event to his master with undisguised pleasure, referring to the deceased as 'the head of all our enemies here'.[163] Nonetheless, the Neapolitans too had their moments. Bertini intrigued with the Genoese exiles (probably some of those enemies here referred to by Panigarola), and the Neapolitan contingent — Bertini's successor Palombaro, Don Federico and his men — rejoiced publicly when they heard the news, inaccurate as it happened, that the uprising in Genoa against Milanese rule in June 1476 had succeeded. They sought to discredit the duke of Milan by spreading the recurrent rumours of his attempts to seek a reconciliation with France behind Charles the Bold's back. Much to Panigarola's chagrin, they mocked the ignominious flight of the Milanese ambassadors on the day of the battle of Grandson.

Perhaps the best example of the bizarre and often desperately Machiavellian character of this rivalry is provided by the fate of Giovanni Palombaro's dispatch of 16 March 1476.[164] In it Palombaro had some very harsh things to say about the duke of Burgundy's military aptitude, but, like many others of the Neapolitans' letters, it was intercepted by the duke of Milan's border guards. Galeazzo Maria immediately sent it on to Panigarola who showed it to Charles on 3 April; Charles was naturally offended by what Palombaro had written about him and he became even less interested in marrying his daughter to Don Federico than before. Panigarola let him have a copy; Charles slipped it between his shirt and his doublet to signify that the matter was close to his heart. Panigarola returned the original to his master on 11 April and shortly afterwards, on Charles the Bold's express instructions, burnt the copy, which no-one but the duke, Matteo de Clariciis and Guillaume de Rochefort had been allowed to see. Despite these precautions the ambassador was reprimanded by his master for indiscretion. By this time Palombaro and Don Federico had come to suspect the worst, but they learnt for certain that the dispatch had been intercepted only towards 10 May, when the bishop of Turin (Jean de Compey-Draillans) let it be known at the Savoyard court that he too had received a copy from the duke of Milan. Palombaro then claimed that his dispatch had been incorrectly deciphered. The lamentations of Palombaro and Federico were pathetic to behold; with tears in their eyes they besought Panigarola to tell them if he knew the fate of the dispatch and to promise not to poison their relations with Charles. Panigarola remained tight-lipped, knowing that he had helped his master to place Milanese influence in the ascendant.

The most routine part of an ambassador's task was the gathering and relaying of information. Detailed information could, in fact, sometimes be used to deceive rather than enlighten. Louis XI, for example, said that he expected his ally Galeazzo Maria to propagate the news he received from his correspondents at the French court throughout Italy in a manner favourable to the French king.[165] One of the reasons why Ferrante sent Bertini to Burgundy, aside from any consideration of making an alliance with Charles, was simply that he — perhaps more than any other ruler in the peninsula — needed a reliable picture of events across the Alps and just could not trust the pro-French version put about by the duke of Milan. When, for example, at the beginning of October 1472 he was waiting to receive a recently arrived Burgundian ambassador (unidentified in our source but quite possibly Antoine de Montjeu), he showed the Milanese ambassador a letter he had received from Charles dated 28 August in which were listed all the towns which the duke had taken from Louis XI in his recent campaigns. When questioned, the Milanese ambassador professed to know nothing of these Burgundian conquests. His embarrassment was manifest, and Ferrante expressed surprise at such ignorance.[166]

Ambassadors were expected to write as fully and as often as possible. As Paul II wrote to Tolentis on 18 October 1469, *'diffusius omnia referes'*. Panigarola's dispatches increased greatly in frequency in the spring and summer of 1476 compared with the previous year, although it was not until 21 March 1476 that he was enjoined by his master to write daily, on pain of death. Two weeks later the duke of Milan reminded his ambassador to put pen to paper every day even if he had nothing of particular moment to report. Before Bembo had left Italy in 1471, by contrast, he had already received his instructions to write daily.[167] Up to a point the gathering of information was fairly straightforward. The ambassador would watch who went in to see the duke and observe how long he stayed. He would engage the duke's advisers in conversation and try to obtain audience with the duke himself as often as possible. In these audiences, as we have seen, Charles was generous with his time and confidences. Indeed, Panigarola's dispatches are noticeably jejune for the period of the duke's illness at Lausanne between the end of April and the beginning of May 1476, when he was unable for a time to gain access to the duke. Sometimes, again, discretion was required. When a French herald came to the duke at Luxembourg around midday on 23 June 1474, his arrival did not escape the attention of the alert Neapolitan ambassador Bertini. Yet, instead of following his immediate impulse to go and ask the duke what news there was, he tried to find out first from his friend Gui de Brimeu, so as not to appear too curious.[168] Nonetheless, Charles was sometimes unobtainable,[169] especially when on campaign, and it was at such times that the ambassador required friends in the ducal entourage who could and would keep him informed.

Moreover, it could on occasions be arduous trying to keep up with the duke. During the Burgundian conquest of Lorraine in the second half of 1475, Panigarola had to make a special outlay from his meagre resources on tents and other articles requisite for camp life. The Milanese chancellery took an unsympathetic view of his expenses. Why could he not just lodge in a village near the camp as was the practice of ambassadors attached to the French and Milanese courts? In a letter written from the Burgundian camp outside Nancy on 31 October 1475, Panigarola explained his reasons with barely concealed exasperation at his master's impercipience. For a start, he wrote, most of the villages nearby were deserted, having been either abandoned by the inhabitants at the approach of Charles the Bold's army or deliberately laid waste at his command; besides, these villages were unsafe because of the ravages of disease which had broken out following the onset of campaigning and because of the hostility of the remaining local population. In any case, Charles himself had issued strict instructions that, for reasons of both safety and discipline, everyone was to lodge in camp. Finally, he explained, it was necessary to be as close to the duke as possible in order to protect his master's interests and to counter the wiles of Don Federico, who had not hesitated to esconce himself in the Burgundian camp.[170]

Although Panigarola found the duke generally frank and open, Rodolfo Gonzaga considered him rather secretive, and Charles could certainly dissimulate when necessary.[171] Sometimes he told Panigarola and his master only what he wished them to know. One is naturally led to suspect that occasionally the information Panigarola obtained from his friends in the ducal retinue was deliberately planted by the duke himself. Certainly Matteo de Clariciis, for example, had his own far from disinterested motives for wanting to ingratiate himself through Panigarola with the duke of Milan, and thus for supplying the ambassador with reliable and useful information. Yet Galeazzo Maria wrote to Panigarola on 17 April 1476 to complain that his two previous dispatches of 12 April and 22 March were as different as night and day, and he admonished him to probe to the bottom of the matters reported (the garrisoning of the Piedmontese passes) and not to believe everything he was told, for he had been duped by Matteo and by everyone else.[172] The duke of Milan was a hard taskmaster. His ambassadors were expected to report the conversations they had, and the information gleaned from them, *in extenso*, but they were not to process it or pass on what were really only their own fallible interpretations of events, nor were they to reply to questions in such a way as to commit their master without specific instructions to do so. Such injunctions could reduce the ambassador's self-reliance and initiative to a minimum, and it was perhaps for that reason that Panigarola on occasions simply handed over to Charles the letters he had received from his master, but he was eventually forbidden to let any of his instructions out of his hands, even if Charles requested them; and, after the battle of Grandson, again acting on instructions, he returned to his master all the papers he had accumulated up till then.[173]

Having obtained his information, whatever its merits, the only remaining problem for the ambassador was to relay it to his master. This task, however, was seldom as easy as he would have wished. Most of the evidence for this comes from the dispatches of Panigarola, but it is clear from other sources that the problem was common to all the Italian ambassadors at the court of Charles the Bold. The use of ciphers was standard practice. Panigarola's consisted of almost two hundred symbols designed to stand not only for individual letters and combinations of letters, adverbs and conjunctions but also for the names of certain rulers or individuals on whose actions he was instructed to report. Most of his dispatches contain coded passages. Sometimes the whole dispatch was coded. In the first half of 1476, however, when he was at the Burgundian court in Savoy, he felt it safe, in view of the reduced distance between himself and Milan which made interception less likely, to risk sending many of them in clear. But in any case — conveniently for the historian — coded and decoded versions of many of them exist side by side in the Sforza archives. Moreover, it is ironical that we are able to know that the non-Milanese ambassadors at court also used ciphers from the fact that several decoded copies of their dispatches are preserved in the Sforza archives and that the keys to their ciphers, now in Vienna, almost certainly originated in the same place. Galeazzo Maria, in fact, customarily had couriers who passed through his lands stopped so that copies could be taken of any letters they were carrying. Before the treaty of Moncalieri, Charles too suffered in this way and after a number of incidents he ordered in 1470 that henceforth all his couriers should take the longer route to Italy through Germany and over the eastern end of the Alps.[174] Yet even Milanese couriers faced the hazard of interception. In the summer of 1475, when the Germans, the League of Constance, the duke of Lorraine and the French king combined to assault Burgundian lines of communication southwards, Panigarola found difficulty in getting news safely to his master. Two Milanese (also two Venetian) couriers were waylaid at that time, and at one stage Galeazzo Maria had to rely for information about the siege of Neuss on his friend the marquis of Mantua, who had his own correspondents, although, being in the German camp, they would present a different picture.[175] Indeed, a correspondent of Guillaume de Rochefort wrote from Padua in June 1475, pressing him as a matter of urgency to relay to Venice the Burgundian version of the siege's progress because at that time only the German side was being reported there.[176]

Panigarola was not only seriously inconvenienced but also given cause to fear for his life when two of his couriers were murdered in the spring of 1476 near the Burgundian camp outside Lausanne.[177] Galeazzo Maria had set up a post at Geneva for the collection of letters sent to and by his ambassadors in Savoy. On the evening of 16 April a courier was found dead in a wood near this spot by two of Panigarola's men; ten stab-wounds were visible. At first it was thought that, although his sword and coat had been taken, all his letters were safe. It was discovered subse-quently, however, that he had been carrying an extremely important letter from the duke of Milan to his ambassador bearing his reply to Charles the Bold's proposals for a joint Burgundian–Milanese partition of Savoy and Piedmont. This loss had diplomatic repercussions, for, while in the missing letter the duke of Milan apparently showed himself favourable to the suggestion, the resulting publicity made him much more timid and Charles never did get another positive reply before the battle of Murten put paid to the plan. Moreover, as a result of the inci-dent Galeazzo Maria ordered Panigarola (and d'Appiano) to be ready to leave at a moment's notice should the outrage be repeated; when the ambassador relayed these instructions to Charles, he was greatly put out and turned white.

There was no shortage of suspects. Charles thought the culprits were agents of the bishop of Geneva, who had been responsible for other attacks, and behind the bishop he suspected ultimately the king of France, who, he said, was anxious to be informed of the state of the Burgundian–Milanese alliance and to exploit any weaknesses in order to create friction between the two dukes. Panigarola himself considered the English soldiers in the Burgundian camp to be the most probable cul-prits, for there had already been several bloody riots between the English and Italian contingents. He felt there were also grounds for suspicion against the French-speaking subjects of the duke of Savoy, because they were displaying the growing dislike of Italians which erupted into savage reprisals after the kidnap of the regent Yolande at the end of June. Finally, he did not rule out the possibility that Don Federico and the Neapolitans, in an attempt to gain revenge for their recent humiliations at Milanese hands, might also be implicated. Charles spared no effort to get to the bottom of the matter. It was in his interest to do so, not only to conciliate his Milanese ally but also to show that he was master in his own camp; previous incidents had caused him grave disquiet about the general lack of discipline among his troops. He was put under pressure by Panigarola to make an example of the culprits if and when they were found; the ambassador understandably feared, as an Italian and as a diplomat, for his own safety. Two weeks later, however, another Milanese courier was found murdered, and although suspects were interrogated under torture the culprit was never discovered. The loss of these couriers impeded Panigarola's communications with Milan, but so also did the flight of those stationed at the Geneva post who had become restive at the new element of risk now injected into their job.

The problem of communications caused the Italian ambassador many other headaches, for couriers were expensive, infrequent and never fast enough for either the ambassador's or his master's peace of mind. In the third quarter of the fifteenth century only Louis XI and Galeazzo Maria had anything like an organised state postal system, and even in these two cases communications outside the ruler's own lands remained hazardous. The Italian ambassador at the Burgundian court was seldom personally allotted couriers. More often he was expected to send his dispatches by way of the couriers sent to him with instructions by his master. But the timing of this system did not always synchronise with his own needs, so that he would find himself compelled to retain the courier until he could give a full and complete account of matters then in hand. Sometimes he would share a courier with a trusted colleague or with a merchant (though this did not give any special guarantee of safe arrival), or indeed with anyone sending a message in the same direction. Milanese ambassadors often found Tommaso Portinari useful in this respect. In October 1475 Panigarola wrote that he had sent his recent letters via the courier of the Venetian ambassador Morosini, who would pass them on in turn to the Milanese ambassador in Venice. On one occasion Lucas de Tolentis sent a letter to Rome by way of Milan, after entrusting it to Panigarola's courier.[178] Sometimes Charles himself would help out. After the murder of Panigarola's couriers in 1476 he provided an armed escort for the ambassador's men taking messages to the post at Geneva, and contributed towards the couriers' expenses. Panigarola did not receive several of his master's letters written between the second half of May and the beginning of August 1475 until the end of October, with the arrival of a Milanese courier who had travelled from Milan with the Burgundian force escorting the duke's returning envoy Salvatore de Clariciis. In 1473 Charles also supplied Bembo with a courier to carry to Venice the ambassador's account of the Burgundian conquest of Guelders; on his arrival this courier was rewarded with pieces of crimson and silver damask decorated with his master's arms, in addition to the sum of 25 gold ducats. But in general it is probable that all the Italian ambassadors' dispatches were full of complaints similar to Panigarola's: if his master wanted more frequent news, he would have to provide more couriers.

In keeping with their hazardous life, couriers expected commensurate remuneration, and this was one of the major items in the ambassador's expenditure. From the scanty information available it is difficult to give adequate figures or attempt a comparative analysis. The only thing that can be said for certain is that ambassadors' complaints about the cost of couriers were one of the most recurrent themes in their dispatches. The papal envoy Aliprandi wrote in 1473 that couriers had cost him fifty *scudi* over the previous two months. He had managed to persuade one of the duke's couriers going to Rome to make a diversion through Milan (taking the precaution of sending the letter coded), but he had to pay him ten *scudi* to do so. Panigarola paid seven ducats for a courier to take a letter from Geneva to Milan in 1475; the courier promised to reach Milan in five days because he, Panigarola explained, could use the 'German route', unlike the Milanese. When Panigarola sent his letters through Germany in 1475 in the custody of the Venetian ambassador's courier, it cost six ducats. In February 1476 he reported that two couriers who had been sent to him by his master had had the effrontery to demand payment for the return trip, since they claimed Galeazzo Maria had only given them enough money for the outward journey.[179]

The speed of communications varied considerably, the two main variables being the location from which the ambassador sent his dispatches and whether the lands through which his courier passed were at peace or war. The dispatches of the Neapolitan ambassadors had the greatest distance to cover. Those, for example, sent by Bertini from the Burgundian camp at Roye on 19 and 20 June 1472 arrived in Naples on or before 15 July; that written at Brussels on 26 February 1473 was received shortly before the end of March.[180] Panigarola experienced difficulties in 1475, but in the following spring communications became much easier. For example, he received his master's letter of 9 April 1476 five days later; the same period elapsed between the sending of his dispatches of 19 and 20 May and his master's receipt of them.[181] This acceleration was due to the fact that he was now geographically closer to Milan, passage through Savoy was generally unhindered, and Galeazzo Maria had instituted a rudimentary postal system between the two. Five or six weeks was not considered slow for communications between Venice and her ambassadors in Burgundy.[182] These times meant that Charles experienced many frustrations in trying to obtain firm commitments of assistance from his Italian allies. By the time an Italian ruler had received his ambassador's dispatch, the situation to which it referred (and perhaps the duke's intentions too) could have changed considerably, and in the meantime the ruler might have obtained a different picture from other sources.

One important point remains to be considered: how significant was the ambassador's personal influence on the relations between his master and the duke? One criterion by which to assess it is the negotiation of treaties, of which there are four instances: the alum treaty with the pope of May 1468, and the treaties of alliance with Naples in 1471, Venice in 1472 and Milan in 1475; of these, only the last was not negotiated at the Burgundian court by the ambassador concerned, for it was rather as a result of the conclusion of the treaty of Moncalieri that Panigarola was sent to Burgundy. As far as the treaty with Ferrante is concerned, we know that the Neapolitan chancery issued Bertini on 4 August 1470 with apparently unrestricted powers to conclude.[183] He was presumably also given more detailed instructions, no longer extant, laying down guidelines which would have limited his personal initiative. The fact that Charles allowed less favourable terms to the king of Naples than, in the following year, to the Venetians,[184] may be attributed as much to Ferrante's weaker bargaining position as to Bertini's softness in negotiation. The Venetian senate, on the other hand, was highly delighted with the terms achieved by Bembo and greatly praised his diligence in persuading the duke to accept the exact conditions it had proposed, namely an obligation to send him money if attacked (rather than to attack his attacker, as he had apparently suggested) and the extraction from him of a promise, of however dubious value, of military and naval assistance against the Turks. Similarly, Tolentis won Charles over to almost complete acceptance of the terms proposed by Pope Paul II for the alum treaty of 1468; here again, though, his success may have been conditioned by the duke's desire at this time to conciliate the Holy See even at the risk of offending many of his subjects.[185]

The restrictions on the ambassador's initiative in such negotiations are illustrated by the events leading up to the conclusion of the Milanese–Burgundian alliance at Moncalieri at the end of January 1475. Its conclusion, and indeed the initiation of negotiations, owed much to the mediation of Yolande, regent of Savoy. Galeazzo Maria was both eager for an alliance and cautious about openly committing himself against France. He took the trouble, therefore, on 27 November 1474 to write in his own hand from Villanova to his representative at the court of Savoy, Antonio d'Appiano, telling him to dissuade Yolande from opening the negotiations with the Burgundian emissary Guillaume de Rochefort until the latter's procuration had arrived;[186] he also saw to it that his enemy, the king of Naples, was excluded from the treaty (even though he was allied to Burgundy). On one occasion the unfortunate Panigarola, who had had nothing to do with these negotiations, fell foul of his master over Charles the Bold's interpretation of the final document. When Charles had the treaty proclaimed publicly in April 1475 he claimed that, if he was attacked by any enemy, Galeazzo Maria was obliged to send up to a thousand troops to his aid. This exaggeration (the treaty in fact mentioned only four hundred men-at-arms) was due, he admitted, to his desire to frighten his enemies. When Galeazzo Maria heard of this, he did not hesitate to vent his anger on Panigarola, although he commanded that his comments should not be passed on but were for the ambassador's eyes only. He seems to have held Panigarola personally responsible for the duke's gaffe, or, at least, to have blamed him for not having remonstrated with him at the time, whereas the wording of Panigarola's letter acknowledging his master's admonitions in fact implies that he himself was unfamiliar with the exact details of the very treaty whose conclusion was the reason for his presence at the Burgundian court.

The ambassador's influence was further restricted by the fact that not all the negotiations between his master and the duke were handled by him alone. Only a month after Bembo's arrival in 1471, Charles sent Guillaume de Rochefort and Antonio dei Corradi di Lignana to Venice to discuss the possibility of recruiting Bartolomeo Colleoni. This duplication of effort, as well as the thorny nature of the negotiations themselves, caused embarrassment all round. Nonetheless, Charles persisted right up to 1475 in sending envoys to Venice on the same matter, even though there was a Venetian ambassador at his court the whole time who could have acted as the necessary channel of communication between the duke and the republic. Similarly, Galeazzo Maria did not feel in 1475 and 1476 that the task of ascertaining his ally's exact requirements of him could safely be left to Panigarola alone. He repeatedly urged the duke to send an embassy to Milan with the appropriate rank and powers to discuss the question. Finally, he lost patience and sent his own embassy to Burgundy in February 1476.

The ambassador was not expected to have to rely unduly on his own initiative, nor was he often left without instructions concerning contingencies. He would receive detailed instructions on how to behave towards the other ambassadors at court. Sometimes he would even be told what to say, especially when confronted with leading questions. In 1473 Bertini was recalled all the way to Naples to receive more detailed briefing on how to deal with the prospect of Mary of Burgundy's betrothal to Don Federico. Conversely, dispatches provide frequent examples of an ambassador reporting that he has had to reply noncommittally to certain questions through lack of instructions. Sometimes, of course, this lack of instructions was deliberate, since rulers might not wish to commit themselves on matters about which they had not yet made up, or could not make up, their mind. On other occasions, however, it is clear that the ambassador's needs in certain situations had not been foreseen, as, for example, when Panigarola met Edward IV in July 1475. The king of England remarked that the duke of Milan, being the ally of Charles the Bold, was his friend too. The ambassador was forced to reply in general terms only, since he had no specific instructions.[187]

There were two areas in which the ambassador might exercise a marginal influence over the course of relations. The first was in his own personal standing with Charles. The duke's immediate impression of the ambassador's master was derived from the behaviour of the ambassador himself, and the latter's winning ways could for a time mask deficiencies in his master's posture towards Charles. In this respect Bertini was probably more successful than Palombaro, Bembo than Morosini, and Panigarola than the Milanese ambassadors sent to Burgundy in 1476. There are important qualifications to be made here, however, for Charles was bound, in the long run, to be influenced more by the actions of his Italian allies themselves than by the interpretation placed on them by their ambassadors at his court. Not a few of the latter tended to be swayed by admiration for the duke and to identify themselves too closely with his interests. Throughout the summer of 1472, for example, Tolentis warned Pope Sixtus IV against the probability of losing the goodwill of the duke through his attempts to placate Louis XI when the success of his overtures to Louis was itself far from assured: '*hic perdere et alibi non capere non est utile*'.[188] Similarly, Panigarola on several occasions urged his master to do everything in his power to conciliate Charles, because his goodwill and might were of inestimable advantage. Yet in both cases this advice, however sound, fell on deaf ears. Sixtus IV and Galeazzo Maria made their own decisions and Charles drew the appropriate conclusions.

The other way an ambassador might exercise some personal influence was in his reporting, one of the fundamentals of his job. The hazards of communication between Italy and the lands of Burgundy, combined with the significance attached by Italian rulers to the actions and intentions of ultramontane princes, lent added value to on-the-spot reports sent from the Burgundian court; the ambassador's own selection and interpretation of news helped determine his master's evaluation of events; and to that extent, therefore, he could condition the policies adopted by rulers. But, again, other factors limited the influence which he might exert in this respect. To start with, he was seldom his master's sole source of information. In the spring of 1476, for example, Galeazzo Maria had two representatives in Lausanne who could report on affairs at both the Burgundian and Savoyard courts, namely Panigarola and d'Appiano. Even though d'Appiano offered to let Panigarola alone report on all the major occurrences, because, he said, events at the Savoyard court depended on decisions taken at the Burgundian court, nonetheless the Milanese chancellor commanded each to write independently of the other so that their master could obtain the fullest information possible.[189] Moreover, as is shown by the large amount of contemporary correspondence extant in the Sforza archives, Galeazzo Maria had many sources of information other than his own diplomats. He was kept abreast of events at the Burgundian court by several of those in the duke's service, sometimes in his immediate retinue, by captains such as Giacomo Galeota and Troilo da Rossano and by Tommaso Portinari. Most of these reports were of course favourable towards Charles, but Galeazzo also received less partisan evaluations from merchants resident in the north or returning to Italy, from Italian soldiers leaving the Burgundian army, and from Francophile (and possibly French-inspired) sources. This abundance of information was probably duplicated, if to a lesser extent, in the sources available to the king of Naples and the Venetian republic. As for the duke of Milan, he certainly did not passively await information but rather sent out agents to gather it.[190]

All in all the conclusion must be that, whether in the strictly occasional business of negotiating treaties or in the day-to-day duties of the resident, the operational parameters within which the diplomat functioned were narrowly drawn. In essence his influence was subject, on the one hand, to the limits to which his master would go in order to conciliate Charles the Bold and, on the other, to the respective value placed by Charles upon his various Italian allies. The ambassador might attempt to extend the former by exhortation and by biased reporting and to influence the latter through the arts of insinuation and flattery; but, however great his efforts, he seldom achieved as much success in determining the course of events as in simply reporting on them.[191]

Daily life

To the Italian ambassador at the Burgundian court, far from home, forced to cope with unfamiliar customs and liable to feel himself surrounded by malice and intrigue, the physical incidentals of his daily routine were doubtless of as much concern as the purely diplomatic aspects. In this context, the duke's fondness for Italian diplomats collectively could be counted as some compensation. The ambassador's life, nonetheless, consisted to an unpleasant degree of a mixture of psychological stress and long periods of boring inactivity coupled with physical discomfort and sometimes real danger.

He was expected first and foremost to follow the court, which had no fixed location. Moreover, Charles spent much of his reign on active campaign and this served only to multiply the fatigue, expense and danger of attendance at court. Let us take as an example the year 1472, most of which Charles spent either engaged in or preparing for war. Of the Italian ambassadors, the Venetian Bembo seems to have been the most diligent. He followed the duke in his campaigns along the Somme and, although he did not accompany him to Normandy, he had good reason for staying behind since he was busy with negotiating the treaty between Burgundy and Venice. The papal legate Tolentis was less venturesome. He was with the duke in camp in June but he too had the excuse of other business to attend to elsewhere, such as overseeing the implementation of the papal alum monopoly and the sale of indulgences. The Neapolitan Bertini did his best to keep up with the duke, and his biographer implied that he shortened his life thereby ('*per istare sempre in peregrinatione*').[192] In 1474 and 1475, however, he did take up quarters in the Burgundian camp outside Neuss for the whole of the siege's ten-and-a-half-month duration. The Venetian ambassador at that time, Morosini, seems to have been absent through illness on more than one occasion between April and June 1475; before April his lodgings were situated ten miles from camp. The Milanese Panigarola was virtually inseparable from the duke during his embassy, although he was parted from him for a few days in June 1476 after the Burgundian army's disorderly flight from the battlefield of Murten.

Even though many of them must have become hardened through previous absences from Italy, they were not immune to homesickness.[193] In the winter of 1473–1474 Bertini enjoyed a brief return to Naples, but this was the only break he had between 1468 and 1475, and the offer he made in October 1475 to return to Italy to help mediate the differences between the duke of Milan and his subject city of Genoa sounds like a disguised plea for recall; in fact, he suffered the ultimate misfortune of dying abroad only a month later. Dandolo persistently requested his recall to Venice on the grounds that he urgently needed to attend to his own private affairs. As well as the length of his embassy (three years), Dandolo's successor Bembo had other pressing reasons to seek his recall, for he had left behind his pregnant young wife Elena Marcello, who early in 1472 bore a son, Carlo, whom he was not to see for another two years. Later in 1472 we find him writing to his brother that he felt it bitter to be far from home and urging him to console Elena. Not surprisingly, his entries in his commonplace book under the heading of UXOR are much concerned with wifely fidelity.

What Queller has said of Venetian diplomacy in the Quattrocento — that it was conducted largely at the cost and the risk of private citizens[194] — applies also to the other Italian powers represented at the court of Charles the Bold. Many of the incidental expenses, such as couriers, were common to most courts of the time, but others were peculiar to Burgundy. We may believe Panigarola, who had experience of both the French and the Burgundian courts, when he complained that the latter was the more expensive; moreover, as Rodolfo Gonzaga had found to his embarrassment some years before, the cost of living at the Burgundian court was much higher than in Italy.[195] The ambassadors were not unpaid, but they usually found themselves having to dip into their own pockets since certain expenses had to be met as they arose; it was then up to them to try to recoup the outlay from their masters afterwards. In October 1472, the Venetian senate sent Bembo five hundred ducats when they learnt of his success in negotiating an alliance with Burgundy. Four months earlier he had been given four hundred ducats to pay the ducal chancellor for the settlement of the formalities of the treaty; the money was probably required as a bureaucratic fee rather than as a bribe.[196]

Yet ambassadors needed to be paid before rather than after the event in order to avoid going into debt. A regular income would have been a godsend. In November 1472, with the triumph of the Burgundian–Venetian treaty still fresh in his mind, Bembo wrote to his friend Bernardo Giustinian asking him to intercede with the senate to give him a salary such as those which, he claimed, others of the republic's ambassadors received.[197] This appeal seems to have gone unanswered. Panigarola had an allowance of fifty *scudi* per month, but this would still have been insufficient even if paid both punctually and regularly. He was certain, he wrote, that the duke of Milan would live up to his reputation for unfailingly rewarding service. Surely the duke did not expect him to consume his own wealth in the duke's service? In any case, he still had no private source of income despite his master's many promises in the past. He could not protect the duke's interests better if he were his own son. He was deep in debt to Tommaso Portinari, Matteo de Clariciis and others; he was too young to die; and so on.[198] Lucas de Tolentis's monthly salary of one hundred and twenty gold ducats had to be paid out of the revenues from the papal alum monopoly and from the sale of indulgences, which it was his duty as papal legate to raise; if he did not do his duty, in other words, he did not get paid. When the duke of Burgundy suspended the alum monopoly in 1473, Lucas hastened to write to Sixtus urging him to relieve him from the poverty and misery into which he had been cast.[199]

The cost of living at court was, in the Italians' opinion, augmented unnecessarily by the courtiers' habit of regularly giving gifts and expecting to receive them in return. Panigarola took it for granted that his master would send and pay for gifts of luxury cloth which the ambassador recommended for potentially useful members of the ducal entourage, but he had, in the first instance, to pay out of his own pocket for the gifts required on festive occasions. As a postscript to his letter written at Nancy on 31 December 1475 he enclosed an itemised list of expenses incurred for gifts given on Christmas Day. The total cost was almost 38 *scudi*, or about three-quarters of his monthly allowance. Among the recipients were twelve trumpeters, ten pipers, twelve heralds and several varlets and grooms of the duke himself; the tambourine players and trumpeters of Anthony of Burgundy; trumpeters and other attendants of Don Federico; and the duke's fool, Monsieur le Glorieux.[200] Panigarola sent a reminder to his master the next month that he needed extra money to pay for these presents, considering their great number and the practice of the court with which, he pointed out, other ambassadors complied.

When the diplomats followed the duke on campaign, their expenditure rose still higher.[201] In the autumn of 1472, Aliprandi claimed that the cost of bread in the Burgundian camp in northern France was exorbitant and that water was fetching prices more usually paid for wine.

Bembo too complained at this time of the additional costs incurred on campaign, which, he wrote, amounted to ten ducats a day. Panigarola bore the most telling witness to such hardships. Camp prices, he soon discovered, were artificially inflated by shortages. He considered it prudent to itemise them in order to convince his master of the difficulties he faced. He complained in October 1475 that he was having to pay up to one-and-a-half ducats for a measure of wine — when it was available. Two months later he reported that the cost of feeding his horses was almost half as much again as the allowance he received for them. From Lausanne in the spring of 1476 he declared the general scarcity to be such that the countryside around for a radius of up to ten miles was being searched for provisions. The shortages experienced on the Swiss campaign were worse than any at Neuss or in Lorraine. Not only were all sorts of food in short supply and overpriced, but also the ambassador had to make additional outlays on extra equipment not required by the normal court routine. In Lorraine, Charles had provided each ambassador with a pavilion at his own expense, but Panigarola complained that he needed extra shelter for his men, twice the number of horses he had, extra couriers and a wagon in which to transport his belongings. The cost of this additional equipment he estimated at one hundred ducats. For a time after the battle of Grandson he thought his wagon had been captured by the Swiss; he eventually recovered it but only after he had paid ninety ducats to the Burgundian soldiers who retrieved it for him. Even so, his losses were almost total. His losses at the battle of Murten, however, were still more comprehensive and he hastened to list them for his master's edification. They included several long robes; hats; two new pairs of shoes; household furnishings such as blankets, plates and candelabra; two horses; and a Spanish mule. His requests for reimbursement went largely unanswered, and three days after the battle of Murten he wrote wryly to his master from the safety of Saint-Claude that he no longer required an extra allowance for these additional camp expenses.

Not only was the ambassador's life expensive, it could also be unpleasant, especially when he was called upon to deal with the rivalry of colleagues. In this context one recalls the Milanese campaign of vilification against the Venetians, the struggle for influence between Panigarola and Bertini, and the intrigues of the various Italian exiles. Such rivalry was sometimes expressed formally in terms of conflicts over precedence on ceremonial occasions. On Christmas Day 1472, for example, Charles the Bold, then holding court at Bruges, invited several of the ambassadors to dine. Bembo insisted that he should precede the papal envoy

Domenico Albergati on the grounds that the latter was only a '*simplex commissarius*' and not, therefore, entitled to the privileges of ambassadorial rank. We know the outlines of the argument from a letter written to the duke of Milan by Pietro Aliprandi, whose sympathies can be gauged from the fact that he referred to Bembo as '*quella bestia*'. It was Aliprandi who tried to refute Bembo's case when the ducal chancellor Hugonet asked him for his opinion; he said that he himself had once, as papal commissioner at the English court, been given precedence over the ambassadors of the duke of Burgundy himself. Bembo took his complaint as far as the duke but the result is not reported.[202]

Not infrequently, the ambassador's health was at stake no less than his *amour propre*. The amount of travelling required could be exhausting. In this respect grey hairs, even if they denoted the wisdom gleaned from experience, could be a liability. Onofrio di Santa Croce twice fell ill on his winter journey to the Burgundian court in 1468; he later excused himself from travelling to a meeting with some of the duke's representatives on the grounds that his aged body could not withstand the inclemency of the season and the difficulties of the route. Tolentis was confined to bed in February 1473 by a fever brought on, he said, by overwork. Morosini was forced by illness to leave the siege of Neuss in the spring of 1475 in order to seek treatment in Bruges. Bertini died prematurely ('*molto giovane*') because of his diplomatic exertions.[203]

The journey between Italy and the Burgundian court could be not only tiring but also perilous. When Bertini returned from Naples in 1474, he was briefly detained at Basel by the municipal authorities, who suspected him of subversive intrigues. It took the intercession of Charles the Bold to secure his release. Nonetheless, his temporary replacement Palombaro showed little sympathy for him and scant faith in the protection afforded by diplomatic status when he commented that Bertini had displayed poor judgement in choosing a route through such a hostile and lawless region.[204] According to the chaplain of Basel, a Venetian ambassador returning to Italy from the Burgundian camp at Neuss in 1474 was detained by Duke Sigmund of Austria in Alto Adige.[205] In February 1476 Pallavicino, Visconti and Grimaldi showed great reluctance to leave Milan, complaining of the perils and discomfort of travelling in winter (as well as of the inadequate provision made for their expenses by their master). Yet their return journey was even more hazardous, for they had to flee across the Alps hotfoot in order to escape the triumphant Swiss, who were rumoured to be pursuing the survivors of the Burgundian rout at Grandson. For a time Visconti was separated from his colleagues, who, when they rejoined him at Susa, sent the duke of Milan what might be termed the typical ambassadorial lament: they had been saved from death only by the grace of God and they therefore begged Him never again to put into Galeazzo Maria's head the idea of giving them such an ill-starred and dangerous mission.

The ambassador placed himself at no small physical risk when he followed Charles on campaign, and the inchoate theory of diplomatic immunity could have provided him with little comfort.[206] Bertini was attacked by Charles the Bold's own soldiers (anxious to vent their discontent about arrears of pay) when the siege of Neuss was lifted. He escaped with his life only when it was discovered he was a priest; this was despite the fact, as Panigarola remarked, that he was the very man who had mediated the truce which made the lifting of the siege possible. Charitable for once towards his arch-rival, Panigarola noted this outrage to a defenceless individual as well as to a member of the *corps diplomatique* with indignation, but he added with some satisfaction that he himself had travelled safely away from Neuss under the protection of the ducal standard. Nine months later the Milanese ambassador dutifully and bravely delayed his flight from the battlefield of Grandson until the last possible moment, but one of his attendants perished. He escaped from the defeat at Murten with only the clothes on his back; this time he lost two of his servants. It might be fitting to conclude this section with the observation that his declarations of willingness to die if necessary in the service of his master were not quite as emptily rhetorical as might at first sight appear.

Similarities and contrasts between Burgundian and Italian diplomatic techniques

If, in the second half of the fifteenth century, Italian diplomatic technique was the most advanced of its day, the last Valois duke of Burgundy was among the first ultramontane rulers to experience prolonged contact with it, both from the Italian ambassadors sent to his court and from the Italians whom he employed as diplomats on his own behalf. For this reason it is worth attempting to discover if he was in any way influenced by Italian methods.

Italian Renaissance diplomacy has acquired among historians a reputation for refined deviousness that makes it possible to consider Machiavelli's advice to rulers to be as much descriptive as prescriptive.

Certainly, one can find instances in diplomatic correspondence of the period of the Italians' conviction of their political sophistication and cultural superiority. Italian ambassadors often professed to find the ultramontanes in general boastful and unrealistic. At Trier in 1473 the Milanese Visconti and the Neapolitan Bertini managed to concur, despite their political differences, in the view that northern rulers, Charles the Bold in particular, lived on fantasies and were given to building castles in the air.[207] Conversely, one can cite utterances by transmontane princes and their courtiers which suggest that they regarded Italians as more deceitful — if not necessarily more clever — than themselves. In 1473, Charles the Bold bitterly referred to '*le tromparie* [sic] *italiane*' after he had let himself be persuaded by King Ferrante to end the papal alum monopoly in his lands for comparatively little benefit.[208] Italian ambassadors were quick to denounce the barbarity and strange customs they found north of the Alps, but in their dispatches they were more sparing than one would expect in extolling their own innate intellectual superiority over the ultramontanes, if only because to do so would have deprived them of excuses should their mission meet with failure. They were not averse to vaunting their cleverness, but this was usually in the context of their surprise and pleasure at having been able to fathom the strange procedures of northern courts and to perceive the realities of power behind the hierarchical façade.

In fact, the stark contrast between Italian cunning and northern naivety becomes less tenable the more one studies the period. Louis XI, for example, had become adept in the intricacies of peninsular diplomacy long before he became king, and although he may not (as was alleged) have followed Italian precepts in dealing with the Public Wealers in 1465, he did express a desire ten years later to learn from the methods of government employed by Ferrante of Naples;[209] as for Charles the Bold, he was no less familiar than Louis with Italian diplomacy and he certainly shared his admiration for Ferrante. After all, deviousness, whether viewed as a vice or, in the context of diplomacy, as a virtue, is common to mankind and not the property of a single nation. As the Milanese ambassador at the French court conceded in 1473, there too men knew how to use deceit ('*usare de le industrie et arte*') when necessary, and in 1474 the same observer was prepared to allow that Charles could be even more perfidious than Louis.[210]

Italians willingly conceded that the ultramontanes were their masters in camouflaging their intentions by raising a smokescreen of conflicting rumours, as the Milanese ambassador in Rome admitted when unable to explain Anthony of Burgundy's reasons for lingering there in the summer of 1475 instead of returning home.[211] The duke of Burgundy's ability to make his enemies believe what he wanted them to was of great advantage in his overall diplomatic strategy. In Italy — at least, before 1475 — it served to paralyse Galeazzo Maria by means of recurrent rumours of a Burgundian expedition against him and thereby, as we saw in Chapter 1, to give the duke of Milan second thoughts about sending help to his French ally against Charles. Moreover, the papal legate Andrea dei Spiriti considered in 1473 that, between Charles and Louis, it was the former who was more capable of stopping 'leaks' other than officially inspired ones; in fact, Charles, he said, was better informed (through disbursing largesse in France) about the king's affairs than was Louis concerning those of the duke. Another legate, Tolentis, complained to Sixtus IV in the same year that it was difficult for him to write of confidential matters, since all the secret information he enclosed in his letters was soon common knowledge at the Burgundian court.

Nonetheless, it cannot be denied that there were important differences between Burgundian and Italian diplomatic techniques. One was the resident embassy, an Italian innovation which Charles, along with other contemporary ultramontane rulers, failed to adopt. Because he did not maintain residents in the peninsula, Charles sought to extract the maximum advantage from those embassies which he did send there by instructing them to follow a circular itinerary that would allow them to visit as many friendly or neutral courts as possible in one trip. This practice had embarrassing consequences in 1475, when Anthony of Burgundy headed an embassy which visited both Milan and Naples, enemies themselves although united to some extent through having a common ally in Burgundy. Galeazzo Maria was most anxious that a solemn Burgundian embassy should be sent formally to congratulate him on the conclusion of the treaty of Moncalieri. Anthony had set out before this alliance had been proclaimed (that is to say, before April) and, after passing through Milan in March, he went on to Naples. Before he was due to return through Milan, Galeazzo Maria told Panigarola to inform Charles that, while he would honour Anthony as befitted his rank, he still insisted on the sending of a separate congratulatory embassy to Milan alone, in accordance with Italian usage. Anthony's mission was insufficient in itself, he wrote, and there was no shortage of critics in the peninsula who would judge that the Milanese–Burgundian alliance rested on insecure foundations if this separate embassy was not sent.[212] His reception of Anthony on his return through Milan in July was noticeably less warm than that given there on his outward journey.

Another contrast lay in the wording of mandates. As a preliminary to negotiations for an alliance between Milan and Burgundy, Guillaume de Rochefort and Orfeo dei Cenni exchanged mandates at Moncalieri on 22 January 1475. Guillaume considered his counterpart's mandate very ample, but Orfeo thought the Burgundian's was rather brief. In it Charles merely stated that he was appointing Guillaume as his proctor empowered to conclude an alliance with Milan, while offering if necessary to send a fuller mandate, provided that Yolande of Savoy, the mediator of the proposed alliance, agreed. Orfeo, who sent a copy of the mandate to Milan presumably for his master's approval, also remarked that Charles had not even signed this document. Clearly the Milanese were on the watch for possible trickery. Guillaume replied that it was not his master's custom to sign letters patent, but, if Galeazzo Maria wanted the document signed, then he could willingly have two or ten signatures; in the meantime he offered to show Orfeo the missives sent to him and to Yolande of Savoy, because these did bear the duke's signature.[213]

As far as diplomatic strategy was concerned, Charles did not go short of the best Italian advice. King Ferrante's right-hand man Diomede Carafa urged the Burgundian ambassadors visiting Naples in February 1472 to advise their master to ally neither with Louis XI nor with Louis' brother Charles of France, but to keep both in hopeful suspense in order to extract the maximum advantage from each. Carafa recommended further that the duke should promise rather than give his daughter's hand in marriage to prospective allies. The duke's record, however, shows that he needed little encouragement to adopt such a policy. He told Ferrante in 1472 that he was not sincere in offering his daughter's hand to Duke Nicholas of Anjou, not least because he was dangling the same prospect before Charles of France at this very time.[214]

The duke of Milan too ventured on occasions to give his Burgundian ally the benefit of his diplomatic wisdom. In April 1475 he advised Charles — then seemingly embroiled irretrievably in the siege of Neuss — that he ought to do as the Italians do when they had a disagreement with three parties: make peace with one, truce with the second and war against the third. In other words, never fight on more than one front at a time. Certainly, Charles managed to isolate Duke René of Lorraine diplomatically before conquering his duchy in the second half of 1475, but it would seem that at this time he was following his habitual policy when preparing territorial expansion rather than his Milanese ally's advice, since he had achieved a similar diplomatic success before the Guelders campaign in 1473.[215] Galeazzo Maria constantly warned him against trusting the king of France but, again, Charles hardly needed such precautionary advice to inflame his suspicions of Louis. The duke of Milan was more nervous than his ally about the outcome of the Swiss campaign. Eventually, towards the end of May 1476, he pleaded with him to avoid armed combat and the risk of leaving his allies exposed; he told him the Swiss were not worth defeating anyway. This advice, which of course Charles did not take, was not, in any case, the product solely of the Italian preference for diplomatic over military methods, for Matthias Corvinus, king of Hungary, had already written to Charles on 7 May urging him to break off the Swiss campaign, since its potential dangers were far greater than any benefits which could be gained; this letter arrived only after the battle of Murten had proved his analysis correct.[216]

Charles, then, was not so easily influenced as some Italians either hoped or feared; instead, as Panigarola noted, he was determined to be his own master.[217] Moreover, although he was on terms of intimacy with men such as Francesco d'Este, Tommaso Portinari and perhaps also Giacomo dei Vischi for several years before his accession in 1467, nonetheless it is true to say that the main influx of Italians did not take place until halfway through his reign and that, therefore, he was exposed to the fullest expression of Italian ideas only comparatively late in life, when he was in his late thirties and when he had already formed his own views on the practice and philosophy of politics through playing a leading part in the Burgundian government for several years — not only, of course, after 1467, but also earlier. Though he was dedicated to the pursuit of fame and glory,[218] his concept of them was not the same as that of the leading Italian rulers of his generation. Theirs was not based solely or even mainly on the achievement of military conquest. It revolved at least as much around the cultivation of the arts of peace, such as the development of a refined and noble mind, the patronage of culture, the foundation and expansion of libraries, and the erection of monuments and buildings. Of course, this sharp contrast can be modified somewhat. Though Charles wished to be remembered most of all as a triumphant soldier, he did have a passion for music and for certain types of literature, and the splendour of his court was designed more to spread his fame than to satisfy any personal craving for luxury. As for the Italians, the ruler of his generation who most set the fashion regarding types of patronage was Federigo da Montefeltro, count and later duke of Urbino, but his patronage was made possible in the first place only by the money he had earned as a mercenary captain, that is to say, from the profits of war.[219] Even so, if we turn again to the two Italians whose correspondence has provided a large amount of the material used in this chapter, namely the duke of Milan and his ambassador at the Burgundian court, we find that, far from encouraging Charles the Bold's desire to emulate the conquerors of classical times, they found it incomprehensible that he should knowingly risk death in battle against the Swiss merely for the sake of vindicating his honour.

This contrast between the duke of Burgundy's idea of true fame and that of the Italians leads us to the point that, if his diplomatic technique differed in important respects from theirs, the reason was that his diplomatic strategy was based on different premises. When studying the development of Renaissance diplomacy in Europe as a whole, the historian is naturally inclined to emphasise the common features, but, in his search for similarities, he should nonetheless not overlook the differences that remained.[220] Diplomacy has sometimes been defined as little more than the extension of war by other means. Such a definition would not have been alien to the age in which Charles lived, but his conception of the relationship between military and diplomatic activity differed significantly from that of contemporary Italian rulers. As between diplomacy and military might, Charles attached more importance than did the Italians to the latter, both because he had the resources to do so and because he had greater opportunities for expansion, especially on his eastern and northern borders. He was wont to justify his wars as defensive, undertaken not from personal or dynastic ambition but in the general interests of his subjects. We should not, however, be misled by such protestations. Vaughan states that, from the sources he studied, it emerges over and over again that Charles the Bold fancied himself as a world conqueror; indeed, while he was engaged in talks with the emperor at Trier in 1473, the view gained ground in distant Piedmont that *'Bergogna debbia signorezare tutt'el mondo'*.[221]

It may be said in conclusion that, from the foregoing comparison between Burgundian and Italian diplomatic techniques, Charles does not emerge unfavourably. That view would probably surprise only those who still regard Valois Burgundy and its dukes as anachronistic political dinosaurs hovering on the verge of extinction as a new age dawned,[222] not to mention those who treat 'Machiavellianism' as if it were solely the product of Renaissance Italy.[223] When this has been allowed, however, one should not overlook the fundamental distinctions remaining between Burgundy and Italy regarding the aims and machinery of diplomacy. In the so-called golden age of peace and independence which Italy enjoyed from about 1454 to 1494 in comparison with earlier and later epochs, diplomacy almost obtained the status of an end in itself for the insecure rulers of the peninsula, who regarded caution as a virtue appropriate to their situation. Charles the Bold, on the other hand, kept the methods of diplomacy, however refined they may by now have become, firmly in their place as a means by which he could help himself to encompass his wider ambitions: territorial expansion, the reduction of urban autonomy, the paralysis or overthrow of his enemies, and election to the imperial throne.

* * *

Three main points emerge from this chapter. With regard to Renaissance diplomacy, it is clear that some sources are more valuable than others for the elucidation of diplomatic practice. If we wish to see how Italian diplomats went about their task at this period, then it is necessary to go beyond treatises and instructions to the actual correspondence of the diplomats themselves in order to gain access to an abundance of evidence of the most direct kind. The survival of large amounts of such material for the reign of Charles the Bold, itself tangible testimony to the intimacy of his relations with the rulers of Italy, gives an invaluable opportunity to study Italian diplomats at work in an ultramontane court. Our sources show that formal speeches and the negotiation of treaties took up far less of the ambassador's time, and were regarded as being less important, than the routine protection of his master's interests on a day-to-day basis in matters such as relations with third parties, commerce, the surveillance of exiles and the relaying of detailed, accurate and up-to-date information. What was required was not so much oratorical ability or social status as the arts of insinuation and persuasion. In order to succeed it was necessary to know which men enjoyed the duke's confidence and to make allies of them. In particular, the ambassador had to win the trust and affection of the duke himself. Nonetheless, the ambassador's power to influence events was subject to strict limits. Although ultimately he was free to exercise his judgement in reporting current affairs, his reaction to them was regulated by detailed instructions from home. Above all, some factors remained beyond his control, namely his master's attitude towards the duke of Burgundy and the duke's assessment of that attitude. Moreover, while Charles showed the Italian ambassadors much formal honour and personal consideration, this was almost certainly outweighed in their eyes by the less pleasant aspects of their calling: malice, intrigue, expense, fatigue and danger.

Secondly, the presence of Italian ambassadors at the Burgundian court and their activities there tell us much about the political situation of the major states of the Italian peninsula. Charles the Bold's reign lay within what was, for Italy, a comparatively peaceful period. Nonetheless, Italian rulers did not then enjoy a state of completely untroubled tranquillity. The need for reliable information was pressing precisely because that tranquillity could be threatened by the pretensions of ultramontane rulers. The intention of the league of the Italian powers formed in the 1450s had been to present a united front to the ultramontanes, but in the years of Charles the Bold's reign that unity showed itself to be far from solid. Italian rulers took sides with ultramontane princes against their neighbours. The rivalry of Milan with first Venice and then Naples was played out at the Burgundian court. Similarly, the presence there of exiles from every part of Italy exhibited for all to see the degree of political instability in the peninsula and the possibility of a welcome being given to outside intervention.

Finally, diplomacy provides one yardstick by which to measure Charles the Bold's susceptibility to Italian influences. Through his contacts with Italy and the Italians, he had an incomparable opportunity to study and imitate Italian methods. Yet, despite his fondness for individual Italian ambassadors and his admiration for certain Italian rulers, his methods were influenced to only a limited extent by theirs. The historian may, of course, choose either to emphasise those areas in which Charles *did* display Italianate characteristics, or insist on the degree to which he remained faithful to Burgundian precedents. But one thing at least is certain: namely, that the question cannot finally be resolved without further research and the discovery of new evidence, some of which this chapter has made a provisional attempt to supply.

Notes

1. The material surviving in Naples from the Aragonese period had already been severely depleted before the further destruction wreaked in 1943: Ilardi, 'Fifteenth-century diplomatic documents', 94–8 [= 'I documenti diplomatici del secolo XV', in his *Studies in Italian Renaissance Diplomatic History*, no. VI (pp. 385–7)]; V. Ilardi and M.L. Shay, 'Italy', in *The new guide to the diplomatic archives of western Europe*, ed. D.H. Thomas and L.M. Case (Philadelphia, 1975), 165–211 (pp. 186–8, 206–7); P.F. Palumbo, *Medio Evo meridionale* (Rome, 1978), 346–50. The best general account of Ferrante's diplomatic

activities in this period is by E. Pontieri, 'La politica estera di Ferrante d'Aragona: dalla fine della prima sollevazione dei baroni alla liberazione di Otranto dai Turchi (1465–1481)', in his *Per la storia del regno di Ferrante I*, 2nd edtn (Naples, 1969), 209–369 [= Chap. IV].

2. On 21 June 1475, Galeazzo Maria wrote from Pavia to Yolande of Savoy that Ferrante, '*non contento de la parte sua, vole mettere el naso per tutto et tenere ambasatori ad casa de caschuno per mostrare de governare ogni homo*' (ASM 492).

3. AOGV, III, 31–2ᵛ, summarised by de Reiffenberg, *Histoire*, 72–3 (Charles) and (Louis); Walsh, 'The coming of humanism', 183 note 157.

4. *Carteggi*, II, no. 376; Eubel, *Hierarchia*, II, 118, and others, assumed that Bertini, because his successor as bishop of Capaccio was not appointed until 22 March 1476, did not die until early in 1476. The date of his birth is not known but it seems that at his death he could be regarded as still relatively young: Vespasiano, *Vite*, I, 290. By way of comparison his brother Domenico was born in about 1417 and died in 1506: S. Andreucci, 'Domenico Bertini e la pieve di S. Giovanni Battista a Gallicano', *La provincia di Lucca*, 10 (1970), 44–51 (pp. 45, 46, 50 note 3).

5. On his return to Naples in 1473 he visited the duke of Milan at Vigevano on 30 November. Shortly after leaving, he learnt of certain seizures by the duke of Lucchese goods — silk cloth — and wrote to him to ask for their release and '*havere per recomendata la mia patria*'. The letter is undated but is filed in Milan, Archivio di Stato, Autografi, 39/7, along with his letter from Novara of 29 November 1473 accepting the duke's invitation to visit him; their meeting is described by Simonetta, *Diarii*, 63. His brother Domenico was born at Gallicano and became a citizen of Lucca in 1448: Andreucci, 'Domenico Bertini', 45.

6. There are brief biographical sketches by F. Snieders in *Dictionnaire d'histoire et de géographie ecclésiastique*, VIII (1935), col. 1613, by I. Walter in *DBI*, IX (1967), 540–2, and by Vespasiano da Bisticci, *Le vite*, I, 289–90.

7. *Fonti aragonesi*, III/2, 127 (no. 863).

8. *Carteggi*, I, no. 164; Vaughan, *Charles*, 8; Molinet, *Chroniques*, I, 171 (however, no Neapolitan ambassador is mentioned in the account of the 1468 meeting by de Reiffenberg, *Histoire*, 49–53).

9. Vespasiano, *Vite*, I, 289; *CSP Milan*, I, 128 (no. 169).

10. Cusin, 'Impero, Borgogna' (1936), 42; Simonetta, *Diarii*, 63. This was not hearsay, because both men had spoken with him personally in November 1473. However, it is certainly a mistake by Bittmann (*Ludwig XI. und Karl der Kühne*, I/2, 570) to say that he did not arrive at the Burgundian court until *after* the conclusion of the alliance between Ferrante and Charles, that is, not until 1471. If Vespasiano was correct in saying that he stayed in England '*alquanto tempo*' before going to Burgundy (*Vite*, I, 289), then Bertini may have been the unnamed Neapolitan ambassador who arrived in London some time in 1467: William Gregory's *Chronicle of London*, in *The historical collections of a citizen of London in the fifteenth century*, ed. J. Gairdner (London, 1876), 55–239 (p. 235). There is some support for this in a letter which Bertini wrote to his friend the cardinal of Pavia (Ammanati-Piccolomini, *Epistolae et commentarii*, 160–2). The letter does not indicate where he was writing from, although he mentions that he is now in farthest Gaul, having only recently left Italy. The date too is

missing, but there is a clue in that he states he had left Italy just after King George Podiebrad of Bohemia had been declared a heretic, an event that took place in December 1466.

11. Simonetta, *Diarii*, 63. For the next sentence see Francesco Maletta to the duke of Milan, Naples, 19 January, 18 March and 3 June 1474 (ASM 225); Bertini to Lorenzo de' Medici, Bolsena, 23 March 1474 (ASF, MAP, XXX, 198); and Vander Linden, *Itinéraires de Charles*, 61.

12. For example, that cited in the previous note and those published in *Carteggi*, I, nos. 203, 219, 259; see also Walsh, 'Vespasiano', 423 note 40.

13. Biographical sketch in Cerioni, *La diplomazia sforzesca*, I, 204–5.

14. Like Giovanni Olzina and perhaps like the Gabriel and Ramon (Raimundo) de Palomar, who were Aragonese lawyers employed by Alfonso in Naples between 1448 and 1454: *Fonti aragonesi*, III/1, 148, 211; A.F.C. Ryder, *The kingdom of Naples under Alfonso the Magnanimous* (Oxford, 1976), 116, 117, 145 note 62, 206. This form was not, however, exclusively Iberian. For instance, a Pietro Palomar was a Genoese merchant engaged in trade with Catalonia in 1404: M. Del Treppo, *I mercanti catalani e l'espansione della Corona Aragonese nel secolo XV* (Naples, 1967), 221, 222, 546. On the grounds of age, lay status and, above all, lack of contemporary comment, it seems unlikely that our ambassador can be identified with the Juan de Palomar, archdeacon of Barcelona, who created such a stir when representing Alfonso at the Council of Basel in the 1430s.

15. The four following examples come from letters of his which have been published: 'Io. Palomer' (1473: Colombo, *Iolanda*, 269); 'Johannes Palomar', 'Jo. Palomar' and 'Jo. Plombari' (1474 and 1476: *Carteggi*, I, nos. 208, 213; II, no. 469).

16. Simonetta, *Diarii*, 55, 60; Zaccaria Saggio to Lodovico Gonzaga, Pavia, 1 October 1473 (AG 1624); Antonio d'Appiano to the duke of Milan, Ivrea, 8 November 1473 (ASM 490); Vander Linden, *Itinéraires de Charles*, 57; Palombaro to the duke of Milan, Thionville, 6 December 1473 (ASM 490). For the next sentence see *Carteggi*, I, no. 213.

17. His activities in this period are mentioned frequently in the dispatches published in *Carteggi* and *Dépêches . . . Charles-le-Hardi*. For what follows see *Carteggi*, II, no. 629; L. Cerioni, 'La politica italiana di Luigi XI e la missione di Filippo di Commynes (giugno–settembre 1478)', *ASL*, 77 (1950), 58–156 (pp. 122–3); and AOGV, IV, f. 31ᵛ.

18. This assumes that the king who sent him to the Burgundian court can be identified as Ferrante of Naples rather than as Ferdinand, son of King John II of Aragon; the king in question is somewhat confusingly described as '*le roy ferant de cecille*' (AGR CC 1924, f. 204ᵛ). He came to Charles '*pour affaires secretz*' and was paid 125 *livres* in September 1469 to defray his expenses for coming from and returning to '*cecille*'.

19. Ferrante to Galeazzo Maria, 19 March 1470 (ASM 218: letters of credence for Antonello); Rodolfo Gonzaga to the marchioness of Mantua, Saint-Omer, 10 July (AG 2100). Bertini was later to remark that Charles seemed to set little store by these and other Neapolitan gifts of horses: Sforza Bettini to Galeazzo Maria, Ham, 17 May 1471 (ASM 538).

20. Again, as with Palomar/Palombaro, the name could suggest either an Italian or an Iberian origin. We can trace his career back to the later years of Alfonso the Magnanimous. For example, in September 1455 he was master of the king's lodgings: Ryder, *The kingdom of Naples*, 81 note 177.

21. Zaccaria Saggio to Lodovico Gonzaga, Milan, 24 March 1470 (AG 1623), reporting conversations with Betes, who had recently arrived in Milan.

22. The duke of Milan to Sforza Bettini in France, Gonzaga, 22 July 1471 (ASM 538); Francesco Maletta to the duke, Naples, 18 November 1471 (ASM 220) and 22 March 1472 (ASM 221); Vander Linden, *Itinéraires de Charles*, 38, 39. For what follows see *Carteggi*, II, no. 393; Simonetta, *Diarii*, 191; Leonardo Botta to the duke of Milan, Venice, 29 March 1476 (ASM 363). Edward IV had maintained good relations with Ferrante almost from the start of his reign, but Betes's two embassies were overlooked by Scofield, *The life and reign of Edward IV*, and also by C. Ross, *Edward IV* (London, 1974), who, in this respect, adds nothing to Scofield. Betes was still alive in June 1484: N. Barone, 'Notizie storiche raccolte dai registri "Curiae" della cancelleria aragonese', *ASPN*, 13 (1888), 745–7 (p. 771).

23. Ryder, *The kingdom of Naples*, especially 228–30 (other references are listed in the index on p. 401); for his career under Ferrante to 1468 see *Codice aragonese*, ed. A.A. Messer (Paris, 1912), 161. The Burgundian embassy of 1474–1476 disproves Ryder's implication (p. 224) that Olzina died in about 1467, unless we are dealing with two separate men with identical names and very similar careers.

24. Ettore Spina, *Lista de quelli vennero con lo Ill.mo D.no Federico de Aragonia*, copy (19th century?) in Naples, Biblioteca della Società Napoletana di Storia Patria, *fascio* XXVI, C5, no. 11, ff. 11–12 (f. 11); I am indebted to Professore Alfredo Parente, Librarian of the Society, for sending me a photocopy. Olzina was described as Federico's treasurer also by Simonetta, *Diarii*, 152.

25. *Carteggi*, I, no. 282, II, nos. 342, 382.

26. ASV, SS, XXIII, ff. 60 (translated in *CSP Venice*, I, no. 407), 77–7ᵛ, 89ᵛ; Gerardo Colli to the duke of Milan, Venice, 31 December 1467 (ASM 353); unsigned letter perhaps to Borso d'Este, from Bruges, written between 12 and 31 December 1467 (Modena, AS, Avvisi dall'Estero, 1, no. 61); Vander Linden, *Itinéraires de Charles*, 6; Perret, *Histoire*, I, 480–1.

27. ASV, SS, XXIII, ff. 147–7ᵛ, 154–4ᵛ; XXIV, ff. 23ᵛ–4, 27–7ᵛ, 34–4ᵛ, 57ᵛ, 61–1ᵛ, 105ᵛ, 114–15ᵛ, 145; Van der Linden, *Itinéraires de Charles*, 16, 25; Perret, *Histoire*, I, 512–13, 523–4, 528–34, 548–9, 555.

28. Biographical sketch by A. Ventura and M. Pecoraro in *DBI*, VIII (1966), 103–9. Additional material, especially on his literary activities, is given by C.H. Clough, *Pietro Bembo's library*, 2nd edtn (London, 1971), 1, 3–4, and 'The library of Bernardo and Pietro Bembo', *Book Collector*, 33 (1984), 305–31; by N.R. Ker, *Medieval manuscripts in British libraries*, 4 vols (Oxford, 1969–92), II (1977), 700–1, 723–4, 741–2, 748, 756–8, 760–5; and by N. Giannetto, 'Un'orazione inedita di Bernardo Bembo per Cristoforo Moro', *Atti dell'Istituto Veneto di scienze, lettere ed arti. Classe di scienze morali, lettere ed arti*, 140 (1981–2), 257–88.

29. ASV, SS, f. 27.

30. London, British Library, Additional MS 41068A, f. 206ᵛ/247ᵛ (old/new foliation). On this manuscript see G. Neilson, 'A Venetian's commonplaces', *Athenaeum*, no. 3556 (21 December 1895), 871–2; E. Levi, 'Lo zibaldone di Bernardo Bembo', *Rassegna bibliografica della letteratura italiana*, 55 (1896), 46–50; and *British Museum. Catalogue of additions to the manuscripts 1921–1925* (London, 1950), 219–20.

31. ASV, SS, XXV, ff. 43–4ᵛ; the section on Venetian commerce in England is translated in *CSP Venice*, I, 129 (no. 436).

32. London, British Library, Add. 41068A, f. 101ᵛ/142ᵛ; Neilson, 'A Venetian's commonplaces', 872; Levi, 'Lo zibaldone di Bernardo Bembo', 49.

33. Perret, *Histoire*, II, 38 note 1. For what follows see ASV, SS, XXV, ff. 76–6ᵛ; Vander Linden, *Itinéraires de Charles*, 61; and Simonetta, *Diarii*, 123.

34. ASV. SS, XXVI, ff. 81–1ᵛ.

35. Simonetta, *Diarii*, 108–9. For what follows see Perret, *Histoire*, II, 59; *Carteggi*, II, no. 342; Vander Linden, *Itinéraire de Charles*, 71; and Simonetta, *Diarii*, 187.

36. Ilardi, 'Fifteenth-century diplomatic documents', 73.

37. To Doge Niccolò Tron, Bruges, 12 December 1472, in ASM 515. Also in ASM 515 are the following letters from the same period: Bembo to his father and brother, both dated Bruges, 13 November 1472; and five letters of Petrus Blanchus (probably Bembo's secretary), all dated Bruges, 17 November 1472, to his mother, father and brother, to Lodovico Stella, secretary to the doge, and to Hieronymus, a scribe in Stella's office. BL, Add. 41068A contains four references to his Burgundian embassy: ff. 43ᵛ/82ᵛ, 101ᵛ/142ᵛ, 206ᵛ/247ᵛ and 252/293 (an apparently admiring reference to Charles from 1472, Bembo's arrival at court in 1471, his departure from Venice in 1471 and Charles's investiture by the emperor with the duchy of Guelders in 1473).

38. *Carteggi*, I, no. 260.

39. The contents of Contarini's letter to Doge Pietro Mocenigo from Besançon, 29 January 1476 (summarised in that of Leonardo Botta to the duke of Milan from Venice, 15 February 1476, in ASM 361) are corroborated by Panigarola's account of Contarini's audience with Charles (*Carteggi*, II, no. 396).

40. Published by Perret, *Histoire*, II, 376–7, from ASV, SS, XXVII, ff. 57ᵛ–8.

41. Leonardo Botta to the duke of Milan, Venice, 23 February 1476 (ASM 361). Giacomo was later ambassador at the papal and imperial courts in 1477 and 1478: Perret, *Histoire*, II, 99 note 2; G. Paparelli, *Callimaco Esperiente* (Salerno, 1971), 142, 143.

42. Botta to the duke of Milan, Venice, 4 June 1476 (ASM 363); Perret, *Histoire*, II, 84–9; ASV, SS, XXVII, ff. 90–90ᵛ.

43. Vaughan, *Charles*, 165.

44. C. Santoro, *Gli uffici del dominio sforzesco (1450–1500)* (Milan, 1947), 9 note 8; G. Chittolini, 'Infeudazione e politica feudale nel ducato visconteo-sforzesco', *Quaderni storici*, 19 (1972), 57–130 (pp. 106, 129–30).

45. *Dispatches*, I, xlv–vii, li.

46. *Carteggi*, I, nos. 157, 159.

47. Vaughan, *Charles*, 74. For what follows see *Carteggi*, I, no. 163.

48. Biographical sketches in *Dépêches . . . Louis XI*, II, 108 note 1, in Cerioni, *La*

diplomazia sforzesca, I, 205–6, in G. Soldi Rondinini, 'Giovan Pietro Panigarola e il "reportage" moderno', *Archiv des historischen Verein des Kantons Bern*, 60 (1976), 135–54 (pp. 137–8) and in *Dispatches*, III, l–lviii. See also Y. Cazaux, 'Charles de Bourgogne devant Jean-Pierre Panigarola, ambassadeur milanais, et devant sa mort', *PCEEB*, 20 (1980), 45–53. Neither the year of his birth nor that of his death is known, although, as we shall see, he was perhaps in his early or mid-thirties in 1475 and he was still alive in 1485 (or 1489, according to Soldi Rondinini). It is worth mentioning that his usual signature was *Panicharolla*, not *Panigarola*.

49. *Carteggi*, I, no. 241.
50. Lodovico il Moro.
51. Simonetta, *Diarii*, 153; *Carteggi*, I, no. 255.
52. *Carteggi*, II, nos. 648, 649; Giovanni Bianchi to the duke of Milan, Turin, 8 September (ASM 496); and the duke to Francesco Pietrasanta, his ambassador in France, from Galliate, 10 September 1476. Panigarola, writing to the duke of Milan from Oulx near Susa on 5 September (*Carteggi*, II, no. 650), gave an interesting account of his departure from the Burgundian court. At first Charles was reluctant to let him go and relented only when he became convinced that Galeazzo Maria had irrevocably ended their alliance. He then gave Panigarola 400 florins, apologising that he was unable to give a sum more commensurate both with his love for Galeazzo Maria and with Panigarola's own deserts. On leaving, Panigarola was allotted 400 men-at-arms and 50 crossbowmen to escort him through Savoy to Dauphiné.
53. *Carteggi, passim.*
54. *Carteggi*, ii, no. 377.
55. Biographical sketches of these in Cerioni, *La diplomazia sforzesca*, I, 184, 203–4, 253–4, and (Alfieri) in Santoro, *Uffici*, 31, 54.
56. *Carteggi*, II, no. 403.
57. *Carteggi*, II, no. 428.
58. *Carteggi*, II, nos. 434, 439, 442, 444, 446, 459. The three ambassadors, plus Alfieri, had reached the comparative safety of Susa by 12 March. Pallavicino and Visconti arrived at Vigevano on 16 March, and Grimaldi probably followed them the next day: Simonetta, *Diarii*, 197. On the embassy see also Dürr, 'Galeazzo Maria Sforza', 339–43, and Zambarbieri, 'Milano e la Borgogna. II', 1–2.
59. Biographical sketch in Cerioni, *La diplomazia sforzesca*, I, 252–3. For what follows see the two articles by Cusin, 'I rapporti tra la Lombardia e l'impero', 255–86, and 'Impero, Borgogna', *passim.*
60. Some of his dispatches are printed in *Dépêches . . . Charles-le-Hardi, passim*, a handful in *Carteggi*; others, mostly from the years 1470–3, by Colombo, *Iolanda*, 239–41, 246–60, 270–4, 295–6; some extracts and translations in *CSP Milan*, I, nos. 291, 304, 311, 314, 330, 323–3. For the originals see ASM 487–97. Biographical sketches by N. Raponi in *DBI*, III (1961), 535–7, and by Cerioni, *La diplomazia sforzesca*. I, 129.
61. Paquet, 'Une ébauche', 62–144.
62. ADN B 2093/66,970; A.I. Cameron, *The Apostolic Camera and Scottish benefices, 1418–1488* (Oxford, 1934), 245. He died on 10 December 1479,

having been promoted bishop of Terni in August 1472 and transferred to Pesaro in May 1475: Eubel, *Hierarchia*, II, 186, 236.

63. F. Saxl, 'A Marsilio Ficino manuscript written in Bruges in 1475, and the alum monopoly of the popes', *JWCI*, 1 (1937), 61–2. This manuscript is now in Florence: Kristeller, *Iter Italicum*, I, 229–30. Albergati died in 1484: Infessura, *Diario della città di Roma*, 121–2; P. Paschini, *Roma nel Rinascimento* (Bologna, 1940), 265.

64. In May 1476 the bishop of Modena's legatine powers were extended so as to cover not only France but also the lands of the dukes of Burgundy, Brittany and Savoy: Schlecht, *Andrea Zamometić*, 155. He seems, however, to have visited Charles only once, briefly, in March 1476: *Carteggi*, II, nos. 472, 478. Andrea dei Spiriti continued to work in the papal bureaucracy under Innocent VIII and Alexander VI: E. Brouette, 'Les clercs "mensiers" de la Chambre apostolique sous les pontificats d'Innocent VIII et d'Alexandre VI (1484–1503)', in *Économies et sociétés au Moyen Age. Mélanges offerts à Édouard Perroy* (Paris, 1973), 581–7 (p. 583 note 10).

65. R.A. Maulde-la-Clavière, *La diplomatie au temps de Machiavel*, 3 vols (Paris, 1892–3), I, 343–52; B. Behrens, 'Treatises on the ambassador written in the fifteenth and early sixteenth centuries', *EHR*, 51 (1936), 616–27. Biographical sources for what follows are those cited in the preceding sections, except where otherwise stated.

66. Cicco Simonetta to Sacramoro in Rome, Milan, 27 April 1472 (ASM 72). Olzina describes himself as 'Johannes Olzina *prothonotarius*' in a document written on behalf of Alfonso the Magnanimous in 1451: J. Ferguson, *English diplomacy 1422–1461* (Oxford, 1972), 226.

67. In the spring of 1474, he complained to the Neapolitan ambassador that John II of Aragon had slighted him, when ratifying his inclusion as a Burgundian ally in the duke's recent truces with Louis XI, by sending a higher-ranking envoy to France than to Burgundy; nor was he mollified by Bertini's explanation that substance mattered more than appearance: *Carteggi*, I, no. 219. There were, of course, other reasons for friction between Charles and John II.

68. '. . . *a me poi aparte disse che ad bon mercatante non conviene si non un bon motto* . . .': *Carteggi*, II, no. 502 (signifying that he would not be averse to Galeazzo Maria seeking to increase his influence in Piedmont). It was as a merchant that Panigarola had first gone to France in 1464.

69. Letters from Venice to Galeazzo Maria by Gerardo Colli, 9 July 1471 (ASM 357) and Leonardo Botta, 10 and 27 March 1474 (ASM 359).

70. T. Frenz, 'Die Gründung des Abbreviatorenkollegs durch Pius II. und Sixtus IV', in *Miscellanea in onore di Monsignor Martino Giusti*, 2 vols (Città del Vaticano, 1978), I, 297–329 (p. 310).

71. Some of the corrections appear to have been written by Onofrio himself: Santa Croce, *Mémoire*, xxix–xxx.

72. F. Di Bernardo, *Un vescovo umanista alla corte pontificia. Giannantonio Campano (1429–1477)* (Rome, 1975), 431.

73. D. Hay, *Italian clergy and Italian culture in the fifteenth century* (London, 1973), 6–7, 10.

74. Vespasiano da Bisticci, *Vite*, I, 290.

75. A. Soría, *Los humanistas de la corte de Alfonso el Magnánimo* (Granada, 1956), 52–5, 97, 129, 162, 244, 277; A.F.C. Ryder, 'Antonio Beccadelli: a humanist in government', in *Cultural aspects of the Italian Renissance. Essays in honour of Paul Oskar Kristeller*, ed. C.H. Clough (Manchester–New York, 1976), 123–40 (pp. 125, 131, 133, 137 note 7, 139 notes 44, 65); Ryder, *The kingdom of Naples*, 224, 229.

76. Santoro, *Uffici*, 13. For the rest of the sentence see *Dispatches*, I, xlv–vii, li, and L. Frati, 'Due umanisti bolognesi alla corte ducale di Milano', *ASI*, 5th ser., 43 (1909), 359–74 (359–67).

77. L. Martines, *Lawyers and statecraft in Renaissance Florence* (Princeton, N.J., 1968), especially Chapters 8 and 11.

78. For Grimaldi see *Carteggi*, II, no. 439. For the Valenciennes speeches see my 'Charles the Bold and the crusade', 55–6, 59, 60, 81–2. Both Bembo and Bertini had already demonstrated in Italy their flair for public speaking. For Bembo (1455, 1462, 1464) see Ventura and Pecoraro in *DBI*, VIII (1966), 104, and Giannetto, 'Un'orazione inedita'. For Bertini see (1452) P. Sambin, 'Il Panormita e il dono d'una reliquia di Livio', *IMU*, 1 (1958), 276–81 (p. 277) — also Kristeller, *Iter Italicum*, I, 320 — and (1465) *Nuovi documenti per la storia del Rinascimento*, ed. T. de Marinis and A. Perosa (Florence, 1970), 118–28.

79. E. Santini, *Firenze e i suoi 'oratori' nel Quattrocento* (Milan etc, 1922), Chap. 4; D. Hay, *The Italian Renaissance in its historical background*, 2nd edtn (Cambridge, 1977), 157.

80. Panigarola also knew Latin and we are indebted to him for recording a quotation of Lucan (*Pharsalia*, I.281) by Charles in 1476: *Dispatches*, III, lvi, 132–5, *Carteggi*, II, no. 477, and Zambarbieri, 'Milano e la Borgogna. II', 12 note 139, correcting my mistaken reading of the dispatch in question in my 'Une citation inexacte de Lucain par Charles le Téméraire et Louis XI', *MA*, 86 (1980), 439–51 (pp. 441–2).

81. P. Ghinzoni, 'Spedizione sforzesca in Francia (1465–1466)', *ASL*, 2nd ser., 7 (1890), 314–345 (pp. 337, 344); Ryder, *The kingdom of Naples*, 310; Francesco Maletta to the duke of Milan, Naples, 26 March 1473 (ASM 223).

82. Alfieri and Panigarola were only secretaries, not members, of the Council: Santoro, *Uffici*, 8, 9, 12, 13, 16, 31, 50. Several members of the Panigarola family served in the Sforza bureaucracy, including his brother Aluise, although the most eminent was probably Gottardo, *spenditore ducale* under Galeazzo Maria. P.F. Visconti served in the regency council set up after Galeazzo Maria's assassination and later he was one of the two *Deputati del denaro* first appointed by Lodovico il Moro in 1480: D.M. Bueno de Mesquita, 'The Deputati del denaro in the government of Ludovico Sforza', in *Cultural aspects of the Italian Renaissance. Essays in honour of Paul Oskar Kristeller*, ed. C.H. Clough (Manchester–New York, 1976), 276–98 (pp. 277–8, 288, 292).

83. *Codice aragonese*, ed. Messer, 46–7; Buser, *Die Beziehungen der Mediceer zu Frankreich*, 407.

84. *Dispatches*, III, 220–1, 223 note 5.

85. In addition to *Dispatches*, III, liii, see G. Balbi, 'Le relazioni tra Genova e la Corona d'Aragona dal 1464 al 1478', in *Atti del I° Congresso storico*

Liguria–Catalogna . . . 1969 (Bordighera, 1974), 465–512 (p. 481), Perret, *Histoire*, II, 3, and L. de' Medici, *Lettere*, I, 485–92.

86. *Dispatches*, III, 150–1, 210–11, 302–5, 340–1.

87. In addition to Ventura and Pecoraro in *DBI* see B. Beffa, *Antonio Vinciguerra* (Bern–Frankfurt, 1975), 20–4, 89–91, and Clough, 'The library of Bernardo and Pietro Bembo', 312. But when Bembo returned to Italy from Burgundy in 1474, he was rated by his friends as something of a diplomatic expert, according to the verses of Cristoforo Landini printed by A. Della Torre, 'La prima ambasceria di Bernardo Bembo a Firenze', *GSLI*, 35 (1900), 258–333 (p. 325). Bembo was the owner of a Memling diptych, perhaps acquired during his embassy to Burgundy, while in his subsequent embassy to Florence he may well have commissioned the portrait of Ginevra de' Benci painted by Leonardo da Vinci: J. Fletcher, 'Bernardo Bembo and Leonardo's portrait of Ginevra de' Benci', *Burlington Magazine*, 131 (1989), 811–16. I am indebted to Dr Lorne Campbell for this reference.

88. Marcora, 'Stefano Nardini', 257, 267. For what follows see *Mémoire du légat Onufrius*, 5–6, and Giovanni di Iuzzo in *Cronache e statuti della città di Viterbo*, ed. I. Ciampi (Florence, 1872), 102 note 1.

89. Gerardo Colli to the duke of Milan, 9 July (ASM 357); ASV, SS, XXV, f. 82ᵛ ('. . . *Bernardum Bembum plurimum laudaverunt de prudentia, modestia, aptitudine et optimis moribus . . .*').

90. *Dispatches*, III, lv note 59; Paravicini, *Guy de Brimeu*, 470 note 79.

91. *Dépêches . . . Charles-le-Hardi*, II, 179.

92. We know that Onofrio was 29 in 1448: Eubel, *Hierarchia*, II, 255. For what follows on Panigarola and Bertini see *Carteggi*, I, nos. 260–1, and Vespasiano, *Vite*, I, 290.

93. *Carteggi*, II, nos. 483, 611, 612.

94. The key to his cipher is in Vienna, Österreichische Nationalbibliothek, Codex Vindobonensis 2398 (copy in ASM 516), f. 76v, reproduced in facsimile in F. Tranchedino, *Diplomatische Geheimschriften*, ed. W. Höflechner (Graz, 1970), f. 76ᵛ, and in Cerioni, *La diplomazia sforzesca*, II, f. 76ᵛ. That Panigarola largely wrote his own dispatches is made clear by those he wrote at Lausanne on 5 April and 17 May 1476 (*Carteggi*, II, nos. 496, 570), where he refers to being interrupted while writing by, respectively, Matteo de Clariciis and Guillaume de Rochefort.

95. A handful of his letters, dated Bruges, 17 November 1472, is in ASM 515. According to D.E. Queller, *The office of ambassador in the Middle Ages* (Princeton, N.J., 1967), 187, it was uncommon for Venetian ambassadors actually to write — as opposed to merely signing — their dispatches.

96. ASV, SS, XXVIII, f. 58; Simonetta, *Diarii*, 187; Queller, *The office of ambassador*, 171–2, 185–90. AGR CC 1824, f. 217 contains a curious reference to payments of 6 *livres* 5 *sous* made in November 1469 to certain trumpeters of Venice as a gift for having recently played before Charles the Bold; perhaps this was connected with Dandolo's second embassy. For what follows on Morosini and Tolentis, see Leonardo Botta to the duke of Milan, 10 March 1474 (ASM 359) and Paquet, 'Une ébauche', 135.

97. What follows is based on A. Schaube, 'Zur Entstehungsgeschichte der ständi-

gen Gesandtschaften', *MIÖG*, 10 (1889), 500–2, F. Ernst, 'Über Gesandtschaftswesen und Diplomatie an der Wende vom Mittelalter zur Neuzeit', *AKG*, 33 (1950), 64–95, G. Mattingly, *Renaissance diplomacy* (London, 1962), 55–118, and Queller, *The office of ambassador*, 76–84.

98. By Martines, *Lawyers and statecraft*, 311–14. Indeed, the very hypothesis that it was the resident embassy as such which marked the transition from medieval to modern diplomacy has been questioned by R. Fubini, 'La figura politica dell'ambasciatore negli sviluppi dei regimi oligarchici quattrocenteschi', *Annali della Facoltà di Scienze Politiche dell'Università di Perugia*, 16 (1979–80), 33–59, and 'Appunti sui rapporti diplomatici fra il dominio sforzesco e Firenze medicea', in *Gli Sforza a Milano e in Lombardia e i loro rapporti con gli stati italiani ed europei (1450–1535)* (Milan, 1982), 291–334. Like Martines, however, Fubini derives his arguments largely from a study of Florentine practice.

99. *Dispatches*, I, vii–x1; III, xv–xxxi.

100. The accounts by Schaube ('Zur Entstehungsgschichte', 524–6) and Mattingly (*Renaissance diplomacy*, 97–8, 305), relying as they do only on published sources, are both inaccurate and incomplete, while the claims made for the primacy in this respect of the court of Charles the Bold by Kirk (*History of Charles the Bold*, II, 156–7) err by exaggeration.

101. For more details of their functions see below, 'Functions at court'.

102. *Carteggi*, II, no. 376. For the next sentence see Domenico Malipiero (1428–1515), *Annali veneti*, 238.

103. A.M. Fobe, 'De Spaanse nalatenschap: de ontstaansredenen van de vroegste residerende gezantschappen vanuit de Nederlanden (1492–1506)', *TG*, 85 (1972), 171–9. The case put by L. Chevailler, 'Un sujet des ducs de Savoie ne fut-il pas le premier ambassadeur des temps modernes?' in *Studi in onore di Edoardo Volterra*, 6 vols (Milan, 1971), III, 705–14, for Eusebio Margaria, sent by Duke Louis I of Savoy to Rome in 1460 to stay until recalled ('*orator et ambaxiator noster continuus*') is unconvincing.

104. Commynes, *Mémoires*, I, 218–21; *Dépêches . . . Louis XI*, II, 125, 151–2; Périnelle, 'Dépêches de Nicolas de' Roberti', 440; Ernst, 'Über Gesandtschaftwesen', 76–85; *Dispatches*, I, vi–vii; III, xxii–iii, xxx.

105. De la Marche, *Mémoires*, IV, 5, 184, 186, 189; see also Commynes, *Mémoires*, 154.

106. Chastellain, *Oeuvres*, V (= *Chronique*), 378. The legate is not here named but he was probably Tolentis rather than Santa Croce, because Tolentis also attended the next meeting of the Order in 1473, while Santa Croce did not arrive in Bruges until June. The Neapolitan ambassador was probably Bertini.

107. The legate, though mentioned by several sources, was not named by them. However, he was probably Santa Croce, because the latter was specially invited by the duke to his wedding (*Mémoire*, 37–40), although Tolentis is suggested by Paquet, 'Une ébauche', 47 note 2.

108. AOGV, reg. III, ff. 5, 6^v, 8^v–9^v, 38^v–9, 41^v–4, 47; de Reiffenberg, *Histoire de l'Ordre*, 77–80; Vaughan, *Charles*, 179; Walsh, 'Charles the Bold and the crusade', 55–6, 59, 60, 81. The presence of the ambassadors of the pope, the

king of Naples and the republic of Venice (though their names are not given) is mentioned also in the account of the Valenciennes chapter meeting in Valenciennes, Bibliothèque Municipale, 776, ff. 62–72ᵛ (f. 66ᵛ).

109. See their letters in *Carteggi*, I, nos. 259–60.

110. *Carteggi*, I, nos. 266, 297, 304.

111. *Carteggi*, I, no. 327; II, no. 331. Charles, though not as tall as his lanky father, was by no means short (Vaughan, *Charles*, 156–7), so perhaps Panigarola's description is evidence that he himself was tall. Bertini too had met Edward IV, both in England in about 1467–1468 and during the king's exile in the Low Countries in 1470–1471, when he wrote admiringly to the cardinal of Pavia of Edward's '*humanitas*', gravity, clemency, liberality and piety: Vespasiano, *Vite*, I, 289; Ammanati-Piccolomini, *Epistolae*, ff. 201–1ᵛ.

112. *Carteggi*, II, no. 385. From the first, Panigarola wrote in May 1475 (*Carteggi*, I, no. 297), Charles had given him '*loco digno*' in the presence of the other Italian ambassadors. For the next sentence see *Carteggi*, II, no. 515.

113. Bittmann, *Ludwig XI. und Karl der Kühne*, I/2, 437; II/1, 161 note 213; Paquet, 'Une ébauche', 106; Kirk, *History of Charles the Bold*, II, 265.

114. Referring to the number of foreign ambassadors who came to the Burgundian court at Bruges in 1472, the anonymous author (Anthonis de Roovere?) of the *Excellente cronike van Vlaanderen* (Antwerp, 1531) emphasised (f. clxiiiᵛ) that Charles had an excellent reputation ('fame') among all the kingdoms of the world. See also Vaughan, *Charles*, 179–80, and, in general, J.R. Hale, 'International relations in the West: diplomacy and war', in *The new Cambridge modern history*, ed. G.R. Potter, I (Cambridge, 1962), 259–91 (p. 265). Ferrante, a ruler of far less sound title or splendid ancestry than Charles, also warmly welcomed foreign ambassadors because he felt their presence conferred a measure of legitimacy on his regime, as was noticed by Pieter Bogaert, the Burgundian ambassador in Naples in 1474, who told the Milanese ambassador there that Ferrante now had what he had always wanted, namely ambassadors at his court from every Christian power, save only for the pope and the emperor: Francesco Maletta to the duke of Milan, 19 March 1474 (ASM 225).

115. For example, Tolentis ('*longus sermo*') and Bembo ('*in sermonibus et collocutionibus vobiscum habitis*'): Paquet, 'Une ébauche', 107–8, and ASV, SS, XXV, f. 67.

116. *Carteggi*, I, no. 219 (translated by Vaughan, *Charles*, 288–90). In February 1472 he wrote how he had visited the duke, who was then receiving ambassadors from Louis XI; Charles came across and whispered confidentially in his ear about the proposals they brought (Bittmann, *Ludwig XI. und Karl der Kühne*, I/2, 571).

117. Panigarola wrote to his master in May 1475 (*Carteggi*, I, no. 297) that, after a discussion with him on Italian affairs, Charles had asked him to let Galeazzo Maria know he would appreciate news on these matters, on which he was receiving conflicting reports.

118. For this and what follows see *Carteggi*, I, nos. 258, 304.

119. Cusin, 'I rapporti', 303–4; *Carteggi*, II, no. 382.

120. *Carteggi*, II, no. 448; Charles had sent for Panigarola at daybreak to tell him of

his plans to reassemble his army after his recent defeat at Grandson and to ask him to pass on to his master an urgent request for Milanese troops.

121. *Carteggi*, I, no. 327. For the next sentence see *Carteggi*, II, nos. 477, 492, 523, 618.
122. *Carteggi*, II, no. 556.
123. *Carteggi*, II, nos. 487, 592. For the next sentence see *Carteggi*, II, no. 612.
124. For what follows see *Carteggi*, II, nos. 400, 646.
125. *Dépêches* . . . *Louis XI*, III, 168–9, 242, 313; IV, 139, 218, 244–5; *Dispatches*, III, xxxix.
126. *Lettres de Louis XI*, III, 264–5, 283–6; Perret, *Histoire*, I, 503–4, 508–9; Bittmann, *Ludwig XI. und Karl der Kühne*, I/2, 271–2; *Dispatches*, III, xviii, lii–iii. For the next sentence see Cristoforo da Bollate to the duke of Milan, Senlis, 1 March 1474 (ASM 541) and Francesco Pietrasanta to the same, Tours, 22 August 1476 (ASM 542).
127. Discussed in more detail in my 'Vespasiano da Bisticci'.
128. *Carteggi*, I, no. 327, II, no. 356. The Venetian republic, however, tried to restrict the acceptance of such gifts and honours by its ambassadors: D.E. Queller, *Early Venetian legislation on ambassadors* (Geneva, 1966), 22, 42–3. Fifty silver marks was also the sum Charles gave to the legate Nanni on his departure in June 1475: *Carteggi*, I, no. 327. Panigarola himself was to receive 400 florins when he left in 1476: *Carteggi*, II, no. 650.
129. *Carteggi*, II, no. 649.
130. *Carteggi*, II, nos. 469, 492, 499, 508, 514.
131. Santa Croce, *Mémoire*, 41–4 (translated by Vaughan, *Charles*, 26–7). For what follows see *Carteggi*, I, no. 163.
132. Sforza Bettini to the duke of Milan from Le Mans, 23 August 1470, and from Beauvais, 6 September 1470, and Cicco Simonetta to Sforza from Parma, 15 September 1470 (all in ASM 537).
133. Walsh, 'Vespasiano', 409–10 (Bertini); above, Chapter 2, 'The search for friends' (Tolentis, Aliprandi, Nanni). It was suggested by Paquet ('Une ébauche', 35 note 5) that Tolentis may have undertaken a mission to Venice on Charles's behalf in 1476, but I have found no trace of it.
134. Francesco Maletta to the duke of Milan, Naples, 23 September 1472 (ASM 222), summarising Bembo's lost letter of 19 August.
135. The letter is in ASM 540.
136. Cusin, 'Impero, Borgogna', 41 (Visconti). Some of Pietrasanta's dispatches are in *Dépêches* . . . *Charles-le-Hardi*, I, no. 107; II, nos. 152, 161, 176, 181, 186, 202, 205, 209, 215, 220, 245, 264. In August 1476 he was sent to France to patch up his master's relations with Louis XI, who initially received him favourably: Kendall, *Louis XI*, 307–8, 440; *Dispatches*, I, x; III, xxii.
137. Ammanati-Picolomini, *Epistolae*, ff. 261, 288; Soldi Rondinini, 'Giovan Pietro Panigarola', 141; Zambarbieri, 'Milano e la Borgogna, II', 6–8; Paquet, 'Une ébauche', 83, 86. For the next sentence see the poem dedicated to Charles by Bembo's Riminese friend Giovanni Aurelio Augurello in 1475 published by Della Torre, 'La prima ambasceria', 268–9, and G. Pavanello, *Un maestro del Quattrocento (Giovanni Aurelio Augurello)* (Venice, 1905), 241–2, and E. Narducci, 'Intorno all'autenticità di un codice vaticano contenente il trattato

di Boezia "De consolatione philiosophiae" scritta di mano di Giovanni Boccaccio', *Atti della Accademia Nazionale del Lincei. Memorie della classe di scienze morali, storiche e filologiche*, 8 (1882), 243–63 (p. 243).

138. Walsh, 'Vespasiano', 410–17.

139. See, for example, Behrens, 'Treatises on the ambassador', and Martines, *Lawyers and statecraft*, Chap. 8.

140. In this respect, Maulde-La-Clavière's *La diplomatie au temps de Machiavel* remains unsurpassed as a mine of insight and information (cf Martines, *Lawyers and statecraft*, 383: '. . . on diplomacy as an art and institution in this period, the most important, if curious book ever written . . .').

141. ASV, SS, regs. XXIII–VII cover the period 1467–1477.

142. The ciphers used by Aliprandi (1472–1473, 1474), Palombaro (1473–1474, 1476), Nanni (1474), Panigarola (1475–1476), Visconti, Pallavicino and Grimaldi (1476), Spiriti (1476) and Don Federico (1476) are contained in Vienna, Österreichische Nationalbibliothek, Codex Vindobonieinsis 2398, ff. 68, 71ᵛ, 72, 75, 76ᵛ, 80ᵛ, 81ᵛ, 82, 82ᵛ, and reproduced in facsimile in Tranchedino, *Diplomatische Geheimschriften*, and in Cerioni, *La diplomazia sforzesca*, II.

143. *Carteggi*, I, nos. 258, 261. For the bishop of Metz's help see also *Lorraine et Bourgogne*, 50.

144. *Carteggi*, I, no. 163.

145. *Carteggi*, I, no. 255. Disorder rather than mere delay was what had struck Prospero da Camogli about Philip the Good's court in 1461: *Dispatches*, II, 342 (but see also Vaughan, *Philip the Good*, 164).

146. Bittman, *Ludwig XI. und Karl der Kühne*, II/1, 160. For what follows see *Carteggi*, II, nos. 439, 444.

147. *Carteggi*, II, no. 482.

148. *Carteggi*, II, no. 439. For what follows see *Carteggi*, I, no. 259 (Bertini); *Dagboek van Gent van 1447 tot 1470*, ed. V. Fris, 2 vols (Ghent, 1901–4), II, 224, and ADN B 3433/118,485 (Milanese ambassadors 1469); *Extrait d'une ancienne chronique*, in Commynes, *Mémoires*, ed. Godefroy and Lenglet du Fresnoy, II, 199 (Bembo 1471); and Neilson, 'A Venetian's commonplaces', 872, and Levi, 'Lo zibaldone di Bernardo Bembo', 49 (Bembo's disconcerting first meeting with the duke's pet lioness at a banquet in August 1471).

149. Venice, Archivio di Stato, Libri Commemoralia, XVI, f. 51.

150. *Carteggi*, I, nos. 262, 265; Francesco Maletta to the duke of Milan, Naples, 1 March and 13 April 1475 (ASM 227).

151. For what follows see *Carteggi*, II, nos. 365, 366, 371. Although the truce of Soleuvre bears the date 13 September 1475, negotiations continued, as Panigarola's dispatches make clear, for several weeks afterwards, the delay being caused by diplomatic fencing between Charles and Louis over the duke of Lorraine and the count of Saint-Pol: Walsh, 'Vespasiano', 406–7; S.H. Cuttler, *The law of treason and treason trials in later medieval France* (Cambridge etc, 1981), 225.

152. For this paragraph see Zaccaria Saggio to the marquis of Mantua, Milan, 22 August 1475 (AG 1625); *Carteggi*, II, nos. 334, 360, 363, 383, 561, 573, 590;

the duke of Milan to Leonardo Botta in Venice, 28 July 1476 (ASM 363); Dürr, 'Galeazzo Maria Sforza', 321–2, 325–6.

153. ASM 519 (= *Dépêches . . . Charles-le-Hardi*, II, no. 208).
154. *Carteggi*, I, no. 269.
155. For what follows see *Carteggi*, I, nos. 246, 247, and Antonio d'Appiano to the duke of Milan, Moncalieri, 16 February 1475 (ASM 492).
156. Similarly, Tolentis obtained news in 1472 not only from Guillaume Hugonet and Anthony of Burgundy but also '*per nonnullos intimos et secretos cubicularios sue celsitudine*': Paquet, 'Une ébauche', 91. For what follows see *Carteggi*, II, nos. 366 (Ducaret), 644 (Matteo).
157. For what follows, see *Carteggi*, I, nos. 269, II, nos. 496, 550, 556, 563, 572, 577; and Gregorio di Lagneto to Matteo de Clariciis from Turin, 4 and 20 May 1476 (ASM 519).
158. For what follows, see *Carteggi*, II, nos. 400, 496, 511, 554, 587, 641.
159. *Carteggi*, II, nos. 460, 462.
160. ASV, SS, XXV, ff. 43ᵛ–4 (16 July 1471); Zaccaria Barbaro to Doge Niccolò Tron, Naples, 21 May 1473 (BNMV 8170/VI, 12). For what follows, see ASV, SS, XXVII, f. 10ᵛ (5 April 1475); and *Carteggi*, I, nos. 255, 327.
161. *Carteggi*, I, no. 165; Cristoforo da Bollate to the duke of Milan, Vendôme, 10 October 1473 (ASM 540; see also Bittmann, *Ludwig XI. und Karl der Kühne*, II/1, 161).
162. *Carteggi*, I, no. 265.
163. *Carteggi*, II, no. 376. For what follows, see *Carteggi*, II, nos. 468, 602. Panigarola alleged Neapolitan encouragement of the Genoese exiles in his dispatches of 24 November 1475 and 25 June 1476 (*Carteggi*, II, nos. 376, 613).
164. *Carteggi*, II, no. 469. For what follows, see *Carteggi*, II, 492, 499, 508, 514; d'Appiano to the duke of Milan, Lausanne, 10, 11, 12 and 13 May 1476 (ASM 495); and Dürr, 'Galeazzo Maria Sforza', 357–9.
165. Cristoforo da Bollate to the duke of Milan, Senlis, 26 February 1474 (ASM 541); see also *Dispatches*, III, xxiii–iv; For an example from 1471, see Bittmann, *Ludwig XI. und Karl der Kühne*, I/2, 509.
166. Francesco Maletta to the duke of Milan, Naples, 1 October 1472 (ASM 223). In the following month Ferrante expressed disbelief of the news from France which had been relayed to him by Galeazzo Maria: Barbaro to the doge, Naples, 12 November 1472 (BNMV 8170/IV, 24).
167. ASV, P, 1, no. 26; *Carteggi*, II, nos. 474, 495; ASV, SS, XXV, f. 43ᵛ.
168. *Carteggi*, I, no. 219 (translation in Vaughan, *Charles*, 288); see also Bittmann, *Ludwig XI. und Karl der Kühne*, II/1, 233. Similarly in 1472, when Bertini, having been told confidentially by Charles that he intended to make peace with Louis XI, who had offered him help against two French princes, thought it indiscreet to ask who these princes were: Bittmann, *Ludwig XI. und Karl der Kühne*, I/2, 583.
169. For example, when Charles spoke to Bertini on 2 January 1472, it was the first time since his mother's death on 17 December 1471: Bittmann, *Ludwig XI. und Karl der Kühne*, I/1, 571.
170. *Carteggi*, II, no. 366.
171. *Carteggi*, II, no. 514.

172. *Carteggi*, II, 520.
173. *Carteggi*, II, nos. 425, 473, 488, 492, 504, 508, 514, 519, 533.
174. Rodolfo Gonzaga to the marchioness of Mantua, Ghent, 23 January 1470 (AG 2100). In an earlier incident, an intercepted Burgundian courier was searched without success because he had concealed his letter in a false bottom in one of his shoes: Gerardo Colli to the duke of Milan from Venice, February(?) 1468 (ASM 354).
175. Lodovico mentioned such sources in his letter to Zaccaria Saggio in Milan, 2 July 1475 (AG 2893, lib. LXXVIII, f. 73ᵛ). Several letters on German affairs, some in German, some in Italian, written by Tristano de Saxoduro (Hartfelsen?) to Marchioness Barbara between 1469 and 1475, are in AG 439. A letter of Tristano describing the battle between the imperial and Burgundian forces fought outside Neuss in May 1475, addressed to Lodovico and dated 3 June 1475, is in AG 2187, no. 1150. Galeazzo Maria mentioned his indebtedness to Lodovico for information about the siege of Neuss in his letters to Leonardo Botta in Venice of 3 and 6 July 1475 (ASM 362).
176. The letter is in Mangin, 'Guillaume de Rochefort', appendix 10.
177. For this and the next paragraph see *Carteggi*, II, nos. 519, 527, 528, 533, 535, 537, 540, 543, 553, 567, 574; and the duke of Milan to d'Appiano from Milan, 27 and 30 April 1476, and d'Appiano to the duke from Lausanne, 13 May 1476 (ASM 495).
178. *Carteggi*, II, nos. 360, 527. In 1472 Tolentis had sent a letter to Rome via Venice: Paquet, 'Une ébauche', 82. For what follows, see *Carteggi*, II, nos. 363, 366, 605; and ASV, SS, XXVI, f. 29.
179. *Carteggi*, I, nos. 192, 247; II, nos. 360, 433.
180. Francesco Maletta to the duke of Milan, Naples, 15 July 1472 (ASM 222) and 30 March 1473 (ASM 223). These figures seem to be fairly typical for Naples, although they may be slightly inflated by the fact that, given the shortage of couriers mentioned above, letters might not be posted until several days after they were written; they might then be sent off together in a batch. For example, Giovanni Palombaro did not receive his master's letters of 13 February and 17 and 20 March 1474 until after 25 April: *Carteggi*, I, no. 212.
181. *Carteggi*, II, nos. 514, 580.
182. On 25 October 1471, for example, the senate acknowledged receipt of Bembo's dispatches of 16 and 20 September, while it thanked Morosini for his letter of 15 December 1474 on 30 January 1475 and Morosini had received this acknowledgement before 9 March: ASV, SS, XXV, f. 67; XXVI, f. 169ᵛ; *Carteggi*, I, no. 260.
183. *Fonti aragonesi*, III/2, 127 (no. 863).
184. For this and what follows see above, Chapter 1, 'The material value of the Italian alliances: provisions', and ASV, SS, XXV, f. 157.
185. Compare his instructions, printed by Paquet, 'Une ébauche', 67–9, with the articles of the treaty itself, printed in *Codex diplomaticus dominii temporalis S. Sedis*, III, 451–5.
186. *Carteggi*, I, no. 228. For the rest of the paragraph, see *Carteggi*, I, nos. 235, 266; II, nos. 335, 363; Zambarbieri, 'Milano e la Borgogna, I', 38, 41.
187. *Carteggi*, II, no. 331.

188. Paquet, 'Une ébauche', 84, 86 and (whence the quotation) 90. For the next sentence see, for example, *Carteggi*, II, nos. 400, 483, 627.
189. D'Appiano to the duke of Milan, Lausanne, 9 and 18 April 1476, and Simonetta to d'Appiano, 1 and 20 April 1476 (ASM 495; d'Appiano 18 April = *Dépêches . . . Charles-le-Hardi*, II, no. 174).
190. '. . . *ha fuori messi e spie in ogni canto et è avisato continuamente de tuti loro* [the ultramontane rulers'] *progressi . . .*': Zaccaria Saggio to Lodovico Gonzaga, 27 March 1476 (AG 1625).
191. A conclusion also reached by Mattingly, *Renaissance diplomacy*, 110.
192. Vander Linden, *Itinéraires de Charles*, 37–47; Paquet, 'Une ébauche', 76–104; Vespasiano, *Vite*, I, 290. Bembo's purchase of manuscripts in 1472 in Vaucluse and Gascony must, from what has been said above, have been done through agents rather than personally, assuming that the date 1472 is correct.: P. de Nolhac, *La bibliothèque de Fulvio Orsini. Contributions à l'histoire des collections d'Italie et à l'étude de la Renaissance*, Bibliothèque de l'École des hautes études, Sciences philologiques et historiques, LXIV (Paris, 1887), 293, 302; Walsh, 'The coming of humanism', 151 and note 17; Clough, 'The library of Bernardo and Pietro Bembo', 310. For the rest of the paragraph, see Vander Linden, *Itinéraires de Charles*, 63–7; Leonardo Botta to the duke of Milan, Venice, 6 April 1475 (ASM 361); and *Carteggi*, I, nos. 266, 283, 304; II, no. 612.
193. For what follows, see *Carteggi*, II, no. 169; Perret, *Histoire*, I, 555 note 4; Levi, 'Lo zibaldone di Bernardo Bembo', 48 note 1; Bembo to his brother from Bruges, 13 November 1472 (copy in ASM 515); and London, BL, Add. 41068A, f. 40 (new foliation).
194. Queller, *Early Venetian legislation on ambassadors*, 17.
195. *Carteggi*, II, no. 336. For Rodolfo see the next chapter. Others who complained of the cost of living at court were Philip of Savoy in 1469 and the abbot of Casanova in 1473: Daviso, *Filippo il Senza Terra*, 68–9, 168; Cusin, 'Impero, Borgogna', 40.
196. ASV, SS, XXV, ff. 141ᵛ (although Queller, *The office of ambassador*, 94 and note 53, regards it as a bribe) and 157ᵛ.
197. Bembo to Giustinian, Bruges, 16 November 1472 (copy in ASM 515).
198. *Carteggi*, II, nos. 336, 369, 386, 433, 482.
199. Paquet, 'Une ébauche', 75, 113, 114.
200. *Carteggi*, II, no. 394.
201. For this paragraph, see Bembo to his brother, Bruges, 13 November 1472 (ASM 515); *Carteggi*, I, no. 176, II, nos. 369, 386, 445, 448, 482, 605, 612. See also Soldi Rondinini, 'Giovan Pietro Panigarola', 152–4.
202. *Carteggi*, I, no. 183. Disputes over precedence also took place in Italy between Burgundian and Milanese ambassadors. See, for example, Francesco Maletta to the duke of Milan, Naples, 27 May 1474 (ASM 225); the duke to Leonardo Bottta in Venice, 11 August 1473 (ASM 358); Botta to the duke, 9 June 1474 (ASM 359); and Niccolò Cattabene to the marquis of Mantua, Venice, 25 June 1474 (AG 1431, no. 1439). In the first of these instances, the Milanese ambassador in Naples tells how he decided not to attend a court wedding in order to avoid the risk of having to give precedence to the Burgundian amabassador Pieter Boghaert.

203. Santa Croce, *Mémoire*, vi–vii, 111; *Carteggi*, I, nos. 185, 266, 283, 304; Vespasiano, *Vite*, I, 290.
204. *Carteggi*, I, no. 212.
205. Knebel, *Diarium*, I, 144–5. For reasons of timing, however, such an ambassador could have been neither Bembo nor Morosini; perhaps the person intercepted was not an ambassador at all but only a courier. For the rest of the paragraph see *Carteggi*, II, nos. 401, 456, 459.
206. For this paragraph see *Carteggi*, I, no. 327, II, nos. 482, 535, 612.
207. Cusin, 'Impero, Borgogna', 41.
208. Cristoforo da Bollate to the duke of Milan, Vendôme, 10 October 1473 (ASM 540).
209. G. Peyronnet, 'La politica italiana di Luigi delfino di Francia', *RSI*, 64 (1952), 19–44; Walsh, 'The coming of humanism', 183 note 157.
210. Cristoforo da Bollate to the duke of Milan, Orléans, 25 October 1473 (ASM 540), in relation to Louis XI's attempts to detach Ferrante from his alliance with Burgundy; and Bittmann, *Ludwig XI. und Karl der Kühne*, II/1. 188 and note 265.
211. '. . . *quisti franciosi et ultramontani de trovate et fictioni ne sono facti li maestri* . . .': Sacramoro to the duke of Milan, Rome, 26 May 1475 (ASM 79). For what follows, see Bittmann, *Ludwig XI. und Karl der Kühne*, I/2, 437; II/1, 161 note 213; Paquet, 'Une ébauche', 106; Kirk, *History of Charles the Bold*, II, 265. On the problem of keeping secrets, see also *Dispatches*, III, 336–9.
212. *Carteggi*, I, no. 299. For the next sentence see Simonetta, *Diarii*, 158, 159, 176; Zaccaria Saggio to the marquis of Mantua, Milan, 10 July 1475 (AG 1625); and, in general, G.P. Lubkin, *A Renaissance court: Milan under Galeazzo Maria Sforza* (Berkeley, 1994) 211–12, 214, 219–20.
213. *Carteggi*, I, 231.
214. In fact, Ferrante was already convinced that the successful suitor, whatever happened in the meantime, would eventually prove to be Maximilian of Austria; see Zaccaria Barbaro to Doge Niccolò Tron, Naples, 19 February and 1 June 1472 (BNMV 8170/II, f. 1^v; III, f. 14) and Bittmann, *Ludwig XI. und Karl der Kühne*, II/1, 444.
215. *Carteggi*, I, no. 278; Vaughan, *Charles*, 118–19, 354. This piece of advice had been handed down by Galeazzo Maria's father and grandfather: L. Collison-Morley, *The story of the Sforzas* (London, 1933), 21.
216. *Carteggi*, II, no. 580; *Dépêches . . . Charles-le-Hardi*, II, no. 192 (= Matthias Corvinus's letter). Galeazzo Maria, when allied to Louis XI, had offered advice to him as well: for two examples, see Bittmann, *Ludwig XI und Karl der Kühne*, I/2, 558–9, 611.
217. *Carteggi*, II, no. 382 (Panigarola to the duke of Milan, 4 December 1475, describing Charles's reaction to the self-assertion of his half-brother Anthony).
218. Vaughan, *Charles*, 107–8, 181–2.
219. See, for example, the studies by C.H. Clough in his *The duchy of Urbino in the Renaissance* (London, 1981), Essays VIII, IX and III: 'Federigo da Montefeltro's patronage of the arts, 1468–1482' [1973], 'Federigo da Montefeltro's artistic patronage' [1978], and 'Towards an economic history of the state of Urbino at the time of Federigo da Montefeltro and of his son, Guidobaldo' [1978].

220. A point made also by Maulde-La-Clavière, *La diplomatie*, I, 7.

221. Vaughan, *Charles*, 181; d'Appiano to the duke of Milan, Montecrevello, 7 October 1473 (ASM 490).

222. The question of modernity is tackled by W.P. Blockmans, 'De Bourgondische Nederlanden: de weg naar een moderne staatsvorm', *Handelingen van de Koninklijke Kring voor oudheidkunde, letteren en kunst van Mechelen*, 77 (1973), 7–26; and see also the review of Vaughan's *Charles the Bold* by H. Kaminsky in *Speculum*, 52 (1977), 175–7, and D. Matthew, *The medieval European community* (London, 1977), 399–400, 404–7.

223. See, for example, the precautionary remarks of M.G.A. Vale, *Charles VII* (London, 1974), 4–5. Comparisons between Machiavelli and Commynes have been drawn by K. Dreyer, 'Commynes and Machiavelli: a study in parallelism', *Symposium*, 5 (1951), 38–61, and by A. Stegmann, 'Commynes et Machiavel', in *Studies on Machiavelli*, ed. M.P. Gilmore (Florence, 1972), 267–84.

CHAPTER SIX

Italian Princes at the Burgundian Court

Italian rulers sent not only diplomats to the Burgundian court but also princes. Leonello d'Este, marquis of Modena and Ferrara, sent his illegitimate son Francesco. Lodovico Gonzaga, marquis of Mantua, sent Rodolfo, the fourth of his five sons. King Ferrante of Naples sent his second son Federico. Galeazzo Maria, duke of Milan, thought for a time of sending his younger brother Lodovico. Of course, the reasons for the presence of Italian princes at the Burgundian court were not so predominantly political as in the case of the diplomats. For the princes and noblemen of western Europe, the Burgundian court represented a form of finishing school where they could learn the arts and etiquette, not only of politics, but also of warfare, chivalry and courtly life.[1] This was certainly true of Francesco d'Este and Rodolfo Gonzaga, although political reasons were uppermost in the case of Federico d'Aragona and of the proposed visit of Lodovico Sforza. There were, in fact, perceptible differences between these princes in terms both of their rank and of the duration and purpose of their visit. Rodolfo Gonzaga and Francesco d'Este were scions of what were only, in political terms at least, second-rank dynasties. Federico d'Aragona, on the other hand, was the son of the only king in the Italian peninsula and of the ruler with whom Charles the Bold had made his first Italian alliance; and though he was only the second of Ferrante's four legitimate sons, he did himself eventually succeed to the Neapolitan throne. Francesco d'Este arrived at the Burgundian court in 1444 and actually made it his home for over thirty years, until at least the middle of 1476. By contrast, Rodolfo Gonzaga stayed just over a year, from September 1469 until November 1470, while Federico d'Aragona, though he was two years away from Naples, spent a mere nine months with Charles. His purpose was almost entirely political, for he hoped to marry the duke's heiress Mary. Rodolfo's, on the other hand, was mainly a courtesy visit designed to cement the amicable relations already existing between Burgundy and Mantua rather than to achieve any specific diplomatic objective. Rodolfo, like Francesco d'Este before him, had probably been instructed to imbibe as much as he could of the rudiments of courtly life; but, as for Francesco, we can only guess at the motives behind the decision to send him to the Burgundian court.

These visits have long been known to historians, yet there is more to be said about each of them. Francesco's was described in some detail by Ernst Kantorowicz, but more information is supplied below both on his time at the court of Philip the Good and of Charles the Bold and, more especially, on his subsequent career. The attempt by Federico to win the hand of Mary of Burgundy formed the subject of an essay by Ernesto Pontieri, but more can be written on the reasons for its failure, on its background from 1471 onwards and on its place in the context of relations not only between Naples and Burgundy but also between Naples, France and Aragon. As for Rodolfo, although his correspondence with his mother from the Burgundian court in 1469–1470 has been used by historians, the visit itself has only recently been given a study of its own. In short, the presence of these three princes at the court of Charles the Bold provides material for a deeper insight into his relations with Italy.

Francesco d'Este (ca. 1429–post 20 July 1486)

The main outlines of Francesco d'Este's life and career were traced sixty years ago by the late Ernst H. Kantorowicz.[2] He was born in or about 1429, the illegitimate son of Leonello d' Este, marquis of Ferrara and Modena from 1441 to 1450; the identity of his mother is not known. On 26 July 1444 he left Ferrara in the company of Jean de Heinsberg, bishop of Liège and a friend of both the marquis of Mantua and the duke of Burgundy, and arrived in Liège on 1 September. It is not known for sure why he left home at this time. Perhaps his father, having just married a daughter of the king of Naples, Maria, felt embarrassed by the presence of a bastard son; or it may be that Leonello, hoping now for legitimate offspring, did not think he would have the resources to offer him satisfactory prospects. Nor is it certain that the intention was for Francesco to make a life for himself beyond the Alps, as in fact eventually happened, rather than simply to pay a visit of limited duration to an ultramontane court. There had already been a variety of contacts between the courts of Ferrara and Burgundy. Philip the Good had sent a deputation to the Council of Ferrara in 1438, thus demonstrating his support for Pope Eugenius IV against the Council of Basel.[3] Ferrara University was popular with students from Philip's lands, especially for law and medicine, and among those who studied there were several who later became councillors of Charles the Bold, notably Antoine de Montjeu and Ferry de Clugny.[4] Conversely, Flemish painting was much admired at the Este court, as were the works of the Franco-Flemish school of music.[5] In fact, although the Ferrarese court was one of the major centres in Italy of the new humanist current in art and learning, it was also perhaps more closely attuned than any of its counterparts in the peninsula to the culture of the north; for instance, Ferrarese courtiers were avid readers of French romances and tales of chivalrous adventure.

Francesco did not long remain with his escort, the bishop of Liège, since, for reasons unrecorded, he was soon transferred to the household of Philip the Good's heir, the count of Charolais (the future Charles the Bold). We know that from at least 1448 he and Charles, his junior by some four years, had a tutor in common, Antoine Haneron. This is alluded to in letters of credence written at Middelburg on 12 June 1454 on behalf of Francesco and his servant Giovanni — they were about to leave for a visit to Ferrara concerning certain of Francesco's affairs — by Charles, who told Marquis Borso d'Este that Francesco '*a puero educatus est in nostra domo*', adding that '*personam eiusdem Francisci valde gratam habeo et acceptam . . . in agendis honeste sempre se habuit in omnibus*'.[6] Three years previously, in a letter written at Brussels on 1 October 1451,[7] Charles had recommended Francesco to Borso as '*bon filz et de bonnes meurs*'. Antoine Haneron was a renowned academic, but perhaps equally important in the formation of the heir's intellectual outlook was the fact that he was brought up and educated with an Italian prince, which was reflected later in his ability to speak Italian and in his fondness for and admiration of Italians.[8] Francesco made a favourable impression also on Philip the Good, who wrote to Borso ('*Magnifico ac potenti principi consanguineo nostro carissimo Marchioni Estensi*') from Brussels on 3 June 1451 deprecating his thanks for the duke's munificent treatment of Borso's relative, '*cum pro suis meritis eum Franciscum commendatissimum habeamus*'. Francesco was appointed ducal chamberlain in 1464. Three years later he was one of twelve princes and bannerets who carried the ducal coffin to its tomb in Brussels after Philip's death at Bruges in June 1467.

By now Francesco had probably become reconciled to the life of an expatriate, but he was not yet entirely cut off from his friends and relations in Ferrara. As just mentioned, he seems to have returned there in 1454; he paid a brief visit (long enough to borrow some books from the Este Library) when he accompanied the Burgundian embassy sent to the Congress of Mantua five years later; and he was there again in March 1462.[9] In 1464 he went to Venice on behalf of Duke Philip and was back in Italy three years later, when he again seems to have paid a visit to his native city. Such visits, however, could only have convinced him that there was no longer a place for him there. In 1466 he addressed three letters to his uncle Borso pleading for the full and speedy remittance of his annual allowance and complaining of previous delays in this regard. He needed the money, he said, in order to maintain his state at the Burgundian court, and, if it was not forthcoming — this reads almost like a threat — he would have to consider returning to Ferrara ('*ale parte de la*'). Though these letters show that he was still eager for news from Ferrara, it is perhaps illustrative of his new allegiances that only one of them (that written from Bruges on 6 May) was in Italian, the others (Brussels, 20 March and 2 October) being in French.[10]

One event in particular had a profound effect on the course of his career during the reign of Charles the Bold. This was the disputed succession to the ducal throne of Ferrara which followed the death of Borso on 19 August 1471. Francesco's grandfather, Marquis Niccolò III, had changed the order of succession in favour of his legitimised bastard son Leonello, who ascended the throne in 1441, thereby debarring Niccolò's younger but legitimate son Ercole. On Leonello's death in 1450 his natural brother Borso was chosen to succeed by virtue of his age and experience. His reign was marked by a scarcely concealed rivalry for the succession between Ercole, whose claims were based on prior descent and legitimacy, and Leonello's son Niccolò, who claimed the throne by virtue of Niccolò III's will, which had settled the succession on his father Leonello and his offspring. On Borso's death Francesco returned to Ferrara to support the claims of his half-brother Niccolò. The attempted *coup d'état*, however, failed and Niccolò was forced into exile. Perhaps because of his Burgundian connections, Francesco himself was treated leniently. Duke Ercole provided him with horses, clothes and money, as well as the promise of a monthly pension of one hundred gold ducats, on condition that he departed from Ferrara for good; Francesco perforce accepted this offer, leaving his native city on 15 September 1471.[11] Charles hastened to recognise

Ercole's succession, since, however great his affection for Francesco, he did not wish to compromise relations with Ferrara.

During Charles the Bold's reign, Francesco settled down to the life of a Burgundian courtier. In Burgundian chronicles and financial records he was usually referred to as '*marquis de Ferrare*'. This appears to have been purely a courtesy title devoid of political overtones, although it does justify calling Francesco, who was, after all, only the bastard son of one of the lesser Italian rulers, a prince. Though greatly trusted and honoured by the duke, he was not among his most influential advisers. Nonetheless, according to the surviving court records known as *escroes*, the bulk of which is preserved at Lille,[12] he was at court almost continuously from the autumn of 1466 until the middle of 1476. He attended several ceremonial occasions and served a number of visitors as a guide to the intricacies of court life. In 1461 he was assigned to accompany the Milanese ambassador Prospero da Camogli, who considered him to be of good judgement and alert mind.[13] In September 1463 he escorted Margaret of Anjou, queen of the deposed King Henry VI of England, when she came to Bruges. He was one of those present at the reception of the Milanese ambassadors in 1469.[14] His advice smoothed the path for Rodolfo Gonzaga when he arrived later that year; he was related to Rodolfo and possibly also to one of his attendants, Rainaldo d'Este.[15] It was to Francesco that Rodolfo's father turned in 1472 and 1473 when he sought assistance with the purchase of certain hounds in France for the Gonzaga breeding kennels. Similarly, when Galeazzo Maria in 1473 sent his leading *cantore*, the Fleming Gaspar van Weerbeke, to Flanders to recruit singers from among his compatriots for the ducal chapel in Milan, he provided him with a letter of recommendation addressed to Francesco.

His military experience was limited. He may first have seen action in September 1444, when he left Liège for the Burgundian court in the company of the bishop's nephews, for the party seized the little town of Herbesthal. He was in the entourage of the count of Charolais during the Ghent campaign in 1452, and he may have followed Charles against Liège, perhaps with mixed feelings, in 1467 or 1468. From 2 September 1469 until 13 June 1473 he was captain of Westerlo.[16] He was also governor and captain of Le Quesnoy between 1 October 1472 and 30 September 1474. These responsibilities did not prevent him spending most of his time at court or on other ducal business, and he had a deputy in Le Quesnoy; this was the provost of the town, Jean de Flandre.[17] During much of 1475 he was in Italy, but he returned for the campaigns in Savoy against the Swiss between April and July 1476,[18] although he does not seem to have held any military command. Indeed, he probably gained most experience of warfare in its quasi-military forms, jousts and tournaments. He took part, for example, in the tilts staged to celebrate the duke's marriage at Bruges in 1468 and in those organised in 1473 at the time of the chapter meeting of the Order of the Golden Fleece at Valenciennes.

The captaincies of Westerlo and Le Quesnoy provided Francesco with a useful source of income. The governorship of Le Quesnoy entitled him to all the proceeds of the legal cases which came within his purview, in addition to the tolls normally exacted by the duke on the burghers of the town and on the markets held in the area.[19] His salary as captain of Westerlo was more strictly defined, at a hundred francs a year.[20] Furthermore, for regular attendance at court, which formed part of his duties as a member of the ducal household, he could expect 36 *sous* per day. He received in addition occasional gifts from Charles: 48 *livres*, for example, in 1468 for his expenses at Brussels after returning with the duke from Liège; eighty *livres* in August of that year to enable him to clothe himself fittingly at the duke's wedding; and a hundred and twenty *livres* in March 1474 for reasons unspecified.[21] Over and above his Burgundian income, he seems to have hoped for some sort of allowance from his relatives in Ferrara. We can make a reasonable guess at the nature of some of his expenses. Clothing for the normal routine of court life and equipment for the occasional campaign would have been a perceptible drain on his resources. He may also have had a sizeable household of his own to maintain. Two members of his suite were certainly Italian. Giovanni da Modena (Jehanin de Modene) was designated to accompany him to Ferrara in the summer of 1454 and was sent by Francesco to convey messages to Borso d'Este in October 1466.[22] A Carlo de Trino ('*Karlo de Tryno serviteur du marquis de Ferrare*') received fifty *livres* in April 1473 when he brought news to Charles in Brussels from his master concerning the marriage of his — apparently Francesco's — daughter.[23]

A diversion from attendance at court would have been provided by diplomatic missions, mostly, as is understandable, to Italy. In 1458 and 1464 Philip the Good sent him to Mantua and Venice respectively. In 1466 Charles the Bold, then count of Charolais, included him among the knights whom he sent to confer with the earl of Warwick at Saint-Omer.[24] In Charles the Bold's reign he went three times to Italy. The first journey, already mentioned, was unofficial and took place in 1471 when he attempted to help his half-brother Niccolò seize the ducal throne of Ferrara. In June 1473 he was sent, together with Guillaume de Rochefort and Antoine de Montjeu, to Venice and Malpaga for negotiations with Bartolomeo Colleoni.[25] His journey to Italy in 1475 was again of an official nature, although its purpose has not hitherto been sufficiently elucidated. He was one of the first to be designated as a companion to Anthony of Burgundy for his mission to Naples to take the insignia of the Order of the Golden Fleece to King Ferrante, following the latter's election in 1473. As early as July 1474 he received some 1,160 *livres*, made up of both gifts and payment of expenses,[26] but, perhaps because of the siege of Neuss, departure was delayed, so that Anthony and his companions did not set out before the beginning of February 1475. Having travelled through Piedmont and the duchy of Milan, they arrived in Naples on 15 April. Anthony, who made no secret of his Milanese sympathies, met with a cooler reception than he expected and hastened to leave in the first week of May.[27]

Francesco, however, remained behind in the capacity of Anthony's attorney to explore certain marriage proposals made by Ferrante in the hope of winning both Anthony's partisanship and, through Anthony, the renewed favour of Charles the Bold. These marital schemes ranged from a match between Anthony's son Philippe, lord of Beveren (who had accompanied his father to Naples), and a daughter either of the duke of Venosa, Francesco del Balzo, or of the prince of Rossano, Marino Marzano, to a wedding between Anthony himself and a daughter of the duke of Venosa.[28] By the second half of May it was being reported that Francesco had progressed as far as agreeing to a marriage between Anthony's son and a daughter of the duke of Venosa, as well as arranging the size of the dowry at 25,000 ducats.[29] Such a match could have had far-reaching political consequences. The duke of Venosa was reputed the greatest lord of the kingdom of Naples,[30] and through his wife Sanzia di Chiaramonte was related to the king, who was married to Sanzia's sister Isabella. Moreover, when Anthony passed through Rome on his return from Naples, he was not only legitimised by Pope Sixtus IV in person but also declared capable of succeeding his half-brother if Charles left no nearer heir; the motives behind this declaration are unclear, but Anthony may have been encouraged to see himself as a rival to Mary of Burgundy for the succession.[31]

By this time Francesco had left Naples. On 20 September he was at Parma, whence he wrote to the duke of Milan asking for safe passage through his lands; by 23 November he was again at the Burgundian court.[32] The marital arrangements he had made in Naples soon came to nothing. For a start, the duke of Venosa objected to the high-handed manner in which his daughter was being disposed of by Ferrante. His reluctance seems to have been connected with the existence of an anti-Burgundian party in Naples, which made much propaganda out of what it regarded as Charles the Bold's treacherous betrayal of the count of Saint-Pol, a cousin of the duke of Venosa, in the autumn of 1475.[33] Charles too was against the marriage. He said that it had been negotiated without his prior knowledge or approval, adding that, despite Anthony's flagrant attempts at self-aggrandisement, he, the duke, was determined to be master in his own house.[34] Anthony himself, an avowed Sforzaphile, was perhaps less concerned about his son's marital prospects than about the risk of incurring Galeazzo Maria's displeasure. At the beginning of December he called Panigarola to his quarters to tell him that the Neapolitan marriage would not, if he had any influence in the matter, take place and that he preferred the friendship of the duke of Milan to that of the king of Naples, even if a marriage with Ferrante's own daughter had been at stake. For the embarrassment caused all round he threw the blame on the unfortunate Francesco d'Este, who, he claimed, had exceeded his instructions. Some months later Anthony confessed himself willing to lose the 5,000-odd ducats already deposited as security for the completion of the match if only he could wash his hands of the whole affair. He alleged that Ferrante was using the prospect of this match as a lever to induce Charles to give his own daughter to Don Federico, but this plan, he said, though devious, had little chance of success, since neither Charles nor Anthony wanted either of those marriages to take place.

Francesco's part in this affair had been that of the victim of events over which he possessed little control. His influence on matters closer to his own heart, namely Burgundian relations with Ferrara, was also slight. In the latter years of his reign his uncle Borso, through his espousal of the Angevins and through his intrigues with Venice against the Sforza of Milan, the Medici in Florence and the Aragonese dynasty in Naples, had become more closely aligned with Burgundy than with France. Ferrara became committed still further to the anti-Milanese bloc in 1471 with the succession of Ercole d'Este. Ercole was backed by the Venetians, whereas Galeazzo Maria had given his support to the losing candidate, Niccolò di Leonello. There were, however, complications. Niccolò's failure was also a setback for the prospects in Ferrara of his half-brother, the Burgundian councillor Francesco, who now became an exile, as well as an affront to Niccolò's uncle, Lodovico Gonzaga, a friend of Charles the Bold. Yet, despite his ties with both Francesco and the marquis of

Mantua, the duke of Burgundy acted on political considerations of his own and lost no time in recognising Ercole. By the end of 1472, Charles was reported to enjoy an '*intelligentia*' with him and was able, in the following months, to benefit from this understanding when Ercole allowed him to recruit troops in his lands.[35] Given the geographical position of the duchy of Ferrara, however, it was understandable that Ercole should be reluctant to place himself completely within any one set of alliances. His original supporters, the Venetians, were offended by his marriage to Leonora, daughter of the king of Naples, in 1473. As a result, the Venetians became somewhat estranged both from Ercole and from Ferrante, whom they regarded as trespassing in their own sphere of influence. This conflict was unfortunate for Charles, since he wished to maintain his Italian partners in harmony.

In the summer of 1473, Charles sent his congratulations to Ercole on his marriage to Leonora d'Aragona through Louis de Néelle, an embassy which has previously escaped the attention of historians. Louis de Néelle, whose frequent attendance at court is recorded in the Lille *escroes*,[36] was a knight and ducal councillor-chamberlain. Little else is known about him, although the reason why he was chosen for this embassy may have been his kinship with Ercole.[37] For the purposes of expenses, his embassy was computed as lasting from 1 May to 9 November 1473,[38] but he cannot have left in May, because on 9 June he received a gift of 336 *livres* to pay for twenty ells of cloth of gold to be made up into a long robe with which to clothe himself on his journey.[39] By the time he arrived at Turin on 27 July, having lost six horses on his passage across the Alps, the wedding had already taken place (4 July). Louis was further delayed by feeling it necessary to ask for a safe-conduct across the duchy of Milan, despite Galeazzo Maria's protestations that ambassadors, especially Burgundian ambassadors, could travel unmolested without one.[40] It was not until 28 August that he finally reached Ferrara and delivered himself of his nuptial felicitations; he left on 15 September.[41] On 9 November he returned to his master's side at Trier.[42] Close on his heels came a Ferrarese ambassador, presumably to reciprocate the Burgundian embassy.

Ercole's defeat of Niccolò di Leonello's attempt to seize the ducal throne in 1471 had offended both the marquis of Mantua and the duke of Milan, while his Neapolitan marriage in 1473 alienated his original protector, the republic of Venice. The struggle between Naples and Venice to establish a dominant influence over this strategically situated duchy was to lead in 1482 to the so-called War of Ferrara. Perhaps

Charles was already worried about his friend's security in 1474. In the summer of that year we find one of his ambassadors in Venice (perhaps Lupo de Garda) anxiously questioning his Mantuan counterparts about Niccolò's continuing intrigues against his uncle. A Ferrarese chronicler recorded that in the following year Charles sent Ercole a mantle of crimson velvet open at one shoulder '*a la borgognona*', together with a gold chain to wear around his neck. Ercole received the gift in a solemn ceremony in Ferrara Cathedral on 19 November 1475. These details may amount to a confused description of the insignia of the Order of the Golden Fleece, although there is no evidence that the duke of Ferrara was ever offered such an honour. There does, however, seem to have been some connection between this gift and Ercole's friendship with, on the one hand, Naples and with Burgundy on the other. It was in November 1475 that Ercole accepted Ferrante's order, that of the *Armellino* or Ermine. A Veronese chronicler noted that in the same month perpetual fraternity was proclaimed between Charles and the kings of Naples, Hungary and England, and Ercole was one of the lesser rulers included in the arrangement.[43]

The year 1476 witnessed a decisive event in Ercole's reign. While the duke was absent from Ferrara at the beginning of September in his palace of Belreguardo, his old rival Niccolò di Leonello again attempted to overthrow him; the Venetians, contrary to their policy in 1471, now gave their support to Niccolò. After initial successes, however, the rising failed miserably, and Niccolò, along with many of his followers, was put to death, although out of respect for his uncle, the marquis of Mantua, Niccolò's head was skilfully sewn back onto his shoulders after decapitation to ensure that his body was buried in one piece.[44] But this time Francesco d'Este was in no way implicated in his half-brother's plans, whose failure did nonetheless mean that he was unlikely ever again to receive a welcome in Ferrara.

Kantorowicz was unable to trace Francesco's career beyond the end of 1475. We can, however, discover that he lived for a further eleven years at least. He received his full salary of 55 *livres* 16 *sous* for service in the ducal household for the month of July 1476, but this was the final occasion on which he is mentioned in the Burgundian accounts; his name does not appear, for example, in the last of the surviving *escroes* for the duke's reign, that for August and September 1476.[45] It is not impossible that he fought at the battle of Nancy in January 1477;[46] nonetheless, the next exact information we have on his movements tells us that he was appointed governor of Montpellier by Louis XI on 7 July 1477.[47] Many of Charles the Bold's former partisans found their way into the French service at this time, but it would be interesting to know if Francesco left the Burgundian ranks before or after the battle of Nancy — that is, whether he served the duke faithfully to the last or sought rather to protect his future prospects by attaching himself to the rising star of the king of France before January 1477. His governorship of Montpellier was marked by intrigue and fluctuating fortunes. Although he was nominated governor on 7 July 1477, the previous incumbent, Regnaud de Chesnay — perhaps reluctant to recognise the claims of one whose devotion to the French crown was of such recent origin — did not surrender the seals of office until August. In May 1483, Regnaud was again named governor of the city. This reversal in Francesco's fortunes may have been the consequence of the onset of his new master's final illness and of the power struggle which ensued; nonetheless, it was not until Christmas Eve that Francesco was completely ousted. By the end of 1484, however, he was again in charge of Montpellier; perhaps he had added his complaints to those expressed by several delegates at the assembly of the French Estates held at Tours earlier that year against the precipitate removal from office after Louis XI's death of many of the former king's nominees. Francesco again fell from power, apparently this time for good, in July 1486. On 3 July François de Marzac, lord of Hauterive, was named governor, although Francesco was himself still using this title over two weeks later. The date of his dismissal may indicate that he had aligned himself with the dissident Orleanist faction, which had been defeated in the autumn of 1485, and had suffered for his political misjudgement (as did Philippe de Commynes). Be that as it may, this is the last documentary reference to Francesco so far uncovered.

We are fortunate in knowing, allowing for a degree of artistic licence, what he looked like.[48] His portrait was painted by Rogier van der Weyden in about 1460; this picture, now in the Metropolitan Museum of New York, was thought, before Kantorowicz's investigations, to represent not Francesco but his father Leonello. He is depicted also on a medallion struck by an unknown artist and now in the Biblioteca Vittorio Emanuele in Rome. Unlike the van der Weyden, the medallion shows Francesco in profile. It was executed before 1476 at the latest and was quite possibly done from life, although it could have been copied from portraits such as that done by van der Weyden. Both representations emphasise Francesco's long, thin and slightly hooked nose and the melancholy expression in the eyes, which, veiled behind long lashes, seem to suggest the habit of looking out on the world with a disillusioned caution, understandably so in view of the vicissitudes of his career. Finally, his portrait may have been painted by Hans Memling.[49] It would be fascinating if a portrait could be unearthed from the period after 1477, so that we might see what physical traces were left on him by the storms of his later years.

Rodolfo Gonzaga (1451/2–1495)

Rodolfo was born in 1451 or 1452, the fourth of five sons of Lodovico Gonzaga, marquis of Mantua, and his wife Barbara of Brandenburg (von Hohenzollern).[50] Being a younger son seems to have been one of the decisive influences in his life. It entailed not only a subordinate role and a degree of frustrated ambition but also, at least until 1478 when the Gonzaga patrimony was partitioned, a certain amount of poverty, for, although Marquis Lodovico made the Mantuan court one of the most brilliant cultural centres of the age, he was not a wealthy ruler. One of the most recurrent themes in Rodolfo's correspondence, both from Burgundy and from courts in Italy which he visited subsequently, was the need for ever more money, not only to maintain the due state which he regarded as both required of him by his sense of honour and expected of him by others, but also simply to meet the most elementary expenses, such as feeding and clothing his companions and servants.

It would be reassuring if we could be certain what he looked like, so that assessment of his character based on documentary evidence might be tested against contemporary pictorial testimony. This, however, is not easily done.[51] Nevertheless, we can reasonably surmise from his position as the second-youngest brother that, without either the resources as yet to contract a good marriage or the inclination to embark on an ecclesiastical career, his thoughts must have turned at an early age to making a living from the trade of arms. This was probably one of the considerations which prompted his father to send him in 1469 to the court of Charles the Bold. Lodovico himself certainly had an adequate knowledge of the French language.[52] Yet, although the Gonzaga had long had family and political contacts north of the Alps, these had usually been with the princes of Germany rather than with those of France or Burgundy; thus in 1469 Rodolfo had a Hohenzollern mother and, through his brother Federico, a Wittelsbach sister-in-law, while on 22 February of that year, shortly before setting out for the Burgundian court, he himself had been knighted by Emperor Frederick III, who was then visiting Italy.

The courts of Mantua and Burgundy had first set their relations on a close and friendly footing in 1459 when Philip the Good, distinguishing himself from most other rulers by his prompt and wholehearted response, sent a splendid embassy under the leadership of the duke of Cleves to the congress held in Mantua by Pope Pius II to discuss plans for the crusade, thereby earning the gratitude no less of the marquis than of the pope. Perhaps also Lodovico was disillusioned about the merits of a German courtly education by the lack of grace and accomplishment displayed by his future daughter-in-law Margarete von Wittelsbach and her escort when they arrived in Mantua in 1463. Certainly, two years later Rodolfo's next elder brother Gianfrancesco was sent to Naples to complete his courtly education.[53] In fact, we know that Rodolfo's parents were considering sending him to Burgundy even before the accession of Charles the Bold. The visit was put off then because of the potential danger to him posed by the likelihood of renewed hostilities between Burgundy and France.[54] The most direct evidence, however, for Lodovico's motives in sending his son to the Burgundian court is the letter he himself wrote to Charles on 19 July 1469. He informed Charles that when he was younger he had wished to offer his services to his father Philip but had been prevented from travelling by the unsettled state of affairs in Italy. Now that Charles had become duke, he had the same claims on Lodovico as his predecessor had had, but, since the marquis himself had passed the age suitable for such an enterprise, he planned to send his son Rodolfo to discharge in his person the obligations earlier incurred by his father.[55] Lodovico clearly had in mind that his son should acquire a general acquaintance with courtly manners and not just learn certain specific skills, such as those of warfare, since he talked of him as '*bonarum omnium institutionum fructus uberrimos consequuturum*'. Rodolfo, he wrote, was already possessed of great affection for the duke, but, should he show himself in any wise deficient, Lodovico begged Charles to correct him as a father would his son or a lord his servant. This was probably the letter of introduction which Rodolfo presented to Charles on his arrival at the Burgundian court, then at The Hague, on 10 September 1469.[56]

Rodolfo, then aged seventeen or eighteen, left Mantua on 13 July 1469. A week later he arrived in Milan, where Galeazzo Maria gave him a warm reception but urged him to delay his departure and even tried to dissuade him from going to Burgundy at all, on the grounds that he would find nothing of value at the court of Charles the Bold, Galeazzo Maria's enemy; in fact, he would have to unlearn all the refinements of speech and manners he had so far acquired if he wanted to fit in there![57] When Rodolfo did leave four or five days later, a throng of people came to see him off, including, as the Mantuan ambassador noted, a large number of ladies anxious to feed their eyes on the handsome young prince. Rodolfo himself does not seem to have been aware of making such an impression; he merely complained to his mother that he needed a change of clothes! After crossing the Alps he passed through 'Biana' (Beaune?), where he was presented by the commune with casks of its finest wine. He was similarly honoured at Valenciennes. After passing through Mons at the end of August he had to spend several days at Brussels in order to rest his men and horses and to gather information regarding the duke's whereabouts. When he left, the young lieutenant of the city, who had already shown him the utmost courtesy, insisted on accompanying him part of the way. He arrived at Antwerp on 5 September, embarking the following day for Holland. Partly because this stage of the journey was by boat and partly because he had heard that provisions for his horses would be difficult to find in Holland, he left the majority of his horses behind. This was a great disappointment, since he had hoped to make his entry with the most splendid mounted cortège possible. Nevertheless, large crowds accompanied him to the harbour prophesying a grand reception by Charles for such a fine lord. Rodolfo arrived at The Hague on 9 September. The following morning, after being briefed by his relative Francesco d'Este on how to deport himself, he was presented to the duke, who at the time was hearing mass.

The exact number of Rodolfo's companions is nowhere recorded, nor are all their names traceable. He is reported to have left Mantua 'con una bela famia', but the chronicler implies that many of them were to return once their charge had been united with the duke of Burgundy.[58] Rodolfo certainly seems to have parted company with some of them at Antwerp. On 27 November he wrote that he had 23 mouths to feed and 21 horses. Among his companions he mentioned by name (on this or subsequent occasions) a Paolo, an Andrea, a Martinello, a Gidino, a boy-servant known as The Blind One ('el ceco'), Antonio del Bolegnino, Iacomo or Giacomo Bocalino, Tommaso da Bologna, Rainaldo d'Este, Niccolò Terzo and Enrico Suardi.

A little background information can be supplied for some of these. Suardi came from a Bergamese family, several of whose members settled in Mantua during the reign of Lodovico Gonzaga. He was Rodolfo's secretary and guardian and accompanied him on several of his peregrinations through Italy after their return from Burgundy.[59] Niccolò Terzo, chamberlain of the marquis of Mantua, had been knighted by the emperor in February 1469 at the same time as Rodolfo and, again like Rodolfo, he was to die fighting against the French at the battle of Fornovo in 1495.[60] He left for Mantua, in the company of Messer Iacomo, shortly after Rodolfo had presented himself to Charles, who paid their expenses; Iacomo and Paolo were to return to Rodolfo in the spring of 1470.[61] Rainaldo d'Este's name suggests he can be identified with Rinaldo (died 1503), the natural son of Niccolò III, marquis of Ferrara, and Anna dei Roberti; if so, he was the half-brother both of Leonello, father of Francesco d'Este, and of Marquis Borso.[62] He was knighted in Milan by Galeazzo Maria in July 1469 on his way to the Burgundian court with Rodolfo; he had left to return to Mantua before the end of November. Tommaso da Bologna and Paolo also departed not long afterwards, carrying letters to the marquis of Mantua. We know that Rodolfo had a servant called Gian Battista (Jehan Baptiste), because the Burgundian accounts record payments to him in September 1469 and in January and June 1470.[63] Rodolfo also had a groom known as 'The Abbot'. In January 1470 this personage came to blows with 'ziacheto', a former servant of Francesco d'Este (hired by Rodolfo as an interpreter) over the respective merits of French and Italian; he seems to have had the best of the encounter, since he almost killed his adversary.

Rodolfo soon settled down to the life of a courtier; as he wrote to his mother on 16 September, '*cosí me ne vado a la corte secondo fano li altri cortesani*', and in fact the *escroes* for the five months from April to August 1470 show that he was paid as a courtier for regular attendance upon the duke.[64] In his letter from The Hague of 3 October 1469,[65] Enrico Suardi described to the marchioness of Mantua her son's daily routine. Like the other courtiers, Rodolfo had to accompany Charles to mass and vespers and attend at the *audience*. He was to have supper with the duke and then listen to the reading aloud of saints' legends, which the duke liked to hear for a couple of hours every evening at this time. Afterwards, for refreshment, the duke would partake of some bread and a drink served by the most worthy person present, which was usually Rodolfo, with whom, Suardi wrote, Charles was well pleased. Rodolfo accompanied him to his chamber to help him undress and to assist him into bed, a process normally lasting an hour. During the day Charles was often alone in his quarters with his menservants. Between vespers and supper, however, several of the lords of the ordinance and members of the ducal household would come to him to pass the time, and when, twice a week, the duke rode a few leagues from the court to hear mass, anyone who wished might accompany him; Rodolfo usually went on these occasions.

Although, to their credit, the Mantuans seem to have made every effort speedily to acclimatise themselves to their new environment, they clearly found much that was unfamiliar. Suardi explained to Rodolfo's mother (from Ghent, 21 January 1470) that, though his charge had ready access to the duke, this could by no means be taken to signify that Rodolfo could easily make a confidential request for Charles to supplement his allowance, as the marchioness, dismayed by her son's spiralling expenses, had apparently suggested. In the matter of access to the duke, Rodolfo was not the object of any favouritism, since most of the Burgundian courtiers of similar rank demanded the same privilege. Rodolfo considered Charles secretive and slightly parsimonious,[66] but he does seem to have admired him for his fortitude in the face of adversity. Amidst rumours of a joint Anglo-French attack against him in 1470, the duke's mood was almost one of elation (*'questo Signore ha animo di difendersi molto bene e sta alegra e di bona voglia e né in vista né in parola pare che non si spaventa di cosa che avenga . . .'*). Rodolfo discovered a keen interest at court in the affairs of Italy and, from the rumours current there, he learnt of the defeat on 23 August 1469 of the papal armies besieging Rimini sooner than from his own family.

Some of the courtiers with whom he had dealings are mentioned by name in his correspondence. On 5 October 1469 Suardi wrote that Guillaume Bische had recently invited Rodolfo to a dinner in order to show him the sumptuous standard of living maintained by the leading courtiers. Shortly afterwards, the lord of Beveren, son of Anthony of Burgundy, took him to dine in the chamber of the lords of the ordinance, as Rodolfo called them (the companies of ordinance as such were not established until 1471). Rodolfo at this time was under the impression that he would have to serve in the army which Charles was then preparing, and the lord of Beveren wanted to show him what to expect if he joined the ranks of the lords of the ordinance, who all asked him to visit and dine with them again often and informally. He seems to have been treated with special kindness by one of the courtiers who was later among the leaders of the embassy to Naples in 1472.[67] The duke's doctor was also mentioned by Rodolfo (though not by name). Some time in September 1469 Rodolfo made a sight-seeing trip across Holland, where he was greatly honoured in four of the towns of the province but where also, unfortunately, the combination of bad weather and a rough journey by boat gave him a heavy cold in the head, which laid him low for several days. Charles took the precaution of sending his own physician to attend him, which he did successfully. It came as a shock to Rodolfo, however, to learn that the doctor expected a consideration for his efforts. He was advised by his relative Francesco d'Este to make a gift in the form of a length of black silk. His illness could, after all, have been more serious, for, as Suardi wrote (The Hague, 5 October), there had recently been an outbreak of the plague locally; Suardi seems to have been surprised by the hardy imperturbability of the inhabitants, who regarded the daily death toll of six or eight people as insufficient reason to prevent them carrying on their business as usual.

Rodolfo's visit to the Burgundian court was basically without political overtones, unlike that of Don Federico six years later, but while he was there he does seem to have had two diplomatic tasks to perform. The first was to make preparations to visit his mother's sister Dorothea, wife of King Christian I of Denmark.[68] In addition, he investigated the possibility of a marriage between his sister Barbarina and Philip of Savoy. He soon discovered that such a match had little chance of success, since, to start with, Charles had his own matrimonial plans for Philip.[69] He felt also that the strength of Philip's situation could be over-estimated, as his income was too dependent on the continuing favour of the duke, while his prospects of wielding power independently in Savoy in the future were uncertain. In any case, he hinted, the dowry which Philip would expect from his bride, probably 30,000 or 40,000 ducats, was likely to be beyond the marquis of Mantua ('. . . *di qua sono li più grandi dotti i più terribili dil mondo . . .*'); for example, Anthony of Burgundy, whose annual income Rodolfo estimated at not more than 10,000 ducats, had provided each of his two daughters with dowries of 30,000 *écus* in ready cash. Undeterred, Lodovico Gonzaga seems even to have hoped to marry his daughter to Prince Philibert, the Savoyard heir-apparent, and took matters as far as approaching the prospective bridegroom's uncle, the king of France, for his approval. Louis XI's reply was not encouraging; although he confessed himself flattered by Lodovico's desire to be related to him, he made no secret of his reluctance to be aligned with one who had sent a son to the court of his arch-enemy.[70]

There is much of interest to historians in the correspondence of Rodolfo and Suardi from the Burgundian court. It tells of the duke's attempts at the end of 1469 to persuade the Frisians to accept Burgundian rule. Reports of the growing uncertainty of events in England, following the flight of the earl of Warwick, and of the decline in King Edward IV's authority are transmitted in detail. Rodolfo saw the connection between apparently isolated events — as they could have seemed to an outsider — such as the dispute which occurred late in 1469 between the duke of Bourbon and Philip of Savoy over territories on the borders of their respective lands, or Louis XI's plans to attack the duke of Brittany, and the general pattern of growing hostility between France and Burgundy. Many of his letters were filled with reports of the imminence of war and with news of Burgundian military preparations. His account of the duke's reception of Louis XI's ambassadors at Saint-Omer on 15 July 1470 is more credible, if less vivid, than Chastellain's.[71] His penultimate letter, written at Hesdin on 15 October, recorded an event which was shortly to change the war of words between Charles and Louis into real hostilities, namely the arrival in Holland of Edward IV after his deposition by the French-backed Henry VI. His last letter, from Ghent on 29 November, described the flight to the French court of the duke's natural brother Baudouin, although Rodolfo's explanation of the reasons for it is not entirely convincing.[72]

Perhaps inevitably, however, the topic which predominates is expenses and the difficulty of making ends meet. Rodolfo found that the cost of living in the Low Countries was higher than in Mantua, which made a mockery of his monthly allowance of 800 Mantuan *lire*.[73] When he arrived in Mons in August 1469, he wrote to his mother that '*maxime in questo paese è caro il vivere*', and his complaints only grew more frequent and strident thereafter. By way of illustration, the 200 ducats sent him by his father for the purchase of three or four long robes only just sufficed to pay for the lining.[74] His mother was incredulous, remarking that for such a price he could have had them lined with sable; but no, Rodolfo replied from Bruges on 10 March 1470, that would have cost another hundred! He had to provide for all the members of his suite from his own pocket, for they were as poor as Job, he said, and not gentlemen with a private income. In a sense the duke's accordance to him of the honours due to one of his rank was an embarrassment, for it obliged him to live beyond his means in a vain attempt to match the lifestyle of those around him. It was not the custom, for example, to wear the same outfit two days running. Rodolfo, though, did not have the resources even to ensure that each of his companions had at least one long robe. As they were not suitably dressed, they could not accompany him to court and there do him honour. Consequently he was unable to take quite as active a part in the life of the court as he would have wished.[75]

Like the Italian ambassadors, he found the necessity of following the court fatiguing and above all costly. At The Hague he suspected being charged exorbitantly for four rooms with eight beds. The innkeeper was so importunate in his demands for rent that it was necessary to go to the duke's *maîtres d'hôtel* to arrange a compromise. Perhaps for this reason he hired an interpreter, a tapestry worker who had once worked in Mantua and who had served Francesco d'Este in the Liège campaigns, 'ziacheto' (Giachetto/Jacquet?). At Ghent Rodolfo talked of lodging in the home of a private family. On 10 July 1470, however, he wrote from Saint-Omer that following the duke sometimes forced him to rent accommodation in three different places at a time. Again like the Italian ambassadors, he found the Burgundian courtiers' expectations of gifts a burden which was easy neither to foresee nor to satisfy.[76] When he first served the duke at supper, he had to pay ten ducats to the *valets de chambre* for the privilege. An offering of six *bistachi* to the master of the ducal chapel was required when he went with the duke to mass. To Anthony of Burgundy he made a gift of four Mantuan yards of gold brocade. He gave pieces of silk to the *maîtres d'hôtel*, one of whom, Guillaume Bische, also asked him for his short mantle of gold brocade which had obviously taken his fancy, despite Rodolfo's protestations to his mother that he had nothing suitable to wear. Even the *argentier* Guilbert de Ruple required a consideration, for it was he who paid the courtiers their monthly allowance for attendance on the duke. To have participated in a tournament planned for February 1470 would have cost fifty ducats.

On top of all the financial burdens of peacetime, Rodolfo soon found himself having to meet military expenses in preparation for the war which was feared imminent between Burgundy and France. He was led to understand that he might be given the command of one of the companies of the ordinance which Charles began to organise in the winter of 1469–1470 on the lines of the French and Venetian armies. He discovered he himself had to make the initial outlay on equipment before he received money from the duke for maintenance. A frantic note now entered his correspondence. He needed more horses and would probably have to buy them locally, since, judging by those he had with him, Mantuan horses were not capable of meeting the demands of Burgundian warfare, in which, he wrote on 27 November 1469, no quarter was given; moreover, the demand caused by war preparations was pushing up prices all the time. He even needed to buy, Suardi wrote in March 1470, new saddles '*al modo di qua*'. He went to Bruges to have a suit of armour made and to raise a loan among the merchants of the city. He had already been forced into debt to the tune of 200 ducats borrowed from Rainaldo d'Este. Now he had to turn to the ubiquitous Tommaso Portinari for a loan of 400 ducats, but even the sympathetic Portinari eventually had to refuse further credit because of the duke's prior claims on his financial resources.[77]

It was presumably this situation which induced the marquis of Mantua on 14 March 1470 to instruct Iacomo Bocalino, then about to return to the Burgundian court, to tell Charles that his master, by sending his son to him, had at last satisfied his desire of old to serve the duke. But now that Charles was preparing for war, and in view of his own financial plight, he could no longer guarantee to meet all his son's requirements and therefore hoped that Charles would be able to help.[78] Some help was in fact given; the Burgundian accounts record a gift of 150 *livres* made to '*monseigneur le marquis de Manthua*' in August 1470 for the purchase of a horse. Iacomo carried with him to the Burgundian court a letter of exchange for 800 ducats and a repeat of the advice previously given that Rodolfo could and should cut down on his expenses by sending some of his servants and mules home. Rodolfo was doubtless grateful for the first (although Suardi had suggested, on 27 November 1469, that 1,000 ducats might not be enough to cover all their projected expenses); but on the second point he had his reservations, for, he argued on 10 March 1470, if war broke out, he preferred to trust himself to his own men rather than to strangers hired locally.

We do not know whether Lodovico Gonzaga had originally intended his son to stay longer than fifteen months, but it seems that Rodolfo's mounting costs and the prospect of his being required to serve in a potentially bloody war against France compelled the marquis to call it a day. On 10 September 1470 he sent a messenger to his kinsman Albrecht, marquis of Brandenburg and burgrave of Nuremberg, requesting him to grant his son safe passage across his lands on his return from the Burgundian court.[79] Rodolfo's instructions to depart took some time in reaching him, as he remarked in his last letter from Burgundy, which he wrote at Ghent on 29 November shortly after taking his leave of the duke at Bruges. He had arrived in Monaco by 11 January 1471, when he wrote to his mother that he had completed the most dangerous part of his journey.[80] He was probably reunited with his family within a week to ten days, although the exact date of his homecoming has not been recorded.

In view of all the problems he had faced, it is possible that he did not greatly enjoy his time at the court of Charles the Bold. On more than one occasion he referred to the fact that he was there in obedience to the wishes of his parents, as if to imply that his own preferences did not tally with theirs; and later, when offered the opportunity to return to Burgundy, he showed no desire to do so. Be that as it may, his visit had a beneficial effect on relations between Burgundy and Mantua. In March 1472, for example, Lodovico Gonzaga braved the misgivings of Galeazzo Maria to invite the embassy led by Philippe de Croy to stop in Mantua on its return from Naples. Louis de Néelle may have passed through Mantua in September the following year on his return from Ferrara. Mantuan troops were certainly among those Italian contingents recruited in the peninsula by the duke of Burgundy in 1473. Indeed, if the marquis of Mantua had had his way, they would have been joined in the Burgundian army by Rodolfo. In 1474 Charles sought to utilise his political credit in Mantua when he urged Rodolfo's elder brother, Cardinal Francesco, to exert his influence in Rome against the registration of the bull of excommunication issued against him in the previous year. Towards the end of 1474 Francesco facilitated the conclusion of the treaty of Moncalieri by helping to convince Galeazzo Maria of Charles the Bold's sincerity in the negotiations, for he was able to show how disillusioned the duke of Burgundy had now become with his Neapolitan alliance.[81] As a result of that treaty, Burgundian ties with Mantua became stronger, because the marquis was already close to Galeazzo Maria and he was among those present when the treaty was proclaimed in Milan Cathedral in April 1475. Against the background of the siege of Neuss, however, he was afraid lest this alliance should compromise him in the eyes of his friends and kinsmen in Germany.[82] Nonetheless, during the summer he invited Anthony of Burgundy to visit him on his return from Naples. On 22 December 1475 the count of Campobasso wrote from Nancy of the Burgundians' affection for the marquis.[83] Lodovico followed the progress of the duke's campaigns with great interest, and after the battle of Murten he sent an extra courier to his ambassador in Milan, so that he could be kept fully informed of events across the Alps.

This ambassador, Zaccaria Saggio da Pisa, supplies some interesting information on the death of the last Valois duke.[84] The duke of Milan's brothers, Lodovico il Moro and Sforza Maria, duke of Bari, had left for France in the late summer of 1476, and in the first letters which they sent home after arriving at the French court they relayed the accounts of the battle of Nancy gleaned by talking to the survivors. They reported that Charles had been struck down by one of his own men, who had not recognised him, while trying to flee. He was then trapped in a ditch by his horse, which had fallen on top of him, and, unable to extricate himself, had been killed by Swiss soldiers, who, however, did not realise who he was. The marquis himself had already received reports from his German sources within two weeks of the battle that Charles had perished, but he was reluctant at first to believe them because, he wrote, reports of small infirmities suffered by great lords were always exaggerated and given the most pessimistic interpretation.[85] In this case, however, he was proved wrong.

Let us return to Rodolfo. For much of the period between his return from Burgundy in 1471 and the year 1478, when he at last obtained lands of his own, he led an unsettled, frustrating and impecunious existence traversing the length and breadth of the Italian peninsula in search of a military command and the status and security that would go with it.[86] By 1473 he was lodged at Cesena in the Papal States commanding a hundred and fifty cavalry of the papal army, but, feeling his conditions of service to be demeaning, he left in May for Venice, where Colleoni, who was recruiting troops in the hope of joining Charles the Bold across the Alps, gave him the command of a hundred and fifty lances, a larger force than that entrusted to him by Sixtus IV. Galeazzo Maria, though, would have none of it. Regarding the duke of Burgundy as his enemy and the marquis of Mantua as his client, he put pressure on Lodovico to command his son to leave Colleoni; and in order to keep Rodolfo out of harm's way he even suggested sending him to serve the king of France in the company of his own captain, Roberto Sanseverino, who, he repeatedly threatened at this time, would join Louis XI if Colleoni went to Burgundy. Nonetheless, despite the political dangers — and because of the urgent need to find occupations for his sons — Lodovico cherished the hope of obtaining a command for Rodolfo in the Burgundian army. He asked his friend Giacomo Galeota, who had visited Mantua in the spring of 1473, to use his good offices on his son's behalf when he returned to the Burgundian court. Rodolfo (at whose feelings over being thus hawked about we can only guess) expressed himself agreeable but reminded his father that, while the necessarily protracted negotiations were being conducted, he would remain unemployed and penniless. Nothing seems to have come of the scheme, even though Antoine de Montjeu and Lupo de Garda told the Mantuan ambassador in Venice in June 1474 that their master was still anxious to have Rodolfo in his army. In 1475 this was finally ruled out, because Rodolfo took service instead with the republic of Florence, in whose service he remained until after Charles the Bold's death.

The rest of his story can be quickly told, for, though interesting, it does not strictly concern us. By the partition of the Gonzaga lands after his father's death in 1478, he became lord of Castiglione delle Stiviere and Solferino. On the death of his brother, Marquis Federico, in 1484 he was accused of trying to impede the succession of his nephew Francesco. In the following year his first wife Antonia Malatesta died in suspicious circumstances; one version states that he had her beheaded for adultery after she was caught *in flagrante delicto* with her dancing teacher. In 1493 he and his descendants were raised by Emperor Maximilian to the dignity of princes of the Holy Roman Empire. Eleven years earlier he had enlisted as a captain in the Venetian army and it was in this capacity that he met his death on 6 July 1495, fighting at the battle of Fornovo against the retreating French army of Charles VIII.[87]

Federico d'Aragona (1451/2–1504)

The general historical opinion of Don Federico d'Aragona was well summed up by Tommaso Persico when he described him as the most amiable and virtuous and yet the most unfortunate of the Aragonese dynasty.[88] His mildness and humanity endeared him to the fractious nobility and the oppressed peasantry of the kingdom of Naples alike, while he was also renowned in later years as the patron and friend of artists and men of letters, and as a connoisseur of women. Although in later life both pictorial and sculptural portraits show him as gaunt and balding, with the stoop of middle age, in his youth he was of handsome appearance, tall, with long straight hair, a characteristic hooked nose and deep-set eyes.[89] His life was marked by those sharp turns of fortune's wheel which provided so much material for the pens of Renaissance moralists and historians. In a downcast moment, just after taking his leave of Charles the Bold in June 1476, he himself complained to the Milanese ambassador about his malign stars.[90] We do not know his date of birth, only that he was baptised on 19 April 1452, among those present being Emperor Frederick III. During much of King Ferrante's long reign he was overshadowed by his elder brother Alfonso, the heir-apparent, with whom he was contrasted as strongly as Charles the Bold was with his father Philip.[91] Yet in the space of two short years, from 1494 until 1496, he witnessed the deaths of his father, his brother and his nephew (Alfonso's son and successor, Ferrandino), which, to general rejoicing, left Federico as king; improbable as this event must at one time have seemed, it had reportedly been predicted several years earlier by

Angelo Cato, patron of Philippe de Commynes.[92] Federico, however, did not long enjoy his unaccustomed eminence. The combined efforts of the French and Spanish rendered him the last of his house to occupy the Neapolitan throne, and in 1501 he left Naples for France, where he died an exile three years later.

For the historian of Burgundy, the main episode of interest in his career was his unsuccessful suit for the hand of Charles the Bold's heiress Mary.[93] It is worth remarking at this point that the Burgundian suit was only one of several which he undertook for diplomatic reasons on his father's instructions; the others will be mentioned in due course. Charles the Bold's use of the prospect of his daughter's hand in marriage as an instrument of diplomacy is amply illustrated in his relations with Naples. Ferrante was already talking of a marriage between Federico and Mary as early as April 1470, and this talk was renewed in November 1471 following the proclamation of the alliance between Naples and Burgundy.[94] The Burgundian ambassadors who visited Naples in February 1472 encouraged Ferrante and his court in their optimism, although, they hinted, the duke himself had not yet made up his mind. The Neapolitans did all in their power at this time to present the prince in an advantageous light, clothing him sumptuously and showering honours upon him in the ambassadors' presence. His sister Leonora even hoped Charles would send for Federico before Easter. This buoyancy, however, collapsed in the summer with the news that the duke had betrothed Mary to Duke Nicholas of Anjou. Ferrante himself took the setback calmly, but the disappointment of those around him, which was all the greater because their estimation of Federico's prospects had been so favourable, was only increased by the fact that the duke of Anjou was regarded as the leading enemy of the Aragonese dynasty. Charles, however, hastened to remedy matters. Ambassadors of his arrived in Naples at the beginning of October to assure the king that their master's alliance with Nicholas was in no way prejudicial to his relations with Ferrante. It must have been some encouragement to Neapolitan hopes that, when the ambassadors departed, they left behind them two young men to teach Federico French. No more was heard of the scheme during the following year, when mutual recriminations came to be voiced by each ruler over the other's failure to fulfil treaty obligations, and when the duke of Burgundy's negotiations with Frederick III seemed to show that he would prefer to marry Mary to Maximilian of Habsburg; for his part, Ferrante investigated the possibilities of an Aragonese match for his son.[95]

Yet by the beginning of 1474, Neapolitan hopes were again high as a result of the failure of the Trier interview. Moreover, the return from the Burgundian court of the Neapolitan ambassador Bertini, bearing the duke's requests for his ally's assistance in the campaigns against Louis XI planned for the coming spring, gave Ferrante the opportunity to try to strike a bargain. He offered a thousand men-at-arms if Charles would not only recommence his war with France and continue it without making any unilateral or compromise peace, but also marry his daughter to Federico. Charles, though, balked at such conditions. If Ferrante sent only this number of troops, he said, the duke of Milan would simply send half as many again to *his* ally, the king of France; but, if Ferrante would not only pay, as well as send, these troops and at the same time declare war on Galeazzo Maria, then he would be willing, he hinted strongly, to give his daughter to Federico and make the latter his heir. The king of Naples, according to the Milanese ambassador, entrusted his agreement with these terms to Bertini, who left Naples to return to the Burgundian court in mid-March.[96] Although the matter must now have appeared to be close to completion, it was not, curiously, until 26 October 1474 that Federico set out from Naples. One reason for this delay was that Ferrante spent some time awaiting the arrival of Anthony of Burgundy, who was due to come to Naples to bring him the insignia of the Order of the Golden Fleece[97] (to which he had been elected as long ago as May 1473); perhaps it was expected also that Anthony would take Federico back with him on his return. Anthony left Malines on 13 July 1474 charged with embassies to England, Brittany, Portugal, Aragon and Venice, as well as to Naples,[98] but nine months elapsed before he arrived at Ferrante's court. In the meantime, Ferrante presumably became impatient and packed off his son to find his own way to Burgundy, so as to force the hand of the duke. The delay could also be explained in terms of the time necessary for the preparation of Federico's expedition.

It would further seem, however, that there was some uncertainty in the king's mind about the welcome his son would receive. It is worth emphasising that no record has been found of Charles explicitly inviting Federico to his court, and the failure of Anthony of Burgundy to arrive in Naples on time might have been interpreted as a sign of the duke's decreasing enthusiasm for the Neapolitan match. To contemporaries it appeared obvious that the object of Federico's mission was simply and solely to seek the hand of the Burgundian heiress. Yet, perhaps to save face if the mission were unsuccessful, Ferrante's agents put it about that his son was going to Burgundy on a mere courtesy visit in order to thank

Charles for the Golden Fleece and to take him in return Ferrante's own order, the Ermine (*Armellino*); so effective was this obfuscation that the Mantuan ambassador in Rome wrote to his master in November that the object of the mission was a mystery.[99] The Milanese ambassador in Naples, as perhaps might have been expected from one of Galeazzo Maria's agents, offered a more detailed and complex explanation, obtained, he said, from an absolutely unimpeachable source. If Federico could not induce Charles to give him Mary's hand at once, he was commissioned by his father at least to make every effort to persuade him to appoint him his lieutenant-general with the command of all the count of Campobasso's troops — with the same salary — and to convince Charles of the count's unreliability on the grounds that, as an Angevin, he was sympathetic to Louis XI. Ferrante's premise was reported to be that, in the role of lieutenant-general, his son could prove his worth and convince not only Charles but also the great Burgundian lords of his fitness to be the duke's successor.

As for Louis XI, he was a cynic. Towards the end of December 1474 he expressed the view that Federico would not go further than Ferrara, but he also took the trouble of resorting to the most devious means in order to ensure this.[100] He had already declared in April that the Neapolitan match would never take place because Charles was only using his daughter as a bargaining counter (*'per la mercantia faceva continuamente lo prefato ducha de soa figliola'*).[101] This trading with his daughter's hand has caused Charles to have a bad press, both among the historians of his own age and among today's. It has been asserted, for example, that 'of the numerous dynastic bidders for the hand of Mary, heiress of Burgundy, none were so completely fooled as the cunning Ferrante and his amiable son Federigo'.[102] But this is not entirely true. Ferrante was nobody's dupe, nor did he win his reputation as a cunning ruler for nothing. As early as 1472 he had forecast that Mary would eventually be wed to Frederick III's son Maximilian.[103] Conversely, as the Milanese ambassador reported, he felt it worthwhile to send his son all the way to the Burgundian court just to neutralise the political threat posed by the duke's confidence in the count of Campobasso, even if Federico did not succeed in his other task of wooing Mary.

In any case, Ferrante too was quite capable of marital *'mercantia'* where his own children were concerned. In March 1474, after months of tortuous negotiation, the ambassadors of the king of Aragon were incensed to learn that Ferrante had all along been negotiating marriage alliances not only with their own master but also with the duke of

Burgundy and the king of France and even with their enemy, the king of Castile.[104] Between 1472 and 1474, when Ferrante's hopes of the Burgundian match for Federico were alternately raised and depressed, he had kept his options open by negotiating with King John II of Aragon for a marriage between Federico and John's daughter Juana. Naturally he expected to reap political advantages from these dealings, in addition to the satisfaction of providing for his son. If his alliance with Charles, from which stemmed the prospects of securing the Burgundian succession, was one way of coping with the threat of Louis XI, the projected Aragonese match was another, for it seems to have been envisaged that Federico should be set up as a semi-independent prince in Roussillon, that trouble-spot which for so long in the second half of the fifteenth century caused friction between the kings of France and Aragon. Ferrante was anxious either to see John II and Louis XI settle their differences or, if this proved impossible, to ensure that the French king was prevented from weakening John II — and therefore from threatening Ferrante himself — through military expansion along the Pyrenees and in Catalonia, as Louis had been trying to do since the early 1460s. He also considered solving the French problem by not discountenancing the intermittent and not totally sincere overtures for a marriage alliance which Louis himself made at this time. The two methods were to be combined in 1478 when Federico married Louis' niece Anne of Savoy as part of a short-lived tripartite settlement involving Ferrante, the rulers of Spain (John II and Ferdinand the Catholic of Aragon and Isabella of Castile) and the king of France. As we shall see later, it was planned at one time that Anne should have Roussillon as dowry. This disputed area would thus have become a neutralised buffer zone between France and Aragon under the rule of Federico.[105]

Such tortuous negotiations were the result not only of Ferrante's consciousness of his political insecurity but also of his own fecundity, having so many children, as the Venetian ambassador in Naples put it; furthermore, he was determined, he said, to leave his sons better provided at his death than he himself had been when his father Alfonso had died in 1458.[106] On the other hand, he had to wed his children wherever he could, nor did his situation allow him to pick and choose, for, with an insecure title to his throne and faced by serious, if mostly latent, opposition both at home and abroad, he hardly found himself in a position of having to fend off a throng of suitors from the ruling houses of Europe. Naturally he wished to do the best he could for Federico, but he was not irrevocably set on the Burgundian match. These considerations, then, had decided him by the middle of July 1474 to send his son away to seek his fortune '*o per Borgogna o per altrove*', and, two months later, to marry him off by one means or another ('. . . *per uno modo o per uno altro vogliono vedere uxorarlo come se dice ad Napoli . . .*'). Federico's Burgundian expedition, moreover, should be seen in the context of his father's overall marital diplomacy at this time. In the summer of 1473 Ferrante had seen his daughter Leonora wed to the duke of Ferrara, and in the following year the negotiations began with Matthias Corvinus which were to make his other daughter, Beatrice, queen of Hungary in 1476. Since his third son Giovanni wished to enter the Church and his eldest, Alfonso, had been married for almost a decade, Federico was the next in line of the royal children to be provided for; Ferrante's youngest son Francesco was only thirteen and Alfonso's son, Ferrandino, was still an infant.

On 18 October 1474, Federico was given the fullest possible powers to travel to the court of Charles the Bold and to negotiate for the hand of his daughter. No limit was placed on the offers of money and troops which he was authorised to make as a *quid pro quo*. Similar powers were accorded to the Neapolitan ambassador at the Burgundian court on 26 November, and both mandates were confirmed by Ferrante's heir-apparent, Alfonso, two days later.[107] Federico finally left Naples on 26 October amidst much speculation throughout Italy about the true purpose of his mission. Coming as it did at a time when Ferrante was having to spend heavily to prepare for his daughter Beatrice's wedding, Federico's expedition placed the Neapolitan monarchy under some financial strain, but the king declared himself resolved that his son should not lack the necessary means, even if he had to imperil his own '*stato*' in doing so.[108] Consequently, the prince was equipped with a magnificent entourage whose composition we know in detail. According to the list made by one of its number, Ettore Spina,[109] Federico's escort comprised over five hundred persons, around a hundred and fifty horses and thirty-five pack-mules. One hundred and fifty-three people, almost a third of the total, were assigned to the prince as personal attendants. His leading advisors were Giulio Acquaviva, duke of Atri; Camillo Pandone, his chamberlain; Giulio d'Altavilla; the baron della Torella; Count Alberico da Lugo; Berlingerio Carafa, his major-domo; Giacomo Conti, the renowned captain; and Giovanni Olzina, described as his treasurer. Among other names of interest are those of the writer Elisio Calenzio, Federico's tutor and secretary; Angelo Cato, remembered today for his association with Philippe de Commynes; and Troilo Caracciolo, whose relative Tristano later wrote a defence of the

Neapolitan nobility which touches briefly on this expedition and on its members' participation in Charles the Bold's wars.[110] Spina's list is not totally comprehensive, since Federico left a number of attendants behind in Ferrara; he replaced them with over a dozen others there, who included not only some pipers and trumpeters but also Duke Ercole's own doctor.

Shortly before departure, Ferrante had declared publicly that, even though he had perhaps more love for Federico than for his other sons, nonetheless he could not provide him with such '*stato*' in Italy itself as he would have wished and that, therefore, he was having to send him away to seek his fortune.[111] It is quite clear that, despite his father's mollifying words and deeds, Federico did not relish leaving. The Milanese ambassador at the court of Savoy noted in February 1475 that he spoke of his forthcoming visit to Burgundy with scant enthusiasm. His reluctance may have been based in part upon both the prospect of a winter crossing of the Alps and the possibility of being attacked by Charles the Bold's enemies. In any case, as we saw with the ambassadors in the previous chapter, Italians seldom enjoyed leaving the peninsula for what they often regarded as the barbaric North. However, the Milanese and Mantuan ambassadors in Rome discovered a more powerful reason than homesickness for Federico's discontent, namely his suspicion that his brother Alfonso, resentful of Federico's popularity in Naples, had lighted upon this ill-fated courtship as a means of getting him out of the way.

His journey to Burgundy, which took him out of Italy by way of Rome, Urbino, Florence, Ferrara, Venice, Milan and Piedmont, did not pass without incident. In Milan, for example, where he stayed from 27 January until 1 February, his reception was decidedly cool, though this did not prevent the duke paying all his expenses. Galeazzo Maria, deeply suspicious by nature and, at that time, profoundly mistrustful of Ferrante in particular, was alarmed by the presence in his guest's entourage of so many soldiers. He agreed to let Federico pass through his lands only after resolving to give him leave to depart as soon as it was requested.[112] It was not until he arrived in Piedmont that Federico came into contact with the representatives of the duke of Burgundy.[113] In Turin he probably met Guillaume de Rochefort, who spent several months at the court of Savoy at this time for the purpose of negotiating the treaty of Moncalieri. Charles assigned as his guide Agostino dei Corradi di Lignana, but Federico preferred the hazards of finding his own way across the Alps to entrusting himself to one of such dubious reputation. His passage over the mountains was fraught with danger, for to the uncertainties of winter was added the explicit intention of the Swiss, now at war with Burgundy, to prevent what they regarded as military reinforcements reaching the enemy; Federico avoided the ambush they prepared for him only by a matter of hours.[114]

Even after arriving safely at Besançon in the county of Burgundy in mid-March, he had to wait several weeks before he could resume his journey, because the next stage, through Lorraine, was hazardous without a strong Burgundian escort.[115] Between January and May the duke of Burgundy wrote repeatedly to his lieutenant in Luxembourg instructing him to do his utmost to receive the prince with every mark of honour and to try to provide an escort for him from Lorraine to Luxembourg. Early in April Charles even sent one Nicolas Rosen called Lembourg to René of Lorraine to ask him to grant Federico passage. René, however, refused, and, as the largest number of troops Charles could spare for an escort was fifty lances, the Neapolitans had to sit tight in Besançon awaiting the end of the siege of Neuss. As Giacomo Conti wrote thence to his brother Andrea in Naples, they could go neither forward through Lorraine nor back through Burgundy, which too had now been overrun by the Swiss. The delay placed a severe strain on Federico's finances, so that in April his father had to send him a letter of exchange for 14,000 ducats. The Neapolitan ambassador Bertini was bitter at this treatment by the duke of an honoured visitor and expressed the wish that Federico had never left Naples. Certainly, Charles himself felt it necessary to write to Ferrante on 9 July asking him to pardon his inability to remedy this delay and not to regret having sent his son (referring to Federico as '*communis filius*') to him. Yet there was to be still further delay, for it was not until early in September that Charles marched into Lorraine. At the same time Anthony of Burgundy moved north into the duchy with the troops available from the two Burgundies. With Anthony came Federico, and it was in Lorraine, at Pont-à-Mousson, that he at last met Charles on 26 September, exactly eleven months after leaving Naples. Initially he was quite satisfied with the warmth of his reception, which, he wrote to the duke of Milan on 18 October, made up for his previous difficulties en route.[116]

During the nine months which elapsed between his arrival and departure, Federico remained steadfastly at the duke's side in both court and camp.[117] As befitted his rank, he was given an honoured place on state occasions. When Charles took formal possession of the duchy of Lorraine at Nancy on 18 December 1475, Federico sat at his left hand.

Immediately after the battle of Grandson Charles appointed him his lieutenant, with the specific task of reorganising the Burgundian army which had performed so lamentably against the Swiss. It was in this capacity that he took the platform in the absence of the duke himself on 14 April 1476, when the treaty between Charles and the emperor was proclaimed at Lausanne. Some measure of the solicitude which the duke showed for his guest can be gauged from the gift of 4,000 *scuti* which he gave him at the end of December 1475. Its purpose was to enable Giulio Acquaviva to re-equip himself in Metz, following a disastrous fire at his lodgings in Nancy in which he had almost perished; Giulio himself was reluctant to accept the gift, but perhaps his young master had a truer appreciation of the state of their finances.

He was also active militarily. He was one of the first to enter the town of Grandson when it fell to the besieging Burgundian army on 21 February 1476. This may have been one of the occasions when he shared the spoils of victory, for, on his return to Italy, a Sienese chronicler noted that he had with him seventy mules laden with his possessions, a part of which had been won in the Burgundian wars. Molinet mentioned '*le prince de Tarente*' as one of the duke's military advisers who, just before the battle of Grandson, urged him to draw up his army in expectation of an imminent Swiss assault. Federico kept close to Charles during that battle, fighting, according to Panigarola, with great valour, and he was well placed to assess the outcome as a setback rather than a defeat. The importance of the Neapolitan contingent to the Burgundian army can be seen in the military ordinances drawn up by Charles in May 1476. These divided the troops into four corps, each consisting of two lines of battle, making eight lines in all. Giulio Acquaviva was placed in overall command of the first corps, and Federico of the second. In the second line of battle, Giulio d'Altavilla commanded six hundred infantry of the ducal household. The Neapolitans, however, did not have the opportunity to test the value of these arrangements, since they left before the duke's next encounter with the Swiss at Murten.[118]

The main purpose of Federico's mission, however, to wed Mary of Burgundy, was not successful. The reasons for this failure have never been completely clarified by historians — despite the work of Ernesto Pontieri[119] — mainly because the dispatches of the Milanese ambassador Panigarola, the most detailed source for this episode, remained so long unpublished in their entirety. As far as the marriage negotiations themselves are concerned, even Panigarola is vague, although in three of his dispatches he does give some fascinating glimpses of these obscure dealings. It seems that within a month of his arrival, Federico had told Charles that the purpose of his visit was to seek Mary's hand and, in exchange, had made certain proposals.[120] In a dispatch written after the battle of Murten,[121] Panigarola described a conversation which he had had tête-à-tête with the duke in his quarters on the evening before that battle. Charles confirmed that he had indeed offered his daughter's hand to Federico — without specifying exactly when that offer was made — not sincerely, however, but as bait to persuade him to stay longer and as a gambit to induce the Neapolitans to name the price they were prepared to pay. They had responded by offering the immense sum of 1,800,000 *scuti* and by sending to Naples for a mandate to conclude on these terms. The reply sent by Ferrante, however, was that Federico himself should return while the Neapolitan ambassador Palombaro remained to tackle the question of such securities as might be found necessary. The duke's answer to this was that no securities were needed on his side other than the person of his own daughter, while from them he wanted the money proffered rather than securities. He told Panigarola that he felt his response had marked the beginning of the end of his Neapolitan alliance; since that time, he knew, the king of Naples had sought an understanding with Louis XI, although he professed himself unable to see what the French king had to offer which could prove more attractive than the possibility of Mary's hand in marriage. Through Panigarola he warned his Milanese ally to beware of Ferrante's intrigues to gain possession of Genoa and Provence; these designs, he claimed, were fostered by Louis and aimed against Galeazzo Maria. He advised the latter to forestall the danger by persuading Ferrante's son and heir Alfonso, Galeazzo Maria's brother-in-law, to declare himself king in his father's stead. Finally, Charles promised him all the help he could muster if the duke of Milan needed his protection against Ferrante.

The third of Panigarola's dispatches which sheds some light on the marriage negotiations was written at Salins on 14 July 1476.[122] The Milanese ambassador stated that Federico, who had by now left the Burgundian court to receive a warm welcome in France, had recently offered Charles the sum of 200,000 *scuti* payable at Bruges for the hand of Mary. The contrast with the much larger amount previously offered is striking, and it may be that by now the Neapolitans were less interested in bringing off the match than in merely keeping open their channels of communication. In any case, the duke rejected the offer with disdain, saying he had no need at present of money; to prove his point he referred Panigarola to the list then being prepared of revenues on which he could lay his hands whenever he wished, and which would enable him to encompass the same great designs as he had in the past.

The time and place of these exchanges is somewhat vague, but the assertion that Federico made a bald offer of money for the duke's daughter is rendered more credible by a reading of the mandate which Ferrante had given his son on 18 October 1474. From this we learn that Federico was empowered to offer Charles in Ferrante's name as much as was necessary in terms of money, goods or troops to persuade him to agree to the marriage.[123] Indeed, shortly after this document was issued, the Mantuan ambassador in Venice told his master how he had heard from the Ferrarese ambassador — a not unreliable report this, since the relations between the Ferrarese and Neapolitan courts were then particularly close — that Ferrante had made allowance for a sum of up to 100,000 ducats to pay for his son to go to Burgundy for the marriage. In addition to routine expenses of bed and board, such an amount was presumably allotted to cover also the sum, or an instalment of it, which would be offered to Charles to induce him to part with his daughter.

It is easier to discover, through Panigarola's dispatches as well as with the aid of other sources, the reasons why the courtship failed, as distinct from the course it took in its advanced stages. There is some evidence to show that Charles, like many fathers before and since, was simply reluctant to give away his only daughter to another man. Even before Federico had arrived, the duke had become agitated in a conversation on the subject with the Milanese ambassador, saying that he had no intention of marrying her off; and after the prince arrived, he still said she was too young and could wait,[124] even though she was in fact eighteen, an age at which many princesses of that epoch were already wives and mothers.

For diplomatic reasons too, Charles was loath to relinquish the hold over his allies, both actual and potential, which was given him by the fact that Mary was his heiress and that her husband would be the duke's effective successor. In October 1475 he told Panigarola that he was in no hurry to make a decision regarding Federico; in the meantime he would hold onto him with fine words.[125] The appointment of the prince as the duke's lieutenant can be interpreted in this light; Charles wanted to raise his hopes without satisfying them.[126] In fact, it was diplomatic reasons which compelled him to seek instead a closer understanding with the emperor from mid-1475 onwards, and in his relations with Frederick III he employed his daughter, as usual, to further his plans. He obviously felt now (and had probably done so at least since 1469, although circumstances had never been so propitious before) that the emperor's alliance had more to offer than that of the king of Naples. We have seen already that Ferrante himself had long feared that Maximilian of Austria would be the successful suitor for the Burgundian heiress, and, although Charles did not sign the formal treaty of engagement between his daughter and the Habsburg prince until 5 May 1476, Federico was reported almost three months earlier to have determined to leave the Burgundian court exactly because of the duke's infatuation with the imperial marriage scheme.[127] Charles might have been less swayed by these political reasons had a bond of sympathy sprung up between himself and Federico. The latter, unfortunately, did not have the qualities the duke was looking for in a son-in-law. Charles was displeased when, at the siege of Murten, the prince and his men preferred, as he saw it, to idle away their time in their tents rather than expose themselves to the dangers posed by the tenacious resistance of the Swiss garrison. In his anger he referred to Federico contemptuously as an unmanly hedonist.[128] The spartan and militaristic duke was temperamentally poles apart from his peace-loving and easy-going guest.

Nor was it the views of the duke alone which had to be considered, for what happened after his death was not of such pressing concern to him as it was to his leading courtiers and advisers. Ferrante, as we have seen, reportedly hoped that his son's appointment as ducal lieutenant would give him the opportunity to convince the Burgundian magnates of his worth. But, try as he might, Federico never won their approval. It was not just because he was Italian;[129] some of the courtiers shared or surpassed their master's interest in and admiration for things Italian.[130] But, unlike for example the duke of Milan, the king of Naples seems to have had few friends at the Burgundian court. In any case, his throne was far from secure and he did not enjoy in Burgundy the reputation of the duke of Milan for wealth, power and influence. In January 1475 three Burgundian lords very close to the duke sent a message to Ferrante warning him not to send his son northwards if he could not equip him in a fashion anything other than splendid, as the custom of the ducal court demanded; otherwise he would suffer great humiliation. They sought also to discourage him with the report that Mary had already been married secretly to the son of the duke of Cleves.[131] This unwelcoming attitude did not change significantly after Federico's arrival, despite the splendour of his suite and the personability of the prince himself. Philippe de Croy complacently described his journey as part of the homage due from the courts of Europe to the magnificence of the Burgundian power arrayed in all its splendour at the siege of Neuss.[132] Panigarola was given to understand by his sources close to the duke that those leading men who accompanied Charles on his Lorraine campaign did not want Federico's enterprise to succeed, regarding his pride as disproportionate to his station. In fact, few of the leading courtiers had anything to do with him. The prince did try to cultivate Anthony of Burgundy, whom he wrongly thought to possess great influence with his half-brother the duke, but Anthony had even less time for the Neapolitans after his marital embroilments with Ferrante in 1475 than before; moreover, he was one of the strongest partisans of the Milanese alliance.[133]

It was perhaps the conclusion of the alliance with Milan in January 1475 which, next to the duke's *rapprochement* with Frederick III, proved to be the most potent political reason for the failure of Federico's courtship. The king of Naples had been the duke's first Italian ally, and for a couple of years he had enjoyed a firm hold on the duke's affections. By 1474, however, Charles had become disillusioned by Ferrante's unwillingness to offer him anything more substantial than encouragement in his campaigns against Louis XI and against his other foes, and through the treaty of Moncalieri he replaced Naples with Milan as the lynchpin of his influence in Italy. Because he believed this alliance would enable him to tap the great military and financial resources possessed by Galeazzo Maria, he now placed his new ally above all his others in the peninsula. The adverse effect on Federico of the treaty, which had not been foreseen when he left Naples and which was concluded while he was en route, was compounded by the fact that Naples and Milan were bitter rivals in Italy, so that in the new situation created by the Milanese alliance Charles was bound to take the side of Galeazzo Maria against Ferrante if the two rulers came into conflict.

It is clear that the duke of Milan, his ambassador Panigarola and his friends at the Burgundian court actively discouraged Charles from marrying his heiress to Federico. Guy de Brimeu seems to have spoken of the possibility of a marriage between Mary and Galeazzo Maria's eldest son Gian Galeazzo, count of Pavia, who was at the time not yet six, and he certainly asked Panigarola if it was likely that his master would accept membership of the Order of the Golden Fleece.[134] Moreover, at his first public audience the Milanese ambassador had promised that his master would shortly be sending his younger brother Lodovico, known as il Moro, to the Burgundian court. Charles was delighted to hear this, and in June 1475 urged Galeazzo Maria to send him without delay as the passage across Lorraine was now safe. In October he said that every day's delay seemed to him like a thousand years; indeed, if circumstances allowed, he would like to travel south himself in order to meet the duke of Milan. By this time, Federico and his companions had convinced themselves, despite their initial apprehension, that their Milanese rival would not set forth from Italy. Yet only a month later the Mantuan ambassador in Milan reported that the list of those who would accompany Lodovico was then in the process of being drawn up. A week later, however, it was all off. Galeazzo Maria made the excuse that he did not wish to expose his brother to friction with Federico (for example, in questions of precedence), but perhaps the real reason was his dissatisfaction with his ally over his dealings with the emperor at this time. It is interesting to recall that in 1469, when he was an avowed enemy of Charles, Galeazzo Maria had told Rodolfo Gonzaga that he would never let anyone whom he wished well travel to Burgundy, whether it be friend, brother or son.

Even if the duke of Milan did not have a candidate of his own for Mary's hand, he still did all in his power to frustrate the plans of Federico, and he fully supported Charles the Bold's delaying tactics.[135] He and his ambassador had the support of the Neapolitan exiles in the duke's service. Some of these held influential positions in the household, bodyguard and army. Federico must have seemed to pose a direct threat to them; one of the aims of his mission, for instance, was to displace the count of Campobasso from his command in the army. It is difficult to specify exactly how they were able to obstruct their enemy, but, as for Campobasso, he told Panigarola shortly after the latter's arrival that he was opposed to Ferrante's schemes for gaining possession of Provence, which he would rather see fall to Galeazzo Maria. Again, by April 1476 the duke's trusted doctor Matteo de Clariciis was urging his master to dismiss the Neapolitans as quickly as possible; indeed, the Neapolitan ambassador Bertini, after complaining bitterly about the hostile influence exercised by Matteo and by his brother Salvatore, the duke's secretary, had already written home so that Ferrante could take reprisals against those of their brothers who had remained in the kingdom of Naples.[136] Federico's relations with these people, whom he knew to be working against him, must have been most unpleasant, especially when, in May 1476, he was put in command of the third line of the Burgundian army in which Troilo da Rossano and his two sons commanded several thousand troops between them; Ferrante had strongly opposed his Burgundian ally's recruitment at the end of 1472 of this Neapolitan mercenary.[137]

Federico sometimes got a measure of his own back against his tormentors.[138] In general, however, the Milanese faction won the battle for influence. Despite his denials, it is clear that the duke of Milan deliberately made life difficult for Federico by means of his agents' interception of communications between Naples and the Burgundian court. The best example is the fate of Giovanni Palombaro's dispatch of 16 March 1476, discussed in the previous chapter.[139] But before this Federico had suffered much inconvenience and anxiety through Galeazzo Maria's actions. In November 1475 both his father and elder brother had fallen seriously ill. Federico was deeply perturbed by the news, not only for understandable family reasons but also because, if the illnesses proved fatal (which at one stage it was rumoured they would), he would have had to return home forthwith to play a part in the regency of his young nephew, who would have been called upon to succeed. It was many weeks before he heard that Ferrante and Alfonso had recovered. By this time, however, he urgently required instructions as to how far he should proceed in his marital negotiations with Charles or whether he should cut his losses and leave. In April 1476 he sent a troop of twenty-five men, followed shortly afterwards by some messengers in disguise, in an effort to evade the attentions of the Milanese border-guards. Yet in May he complained that his secretary Giovanni Battista had been detained by the duke of Milan on his return from Naples. Panigarola ascribed the prince's disquiet to the fear that, through interrogation, Giovanni Battista might reveal Ferrante's dealings with Louis XI and his intrigues against Galeazzo Maria. Federico finally received his instructions to leave from a messenger who had taken the longer but safer sea route from Naples, and thence to the Burgundian camp from Nice overland through Savoy.

Partly as a result of this constant Milanese hostility, Federico was made to suffer for his father's sins, as Charles saw them. After Charles had received his acceptance as ruler by the Estates of Lorraine at Nancy on 18 December 1475, he descended from his throne to ask the Milanese ambassador for a copy of Galeazzo Maria's acceptance of his inclusion in the truce of Soleuvre as a Burgundian ally. Panigarola produced it instantly. Thereupon Charles made a rousing declaration of his devotion to the duke of Milan. This theatrical performance, so characteristic of Charles, was intended primarily for the benefit of two people: the French ambassador, the bishop of Evreux, whose master had unceasingly sought to sow dissension between the two allied dukes ever since the conclusion of the treaty of Moncalieri at the beginning of that year; and Federico, whose father, in Charles the Bold's view, had shown himself to be an increasingly unreliable ally. The drama had its desired effect. The bishop of Evreux hastily excused himself on the pretext that he felt the onset of a nosebleed. Federico, who was unable to match Panigarola's gesture of support for Charles, since his father had not yet ratified his own inclusion as a Burgundian ally in the Soleuvre truce, understandably turned completely pale at such a public humiliation.[140] He also fell into disfavour through the duke's dislike of Ferrante's schemes for extending his influence in Savoy and Provence, both of which Charles himself attempted to bring under his own control in the first half of 1476. Federico was empowered to try to persuade him to use his influence in Savoy and Provence, firstly to secure Yolande of Savoy's agreement to a marriage between his younger brother Francesco and one of Yolande's daughters (probably Anne, who, ironically, was later to marry Federico himself) and, secondly, to induce King René to cede Provence — and the claims to the Neapolitan throne which went with it — to Yolande's daughter as a dowry. In this way, Ferrante hoped to neutralise the hostility of the French king to both branches of the Aragonese dynasty; he had by this time become disillusioned with his Burgundian ally's willingness to block the French menace by continuing hostilities with Louis XI, a method on which he had relied since 1471. Federico's invidious part in these negotiations only widened the breach between himself and Charles, who said in April 1476, after yet another audience on the subject, that he was only awaiting a suitable opportunity for dismissing the Neapolitans.

In view of all this frustration and unpleasantness, it may indeed be thought 'strange that Federigo should have stayed so long in the Burgundian camp'.[141] The reason seems to have been not that the Neapolitans continued too long to cherish hopes of success, but that the arrival of the instructions to depart which they so eagerly awaited from Naples were long delayed. The explanation of this delay can be found in the duke of Milan's obstruction of communications between Ferrante and his son; in the simultaneous illnesses of Ferrante and his eldest son at the end of 1475, which postponed the taking of a decision in Naples about Federico's future for several weeks; in Ferrante's need to keep his son in Burgundy to pursue the negotiations over Provence; and in Charles the Bold's ability to make it difficult, through cajolery, for Federico to leave until Charles himself wished him to.

We have seen that the Neapolitans were already disillusioned about the duke's intentions only weeks after their arrival, but, though there was soon talk of an imminent departure, it was not planned that Federico should go directly back to Naples. There were two alternatives: a return through France or through Aragon. His visit to the French court after leaving the duke of Burgundy set in motion the negotiations which led to his marriage with Louis XI's niece, Anne of Savoy, in 1478; yet there is little evidence that the prince or his father seriously considered the possibility of such a match during his stay in Burgundy. The journey through France was necessitated basically by geography, in the context of Federico's wish to travel to the Aragonese court, but courtesy dictated that he should pay his respects to Louis on the way; political events too urged this course of action, for Ferrante wanted to dissuade Louis from continuing to support King Alfonso V of Portugal and Juana la Beltraneja against Ferdinand the Catholic and his wife Isabella in the war then raging over the Castilian succession.

Federico's proposed visit to the Aragonese court arose from the long-continuing negotiations for a marital alliance, which was designed to strengthen the close political and family ties already existing between the two branches of the Aragonese dynasty. Two matches were under discussion: a marriage between the infanta Isabella and the prince of Capua, Ferrandino, the eldest grandchildren respectively of John II and of Ferrante; and one between John's daughter Juana and either Ferrante himself or Federico. Ever since the end of 1471, this Juana had been viewed as an alternative wife for Federico if Mary of Burgundy proved unobtainable. Six months before Federico even arrived at the Burgundian court, the Neapolitan ambassador told Panigarola that the purpose of his coming was to arrange a marriage in Spain and that the visit to Charles was only a stage on that journey.[142] Of course, these words could be interpreted as a verbal smokescreen designed to provide an excuse if the Burgundian courtship proved unsuccessful, as indeed the unenthusiastic Bertini seems to have suspected all along would be the case. Yet just over three weeks after Federico's arrival, Bertini told Panigarola that they had received Ferrante's instructions to set out as soon as possible for Aragon; he said they were waiting only for a suitable opportunity to take their leave of Charles, which they hoped to do when the duke returned from Lorraine to Flanders; they would ask him to obtain a safe-conduct from Louis XI for their journey across France, though they were prepared to set off without one; indeed, they had been completely disappointed with their reception at the Burgundian court, and, if the siege of Neuss had not been raised in time to make available a Burgundian escort for Federico across Lorraine, they would just have gone straight on to Aragon without even visiting Charles. Towards the end of January 1476 Federico spoke as if his speedy departure were merely a formality. When his father had recovered, he said he expected him to send an ambassador to replace Bertini (who had died in the previous November), so that Ferrante would be represented at the meeting between the duke and the emperor which had been planned to take place at Utrecht in the coming May; this would leave Federico free to travel to France and Aragon and thence back to Italy.[143]

The prince remained in the Burgundian camp for a further five months after this last conversation. It was a period marked by the cold behaviour towards him of the duke and his courtiers and by the harassment and hostility of the friends and agents of the duke of Milan. Although his self-esteem was assuaged to some extent by his appointment as ducal lieutenant, Federico was clearly resigned to the impossibility of becoming Charles the Bold's son-in-law. At the beginning of June 1476 five galleys left Naples to bring him home.[144] Count Alberico da Lugo, one of his companions who had returned to Naples for instructions and who had travelled on these galleys, arrived in the Burgundian camp during the morning of 18 June. On the evening of the following day Federico showed Charles a letter from Ferrante informing him that he had sent galleys to bring his son back to Italy; it was hoped he would be able to return quickly as he was due to attend the wedding in Rome of his sister Beatrice to the king of Hungary arranged for 8 July and to accompany her to her new homeland. He asked, therefore, for immediate licence, so that he could depart the following day. He told Panigarola later that he had been afraid that Charles might refuse, but, although the duke was annoyed by the suddenness and importunity of the request and though Panigarola again urged delay, Charles felt he could not in the circumstances refuse without unnecessarily offending the king of Naples, who was still his ally after all, if only nominally; in any case, he may have been relieved to let him go.

That appearances were maintained is suggested by Molinet's account of the leave-taking, but Panigarola's dispatches tell a different story. On the evening of 20 June the Milanese ambassador met Federico, who was mounted up and preparing to leave. The prince complained of the malignity of his stars, which had condemned him not only to travel to such a wild place as Hungary without even returning first to Naples, but also to leave the Burgundian court in such a way as to cause the duke and his men to level accusations of cowardice, for everyone knew a battle with the Swiss was imminent.[145] He apologised for the manner in which he had earlier denounced Galeazzo Maria's interception of his couriers, although he still remained convinced that such interception had taken place. Panigarola, however, rejected the charge and chided Federico for his overt rejoicing at the rumours of the Genoese uprising. The prince's explanation of his actions did not satisfy Panigarola, who remarked that, even if Federico were, as he protested so vehemently, grieved to leave, his companions were not, nor would the Burgundians' suspicions of them cease until they were safely embarked at Nice. This last jibe is apparently borne out by the duke's hints to Panigarola that he would not be displeased if his master made some attempt to detain Federico, either on his way through Savoy or after he had boarded the galleys sent to fetch him. The advantage of this, he thought, was that Ferrante would not proceed either with his negotiations with Louis XI (of which Charles was deeply suspicious) or with his intrigues against Genoa until he was assured of his son's safety.[146]

Federico finally left on Friday, 21 June, the eve of the battle of Murten. No-one could have been surprised at his rather downcast departure in itself, although the precipitate manner in which he took his leave did undoubtedly cause some raising of eyebrows and unflattering comment. Philippe de Commynes ascribed this hastiness to Federico's having heeded Angelo Cato's prediction that, in his impending battle with the Swiss, Charles would be defeated.[147] It is intriguing to find some corroboration of this story in a contemporary source.[148] Perhaps this episode explains why Federico in later life placed such trust in astrologers.

Some weeks before his departure he had begun to make arrangements for the safe transport of his possessions as soon as he should be able to leave. But his planned journey into France was delayed by the disruption of communications which followed the battle of Murten and by the need to obtain a safe-conduct from Louis XI. In fact, after the battle both the Neapolitans and Charles sought refuge in Gex, where Federico and his men were placed in the embarrassing position of having to avoid the duke.[149] They seem to have felt bitter at his behaviour over his daughter's marriage.[150] It was not until 26 June that Federico was able to leave Gex. He had had to ask Yolande of Savoy to intercede with her brother Louis XI for a safe-conduct; when it arrived it was found to contain, in addition to the standard formulae, three courteous lines written in the king's own hand. Little information has survived on Federico's visit to Louis XI, not least because the series of dispatches sent from Naples and France by the Milanese ambassadors is somewhat truncated for 1476; we do know, however, that towards the end of July Charles himself commented wryly on the contrast between the reasons the prince had given him for having to leave in such haste, and his subsequent prolonged stay in France amidst much courtesy and junketing.[151]

Ferrante had long regarded Louis XI as the most dangerous long-term threat to his throne, but he should not be judged as having dropped his guard in allowing his son to go to the French court. We have seen that, for the purpose of containing French hostility, he had for some time considered *détente* as an alternative to confrontation, and ever since 1472 the lines of communication between the two kings had been kept open. The possibility of a marriage alliance, however, had usually been discussed only in terms of a match between the dauphin and a Neapolitan princess; the prospect of Federico's inclusion in the negotiations through a marriage with a French princess was based on only very flimsy foundations.[152] But the approach of the Neapolitan prince now gave Louis XI an opportunity to improve relations with Naples. On 12 July 1476, the day before Federico was due to arrive in Lyon, Louis held in that city a council meeting whose import was recorded by the Milanese ambassador.[153] Louis declared himself weary of supporting the king of Portugal in the war of the Castilian succession, and, as this support had been given only as a means of implementing his wider policy of opposition to the king of Aragon, he was now, in effect, proposing a compromise settlement. He said he wished to make a league with John II, as well as with John's son Ferdinand and nephew Ferrante. The method he put forward was to marry Federico to a sister of the duke of Savoy; as dowry the bride would be given the county of Roussillon or lands of similar value. Louis reserved his decision until he had seen Federico the following day. It was planned that, if the two of them hit it off, Federico would return forthwith to Naples to expedite the necessary arrangements. Federico was given a warm welcome by Louis and seems to have been very favourably impressed by him.[154] Such was the cordial atmosphere of his sojourn in France that he even spent a pleasant few days in Provence at the court of King René before embarking, probably at Marseille, in the company of Cardinal Giuliano della Rovere, who was also returning to Italy following his legation to France.[155]

Presumably because of the success of this trip, no more was now spoken about one to Aragon; indeed, the basis for it had been removed by the signature on 5 October 1476 of a contract of marriage between Doña Juana and, not Federico, but his father Ferrante. In any event, Federico returned home on 21 October with something to show for his experiences, despite his failure in Burgundy, and his fervent plea that he be allowed to stay in Naples and not be sent away with his sister to the wilds of Hungary was granted, thanks partly to the intercession of the duke of Urbino; the latter let his sympathy for him overrule his apprehension at the possible displeasure of Duke Alfonso of Calabria, who was reported to be jealous of his more attractive younger brother.[156]

Since Federico's subsequent French marriage arose indirectly from his stay at the Burgundian court and since it throws light on his father's relations with both Charles and Louis, it is worth pursuing the story past 1477. Little more was heard of the French marriage for over a year, until on 23 March 1478 Ferrante gave powers of proxy to two envoys to conclude the match between his son and Anne of Savoy.[157] Louis XI's permission was necessary because Anne was his niece and was then residing at the French court, where she had been brought up. Curiously enough, the agent on the Savoyard side was none other than the ubiquitous abbot of Casanova, who had returned to the service of Savoy after the duke of Burgundy's death and whose participation in the negotiations aroused only suspicion and mistrust. The contract of marriage was signed by the French and Neapolitan representatives at La Lande in the diocese of Chartres on 1 September 1478. On 9 October Louis reached agreement with Ferdinand and Isabella at Saint-Jean de Luz; he abandoned his support for Alfonso V of Portugal, while they renounced their ties with Burgundy; and on this basis the old French–Castilian alliance was renewed.

Federico did not leave Naples until shortly after the middle of February 1479. Travelling by sea, he landed on the Provençal coast some time in April and was formally received by Louis at the French court, then at La Motte d'Egry, towards the end of May. He had been provided by the shrewd and experienced Diomede Carafa, count of Maddaloni, with a manual instructing him how best to deport himself. In general, Carafa advised him to keep a low profile, to ignore the insults which were bound to come his way, to adopt a gradual approach towards winning the goodwill of the king and his courtiers, and to avoid any action which might further inflame the naturally haughty temper of the French nation. Unknown to Federico, some members of his entourage had been deputed to treat with Louis on matters of interest to Ferrante, the advantage of this being that no dishonour would attach to Federico himself if these envoys were occasionally treated by Louis with disdain, as it was obviously envisaged they would be. Such counsels and stratagems seem to have been directly influenced by memories of what had befallen at the Burgundian court, and, with the benefit of his earlier experiences, Federico did all that could have been expected of him. According to the Ferrarese ambassador, his courtesy and self-effacement gave no offence to those ill-disposed towards him, while his natural charm and grace won him friends among neutral observers.

Nonetheless, his time at the French court was by no means easy, for, regardless of his own actions, the general diplomatic situation was bound to affect Louis XI's attitude towards him. Anxious as Louis was for a settlement with the Aragonese in both Spain and Naples, he was alarmed by Ferrante's apparent intention to establish his domination over the powers of the Italian peninsula. In the wars following the Pazzi conspiracy, the Neapolitan–papal party seemed likely to overcome the French-influenced triple alliance of Florence, Milan and Venice. Louis could hardly appear to be in favour of strengthening ties with Naples at such a time. These considerations lay behind Louis' alternately cordial and hostile treatment of Federico and his sporadic fulminations against his father. Ferrante, for his part, was quite capable of exerting pressures of his own on the king of France. One of Louis's motives for agreeing to Federico's marriage with Anne of Savoy may have been to forestall a match provisionally arranged at the end of 1477 between Federico and Emperor Frederick III's daughter Kunigunde. The plan, if successful, would have had wide diplomatic repercussions. It was envisaged that Federico would be installed as imperial vicar in Milan, following the overthrow of the Sforza regime, which had remained seriously weakened since the assassination of Galeazzo Maria in December 1476. In this way Ferrante might have been able to dominate Italy and block the gateway south for any would-be invaders from France. Ferrante's son-in-law Matthias Corvinus, king of Hungary, then temporarily reconciled with the emperor, hoped the deposition of the Sforza would weaken and isolate his major rival for influence in the Adriatic, the republic of Venice; while the Habsburgs were glad not only to strike at the friends of France, as the Sforza were usually considered, but also to revive their own prospects of again effectively integrating the valuable duchy of Milan within the Empire.[158]

It was against this stormy background that Federico's marriage to Anne of Savoy was consummated in the summer of 1479. The details of the arrangement made remain obscure, but we know that the prince did not long enjoy the pleasures of matrimony, for Anne died in March the following year while giving birth to a daughter later christened Charlotte. The marriage thus not only ended prematurely in tragic circumstances but also — and this probably concerned Ferrante more — it failed to yield the material benefits originally promised. Anne did not receive Roussillon as a dowry, since Ferdinand the Catholic, unlike his late father (King John of Aragon had died on 9 January 1479), could not be persuaded to renounce his rights to that county. Federico returned to

Naples on 22 May 1482, but not for long. On the journey back he was accompanied by one of Louis XI's *maîtres d'hôtel*, who had been commissioned to ask Francesco di Paola, the renowned Calabrian hermit (later canonised), to travel to France in order, as Commynes, put it, to mediate with God to extend the span of the ailing king's life. After some hesitation, Francesco was persuaded to agree, and in February 1483 he left Naples with an escort led by Federico. They travelled by sea, but Federico returned to Italy immediately after setting his charge down on the French coast near Marseille.[159] Thus for about half of the period between 1474 and 1483, Federico was out of Italy, in Savoy, Burgundy, Lorraine and France, and his experiences there, particularly in France, seem to have had a strong influence on his cultural and perhaps also his political sympathies.[160]

The rest of his life can be briefly recounted. On 28 November 1487 he married again, but, as so often, the match was dictated by the political considerations of his father. Pirro del Balzo, duke of Venosa and prince of Altamura, had been imprisoned for his part in the Barons' Rebellion a year or so previously; the marriage to Federico of his daughter Isabella therefore brought yet more of the lands possessed by the semi-independent Neapolitan nobility under the control of the grasping and calculating King Ferrante. Isabella, unlike Anne of Savoy, lived long enough to bear Federico five children; but, as one of the *tristi reyne* celebrated in Neapolitan legend, she survived not only the fall of the Aragonese dynasty but also her husband's death as an exile in France.[161] In 1496 the demise in quick succession of his father, brother and nephew brought Federico to the throne of Naples, an event which aroused hopes that the refined new king, amiable and popular, would be able to lay the foundations on which the prosperity of the *Regno* might be rebuilt. Yet it was not to be. Louis XII burned to emulate his predecessor Charles VIII's conquest of Naples; worse still, Federico's cousin Ferdinand the Catholic, on whom so many hopes of succour rested, not only did not assist him but also made an agreement with the French to partition the kingdom between himself and Louis. After a brave but vain resistance, Federico was forced to concede. The last Aragonese king of Naples, he left for France accompanied by his wife and by his friend, the poet Jacopo Sannazaro, in 1501. In February 1504 he contracted what proved to be a fatal illness.[162] Yet destiny still refused him a peaceful end. In September his house in Tours was burned down around him and he was carried on his sickbed, only just in the nick of time, to safety. In the presence of St. Francesco di Paola and the faithful Sannazaro, he died on 9 November. His body was buried in the Minorite church in Tours. By his orders his most cherished possessions were enclosed in his tomb, so that his widow or sons might later, if necessary, retrieve them; his widow Isabella placed beside them some locks of her own hair. Even now Federico found no undisturbed rest, for in 1562 the tomb was ransacked either by Huguenots fired by religious zeal or by robbers misled by exaggerated tales of buried treasure. We can hardly disagree with the eminent Neapolitan historian Luigi Volpicella who wrote almost a century ago that, if we did not know the facts of Federico's life, we should dismiss the story recounted above as the invention of a romantic novelist.

Notes

1. Vaughan, *Philip the Good*, 162–3, and *Charles*, 61, 165, 240–7.
2. E.H. Kantorowicz, 'The Este portrait by Roger van der Weyden', reprinted, with improved illustrations, from *JWCI*, 3 (1939–40), in his *Selected studies*, ed. M. Cherniavsky and R.E. Giesey (Locust Valley, N.Y., 1965), 366–80. Information from this article is used in the following pages without further indications, although sources will be cited for points on which I have supplemented or disagreed with it. On Kantorowicz's relatively overlooked work in the field of Burgundian history see my Ph.D. thesis, 'Charles the Bold, last Valois duke of Burgundy 1467–1477, and Italy' (Hull University, 1977), 595–6. See also R.E. Giesey, 'Ernst Kantorowicz — scholarly triumphs and academic travails in Weimar Germany and the United States', *Leo Baeck Institute Yearbook*, 30 (1985), 191–202 (p. 195).
3. Vaughan, *Philip the Good*, 211–12.
4. Walsh, 'The coming', 186–7. Another law student, 'Messire Philippo de Borgogna', was knighted personally by Duke Ercole on 21 January 1476: B. Zambotti, *Diario ferrarese dall'anno 1476 sino al 1504*, ed. G. Pardi (Bologna, 1934), 4.
5. Most historians accept (though Kantorowicz did not) that Roger van der Weyden visited Italy in 1450. He certainly had connections with Ferrara and possibly visited it at that time: A.M. Schulz, 'The Columba altarpiece and Roger van der Weyden's stylistic development', *Münchner Jahrbuch der bildenden Kunst*, 3rd ser., 22 (1971), 63–116 (pp. 69, 108–10). Guillaume Dufay visited Ferrara certainly once (1437) and possibly twice (1433) during Francesco d'Este's childhood: L. Lockwood, 'Dufay and Ferrara', *Papers read at the Dufay quincentenary conference, Brooklyn College, December 6–7, 1974*, ed. A.W. Atlas (New York, 1976), 1–25. For the rest of the paragraph see W.L. Gundersheimer, *Ferrra. The style of a Renaissance despotism* (Princeton, N.J., 1973), 276–8, and G. Bertoni, *Studi su vecchie e nuove poesie e prose d'amore e di romanzi* (Modena, 1921).
6. The letters of Charles and Philip cited in this paragraph are in Modena, AS, Minute di lettere ducali di principi e signorie in Italia e fuori d'Italia, 1563 A/8.
7. The year is missing, but between 1450 and 1456 Charles was at Brussels on 1

October only in 1451: H. Vander Linden, *Itinéraires de Philippe le Bon, duc de Bourgogne (1419–1467), et de Charles, comte de Charolais (1433–1467)* (Brussels, 1940), 286.

8. This point is also taken up by Vaughan, *Valois Burgundy*, 188. Described as 'le marquis de Ferrare', Francesco was listed in the *escroe* of 11 November 1450 as receiving 21 *sous* 4 *deniers*: Paravicini, 'Soziale Schichtungen', 161.

9. A. Belloni, 'Un lirico del Quattrocento a torto inedito e dimenticato: Giovan Francesco Suardi', *GSLI*, 51 (1908), 147–206 (p. 181); and *Dispatches*, II, 235.

10. Similarly, the form of signature for the two letters he signed (20 March and 6 May 1466) was French: 'Francisque de Est M.', the 'M.' presumably standing for 'marquis', 'marchese' or 'marchio'. The letters are in Modena, AS, Casa e stato: Principi non regnanti, 130, 1676/1–3, and appear to be the only ones of his extant in Modena.

11. *Diario di Ugo Caleffini (1471–1494)*, ed. G. Pardi, 2 vols (Ferrara, 1938–40), I, 5. In the person of Borso, the rulers of Modena and Ferrara had been raised from marquis to duke by Frederick III in 1450, for Modena, and, for Ferrara, by Paul II in 1471.

12. ADN B 3431–40 cover, with some gaps, the period of Charles the Bold's reign. There are duplicates of some of these in Brussels and Paris.

13. *Dispatches*, II, 187, 235.

14. *Carteggi*, I, no. 163.

15. The first wife of Francesco's father was the sister of Rodolfo's father, while Rainaldo may have been a half-brother of Francesco's father. For what follows see Lodovico Gonzaga to Francesco, 31 March 1472 (AG 2187, no. 764) and 10 June 1473 (AG 2892, no. 40), and Motta, 'Musici alla corte degli Sforza', 308 note 4.

16. ADN B 17711: letter of Charles the Bold from the camp at Montfoort in Guelders, 13 June 1475, ordering his *commis sur le fait des demaines et finances* to pay four years' salary at 100 francs per annum (as from 2 September 1469) to '*nostre amé et féal chevalier, conseillier et chambellain messire Francisque de Est, marquis de Ferrare*'.

17. Jean's accounts constitute ADN B 11391–2.

18. ADN B 3333, ff. 24ᵛ, 46ᵛ, 86ᵛ; 3377/113,555.

19. ADN B 11391, f. 1.

20. There may, however, have been some delay in paying him. On 6 June 1475 the *commis sur le fait des demaines* gave their consent (the addressee of the letter, in ADN B 17717, is not given) to the payment of certain wages previously granted to him as captain of Westerlo. The document probably refers to his captaincy between 1469 and 1473. Kantorowicz, 'The Este portrait', 375 and note 68, however, relying on the printed inventory, thought he was still captain of Westerlo in 1475.

21. AGR CC 1923, ff. 46ᵛ–7, 215; ADN B 2100.

22. Letters of Charles and Francesco to Borso, in Modena, AS, respectively, Minute di lettere di principi e signorie in Italia e fuori d'Italia, 1563 A/8, and Casa e stato: Principi non regnanti, 130, 1676/1–3.

23. ADN B 2096/67,179 ('. . . *touchant le mariage de sa fille . . .*'). This vague ref-

erence is the only information we have about Francesco's private life. If he married at all, the date of the wedding and the name of his wife are alike unknown. Kantorowicz, 'The Este portrait', 376 note 69, prompted by the fact that this portrait was in the possession of the Courcelles family, conjectured that Francesco may have been related to it.

24. Francesco to Borso d'Este, 2 October 1466 (AS Modena, Casa e stato: Principi non regnanti, 130, 1676/1–3).

25. Instructions published in Plancher, *Histoire générale et particulière de Bourgogne*, IV, cccxxiii–xxvi. On his return he passed through the lands of Galeazzo Maria, though he felt it prudent to apply first for a safe-conduct: Francesco to the duke of Milan 'ex Ipporigia', 6 October 1473 (ASM 490); the duke to Cristoforo da Bollate, his ambassador in France, from Pavia, 20 October 1473 (ASM 540).

26. ADN B 2100. He was present at court between the middle of September 1474 until 4 February 1475: ADN B 3438–9.

27. Francesco Maletta to the duke of Milan, Naples, 15 April and 1 and 9 May 1475 (ASM 227).

28. Leonardo Botta to the duke of Milan, Venice, 2 June 1475 (ASM 361). Botta received his information directly from Anthony himself. Perret, *Histoire*, II, 41 note 2, relying solely on this dispatch, was able to tell only half the story.

29. Francesco Maletta, postscript to his letter of 17 May 1475 to the duke of Milan from Naples (ASM 227).

30. Same to same from same, 1 June 1475 (ASM 227).

31. Anthony's legitimisation is described by Vaughan, *Charles*, 237, who does not, however, comment on its potential significance.

32. Milan, Archivio di Stato, Autografi, 63, A30; and ADN B 3439/119,225. He does not seem to have visited Modena or Ferrara during his time in Italy in 1475.

33. *Carteggi*, II, no. 506. At the head of the anti-Burgundian party, apparently, was the Neapolitan heir-apparent Alfonso, who may have been motivated in part by jealousy of his younger brother, Federico, who was then at Charles the Bold's court. Saint-Pol's mother Margherita del Balzo was the sister of the duke of Venosa's father Guglielmo.

34. *Carteggi*, II, no. 363. For what follows see *Carteggi*, II, nos. 382 (PS), 506, 586.

35. Matteo d'Herboi to the duke of Milan from Ostíglia, 11 November 1472 (ASM 395); and above, Chapter 1, 'The material value of the Italian alliances: fulfilment'.

36. For 1471–5, see ADN B 3434–9.

37. Antonio d'Appiano, writing to the duke of Milan from Turin, 27 July 1473 (ASM 490), described Louis as Ercole's '*parente*'. Moreover, Ludovico I, marquis of Saluzzo, writing to the duke of Milan from Saluzzo, 28 July 1473, asking for a safe-conduct for Louis (ASM 490), described him as the son, by one of his sisters, of the count (in fact, lord) of Offemont. These clues enable us to identify Louis a little more precisely. Of Ludovico's sisters, Giovanna married Guy de Néelle (of the Clermont-en-Beauvaisis branch of that family), lord of Offemont, in 1429, while Riccarda married Niccolò II d'Este, marquis of Modena and Ferrara, in 1431 and, by him, became the mother of Duke

Ercole. For Riccarda see W.K. von Isenburg and F. von Loringhoven, *Stammtafeln zur Geschichte der europäischen Staaten*, 4 vols (Marburg, 1953–8), II (1956), table 123, and, for Giovanna, Père Anselme (Pierre de Guibours), *Histoire généalogique de la maison royale de France* . . ., 9 vols, 3rd edtn (Paris, 1726–33), VI (1730), 52, and F.A. Aubert de La Che(s)naye-Desbois, *Dictionnaire de la noblesse* . . . *de la France*, 19 vols, 3rd edtn (Paris, 1863–76), V (1864), 926–7. Louis was thus, through his mother, first cousin of the duke of Ferrara. Moreover, the letter of the marquis of Saluzzo mentioned above makes it clear that he was legitimate. Yet he is mentioned by neither Anselme nor Aubert, both of whom state that Guy de Néelle had only one son, Jean, who succeeded Guy as lord of Offemont some time in 1473. However, both Guy and Jean were in the service of the French crown, unlike our Louis.

38. For which he was paid 1,100 *livres*: he had between 24 and 26 companions (ADN B 2096/67,162).

39. ADN B 2096/67,163. On 27 April Charles had paid 16 *livres* 6 *sous* to a craftsman of Bruges for two lady's saddles, decorated with the device of his wife Margaret, which he meant to give as a wedding-present to Ercole's bride Leonora (ADN B 2096/67,238). Although, in the event, Louis was woefully late, his mission had been planned months in advance and was known to the Neapolitan ambassador Bertini when he wrote to Ferrante from the Burgundian court on 21 March 1473; this letter, now lost, was referred to by Zaccaria Barbaro writing to Doge Niccolò Tron from Naples on 15 April 1473 (BNMV 8170/V, 35).

40. Antonio d'Appiano to the duke of Milan, Turin, 27 and 29 July 1473, and the marquis of Saluzzo to the duke, Saluzzo, 28 July 1473 ASM 515); *Carteggi*, I, no. 202 (the duke to Louis de Néelle, 1 August 1473); and Cusin, 'Impero, Borgogna', 41.

41. Caleffini, *Diario*, I, 41. During this time he seems to have paid a visit to the marquis of Mantua or, at least, the marquis made preparations to receive him: Lodovico Gonzaga to Ercole d'Este and to the vicar of Bozzolo, 6 and 9 September (AG 2892, lib. LXXI, ff. 48, 51).

42. There appears to have been some delay in paying all that was due to him, because Charles felt it necessary to write from the camp at Neuss on 28 October and 16 December 1474 to his receiver-general Pierre Lanchals and to '*noz améz et féaulx les trésoriers sur le fait de nostre demaine*' ordering them to pay what was owed to Louis '*du voyaige par lui dernièrement fait depars nous ou pays d'Italie*' (ADN B 17713: dossier entitled 'Néelle (Louis de) chambellain'). For the next sentence see *Extrait d'une ancienne chronique*, in Commynes, *Mémoires*, ed. Godefroy and Lenglet du Fresnoy, II, 209, and Vander Linden, *Itinéraires de Charles*, 57.

43. Jacobus de Palazzo to Lodovico Gonzaga, Venice, 30 June 1474 (AG 1431); Caleffini, *Diario*, I, 109–10; Ercole to the duke of Milan, 4 November 1475, and the duke to Ercole, 20 November 1475 (ASM 323); *Cronaca di Anonimo Veronese 1446–1488*, ed. G. Soranzo (Venice, 1915), 316. The insignia and alliances mentioned as being received by Ercole at this time could, of course, refer instead to the Order of the Garter to which he had been elected in August 1474, although the far-from-impartial Hans Knebel (*Diarium*, I, 158–9, 200)

wrote that Ercole did send troops to Charles at Neuss, and that in April 1475 he was one of several Italian rulers allied with him against the emperor and the League of Constance.

44. A. Cappelli, 'Niccolò di Leonello d'Este', *Atti e memorie della R. Deputazione storica per le province modenese e parmensi*, 5 (1868), 413–38 (pp. 424–7); A. Morselli, 'Vela e diamante', *Atti e memorie della Accademia di scienze, lettere e arti di Modena*, 5th ser., 9 (1950–1), 233–45; Gundersheimer, *Ferrara*, 180–3.

45. ADN B 3333, f. 86ᵛ, and 3440.

46. Bernardino Zambotti noted in his *Diario* for January 1477 that Charles died in the battle, adding '*è così se ha lettere*'; the editor, Giuseppe Pardi, suggested that such letters may have been written by Francesco (p. 30 and note 7).

47. For what follows, see Dupont-Ferrier, *Gallia Regia*, IV, 207–8. Another appearance of Francesco after the battle of Nancy is as a friend of the Venetian ambassador Bernardo Bembo in 1477 — they shared an interest in classical literature: Fletcher, 'Bernardo Bembo', 815.

48. For what follows, see Kantorowicz, 'The Este portrait', figs 1–3. The portrait may once have been in England, in the first quarter of the nineteenth century: L. Campbell, 'Lord Northwick's collection and Rogier van der Weyden's portrait of Francessco d'Este', *Burlington Magazine*, 144 (2002), 696.

49. Kantorowicz, 'The Este portrait', 378, thought that Francesco was Memling's *Man with the arrow* (National Gallery, Washington) and that the picture was painted in about 1468–9, basically because of the similarity, discounting a greater stoutness due to advancing years, between the sitter and that of Roger's portrait. However, M. Cinotti, *The great galleries of the world. The National Gallery of Art of Washington and its paintings* (Edinburgh, 1975), p. 42 and fig. 71, apparently unaware of Kantorowicz's researches, wrote that the portrait (which she dates to about 1470) presumably depicts a member of a corporation of archers who has won some archery competition, his victory being symbolised by the golden arrow.

50. Compare Litta, *Famiglie celebri italiane*, III, fasc. 'Gonzaga di Mantua', part 4, tables XVI, XVII (1451) and P. Savy, 'A l'école bourguignonne. Rodolfo Gonzaga à la cour de Bourgogne (1469–1470)', *Revue du Nord*, 84 (2002), 343–66 (p. 344: 18 April 1452) (cf. below, 'Bibliographical Supplement', n. 7). The eldest, Federico, succeeded his father as marquis in 1478. The second and fifth sons, Francesco and Lodovico, entered the Church. Gianfrancesco and Rodolfo lived in part by the trade of arms and, after 1478, founded cadet branches of the Gonzaga line possessing lands on the periphery of the marquisate of Mantua. According to local experts, it was Rodolfo's house in the Via R. Ardigò in Mantua (Number 11) that now contains the Archivio di Stato: Brinton, *The Gonzaga*, 244.

51. Mantegna's picture of Marquis Lodovico's court in the *Camera degli Sposi* (*Camera Picta*) of the Gonzaga palace in Mantua included portraits from life: A. Tissoni Benvenuti, 'Un nuovo documento sulla "Camera degli Sposi" del Mantegna', *IMU*, 24 (1981), 357–60. It is usually assumed that Rodolfo's is among them, but there is no consensus on which one it is. Some, such as R. Signorini, 'Lettura storica degli affreschi della "Camera degli Sposi" di A. Mantegna', *JWCI*, 38 (1975–6), 109–35 (p. 123 note 75), and R.W.

Lightbown, *Mantegna: with a complete catalogue of paintings, drawings and prints* (Oxford, 1986), 105, have seen him in the rather chubby young man standing behind his mother. On the other hand, from what is known of Rodolfo from other sources, a claim could be made for the more truculent-looking youth standing arms akimbo in front of the pillar to the right of the family group: P. Kristeller, 'Barbara von Brandenburg, Markgräfin von Mantua', *Hohenzollern Jahrbuch*, 3 (1899), 66–85 (p. 77); *Andrea Mantegna*, trans. S.A. Strong (London, 1901), 244.

52. Giovanni Pietro Arrivabene to Lodovico, Rome, 1 February and 13 March 1476 (AG 845, the first used by A. Luzio, *L'Archivio Gonzaga di Mantova*, II (Verona, 1922), 115 note 2). For what follows, see G. Coniglio, *I Gonzaga* (Milan, 1967), 50–2, 75–6, 80–3, 88–9, and A. Schivenoglia, *Cronaca di Mantova dal MCCCCXLV al MCCCCLXXXIV*, ed. C. d'Arco, in *Raccolta di cronisti e documenti storici lombardi inediti*, II (Milan, 1856), 121–94 (p. 162).

53. Schivenoglia, *Cronaca*, 139–40, 153; G.L. Fantoni, 'Un carteggio femminile del sec. XV: Bianca Maria Visconti e Barbara di Hohenzollern-Brandenburgo Gonzaga (1450–1468)', *Libri e documenti*, 7 (1981), 6–29 (pp. 6, 14 note 4); R. Signorini, '"Manzare poco, bevere aqua asai et dormire manco": suggerimenti dietici vittoriniani di Ludovico II Gonzaga al figlio Gianfrancesco e un sospetto pitagorico', in *Vittorino da Feltre e la sua scuola . . . Atti del Convegno . . . 1979*, ed. N. Giannetto (Florence, 1981), 115–48 (p. 117).

54. Cardinal Francesco Gonzaga to Marchioness Barbara, Rome, 2 March 1467 (AG 843); I am indebted to Professor Elisabeth Swain for a transcript of this letter.

55. AG 2187, f. 383. A similar formula was used by Ferrante of Naples in October 1474, when he sent his son Federico to the Burgundian court: Calmette, 'Le projet de mariage bourguignon–napolitain', 464.

56. *Cronycke van Hollandt, Zeelandt ende Vrieslandt . . . tot de jare MCCCCC ende XVII* (Leiden, 1517), f. cccxxii, and especially Rodolfo to Marchioness Barbara, The Hague, 16 September 1469, in AG 2100. This *busta* contains the following letters from Rodolfo to his mother used in subsequent pages for details of his visit: from Bozzolo, 19 July 1469; from Milan, 24 July 1469; from Mons, 29 August 1469; from The Hague, 16 September and 4 and 20 October 1469; from Brussels, 27 November 1469; from Brussels, 30 November 1469 (with a postscript from Ghent, 28 December); from Ghent, 23 January 1470 (two); from Bruges, 10 March 1470; from Saint-Omer, 10 (two) and 15 July 1470; from Hesdin, 2, 12 and 15 October 1470; and from Ghent, 29 November 1470. Most are written in the hand of his secretary and guardian Enrico Suardi. Suardi's five letters to Barbara from 1469–1470 are in AG 567. The existence of this correspondence was first brought to the attention of historians by Luzio, *L'Archivio Gonzaga*, II, 115, 124 note 2. It has since been used by Kantorowicz, 'The Este portrait', 373, 374; by Bittmann, *Ludwig XI. und Karl de Kühne*, I/2, 424, 434; and by Vaughan, *Charles*, 59, 65, 74–5, 191–2, 211, 238.

57. Schivenoglia, *Cronaca*, 161, and Rodolfo, 26 July 1469 ('. . . *se in me fusse alcuno bon costume, alcuna bona manera per la praticha e per la conversacione, loro tutte*

me le converà lasciare . . .'). For details of Rodolfo's journey see, in addition to the letters listed in the previous note, those from Milan of Rodolfo and Suardi to the marchioness of Mantua, 23 and 26 July 1469, and of Zaccaria Saggio to the marquis, 26 July 1469 (AG 1623), and of Lorenzo Mareschalcho to the marchioness from Antwerp, 7 September 1469 (AG 567).

58. Schivenoglia, *Cronaca*, 161.
59. He wrote verses, and was presumably related, to the poet Giovan Francesco Suardi (died 1468/9): Belloni, 'Un lirico del Quattrocento', 206 notes 4, 5; I follow Belloni (p. 154 note 1) in using the form Suardi rather than Suardo.
60. Schivenoglia, *Cronaca*, 162; R. Truffi, *Giostre e cantori di giostre* (Rocca S. Casciano, 1911), 172; A. Bernardi, *Cronache forlivesi dal 1476 al 1517*, ed. G. Mazzatinti, 2 vols (Bologna, 1895–7), I/2 (1896), 61.
61. AGR CC 1924, f. 206ᵛ; AG 2187, ff. 475–6 (Lodovico Gonzaga's instructions for Iacomo, who was about to leave for Burgundy, dated 14 March 1470); Suardi, 16 September 1469; Rodolfo, 10 July 1470.
62. Caleffini, *Diario*, I, 22; C. von Chłedowski, *Der Hof von Ferrara*, translated from the Polish by R. Schapiro (Munich, 1919), 210; Modena, AS, Casa e Stato: Principi non regnanti, 49,130/10 (correspondence of Rainaldo di Niccolò III d'Este); Walsh, 'The coming', 159.
63. AGR CC 1924, f. 209ᵛ; 1925, ff. 46ᵛ–7, 336, 370.
64. ADN B 3434; Brun-Lavainne, 'Analyse', 202.
65. Much of it translated by Vaughan, *Charles*, 192.
66. Rodolfo, 23 January 1470, and, for what follows, 15 October 1470 and 4 October 1469.
67. He may perhaps be identified as Philippe de Croy, lord of Quiévrain. In 1472 it was at Rodolfo's special request that the marquis of Mantua invited the Burgundian ambassadors to visit him on their return from Naples. The invitation threatened to compromise the marquis in the eyes of his powerful Milanese neighbour, but Galeazzo Maria deigned to overlook the implied insult to his ally Louis XI by choosing to regard the invitation as a purely personal, rather than political, matter. The ambassadors arrived in Mantua at the end of March and stayed for several days. See the letters of Rodolfo from Mantua to his father, 2 September 1471, and to his mother, 2 December 1471 (AG 2100), and to his father, 19 March 1472 (AG 2101), and of the marquis to the duke of Milan, 7 and 30 March 1472, and of the duke to the marquis, 10 March 1472 (ASM 395).
68. For this and what follows, see Rodolfo, 23 January 1470. It does not appear that Rodolfo ever went to Denmark, but Christian and Dorothea visited Mantua in 1474 and 1475 respectively.
69. Rodolfo did not specify what these plans were, but in any event they were never realised, and it was mainly for material reasons that Philip left Charles the Bold's service towards the end of 1470 for that of Louis XI, who gave him in marriage one of his own nieces, Marguerite de Bourbon: Vaughan, *Charles*, 243.
70. '. . . *più voluntiera faria parentato con uno cane rabiato che con alcuno amico d'esso duca de Bergognia* . . .': the bishop of Novara to the duke of Milan, Montrichard, 12 October 1470 (ASM 537). In 1474 Charles apparently

suggested a marriage between Rodolfo's sister Paola and a scion of the ducal family of Guelders: Cardinal Francesco to Lodovico Gonzaga, 9 May 1474 (AG 845) and see also the letters of credence for Lucas de Tolentis addressed by Charles to Francesco dated Vesoul, 23 March 1474 (AG 2187/1121).

71. Vaughan, *Charles*, 65–6.

72. Vaughan, *Charles*, 238–9. Baudouin was involved in intrigues with Louis XI but not to the extent, as Rodolfo wrote, of plotting to capture Charles and hand him over to the French king.

73. Schivenoglia, *Cronaca*, 161. From the graphs drawn up by Tits-Dieuaide, *La formation des prix céréaliers*, between pp. 368 and 369, it emerges that cereal prices in Brabant and Flanders were around 25 per cent higher in 1469–1470 than the average for the preceding ten years, but this rise seems insufficient by itself to account for the discrepancy noticed by Rodolfo. Two Italian pieces of evidence may be cited concerning the Burgundian court's standards of consumption. On 2 January 1472 Francesco Maletta wrote to the duke of Milan from Naples (ASM 221) that Ferrante was reluctant to pay the expenses of the recently arrived Burgundian embassy '*perché dice è difficile cosa contentarli de loro manzare*'. When Anthony of Burgundy arrived in Milan from Naples in July 1475, it was considered fitting to give him '*uno dignissimo presente de cose mangiative*': Simonetta, *Diarii*, 176.

74. Lodovico Gonzaga to Suardi, 10 December 1469 (AG 2891, lib. LXIV, f. 43^v).

75. These frustrations burst out in his letters of 20 and 27 November 1469: '. . . *essendome fatto grande honore me ne vene a resultare grande vergogna . . . me bisogna più tosto stare a vedere che interponerme a cosa che sia e questo perché i poveri homeni mai non fanno bene . . .*' Even allowing for the possibility of exaggeration arising from the ambition and extravagance of youth, Rodolfo's laments were borne out implicitly by Garzia Betes, the Neapolitan ambassador who returned from England via the Burgundian court shortly after Christmas 1469. '*Bello como un perla e tuto gentille*' was how Betes described Rodolfo to the Mantuan ambassador in Milan, who wrote to his master after this conversation that '*di lui dice bene assai e tuta quella corte lo comenda assai et ogniuno ne parla bene e degnamente e tanto meglio se ne diria quanto più l'havesse da spendere, che in vero è il fondamento di far ben dir di sé*': Saggio to Lodovico Gonzaga, 24 March 1470 (AG 1623).

76. For what follows, see Rodolfo, 20 October and 27 November 1469 and 23 January 1470.

77. Rodolfo, 10 July 1470. Rodolfo's debts to Portinari were mentioned also by Saggio, writing to Lodovico Gonzaga from Milan on 28 December 1470 (AG 1623).

78. AG 2187, ff. 475^v–6. For the next sentence, see AGR CC 1925, ff. 379–80.

79. B. Hofmann, 'Barbara von Hohenzollern', *Jahresberichte des historischen Vereins für Mittelfranken*, 41 (1881), 1–51 (p. 46).

80. The letter is in AG 2100.

81. Sacramoro to the duke of Milan, Rome, 5 November 1474 (ASM 76).

82. Simonetta, *Diarii*, 163; Lodovico Gonzaga to Saggio in Milan, 30 June 1475 (AG 2893, lib. LXXVIII, f. 70^v). Indeed, Hans Knebel (*Diarium*, I, 200) listed the marquis among those Italian rulers who, he claimed, were allied with Charles against the emperor and the Germans in 1475. For the next sentence,

see Leonardo Botta to the duke of Milan, Venice, 21 and 23 June 1475 (ASM 361).

83. '. . . *io cognoscendo la gran partialità de tuti de casa de esso Illustrissimo Signore essere più verso Vostra Illustrissima Signoria che ad altro signore de Italia*' (AG 629, no. 67). For the next sentence see Lodovico to Saggio, 1 July 1476 (AG 2894, lib. LXXXI, f. 4).

84. For what follows, see his letter to the marquis of 26 January 1477 (AG 1626).

85. To Giovanni Alberto Brugnolo in Milan, 17 January 1477 (AG 2188). His agent in Rome, Arrivabene, did not mention the rumours of the duke's death until 8 February, when he wrote to his master (AG 846) that, if they were true, then the influence of Louis XI would increase; however, some Burgundians in Rome refused to believe them, insisting that Charles was still alive, having won the battle and retaken Nancy. For further instances of Mantuan interest in the duke's death, see Walsh, 'Vespasiano', 416, 424 note 53, 426 note 79.

86. For this paragraph, see Schivenoglia, *Cronaca*, 166, 172–4; Rodolfo to his mother, Cesena, 15 March, 12 April, 28 May and 13 June 1473 (AG 2101); the duke of Milan to the marquis of Mantua, 10 May 1473 (AG 1607); the marquis to Saggio in Milan, 20 May 1473, and Saggio to the marquis, 10 July 1473 (AG 1624); Giacomo Galeota to the marquis, Jussey, 29 September 1473 (AG 629); *Carteggi*, I, no. 206; Francesco Gonzaga to the marquis, Rome, 9 May 1474 (AG 845); and Niccolò Cattabene to the same, Venice, 25 June 1473 (AG 1431).

87. Schivenoglia, *Cronaca*, 185, 190, 192; B. Arrighi, *Storia di Castiglione delle Stiviere sotto il dominio dei Gonzaga*, 2 vols (Mantua, 1853–5), I, 12–14; F. Kenner, 'Die Porträtsammlung des Erzherzogs Ferdinand von Tirol. Die italienischen Bildnisse', *Jahrbuch der kunsthistorischen Sammlungen des allerhöchsten Kaiserhauses*, 17 (1896), 101–275 (pp. 226–33); Luzio, *L'Archivio Gonzaga*, II, 263–4; Brinton, *The Gonzaga*, 102–3; *Cronaca di Anonimo Veronese*, 368 and note 2, 441; *Cronaca universale della città di Mantova*, ed. G. Amadei, E. Morani and G. Praticò, 4 vols (Mantua, 1953–7), II (1955), 236, 260–1, 266–8, 308–11, 318–23; Coniglio, *I Gonzaga*, 90; A. Benedetti, *Diario de Bello Carolino*, ed. and trans. D.M. Schullian (New York, 1967), 99, 141, 291 note 18. P. Pieri, *Il Rinascimento e la crisi militare italiana* (Turin, 1952), 350 note 1 (on p. 351), discussing the battle of Fornovo in a section on the use of the reserve in Italian warfare, talks of Rodolfo being an expert, a veteran of the Burgundian wars, and the apparent author of the plan of battle.

88. T. Persico, *Diomede Carafa* (Naples, 1899), 212. Much of the basic biographical information about Federico used in subsequent pages is taken without further reference from L. Volpicella, *Federico d'Aragona e la fine del regno di Napoli nel MDI* (Naples, 1908), from the same, in his editorial notes to *Regis Ferdinandi Primi instructionum liber* (Naples, 1916), 234–40, and from A. Archi, *Gli Aragonesi di Napoli* (Bologna, 1968), 113–34.

89. Hill, *A corpus of Italian medals*, I, 78, and II, no. 312 (famous portrait medal attributed to Francesco di Giorgio, ca. 1480); G.L. Hersey, *Alfonso II and the artistic renewal of Naples, 1485–1495* (New Haven–London, 1969), 28 note 7, 124, fig. 171. More stylised and less skilful representations of Federico in later life can be found in *Una cronaca napoletana figurata del Quattrocento*, ed. R.

Filangieri di Candida (Naples, 1956), 88, 101, 191, 241, 246, 249, 254; see also the portrait medals of uncertain authority, in Hill, *Corpus*, I, 78, 79, 81, 82; II, figs. 311, 315, 327–8, 330–2.

90. *Carteggi*, II, no. 582 (PS).

91. C. Porzio, *La congiura de'baroni del regno di Napoli contra il re Ferdinando Primo*, ed. E. Pontieri (Naples, 1958), 78–9, and, on Charles and Philip, Wielant, *Recueil des antiquités de Flandre*, 52–8 (on which see also the critical comments of Vaughan, *Charles*, 158–9).

92. Commynes, *Mémoires*, III, 34.

93. The standard work is E. Pontieri, 'Sulle mancate nozze tra Federico d'Aragona e Maria di Borgogna (1474–1476)', reprinted from *ASPN*, 63 (1939) as Chap. III (pp. 161–208) of his *Per la storia del regno di Ferrante I d'Aragona re di Napoli*, 2nd edtn (Naples, 1969).

94. For this paragraph, see L. de' Medici, *Lettere*, I, 168; Zaccaria Barbaro to Doge Niccolò Tron, Naples, 17 November 1471 and 28 September 1472 (BNMV 8170/I, 14, and III, 44); and Francesco Maletta to the duke of Milan, Naples, 17 February, 5 June and 23 December 1472 (ASM 222).

95. The possibility of an Aragonese match for Federico is mentioned by Calmette, *Louis XI, Jean II*, 371 note 3, by J. Vicens y Vives, *Juan II*, 342, and by M.I. del Val, *Isabel la Católica* (Valladolid, 1974), 254–5, 309; the prospective bride was John II's daughter Juana. None of these authors, however, uses the main source for the Italian side of the negotiations, namely the dispatches from Naples of the Milanese and Venetian ambassadors, Francesco Maletta and Zaccaria Barbaro, in ASM 224–5 and BNMV 8170/V–VI respectively.

96. The only source for this transaction is Francesco Maletta's dispatch to the duke of Milan from Naples of 3 June 1474 (ASM 225); Maletta, however, claimed his source was impeccable, and certainly, as we saw in Chapter 1 ('The material advantage'), Charles did ask at this time for troops and money.

97. Antonio Cincinello to Ferrante, Milan, 11 July 1474 (ASM 226), referring to letters from the Burgundian court of Francesco Bertini informing his master of Anthony's mission.

98. ADN B 2105/67,598.

99. Giovanni Pietro Arrivabene to the marquis, 1 October and 13 November 1474 (AG 845). For what follows, see Francesco Maletta to the duke of Milan, 28 October 1474 (ASM 226).

100. Between October 1474 and January 1475, he sent agents to Italy to propose a marriage between the dauphin Charles and a daughter of Federico's brother Alfonso, a proposal designed more to create dissension between Naples and Burgundy than to produce amity between Naples and France. He also sent an envoy purporting to have been sent by Charles himself to warn Federico not even to set out, as his safe passage as far as the Burgundian court could not be guaranteed. See Francesco Maletta to the duke of Milan, Naples, 24 October and 2 December 1474 (ASM 226); Cristoforo da Bollate to the same, Paris, 27 December 1474 (ASM 541) and 13 January 1475 (ASM 542); and L. de' Medici, *Lettere*, II, 491–2.

101. Cristoforo da Bollate to the duke of Milan, Senlis, 29 April 1474 (ASM 541). But Louis was more eager to imitate than condemn, for, as he had told da Bollate

the previous year, he intended '*fare anche me como fa lo duca de Burg[ogn]a de sua figliola*': same to same, Chartres, 23 December 1473 (ASM 540).

102. C.A.J. Armstrong, in his introduction to his edition and translation of Mancini, *The usurpation of Richard the Third. Dominicus Mancinus ad Angelum Catonem De occupatione regni Anglie per Riccardum tercium libellus*, 2nd edtn (Oxford, 1969), 34.

103. Zaccaria Barbaro to Doge Niccolò Tron, Naples, 19 February and 1 June 1472 (BNMV 8170/II, f. 1ᵛ; III, f. 1ᵛ); Bittmann, *Ludwig XI. und Karl der Kühne*, II/1, 444.

104. Maletta to the duke of Milan, Naples, 19 March 1474 (ASM 225).

105. Indeed, just before Federico left Naples in October 1474 Ferrante sent envoys to Aragon empowered to negotiate a marriage with John II's daughter Juana either for himself or for Federico: Vives, *Fernando el Católico*, 323–5. He was thus already hedging his bets. For earlier projects see Cristoforo da Bollate to the duke of Milan, Orléans, 25 October 1473 (ASM 540), and Senlis, 29 March 1474 (ASM 541), and Sacramoro to the same, Rome, 27 September 1474 (ASM 76).

106. C. Canetta, 'La morte del conte Jacomo Piccinino', *ASL*, 9 (1882), 252–88 (p. 264 = 1465), and Barbaro to the doge, Naples, 13 October 1472 ('*lui havendo tanti figliuoli*') and 17 November 1471 (BNMV 8170/IV, 9, and I, 4). For what follows, see Maletta to the duke of Milan, Naples, 14 July and 4 September 1474 (ASM 226).

107. The documents were published by Calmette, 'Le projet de mariage bourguignon–napolitain', 464–72.

108. Maletta to the duke of Milan, Naples, 4 August 1474 (ASM 226); Arrivabene to the marquis of Mantua, Rome, 7 November 1474 (AG 845).

109. Naples, Biblioteca della Società Napoletana di Storia Patria, *fascio* XXVI, C5, no. 11, ff. 11–12.

110. T. Caracciolo, *Nobilitatis Neapolitanae defensio*, in his *Opuscoli storici*, ed. G. Paladini (Bologna, 1934), 141–8 (pp. 143–4). For the next sentence, see Leonardo Botta to the duke of Milan, Venice, 6 January 1475 (ASM 359).

111. Arrivabene to the marquis of Mantua, Rome, 7 November 1474 (AG 845). For the rest of the paragraph, see Antonio d'Appiano to the duke of Milan, Turin, 11 February 1475 (ASM 495) and Sacramoro to the same from Rome, 5 November 1474 (ASM 76), from Milan, 8 February 1476 (ASM 80) and from Foligno, 7 October 1476 (ASM 82).

112. Simonetta, *Diarii*, 151–3; *Codice Visconteo-Sforzesco*, ed. C. Morbio (Milan, 1846), 438; the duke of Milan to Cristoforo da Bollate in France from Vigevano, 3 December 1474 (ASM 541); and Saggio to the marquis of Mantua, Milan, 17 January 1475 (AG 1625). Galeazzo Maria's disquiet may have been due also to a suspicion that Federico's arrival represented a last-minute Neapolitan attempt to prevent the conclusion of the treaty of Moncalieri between Milan and Burgundy.

113. For what follows, see Antonio d'Appiano to the duke of Milan, Turin, 5, 11 and 13 February 1475 (ASM 492) and *Carteggi*, I, no. 249.

114. D'Appiano to the duke of Milan, Moncalieri, 17 January 1475 (ASM 492); *Eidgenössische Abschiede*, 526 (no. 776); Saggio to the marquis of Mantua,

Milan, 23 February 1475 (AG 1625); Knebel, *Diarium*, I, 158; T. von Liebenau, 'Ueber eine geheime Mission des Gabriel Morosini', *BSSI*, 23 (1901), 96–100 (p. 100 note 1).

115. For what follows see M. Rey and R. Fiétier, 'Le moyen âge du XIIᵉ au XVᵉ siècle', in *Histoire de Besançon*, ed. C. Fohlen, 2 vols, 2nd edtn (Besançon, 1981–2), I, 329–572 (pp. 521–2); Knebel, *Diarium*, I, 204–5; *Recueil de choses advenues du temps et gouvernement de très haulte mémoire feu Charles, duc de Bourgogne, estant le seigneur du Fay gouverneur au pays de Luxembourg*, in *Publications de la Société pour la recherche et la conservation des monuments historiques dans le Grand-Duché de Luxembourg*, III (Arlon, 1847), 85–153 (pp. 103, 106–7, 109–10, 116); ADN B 2106/67,763; Arrivabene to the marquis of Mantua, Rome, 9 June 1475, summarising Conti's letter (AG 845); Maletta to the duke of Milan, Naples, 18 April 1475 (ASM 227); *Carteggi*, I, no. 283; AG 2187, f. 1154 (Charles's letter to Ferrante *'ex castris apud flumen Harnufan'*); and *Chronique de Lorraine*, 165.

116. Published by Pontieri, 'Sulle mancate nozze', 188 note 60, who reads the date as 1476, although the content means it can only be 1475, but it is filed in ASM 228 (not 225 as Pontieri states), the *carteggio* for 1476, rather than 227 (= 1475).

117. For what follows, see *Carteggi*, II, nos. 385 (part translated by Vaughan, *Charles*, 170–1), 468, 515, 388.

118. Camillo Pandone to Ferrante, Lausanne, 13 March 1476 (ASM 518); A. Allegretti, *Diarj sanesi*, ed. L.A. Muratori (Milan, 1723), 762–860 (pp. 776–7); Molinet, *Chroniques*, I, 139 (though this description fits better what we know about the council of war held before the battle of Murten); *Carteggi*, II, no. 445; *Dépêches . . . Charles-le-Hardi*, I, no. 140; II, no. 200.

119. Pontieri, 'Sulle mancate nozze', 192–208, who stresses that, while Ferrante sought an ally against France, Charles was more concerned with the Empire, hence his preference for Maximilian of Habsburg over Federico.

120. *Carteggi*, II, no. 366.

121. *Carteggi*, II, nos. 612, 613.

122. *Carteggi*, II, no. 637.

123. See the document published by Calmette, 'Le projet de mariage bourguignon–napolitain', 466. Calmette (p. 463 note 2) confessed to being unable to shed any light on the course of the negotiations; Pontieri too could shed no light on them. For the rest of the paragraph see Niccolò Cattabene to the marquis of Mantua, Venice, 2 November 1474 (ASM 1431).

124. *Carteggi*, I, no. 265, and II, no. 360.

125. *Carteggi*, II, no. 366. Similarly, Guillaume de Rochefort had told the Milanese ambassador at the Savoyard court earlier that year that Federico would be a means to enable Charles to string Ferrante along (*'intertenire'*): d'Appiano to the duke of Milan, Moncalieri, 16 February 1475 (ASM 492).

126. But such action could also be useful in putting pressure on Ferrante's rival Galeazzo Maria to be more amenable towards the duke of Burgundy. For a similar, though less momentous, example of Charles the Bold's balancing between Naples and Milan, see R.J. Walsh, 'Music and Quattrocento diplomacy: the singer Jean Cordier between Milan, Naples and Burgundy in 1475', *AKG*, 60 (1978), 439–42.

127. Arrivabene to the marquis of Mantua, Rome, 16 February 1476 (AG 845).

128. *Carteggi*, II, no. 601.

129. In 1466, Louis XI had suggested that Galeazzo Maria might seek Mary's hand but warned that, even if he succeeded, his future Burgundian subjects '*non soffrirano governo italiano*': *Dépêches . . . Louis XI*, IV, 302.

130. Walsh, 'The coming', 185–92.

131. Maletta to the duke of Milan, Naples, 27 January 1475 (ASM 227). One of these lords had been with the embassy to Naples of 1472 (Philippe de Croy?). They said the duke had no intention of agreeing to the marriage; he wanted Federico sent to him merely to demonstrate to Louis XI the strength of his Neapolitan alliance and to frighten Galeazzo Maria out of sending troops to the French king against him (the treaty of Moncalieri had not yet been concluded).

132. The letter is printed in Haynin, *Mémoires*, II, 183–4, and in Chastellain, *Oeuvres*, VIII, 268. For the next sentence, see *Carteggi*, II, no. 360.

133. *Carteggi*, II, nos. 360, 393, 409.

134. *Carteggi*, I, nos. 258, 310. For what follows, see *Carteggi*, I, nos. 256, 259, II, no. 366; Saggio to the marquis of Mantua, Milan, 18 and 25 November 1475 (AG 1625); and Enrico Suardi to the marchioness of Mantua, Milan, 23 July 1469 (AG 1625).

135. *Carteggi*, II, no. 580.

136. For these examples, see *Carteggi*, I, no. 256, and II, nos. 331, 496.

137. The Urbinese ambassador at the Neapolitan court, reflecting the views held there of Troilo, described him to the Venetian ambassador as '*un mato spazado*': Barbaro to Doge Niccolò Tron, 15 December 1472 (BNMV 8170/IV, 41).

138. For example, over the revolt of Genoa against Milanese rule and the ignominious flight of the Milanese ambassadors from the Burgundian camp before the battle of Murten: *Carteggi*, II, nos. 376, 468, 613.

139. For what follows, see *Dépêches . . . Charles-le-Hardi*, I, no. 86; and *Carteggi*, II, nos. 393, 395, 512, 526, 583, 597, 604, 609.

140. *Carteggi*, II, no. 385. For what follows, see *Carteggi*, II, nos. 469, 493, 496. Charles told the Milanese ambassador that he had made Federico his lieutenant solely in order to beguile him while he completed his own plans in Provence (*Carteggi*, II, no. 492: Panigarola, 3 April 1476). There appears to have been no connection between the duke's appointment of Federico as his lieutenant and the departure some months before of the count of Campobasso on, so he claimed, a pilgrimage to Compostela.

141. Armstrong, in Mancini, *The usurpation of Richard III*, 34.

142. *Carteggi*, I, no. 258. Shortly before, the Milanese ambassador in Naples had been given to understand by Alfonso of Calabria that Ferrante was waiting to see if Federico succeeded in Burgundy before he went ahead with the Aragonese match: Maletta to the duke of Milan, 1 March 1475 (ASM 227).

143. *Carteggi*, II, nos. 360, 395, 565. As regards the other Neapolitan–Aragonese marriage proposal under consideration, a contract was signed on 3 May 1476 for a marriage between Isabella, daughter of the Catholic Kings, and Ferrandino, eldest son of Alfonso of Calabria: Vicens y Vives, *Juan II*, 361.

144. For this and the next paragraph, see Perotto de Vesach to the duke of Ferrara, Naples, 1 June 1476 (Modena, AS, Cancelleria, estero: Carteggi degli ambasciatori, Napoli, 1, 161); *Carteggi*, II, nos. 604, 607–8, 613; and Molinet, *Chroniques*, I, 164.

145. *Carteggi*, II, no. 582 (PS).

146. Galeazzo Maria may have heeded this advice, since he invited Federico to pass through the duchy of Milan on his return. See his letters to Federico and to Cristoforo da Bollate, whom he sent as messenger to Federico, both dated Pavia, 26 June 1476 (ASM 495).

147. *Mémoires*, II, 118. As is pointed out by Armstrong (in Mancini, *The usurpation of Richard III*, 26–8), Commynes showed caution by suggesting that Cato's prediction was based on rational forecasts rather than astrology, in which he was adept, according to contemporaries. In this context it may be of interest to remark that the Milanese ambassador in Naples, Maletta, writing to his master on 22 December 1474 (ASM 226), had recommended Cato as a most reliable source of information both on Neapolitan affairs in general and on the reasons for Federico's visit to Charles the Bold.

148. As a postscript to his dispatch of 2 July 1476 (ASM 495), the Milanese ambassador in Turin, Francesco Pietrasanta, wrote to his master about reports reaching him of the predictions made by Federico's astrologer, namely that Charles would be defeated, and it was for this reason that Federico had left, but the astrologer had also predicted that Charles would be successful if he waited until after the calends of August. For the next sentence, see Brinton, *The Gonzaga*, 60 note 1, citing the second book of Mario Equicola's history of Mantua (1521), where several examples besides that of Federico are given; Equicola (ca. 1470–1525) had studied at the University of Naples.

149. D'Appiano to the duke of Milan, Gex, 30 May and 24 June 1476 (ASM 495); *Dépêches . . . Charles-le-Hardi*, II, nos. 223, 253.

150. See, for example, B. Croce, 'Elisio Calenzio', in his *Varietà di storia letteraria e civile. Prima serie*, 2nd edtn (Bari, 1949), 7–29 (pp. 21–3), Pontieri, 'Sulle mancate nozze', 207–8, and T. Caracciolo, *De varietate fortunae*, in his *Opuscoli storici editi e inediti*, 73–105 (p. 93). See also Walsh, 'Vespasiano', 414.

151. *Dépêches . . . Charles-le-Hardi*, II, no. 253; d'Appiano to the duke of Milan, Gex, 26 June 1476 (ASM 495); *Carteggi*, II, nos. 629, 637, 643.

152. Writing to the duke of Milan on 29 July 1475 (ASM 227), Maletta announced the arrival in Naples of the French king's emissary, Tommaso Taquino, bearing a proposal for a marriage between Louis' eldest daughter Anne and Federico. On 19 June 1476, Panigarola wrote that he had learned from a reliable source that Federico would soon leave for France to marry Louis' younger, hunchbacked daughter Jeanne (*Carteggi*, II, no. 607). However, neither report seems worthy of much credence. Anne had been betrothed to Pierre de Beaujeu since 1473, when she was twelve, while the contract of marriage between Jeanne and Duke Louis of Orléans (later King Louis XII) was to be completed towards the end of August 1476, when Jeanne too was twelve, but Louis had already decided on this match three years earlier. See *Lettres de Louis XI*, III, 173 note 1, and X, 350 and note 1, and Isenburg and Loringhoven, *Stammtafeln*, II, table 16. Armstrong (in Mancini, *The usurpation of Richard III*, 34) wrote of

Federico's marriage in 1479 to Anne of Savoy that he transferred too late from the Burgundian to the French court to receive more than a modest matrimonial reward from Louis XI, but it is difficult to see how he could have made a better French match, since Louis' two daughters had already been provided for, as stated above; and, in any case, Jeanne was correctly thought by her father to be infertile.

153. Francesco Pietrasanta to the duke of Milan, Lyon, 18 July 1476 (ASM 542), naming his source as Lionetto de' Rossi, the manager of the Lyon branch of the Medici bank. See also L. de' Medici, *Lettere*, II, 229–30, and Vicens y Vives, *Fernado el Católico*, 324.

154. Sacramoro to the duke of Milan, Foligno, 1 October 1476 (ASM 82); T. de Marinis, *La biblioteca napoletana dei re d'Aragona*, 4 vols (Milan, 1947–52), II (1947), 311; and Passero, *Storie*, 31, 35–6.

155. Perotto de Vesach to the duke of Ferrara, Naples, 21 August 1476 (Modena, AS, Cancelleria, estero: Carteggi degli ambasciatori, Napoli, 1, 164 and 167); *Les comptes du roi René*, II, no. 2314; Labande, *Avignon au XVᵉ siècle*, 228; G. Arnaud d'Agnel, *Politique des rois de France en Provence. Louis XI et Charles VIII*, 2 vols (Paris–Marseille, 1914), I, 57–8.

156. Sacramoro to the duke of Milan, Foligno, 7 October 1476 (ASM 82).

157. For details of the marriage and general diplomatic background, see J.B.M.C. Kervyn de Lettenhove, *Lettres et négociations de Philippe de Commynes*, 3 vols (Brussels, 1867–8), I, 212–13, 244–6, 264–5, 271–2, 325, and III, 53; *Lettres de Louis XI*, VII, 160–2, and VIII, 33, 80, 163 note 2, 270–1; Perret, *Histoire*, II, 136–7, 142, 186–92, 196, 201; Persico, *Diomede Carafa*, 213–16; Périnelle, 'Dépêches de Nicolas de' Roberti', 158–9, 166, 179, 196, 199–200, 202, 428–9, 432–3, 435, 437, 441, 463, 471; Volpicella, *Federico d'Aragona*, 51 note 1; *Regis Ferdinandi Primi instructionum liber*, 234–5; C. De Frede, 'Un memoriale di Ferrante I d'Aragona a Luigi XI (1478)', *RSI*, 60 (1948), 403–19; Cerioni, 'La politica italiana di Luigi XI e la missione di Filippo di Commynes', 59–156; Vicens y Vives, *Juan II*, 363–4; and L. de' Medici, *Lettere*, II, 447–8, and III, 214–15. There are two editions of Carafa's *Memoriale* for Federico on this trip, by A. Altamura in *Testi napoletani del Quattrocento* (Naples, 1953), 35–49, and by L. Miele, *Memoriale a Federico d'Aragona in occasione della sua andata in Francia* (Naples, 1972).

158. For the imperial marriage see, in addition to the works cited in the previous note, W. Fraknói (Frankl), *Mathias Corvinus* (Freiburg im Breisgau, 1891), 196–203; L. Sorricchio, 'Angelo ed Antonio Probi, ambasciatori di Ferdinando I d'Aragona (1464–1482)', *ASPN*, 21 (1896), 148–69 (pp. 150–1, 161–5); Cusin, 'I rapporti tra la Lombardia e l'impero', 306–16; Pontieri, 'La politica estera di Ferrante d'Aragona', 266–73; and K. Nehring, *Matthias Corvinus, Kaiser Friedrich III. und das Reich* (Munich, 1975), 91–5, 107–11.

159. Notar Giacomo, *Cronica di Napoli*, ed. P. Garzill (Naples, 1845), 148; Commynes, *Mémoires*, II, 294–5; F. Flamini, 'Francesco Galeota, gentiluomo napolitano del Quattrocento e il suo inedito canzoniere', *GSLI*, 20 (1892), 1–90 (pp. 8–11, 72–8); Pontieri, 'Un monarca realista e un asceta del Quattrocento: Ferrante d'Aragona, re di Napoli, e S. Francesco di Paola', in his *Per la storia*, 371–443 (pp. 427–40); and especially G. Roberti, *S. Francesco*

di Paola, 2nd edtn (Rome, 1963), 349, 363–4, 380–1, who corrects those authors who state that the saint's journey to France took place in 1482.

160. See, for example, P. de Vigneulles, *Gedenkbuch aus den Jahren 1471 bis 1522*, ed. H. Michelant (Stuttgart, 1852), 24; B. de Mandrot, *Ymbert de Batarnay* (Paris, 1886), 322–3; Volpicella, *Federico d'Aragona*, 10–11; and Commynes, *Mémoires*, III, 34.

161. Isabella died at Ferrara in 1533 aged 69, having returned from France in 1511. She had two daughters by Federico: Isabella and Giulia, and three sons: Ferdinando (or Ferrante/Fernando/Ferrando), Alfonso and Cesare. Not much is known about them, but clearly the male line died out with Federico's sons. Alfonso died at Grenoble in 1515. The eldest, Ferdinando, passed the bulk of his life in gilded captivity in Spain, dying in a monastery probably in 1559; he had been married twice, but both his wives had been chosen for him on the basis of their known infertility. See F. Carabellese, 'Andrea da Passano e la famiglia d'Isabella del Balzo d'Aragona', *ASPN*, 24 (1889), 428–43; B. Croce, 'Isabella del Balzo', in his *Storie e leggende napoletane*, 4th edtn (Bari, 1948), 183–212; de Marinis, *La biblioteca napoletana*, II, 198; M. del Carmen Pescador del Hoyo, 'Tres documentos de Federico de Napoles en los fondos del Archivo Histórico Nacional de Madrid', in *Studi in onore di Riccardo Filangieri*, 2 vols (Naples, 1959), II, 249–60; R. Silvestri Baffi, 'Di Isabella del Balzo e del suo viaggio attraverso la Puglia', in *Studi di storia pugliese in onore di Giuseppe Chiarelli*, ed. M. Paone, 2 vols (Galatina, 1972–3), II, 321–51 (pp. 328 and note 9, 349–51); and Archi, *Gli Aragonesi di Napoli*, 126–34. Ciarlotta, as the Neapolitan sources describe her, Federico's daughter by his first marriage, died in 1505, only a year after her father.

162. For what follows, see — in addition to the works already cited — Roberti, *S. Francesco di Paola*, 515–16, 634, and Volpicella, *Federico d'Aragona*, 81.

CHAPTER SEVEN

Italian Troops in Charles the Bold's Army

Perhaps the single most striking feature of Charles the Bold's relations with Italy and of his interest in things Italian was the large number of Italian mercenaries in his army. That army was cosmopolitan and, besides his own subjects, comprised troops of many nationalities, but by 1476 the Italians were probably the most numerous of these outsiders and were certainly the most important in terms of rank. As we saw in Chapter 1, the duke's attempts through diplomacy to augment his armed forces with contingents from the armies of Naples, Venice and Milan, despite what is sometimes assumed, met with only limited success. Since, therefore, this phenomenon of large numbers of Italian troops serving in the Burgundian army during his reign can be explained only partially by reference to the terms of his treaties with his allies in the peninsula, it is appropriate to consider it more fully here as a separate topic. This chapter will attempt to show how, when and why these mercenaries came to be in the ducal army, to estimate their numbers and to assess their military value and influence.

Charles the Bold's motives for recruiting Italian troops

The last Valois duke of Burgundy was not alone in his admiration of Italian troops. Ultramontanes had been able to appreciate them at close quarters, both in Italy itself — during their own campaigns there in the middle decades of the fifteenth century and earlier (for example, those of the Angevins in Naples, or of the French under Charles VII in northern Italy) — and in their own lands (for instance, the Milanese troops who came to the aid of Louis XI in the War of the Public Weal). A high regard for Italian military expertise and a desire to learn from it were among the few things Louis XI and Charles the Bold had in common.[1]

In addition to these general motives, there were short-term reasons why the duke recruited his Italian mercenaries when he did (mostly in the period between the autumn of 1472 and the early summer of 1473). In the first half of his reign, Charles felt himself to be at a disadvantage in relation to the French king, because Louis always had the initiative on the outbreak of hostilities through the possession of a permanent or standing army.[2] As early as the beginning of 1469, we find Charles complaining of the deficiencies of the traditional Burgundian military machine, notably the delay in assembly of those called upon to serve and the weakness, in terms of both numbers and quality, of the army produced by such means.[3] These deficiencies had almost proved fatal when Louis attacked suddenly across the Somme in January 1471, for Charles had then been unable for a short but vital space of time to retaliate. In order to increase his preparedness, he had attempted since the autumn of 1469 to establish an army based, like its French exemplar, on companies of ordinance made up of full-time, salaried professionals. But by the time he signed a five-month truce with Louis on 3 November 1472, this new organisation was still not complete, and as that truce was regarded by both parties as likely to be only a respite before the resumption of hostilities in the next campaigning season, the duke began to recruit foreign mercenaries on a large scale in order to bring his army up to the requisite numerical strength and state of readiness. The addition of these contingents, he hoped, would not only enable him to defend himself if attacked, but also give him a striking force capable of taking the offensive (*'piutosto apto ad avanzare che cedere'*).[4]

Italians were not the only foreign troops he enlisted at this time, for he also recruited Englishmen, Germans and troops from other parts of western Europe. The Italians, however, did have certain qualities to recommend them. In the winter of 1472–1473 they were, above all, readily available and easily obtainable in large numbers. The timing of this recruiting shows again how important the duke's attitude to France was in determining the course of his relations with the peninsula. It was apprehension of Louis XI which impelled him to try — in vain, as it proved — to secure the services of the Venetian captain-general Colleoni.[5] It is interesting, by way of comparison, to find Louis himself asking Galeazzo Maria at the end of 1473 for the loan of the services of that ruler's leading captain, Roberto Sanseverino, on similar grounds: namely, that the enlisting of Italian troops was the speediest means of preparing himself for war.[6]

Moreover, when Charles entered the market for foreign troops, he had military, rather than merely logistical, reasons for giving priority to recruiting Italians. He wanted to enlist Colleoni, as his envoy Giovanni di Candida told the Venetian senate early in 1473, '*ob virtutes, famam et constantem fidem suam*'.[7] He probably felt a proportional degree of warm admiration for the less prominent Italian mercenaries, since in his opinion the Italians were indisputably pre-eminent in the arts of war, possessing experience, expertise, discipline and organisation. The chronicler Jean Molinet reports Charles as saying to his Italian troops at the siege of Neuss that it was these qualities which had persuaded him to bring them from Italy and to promote them to the leading positions of command in his army, even in preference to his own relatives, subjects and vassals; similarly, when he sent Hugues de Chalon to Italy in April 1476 to recruit troops, the Milanese ambassador wrote that the duke wanted Italians because they were more suited to the trade of arms and alert to his wishes.[8] Certainly he hoped that some of their prowess would rub off onto his own subjects, who, as he told Troilo da Rossano (one of his leading Neapolitan captains) after the battle of Murten, had grown rusty in the practice of arms because of the long years of peace they had enjoyed in the reign of Philip the Good.[9] In the event, however, this early experiment in military education, which by May 1476 had made the Burgundian army, in Vaughan's words, 'predominantly Italian', certainly as far as its senior officers were concerned,[10] was cut short by the duke's death less than a year later.

Chronology of recruitment

Given, on the one hand, the heterogeneous geographical origins of the troops who served in the Burgundian army and, on the other, the desire for travel and adventure of the European knightly class during the late Middle Ages, it is probable that Charles the Bold's army contained from the time of his accession at least some Italian soldiers (as had the French army for many years[11]). For example, a contingent of 'Lamparter' (presumably Italians or 'Lombards') travelled through the Black Forest and Breisach to join the Burgundian governor of Alsace in 1470.[12] Giacomo dei Vischi of the counts of San Martino in Piedmont had a connection with the Burgundian court reaching back into the reign of Philip the Good, making him, in other words, readily available when military commanders were needed, so that Charles did not have to look far if he wanted an experienced Italian captain. In this context we first find him mentioned in the financial records of the reign towards the end of 1471, when he was in charge of between forty and sixty men-at-arms. Between February and April of the following year he was described as a *conducteur* of a hundred lances of the ordinance stationed at Corbie in Picardy.[13] Antonio dei Corradi di Lignana, elder brother of Pietro and later one of the duke's most trusted Italian mercenaries, probably took part in the Burgundian campaigns along the Somme in the early months of 1471.[14]

The bulk of the Italian mercenaries, however, were recruited in the winter of 1472–1473. Charles enlisted the captains first; he then made an advance payment to enable them to furnish the troop quotas allotted. The first such contract from this period was that made with Troilo da Rossano and his two sons, Alessandro and Gianfrancesco, on 29 September 1472; Troilo was given just over six months in which to recruit troops in Italy and have them ready for muster in Burgundy or Lorraine.[15] The contract with perhaps the most famous (or infamous) of all the mercenary captains — Cola di Monforte, count of Campobasso — bears the date 10 November 1472.[16] By mid-November, Charles had also arranged to take into his service, as captains, the Piedmontese brothers Antonio and Pietro dei Corradi di Lignana, although the contract with Giacomo dei Vischi and his two sons, Filippo and Battista, had to wait until 12 March 1473.[17] Cola di Monforte's friend and fellow-Neapolitan, Giacomo Galeota, was probably enlisted formally in January 1473; in order to start his recruiting campaign, he had presented himself at the Savoyard court in Vercelli towards the end of that month.[18] And it was precisely at this time that the duke's hopes of enlisting Colleoni were at their height. Charles seems originally to have planned that his new contingents would have reached his lands by the beginning of April 1473, so that he might enjoy the benefit of their services when his truces with Louis XI expired. However, the delays which they experienced in Italy — and which probably owed not a little to the obstruction of the duke of Milan and the republic of Venice — disrupted his timetable, and perhaps this fact contributed something towards his decision to renew the French truce. Giacomo Galeota, for example, was still at Reggio in mid-May, while Giacomo dei Vischi had for some reason travelled on to Rome, where he had been detained by illness; he was still in Piedmont in October, although the company he had assembled had crossed the Alps in time to take part in the siege of Nijmegen in July. But most of the new recruits had probably arrived in

Dijon by the beginning of June, when the question of payment due to them caused the local authorities no little trouble.[19]

Charles made no further large-scale attempt to augment his army with Italian mercenaries until the spring of 1476. It is possible, though, that more did join him in the intervening period on their own initiative. Such enlistment, of course, is by its very irregularity difficult to trace, but some examples can be found. At the beginning of 1474, a Giovanni and a Fabrizio, both of Capua, left the kingdom of Naples for Burgundy.[20] Ameo or Amedeo di Valperga first appeared in the duke's service as a squire in May 1474; later, during the siege of Neuss, he was given charge of a hundred lances of the ordinance.[21] He was accompanied, or joined subsequently, by his brothers Arduino and Arrighino, whose earliest recorded exploits were at the siege of Neuss.[22] The young Agostino Fregoso was in the Burgundian service by the early summer of 1474, although he is not recorded in the *escroes* until October that year.[23] It is possible that Italians were among the hundred men-at-arms whom Guillaume de Rochefort was empowered in December 1474 to recruit in the lands of the duke of Savoy. Similarly, the 68 soldiers enlisted in the duchy of Savoy by Anthony of Burgundy on his return from Naples in the second half of 1475 may have included some Italians.[24] In general, however, it seems reasonable to conclude that Italian additions to the Burgundian army between the summer of 1473 and the spring of 1476 were numerically marginal, and they were probably only to a very small extent the result of direct activity by Charles himself.

His next and final recruiting drive in the peninsula took place between the middle of April and the end of June 1476, and was conducted by Hugues de Chalon, lord of Châteauguyon. This time Charles wanted to enlist troops individually or in small units (*lanze spezzate*[25]), and directly, rather than through captains commanding several hundred men each; presumably he felt this method would improve quality and discipline while reducing costs. Hugues stayed at Turin for over ten weeks, entering into negotiations with many soldiers both renowned and disreputable, but those whom he showed an interest in recruiting were often unable to produce the necessary papers or financial sureties. Although this mission aroused much interest, excitement and trepidation throughout northern Italy, it did not significantly increase the size of the Burgundian army before defeat at the battle of Murten, followed by Hugues' brief arrest at the hands of the Piedmontese authorities, brought it to a premature close.

Numbers

Attempts to estimate the number of Italian troops in the duke's army are beset by several obvious difficulties. Nowhere in the Burgundian records, for instance, can we find a complete head-count of all the troops such as would make possible an enumeration of just the Italian names. On the contrary, payments were made to individual divisions, and, even when these were commanded by Italian captains, they may not have been composed entirely, or even mainly, of Italian rank-and-file. Again, increases in numbers through recruiting were doubtless offset, to an extent difficult to determine exactly, by losses from deaths or desertion.

We may start by totalling the numbers of Italians enlisted in the first recruiting drive of 1472–1473. From the contracts made with the major captains, we learn that the count of Campobasso was to bring 400 lances (each consisting of four horsemen), 100 mounted crossbowmen, 200 infantry of the type known as *provisionnaires* (*provisionati* in Italian) and 100 cavalry of the type known as *jennetaires* (*genectarii* in the contract); [26] Troilo da Rossano was allotted 150 six-man lances, 100 mounted crossbowmen and 200 *provisionnaires*; Galeota's quota was 150 four-man lances and 300 *provisionnaires*; the Corradi di Lignana brothers were to furnish between them 200 lances (presumably consisting each of the usual four men, although their contract did not specify this); and, finally, Giacomo dei Vischi was required to enlist 100 lances (again, presumably, of four men, although the number was not stated). Some qualifications have to be made. We may assume that the captains produced the number of troops for which they had received advance payment, since Charles seems to have been pleased with the results of their efforts, [27] but these contingents probably included a small number of non-combatants, such as trumpeters, doctors, secretaries and notaries. Moreover, some of the troops may not have been Italian at all; according to one eye-witness, most of Campobasso's troops were from Catalonia. [28] If we accept the figures at their face value, however, we arrive at the following totals: 4,600 cavalry (850 four-man and 150 six-man lances, plus 100 *jennetaires* and 200 mounted crossbowmen) and 700 infantry, a grand total of 5,300 troops. [29] Moreover, the proportion of Italians in the Burgundian army at this time is interesting. Early in 1473, Charles told the States General that he was aiming at a standing army numbering about 10,000 men, a figure which did not include the army in the two Burgundies or the artillery corps. [30] Thus our estimated 5,300 Italians represented something between a third and a half of the whole army.

Between 1474 and 1476 the army was slightly augmented, as we have seen, by new recruits from the peninsula, but these accretions of manpower were to some extent — even, perhaps, completely — offset by losses through casualties or desertion. Desertion may have been encouraged by the practice of giving the newly recruited mercenary company leaders payments in advance to enable them to prepare themselves and their men for review by the duke's officers up to three months later; Galeota was one commander who suffered from this problem.[31] Casualties resulting from actual hostilities were probably more numerically significant than desertions. Campobasso's company suffered severe losses in 1474 and 1475, especially at the siege of Neuss, so that by the beginning of 1476 its original strength had been almost halved.[32] The Italians who remained at this time to defend the borders of Burgundy and Franche-Comté against the Swiss and the French were similarly afflicted. As one of the duke of Milan's correspondents (possibly Troilo) put it, the war there was nothing but fire and blood.[33] Certainly Troilo complained of a shortage of manpower, while already in June 1474 the musters held in Luxembourg revealed that Giacomo dei Vischi's company was almost 15 per cent under strength.[34]

The records of the reviews held in the summer of 1475 enable us to discover the strength of the Italian contingents after two years in the Burgundian service. Troilo's company, which was reviewed in Burgundy in April, July and September, was still composed of 150 six-man lances, 100 mounted crossbowmen and 200 infantry. The review of Giacomo dei Vischi's contingent showed not only that it was back to strength after the decline in 1474, but also that it may have been larger than it had been in 1473, since each of its hundred lances now definitely consisted of six and not four men. In addition, Giacomo commanded three hundred archers; shortly after the review, however, his company was among the Burgundian forces who suffered heavy losses fighting against the Swiss near Château Chinon.[35] According to the review of Campobasso's company at Neuss on 8 June, he had under his command 237 men-at-arms (mostly Italians, judging by the list of names given in his receipt), 132 mounted crossbowmen and 164 infantry. Added to these were 27 German artillerymen ('*culevriniers almans*') and 13 assorted non-combatants. The review in the following month accounted for a further ten soldiers and 329 German infantry. Galeota's company, as reviewed at Neuss on 7 June, comprised 144 men-at-arms, 294 infantry and 25 non-combatants. Finally, the review of the Corradi di Lignana brothers' company made at the same time as the others, and also at Neuss, gives the following figures for combatants: 169 men-at-arms (a term, like 'lances', usually referring to cavalry), 51 mounted crossbowmen, 285 infantry and 66 'culevriners', also on foot (see Figure 2).[36]

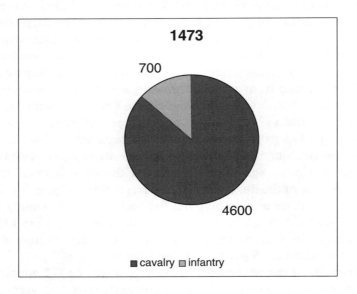

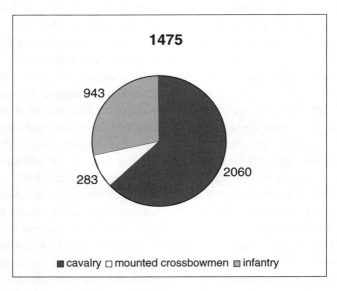

Figure 2. Numbers of Italian troops in Charles the Bold's army, (a) 1473 and (b) 1475.

Some of these Italian captains were in charge of German troops, and it is probable that not all the other troops who belonged to the companies commanded by Italians were themselves Italian. For example, Molinet tells us that at the siege of Neuss the comparative newcomer Ameo di Valperga was placed in command of a hundred lances formerly under Josse de Lalaing.[37] The figures derived from the 1475 reviews may not tell the whole story for another reason, namely that additional groups of Italians were quite possibly engaged in garrison duty in the Low Countries or on the borders with northern France.[38] To take them at their face value, however, we find that the Italian troops thus listed amounted to 2,050 cavalry, 283 mounted crossbowmen and 943 infantry, or 3,276 in all. Compared with the figures for two years previously, the infantry and mounted crossbowmen had increased substantially, but these gains were more than outweighed by losses in cavalry. On the other hand, this balance could have been in part the result of organisational changes introduced by Charles to meet revised military preferences. In any case, these figures tally fairly closely with those of a German student of the duke's army who, on the basis of published sources, estimated that Charles had about 3,000 Italian troops at the siege of Neuss.[39]

Between the battles of Grandson and Murten, the duke tried to reinforce his army in Savoy by further Italian recruiting conducted in Piedmont by Hugues de Chalon, but with apparently little significant result. The accounts of the *trésorier des guerres* for 1476, Hues de Dompierre, record advance payments made to several Italian captains, who were to use the money to prepare themselves for review in the Burgundian camp in the first half of July. In the case of only some of these captains are the figures recorded for how many men they were to bring with them; given this qualification, the figures would have totalled at least 254 men-at-arms and 300 infantry.[40] From the dispatches sent to the duke of Milan by his representatives in Piedmont and at the Burgundian court, we can calculate further that the numbers which would have been commanded, both by these captains whose quota is given in Hues de Dompierre's account and by those not mentioned at all in that account but who are reported by the Milanese observers to have received advance payment, would have amounted to about 250 lances, 500 infantry and 50 mounted crossbowmen.[41] Altogether the projected reinforcements could have totalled 2,500 combatants, or just under half the number recruited three years before. A Milanese exile and agent of the duke at the Savoyard court, Antonio Matteo da Iseo, told the Milanese ambassador in Turin that Charles wanted to enlist up to

1,420 troops of one sort or another.[42] But it was not to be. By the time that the battle of Murten struck a disastrous blow to Burgundian influence in Savoy, the contracts with most of the would-be captains remained unsigned. At the end of June, Hugues de Chalon received instructions to send off at once all those with whom he had reached agreement over terms, but there is no record, either in Burgundian accounts or in Panigarola's dispatches, of any of the troops actually arriving in the Burgundian camp after the battle, despite some assertions by contemporaries to the contrary.[43] Moreover, it is almost certain that, between the battles of Grandson and Murten, the overall number of Italians in the ducal army suffered an absolute decline, largely through desertion. At the beginning of June 1476, the Milanese ambassador in Turin reported that Italians fleeing from the Burgundian camp were returning home through Piedmont every day. Arrears of pay and shortages of supplies in the Burgundian camp were the major reasons for their flight, although a lack of confidence in the duke's military prospects against the Swiss may have been a contributory factor. One of the captains who left at this time was Count Giberto da Correggio, who returned to his homeland accompanied by fifty lances.[44]

At the battle of Murten the duke's army suffered more severe casualties than in any previous encounter. The losses of the Italian contingent may have been disproportionately heavy. Partly this was because, if the survivors are to be believed, they had exposed themselves to the Swiss assaults with especial bravery,[45] but the benefit to their master of such courage was diminished by the fact that several of the survivors subsequently deserted. Another reason for their heavy losses was that, before the battle, some Italian contingents had been recalled to Savoy from postings elsewhere, so that most of the Italians in the duke's pay fought in the battle and were disproportionately represented there; one of the recalled captains was Angelo di Monforte, son of the count of Campobasso, who arrived in Savoy from Lorraine where he had been engaged on garrison duty.[46] Among the fatalities were Antonio dei Corradi di Lignana and three-quarters of his company (his brother Pietro having been killed at the battle of Grandson), and Troilo's son Gianfrancesco. Shortly after the battle, the duke lost also the services of Lodovico Tagliante d'Ivrea, one of his *conducteurs* of a hundred lances of the ordinance. As a Piedmontese subject of the duke of Savoy, Lodovico had deliberately foiled Charles the Bold's attempt on the night of 26–27 June 1476 to kidnap Yolande of Savoy together with her children; helped by compatriots, he had smuggled the young Duke Philibert and one of his brothers to the safety of

Geneva. Naturally, he later refused to return to the Burgundian army, even though, he said, Charles was prepared to forgive him and had invited him back.[47] Lodovico's action probably had a more significant effect on the ultimate fortunes of the last Valois duke than did even the count of Campobasso's famous defection before the battle of Nancy: without having the young duke actually in his hands, Charles lost all hope of controlling Savoy, whereas, had he managed to retain Savoy, he might never have had to fight that last fatal encounter. Nonetheless, Lodovico's flight was probably not followed by that of many of his comrades-in-arms; for example, his *chef de chambre*, Filippo da Pietrasanta, remained in the army as Giacomo dei Vischi's chancellor.[48]

The fragmentary nature of the sources renders hazardous attempts to assess accurately the number of Italian troops serving in the months before the battle of Nancy.[49] The difficulty, for example, recurs of having to decide whether or not the troops commanded by Italian captains were themselves Italian. Not all necessarily were. This is probably true, for instance, both of the reinforcements brought by Campobasso from Lorraine in the autumn of 1476, and of the right wing of Charles the Bold's line of battle commanded by Galeota at Nancy in January 1477. Oliviero da Somma from the kingdom of Naples was another of the captains of a hundred lances of the ordinance whose troops may not all have been Italian, though probably many were.[50] There are some clues, however. By the end of July 1476, Troilo was reported to have reassembled 800 of the one thousand men who had been under his command before the battle of Murten; the rest had either perished or departed. The duke was so pleased with this effort that he promised to place the Neapolitan captain in charge of a column comprising two thousand infantry and three hundred lances.[51] The one hundred lances captained at this time by Troilo's son Alessandro were probably part of, not additional to, those under the overall command of his father. Although Pietro dei Corradi was dead, the remnants of his company, consisting of one hundred lances of the ordinance and including several English archers, continued to serve the duke under the command of his son Guglielmo, while another son, Giorgio, had the charge of some ninety men in the company of Alessandro di Troilo.[52] As captains of one hundred lances of the ordinance, both Ameo di Valperga and his brother Arduino participated in the campaigns leading up to the siege and battle of Nancy.[53] The 120 men-at-arms led away from the Burgundian army on the Friday before that battle by Giovanni and Angelo di Monforte, as also the 180 soldiers with whom their father, the count of Campobasso, had defected two days before, are likely in the main to have been Italian and probably represented the greatly diminished remnants of the 400-lance company led across the Alps by the count almost four years previously.[54]

In addition, Charles seems to have enjoyed the services on his last campaign in Lorraine of a number of Italians who had not fought in Savoy because they were then discharging garrison duty elsewhere. Ruggerone Accrocciamuro, count of Celano, who had first come to the Burgundian army through enlistment with his friend the count of Campobasso, was recalled from guarding Saint-Quentin in August 1476, where he commanded at that time 100 lances of the ordinance. He probably fought at the battle of Nancy since some accounts say he was taken prisoner there, and he appears briefly to have remained in the service of Mary of Burgundy for a few months thereafter.[55] Similarly, the one-hundred-lance company of Giacomo dei Vischi was transferred from garrison duty in Guelders to join Campobasso in Lorraine in September 1476.[56] The company was in fact commanded by his sons Filippo and Battista, since Giacomo himself seems to have been otherwise engaged: towards the end of May he had been sent to Italy on behalf of the duke; he had returned to court by the middle of July; but in the last week of November he was in Piedmont.[57] Neither chronicle sources nor the accounts of the *trésorier des guerres* tell us whether Filippo and Battista fought at Nancy. Finally, the account of the *trésorier des guerres* records that Mary of Burgundy paid off in April 1477 55 loyal Italian troops who had fought in all of her father's last three battles and who had returned to the Burgundian service after the disaster at Nancy.[58] The strength of the Burgundian army at Nancy was less than that at any other of the duke's battles, and has been calculated as amounting to not much more than five thousand men.[59] Even allowing for the fact that the Italian companies may have been under strength, that the lances composing them may have contained only the Italian unit-measure of four, rather than six or nine, combatants, and that troops commanded by Italian captains may not themselves have belonged to that nationality — not to mention the defection of the count of Campobasso and his sons and their followers — it still seems reasonable to conclude that Italian soldiers formed a relatively high proportion of the Burgundian army in that last battle (just as they had at Grandson and Murten), if only because Charles then deployed all the Italians available to him, while the troops from other sources were now sadly diminished.

Numerically, Italian troops had played a most important role in the duke's campaigns since the summer of 1473. Certainly, in numerical comparison with other foreign contingents in the army, the Italians were pre-eminent. Moreoever, whereas other foreign troops were esteemed primarily for one particular skill — the Germans, for instance, were valued for their proficiency with artillery and the English as archers — the Italians were more versatile. They comprised cavalry, infantry and crossbowmen (both mounted and on foot); in such roles they excelled on the field of battle and, at sieges, as sappers and engineers. Above all, because of their comprehensive expertise in all branches of the military art and because of their skill as generals in tactics and strategy, Charles placed them in the highest positions of command, out of proportion to their numbers.

Some personal characteristics

What might be termed the sociological structure of Italian mercenary companies is a fruitful field for research.[60] In this context, it is worth attempting a similar analysis of Charles the Bold's Italian mercenaries, though what follows must be regarded as tentative, since the evidence is scattered and fragmentary, and the bulk of the information available concerns the higher-ranking officers; the mass of the rank-and-file remain largely anonymous.

Geographical origins present few problems. The count of Campobasso and his two sons, Giacomo Galeota, the count of Celano, Troilo da Rossano and his two sons, and Oliviero da Somma were all originally subjects of the kingdom of Naples. The Piedmontese were the next most numerous group among the higher-ranking officers; such were Antonio and Pietro dei Corradi di Lignana and Pietro's two sons, Giacomo dei Vischi and his two sons, and the brothers Ameo, Arrighino and Arduino di Valperga. In contrast, the other major states of the peninsula — Milan, Venice, Florence and Rome — seem to have provided very few, if any, captains. The 'comes Ursus Angwillarius' or 'de Angwillis' who perished in a sally by the Neussers at Christmas 1474 may well have belonged to the Roman family of Anguillara.[61] The Genoese influx into the Burgundian camp in the winter of 1472–1473 was particularly marked, but in terms of rank they were not especially noteworthy. The lesser states of Ferrara and Mantua also provided a small number of officers of middle rank. The reasons for this geographical distribution are fairly clear. Largely from political motives, the duke of Milan and the republic of Venice were reluctant to allow their subjects to serve in other rulers' armies and, even when these powers were allied to Charles, were anxious not to be compromised in the eyes of hostile neighbours by too close association with his campaigns. Florence always held Charles at arm's length and, in any case, was not noted as a breeding ground for generals. On the other hand, Yolande of Savoy, Lodovico Gonzaga and Ercole d'Este seem to have been quite happy to see their subjects enlist in the Burgundian army, while the Neapolitan and Genoese malcontents were, by the fact of their exile, able to act as free agents, regardless of the misgivings felt by Ferrante and Galeazzo Maria. Piedmont, Liguria and the Mezzogiorno were, in addition, regions which traditionally maintained close links with transalpine Europe; their nobility was at once prolific and, in many cases, impoverished; and frequent political upheavals provided a further incentive to seek a living through the trade of arms outside the homeland.

Ascertaining the geographical origins of the rank-and-file, most of whose names — which might offer some guidance — we do not even know, is more difficult. In the case of the recruiting campaign of 1473, which brought the largest single accretion of peninsular troops to the Burgundian army during Charles the Bold's reign, the place of recruitment provides some clues. Thus, the Neapolitan commanders (Campobasso, Galeota and Troilo), after passing with only light escorts through Piedmont and the duchy of Milan, set up enlistment centres in north-central Italy — for example, at Reggio in the lands of the duke of Ferrara — before returning to Charles through the territories of the Venetian republic, where more recruits may have joined them, though probably not in large numbers. On the other hand, it could be misleading to suggest that all, or even most, of the Italian troops recruited at this time came from the lands of the duke of Ferrara, the marquis of Mantua and the republic of Venice, for the simple reason that the prospect of Burgundian pay probably attracted many others from much further afield. It is true that this pattern does not seem to have applied, for instance, to the Corradi di Lignana brothers, who, as far as one can tell, enlisted their men only in their homeland of Piedmont. Yet against this we have the assertion of Yolande of Savoy in May 1473 that not more than a hundred men had been recruited in her lands by Charles the Bold's mercenary captains. The assertion needs, however, to be treated with caution, since it was designed to mollify Galeazzo Maria, who, alarmed by all the recent bustle on his borders, had protested to Yolande about it.[62]

But, at least in the case of the Neapolitan captains, it is probable that the geographical origins of most of their men did not correspond with theirs. When Campobasso and Galeota left the service of Duke John of

Anjou for that of Charles the Bold towards the end of 1472, they probably brought with them a number of their compatriots who, like them, had left Naples eight or so years previously. The number could not have been large, though, or Charles would not have required these captains to go to Italy to fill the troop quotas he allotted them. We have a list of 237 men-at-arms serving under Campobasso in June 1475.[63] Of the names that are legible, some are merely patronymics or nicknames, but, of the remaining toponymic surnames, by no means the majority testify to a Neapolitan origin. For example, against Rizarda de Campebassa, Rosarata de Tarento, Angello de Campobasso, Antonelo de Troya and Jehan de Tarente can be set Jacobo de Verona, Laurento de Modena, Salvator de Novara, Domenico Lombardo, Lo Firentino, Jehan de Brexa, Modenesse, Caross de Ferrara, Jehan d'Alexandrie, Anthonio de Ivrea, Franciscus de Verona, Paulo de Modena, Petro d'Alexandria and Alberto dela Mirandola, not to mention such non-Italians as Pablo, Jehan de Chalon and Nicolò Albanesse. It seems reasonable to conclude, therefore, that the bulk of the rank-and-file were natives of northern Italy, while, in addition, there may have been a minority from central and southern Italy. In particular, it is improbable that the Neapolitan preponderance among the captains was reflected in the ranks.

It has been suggested that one of the main cohesive forces in Italian mercenary companies of this period was the degree of inter-relatedness of many of their members.[64] Certainly, the evidence appears to confirm that this was to a large extent true of Charles the Bold's Italian mercenary companies. Giacomo dei Vischi, Campobasso, Troilo[65] and possibly Pietro dei Corradi di Lignana all had two sons each serving with them. Giacomo da Mantua took over his father Biagio's hundred-lance company some time in the summer of 1475 after his father's death.[66] Antonio and Pietro dei Corradi di Lignana were, of course, brothers; so also were Ameo, Arrighino and Arduino di Valperga. Oliviero da Somma had a brother, Aloise ('Aloys'), of whom we know only that he received moneys due to Oliviero on his brother's behalf in March or April 1477; Oliviero had not yet been released after being captured at the battle of Nancy.[67] Giovanni Pietro da Pietrasanta was the brother of Filippo, chancellor of Giacomo dei Vischi. Rainieri Mancella, the Neapolitan governor of Nijmegen, was the son-in-law of Galeota, while Lodovico Tagliante was the nephew of Giacomo dei Vischi. Galeota too had a nephew with him.[68] Friendships formed through shared experience of past hardship may have been just as important as kinship. Galeota, as he said himself, had been saved from starvation at the time of the defeat of the Angevin cause in 1464 only by the solicitude of the count of Campobasso, while it was through the latter that the count of Celano was recruited into the Burgundian army in 1473. It is quite probable that ties of blood and affection such as these were repeated down through the ranks.

The leading captains were not without social standing. Some were counts: Cola di Monforte (Campobasso), Ruggerone Accrocciamuro (Celano) and 'Ursus' (Anguillara?). Others had comital or similar status. Giberto da Correggio shared the title of count with his brother Borso after the death of their father Manfredo in 1474.[69] Giacomo dei Vischi shared the title of count of San Martino with several relatives, although Burgundian sources often termed him *the* count of 'Saint-Martin'. The father of the Valperga brothers — Giacomo, murdered in 1462 — had been count of Masino. Uguccione Rangoni, lord of Spilamberto, one of those whose sons joined the Burgundian army in 1473,[70] bore the title of marquis. Fabrizio da Capua, who enlisted in the spring of 1474, was the brother of Francesco, count of Altavilla. Galeota's family belonged to the Capece clan of Naples, many of whose members had won renown in politics and letters from the twelfth century onwards, and his wife may have been related to the Sforza,[71] while Troilo was certainly related by marriage to Galeazzo Maria.[72]

Often for political reasons, however, the social pretensions of some of these men outstripped financial realities. Galeota and Campobasso had lost all they possessed by their rebellion against Ferrante and by their subsequent flight from Naples. In 1476 Campobasso described himself as a '*povre gentilhomme*', while Louis XI referred to him disdainfully as a count without a county.[73] Accrocciamuro had similarly lost the county of Celano from which he derived his title, although he seems to have retained certain lands in the kingdom of Naples, which were protected in part by their status as papal fiefs.[74] Others who had lost lands were the Valperga brothers, sons of the former count of Masino. Troilo must have learned early in life that his connection with the Sforza did not preclude the necessity of making his own way in life. In 1468, for example, we find him described as '*colericho et mezo disperato*' over arrears of pay owed him by the Venetians, in whose service he then was, and offering to fight in Greece against the Turks, while three years later his son Alessandro wrote to the duke of Milan for help with *his* debts.[75] In the spring of 1472 Troilo penned three pathetic letters from Ferrara to Lorenzo de' Medici pleading to be taken into his service so that he could provide for those who depended on him, as he himself was penniless.

To men in such a plight, therefore, the Burgundian recruiting must have come as manna from heaven. Service with Charles promised high pay, continuity of employment and, not least, adventure. These rewards were sufficient to attract Campobasso and Galeota away from the service of Nicholas of Anjou (though probably not without his consent) in the winter of 1472–1473. If Venice attempted to encourage fidelity and permanence of service among her mercenaries by concentrating on providing security of employment rather than promising initially attractive prospects of high pay and rapid promotions, Charles could offer similar security. If his arrangements with all his mercenary captains resembled those he made with Campobasso, then it would seem that, in the first instance, he offered them a three-year contract on which he retained an option to renew. But he never appeared likely to spend long periods in peace and idleness such as would have allowed him to reduce the size of his army. When, at the end of 1475, he appointed his captains for the following year, some of the Italians suffered a certain loss of status and a reduction in pay, but he sought to reassure them with the forecast that he would always have need of men-at-arms and probably of more, rather than fewer, than he then had. Troilo, for one, reportedly expressed the wish to stay in his service for as long as he lived.[76] In the context of their previous experiences, the Italian mercenaries may have found Burgundian rates of pay generous. Campobasso, for example, seems to have delighted in recounting to any who would listen the details of his own lucrative contract with Charles.[77] The money he was able to dispense in the early months of 1473 brought a crowd of would-be recruits flocking to him in his quarters in Vercelli. In 1476, some of those who had served under the recently deceased Colleoni made the pretence of negotiating for a Burgundian command in order to extract better terms from their Venetian paymasters.

The duke's Italian captains were men of both expertise and experience, but, as Louis XI pointed out just a few days before his rival's death, Charles did not succeed in enlisting the cream of the peninsula's military commanders. Louis described the duke's Italian recruits as people who could not find employment elsewhere. He considered Campobasso to be fitted to hold only a lesser rank (*'non era bono se non per uno cancelleri'*), and dubbed Galeota *'uno simplice homodarme'*. Had Charles, however, managed to recruit such men as Federigo da Montefeltro, Orso Orsini or Roberto Sanseverino, Louis conceded that he would have deserved real commendation.[78] Similarly, when Charles sent Hugues de Chalon to Piedmont in the spring of 1476 to recruit further Italians for his army, Galeazzo Maria warned him that the results might not match expectations: since the best troops in the peninsula were already serving himself, the king of Naples or the republics of Florence and Venice, the only soldiers who would be available were those whom no other ruler wished to employ.[79] This was not entirely correct, however, for a sufficient number of troops left Galeazzo Maria's own service to join the Burgundian army to prompt him to write to Panigarola instructing him to ensure that Charles accepted none of them unless they could prove in writing that they had their master's permission.

Certainly, some of the recruits had their own motives for joining Charles, and probably few had impeccable backgrounds. Some were adventurers whom poverty or malice could drive to desperate measures. Troilo da Rossano, for example, can perhaps be identified with the Troilo who suffered ten years' imprisonment following an attempt in 1443 to betray Francesco Sforza to King Alfonso of Naples, whose service he later entered,[80] and who later fled from the Milanese army engaged against Colleoni in 1467. Our Troilo was undoubtedly accused of harbouring fantastic designs against the Medici regime in 1470, while only a few months later he tried to persuade the authorities of Padua, now ruled by his former paymasters the Venetians, to return to Milanese rule.[81] Ugo Sanseverino's attempts to secure a Burgundian command in 1476 may have been prompted in part by the fact that he was in dispute with Galeazzo Maria over certain lands confiscated from him by the latter. Another of those who negotiated unsuccessfully with Hugues de Chalon at this time, Boccalino dei Guzzoni d'Osimo, was later to obtain a dubious kind of fame by taking advantage of the chaos in the Mezzogiorno arising from the revolt of the Neapolitan barons in the mid-1480s to seize his native town and hold it by force for two years against the army of the pope; he threatened that, if his rule in the city were not ratified, he would place Osimo in the hands of the Turkish sultan![82]

Italian rulers were sometimes far from pleased to see their subjects leave to join the Burgundian army, especially if they were deserters or fugitives from justice. The latter case is illustrated by the duke of Milan's detention in the summer of 1475 of Troilo's son Alessandro, who was then in Lombardy, as a reprisal for his father's acceptance into his company of Milanese fugitives; one of them was a deserter, while another had fled to avoid punishment after committing murder.[83] On other occasions, though, Italian rulers were quite glad that the Burgundian army could rid them of potential nuisances, whether criminal or political. Galeazzo Maria was willing, perhaps eager, to give his illegitimate half-brother Sforza Secondo the necessary licence to join up, with the sole proviso that he could not guarantee Sforza's good behaviour.[84] When the count of Celano applied to be taken into the company commanded by Campobasso, he was in possession of letters from the king of Naples recommending him to the Venetians, while in the previous year he had made overtures to the duke of Milan for a command.[85] The fact that Ercole d'Este, duke of Ferrara, was prepared to stand surety for the fulfilment of the contract between his subject Count Giberto da Correggio and the count of Campobasso in 1473[86] may have been due in part to the fact that he was pleased to see Giberto on the other side of the Alps, for the disputes between the counts of Correggio and their neighbours could involve Ercole in unwanted quarrels with *his* neighbours, such as the duke of Milan and the marquis of Mantua.

Doubtless, some Italian troops regarded the Burgundian army as a source of military education and adventure, which were becoming increasingly difficult to find in their homeland owing to the comparatively settled condition of relations between the states of the peninsula — especially in the first half of the 1470s — and to the reluctance of Italian rulers to maintain large, expensive armies over protracted periods, a reluctance only fortified by this unaccustomed era of goodwill. Such was presumably the case with the son of the count of Montone sent to Burgundy in 1473;[87] here the master–pupil relationship in military matters between Italy and the ultramontanes was reversed, for this young man was the grandson of Braccio da Montone, known as Fortebracci, one of the most renowned *condottieri* of them all. In the summer of 1475, a former follower of Colleoni asked for a safe-conduct across the lands of the duke of Milan so that he could travel to enlist with Charles, describing himself as a poor soldier made redundant by the peace of Italy. An eloquent expression of such motives came from Leonello Brandolini, whose father Tiberto had been imprisoned in 1462 for plotting against Francesco Sforza (and whose death shortly afterwards was not widely thought to have been due to natural causes). In 1475, Leonello asked the duke of Ferrara for permission to travel to him in order to await there the arrival of Anthony of Burgundy, who was expected shortly and through whom he wished to enlist in the Burgundian army. Having resigned from service under Colleoni and thirsting for action, he wanted to test himself in Burgundy.[88]

Finally, anyone who considers the ages of the duke's leading mercenary captains might well conclude that the rigours of camp life were conducive to longevity. When, for example, Campobasso joined up in

October 1472, he must have been about fifty years old. Antonio and Pietro dei Corradi di Lignana were probably in their forties, since they had held commands in the Savoyard army as early as 1457 and Pietro was, it seems, the father of sons who could be treated as adults by 1476. Giacomo dei Vischi may have been slightly older, having already held an important military command from Filippo Maria Visconti, duke of Milan, who died in 1447. Perhaps the oldest was Troilo, described in November 1472 as about sixty.[89] Further indications as to age are provided by the fact that several captains had adult sons fighting beside them.

Military value

Apart from the additional numerical strength the Italians brought to the Burgundian army, their primary military qualities were experience and expertise. In his leading captains recruited from the peninsula — and probably also in the bulk of the rank-and-file — Charles possessed a vast and valuable fund of experience. Both Antonio dei Corradi di Lignana and Troilo da Rossano had held commands in the Venetian army in the late 1460s;[90] Troilo had also served under Francesco Sforza and Alfonso the Magnanimous in southern and central Italy, while Giacomo dei Vischi was conversant with Milanese military practice. The count of Celano had spent a period in the service of the papacy.[91] Campobasso and Galeota had been closely involved with the campaigns of the war of the Neapolitan succession in the early 1460s, and had later fought for the Angevin cause in both France and Catalonia. Through these men, Charles could tap a source of knowledge derived not only from some of the major campaigns of the previous thirty years but also from the contrasting military practices of the different states of the peninsula.

Expertise was their other major asset. They needed no prior training before they were ready to fight, in contrast to the majority of the duke's own subjects. They knew how to respond to orders and to handle their weapons; in general, they were familiar with the routine of camp life; and, in several respects, they may well have been better equipped than some of the duke's own best troops. Evidence for this is not hard to find in the campaigns after 1473. Galeota and Campobasso played the leading role in the battle against the German army fought outside Neuss on 23 May 1475; Galeota also commanded one of the two wings of the Burgundian army at the battle of Nancy.[92] Italians were equally prominent and proficient in the numerous encounters which were both more humdrum and more typical than set-piece battles. At the siege of Neuss, for instance, Campobasso (described by Molinet as '*experimenté en armes autant que nul de son temps*') was placed by Charles in charge of organising in the most efficient manner possible the positions to be taken up by the besiegers.[93] Thereafter, he exercised great ingenuity in devising ways to encompass the fall of the town. In the autumn of 1474 his men established a temporary beach-head on one of the islands in the Rhine facing Neuss, after one of them had swum out to it with a rope and tub which were then used to transfer the others across the river. He also supervised attempts to take the town by sapping and mining, and by the construction of siege-engines which protected the besiegers as they approached the walls.

The duke's faith in the skill of his Italian commanders can be seen in the prominent place he gave them in the ordinances he drew up in May 1476. These divided the army into four main sections, each comprising two separate lines. The first section was commanded by Giulio d'Acquaviva, duke of Atri, while in its second line he and another Neapolitan, Giulio d'Altavilla, were each placed in charge of three hundred troops of the ducal household. The second section was an almost completely Italian affair. Its chief was Don Federico; the captains of its two lines were Troilo da Rossano and Antonio dei Corradi di Lignana; subsections were placed in the charge of Troilo's two sons and of Guglielmo dei Corradi di Lignana; and the soldiers who made up this section came mainly from the Italian companies captained by Antonio and Troilo. The captain of the first line of the third section was Galeota, whose troops comprised its right wing, while the two wings of its second line were commanded, respectively, by Oliviero da Somma and Angelo da Campobasso, both Neapolitans. But other indications of the duke's faith in them might be mentioned. After the battle against the Germans at Neuss in May 1475, he knighted Arrighino di Valperga, the Genoese Agostino Fregoso, a son of the count of Campobasso and a son of Troilo da Rossano.[94] He placed Italian garrisons in key border areas, such as Picardy, Burgundy and Guelders, while among his military governors were Francesco d'Este in Westerlo and Le Quesnoy, Rainieri Mancella in Nijmegen and Ameo di Valperga in Vaudémont. His trust extended to placing Italians among his bodyguard, such as the 'Nicole Maria Lapolitain' (Neapolitan?), Hannibal Ayosa, Pietro da Diarino and Antonio da Pando who appeared regularly in the accounts of the ducal household from at least as early as 27 September 1474;[95] Hannibal and 'Nicole Maria', together with Fabrizio da Capua, were still in his household at the time of the battle of Murten.

Of course, the Italians were not without their faults. Some of these were probably common to all soldiers of the time, especially to mercenaries serving in a foreign land under a ruler to whom they felt no natural loyalty, but others may have been peculiar to the Italians. After his unfortunate experiences in the early part of his reign with his own conscripted feudal levies and civic militias, Charles seems to have cherished great hopes for the Italians' reportedly unique standards of discipline and prompt obedience, and when they lapsed from these exacting standards he suffered a correspondingly deep sense of disappointment. One area where there is some evidence of misbehaviour is when Italians were billeted in towns as garrisons. In 1474, compensation was paid by the town of Dijon for effects seized from certain Lombards stationed nearby by inhabitants of the town who had wrongly accused them of cattle-rustling, and who had been over-hasty in seeking redress, but in the same year the city authorities refused to have a Lombard garrison. Their magistrates complained to Charles in April 1475 that recently some Italian troops (possibly belonging to Troilo's company) had violently released one of their compatriots from gaol. Perhaps the trouble went back to the summer of 1473, when the duke's new Italian troops streamed across the Alps into Burgundy only to find the local authorities unable or unwilling to pay for their upkeep; on 1 July two officials had written to Charles from Dijon that the newcomers *'font de grans maulx e dommaiges en foulant merveilleuzement vos subgez'*.[96] Certainly, Anthony of Burgundy considered the town of Moudon in Savoy to have acted quite reasonably shortly after the battle of Grandson in refusing to have a Burgundian garrison which included Italian troops, feeling that the townspeople could not be blamed for suspecting that the garrison would have plundered rather than guarded them. In mitigation, however, it might be said that charges of misconduct laid by communities against soldiers billeted on them against their will and at their expense were a commonplace of the times, and need not be laid only at the door of the duke's Italian mercenaries.

Quarrels among the soldiers themselves could also have serious repercussions. While Charles was hurriedly rebuilding his army in Savoy at Lausanne in the spring of 1476, his Italian contingents were involved in a number of unseemly and bloody riots with troops of other nationalities.[97] There was particularly bad feeling between the Italians and the English, both of whom claimed pre-eminence in the art of war; the two Milanese ambassadors, Panigarola and d'Appiano, expressed fears for their own safety in this situation where, as they wrote, men were being killed daily, where the violence was worse than among the Turks and where, Panigarola suspected, the duke himself seemed to take the side of the English, whom he regarded as almost his own subjects and who regarded themselves as superior to all other races. On one occasion, during the first week of May 1476, the English teamed up with their colleagues from Picardy, Liège and Guelders in an attempt to sack the Italians' quarters. These incidents were serious not only because of the loss of life incurred, but also because of the more general threat they posed to camp discipline, and in particular to the authority of Charles himself, for he had sometimes to intervene personally in order to quell the rioters. Again, though, the blame was not the Italians' alone. The overall unpleasantness of camp life during these weeks — arrears of pay, shortage of food, inadequate accommodation — was sufficient to have provoked restiveness among the best-behaved troops. In such conditions, tensions could erupt into violence as a result of comparatively small irritations, such as quarrels over women or disputes about national pride.

As mercenaries, the Italians were naturally upset as soon as their pay fell into arrears.[98] Charles paid the penalty in desertions. Arrears of pay were reported by Francesco Pietrasanta to have been the major reason for Giberto da Correggio's departure in 1476 and, according to Molinet and de la Marche, they contributed towards the defection of Campobasso. It should not be thought that the duke was unaware of this attitude; on the contrary, as he told Panigarola in May 1476, he meant to meet his obligations but he was reluctant to pay off in one lump sum, rather than in small instalments, the large arrears which for various reasons had built up during his campaigns in Savoy, because as soon as troops, especially Italians, had their pockets full of money they tended to rush off in order to spend it. In this context, the initial stages of recruiting could be particularly vexatious. The new recruits were customarily paid in advance in order to prepare themselves for musters arranged for a few months in the future; it was a great temptation simply to keep the money without appearing at the musters; and Galeazzo Maria was requested by Charles on more than one occasion to send back across the Alps troops who had thus fled to Milan from the companies of Galeota and Campobasso or, at least, to ensure the return of money paid them.

The *condottiere* system under which the Italian mercenaries operated may have had some faults peculiar to itself. By the terms of the contracts made in the winter of 1472–1473, the duke paid the captains a certain amount for the wages and upkeep both of themselves and of the number of men allotted to them; the captains were then responsible for paying their men out of this sum. There was an obvious temptation to pocket some of the money due to those under them and, at least in the cases of Galeota and Campobasso, this seems to have happened.[99] Another defect was that discipline and efficiency depended too much, under such a system, on the efforts of the commander, and the performance of Campobasso's men deteriorated alarmingly when illness forced him to leave the siege of Neuss for a few weeks in the spring of 1475. It was such weaknesses that the duke presumably wished to remedy with his new military ordinances inaugurated at Nancy towards the end of December 1475. All troops were now taken under his personal command, and were to be paid individually by his financial officers; the captains, as in the French king's *compagnies d'ordonnance*, were to receive a regular but separate provision for themselves. These measures had the overall effect on the captains of reducing both their pay and their status, and some of them — Panigarola mentioned Campobasso and Troilo by name — were greatly disgruntled. It is noticeable also that when Charles tried a few months later to augment his army by further Italian recruiting, he attempted to do so by enlisting small units of troops (*lanze spezzate*), and not by hiring captains who would then subcontract for him, as in 1472–1473.[100]

Other deficiencies displayed by the Italians may have been peculiar to soldiers of that nationality at that epoch. As mercenaries, they served primarily for money rather than loyalty, and expected to be treated with the same consideration they demanded from employers at home. Charles, on the other hand, was a harsh disciplinarian who expected instant and complete obedience from his men. One Milanese ambassador noted the contradiction and predicted dire consequences if the duke persisted with his traditional methods in his treatment of his Italian soldiers.[101] Again, it may be that, as mercenaries, the Italians were less willing than others to be used as cannon-fodder, or to take the risks with their lives that the duke's strategy and tactics sometimes required of them. Many factors induced them to think less of their master's greater glory than of their own self-preservation: fighting was a career which they wished to live to pursue as long as possible; they were reluctant to sacrifice needlessly the lives of their relations, friends and compatriots serving with or under them; and their contracts with the duke, which were of fixed but short duration, did not effectively counterbalance their strong desire to return to Italy when circumstances there were more favourable.

Criticism of the excessive self-interest of mercenaries was a commonplace in Renaissance Italy. There is some evidence from their behaviour in the army of Charles the Bold to substantiate such charges. Through a lack of alertness and application, at the siege of Neuss the Italians of Campobasso's company failed to hold important mines which had taken months to tunnel. D'Appiano reported that the loss of Vaudémont to the duke of Lorraine in April 1476 was attributed largely to the frivolous behaviour of its governor, Ameo di Valperga, who — in his desire to play the courtier in Savoy — had irresponsibly absented himself from duty. At the siege of Murten in June of that year, Charles bitterly and humiliatingly reproached his leading captains, including Troilo and Antonio dei Corradi di Lignana, for insufficient vigour in pushing their positions closer to the walls of the town; for the same reason he accused Don Federico of unmanly conduct.[102] On the other hand, it cannot be denied that the men of Campobasso's company showed admirable bravery in attempting to advance the siege of Neuss, while at the siege of Murten not all the men under the command of the chided captain Antonio dei Corradi di Lignana were Italians, for some were English and others Picards. Don Federico's solicitude for the safety of himself and his companions could be excused on the grounds that he was a prince who was expecting any minute his father's instruction to return to Naples. In any case, non-Italian captains too agreed with Troilo's misgivings about the duke's insistence on the priority of taking Murten; they argued that it was better to avoid unprofitable losses in besieging the town and instead to save the men for the main encounter with the full Swiss army, whose arrival was then believed to be imminent; for if that were defeated, then the town would fall of itself. Moreover, the losses suffered by the Italians in the duke's campaigns are evidence enough that they did not shirk their duty. A comparison with his English mercenaries is instructive. They too suffered heavy casualties, but they would not fight when the situation was irretrievably lost; seeing no hope of relief, the English garrison at Nancy forced the Burgundian commander to surrender on terms to the duke of Lorraine in October 1476, as this was the only way open to them of saving their lives without necessarily sacrificing their honour. Discretion, no less than valour, was an essential component of warfare at this time.

The debate over the value of foreign mercenaries relative to national conscripts is an old one. It was being conducted in Renaissance Italy between the proponents of the *condottiere* system and those of the civic militias, and it has been argued since by historians. Charles the Bold's army, which, as Vaughan puts it, had been gradually transformed into a standing army of mercenaries, might be regarded as outmoded in comparison to the forces which were thrown against it by the Swiss and their allies, which beat it in three successive battles; whereas the Burgundian army was of a heterogeneous nature, that of the Swiss was united by a common purpose.[103] At a time when the composition of the armies of France, England and Spain was increasingly coming to reflect the emerging national consciousness of those countries, Charles looked to foreign, especially Italian, troops to improve the efficiency and augment the size of his. On the other hand, his intention — as shown by his words to Troilo in 1476[104] — was clearly not to replace his own subjects entirely by mercenaries, but to recruit those foreigners so that they could teach his subjects the rudiments and refinements of warfare; the use of mercenaries was to that extent simply a provisional or stopgap measure. In any case, it would be foolish to award or deduct points according to a scale designed anachronistically to measure 'modernity' on the basis of a search for early manifestations of national feeling. Mercenaries continued for a long time to play an important role in the armies of the early modern period; indeed, in the generation or so before the Reformation, it was Charles the Bold's victorious foes, the Swiss, who were Europe's most successful mercenaries.

The argument, in short, has to be decided in its proper context. The duke's use of foreign mercenaries was a rational response to a specific military problem: the need for trained and expert soldiers ready to serve in large numbers at short notice. This applies particularly to his Italian recruits. They had their faults, but they also possessed qualities otherwise unobtainable. Charles the Bold's high valuation of the peninsula's soldiery remained constant until the end of his reign, judging by his words to Troilo in 1476, and if he himself did not waver in his satisfaction at the decision to enlist Italian troops, then the historian should not be too hasty in disagreeing with the duke's own assessment. Indeed, his successive defeats and eventual death at the hands of the Swiss did not in the short run convince Italian opinion that the Burgundian army and, by implication, the Italian military expertise on which he had relied so noticeably had been proved inferior to that of the Swiss;[105] rather, informed Italians ascribed these disasters to the duke's faulty generalship or even to the intervention, provoked by his cruelty, of divine providence. An interesting sidelight on his wisdom in relying so heavily on Italian mercenaries is provided by the opinions of Louis XI, to fight against whom was the original purpose, in the main, of their recruitment by Charles. Louis was not averse to trying to hire Italian troops himself, although his comments about those enlisted by the duke were largely derogatory.[106] Yet his actions, despite what he told his Swiss allies in February 1477, rather belied his words. He probably tried to seduce Campobasso from his Burgundian allegiance in June 1476; he was reported to have made a wholesale attempt to recruit the Neapolitans remaining in the Burgundian army after the battle of Nancy; he certainly made friendly overtures to Troilo's son Alessandro in June 1477 when he was contemplating returning to Italy; and he hastened to snap up the services of Galeota in the summer of 1478 when this redoubtable Neapolitan was given leave to depart by Mary and Maximilian.

Loyalty: the case of the count of Campobasso

The argument over the value of the duke's Italian mercenaries and about his wisdom in using them revolves to a great extent around the question of loyalty. In this context, the behaviour of the count of Campobasso has tended to overshadow all else. It was not common in the later Middle Ages for a ruler to die on the battlefield, and the dramatic end of the last Valois duke of Burgundy has been rendered all the more piquant by the tradition that his death could be attributed in some part to treachery. The episode has provided material for both novelists and playwrights, while historians, relying above all on the account given by Philippe de Commynes, have continued to recount, and in some cases embellish, his version right up to our own day.[107]

There are two main parts to the charge of treachery against Campobasso, which, though distinct, are sometimes confused. The first is that on Wednesday, 1 January 1477, four days before the fatal battle of Nancy, Campobasso left the besieging Burgundian army with about 180 men and transferred to the approaching army of the duke of Lorraine; two days later his two sons Giovanni and Angelo, together with about another 120 soldiers, followed suit. All the available chronicle sources agree fairly closely on the timing of the event and on the number of troops concerned. Most sources say Campobasso and his sons left stealthily, which might be regarded as compounding their offence. Against these, however, it is worth noting that Thomas Basin recorded that the count first asked the duke for leave to depart and was given it.[108] Moreover, a nearly contemporary French version, recorded in an Italian ambassador's dispatch shortly after the battle, tells how he was in fact dismissed by Charles ('. . . *havendo havuto parole insieme et havendoli dato licentia, esso Conte Colla si partitte . . .*');[109] a similar version, much embellished, was given by a chronicler from the kingdom of Naples, writing in about 1479 and emphasising the bad feeling between the duke and the count.[110]

Yet the simple act of leaving the duke, whether in secret or openly, does not of itself amount to the black treachery with which the count's name has so long been associated. Other Italians had left the Burgundian army at various times over the previous three years, for financial and other personal reasons, and it was natural, with an enemy so near, that Campobasso should place himself in the hands of the duke of Lorraine, for otherwise he might have been regarded as still attached to the Burgundian cause and engaged on some matter of aggression or reconnaissance. If he had really wished to wreak the utmost havoc, as Commynes alleged he did,[111] he could have delayed his desertion until the battle itself, as Lord Stanley did at Bosworth. As far as the logistical effects of his desertion are concerned, they were not insignificant but neither were they at all decisive, for the three hundred men he and his sons led away from the Burgundian camp represented perhaps only 6–7 per cent of the duke's total forces in his last battle; in any case, the duke was not favourably placed to meet his enemies' attack, and the fact that he was already heavily outnumbered made defeat almost inevitable, regardless of Campobasso's desertion.

The main burden of the charge against him is that after leaving Charles, he united his forces with those of the duke of Lorraine and fought against his former colleagues in the battle. If his defection could be presented as excusable on the grounds of prudence or from motives of self-preservation, the act of fighting on the opposite side to his erstwhile comrades-in-arms betrays a rancour against the duke of dramatic intensity. Yet it is interesting and significant that Commynes, who otherwise neglects no slander or literary artifice to blacken the count's name, makes no mention of his part in the final battle. Indeed, it should not be overlooked that the part he actually played in the battle is not entirely clear. Some accounts merely record that he fought on the side of Duke René. The most interesting of these is the Neapolitan chronicler, who claimed to have been told — by whom, one wonders — that at one stage Charles actually found himself engaged in hand-to-hand fighting with his former captain.[112] Other sources say that the count was stationed at the bridge over the River Meurthe at Bouxières-aux-Dames, thereby blocking the Burgundians' escape northwards to Metz; one of them, Jean de Margny, who was at the battle, said he saw Campobasso's men attacking the fugitives at the bridge. Most of them, however, suggest that the reasons for this positioning were, in part, Duke René's reluctance to be closely associated with the count and, more important, the latter's desire to take prisoners, presumably for ransom, rather than that he was motivated by a revengeful urge to ensure Charles the Bold's death, as Commynes alleged.[113] In fact, the desire to take prisoners for ransom would have ruled out the exaction of revenge by killing fugitives. But losses were bound to occur, because fugitives unlikely to yield good ransoms tended not to qualify for quarter; the delays in crossing the bridge at Bouxières-aux-Dames allowed the pursuers to catch up; and many Burgundians drowned in the Meurthe in a futile attempt to swim to safety. For these heavy casualties other reasons can be adduced which lessen the importance of Campobasso's alleged vendetta-inspired blood-lust. Basin attributed them to the fact that René was enabled by his intimate knowledge of the terrain to block all escape-routes, something the Swiss had attempted at Murten,[114] while a German mercenary who for a time served under Charles ascribed the high death toll to the fact that the Swiss and the duke of Lorraine followed up their victory by a determined pursuit, which had not happened at Grandson or Murten.

Still, even after these qualifications have been made, it remains indisputable that the count played some part in a bloody battle where many who had been his colleagues less than a week before lost their lives. The rapidity of this tergiversation and its consequences have understandably caused his reputation to be stained with the stigma of infamy ever since.

Nonetheless, the reasons that led him to such an act remain, even now, the subject of controversy. The explanation which was long accepted and even elaborated by historians was that provided by Commynes, according to whom the count's final act of betrayal was the climax of long-planned treachery, and the last in a series of acts which had previously included wilful neglect in prosecuting the sieges of Nancy in 1475 and 1476, clandestine offers to Louis XI to kill or capture Charles, and attempts to ensure that the duke was indeed killed or captured at the battle of Nancy. Commynes asserted that his motives were threefold: he was a lifelong supporter of the house of Anjou, to which he was more devoted than to Charles; he was congenitally treacherous and wicked, so that his departure from the Burgundian camp before the battle of Nancy constituted almost the classic gratuitous crime; and, by behaving in this way, he was unwittingly serving as the instrument of divine providence, sent to punish the duke for his crimes and follies.[115] This version, though, has many weaknesses. It is impossible to corroborate, though less difficult to refute, from other sources; and this uniqueness, which was once seen as deriving from Commynes' inside knowledge and which recommended itself for that reason, tends now to be regarded rather as a fabrication by a writer anxious to prove treachery in others in order to divert his readers' attention away from his own defection from Charles to Louis in 1472.[116]

Contradicting Commynes, the Neapolitan historian, philosopher and statesman Benedetto Croce sought, over sixty years ago, to redeem his compatriot's reputation. He portrayed Campobasso's defection as an act more of impulse than of long-meditated perfidy. Relying on the testimony of the *Chronique de Lorraine*, he argued that Campobasso decided to leave after Charles had struck him with his gauntlet in angry reaction to his intercession with the duke on behalf of a captured messenger of the duke of Lorraine, whom Charles wished to hang. This humiliating blow was the final straw, because the count already nurtured a number of other grievances — borne out by several chroniclers — such as arrears of pay and a loss of status due to the duke's reallotment of commands in his army.[117] While not whitewashing the count, Croce does make his offence more understandable and less heinous. Yet this version, well-grounded historically as it is, does not entirely eliminate the charge levelled for different reasons by Commynes: that of premeditation: Campobasso did not leave immediately after being struck by the duke, but instead waited to choose his moment, and, if the blow was the final straw on top of his other grievances, he must for some time previously, because of those other grievances, have been considering the possibility of defection. Croce's version, though it has far more to recommend it than that of Commynes, has not stilled controversy.[118] It should be noticed also that, if our only choices were the testimony of Commynes and that of the *Chronique de Lorraine*, we should be on very uncertain ground. Richard Vaughan has described the Lorraine chronicle as largely fanciful and as one of the most imaginative chronicles of the age, while for Commynes he shows even less respect, accusing him of unparalleled mendacity.[119] Regrettably, we cannot, for the siege and battle of Nancy, supplement the chroniclers with the shrewd reports contained in Italian diplomatic dispatches written by eyewitnesses, because in the last months of the duke's life there were no Italian ambassadors at his court.

Italian evidence from earlier periods of his reign, however, does provide a good deal of relevant and hitherto largely unutilised information on the background to Campobasso's actions; yet, while it helps give a clearer picture of the *condottiere* mentality, it does not make it any easier to pronounce with certainty for or against Campobasso's guilt; and some points can be made in favour of Commynes and against Croce. There is, for instance, some plausibility in the general picture of intrigue and subversion painted by Commynes; this was not simply the literary product of a feverish imagination. In March 1473, while Campobasso was still in Italy recruiting troops for the Burgundian army, Louis XI told the Milanese ambassador that he had received approaches from the count asking to be taken into his service. Louis, however, felt he could not be certain of their sincerity, because the count himself would not reveal his intentions until he was sure of Louis. In fact, the king suspected the whole thing was a trick. Consequently, he wanted his ally the duke of Milan to sound out the count to ascertain whether he really could be induced to change sides or, if this seemed unlikely, to have a 'tough guy' ('*manesco*') recruited into the Burgundian army to do away with him; Louis promised such a double agent would be well rewarded if he succeeded.[120] There followed over the next year or so a series of attempts to foment subversion in the Burgundian army, although it is worth pointing out that Campobasso was implicated in none of them. In April 1473, for example, the duke of Milan considered sending troops to join the Burgundian army in Troilo's company in order to spy for him and his French ally; these men would have averted suspicion by pretending to have fled from Galeazzo Maria.[121] Not long afterwards, he did send a Giovanni Pietro dei Crotti to join the company of Pietro dei Corradi di Lignana to keep him informed of events and, if possible, to persuade some of his compatriots to defect to Louis XI. Giovanni Pietro could pass on little news of value, so, prompted partly by arrears of pay, he chose the latter course. During the night of 15 October 1473, he and some two hundred companions left their post on the border with France and crossed over into Bar. The coup, however, misfired. The deserters were arrested by the agents of Louis XI — who had not been forewarned of their intentions — and Galeazzo Maria was forced to intercede for their release.[122] It was perhaps this episode that encouraged Louis to express the hope shortly afterwards that some of the duke of Burgundy's Italian troops would betray an important fortress to him. Certainly, in July 1474 a Lombard soldier from the company of Antonio dei Corradi di Lignana travelled to Galeazzo Maria to say he had been commissioned by about forty of his companions to offer him their loyalty; if war broke out between Charles and Louis and if Galeazzo Maria so commanded, they would either desert to Milan or join the French army. In October that year, one of Galeota's men-at-arms wrote to the duke of Milan listing a number of his compatriots (commanding between them over a hundred troops) who were willing to serve his interests, perhaps by joining the French army or by helping to betray important positions, such as the town of Abbeville, to Louis' men.[123]

Commynes's allegation that the count acted as he did partly because of his deep-rooted Angevin loyalties is, though not necessarily true, at least credible. The conflict between the Aragonese and Angevin dynasties in the fifteenth century was very real, and the reality of the conflict was not lost on one of those most closely concerned, King Ferrante of Naples. Ferrante was alarmed by his Burgundian ally's choice of Neapolitan exiles among the Italian mercenaries who enlisted in his army in the winter of 1472–1473. He asked Charles to dismiss them. He was particularly fearful of the count of Campobasso, because, as his adviser Diomede Carafa put it, the count was unlikely to be more faithful to his adopted lord, Charles, than he had been to his natural lord Ferrante, whom he had betrayed. The duke refused, however, explaining with perhaps a greater degree of insouciance than was tactful that he was more likely to persuade the exiles to a love of Ferrante than they were to induce him to hate his Neapolitan ally.[124] Nonetheless, Ferrante was not mollified, and, according to one well-informed source, among his reasons for sending his son Federico to the Burgundian court in October 1474 was his wish to see the prince replace Campobasso as the duke's lieutenant. Federico was instructed to deploy the argument — doubtless one calculated to weigh strongly with a ruler like Charles, who viewed Louis XI with such suspicion — that, as an Angevin, Campobasso was incorrigibly Francophile.[125]

Yet, if there is circumstantial evidence at least to bolster the plausibility of Italian subversion in the Burgundian army and of the Angevin loyalties which Commynes ascribed to Campobasso, the question remains whether the particular charges levelled by Commynes against him can be justified. That Campobasso was reluctant in 1475, 1476 and 1477 to fight against his former employer, the house of Anjou, is possible, especially since material ties were added to those of sentiment, for between 1465 and 1472 he was rewarded for his service to the Angevins with a lifetime title to the revenues of the lordship of Einville-au-Jard in Lorraine, an annual pension from the receipt-general of the duchy of Bar and the lordship of Commercy in Bar, together with the castle of Pierrefort.[126] On the other hand, such considerations were probably not those which weighed most heavily with him. He did not hesitate to leave the Angevin for the Burgundian service before (not after, as Commynes states) the death of Duke Nicholas in 1473; he hastened to return to Italy after the battle of Nancy; and his son Angelo sold Commercy back to King René in 1479, only a year after his father's death.

According to Commynes, Campobasso made repeated offers to the French king to kill or capture Charles for him. Regarding this charge we have only his testimony, although it may be that in this he was misled by Louis himself.[127] Ferrante of Naples, for one, as we have just seen, warned that Campobasso's Angevin loyalties might cause him to betray the duke to the king, while Louis himself claimed in March 1473 that Campobasso had made overtures to him, although he remained unconvinced by them. The only other evidence of contacts between the two came in June 1476, when Louis ordered one of the count's captured heralds to be released so that he could ask his master to change sides; the impetus, in other words, came from the king, not the count.[128] Circumstantial evidence to support an interpretation along these lines is provided by the fact that, shortly before, Louis seems to have made similar covert approaches to Galeota.[129] One curious aspect of all this is that, if the king was eager for the count's services, then that is not easy to reconcile with the disparaging remarks he made about him in December 1476; indeed, he had no particular reason to cherish the count, since he blamed him for the loss of Catalonia to the king of Aragon in 1472.[130] In short, such evidence as there is does not support Commynes' allegation of underhand dealings with Louis. Similarly, while it has been suggested that the duke of Lorraine too was in contact with Campobasso in 1476,[131] the initiative, as with Louis XI two months previously, did not come from the count's side. Of course, it may be that Campobasso had been unable or unwilling to hide a growing sense of grievance, and that this had given Charles the Bold's enemies the impression that his captain was open to offers or appeals. Even so, it is striking, in the light of Commynes' assertions of long-planned betrayal, that no account portrays René as having been prepared for, rather than surprised by, Campobasso's eventual defection.

Perhaps the most serious of Commynes's charges is the suggestion that from about the latter part of 1475 onwards, Campobasso systematically attempted to sabotage his master's war effort. The evidence, however, is circumstantial rather than convincing. For example, it was Campobasso's son Giovanni who was in charge of the defence of Lunéville when it surrendered to the duke of Lorraine in July 1476, but the surrender took place with the consent of the lord of Bièvres, one of the leading Burgundian commanders in Lorraine, because further resistance was futile; and it was made in such a way, and in order, that the lives of the garrison might be saved. Similarly, the fall of Nancy in October was due largely to the failure of supplies and reinforcements to arrive in time, the responsibility for which was Campobasso's, but his delay can be explained simply in terms of the obstacles presented by the route recommended to him by his subordinates.[132]

If we turn from Commynes to Croce, we find an explanation based on a gradual growth of dissatisfaction in the count, reaching a flashpoint when he was struck by the duke of Burgundy for interceding on behalf of Siffredo dei Baschi. In tracing these grievances we return to firmer historical ground. Like most mercenaries, Campobasso was very sensitive in matters of payment, and he deeply resented the loss of income caused by the duke's reorganisation of the command structure of his army at the end of 1475, as a result of which the companies that had formerly been subject to Charles indirectly through his mercenary captains were now placed directly under his command. Moreover, in Campobasso's case, as chroniclers make clear, the remnants of the four-hundred-lance company with which he had originally been entrusted, and which was now sadly diminished, were redistributed among the count's sons and among other companies; in other words, his command was plundered in order to bring others up to strength. These changes, then, entailed a loss of both income and authority. Campobasso had already mentioned to the duke of Milan in mid-1475 (as had Galeota) the possibility of returning shortly to Italy in order to be taken into his service when his Burgundian contract expired, and his loss of status now provoked him in a fit of pique to leave the Burgundian camp on the pretext of undertaking a pilgrimage to Santiago de Compostela. Moreover, we learn from others that arrears of pay continued to rankle with him even after his return to active service in the second half of 1476. It is not, however, easy to assess the justice of his complaint; certainly, others of the duke's Italian mercenaries grumbled about arrears of pay at this time, but we do know also that the count and his sons did receive some money during their last twelve months in the ducal army, even if these payments were neither up-to-date nor complete.[133]

Such grievances over pay and status did not trouble only the count. This is an important point which, though sometimes overlooked, nonetheless requires an explanation. The reasons put forward by Commynes to show why Campobasso reacted differently from his compatriots have been examined and found wanting, while Croce did not really tackle the problem. Perhaps the answer may be that Campobasso was affected to a greater degree by these grievances than were his colleagues. Loss of status caused him a particularly intense resentment because he was the duke's leading Italian mercenary captain. He did not hide his pretensions, which indeed seem to have been justified to some extent from the end of 1472, because of the higher pay he received and the larger number of troops placed under his command in comparison with his colleagues. He admitted he was not desirous, for example, that Charles should succeed in his attempts to enlist Colleoni because, in that case, he would have had to take second place to the Venetian general.[134] In the contract he made with the duke in November 1472, it was stipulated that he should be responsible only to the duke and that he should be placed under the command of no other general, unless Colleoni joined the Burgundian army; that, if Colleoni *were* recruited, Campobasso would still retain the pay and conditions allowed him in the contract; and that his troops would not be distributed among other captains, unless Colleoni were recruited. This last condition, as we have seen, was disregarded when the three-year contract expired at the end of 1475. The receipt given by the count for payment after the reviews made at Neuss in June 1475 may be another example of his self-esteem, for he signed himself *'nous'*, whereas the other Italian mercenaries used the simple *'je'*.[135]

The status of all the mercenary captains had been reduced by the changes made at the end of 1475, and the duke's intention to phase out the *condottiere* system of subcontracting became even clearer through his methods of recruiting in the spring of 1476. Yet, while Campobasso, for the reasons outlined, perhaps felt the force of these reforms more keenly than his colleagues, some of the latter may, conversely, have been slightly less perturbed than he was, owing to the fact that, in comparison with him, they had risen relatively higher in the duke's esteem since 1473; in other words, the prestige differential between Campobasso and his junior colleagues had been eroded. Accounts reaching Milan of the battle fought against the Germans at Neuss in May 1475 all agreed in attributing its success to Galeota, rather than to Campobasso, and the duke's Italian secretary Salvatore de Clariciis wrote after the battle that his master considered Galeota the most valiant soldier he had with him. Similarly, Charles made much of Troilo after the battle of Murten for his success in reassembling his company, and he promised to entrust him with an even larger command in future. It may be that a certain amount of rivalry existed among the duke's Italian captains; of Troilo, for example, the Neapolitan ambassador remarked in 1473 that he had many Italian rivals.[136]

This brings us back to the immediate cause of Campobasso's desertion, according to the Lorraine chronicler: the blow given him in anger by the duke when he interceded for Siffredo dei Baschi, an event which can probably be dated, if indeed it did take place, to December 1476. Siffredo had been sent by Duke René to tell the defenders of Nancy the good news that the Swiss, meeting at Zürich, had at last agreed to send help. Charles wanted to hang him, presumably on the grounds that he was breaking the laws of war which refused him entry to the town now that the Burgundians had begun their siege.[137] It will at once be apparent that the account of this episode given by Commynes is entirely different from, and irreconcilable with, that in the *Chronique de Lorraine*. According to Commynes, Campobasso reinforced the duke's determination to hang Siffredo and sought to prevent intercession for him, lest his own treacherous dealings with René and Louis XI should at this late hour be revealed by the messenger, whom he suspected of knowing about them; yet even one of Commynes's more recent defenders concedes that the Lorraine chronicler's version is the more plausible.[138]

The Lorraine chronicler was not one of the most reliable of his time; yet, even if the Siffredo affair did not take place at all, nonetheless the motives from which he portrayed Campobasso as having acted in interceding for Siffredo were unlikely to have been alien to him, and they assume verisimilitude when we consider other accounts of his behaviour in the preceding year. According to the chronicler, not only Campobasso but also Galeota, the first men in the Burgundian camp to recognise Siffredo, pleaded for him, initially because he was a fellow Italian and one of good family. This would tie in with what we know of the strength of the social bonds among Italian mercenaries in the Burgundian army, especially, perhaps, among the upper ranks and classes.[139] A further reason why Campobasso and Galeota reportedly urged clemency was that of humanity, for if Siffredo were put to death, reprisals would inevitably be taken against Burgundian prisoners held by the Lorrainers in Nancy and elsewhere, a prediction which proved correct.[140] Behind this argument, we can detect the Italians' dislike of the terror tactics sometimes employed by Charles in pursuit of quick results in his campaigns. There was a clear divergence of opinion between the duke and the bulk of Italian military opinion, with the latter seeking in general to out-manoeuvre rather than annihilate an enemy; a certain professional self-interest linked Italian mercenaries, even when on opposing sides, in a reluctance to go to extremes. Exemplary cruelty, as practised by Charles on occasions, seemed to them to be unwise militarily as well as morally.

The most obvious cause for complaint by Campobasso was the humiliation and possibly physical hurt suffered as a result of the blow from his master's (probably mail) gauntlet. That Charles could strike one of his leading advisers, especially during what proved to be the last weeks of his life when the strain of adversity began to take its toll, is quite plausible, for other sources tell of threats, verbal assaults and even blows directed by him, both then and earlier in his reign, against some of his captains, Italian and non-Italian alike.[141] Humiliation too was inflicted on the count by the public and derisory rejection of his advice, advice prompted by military no less than by ethical considerations. To Campobasso, on whose counsel the duke had once so willingly relied, this indifference now must have confirmed that loss of ducal esteem which had been adumbrated by the military reforms of December 1475. Other sources suggest that his awareness of his inability any longer to influence the duke was a major reason for his desertion.[142] He was not alone in despairing of the duke's apparent unwillingness to face what seemed to be simple and stark military reality. His leading generals, for example, advised strongly and in vain that he should withdraw from Nancy with the bulk of his forces to Luxembourg for the winter, rather than risk his own person in a siege which could not now be brought to a speedily successful conclusion.[143]

Perhaps, above all, it was Campobasso's determination not to be dragged down in the wake of a ruler who seemed doomed, by his mistakes or by his fortune, to destruction that left an invidious defection as his only escape. This was more than an instinct of sheer self-preservation. If Charles had taken the advice to retire to Luxembourg for the rest of the winter, Campobasso would still have remained in the firing line, since it was proposed that he and the count of Chimay should stay behind with a token force to continue the siege of Nancy. With the rejection of this plan, it must presumably have seemed pointless for him to remain any longer. Already in the spring of 1476, during his return journey from Santiago de Compostela, he had reportedly expressed (to the duke of Brittany) disillusionment with Charles, whom he described as cruel, obstinate and persistently unsuccessful as a general.[144] The events of December 1476 can have served only to confirm him in this judgement. In addition, he had the lives of his men to consider. Self-interest, certainly, was involved to some extent, since his value to any future employer depended in part on the number of men he could bring with him. Yet it would be hard to deny him any humanitarian motive, for, as one reviewer of Croce's essay put it, he had some care for the lives of his men, declining to throw them away in a senseless war.[145]

In the end, then, it was a question of personal choice and individual psychology. Yet, by the same token, it is important not to let Campobasso's behaviour blacken by association the reputation of the other Italian mercenaries. In fact, his behaviour was by no means typical, as Commynes himself was at pains to make clear, contrasting him in particular with Galeota, whom he considered to be as trusty and valiant as his fellow Neapolitan was traitorous.[146] Galeota himself was not unaware of this reputation for loyalty; in 1478 he wrote to Lorenzo the Magnificent that he had always striven to keep his reputation immaculate. He was perhaps the last of the Italian soldiers to leave the Burgundian service. This he did in August 1478, but not before obtaining permission from his new master, Maximilian of Austria; he wanted to return to Italy and wrote to Lorenzo for a command in the Florentine army; after the failure of this application, he was attracted by the offers of Louis XI, but his decision to join the old enemy of his former master cannot be reproached, for it was made only when a period of truce prevailed between France and Burgundy.[147] Galeota was undoubtedly more typical than Campobasso of Charles the Bold's Italian mercenaries. It is true that some of them fled from time to time through dissatisfaction with pay and conditions, but there was nothing on a scale to match Campobasso's desertion. On the contrary, the bulk of them fought with much bravery and persistence. Both the Corradi di Lignana brothers, for example, died in battle, Pietro at Grandson and Antonio at Murten. At the battle of Nancy the count of Celano was taken prisoner; after his release he may have served Mary and Maximilian for a time before being paid off.[148] Troilo too was captured in that battle, but he was less fortunate than Celano, for he was still languishing in a Lorraine gaol in June 1480, by which time his surviving son Alessandro had probably been paid off by Mary and had returned to Italy.[149] A number of other Italians, who constituted the remnants of several companies decimated at Grandson, Murten and Nancy, returned to the Burgundian service after the last battle only to be paid off by Mary, who seemingly did not have the money to continue paying them.[150] Ironically, one of those who was for a time retained was none other than Giovanni di Monforte, younger son of the count of Campobasso. He was a member of Maximilian's household in September 1477, although it is probable that, like his brother Angelo, he left the Burgundian service shortly afterwards to return to Italy to be with his father.

Finally, while some Italian troops, particularly those with Milanese loyalties, actively engaged in subverting their colleagues, as we saw earlier in this section, this again was far from typical. Charles did not hide his suspicion that, for example, the disgraceful flight of his army at Grandson was caused by treachery in the ranks, and he believed the reluctance of some of his captains to risk a second contest with the Swiss was the result of treason rather than military caution. Yet the Italians were the last people whom he then thought of blaming. His wrath was directed rather against those of his French-speaking subjects who were aware and glad of his temporary inability to return to the fray, because they — the principal captains, the Burgundian and Picard nations, and the principal officials and administrators of his camp — did not want his power to increase relative to that of Louis XI.[151] As usual, the duke's main fear was of Louis XI, in comparison with whom the count of Campobasso must have seemed small fry indeed.

Italian military influence on Charles the Bold

There is a strong *prima facie* case for assuming that Charles was influenced by Italian military practice. After all, from 1473 onwards he increasingly placed Italians in many of the more important positions of command in his army, out of proportion to their numbers; he was keenly interested in Italian military practice and theory; and he wanted his subjects to learn the art of war from his Italian mercenaries. Moreover, he could receive Italian military advice not only from his mercenaries, but also from the Italian ambassadors at his court and, through them, from the ambassadors' masters and their masters' leading advisers.

The evidence is particularly strong regarding the organisation of his army. The use of the term *conducteur* for the commander of a company of the ordinance may have been one such innovation; *conducteur*, of course, resembles the Italian *condottiere*, but it is striking that, after the death of the italophile Charles, the normal term employed changed back to *capitaine*.[152] His bestowal on the *conducteurs* of a captain's baton as the symbol of their authority, in a formal ceremony which took place annually after 1473 (see Plate 4), may have owed something to an imitation of Italian, particularly Venetian, practice. It is possible also that his fastidious attention to the minutiae of military organisation — a capacity for and love of detail that have earned him the tentative description of the inventor of drill[153] — may have been influenced to some extent by the professional outlook of his Italian mercenaries. His determination from at least 1469 onwards to base his army on permanent companies of the ordinance arose from a desire to emulate not only the French *compagnies d'ordonnance*, as is usually accepted, but also the *lanze spezzate* of the Venetian republic.[154] Molinet connected the reorganisation of the companies of the ordinance after 1473 — they were then divided into squadrons (*escadres*) of twenty-five men rather than of ten — with the influx of Italian mercenaries into the Burgundian army during that year;[155] and the remarkable military ordinance issued by Charles while he was at the abbey of St. Maximin outside Trier in the autumn of 1473 has been regarded as betraying a strong Italian influence.[156]

There is also some evidence — though less than that concerning the organisation of his army — of Italian influence on the duke's use of his troops: in other words, on his tactics and strategy. For example, the count of Campobasso, together with a number of other Italians such as Giacomo Galeota and Ameo di Valperga, were given a major role in the conduct of the siege of Neuss, while according to one Italian eyewitness, Charles sent his troops against the German forces in the battle fought outside Neuss in May 1475 in an Italian manner ('*Italici generis*').[157] The duke was certainly willing to hear and request advice. He sought the counsel of his generals, some of whom were Italian, before drawing up his famous military ordinances of May 1476, and again on the eve of the battle of Murten in June.[158] Of course, it could be added that he did not take enough of this advice for his own good; in the opinion of his best modern biographer, his very personal role in military affairs is obviously linked to the fact that he contrived to be defeated, often disastrously, in almost all his major battles; and some chroniclers felt he could have avoided defeat at Grandson and Murten had he listened more closely to Galeota.

The evidence for the improving influence of the Italian mercenaries is mixed. Don Federico considered the Burgundian army before the battle of Murten, as he told Commynes shortly afterwards, to have been the finest he had ever seen in his life; indeed, in June 1476 the duke's Italian captains paid it the highest possible compliment by comparing it favourably with that once commanded by Francesco Sforza. Others, however, had reservations. The Milanese ambassador d'Appiano was not impressed by the army when it was passed under review and muster by Charles in May that year, while the shrewd Burgundian nobleman Philippe Pot, lord of La Roche and member of the Order of the Golden Fleece, was prepared to concede in June that the Milanese army was far superior to any he had seen north of the Alps.[159]

The extent of Italian influence on the duke was limited by the fact that Italy did not provide his only military schooling. He also turned for instruction to accounts of the heroes of antiquity, taking particular pleasure in the deeds of Pompey and Caesar, of Hannibal and Alexander the Great as recounted by, among others, Valerius Maximus and Livy. He and his advisers were apt to sprinkle their speeches with classical allusions, as, for example, at Nancy in December 1475 when Guillaume de Rochefort, speaking on the duke's behalf, reminded the assembled captains that the skill and obedience of soldiers were necessary for the well-being of states, adducing many authorities and examples from both Roman emperors and civil law.[160]

But the question of the extent to which he was influenced by classical authors in military matters has itself provoked controversy. For instance, the siege of Neuss was a splendid set-piece affair which should have provided him with the perfect opportunity to try out the theories and stratagems picked up from his classical reading; yet one close study of his campaigns which considers the question finds very little evidence of such influence there.[161] As Wielant noted, the duke's heavy reliance on foreign mercenaries was one of several characteristics in which he differed so markedly from his father; yet it did not escape Molinet's attention that this preference conflicted with the advice of another classical author whose writings were probably known to Charles, namely Vegetius.[162]

On the other hand, it was argued long ago that the duke was indeed influenced by Vegetius, Xenophon and the rest, if only to the extent that he mastered the sergeant's skills of drill and organisation (without the poor quality of his generalship having been in any way improved thereby). More recently, a detailed if not entirely convincing attempt has been made to trace the influence on his military organisation and conduct of Vasco de Lucena's French version of Xenophon's *Cyropaedi*.[163] A nineteenth-century German historian produced a detailed study comparing the wars between the Greeks and the Persians with those between Charles and the Swiss, while more recently it has been argued that at the battle of Grandson, Charles the Bold attempted the classic double envelopment of Hannibal at Cannae. The second example is interesting because, when Charles was warned in January 1476 about the difficult terrain which he was likely to encounter in his forthcoming campaign in Savoy, he replied that similar difficulties had not deterred Hasdrubal, and that military discipline and human courage could overcome all such problems.

Yet if there is evidence that Charles was to some, not precisely quantifiable, extent influenced by Italian military science, it is impossible to overlook the fact that in both minor and major matters there were marked divergences of outlook. Some of these have been noted already. It may be, for example, that the duke's idea of military discipline was somewhat harsher than that of his mercenaries. Similarly, on the question of remuneration: he thought in terms of delaying payment in order to induce his hired troops to stay in his service, rather than in terms of paying promptly to prevent them becoming so dissatisfied as to leave it; and he expected the same degree of loyalty from them as he demanded from his subjects.[164] Perhaps more significant than these differences of view regarding the management of troops — differences which, after all, were only to be expected where foreign mercenaries were concerned — were those disagreements which took place over tactics. One such was the duke's arguably fateful neglect of Giacomo Galeota's advice in relation to the battles of Grandson and Murten.[165] Another is the fearsome upbraidings he gave to Antonio dei Corradi di Lignana and Troilo da Rossano on more than one occasion towards the middle of June 1476 for their failure to take the town of Murten as quickly as he would have liked. The captains' argument was that they wanted to save their best men for the battle against the full Swiss army which was expected to arrive shortly, for, if that force could be defeated, then Murten would fall or surrender with little further expenditure of blood and toil. Charles, however, was angry because he wished to march on Bern and did not therefore want to leave a Swiss garrison at his rear.[166]

This episode may have been simply a failure of communication rather than a basic conflict of opinion. The fundamental difference of outlook is better illustrated by the Italians' opposition to winter campaigning, which they both disliked for obvious personal reasons of convenience, and disapproved on military grounds. Francesco Bertini, for example, thought Charles was breaching the rules of military science ('*lex militaris*') in not retiring from the siege of Neuss to winter quarters at the end of 1474, while in 1468 the legate Onofrio had assumed that the duke would not attack Liège in winter.[167] It may be that winter campaigning was something that divided the Italians not only from the duke of Burgundy, but also from other ultramontane rulers as well. For example, at the end of 1476 Louis XI, with pointed reference to the duke's continuing siege of Nancy, told the visiting Milanese prince Lodovico il Moro that he himself never campaigned beyond October because he understood this to have been the practice also of his military mentor, the late Francesco Sforza, Lodovico's father; in fact, however, the king had allowed his troops to besiege Perpignan throughout the winter of 1474–1475, a decision which initially brought him nothing but scorn in Rome.[168]

One aspect of the duke's military conduct which, judging by the repeated criticisms made of it by Italians, differed most markedly from

Italian practice was his cold-blooded cruelty, employed as deliberate terror tactics. The sack of Nesle in 1472 and his mass executions of prisoners in 1475 and 1476 were roundly condemned by Italians both in his entourage and in the peninsula itself; they made a significant contribution to the decline in his reputation in Italy in his latter years, and to the fear and loathing with which some Italians came to regard him. Taken together, these individual differences of opinion amount to a fundamental disagreement in military philosophy. Indeed, as far as the art of war was concerned, they reveal the strict limitations on the possibility of Italian influence on Charles; these limitations derived from the fact that, as between the duke and the rulers of the peninsula, there was a basic cleavage in the roles they assigned to their respective armies and in the expectations they had of them.

Italy evolved her own style of warfare as a response to the restricted opportunities for territorial expansion to be found there, to the particular political and financial strengths of rulers, and to the qualities of the troops available. Between about 1454 and 1494, there existed in Italy a degree of peace and interstate stability such as had not been seen for centuries previously; the peninsula was dominated by five major powers — Venice, Milan, Florence, the Papal States and the kingdom of Naples — who in turn dominated their lesser neighbours; and the relative equality between these powers, or between varying combinations of them, helped to discourage attempts to upset the balance. Such a situation was not conducive to territorial expansion. The risks involved were far greater than any possible benefits. Because rulers relied in general on mercenary troops, campaigns were expensive and tended to be short, while the inability of most states, apart from Venice and perhaps also Milan, to maintain standing armies deprived them, when preparing for war, of the important advantage of surprise which could have facilitated major conquests. Moreover, the outcome of military action was always unpredictable, not because Italian soldiers were short of skill but because they lacked the burning motivation necessary. A mercenary captain's prime concern was always to preserve intact his company, on which his status and income depended. His professional outlook made him at times merciful towards his enemies, for this helped ensure his own survival in the event of some future defeat. An example of this attitude is the intercession, according to the Lorraine chronicler, of the count of Campobasso for Siffredo dei Baschi in 1476, but his action reportedly only angered Charles. The process by which soldiering was refined into an art, it has been argued, tended to lessen its effectiveness.[169] The dominance of this outlook was ensured when Francesco Sforza, himself one of the leading mercenary captains of his day, seized the ducal throne of Milan in 1450 and set the style for Italian military thinking. Indeed, because some states were ruled by dynasties whose juridical title was insecure and whose political strength was undermined by the existence of enemies at home and abroad — notably the Sforza in Milan, the Aragonese in Naples and the Medici in Florence — warfare was often eschewed, because the political danger of military defeat was so great. The lack of faith in the efficacy of military action alone displayed by Italians in this period was both cause and consequence of their leadership of the rest of Europe in the techniques of diplomacy.

The type of warfare evolved by the Italians in this situation has been characterised as a combination of defensive and counter-offensive.[170] It was Fabian and cautious, seeking above all to preserve one's own army rather than to destroy the enemy's, to avoid defeat rather than take risks in order to win a victory.[171] The contrast with the last Valois duke of Burgundy is marked. Unlike, for example, Galeazzo Maria, Lorenzo the Magnificent or Ferrante, he had been trained for warfare since childhood; by the time he became duke in 1467 he had already gained experience in numerous campaigns in the Low Countries and France; and one of the most striking features of his character was his love of the military life. As the representative of one of the most splendid and seemingly secure princely houses in Europe, he did not need to fear the overthrow of his dynasty by internal or exiled rivals as soon as he encountered defeat in the field.[172] His attitude towards his troops differed accordingly from that of Italian rulers. Where they might persuade or plead, he would command and expect obedience. Some of his victories might have seemed Pyrrhic in Italian terms, but he was not constrained by reliance on independent-minded mercenaries to hoard his men in an ultra-cautious fashion or to place avoidance of defeat before pursuit of victory. Having lost the bulk of one army at Murten, he immediately set about raising another from among the inhabitants of his own rich and numerous lands, and he was able to claim with some conviction that his campaigns were undertaken to defend his subjects;[173] in this he differed from several Italian rulers, for in some states of the peninsula the degree of sympathy and awareness of mutual interest between the ruler and his subjects was often far smaller.

Yet many of the duke's campaigns were not defensive, but were offensive wars of conquest. Here, the contrast with Italian rulers is most marked. Like most other ultramontane princes of his time, Charles could not afford to neglect opportunities for territorial expansion, and, fortunately for him, there was no shortage of such opportunities, notably in the lands of the Empire, where the bulk of his and his predecessors' annexations and conquests took place.[174] This expansion was certainly prepared and facilitated by shrewd diplomacy, but would have been impossible without substantial force of arms, and no Italian ruler could realistically have cherished territorial ambitions on the same scale.

In short, Charles may to a significant extent have adopted and utilised the skill, organisation and advice of Italians, but the manner in which he actually employed his army for the furtherance of his policies could never become completely Italianate for the reason that, considered in the context of the interrelationship of military power, diplomacy and dynastic interest, fifteenth-century Italy and Valois Burgundy were poles apart.[175]

Apart from their military influence, the duke's Italian mercenaries made some impact also on the financial and constitutional history of the reign. It has been suggested, for example, that one reason for the sharp increase in the issue of silver (as opposed to gold) coins in his reign was his maintenance of a large standing army and his need to find ready cash in smallish denominations to pay it.[176] This army, of course, comprised an ever-larger number of mercenaries, of whom the Italians formed the most sizeable foreign contingent. The development of the institution of the States General may also have been indirectly influenced by the duke's recruitment of several thousand Italian mercenaries. The evolution of the States General under the Valois dukes of Burgundy was a major contributory factor in the gradual unification of the Low Countries in the early modern period; its evolution was given a great stimulus by the extraordinary taxation of Charles the Bold; and this extraordinary taxation in turn was partly prompted by the financial pressures which the payment of a large standing army placed on him. When, therefore, he wished in 1473 to obtain from his subjects a grant of 500,000 crowns yearly for six years to pay for the upkeep of the additional companies of the ordinance which he wanted to create, and of which many were to be manned by the Italian mercenaries he was then recruiting, he took the unusual step of summoning the States General as a body, rather than approach the Estates of each territory separately, as had often happened on similar occasions previously. Moreover, Charles had to make some not insignificant concessions to his subjects in order to obtain their agreement to the grant.[177] Perhaps also his subjects were suspicious not only of the behaviour of his mercenaries but of the very principle they represented, for Charles was one of the first rulers of his day to keep a large standing army, an institution which, with all its financial and constitutional implications, was to provide over the next two centuries a notable bone of contention between rulers and subjects; already in early 1473, while his request for a six-year grant was still under discussion, he put pressure on the deputies to agree by a public display of his military power.[178] Certainly, after his death, the States General lost no time in seeking to limit the numbers of the ducal army by financial means, to keep a tight rein on the discipline of those remaining and to end their ruler's power to declare war without the consent of her subjects.

We have now traced the limits of Italian military influence in the reign of Charles the Bold. To conclude, it might be suggested further that, on a larger time-scale than that provided by the decade of his reign, this influence was short-lived and almost negligible. The reason for that was simply the lack of continuity in personnel between Charles and his successors. It is likely that, by January 1477, the number of Italians in his army was smaller than at any time since the spring of 1473; death and desertion had taken a heavy toll. Very few of the remaining Italians stayed in the Burgundian service after the battle of Nancy for longer than was necessary for them to be paid off, and even someone as faithful as Galeota lingered only eighteen months. On the one hand, many Italians may now have wished to return to their homeland. On the other, Mary and Maximilian lacked the financial resources for a standing army, and perhaps their subjects raised objections of a political nature; certainly, the late duke's successors did not share his great enthusiasm for things Italian. It is significant in this context that no Italians are recorded among the captains of fifty and a hundred lances of the ordinance in the account of the *trésorier des guerres* for 1478.[179] This may serve as a fitting epitaph on the ephemeral nature of many of Charles the Bold's achievements and, in particular, on what might be called, in military history, the Italian experiment of his reign.

* * *

The discussions and conclusions above, though sometimes tentative, are now summarised. The reasons why Charles recruited Italian mercenaries are clear enough. He had gradually become determined to form a standing army so that he would not be left unprepared if attacked by that of Louis XI. He put his plans into action during the truces with the French king in the winter of 1472–1473. Since he felt he could not obtain the quantity and quality required from among his own subjects, he turned to foreign mercenaries. The largest single contingent was provided by Italy. Italian soldiers were admired by several rulers north of the Alps, but this admiration was perhaps more marked in the duke of Burgundy than in most. Although Italian soldiers were to be found in the Burgundian army in the first half of his reign, the main influx came in the recruiting drive which lasted from the end of 1472 to about the middle of 1473. Over the next three years, more Italians probably joined up, but this took place in terms of enlistment by individuals and small groups on their own initiative, rather than as the result of canvassing by Charles himself. In the spring of 1476 he did plan another large-scale recruiting drive designed to add to his array perhaps as many as 2,500 Italian mercenaries, but, as far as one can tell, the scheme was almost completely unsuccessful.

It is difficult to assess numbers with confidence. We do not have a complete list of individuals which would enable us to determine numbers on the basis of names and their likely geographical origins, nor, it should be stressed, can we always be certain that companies commanded by Italians were themselves composed, to a greater or lesser degree, of Italians. The best we can do is to compute the numbers recruited in 1472–1473 and then, on the basis of these figures, estimate later variations. Assuming that the quotas allotted to the mercenary captains in 1472–1473 were filled, and with Italians, then about 5,300 (possibly 5,500) troops were recruited at that time: 4,600 (possibly 4,800) cavalry and 700 infantry. This represented somewhere between a third and a half of the ducal army. Perhaps this number held steady until about the latter part of 1474, with losses through casualties and desertion being offset by the arrival of new enlisters. Thereafter, the Italian strength declined. Reviews held in mid-1475 listed only about 3,300 Italians (the bulk, over 2,000, being cavalry), a figure which reflects losses at the siege of Neuss and in the fighting against the League of Constance in Franche-Comté, but which may be slightly distorted as it probably overlooks some Italian garrisons stationed in the Low Countries. Nonetheless, after the battle of Grandson Charles sought to recruit more Italians, perhaps with the intention of restoring their numbers to the level of 1473; this restoration, however, did not take place. During 1476, there seem to have been increasing desertions. Moreover, Italian losses in combat may have been more severe than previously, because for the battles of Murten and Nancy some Italian companies were recalled from garrison duty to service with the main frontline army. Impressionistic evidence is provided by the case of the count of Campobasso. In January 1477, Campobasso and his two sons deserted with about 300 men. Yet, when he had joined the

Burgundian army over four years before, he had been placed in charge of about 2,000. Even allowing for the possibility that he did not manage to induce all the men under his command to defect with him, and taking into account also the fact that men once under his command had been re-allotted to other companies, the difference between 2,000 men in 1473 and 300 in 1477 represents a sharp reduction.

We can discover a little about these soldiers as people, though less so regarding the rank-and-file than the captains. Neapolitans and Piedmontese were particularly prominent among the captains. Their ages ranged from perhaps the early thirties to the sixties. Many brought relatives with them, including close relations such as brothers, sons and nephews; war was to some extent a family affair. The captains were often of noble birth, with the title of count being not uncommon, but political and financial circumstances dictated that rank was not always accompanied by status and possessions. In terms of geographical origins, the rank-and-file differed from their superiors, for most seem to have come from northern Italy, with some additions from central Italy, and fewer still from the South. For both groups, however, the decision to serve in the Burgundian army was a question of both pull and push: fighting for Charles offered an opportunity to escape from unemployment, political vendettas, justice and boredom.

Was Charles justified in relying so heavily on Italian mercenaries? Certainly they were not without faults. They may have misbehaved on garrison duty, although this was not a uniquely Italian failing. Perhaps more peculiarly Italian was their reluctance to support the duke's methods of warfare where these entailed arrears of pay or what they regarded as unacceptable casualties. Charles had high hopes of their reputed readiness to obey orders. Sometimes he was disappointed, but he sought to remedy the situation by exhortation and, more practically, by taking the mercenaries directly under his own command, whereas, before the end of 1475, he had allowed a measure of intermediate authority to the mercenary captains. What he prized above all, however, was their military experience and professional expertise. The fact that he still wanted to recruit in the peninsula in 1476 shows that he felt the advantages outweighed the risks. He also hoped that his subjects, by prolonged contact with the Italians, would assimilate the soldierly virtues which they had forgotten in the comparatively peaceful reign of his father. But, until they did complete their military education, he had to base his army on mercenaries, and he paid the Italians the compliment of regarding them as the best available.

A test case for his wisdom in placing such confidence in Italian mercenaries is often thought to have been provided by the behaviour of the count of Campobasso in January 1477. In fact, the main charge against the count should be not his defection — other Italians had deserted over the previous three years, though none, admittedly, in such fateful circumstances — but the part he played in the subsequent fighting. It seems unlikely that he actually fought alongside the duke of Lorraine's army at the battle of Nancy, but he probably did station himself in such a way as to impede the Burgundians' retreat, and in this way he contributed to the high level of casualties. The reasons why he left Charles may never be fully clarified. There seems to be little justification for Commynes's explanation, which sees the defection as the culmination of a treacherous plot which had begun as soon as the count entered the Burgundian army; this does not mean, however, that one should overlook the historical plausibility of Commynes's allegations of subversive activities and of Angevin, or Francophile, loyalties, for these were not unknown among the other Italian mercenaries, although such accusations cannot be proved with regard to Campobasso. A more convincing explanation was provided by Croce, who argued that his defection was the result of grievances which had gradually built up over the previous two years or so, particularly over arrears of pay and loss of status, and was therefore almost excusable. Yet Campobasso was the only one of the major Italian commanders to defect, even though others had also been affected by the same grievances. Campobasso reacted differently from his colleagues because he, as the duke's leading Italian captain, had more to lose than they. The immediate cause of his defection in January 1477 is uncertain. The evidence for the Siffredo dei Baschi affair is contradictory and far from reliable. It is probable, nonetheless, that the count was provoked beyond recall by a single incident, perhaps a disagreement with the duke over whether to end or continue the siege of Nancy. But, whatever his reasons, it is important to distinguish Campobasso from the other Italian commanders, who served Charles loyally to the end, some of them being taken prisoner at the battle of Nancy itself.

Charles was certainly susceptible to Italian military influence. This was particularly noticeable with regard to organisational details; perhaps this very attention to detail was the result of imitating the professionalism of his mercenary captains. Sometimes it is difficult to decide whether certain aspects of his military practice resulted from Italian influence or from emulation of the heroes of antiquity. Overall, however, he was less influenced on tactics and strategy. This was because his concept of war and of the relationship between military power and diplomacy differed fundamentally from that of the Italians. Another factor limiting their influence was the short duration of their Burgundian service. Their main influx came only after the middle of the duke's reign, and their presence did not last long after his death, because most of those who had not already left seem to have been quickly paid off by his successor, Mary.

Notes

1. See, for example, *Dépêches* . . . *Louis XI*, IV, 161, 169–70, 218, 244–5, 259, and *Dispatches*, III, xxxix.

2. See, for example, Guillaume Hugonet's speech, on behalf of Charles, to the States General held at Bruges in January 1473, referring to Louis XI's '*puissance de gens d'armes, toujours preste*': *Actes des États Généraux des anciens Pays-Bas*, I, ed. J. Cuvelier, J. Dhondt and R. Doehaerd (Brussels, 1948), 184.

3. Zannono Coiro from the French court to the duke of Milan, 15 January 1469 (ASM 536). For a report in October 1472 of similar complaints see Bittmann, *Ludwig XI. und Karl der Kühne*, II/1, 40–1 and note 41 (Bernhard von Gilgenberg to Peter von Hagenbach). In general, Commynes thought (*Mémoires*, II, 102), Charles preferred foreign troops to his own subjects because he could afford to hire good ones in large numbers.

4. Angelo Probi d'Atri to the king of Naples, Venice, 11 March 1473 (ASM 358), reporting a conversation with Guillaume de Rochefort. See also Vaughan, *Charles*, 214 for an observation by a German official of Charles the Bold linking the duke's desire for foreign mercenaries with his disappointment at the setbacks experienced in the campaign of summer 1472.

5. '. . . *per havere el re di Franza fatto i suoi preparimenti in tal modo che questo capitanio et tute altre zente italiane havea conducto quel Signor li erano necessarissimo* . . .': Barbaro to Doge Niccolò Tron, Naples, 26 March 1473 (BNMV 8170/IV, 20).

6. '. . . *maxime per essere più presto in termini di guerra che de pace deliberava ad omne modo havere succorso et adiuto de gente italiane* . . .': Cristoforo da Bollate to the duke of Milan, Tours, 14 December 1473 (ASM 540).

7. ASV, SS, XXVI, 2.

8. Molinet, *Chroniques*, I, 80–1; *Carteggi*, II, no. 491. On 25 March 1476 (*Carteggi*, II, no. 479), Panigarola had reported that Charles had rebuked his Italian mercenaries, after they had been involved in a riot, for not living up to their universal reputation for good order and obedience. A hitherto unnoticed piece of evidence for the duke's views on the need for military discipline is in ASM 520, filed after Panigarola's dispatch of 27 July 1476. It is an Italian copy of an edict published by Charles at La Rivière on 26 July, outlining his plans for a standing army of 2,000 men to be reinforced as required by other troops and to be divided equally between a company of the ordinance and a household company. The qualifications sought by him can be seen in the section which reads '*ha a fare di gente chi sapiano et siano experti di fare il mestiere loro et de vivere honestamente, bene et con ogni obedientia, lassando tuti li appetiti et volontà loro per seguire la soa* [the duke's] *et exequirla*'.

9. *Carteggi*, II, no. 647 (partly translated in Vaughan, *Charles*, 166); Troilo's family name was de Muris, but his Christian name by itself appears to have been his standard appellation.

10. Vaughan, *Charles*, 216.

11. Contamine, *Guerre, état et société*, 154, 162, 253, 308, 457; B.G.H. Ditcham, 'The employment of foreign mercenary troops in the French royal armies, 1415–1470' (Ph.D. thesis, University of Edinburgh, 1978), *passim*; Ditcham's fascinating study tackles, for France, many of the questions that are considered in this chapter for Burgundy, such as numbers, recruitment, background, integration and military value.

12. Brauer-Gramm, *Der Landvogt Peter von Hagenbach*, 188. Payments to a Jehan de Piedmont to equip himself for the Bugundian army are recorded in the accounts of the receiver-general for 1470: AGR CC 1925, ff. 339, 358ᵛ, 394.

13. ADN B 3540/125,832; AGR CC 25542, ff. 7ᵛ, 8; H.L.G. Guillaume, *Histoire des bandes d'ordonnance des Pays-Bas* (Brussels, 1873), 13.

14. A letter of his to Pietro, dated 20 March 1471 and describing recent fighting around Amiens, is in ASM 538.

15. Vaughan, *Charles*, 214–15.

16. Latin copies are in ASM 515 and in AGR, Manucrits divers, 1173, ff. 191–2.

17. Petrus Blanchus, secretary of the Venetian ambassador Bembo, to Hieronymus (?) presumably in Venice, from Bruges, 17 November 1472 (ASM 515), and Vaughan, *Charles*, 215.

18. D'Appiano to the duke of Milan, Vercelli, 30 January 1473 (ASM 496). A five months' advance payment made to Galeota had run out by June 1473: see the letter concerning the various Italian recruits and the concomitant financial problems written by Jean Jouard and Jean de Le Scaghe (respectively president of the Parlements, and receiver-general, of Burgundy) to Charles from Dijon, 1 July 1473, in ADN B17711. The Neapolitan form of the name is more usually Galeota (Perret, 'Jacques Galéot', 591 note 3, and Tourneur, 'Jehan de Candida', 261), although much secondary literature and some contemporaries use the form Galeotto.

19. Galeota to the duke of Milan, Reggio, 16 May 1473 (ASM 323); Lodovico Tagliante to Giacomo dei Vischi, Dijon, 28 August 1473 (ASM 540); d'Appiano to the duke of Milan, Montecaprello, 10 October 1473 (ASM 490); P. de Vigneulles, *Chronique*, ed. C. Bruneau, 4 vols (Metz, 1927–33), II (1932), 12; the letter of Jouard and Le Scaghe cited in the previous note.

20. Francesco Maletta to the duke of Milan, Naples, 19 January and 25 April 1474 (ASM 225).

21. AGR CC 25543, ff. 26, 26ᵛ.

22. Arduino was in the camp at Neuss on 28 January 1475 when he wrote a letter to 'monsignor d'Ales' praising the splendour of the siege works (ASM 492). Arrighino was one of 28 soldiers grouped around the ducal standard in the battle fought against the imperial forces there in May 1475 and, after the battle, he was one of those knighted by Charles: *Carteggi*, I, no. 306, and Molinet, *Chroniques*, I, 98; Molinet, presumably incorrectly, also mentions (I, 34) a Giacomo ('Jacques') di Valperga.

23. Sacramoro to the duke of Milan, Rome, 2 May 1474 (ASM 76); ADN B

3438/119,105. For the next sentence, see Mangin, 'Guillaume de Rochefort', 30.

24. AGR CC 25543, f. 121ᵛ; see also Vaughan, *Charles*, 237, who further suggests (pp. 306, 359, 364) that the Italian troops attacked by Bern and her associates as they passed through Aigle in Lower Valais on 16 August 1475 were new recruits travelling north from Italy. According to the *Cronycke van Hollandt*, xlvᵛᵒ, the Venetians had sent 8,000 (*sic*) troops to Charles at Neuss.

25. *Dépêches . . . Charles-le-Hardi*, II, no. 181.

26. The former were mercenary infantry usually charged with garrison duty; the latter were heavy cavalry mounted on *jennets*, a Spanish breed of horse.

27. Tourneur, 'Jehan de Candida', 296. For the rest of the sentence, see Knebel, *Diarium*, I, 163, reporting a reference to the '*magnum numerum peditum et inutilium*' (my emphasis) by a canon of Cologne writing to Johannes Helmich early in 1475 about the 'Lombardi' in the Burgundian camp at Neuss.

28. Raphael Cataneii to the marquis of Mantua, Turin, 7 May 1473 (AG 731). But this could simply mean that the men were those whom Campobasso brought into the Burgundian army from among comrades who had fought with him in the earler Angevin campaigns in Catalonia, which does not of itself rule out their being Italian.

29. The figure of 1,000 lances as the duke's aim and achievement is confirmed by Bittmann, *Ludwig XI. und Karl der Kühne*, II/1, 41 note 41 (letter of Bernhard von Gilgenberg to Peter von Hagenbach, October 1472) and J. Calmette, 'L'origine bourguignonne de l'alliance austro–espagnole', in his *Études médiévales* (Toulouse, 1946), 215–39 (p. 235 note 35: letter of Charles to the king of Aragon, 28 March 1473). In 1475, as we shall see shortly, the lances commanded by Giacomo dei Vischi definitely consisted of six, rather than four, men. If this had been the case from the start, then our figures would need to be amended. The cavalry would number 4,800 and the grand total of troops recruited would rise to 5,500.

30. *Actes des États Généraux des anciens Pays-Bas*, I, 186, 188.

31. Salvatore de Clariciis's mission to Milan in 1474 was designed to procure the return of Italian troops who had thus fled from Galeota's company (*Carteggi*, I, no. 220).

32. Molinet, *Chroniques*, I, 39, 81, 129; Knebel, *Diarium*, I, 163.

33. *Carteggi*, I, no. 289.

34. *Carteggi*, II, no. 346; and J. de La Chauvelays, 'Mémoire sur la composition des armées de Charles le Téméraire dans les deux Bourgognes d'après les documents originaux', *Mémoires de l'Académie des sciences, arts et belles-lettres de Dijon*, 3rd ser., 5 (1879), 139–369 (pp. 328–9).

35. La Chauvelays, 'Mémoire', 342; J.R. de Chevanne, *Les guerres en Bourgogne de 1470 à 1475* (Paris, 1934), 202, 286; Roye, *Journal*, I, 335; and Giovanni Pietro da Pietrasanta to his brother Filippo from Crasse (?), 23 June 1475 (ASM 516).

36. For these reviews at Neuss, see ADN B 2107/67, 865–8.

37. Molinet, *Chroniques*, I, 64.

38. Francesco d'Este served as governor of Westerlo and Le Quesnoy, while Rainieri Mancella was for a time governor of Nijmegen. In 1475, troops under

the command of Antonio dei Corradi di Lignana and Tommaso da Capua were stationed in the principality of Liège and in Guelders respectively, while Giacomo dei Vischi's company was stationed in Guelders in 1476: Paravicini, *Guy de Brimeu*, 299 note 211 and 355 note 442d; AGR CC, f. 14; Molinet, *Chroniques*, I, 148–9.

39. D. Schmidt-Sinns, 'Studien zum Heerwesen der Herzöge von Burgund 1465–77' (unpublished thesis, Georg-August Universität, Göttingen, 1966), 149.

40. AGR CC 25543, ff. 258–60.

41. *Carteggi*, II, nos. 604, 608.

42. For this and what follows, see Francesco Pietrasanta to the duke of Milan, Turin, 19 and 28 June 1476 (ASM 495) and *Dépêches . . . Charles-le-Hardi*, II, no. 264. On Iseo see above, Chapter 1 n. 168.

43. For example, Commynes, *Mémoires*, II, 102, 121, and *Cronycke van Hollandt*, lxiii. Perhaps some of the recruits did actually leave Italy but simply failed to reach the Burgundian camp through being waylaid by the Swiss, as is reported to have happened in April 1476 by Knebel, *Diarium*, I, 406–17, 412–13; see also H.S. Offler, 'The heroic age', in E. Bonjour, H.S. Offler and G.R. Potter, *A short history of Switzerland* (Oxford, 1952), 107–40 (p. 131).

44. *Dépêches . . . Charles-le-Hardi*, II, nos. 161, 220.

45. *Dépêches . . . Charles-le-Hardi*, II, no. 264. For the next sentence see Knebel, *Diarium*, II, 11–12, 40, 43–4, 51–2, 445.

46. *Carteggi*, II, no. 535; and AGR CC 25543, ff. 210^v–11. For the next sentence, see *Carteggi*, II, nos. 446, 643, and *Dépêches . . . Charles-le-Hardi*, II, no. 263.

47. AGR CC 25543, ff. 208, 217; and Giovanni Bianchi to the duke of Milan, Turin, 21 September 1476 (ASM 496).

48. AGR CC 25543, f. 222^v.

49. During the last four months of the duke's life, there were no Italian ambassadors at his court to send home the informative dispatches which provide such a useful source for other periods of his reign, while even the account of the *trésorier des guerres* for 1476–1477 does not record all the forces at the duke's disposal in his last campaign: Vaughan, *Charles*, 427–8.

50. *Dépêches . . . Charles-le-Hardi*, II, no. 200; and AGR CC 25543, ff. 40, 40^v, 113^v, 115^v. We know that Oliviero was recruited by the count of Campobasso in the spring of 1473 to command 60 men (30 *elmetii* and 30 *provisionati*): *Carteggi*, I, no. 199. But the sources, both Burgundian and Italian, are silent until 1476, when he was listed in the account of the *trésorier des guerres*.

51. *Carteggi*, II, nos. 643, 647. For the next sentence see AGR CC 25543, ff. 39, 84–5^v.

52. AGR CC 25543, ff. 84, 84^v, 209^v. That Guglielmo was the son of Pietro is a reasonable inference from indirect evidence: *Dépêches . . . Charles-le-Hardi*, II, 351 note 4. For Giorgio (ff. 84, 84^v) it is only supposition. However, we know that Pietro had a wife and more than one son in 1473 and that, after his death at Grandson, Charles asked Galeazzo Maria to take them into his special favour: d'Appiano to the duke of Milan, Vercelli, 18 and 23 March 1473 (ASM 490) and Simonetta, *Diarii*, 199–200. But there is no evidence that Antonio had a wife and family. There were at least two other brothers: Giovanni,

provost of San Cristoforo in Vercelli; and Cristoforo, admiral of the Knights of St John of Jerusalem on the island of Rhodes.

53. AGR CC 25543, ff. 18ᵛ–19, 26, 26ᵛ, 73ᵛ–4; Molinet, *Chroniques*, I, 149.

54. For the timing and numbers, see especially F. Mugnier, 'La desconfiture de Charles le Téméraire', *Mémoires et documents publiés par la Société savoisienne d'histoire et d'archéologie*, 40 (1901), 145–69 (p. 156), and Molinet, *Chroniques*, I, 163–5.

55. Simonetta, *Diarii*, 115–16; Molinet, *Chroniques*, I, 148–9; Mugnier, 'La desconfiture', 165; AGR CC 25543, ff. 16–17ᵛ, 40, 87.

56. AGR CC 25543, f. 14, and Molinet, *Chroniques*, I, 148–9. These Italian troops may be the same as those referred to, but not named, in *Dépêches . . . Charles-le-Hardi*, II, no. 181, and P. Gorissen, *De Raadkamer van de hertog van Bourgondië te Maastricht, 1473–1477* (Louvain–Paris, 1959), 212–13.

57. *Carteggi*, II, nos. 581, 641; and Tallone, *Parlamento sabaudo*, V/1, 187.

58. AGR CC 25543, f. 40ᵛ.

59. Vaughan, *Charles*, 428.

60. See especially M. Del Treppo, 'Gli aspetti organizzativi economici e sociali di una compagnia di ventura italiana', *RSI*, 75 (1973–4), 253–75, which is based on the account books of the company of Michelotto degli Attendoli for the years 1425–1449; also suggestive is M.E. Mallett, *Mercenaries and their masters. Warfare in Renaissance Italy* (London etc, 1973), Chap. 8 ('Soldiers and society'). For Burgundy there is a useful sketch by G. Soldi Rondinini, 'Condottieri italiens au service de Charles le Hardi, pendant les guerres de Suisse (1474–1477)', *PCEEB*, 20 (1980), 55–62.

61. Knebel, *Diarium*, I, 158–9, 164, and Molinet, *Chroniques*, I, 44. Perhaps our 'Ursus' may be identified with Orso, one of two sons of Dolce, count of Anguillara (died 1449), about whom little is known other than that he was probably still alive in 1474: V. Sora, 'I conti di Anguillara dalla loro origine al 1465', *Archivio della Società romana di storia patria*, 29 (1906), 397–442, and 30 (1907), 53–118 (p. 98). The family had held lands in the Papal States until driven out by Pius II and Paul II. The anonymous biographies of various members of the family in *DBI*, III (1961), 300–3, say nothing about Orso. Knebel (*Diarium*, I, 158 and note 3) confused 'Ursus' with Orso's uncle Everso di Anguillara, count of Ronciglione, who had died ten years before. For what follows on the Genoese, see Bittmann, *Ludwig XI. und Karl der Kühne*, II/1, 86. As for the Milanese, there is evidence, as we shall see below ('Loyalty'), that perhaps several hundred troops professing allegiance to Galeazzo Maria were serving in the Burgundian army in 1473–1474, some of whom, in fact, may have been deliberately planted there for subversive purposes by the duke of Milan himself.

62. Gabotto, *Lo stato sabaudo*, II, 106 note 3.

63. For what follows, see ADN B 2105/67,695. I give the names as they stand, apart from the addition of apostrophes, accent marks and majuscules.

64. Del Treppo, 'Gli aspetti organizzativi', 270.

65. Troilo's sons were Alessandro and Gianfrancesco; Panigarola's reference in June 1475 (*Carteggi*, I, no. 306) to a Lodovico, son of Troilo, is corroborated by A. Sablon du Corail, 'Les étrangers au service de Marie de Bourgogne: de

l'armée de Charles le Téméraire à l'armée de Maximilien (1477–1482)', *Revue du Nord*, 84 (2002), 389–412 (p. 390), who cites payments to Lodovico by Mary of Burgundy in 1477 for staying in the Burgundian army after the death of Charles the Bold.

66. AGR CC 25543, f. 41.

67. AGR CC 25543, ff. 40, 40ᵛ. For what follows on Pietrasanta, Mancella and Tagliante, see Giovanni Pietro da Pietrasanta to Filippo, Crasse(?), 23 June 1475 (ASM 516); *Carteggi*, I, no. 248; and Giacomo dei Vischi to the duke of Milan, Dijon, 11 June 1475 (ASM 542).

68. D'Appiano, writing to the duke of Milan from Vercelli on 16 March 1475 (ASM 490), mentions a nephew without naming him. Molinet (*Chroniques*, I, 51) says he had two nephews at the siege of Neuss, naming them as Campanel and Rondelet; the latter, described also as Louis de Boucquan, was still with his uncle in 1478 (I, 221, 242). At this time, Molinet says Galeota had another relative serving with him called Prudence (I, 256); Jean de Roye (*Journal*, II, 373), however, merely calls Prudence Galeota's lieutenant. The nephews, if such they were, may have been the sons of Galeota's elder brother Rubino, himself a noted general in his time. In a rare slip, Bittmann, *Ludwig XI. und Karl der Kühne*, II/1, 41 talks of the Galeotto *brothers* serving in the duke's army. A nephew of Galeota had earlier served with him in Catalonia: Solsona Climent, 'Aspectos de la dominación angevin en Cataluña', 36. For what follows, see Croce, 'Il conte di Campobasso', 87, and Simonetta, *Diarii*, 15–16.

69. Litta, *Famiglie celebri d'Italia*, II, fasc. 'Da Correggio', table 3.

70. *Carteggi*, I, no. 199; which of Uguccione's sons this was is not stated. For the next sentence, see Francesco Maletta to the duke of Milan, Naples, 25 April 1474 (ASM 225).

71. Flamini, 'Francesco Galeota', 2–4; Perret, 'Jacques Galéot', 609 note 4. In the *Cronycke van Hollandt*, f. ccciii, Galeota is described, for reasons which I cannot explain, as count of Cremona.

72. Troilo's wife was Buonacaterina, daughter of Marco Fogliano and Lucia da Torsano; Lucia's illegitimate son by Muzio Attendolo Sforza, born prior to their marriage, was the famous Francesco Sforza. Troilo, therefore, was married to the half-sister of Galeazzo Maria's father and, on one occasion, we find him referred to as Galeazzo Maria's uncle (*barba*): D.G. Valeri, 'Della signoria di Francesco Sforza nella Marca', *ASL*, 11 (1884), 35–78, 252–304 (pp. 281 note 1, 289 note 1, 300 note 1), and Vanoxio to Evangelista della Scroffa, monk of Padua, 17 November 1472 (ASM 515).

73. Molinet, *Chroniques*, I, 163; Francesco Pietrasanta to the duke of Milan, Tours, 31 December 1476 (ASM 542).

74. M. Manfredi, 'Accrocciamuro, Ruggerone', in *DBI*, I (1960), 123, and instructions for Alessandro Spinola, Milanese ambassador-designate to France, 10 February 1470, printed by A. von Reumont, *Della diplomazia italiana dal secolo XIII al XVI* (Florence, 1857), 374, and by Chmel, 'Briefe und Aktenstücke', 58.

75. Gerardo Colli to the duke of Milan, Venice, 13 May 1468 (ASM 354); ASV, SS, XXIII, f. 125; Alessandro di Troilo to the duke of Milan, Montagniane, 18 April 1471 (ASM 357). In 1467, Troilo had been given the fief of Maleo

near Cremona by Galeazzo Maria: Soldi Rondinini, 'Condottieri italiens', 58–9. For the next sentence, see ASF, MAP, XXVII, 86, 157, and XXIV, 125 (12 February, 9 March and 11 April 1472).

76. *Carteggi*, II, no. 388, and Matteo d'Herboi to the duke of Milan from Castiglia, 11 November 1472 (ASM 395). For the allusion to Venice, see M.E. Mallett, 'Venice and its condottieri 1404–1454', in *Renaissance Venice*, ed. J.R. Hale (London, 1973), 121–45 (p. 127).

77. Saggio to the marquis of Mantua, Milan, 28 February 1473 (AG 1624). The favourable nature of the terms of Campobasso's contract was alluded to by Cardinal Francesco Gonzaga, writing to his father from Rome on 9 May 1474 in the context of his brother Rodolfo being considered for a command in the Burgundian army (AG 845). For the rest of the paragraph, see d'Appiano to the duke of Milan, Vercelli, 5 March 1473 (ASM 490) and Pietrasanta to the same, Turin, 22 May 1476 (ASM 495).

78. Pietrasanta to the duke of Milan, Tours, 31 December 1476 (ASM 542).

79. *Carteggi*, II, no. 513. For the next sentence, see *Carteggi*, II, no. 406.

80. For this obscure episode, see G. Simonetta, *Rerum gestarum Francisci Sfortiae Mediolanensium ducis commentarii*, ed. G. Soranzo (Bologna, 1959), 120, 123, 126–7, 131–2; *Cronache e statuti della città di Viterbo*, ed. I. Ciampi (Florence, 1872), 197, 244; F. Gabotto, *Un condottiere e una virago del secolo XV* (Verona, 1890), 15–19; and G.F. Ryder, 'La politica italiana di Alfonso d'Aragona (1442–1458)', *ASPN*, 77 (1958), 43–106 (pp. 59–60). For Troilo's service with Alfonso see G. Soldi Rondinini, 'Milano, il Regno di Napoli e gli aragonesi (secoli XIV–XV)', in *Gli Sforza a Milano e in Lombardia e i loro rapporti con gli stati italiani ed europei (1450–1535)* (Milan, 1982), 229–90 (pp. 264, 271). For the rest of the sentence see M. Palmieri, *Liber de temporibus*, ed. G. Scaramella (Città di Castello, 1906), 185.

81. Letters to the duke of Milan from Venice of Nicolaus Bononsiensis, 12 December 1470 (ASM 356) and Gerardo Colli, 26 March 1471 (ASM 357). For the next sentence, see *Dépêches . . . Charles-le-Hardi*, II, 117 note 6, 275 note 4.

82. *Carteggi*, II, no. 557; F.T. Perrens, *The history of Florence under the domination of Cosimo, Piero, Lorenzo de' Medicis*, trans. H. Lynch (London, 1892); Bernardi, *Cronache forlivesi*, I/1, 160–8.

83. *Carteggi*, II, no. 347; see also *Lorraine et Bourgogne*, 77.

84. *Carteggi*, II, no. 387. Earlier in the year, Sforza Secondo had talked of wanting to enlist in Louis XI's army: the duke of Milan to Cristoforo da Bollate, Milan, 5 January 1475 (ASM 542).

85. Simonetta, *Diarii*, 15–16, and Pietro Riario to the duke of Milan, Rome, 24 May 1472 (ASM 70).

86. Modena, Archivio di Stato, Epistolae, vol. III, f. 108. For examples of the disputes mentioned in what follows, see Arata, *Niccolò da Correggio*, 18–22, and Modena, AS, Registrum delle Lettere, I, ff. 82–3.

87. Cusin, 'Impero, Borgogna', 39. Carlo, count of Montone is known to have had three sons: Braccio, the youngest; Antoniazzo; and Bernardino (born ca. 1459), who was probably the eldest. There is no evidence to identify which of these was the one who joined Charles, but Bernardino seems the most likely candidate. I am indebted for this information to Dr Michel Mallett of the Department of

History, University of Warwick. The decision to send him to Burgundy may have had something to do with the fact that the count of Montone was for some time second-in-command to Bartolomeo Colleoni, whom Charles sought eagerly but in vain to recruit. Bernardino took over the command of his father's company after Carlo's death in 1479. See Dr Mallett's 'Some notes on a fifteenth-century *condottiere* and his library: Count Antonio da Marsciano', in *Cultural aspects of the Italian Renaissance. Essays in honour of Paul Oskar Kristeller*, ed. C.H. Clough (Manchester–New York, 1976), 202–15 (pp. 206, 207). Dr Mallett suggests that, after the battle of Nancy, Bernardino may well have returned to Italy to rejoin his father in the company of the count of Campobasso, who took service with the Venetian republic in the summer of 1477.

88. For these two examples, see Pietro Sacardo to the duke of Milan from Montagnima, 6 August 1475 (ASM 362) and Leonello Brandolini to Duke Ercole from Venice, 15 March 1475 (ASM 322); Leonello tried to obtain a command in the Burgundian army in 1476 (*Carteggi*, II, no. 479), but there is no evidence that he succeeded. For Gerolamo Olgiati, whom curiosity impelled to seek to visit the Burgundian court in 1476, see Lubkin, 'The court of Galeazzo Maria', 258, 300 note 26. In 1476 Diomede Carafa complained that '*per la pace de la Italia*' young men were growing up there without any experience of the art of war: P. Petrucci, 'Per un'edizione critica dei *Memoriali* di Diomede Carafa'. *ASPN*, 94 (1976), 213–34 (p. 229). This is reminiscent of Charles the Bold's complaint that the long years of peace under his father had made his subjects grow rusty in the practice of arms: *Carteggi*, II. no. 647.

89. Matteo d'Herboi to the duke of Milan, Ostíglia, 11 November 1472 (ASM 395). His active military career certainly stretched back as far as the late 1430s, when he served Francesco Sforza: *Documenti diplomatici tratti dagli archivi milanesi*, ed. L. Osio, 3 vols (Milan, 1864–72), III, 158, 160, 274, 288, 403. For Campobasso, the Lignanas and Vischi, see Croce, 'Il conte di Campobasso', 61; H. Ferrand, *Jacques Valperga de Masin* (Paris, 1862), 71, 75; and La Marche, *Mémoires*, II, 204.

90. ASV, SS, XXIII, ff. 103^v, 125, and XXIV, f. 22.

91. Pietro Riario to the duke of Milan, Rome, 24 May 1472 (ASM 70).

92. Vaughan, *Charles*, 201–2, 204, and Molinet, *Chroniques*, I, 166.

93. For this and what follows see Molinet, *Chroniques*, I, 34, 37–9, 43–7. Yolande of Savoy acknowledged the superiority of the 'Lombardi' over the ultramontanes in taking cities by siege (*Dépêches . . . Charles-le-Hardi*, I, no. 28), one of the major arts of medieval warfare, although, twenty years on, Commynes thought otherwise (*Mémoires*, II, 272–3).

94. *Carteggi*, I, no. 306, and Molinet, *Chroniques*, I, 98. For the May ordinances see *Dépêches . . . Charles-le-Hardi*, II, no. 200.

95. ADN B 3438/119,098. See also A. de Lannoy, 'La garde de Charles le Téméraire à Nancy en 1477', *Intermédiaire des généalogistes*, 21 (1966), 120–6 (p. 124). For the next sentence see ADN B 3333, ff. 87, 93, and 3377/113, 555.

96. *Inventaire sommaire des Archives Départementales de la Côte d'Or. Série B*, ed. C. Rossignol and others, 6 vols (Dijon, 1863–94), II, 64, 69; Chevanne, *Les guerres en Bourgogne*, 180; the letter of Jean Jouard and Jean de Le Scaghe to Charles the Bold from Dijon, 1 July 1473, ADN B 17711. For the next

sentence see *Dépêches . . . Charles-le-Hardi*, II, no. 149. For examples of misbehaviour in Lorraine see J. Schneider, 'Campobasso en Lorraine', *Le pays
lorrain*, 63 (1982), 5–24 (pp. 11–13). But there had been complaints about
misbehaviour by the duke's troops even before the arrival of the Italians, and
sometimes the Italian troops were themselves the victims of misappropriation
of property, as one of Troilo's men complained against the town of Thézey in
1475: *Handelingen van de Leden en van de Staten van Vlaanderen (1467–1477)*,
ed. W.P. Blockmans (Brussels, 1971), 129, 145, 165–7, 175, 186–9, and
Lorraine et Bourgogne, 103. For a comparison with France, see P.D. Solon,
'Popular response to standing military forces in fifteenth-century France', *SR*,
19 (1972), 78–111 (pp. 85, 87–91, 96–110), and Ditcham, 'The employment
of foreign mercenary troops', Chaps. 7–9.

97. For this paragraph see d'Appiano to the duke of Milan, Lausanne, 13 and 20
April 1476 (ASM 495); *Dépêches . . . Charles-le-Hardi*, II, nos. 179–80; *CSP
Milan*, nos. 330, 332; *Carteggi*, II, nos. 527, 553; J. de Margny, *L'Aventurier*,
ed. J.R. de Chevanne (Paris, 1938), 86–7.

98. For this paragraph see *Dépêches . . . Charles-le-Hardi*, II, nos. 161, 220;
Carteggi, I, no. 304; Molinet, *Chroniques*, 1, 129, 162–3; La Marche, *Mémoires*,
II, 238–9; and the duke of Milan from Pavia to Antonio dei Bracelli and
Francesco Maletta in Naples, 29 March 1473 (ASM 224).

99. *Carteggi*, I, no. 304; see also Molinet, *Chroniques*, I, 81, who records that
Campobasso's men complained at Neuss that they had been forced by poverty
to sell some of their weapons and equipment. For the next sentence, see
Molinet, *Chroniques*, I, 80–1, 84.

100. *Carteggi*, II, nos. 388, 393.

101. D'Appiano to the duke of Milan, Lausanne, 17 and 18 April 1476 (ASM 495;
18 April = *Dépêches . . . Charles-le-Hardi*, II, no. 174).

102. For this and the rest of the paragraph, see Molinet, *Chroniques*, I, 79–82,
150–1; d'Appiano to the duke of Milan, Lausanne, 21 April 1476 (ASM 495);
Carteggi, II, nos. 599, 601, 608; and Vaughan, *Charles*, 217, 322.

103. Vaughan, *Charles*, 213, 397–8.

104. *Carteggi*, II, no. 647.

105. F.L. Taylor, *The art of war in Italy 1494–1529* (Cambridge, 1921), 34–5; Pieri,
Il Rinascimento e la crisi militare italiana, 304–19. For the next sentence, see
Walsh, 'Vespasiano', 414–17.

106. Pietrasanta to the duke of Milan, Tours, 31 December 1476 (ASM 542). For
what follows, see Knebel, *Diarium*, II, 134–5; Caracciolo, *Nobilitatis
Neapolitanae defensio*, 143; Croce, 'Il conte di Campobasso', 140, note 2; and
Perret, 'Jacques Galéot', 597–8.

107. The development of this historico-literary tradition is well sketched by Croce,
'Il conte di Campobasso', 49–51, 133–52. As for Commynes, Croce and
Dufournet argue that he emphasised Campobasso's treachery in order to divert
attention from his own defection in 1472. Another bias detectable in his treatment of Campobasso was his desire to minimise Duke René of Lorraine's reputation as a general. This effect too could be achieved by emphasising the
decisive influence on the outcome of the battle of Nancy of Campobasso's defection. See J. Dufournet, *Études sur Philippe de Commynes* (Paris, 1975), 89–94.

108. Basin, *Histoire de Louis XI*, II, 340.
109. Zaccaria Saggio to the marquis of Mantua, Milan, 26 January 1477 (AG 1626), relaying the reports sent by Galeazzo Maria's brothers Lodovico and Sforza Maria, who were then on a visit to the French king and who had obtained these details from two of the king's captains. Saggio's source, in other words, was very similar to, almost contemporaneous with, and in some respects more detailed than, the often used *Desconfiture de monseigneur de Bourgogne faite par monseigneur de Lorraine*, published by, among others, Mugnier, in *Mémoires et documents publiés par la Société savoisienne d'histoire et d'archéologie*, 40 (1901), 145–69.
110. Angelo de Tummulillis da Sant'Elia (*Notabilia temporum*, ed. C. Corvisieri (Rome–Livorno, 1890), 226) wrote that Charles flew into a rage in the camp outside Nancy when, having asked his captains for advice, he was urged by Campobasso not to risk battle. The duke, suspecting cowardice or deception, accused him of being afraid and sent him packing, refusing also to pay the arrears of pay which Campobasso claimed.
111. Commynes, *Mémoires*, II, 151. For what follows, see Vaughan, *Charles*, 425, 428, who writes that his defection did not affect the main issue, and that Charles can only have had around 5,000 men at the battle.
112. *Histoire de Charles, dernier duc de Bourgogne*, in J. de Waurin, *Anchiennes chroniques d'Engleterre*, ed. E. Dupont, 3 vols (Paris, 1858–63), III, 263–334 (p. 317: '. . . le comte . . . retourna contre luy à cette heure . . .'); Saggio to the marquis of Mantua, Milan, 26 January 1477 (AG 1626: '. . . si mise insieme col duca di Lorena col quale venne a far quello che è seguito . . .'); A. d'Oudenbosch (d. 1482/3), *Chronique*, ed. C. de Borman (Liège, 1902), 241 ('. . . dimisit ducem et associavit se parti adversae . . .'); and Tummulillis, *Notabilia temporum*, 226. Tummulillis, although his idiosyncratic grammar sometimes obscures his meaning, seems to suggest that Charles had Campobasso at his mercy but instead advised him to flee and that, while this exchange was taking place, the pursuing Swiss caught up with the duke. A curious article by P.-C. Doyere, 'Un grand mystère historique', *Nouvelle revue franc-comtoise*, 15 (1976) [but actually dated 1952], 9–26, attempts to prove that Charles did not die in the battle but was captured by Campobasso, who handed him over to Louis XI, by whom he was imprisoned until his death, which took place before Louis' death.
113. Margny, *L'Aventurier*, 70; Mugnier, 'La desconfiture', 163; *Chronique de Lorraine*, 301–2; *Excellente cronike van Vlaanderen*, f. clxxvii; C. Pfister, *Histoire de Nancy*, 3 vols (Paris, 1902–9), I, 480, 499–50; Commynes, *Mémoires*, II, 142, 151–2.
114. Basin, *Histoire de Louis XI*, II, 340, Daviso, *Iolanda*, 245. In a letter written to his father from Luzern on 23 January 1477 (ASM 594), one M. Conradus Schoch, who describes himself as '*capellanus ducalis*' (of the duke of Lorraine?), reported that the Burgundians had fled almost at the first attack, but that their attempts to escape had been foreseen and were prevented by the shrewd positioning of men to block their passage. For the next sentence, see Wilwolt von Schaumburg, *Die Geschichten und Taten*, ed. A. von Keller (Stuttgart, 1859), 32.
115. Commynes, *Mémoires*, II, 8, 89–90, 95–7, 136–9, 141–3, 149–52.

116. Vaughan, *Charles*, 233–4. While many changed their allegiance as between Burgundy and France in the 1460s and 1470s, it has long been remarked that the duke's irritation at Commynes's defection was particularly strong, for along with three others — of whom two (Baudoin of Burgundy and Jean de Chassa) had been accused by Charles of plotting to kill him — Commynes was specifically excluded from the truce of Soleuvre in September 1475. But the duke's reasons for singling him out in this way have never been fully clarified, although he obviously felt that Commynes' defection placed him on a level with would-be assassins. This suggests that Commynes was perhaps more valued by the duke than has been supposed. Yet, because of the scantiness of the evidence and the reticence of the *Mémoires*, it has usually been assumed that he was only a minor figure in the ducal entourage; for example, S. Kinser, in his edition and translation with I. Cazeaux of the *Memoirs* (2 vols, Columbia, S. Ca, 1967–73), described him as a minor Burgundian nobleman (I, 3). A hitherto unutilised Italian document (see Plate 3), however, if it indeed refers to Commynes (he is not actually named in it, although the date and circumstances make the attribution plausible), suggests a new reason — betrayal of military secrets — for the duke's anger at his defection, and also portrays the fugitive as a much more important figure than previously allowed. At the beginning of October 1472, the king of Naples discussed with the Milanese ambassador the contents of a long letter from Charles dated 28 August, in which the duke listed for his Neapolitan ally his military successes in his war with Louis XI. Relating the discussion to his master, the ambassador continued: '*Item me disse como era fugito dal duca el più caro et secreto creato ch'el havesse, al quale lo dì denanti de la partita sua havea aperto tuto el cuore et intrinseco suo de tuto el progresso ch'el intendeva fare contra el prefato re de Franza, di che esso duca stava molto dolerato et malcontento*'. See Francesco Maletta to the duke of Milan, Naples, 1 October 1472 (ASM 223). If this ducal confidant was not Commynes, who was he?

117. Croce, 'Il conte di Campobasso', 128–31; *Chronique de Lorraine*, 257–62, 285.

118. J. Calmette, 'Campobasso et Commynes', *AB*, 7 (1935), 172–6 (reprinted in his *Études médiévales*, Toulouse, 1946), and Vaughan, *Charles*, 418–19 and 419 note 1, have voiced criticisms of Croce, who, however, is defended by J. Dufournet, *La destruction des mythes dans les Mémoires de Ph. De Commynes* (Geneva, 1966), 54–64. Of course, almost since the first appearance of the *Mémoires* there have been those who were sceptical of Commynes' veracity, but not until Croce contributed to the discussion did this scepticism extend to a rehabilitation of Campobasso.

119. Vaughan, *Charles*, 233–4, 353 note 2, 419.

120. Cristoforo da Bollate to the duke of Milan, Tours, 10 March 1473 (ASM 540; understandably this dispatch was sent in code!).

121. The duke of Milan to Cristoforo da Bollate, 27 April 1473 (ASM 540).

122. Johannes Petrus de Crottis to the duke of Milan, Lyon, 24 November 1473; the duke to Cristoforo da Bollate, Vigevano, 3 December 1473; and Cristoforo to the duke, Tours, 3 December 1473 (all in ASM 540).

123. Da Bollate to the duke of Milan, Senlis, 20 February 1474 (ASM 541); Simonetta, *Diarii*, 126–7; a memorandum of Symon Rigono de Valsassina presumably for the duke of Milan, dated Pavia, 9 October 1474 (ASM 541).

124. Barbaro to Doge Niccolò Tron, Naples, 15 December 1472 and 25 April 1473 (BNMV 8170/IV, 42, and /VI, 3).
125. Maletta to the duke of Milan, Naples, 28 October 1474 (ASM 226).
126. For this and what follows, see Schneider, 'Campobasso en Lorraine', 9, 12, 14, 21–3, and *Lorraine et Bourgogne*, 72–3, 201–2.
127. A defence suggested by Calmette, 'Campobasso et Commynes', 176, though disputed by Dufournet, *La destruction des mythes*, 61.
128. *Lettres de Louis XI*, VI, 62–3. For this interpretation of the letter, see Croce, 'Il conte di Campobasso', 139–40, and Dufournet, *La destruction des mythes*, 61.
129. *Carteggi*, II, no. 477. Louis may already have made approaches to Galeota and others in 1474: Cristoforo da Bollate to the duke of Milan, Senlis, 20 February 1474 (ASM 541).
130. Francesco Pietrasanta to the duke of Milan, Tours, 31 December 1476 (ASM 542), and Cristoforo da Bollate to the same, Tours, 11 February 1473 (ASM 540). However, Campobasso's record in Catalonia has been upheld by Calmette, *Louis XI, Jean II*, 328.
131. Kervyn de Lettenhove, *Lettres et négociations de Philippe de Commynes*, I, 115 note 8 (on p. 116), 148 note 2. But compare *Lorraine et Bourgogne*, 159 and 160 note 2.
132. Schneider, 'Campobasso en Lorraine', 18; Molinet, *Chroniques*, I, 148–50. However, Vaughan, *Charles*, 418–19, is inclined to accept Commynes' charges of treachery in this instance, while a later source, Philippe de Vigneulles, who at the time was a mere child (born in 1471, Vigneulles being some 25 miles from Metz), reports the lord of Bièvres, after leaving Nancy and meeting Campobasso on the road to Metz, as calling him a traitor to his face — as, Vigneulles, adds, he showed himself to be later: *Chronique*, III, 48.
133. For this paragraph, see Molinet, *Chroniques*, I, 129, 162–3; Knebel, *Diarium*, I, 163; *Carteggi*, I, nos. 304, 307, II, nos. 388, 393; la Marche, *Mémoires*, III, 238–9; Caracciolo, *De varietate fortunae*, 93; Tummulillis, *Notabilia temporum*, 226; and AGR CC 25543, ff. 19^v, 20, 37^v, 41^v, 210^v–11 (payments made in August, September and October 1476).
134. Croce, 'Il conte di Campobasso', 106.
135. ADN B 2107/67, 865. According to Roye, *Journal*, II, 11–12, Campobasso visited Brittany in the first half of 1476 and there claimed to be related to the Breton Montforts, the ducal house of Brittany, a claim refuted by Croce, 'Rettificazione di dati biografici intorno a Cola di Monforte', 220–7.
136. Saggio to the marquis of Mantua, Milan, 24 June 1475 (AG 1635); *Carteggi*, I, nos. 203, 324, II, no. 647.
137. *Chronique de Lorraine*, 259–63. The details of the duke's reasoning are supplied by Commynes, *Mémoires*, II, 137. His interpretation of the laws of war, however, was not unduly harsh or eccentric: M. Keen, *The laws of war in the late Middle Ages* (London–Toronto, 1965), 121 note 1.
138. Commynes, *Mémoires*, II, 137–9; Calmette, 'Campobasso et Commynes', 172–5. It is important to note that there is no other independent version of the Siffredo episode. The *Cronycke van Hollandt*, f. ccclxiii^v mentions that, just before the battle of Nancy, the duke struck on the cheek the captain of the 'lombaerdē' when he became too importunate in seeking arrears of pay,

but there is no mention of the Siffredo episode. In any case this is a later source (first published in 1517 and usually attributed to Cornelius Aurelius, born ca. 1460, died after 1523), and is therefore most probably derivative.

139. Above, 'Some personal characteristics'. In fact Siffredo's family, as far as is known, originated in Todi in Umbria: Croce, 'Il conte di Campobaso', 125 note 3. But Siffredo himself had been in the service of the Angevins for several years (L. Caillet, 'Donation par le roi René à Siffroy de Baschi, son écuyer, de plusieurs châteaux des baylies de Digne et de Sisteron (1470)', *Revue de l'Anjou* (1913), 197–201), so it could well have been during that period that Campobasso first met him.

140. *Chronique de Lorraine*, 265–7. But savagery in both sides' treatment of prisoners had already been in evidence in the Lorraine campaign for some months previously; see, for example, Knebel, *Diarium*, II, 40, 43–4, 88, 99, 110–13. For what follows, see Walsh, 'Vespasiano', 405–8.

141. La Marche, *Mémoires*, III, 235–6; Molinet, *Chroniques*, I, 113–14; *Dépêches . . . Charles-le-Hardi*, I, no. 196; *Carteggi*, II, nos. 599, 600, 608; Belotti, *La vita di Bartolomeo Colleoni*, 488; Vaughan, *Charles*, 172, 173, 174–5.

142. Basin, *Histoire de Louis XI*, II, 340; Saggio to the marquis of Mantua, Milan, 16 January 1477 (AG 1626); Tummullilis, *Notabilia temporum*, 226.

143. Molinet, *Chroniques*, II, 154, 164; Commynes, *Mémoires*, II, 150. In fairness to Charles, however, it should be said that his persistence with the siege was not the result solely of irrational obstinacy, because he did have grounds for believing that Nancy would be forced by lack of supplies to surrender before relief could arrive: E. Motta, 'Un documento per la battaglia di Nancy (1477)', *BSSI*, 10 (1888), 191–2; *Excellente cronike van Vlaenderen*, f. clxxxvi[v]; Knebel, *Diarium*, II, 90, 99; and Vaughan, *Charles*, 420–2.

144. Roye, *Journal*, II, 12.

145. E.M. J[amison] in *EHR*, 51 (1936), 732–3 (p. 733).

146. Commynes, *Mémoires*, II, 8, 96, 97. The same contrast is made by Schneider, 'Campobasso en Lorraine', 23–4, while the literary effect achieved by such a contrast is well explained by Dufournet, *La destruction des mythes*, 58.

147. Galeota to Lorenzo, Bruges, 18 August 1478 (ASF, MAP, XXXVI, 1063). This letter makes it clear that Galeota did not leave without permision, and is the only direct evidence on the matter, although Roye, *Journal*, II, 377–8, and *Lettres de Louis XI*, VII, 136–7, point to the same conclusion. Perret, 'Jacques Galéot', 597, Tourneur, 'Jehan de Candida', 33, and Croce, 'Il conte di Campobasso', 163, knew of no such evidence but were prepared to allow Galeota the benefit of the doubt. Lorenzo described Galeota in February 1479 as a '*valente homo*' (L. de' Medici, *Lettere*, III, 400).

148. Mugnier, 'La desconfiture', 165; Molinet, *Chroniques*, II, 168; AGR CC 25543, ff. 16–17, 40.

149. Pfister, *Histoire de Nancy*, I, 508; Croce, 'Il conte di Campobasso', 140 note 2; Périnelle, 'Dépêches de Nicolas de' Roberti', 470; AGR CC 25543, f. 19.

150. AGR CC 25543, f. 40[v]. For what follows, see Gachard, 'Analectes historiques. Cinquième série', 118, and Croce, 'Il conte di Campobasso', 155–6.

151. *Carteggi*, II, 477. Earlier in this conversation, Charles explained to Panigarola why he could not accept Galeazzo Maria's advice not to risk his life by taking personal command in battle, especially against the Swiss: he lacked confidence in both the devotion and the ability of his commanders, so could not delegate the task. Before the battle of Murten he talked of '*traditori francesi*': *Carteggi*, II, no. 612. On the clash of loyalties between Burgundy and France felt by some of his more powerful subjects, see Bittmann, *Ludwig XI. und Karl der Kühne*, I/1, 269–70 and I/2, 407, 479; Vaughan, *Charles*, 231–4; and M. Harsgor, 'Fidélités et infidélités au sommet du pouvoir', in *Hommages à Roland Mousnier*, ed. Y. Durand (Paris, 1981), 259–77 (especially pp. 267–77).

152. Guillaume, *Histoire des bandes d'ordonnance*; F. Lot, *L'art militaire et les armées au Moyen Age en Europe et dans le Proche Orient*, 2 vols (Paris, 1946), II, 116 note 2.

153. Vaughan, *Valois Burgundy*, 227.

154. Rodolfo Gonzaga to his mother, The Hague, 4 October 1469, and Brussels, 27 November 1469 (AG 2100), and Sforza dei Bettini to the duke of Milan, Tours, 8 December 1469 (ASM 536). See also C. Brusten, 'Les compagnies d'ordonnance dans l'armée bourguignonne', in *Grandson — 1476*, ed. D. Reichel (Lausanne, 1976), 112–69.

155. Molinet, *Chroniques*, I, 95, a view shared by de la Chauvelays, 'Mémoire', 355.

156. Lot, *L'art militaire*, II, 116, 255, and see the long review of Lot by G. Peyronnet, 'Riflessioni sul valore della storia militare a proposito d'un recente lavoro', *ASI*, 109 (1951), 68–83 (p. 76); neither author, however, really specifies of what he thinks this influence consisted.

157. Molinet, *Chroniques*, I, 33–4, 37–9, 43–51, 64–5, 80–6; Ammanati-Piccolomini, *Epistolae*, f. 295ᵛ (letter of Francesco Bertini of 7 June 1475).

158. *Carteggi*, II, nos. 561, 612, For what follows, see Vaughan, *Charles*, 204, 205; Molinet, *Chroniques*, I, 165; Haynin, *Mémoires*, II, 218; and Margny, *L'Aventurier*, 70.

159. Commynes, *Mémoires*, II, 121; *Carteggi*, II, no. 596; *Dépêches . . . Charles-le-Hardi*, II, nos. 196, 220.

160. Vaughan, *Charles*, 165; *Carteggi*, II, no. 388; see also my 'The coming of humanism', 181, and 'Une citation inexacte de Lucain', 439–42, 446–50. In a review article dealing with, among others, M.G.A. Vale's *War and chivalry. Warfare and aristocratic culture in England, France and Burgundy at the end of the Middle Ages* (London, 1981), T.B. James, 'Chivalry: fact or fantasy?', *Literature and history*, 9 (1983), 102–5, remarks (p. 104) 'because of this [Renaissance] immersion in classical ideals, paradoxically in 1473 Charles the Bold of Burgundy's great military ordinance differentiated his army by insignia, the first time since the fall of the Roman Empire that such differentiation had been made without reference to social status'.

161. Schmidt-Sinns, 'Studien zum Heerwesen der Herzöge von Burgund', 151–2 (but see also p. 167 and note 3, where he seems to admit such influence). 'What could he have found in them which might have influenced his conduct?', asks Vale, *War and chivalry*, 17, but provides no answer. It has been suggested also that in a slightly later period, the military writings of antiquity had little of value to offer to practical soldiers, although they appealed to men of letters and

theorists: Taylor, *The art of war in Italy*, 176–9; Mallett, 'Some notes on a fifteenth-century *condottiere*', 202–3, 208–9, 210–12; J.R. Hale, 'The military education of the officer class in early modern Europe', in his *Renaissance war studies* (London, 1983), 225–46 (p. 232). But in 1476, Diomede Carafa was already advising Don Federico's younger brother Francesco that the art of war was learnt by experience, not by reading: Petrucci, 'Per un'edizione critica', 228, 230.

162. Wielant, *Recueil des antiquités de Flandre*, 54; Molinet, *Chroniques*, I, 61–2. See also C.T. Allmand, 'Did the *De re militari* of Vegetius influence the military ordinances of Charles the Bold?', *PCEEB*, 41 (2001), 135–43, who answers his question in the affirmative and provides examples.

163. Guillume, *Histoire des bandes d'ordonnance*, 165–6; D. Gallet-Guerne, *Vasque de Lucène et la Cyropédie à la cour de Bourgogne (1470)* (Geneva, 1974), 41–54. For what follows, see H. Delbrück, *Die Perserkriege und die Burgunderkriege* (Berlin, 1887); T. Wise, *Medieval warfare* (London, 1976), 127; and Vaughan, *Charles*, 367.

164. Examples of Italian views on these matters from 1471, 1476, 1477 and 1478 are G. Zorzi, 'Un vicentino alla corte di Paolo Secondo (Chierigino Chiericato e il suo Trattato della Milizia)', *Nuovo archivio veneto*, no. 30 (1915), 369–434; Petrucci, 'Per un'edizione critica', 232; B. Croce, 'Un memoriale militare di Cola di Monforte, conte di Campobasso', *ASPN*, 58 (1933), 371–2; and P. Pieri, 'Il "Governo et exercitio de la militia" di Orso degli Orsini e i "Memoriali" di Diomede Carafa', *ASPN*, 58 (1933), 99–212.

165. Molinet, *Chroniques*, I, 165; Haynin, *Mémoires*, II, 218; Margny, *l'Aventurier*, 70.

166. *Carteggi*, II, nos. 599, 600, 608. For Charles's intentions regarding the Swiss, see *Carteggi*, II, no. 596, and Vaughan, *Charles*, 386, 389.

167. Letter of Bertini from the camp at Neuss, 28 October 1474 in Ammanati-Piccolomini, *Epistolae*, ff. 287ᵛ–8; Santa Croce, *Mémoire*, 84.

168. Pietrasanta to the duke of Milan, Tours, 31 December 1476 (ASM 542); Battista di Giovanni to the same, Rome, 11 October 1474 (ASM 77: Louis XI '*se credeva de buttare in un altro Carlomagno*'). For what follows, see my 'Vespasiano', *passim*.

169. Del Treppo, 'Gl aspetti organizzativi', 275.

170. Pieri, 'Il "Governo"', 120: *difensiva-controffensiva*.

171. Perception of the risks of battle was not, of course, confined to Italy. While Carafa (Pieri, 'Il "Governo"', 208) advised against battle unless one had all possible advantages, Commynes (*Mémoires*, I, 108) advised against putting one's state at risk through battle, which should be avoided if possible, while la Marche's Fortune (K. Heitmann, 'Olivier de la Marche, "Le Debat de Cuidier et de Fortune". Eine dichterische Meditation über den Untergang Karls des Kühnen', *AKG*, 47 (1965), 266–305 (p. 289)) warns that war is a game of chance.

172. However, it is important not to overlook his relations with his elder, illegitimate half-brother Anthony. Anthony served him well (Vaughan, *Charles*, 235–8), but there is some evidence of friction between them, because Charles seems to have felt that Anthony had ideas above his station, and he was deter-

mined not to allow him to overreach himself. For examples from 1470, 1473, 1475 and 1476, see Commynes, *Mémoires*, I, 179; Cusin, 'Impero, Borgogna', 35; Sacramoro to the duke of Milan, Rome, 26 May 1475 (ASM 79) and Rome, 29 April 1476 (ASM 80); *Carteggi*, II, no. 363; and Vaughan, *Charles*, 244–5. As it happened, Anthony was captured at the battle of Nancy and thus could not dispute, had he so wished, Mary's succession or her choice of husband. But one is bound to speculate about the motives behind Sixtus IV's legitimisation of Anthony in 1475.

173. Vaughan, *Charles*, 405, and *Carteggi*, II, nos. 629, 634.

174. Vaughan, *Charles*, 84, 124.

175. '. . . *certo queste guerre non hanno a fare cum le guerre de Italia* . . .': *Dépêches* . . . *Charles-le-Hardi*, II, no. 174 (d'Appiano, April 1476). Perhaps, though, the divergence was becoming less marked by the last quarter of the fifteenth century, especially in the case of Venice, although not, at the other extreme, of Florence: M.E. Mallett, 'Preparations for war in Florence and Venice in the second half of the fifteenth century', in *Florence and Venice: comparisons and relations*, ed. S. Bertelli, N. Rubinstein and C.H. Smyth, 2 vols (Florence, 1979), I, 149–64, and 'Diplomacy and war in later fifteenth-century Italy', *Proceedings of the British Academy*, 67 (1981), 267–88.

176. P. Spufford, *Monetary problems and policies in the Burgundian Netherlands 1433–1496* (Leiden, 1970), 51.

177. Vaughan, *Charles*, 189; R. Wellens, *Les États généraux des Pays-Bas des origines à la fin du règne de Philippe le Beau (1464–1506)* (Heule, 1974), 138–42; J. Bartier, 'Un discours du chancelier Hugonet aux États Généraux de 1473', *BCRH*, 107 (1942), 127–56 (pp. 132–4).

178. Bittmann, *Ludwig XI. und Karl der Kühne*, II/1, 50, 54, 57; Vaughan, *Charles*, 404. For what follows, see Wellens, *Les États généraux*, I, 163, 164.

179. Guillaume, *Histoire des bandes d'ordonnance*, 54–5; see also Commynes, *Mémoires*, II, 249–50. The change in the geographical origin of the foreign elements in the Burgundian army after 1477 — particularly the departure of the Italians — is considered by Sablon du Corail, 'Les étrangers au service de Marie de Bourgogne'.

Conclusion

Charles the Bold's interest in Italy has, as stated at the outset, long been known to, and the subject of comment by, historians, but the evidence offered in the preceding pages will, it is hoped, make possible a fuller understanding of that interest. Indeed, to exaggerate slightly, Charles could be described as having surrounded himself with Italians almost from the cradle to the grave. One of his numerous illegitimate half-brothers, the cleric Raphael de Marcatellis (1437–1508), had an Italian mother.[1] Those with whom Charles, from his early teens, was brought up and educated included Francesco d'Este. During his father's reign he became familiar with Tommaso Portinari and probably also with others less well known today, such as Giacomo dei Vischi. After he had become duke himself, he retained several Italian squires; he had his letters written by Italian secretaries; when he fell ill he placed his trust in Italian doctors; and he may even occasionally have worn Italian-style clothes.[2] He liked to converse with Italian diplomats, whose language he could speak.[3] Italian soldiers constituted the largest group of foreign mercenaries in his army, and he gave them important commands out of proportion to their numbers. The memory of his last battle is forever associated with the defection of one of his Italian generals, the count of Campobasso, and, after his death at Nancy, it was an Italian manservant who located his body.

Richard Vaughan characterised Charles as innovatory, but perhaps to a fault, being ahead of his time and too progressive to be a successful ruler.[4] The duke's fondness for Italians was one aspect of his tendency to innovation. For example, the chronicler Philippe Wielant, contrasting father and son, noted that, while Philip the Good had chosen his military captains from among his own subjects, Charles preferred foreigners, *'Italiens, Néapolitains, Anglois et tels autres'*.[5] Louis XI too remarked in

January 1474, though probably ironically, on Charles the Bold's devotion to Italian customs, manners and methods of government ('. . . *in tutto dato alli costumi, modi et governi italiani* . . .').[6] Were, then, the duke's Italophile tendencies connected with, perhaps even the cause of, his eagerness for change and reform? Support for this hypothesis can be found in some of his own utterances. For example, at the end of 1472 the papal envoy Pietro Aliprandi reported him as declaring a wish to be able to dispose of ecclesiastical benefices as freely in his own lands as he felt Italian rulers did in theirs, and four years later Charles himself told his Neapolitan captain Troilo da Rossano that he had recruited Italian mercenary soldiers so that they might teach his subjects the art of warfare.[7]

Despite such testimony, however, Italian influence on the duke should not be overestimated. Italian methods in diplomacy, administration and warfare were the product of the circumstances and opportunities obtaining in the peninsula. Charles the Bold's circumstances and opportunities were different, and for this reason his own methods differed from those of Italian rulers. Although, as we have seen, he borrowed a certain amount from them, there were limits to what he could usefully adopt. In diplomacy, for instance, he did not follow the Italians in their employment of the resident ambassador. In warfare, despite organisational changes along Italian lines, Charles clearly diverged from conventional Italian opinion on significant points of tactics and strategy. As for administration, it is striking that, although he surrounded himself with Italians at court, entrusting them with a variety of functions, he did not place them in the central posts of the Burgundian bureaucracy. Nor was even Tommaso Portinari an exception to this rule, for his prominence under Charles the Bold stemmed more from his personal intimacy with the duke and from his custodianship of the Bruges branch of the Medici bank than from any administrative office. Of course one may, depending on the approach chosen, prefer either to emphasise those of the duke's procedures which could fairly be described as Italianate, or instead to draw attention to the areas in which he remained faithful to Burgundian precedents. Without further research it may seem prudent to take the more cautious course. Yet, insofar as Charles did imitate foreign exemplars, then clearly we shall now have to take account not only of France, as has long been recognised, but also of Italy.

What of the more general impact made by these Italians during the duke's reign in his lands and on his subjects? In cultural terms, their presence did make itself felt to a certain degree, as I have tried to demonstrate elsewhere.[8] Several of the Italians in his entourage represented some of the typical elements of the burgeoning humanist movement. Such men found a sympathetic audience among some of his courtiers, and a number of those courtiers could be, and occasionally were, described as Italianate. Again, however, this influence was limited. The Italians were concentrated at court, which restricted their influence elsewhere. Since Charles did not have a fixed capital, his court was peripatetic, but this fact, while it perhaps broadened the Italians' contact with the duke's subjects, at the same time dissipated their impact. In any case, during the last three years of his reign, when the Italian presence was at its strongest, Charles spent most of his time outside his own lands, notably in Germany, Lorraine and Savoy.

Italian influence was limited not only geographically and socially, but also chronologically. Charles the Bold ruled for only ten years, and the bulk of the Italians in his entourage did not arrive until the second half of his reign. Their numbers had passed their peak by the second half of 1476, and comparatively few seem to have remained after January 1477. There were several reasons for this. Diplomats and princes were recalled by their masters. Soldiers deserted or were killed in combat. Some of those in the ducal household predeceased the duke. Moreover, Charles himself, though generous in other ways, did not give them the grants of lands and lordships which would have encouraged them to settle; and, even if he had, few showed any desire to put down permanent roots north of the Alps. Finally, it seems that some of the inhabitants of the Valois Low Countries resented these outsiders, perhaps because they associated them with the duke's authoritarian policies, and after 1477 they were in a stronger position than before to make their dislike felt.

The chronological limitation of the Italians' impact raises the question of continuity in the Burgundian state from the Valois to the Habsburg period. Maximilian of Habsburg was deeply flattered by his Burgundian inheritance, admiring its traditions and cherishing the memory of his late father-in-law. The dispersal of the Italians may have been due in no small measure to factors beyond his control, such as the desire of the Italians to return sooner or later to their homeland and the willingness of the people of the Burgundian lands to see them go. Yet, although we should bear in mind that far less research has been done on the period 1477–1482 than on the reign of the last Valois duke, it would appear to be indisputable that, at least in his early years, Maximilian simply did not share the fondness for Italians displayed by Charles the Bold. In this respect, then, there was a sharp distinction between the last of the Valois dukes of Burgundy and the first of his Habsburg successors.

Turning to wider issues, we can see how the Italian presence at the court of Charles the Bold played some part, albeit restricted, in the general transmission of Italian Renaissance ideas north of the Alps. The Burgundian stage of that process has too often been overlooked by historians of ideas and literature. This may be partly because, as I would like to think the amount of new material presented in this book suggests, not enough has been known hitherto to enable them to pronounce with confidence. Another reason is methodological. Scholars have expended immense efforts on the discovery and location in northern libraries of the fourteenth and fifteenth centuries of the works of Italian humanist writers, particularly those of Boccaccio and Petrarch. Yet, even were every pertinent manuscript to be traced, that would still not tell the whole story, simply because Italian ideas were spread not only through written works but also by personal contact. Moreover, when investigating personal contacts, one should not limit the inquiry only to professional men of letters. Other groups, notably diplomats and administrators or even soldiers, could equally boast among their ranks those who were *letterati* and heralds of humanist ideas. In other words, diplomatic events should not be overlooked as a means of elucidating intellectual history. Thus, one of the most cultured courts of the last quarter of the fifteenth century was that of Matthias Corvinus, king of Hungary 1458–1490; the tone of his court owed much to the Italians in the royal entourage and government; and their presence stemmed largely from the marriage in 1476 between Matthias and Beatrice, daughter of King Ferrante of Naples. Similarly, one could examine the numerous Italians in the entourage of Louis XI, who, like those around Charles the Bold, went to the French court for largely political reasons, even though their presence there was probably not without consequence in the cultural field.[9] Literary and artistic history can occasionally illuminate political history. Equally, however, the contribution which political history can make to the understanding of cultural events should not be neglected, especially at a time when historians are exhorted to be interdisciplinary.

If we consider the Italians themselves, we find that many of them still remain somewhat shadowy figures, and that controversy continues to rage around the more prominent, such as Tommaso Portinari and the count of Campobasso. Nonetheless, we now know more both about these famous figures and about the less renowned. We can see how the diplomats went about their work and why so many Italians entered the service of Charles the Bold. While this book has sought to assess the extent of Italian influence on Charles, it has also, if only in passing, illustrated the impact which Charles made on Italy. The rivalry between the duke of Burgundy and the king of France was superimposed on the pattern of opposing alliances already obtaining in the peninsula. Italians were divided between their fear of the duke and their admiration of him, but all shades of opinion took a keen interest in his career. Diplomats and others attempted to give a detailed account of his deeds and plans, while some even composed verses about him. These writings testify both to the rise and to the decline of his reputation in Italy. One might mention too that what Italy took from the north in the cultural field was in many cases transmitted by those born subject to the duke, for example painters, musicians and printers. The Burgundian impact on Italy could prove, on further investigation, to be almost as large a subject as the Italian impact on Burgundy.[10]

Finally, although it is all too easy for a writer to attempt to deflect criticisms of the provisional nature of his conclusions by citing the need for further research, a word of caution is on this occasion justifiable. It is difficult in a work such as this, where the intention has been not only to synthesize the mass of published work but also to break new ground in a subject that has not hitherto received a fully rounded treatment, to avoid developing a sort of tunnel vision or intensity of focus in investigating relations between Charles the Bold and Italy which risks the blurring or even exclusion of wider perspectives. I have tried to avoid this danger, but the absence of other comparative studies has been a handicap throughout. After all, the duke's relations with England were no less close than those with Italy. Exiles from both the Lancastrian and the Yorkist factions found refuge at his court; he could speak their language and more than once declared his love for their nation; and the English were, after the Italians, the largest foreign contingent in his army. Similar observations apply, if not quite to the same extent, to the Portuguese or Germans. The Italians have been easier to study because of the wealth of documentary material they left behind. Nonetheless, we cannot properly place the Italians in context until these other groups have been studied to the same degree.[11]

Notes

1. Meersseman, 'La raccolta dell'umanista fiammingo Giovanni de Veris', 252–5.
2. M. Beaulieu and J. Baylé, *Le Costume en Bourgogne 1364–1477* (Paris, 1956), 187 and note 1. Louis XI thought an Italian mantle a suitable gift for Charles in 1468 (Bittmann, *Ludwig XI. und Karl der Kühne*, I/2, 249 and note 9), while in 1473 a Metz chronicler described him as dressed at his meeting with the emperor in

Trier '*à la mode de Lombardie*': *Journal de Jean Aubrion, bourgeois de Metz, avec sa continuation par Pierre Aubrion 1465–1512*, ed. L. Larchey (Metz, 1857), 65.

3. He told the papal legate Nanni in 1475 that it was less difficult for him to speak at length in Italian than in Latin (*Carteggi*, I, no. 297).

4. Vaughan, *Charles*, 190.

5. Wielant, *Recueil des antiquités de Flandre*, 53–4.

6. For the context, see O. Cartellieri, *Am Hofe der Herzöge von Burgund. Kulturhistorische Bilder* (Basel, 1926), 188, 301, and Vaughan, *Charles*, 164–5. Louis XI's comment was made at a time when he was sending Charles a very beautiful book written in the Italian language and in the Italian script containing the life and deeds of Charlemagne and of some other kings of France. Louis was then optimistic about at last securing an enduring settlement with Charles, hence the gift: Bittmann, *Ludwig XI. und Karl der Kühne*, II/1, 176–7. In the light of Louis' character, however, we can detect also, as Bittmann points out, a touch of irony in the choice of the gift. Louis tended to be slighting of the duke's grandiose ambitions and of his desire to emulate the heroes of antiquity and of earlier medieval history. He was also well aware of Charles's attempts to oppose Burgundian to French influence in Italy, and he knew that the duke had recruited Italian mercenaries for the purpose of strengthening his military capability against France. It has been suggested by Gallet-Guerne, *Vasque de Lucène*, 98 note 5, that the work in question was the Italian version of Einhard's *Vita Caroli* done by Donato Acciaiuoli and presented by him to Louis XI during his embassy to France in 1461. It is not without interest to note that, as we saw in Chapter 3 ('Diplomatic relations with Florence'), Donato's exiled cousin Neri di Agnolo Acciaiuoli seems to have found his way to the Burgundian court briefly in 1473.

7. *Carteggi*, I, no. 183, II, no. 647.

8. Walsh, 'The coming of humanism to the Low Countries'.

9. Vincent Ilardi informs me that his late colleague Professor Paul Murray Kendall once thought of devoting a volume to the subject of Louis XI and Italy.

10. For some further comments, see my 'Vespasiano da Bisticci', 410–19, and 'Relations between Milan and Burgundy', 384–91.

11. In the last decade, Jacques Paviot has published a wealth of studies on relations between Valois Burgundy and Portugal: for details, see the Bibliographical Supplement.

Bibliography

Archive sources

BRUSSELS. Archives Générales du Royaume (Algemeen Rijksarchief):

Chambre des Comptes:
1923–5, accounts of the *argentier* Guilbert de Ruple for 1468–70
25542, account of the *trésorier des guerres* Guilbert de Ruple for 24 March–31 August 1472
25543, account of the *trésorier des guerres* Hues de Dompierre for 1 January 1475–31 August 1477

Manuscrits divers:
1173, nineteenth-century transcriptions of medieval Italian documents, including some fifteenth-century diplomatic dispatches

Trésor des Chartes:
2007, preliminary draft of the treaty of alliance between Charles the Bold and King Ferrante of Naples made at Arras on 14 February 1471 (confirmed, with subsequent modifications, by Charles at Abbeville on 15 August 1471)

FLORENCE. Archivio di Stato:

Carte di Corredo — legazioni e commissarie, 61
Consulte e pratiche, 60
Copiari di lettere responsive, 1–2
Lettere originali responsive alla Signoria, 7–8
Registri di lettere esterne alla Repubblica, 8
Signori — legazioni e commissarie — risposti verbali di oratori, 2
Signori — missive — Prima Cancelleria, 45–7

Mediceo avanti il Principato:
XXI, 408, letter of Tommaso Portinari to Lorenzo de' Medici from Bruges, 8 August 1473
XXIV, 125, letter of Troilo da Rossano to Lorenzo de' Medici from Ferrara, 11 April 1472
XXVII, 86, 157, letters of Troilo da Rossano to Lorenzo de' Medici from Ferrara, 12 February and 9 March 1472
XXX, 198, letter of Francesco Bertini to Lorenzo de' Medici from Bolsena, 23 March 1474
XXXVI, 1063, letter of Giacomo Galeota to Lorenzo de' Medici from Bruges, 18 August 1478

FLORENCE. Biblioteca Nazionale Centrale:

Fondo Principale/Fondo Nazionale, II.V.13, ff. 152^v, letter of Bernardo Bembo to Doge Niccolò Marcello from Dijon. 16 February 1474

LILLE. Archives départementales du Nord:

Série B:
334/16206, provisions of the treaty of alliance between Charles the Bold and King Ferrante of Naples made at Arras on 14 February 1471, as confirmed by Charles at Abbeville on 15 August 1471
2064, account of the receiver-general Barthélemy Trotin for 16 June–31 December 1467
2065–6, accountable receipts and vouchers (*pièces comptables*) of the receiver-general Barthélemy Trotin for 16 June–31 December 1467
2067, account of the receiver-general Barthélemy Trotin for 1468
2068, account of the *argentier* Guilbert de Ruple for 1468
2069–71, accountable receipts and vouchers of the receiver-general Barthélemy Trotin for 1468
2072, account of the receiver-general Barthélemy Trotin for 1469
2073, account of the *audiencier* Jean Gros the Younger for 1469
2074–6, accountable receipts and vouchers of the receiver-general Barthélemy Trotin for 1469
2077–8, account of the receiver-general Barthélemy Trotin for 1470
2079, account of the *contrôleur* Jean Gros the Younger for January 1471–March 1472
2080–3, accountable receipts and vouchers of the receiver-general Barthélemy Trotin for 1470

2084, account of the *argentier* Guilbert de Ruple for January–July 1471 and for September 1471–March 1472

2085–8, accountable receipts and vouchers of the *argentier* Guilbert de Ruple for January–July 1471 and for September 1471–March 1472

2089, account of the *argentier* Nicolas de Gondeval for August 1471

2090, account of the receiver-general Pierre Lanchals for 24 March 31 December 1472

2091–3, accountable receipts and vouchers of the receiver-general Pierre Lanchals for 24 March–31 December 1472

2094, account of the receiver-general Pierre Lanchals for 1473

2095–8, accountable receipts and vouchers of the receiver-general Pierre Lanchals for 1473

2099, account of the receiver-general Pierre Lanchals for 1474

2100, account of the *argentier* Nicolas de Gondeval for 1474

2101–3, accountable receipts and vouchers of the receiver-general Pierre Lanchals for 1474

2104, 2105[bis]–7, account of the receiver-general Pierre Lanchals for 1475

2105, account of the *argentier* Nicolas de Gondeval for 1475

2108, account of the receiver-general Pierre Lanchals for January 1476–February 1477

2109–14, accountable receipts and vouchers of the receiver-general Pierre Lanchals for 1476–7

3333, accounts of the ducal household for 1475–6

3377, *Chambre aux deniers des ducs de Bourgogne* for 1471–8

3431–41, *États journaliers de l'hôtel ducal (escroes)* for 6 April 1466–December 1477 (with some gaps)

3539, account of the *trésorier des guerres* Barthélemy Trotin for January 1470–23 March 1472

3540, account of the *trésorier des guerres* Barthélemy Trotin for September 1472–December 1474

11391–2, accounts of Jean de Flandre, deputy for Francesco d'Este as governor of Le Quesnoy, for October 1472–September 1474

17702–25, *Lettres reçues et dépêchés*, 1467–77

18842, *Lettres missives*, 1403–77

LONDON. British Library:

Additional MSS:

41068A, commonplace book of Bernardo Bembo

541569, ff. 362–83, unpublished fragment of George Chastellain's chronicle describing the journey of the Burgundian embassy to the Congress of Mantua

MANTUA. Archivio di Stato:
[Descriptions for this section come from Luzio's inventory; see the Bibliography]

Archivio Gonzaga:
439, Affari in corte cesarea. Carteggio degli inviati e residenti
563, Danimarca
567, Fiandre. Carteggio degli inviati e diversi
626, Francia. Lettere dei re di Francia ai Gonzaga
629, Francia. Carteggio degli inviati e diversi
723, Svizzera. Carteggio degli inviati e diversi
731, Savoia. Carteggio degli inviati e diversi
745, Monferrato. Carteggio degli inviati e diversi
805, Napoli e Sicilia. Carteggio degli inviati e diversi
843–6, Roma. Carteggio degli inviati e diversi
1100–1, Firenze. Carteggio degli inviati e diversi
1228, Ferrara. Carteggio degli inviati e diversi
1402, Trento. Lettere dei principi vescovi ai Gonzaga
1431, Venezia. Carteggio degli inviati e diversi
1599, Brescia. Lettere da Brescia ai Gonzaga
1607, Milano. Lettere dei signori di Milano ai Gonzaga
1623–6, Milano. Carteggio degli inviati e diversi
2100–1, Lettere originali dei Gonzaga
2187–8, Minute della Cancelleria
2891–4, Copialettere dei Gonzaga; ordinari, misti

MILAN. Archivio di Stato:

Autografi:
39/7, letter of Francesco Bertini to Galeazzo Maria from Novara, 29 November 1473
54 D3, letters of Charles the Bold to Galeazzo Maria from Malines, 10 July 1474 (letter of credence on behalf of Salvatore de Clariciis), and from the camp outside Nancy, 28 November 1475
63 A30, letter of Francesco d'Este to Galeazzo Maria from Parma, 20 September 1475

Fondo Visconteo-Sforzesco, Potenze Estere:
62–83, Roma
216–28, Napoli
322–4, Ferrara
353–64, Venezia
395–6, Mantova
482–98, Savoia e Piemonte
, 514–21, Borgogna e Fiandra
533–43, Francia
593, Svizzera

MODENA. Archivio di Stato:

Avvisi dall'estero, 1 (5157/101)
Cancelleria, Documenti di stati esteri, 1 (5301/101)
Cancelleria, Estero: Carteggi degli ambasciatori: Germania, 1; Milano, 1; Napoli, 1; Venezia, 1

Casa e stato: Principi non regnanti:
49, 130/10, correspondence of Rainaldo di Niccolò III d'Este
130, 1676/13, letters of Francesco d'Este to Borso d'Este from Brussels, 20 March 1466, from Bruges, 6 May (1466), and from Brussels, 2 October (1466)

Documenti e carteggi degli stati e città d'Italia e fuori d'Italia, 173/9
Epistolae, III
Minute di lettere ducali a principi e signorie in Italia e fuori d'Italia, 1626/1
Minute di lettere ducali di principi e signorie in Italia e fuori d'Italia, 1563 A/8
Registri delle lettere, 1–3

NAPLES. Biblioteca della Società Napoletana di Storia Patria:

fascio XXVI, C5, no. 11, ff. 11–12, nineteenth-century (?) copy of Ettore Spina's *Lista de quelli vennero con lo Illmo D.^no Federico d'Aragonia*

VALENCIENNES. Bibliothèque municipale:

MS 776, ff. 62–72^v, anonymous account of the chapter meeting of the Order of the Golden Fleece (Toison d'Or) held at Valenciennes in May 1473

VENICE. Archivio di Stato:

Capi del Consiglio dei X, Lettere, I
Consiglio dei X, Misto, XVII–XVIII
Collegio, Notatorio, XI
Collezione del Cardinale Lodovico Podocataro, Atti della Curia Romana, 1
Documenti ed atti diplomatici, Miscellanea
Libri Commemoralia, XIV–XVI
Senato Secreta, Deliberazioni, XXIII–XXVII

VENICE. Biblioteca Nazionale Marciana:

MS 8170 (= Classe Italiani, VII, codice 398), copies of the dispatches of Zaccaria Barbaro, Venetian ambassador in Naples, to Doges Niccolò Tron (died 28 July 1473) and Niccolò Marcello for the period 1 November 1471–7 September 1473 (in six separately paginated registers)

VIENNA. Archiv des Ordens vom Goldenen Vliesse:

Registers of the proceedings of the chapter meetings of the Order of the Golden Fleece (Toison d'Or), II–IV (1468, 1473, 1478)

Published primary sources and cited secondary works

ACTES des États Généraux des anciens Pays-Bas, I, ed. J. Cuvelier, J. Dhondt and R. Doehaerd, Commission royale d'histoire, Recueil des Actes des États Généraux (Brussels, 1948)

Adorno (Adournes), A., *Itinéraire d'Anselme Adorno en Terre Sainte (1470–1471)*, ed. and trans. J. Heers and G. de Groer, Sources d'histoire médiévale publiées par l'Institut de Recherche et d'Histoire des Textes (Paris, 1978)

Allegretti, A., *Diari sanesi*, ed. L.A. Muratori, in RIS, XXIII (Milan, 1723), 762–860

Allmand, C.T., 'Did the *De re militari* of Vegetius influence the military ordinances of Charles the Bold?', *PCEEB*, 41 (2001), 135–43.

Ammanati-Piccolomini, I., *Epistolae et commentarii* (Milan, 1506)

Andreucci, S., 'Domenico Bertini e la pieve di S. Giovanni Battista Gallicano', *La Provincia di Lucca*, 10 (1970), 44–51

Anonimo Veronese: see *Cronaca di Anonimo Veronese*

Anselme, Père (Pierre de Guibours), *Histoire généalogique de la maison royale de France, des pairs, grands officiers de la mason du roy, et des barons du royaume*, 9 vols, 3rd edtn (Paris, 1726–33)

Anstruther, G., 'The last days of the London Blackfriars', *Archivum Fratrum Praedicatorum*, 45 (1975), 213–36

Arata, A., *Niccolò da Correggio nella vita letteraria e politica del suo tempo (1450–1508)* (Bologna, 1934)

Archi, A., *Gli Aragonesi di Napoli* (Bologna, 1968)

Armstrong, C.A.J., *England, France and Burgundy in the fifteeenth century*, (Hambledon) History Series, 16 (London, 1983); contains, among others, 'Had the Burgundian government a policy for the nobility?' (pp. 213–36; first published 1964) and 'La politique matrimoniale des ducs de Bourgogne de la maison de Valois' (pp. 237–342; first published 1968)

Armstrong, C.A.J., ed., D. Mancini, *The usurpation of Richard the Third*: see under Mancini, D.

Arnaud d'Agnel, G., *Politique des rois de France en Provence. Louis XI et Charles VIII*, 2 vols (Paris–Marseille, 1914)

Arrighi, B., *Storia di Castiglione delle Stiviere sotto il dominio dei Gonzaga*, 2 vols (Mantua, 1853–5)

Aru, C., and E. de Géradon, *La Galerie Sabauda de Turin*, Les primitifs flamands, sér. 1: Corpus de la peinture des anciens Pays-Bas méridionaux au quinzième siècle, 5 (Antwerp, 1962)

Aubert de La Che(s)naye-Desbois, F.A., *Dictionnaire de la noblesse . . . de la France*, 19 vols, 3rd edtn (Paris, 1863–76)

Aubrion, J., *Journal de Jehan Aubrion, bourgeois de Metz, avec sa continuation par Pierre Aubrion 1465–1512*, ed. L. Larchey (Metz, 1857)

BALBI, G., 'Le relazioni tra Genova e la Corona d'Aragona dal 1464 al 1478', in *Atti del I° congresso storico Liguria–Catalogna–Ventimiglia–Bordighera–Albenga–Finale–Genova, 14–19 ottobre 1969* (Bordighera, 1974), 465–512

Ballard, M., 'An expedition of English archers to Liège in 1467, and the Anglo–Burgundian marriage alliance,' *Nottingham Medieval Studies*, 34 (1990), 152–74

Barone, N., 'Notizie storiche raccolte dai registri "Curiae" della cancelleria aragonese', *ASPN*, 13 (1888), 745–71; 14 (1889), 5–16, 177–203, 397–409; 15 (1890), 209–32, 452–71, 702–23

Bartier, J., 'Un discours du chancelier Hugonet aux États Généraux de 1473', *BCRH*, 107 (1942), 127–56

Bartier, J., 'Karel de Stoute', in *Algemene geschiedenis der Nederlanden*, ed. J.A. van Houtte, J.F. Niermeyer, J. Presser, J. Romein and H. van Werweke, 12 vols (Utrecht, etc.), 1949–58), III: *De late Middeleeuwen 1305–1477* (1951), 272–98

Bartier, J., *Légistes et gens de finances au XVe siècle. Les conseillers des ducs de Bourgogne Philippe le Bon et Charles le Téméraire*, Mémoires de l'Académie royale de Belgique, Classe des lettres et des sciences morales et politiques, L (Brussels, 1955)

Bartier, J., 'Quelques réflexions à propos d'un Mémoire de Raymond de Marliano et de la fiscalité à l'époque de Charles le Téméraire', *BMGN*, 95 (1980), 349–62

Basin, T., *Histoire de Louis XI*, ed. and trans. C. Samaran and M.C. Garand, Les Classiques de l'histoire de France au moyen-âge, 26, 27, 30, 3 vols (Paris, 1963–72)

Bauer, E., *Négociations et campagnes de Rodolphe de Hochberg, comte de Neuchâtel et marquis de Rothelin, gouverneur de Luxembourg, 1427(?)–1487*, Recueil de travaux publiés par la Faculté des Lettres, XI (Neuchâtel, 1928)

Beaulieu, M., and J. Baylé, *Le Costume en Bourgogne 1364–1477* (Paris, 1956)

Beffa, B., *Antonio Vinciguerra Cronico, segretario della Serenissima e letterato*, Pubblicazioni universitarie europee, Sezione IX: Lingua e letteratura italiane, 5 (Bern–Frankfurt, 1975)

Behrens, B., 'Treatises on the ambassador written in the fifteenth and early sixteenth centuries', *EHR*, 51 (1936), 616–27

Belloni, A., 'Un lirico del Quattrocento a torto inedito e dimenticato: Giovan Francesco Suardi', *GSLI*, 51 (1908), 147–206

Belotti, B., *La vita di Bartolomeo Colleoni* (Bergamo, 1923)

Benedetti, A., *Diaria de Bello Carolino*, ed. and trans. D.M. Schullian, Renaissance Society of America, Renaissance Text Series, I (New York, 1967)

Benoît, P., *Histoire de l'abbaye et de la terre de Saint–Claude*, 2 vols (Montreuil-sur-Mer, 1890–2)

Berchen, W. van, *Gelderse kroniek*, ed. A.J. de Mooy, Werken uitgegeven door Gelre Vereeniging tot Beoefening van Geldersche Geschiedenis, Oudheidkunde en Recht, 24 (Arnhem, 1950)

Berlière, U., 'La conmende aux Pays-Bas', in *Mélanges Godefroid Kurth. Recueil de mémoires relatifs à l'histoire, à la philosophie et à l'archéologie publié par la Faculté de Philosophie et Lettres de l'Université de Liège*, Bibliothèque de la Faculté de Philosophie et Lettres de l'Université de Liège, Série grande in–8⁰, I–II, 2 vols (Paris, 1908), I, 185–201

Bernardi, A., *Cronache forlivesi dal 1476 al 1517*, ed. G. Mazzatinti, R. Deputazione di storia patria per le province della Romagna, Monumenti istorici, 3rd ser., 2 vols (Bologna, 1895–7)

Bertolotti, A., 'Spedizioni militari in Piemonte sconosciute o poco note di Galeazzo Maria Sforza, duca di Milano', *ASL*, 10 (1883), 548–646

Bertoni, G., *Studi su vecchie e nuove poesie e prose d'amore e di romanzi* (Modena, 1921)

Besson, L., *Mémoire historique sur l'abbaye de Cherlieu* (Besançon, 1847)

Bianchi, J. de', *Cronaca modenese di Jacopino de' Bianchi detto de' Lancelloti*, ed. C. Borghi, Monumenti di storia patria delle province modenesi, Serie delle cronache, I (Parma, 1861)

Bisticci, V. da: see Vespasiano da Bisticci

Bittmann, K., *Ludwig XI. und Karl der Kühne. Die Memoiren des Philippe de Commynes als historische Quelle*, Veröffentlichungen des Max-Planck-Instituts für Geschichte, 9, vols I/1–2 and II/1 (Göttingen, 1964–70) — no more published

Blockmans, W.P., 'De Bourgondische Nederlanden: de weg naar een moderne staatsvorm', *Handelingen van de Koninklijke Kring voor oudheidkunde, letteren en kunst van Mechelen*, 77 (1973), 7–26

Blockmans, W.P., *De volksvertegenwoordiging in Vlaanderen in de overgang van Middeleeuwen naar nieuwe tijden (1384–1506)*, Verhandelingen van de Koninklijke Academie voor Wetenschappen, Letteren en Schone Kunsten van België, Klasse der Letteren, 90 (Brussels, 1978)

Blum, S.N., *Early Netherlandish triptychs. A study in patronage*, California Studies in the History of Art, 13 (Berkeley–Los Angeles, 1969)

Boehm, L., *Geschichte Burgunds. Politik — Staatsbildungen — Kultur*, 2nd edtn (Stuttgart, etc., 1979)

Boehm, L., 'Burgundy and the Empire in the reign of Charles the Bold', *International History Review*, 1 (1979), 153–62

Boeren, P.C., *Twee Maaslandse dichters in dienst van Karel de Stoute* (The Hague, 1968)

Bonello Uricchio, C., 'I rapporti fra Lorenzo il Magnifico e Galeazzo Maria Sforza negli anni 1471–1473', *ASL*, 9th ser., 4 (1964–5), 33–49

Bonenfant, A.M., and P. Bonenfant, 'Le projet d'érection des états bourguignons en royaume en 1447', *MA*, 45 (1935), 10–23

Bonenfant, P., 'Actes concernant les rapports entre les Pays-Bas et la Grande-Bretagne de 1293 à 1468 conservés au château de Mariemont', *BCRH*, 109 (1944), 53–125

Brauer-Gramm, H., *Der Landvogt Peter von Hagenbach. Die burgundische Herrschaft am Oberrhein 1464–1474*, Göttinger Bausteine zur Geschichtswissenschaft, 27 (Göttingen, 1957)

Brinton, S., *The Gonzaga — lords of Mantua* (London, 1927)

British Museum. Catalogue of additions to the manuscripts 1921–1925 (London, 1950)

Brouette, E., 'Les clercs "mensiers" de la Chambre apostolique sous les pontificats d'Innocent VIII et d'Alexandre VI (1484–1503)', in *Économies et sociétés au Moyen Age. Mélanges offerts à Édouard Perroy*, Publications de la Sorbonne, Série "Études", 5 (Paris, 1973), 581–7

Brun-Lavainne, J., 'Analyse d'un compte de dépense de la maison du duc Charles de Bourgogne', *Bulletin de la Commission historique du département du Nord*, 8 (1865), 189–232

Brusten, C., 'Les compagnies d'ordonnance dans l'armée bourguignonne', in *Grandson — 1476. Essai d'approche pluridisciplinaire d'une action militaire du XVᵉ siècle*, ed. D. Reichel, Série recherches de sciences comparées, II (Lausanne, 1976), 112–69

Bueno de Mesquita, D.M., 'The Deputati del denaro in the government of Ludovico Sforza', in *Cultural aspects of the Italian Renaissance. Essays in honour of Paul Oskar Kristeller*, ed. C.H. Clough (Manchester–New York, 1976), 276–98

Buonaccorsi (Callimachus), F., *Epistulae selectae*, ed. I. Lichońska, G. Pianko and T. Kowalewski, Bibliotheca Latina medii et recentioris aevi, 16 (Wratislawa, etc., 1967)

Die Burgunderbeute und Werke burgundischer Hofkunst (catalogue of an exhibition held at the Bernisches Historisches Museum, 18 May–20 September 1969), 2nd edtn (Bern, 1969)

Buser, B., *Die Beziehungen der Mediceer zu Frankreich während der Jahre 1434–94, in ihrem Zusammenhang mit der allgemeinen Verhältnissen Italiens* (Leipzig, 1879)

But, A. de, *Chronique d'Adrien de But complété par les additions du même auteur*, in *Chroniques relatives à l'histoire de la Belgique sous la domination des ducs de Bourgogne (textes latins)*, ed. J.B.M.C. Kervyn de Lettenhove, 3 vols (Brussels, 1870–6), I, 211–717

CAILLET, L., 'Donation par le roi René à Siffroy de Baschi, son écuyer, de plusieurs châteaux des baylies de Digne et de Sisteron (1470)', *Revue de l'Anjou* (1913), 197–201

Caleffini, U., *Diario (1471–1494)*, ed. G. Pardi, R. Deputazione di storia patria per l'Emila e la Romagna, Sezione di Ferrara, Serie Monumenti, I/1, II/2, 2 vols (Ferrara, 1938–40)

Calendar of state papers and manuscripts existing in the archives and collections of Milan, ed. A.B. Hinds, one volume only published = 1385–1618 (London, 1912)

Calendar of state papers and manuscripts, relating to English affairs, existing in the archives and collections of Venice and in other libraries of northern Italy, 38 vols (London, 1864–1947); I = 1202–1509, ed. R. Brown

Callimachus: see Buonaccorsi

Calmette, J., *Louis XI, Jean II et la révolution catalane (1461–1473)*, Bibliothèque méridionale, 2nd ser., 8 (Toulouse, 1903)

Calmette, J., 'Le projet de mariage bourguignon–napolitain en 1474 d'après une acquisition récente de la Bibliothèque Nationale', *BEC*, 72 (1911), 459–72

Calmette, J., *Études médiévales* (Toulouse, 1946); contains, among others, 'L'origine bourguignonne de l'alliance austro–espagnole' (pp. 215–39; first published 1905) and 'Campobasso et Commynes' (pp. 208–14; first published 1935)

Calmette, J., *La question des Pyrénées et la marche d'Espagne au moyen-âge*, La Roue de Fortune (Paris, 1947)

Calmette, J., and G. Périnelle, *Louis XI et l'Angleterre (1461–1483)*, Mémoires et documents publiés par la Société de l'École des Chartes, XI (Paris, 1930)

Cameron, A. I., *The Apostolic Camera and Scottish benefices, 1418–1488*, St Andrews University Publications, XXXV (Oxford, 1934)

Campbell, L., 'Cosmè Tura and Netherlandish art', in *Cosmè Tura. Painting and design in Renaissance Ferrara* [catalogue of the exhibition at Isabella Stewart Gardner Museum], ed. A. Chong (Boston, 2002), 71–105.

Campbell, L., 'Lord Northwick's collection and Rogier van der Weyden's portrait of Francesco d'Este', *Burlington Magazine*, 144 (2002), 696.

Candida Gonzaga, B., *Antico manoscritto di Carlo de Lellis sulla famiglia Filangieri* (Naples, 1887)

Canetta, C., 'La morte del conte Jacomo Piccinino', *ASL*, 9 (1882), 252–88

Cappelli, A., 'Niccolò di Leonello d'Este', *Atti e memorie della R. Deputazione storica per le province modenesi e parmensi*, 5 (1868), 413–38

Carabellese, F., 'Andrea da Passano e la famiglia d'Isabella del Balzo d'Aragona', *ASPN*, 24 (1899), 428–43

Caracciolo, T., *Opuscoli editi e inediti*, ed. G. Paladino, RSI, XXII/1 (Bologna, 1934)

Carafa, D., *Memoriale a Federico d'Aragona in occasione della sua andata in Francia* — (1) in *Testi napoletani del Quattrocento*, ed. A. Altamura, Collezione novantiqua, Romanica, 4 (Naples, 1953), 35–49; (2) ed. L. Miele (Naples, 1972)

Carteggi diplomatici fra Milano sforzesco e la Borgogna, Fonti per la storia d'Italia pubblicate dall'Istituto storico italiano per l'età moderna e contemporanea, ed. E. Sestan, 2 vols (Rome, 1985–7)

Cartellieri, O., *Am Hofe der Herzöge von Burgund. Kulturhistorische Bilder* (Basel, 1926)

Catalano, F., 'Il ducato di Milano nella politica dell'equilibrio', in *Storia di Milano*, 16 vols (Milan, 1953–62), VI (1956), 227–418

Cauchies, J.-M., 'Messageries et messages en Hainaut au XVe siècle', *MA*, 82 (1976), 89–123, 301–41

Cauchies, J.-M., *Louis XI et Charles le Hardi. De Péronne à Nancy (1468–1477): le conflit*, Bibliothèque du Moyen Age, 8 (Brussels, 1996)

Cazaux, Y., 'Charles de Bourgogne devant Jean–Pierre Panigarola, ambassadeur milanais, et devant sa mort', *PCEEB*, 20 (1980), 45–83

Cerioni, L., 'La politica italiana di Luigi XI e la missione di Filippo di Commines (giugno–settembre 1478)', *ASL*, 77 (1950), 58–156

Cerioni, L., *La diplomazia sforzesca nella seconda metà del Quattrocento e i suoi cifrari segreti*, Fonti e studi del *Corpus membranarum italicarum*, VII, 2 vols (Rome, 1970)

Chastellain, G., *Oeuvres*, ed. J.B.M.C. Kervyn de Lettenhove, Publications de l'Académie royale, Collection des grands écrivains du pays, XIII, 8 vols (Brussels, 1863–8)

Chauvelays, J. de la: see La Chauvelays, J. de

Chevailler, L., 'Un sujet des ducs de Savoie ne fut-il pas le premier ambassadeur permanent des temps modernes?', in *Studi in onore di Edoardo Volterra*, Pubblicazioni della Facoltà di Giurisprudenza della Università di Roma, XL–XLV, 6 vols (Milan, 1971), III, 705–14

Chevanne, J.R. de, *Les guerres en Bourgogne de 1470 à 1475* (Paris, 1934)

Chittolini, G., 'Infeudazioni e politica feudale nel ducato visconteo-sforzesco', *Quaderni storici*, 19 (1972), 57–130, reprinted in his *La formazione dello stato regionale e le istituzioni del contado*, Piccola Biblioteca Einaudi, 375 (Turin, 1979), 36–100

Chłedowski, C. von, *Der Hof von Ferrara*, translated from the Polish by R. Schapiro (Munich, 1919)

Chmel, J., 'Briefe und Aktenstücke zur Geschichte der Herzöge von Mailand von 1452 bis 1513 aus den Originalen', *Notizenblatt. Beilage zum Archiv für Kunde österreichischer Geschichtsquellen*, 6 (1856), 30–8, 56–64, 77–88, 109–12, 129–36, 156–60, 170–84, 193–201, 217–27, 245–56, 271–80, 298–302, 325–30, 346–52, 370–6, 395–400, 420–4, 443–8, 466–72, 484–94

Chronique de Lorraine, ed. L. Marchal, Recueil de documents sur l'histoire de Lorraine, V (Nancy, 1859)

Chronologische lijsten van de geëxtendeerde sententiën en Procesbundels (dossiers) berustende in het archief van de Grote Raad van Mechelen, ed. J.T. de Smidt, J. van Rompaey *et al.*, Werken der Vereeniging tot Uitgaaf der Bronnen van het Oudvaderlandsche Recht, 3rd ser., XXI, 3 vols (Brussels, 1966–79); I = 1465–1504

Cinotti, M., *The great galleries of the world. The National Gallery of Art of Washington and its paintings* (Edinburgh, 1975)

Clough, C.H., *Pietro Bembo's library as represented particularly in the British Museum*, 2nd edtn (London, 1971)

Clough, C.H., *The duchy of Urbino in the Renaissance*, (London, 1981); contains, among others (all reprinted with original pagination), 'Towards an economic history of the state of Urbino at the time of Federigo da Montefeltro and of his son, Guidobaldo' (first published 1978); 'Federigo da Montefeltro's patronage of the arts, 1468–1482' (first published 1973); 'Federigo da Montefeltro's artistic patronage' (first published 1978)

Clough, C.H., 'The library of Bernardo and Pietro Bembo', *Book Collector*, 33 (1984), 305–31

Codex diplomaticus dominii temporalis S. Sedis. Recueil de documents pour servir à l'histoire du gouvernement temporel des États du Saint–Siège extraits des archives du Vatican, ed. A. Theiner, 3 vols (Rome, 1861–2)

Codice aragonese, o sia lettere regie, ordinamenti ed altri atti governativi de' sovrani aragonesi in Napoli riguardanti l'amministrazione interna del reame e le relazioni all'estero, ed. F. Trinchera, 3 vols (Naples, 1866–74)

Le Codice aragonese. Étude générale. Publication du manuscrit de Paris. Contribution à l'histoire des aragonais de Naples, ed. A.A. Messer, Bibliothèque du XVe siècle, XVII (Paris, 1912)

Collison-Morley, L., *The story of the Sforzas* (London, 1933)

Colombo, E., *Iolanda duchessa di Savoia (1465–78): studio storico* (Turin, 1893)

Combet, J., *Louis XI et le Saint-Siège, 1461–1483* (Paris, 1903)

Commynes, P. de, *Mémoires*, ed. D. Godefroy and N. Lenglet du Fresnoy, 4 vols (Paris, 1747)

Commynes, P. de, *Mémoires*, ed. J. Calmette and C. Durville, Les Classiques de l'histoire de France au moyen-âge, 3, 5, 6, 3 vols (Paris, 1924–5)

Commynes, P. de, *Memoirs*, ed. S. Kinser, trans. I. Cazeaux, 2 vols (Columbia, South Carolina, 1969–73)

Les Comptes du roi René, ed. G. Arnaud d'Agnel, 3 vols (Paris, 1908–10)

Coniglio, G., *I Gonzaga*, Grandi famiglie (Milan, 1967)

Contamine, P., *Guerre, état et société à la fin du moyen âge. Étude sur les armées des rois de France 1337–1494*, École Pratique des Hautes Études, VIᵉ Section: Sciences économiques et sociales, Centre de recherches historiques: Civilisations et sociétés, 24 (Paris–The Hague, 1972)

Corps universel diplomatique du droit des gens, contenant un recueil des traitez d'alliance, de paix, de trêve . . . depuis le règne de . . . Charlemagne jusques à présent, ed. J. Dumont, 8 vols in 16 parts (Amsterdam, 1726–31)

Correspondance de la filiale de Bruges des Medicis, ed. A. Grunzweig, one volume only published (Brussels, 1931)

Coste, M.E. de la, *Anselme Adorne, sire de Corthuy, pèlerin de Terre–Sainte, sa famille, sa vie, ses voyages et son temps. Récit historique* (Brussels, 1855)

Croce, B., 'Un memoriale militare di Cola di Monforte, conte di Campobasso', *ASPN*, 58 (1933), 371–2

Croce, B., 'Il conte di Campobasso, Cola di Monforte', in *Vite di avventure di fede e di passione*, Scritti di storia letteraria e politica, XXX, 2nd edtn (Bari, 1947), 47–186 (first published 1933–4)

Croce, B., 'Isabella del Balzo regina di Napoli', in *Storie e leggende napoletane*, 4th edtn (Bari, 1948), 183–212

Croce, B., 'Elisio Calenzio', in *Varietà di storia letteraria e civile. Prima serie*, Scritti di storia letteraria e politica, XXIX, 2nd edtn (Bari, 1949), 7–29

Croce, B., 'Rettificazione di dati biografici intorno a Cola di Monforte conte di Campobasso e alla sua familia', in his *Aneddoti di varia letteratura*, I, Scritti di storia letteraria e politica, XLI, 2nd edtn (Bari, 1953), 220–55

Cronaca di Anonimo Veronese 1446–1488, ed. G. Soranzo, Monumenti storici pubblicati dalla R. Deputazione veneta di storia patria, 3rd ser.: Cronache e diarii, IV (Venice, 1915)

Una Cronaca napoletana figurata del Quattrocento, ed. R. Filangieri di Candida (Naples, 1956)

[425]

Cronaca universale dellà città di Mantova, ed. G. Amadei, E. Morani and G. Praticò, 4 vols (Mantua, 1955–7)

Cronache e statuti della città di Viterbo, ed. I. Ciampi, Documenti di storia italiana pubblicati a cura della R. Deputazione sugli studi di storia patria per le province di Toscana, dell'Umbria e delle Marche, V (Florence, 1872)

Cronycke van Hollandt, Zeelandt en de Vrieslandt . . . tot de jare MCCCCC ende XVII . . . (Leiden, 1517)

Curibus Sabinis, A. de, *De excidio civitatis Leodiensis*, in *Veterum scriptorum et monumentorum historicorum, dogmaticorum, moralium, amplissima collectio* . . ., ed. E. Martène and U. Durand, 9 vols (Paris, 1729–33), IV (1729), cols 1379–1500

Cusin, F., 'I rapporti tra la Lombardia e l'impero dalla morte di Francesco Sforza all'avvento di Ludovico il Moro', *Annali della R. Università degli Studi Economici e Commerciali di Trieste*, 6 (1934), 213–322

Cusin, F., 'Impero, Borgogna e politica italiana (l'incontro di Treviri del 1473)', *Nuova rivista storica*, 19 (1935), 137–72; 20 (1936), 34–57

Cuttler, S.H., *The law of treason and treason trials in later medieval France*, Cambridge Studies in Medieval Life and Thought, 3rd ser., 16 (Cambridge, 1981)

DAGBOEK van Gent van 1447 tot 1470, ed. V. Fris, 2 vols (Ghent, 1901–4)

Daviso di Charvensod, M.C., *La duchessa Iolanda*, Collana storica sabauda (Turin, 1935)

Daviso di Charvensod, M.C., *Filippo II il Senza Terra*, Collana storica sabauda (Turin, 1941)

De Frede, C., 'Un memoriale di Ferrante I d'Aragona a Luigi XI (1478)', *RSI*, 60 (1948), 403–19

Degryse, R., 'De admiraals en de eigen marine van de Bourgondische hertogen 1384–1488', *Mededelingen der Akademie van Marine van België*, 27 (1965), 139–225

Delaborde, H.F., *L'expédition de Charles VIII en Italie. Histoire diplomatique et militaire* (Paris, 1883)

De la Coste, M.E.: see under Coste

De Lannoy, A.: see under Lannoy

Delbrück, H., *Die Perserkriege und die Burgunderkriege* (Berlin, 1887)

Del Carmen Pescador del Hoyo, M.: see under Pescador

Della Chiesa, F.A., *S.R.E. cardinalium, archiepiscoporum, episcoporum et abbatum Pedemontane regionis chronologica historia* (Turin, 1645)

Della Torre, A., 'La prima ambasceria di Bernardo Bembo a Firenze', *GSLI*, 35 (1900), 258–333

Del Treppo, M., *I mercanti catalani e l'espansione della Corona Aragonese nel secolo XV*, Università di Napoli, Seminario di storia medioevale e moderna, 4 (Naples, 1967)

Del Treppo, 'Gli aspetti organizzativi economici e sociali di una compagnia di ventura italiana', *RSI*, 75 (1973–4), 253–75

Delumeau, J., *L'alun de Rome, XVe–XIXe siècle*, École Pratique des Hautes Études. VIe Section: Sciences économiques et sociales, Centre de recherches historiques: Ports–routes–trafics, XIII (Paris, 1962)

Del Val, M.I.: see under Val

De Marinis, T.: see under Marinis

De Moreau, R.E.: see under Moreau

Dépêches des ambassadeurs milanais en France sous Louis XI et François Sforza, ed. B. de Mandrot and C. Samaran, Société de l'histoire de France, 4 vols (Paris, 1916–23)

Dépêches des ambassadeurs milanais sur les campagnes de Charles-le-Hardi, duc de Bourgogne, de 1474 à 1477, ed. F. de Gingins La Sarra, 2 vols (Paris–Geneva, 1858)

De Reiffenberg, F.A.F.T.: see under Reiffenberg

De Roover, R.: see under Roover

De Schryver, A.: see under Schryver

Desimoni, C., and L.T. Belgrano, 'Documenti ed estratti inediti o poco noti riguardanti la storia del commercio e della marina ligure. I. Brabante, Fiandra e Borgogna', *Atti della Società ligure di storia patria*, 5/III (1871), 355–547

Deutsche Reichstagsakten unter Kaiser Friedrich III. Achte Abteilung, erste Hälfte 1468–1470, ed. I. Most-Kolbe, Deutsche Reichstagsakten herausgegeben durch die Historische Kommission bei der Bayerischen Akademie der Wissenschaften, XXII/1 (Göttingen, 1973)

De Vocht, H.: see under Vocht

Diario ferrarese dall'anno 1409 sino al 1502 di autori incerti, ed. G. Pardi, RSI, XXIV/7/i (Bologna, 1928)

Di Bernardo, F., *Un vescovo umanista alla corte pontificia, Giannantonio Campano (1429–1477)*, Miscellanea Historiae Pontificiae, 39 (Rome, 1975)

Dina, A., 'Lodovico il Moro prima della sua venuta al governo', *ASL*, 2nd ser., 3 (1886), 737–76

Dispatches with related documents of Milanese ambassadors in France and Burgundy, 1450–1483, 3 vols so far published: I–II ed. and trans. V.

Ilardi and P.M. Kendall (Athens, Ohio, 1970–1); III ed. and trans. V. Ilardi and F.J. Fata (Dekalb, Illinois, 1981)

Dizionario biografico degli italiani (Rome, 1960–)

Documenti diplomatici tratti dagli archivi milanesi, ed. L. Osio, 3 vols (Milan, 1864–72)

Documents inédits sur l'érection des nouveaux diocèses aux Pays-Bas (1521–1570), ed. M. Dierickx, Publications de l'Académie royale de Belgique, Commission royale d'histoire, 3 vols (Brussels, 1960–2)

Doyere, P.-C., 'Un grand mystère historique', *Nouvelle revue franc-comtoise*, 15 (1976), 9–26

Dreyer, K., 'Commynes and Machiavelli: a study in parallelism', *Symposium*, 5 (1951), 36–61

Dürr, E., 'Galeazzo Maria Sforza und seine Stellung zu den Burgunderkriegen. Eine Untersuchung über die südfranzösisch-italienische Politik Karls des Kühnen', *BZGA*, 10 (1911), 259–415

Dürr, E., 'Karl der Kühne und der Ursprung des habsburgisch-spanischen Imperiums', *Historische Zeitschrift*, 113 (1914), 22–55

Dürr, E., 'Ludwig XI., die aragonesisch–castilianische Heirat und Karl der Kühne', MIÖG, 35 (1914), 297–332

Dürr, E., *La politique des Confédérés au XIVᵉ et au XVᵉ siècle. La Confédération, grande puissance politique au temps des guerres d'Italie*, trans. V. Moine (Bern, 1935)

Dufournet, J., *La destruction des mythes dans les Mémoires de Ph. de Commynes*, Publications romanes et françaises, LXXXIX (Geneva, 1966)

Dufournet, J., *Études sur Philippe de Commynes*, Bibliothèque du XVᵉ siècle, XL (Paris, 1975)

Dupont-Ferrier, G., *Gallia Regia ou état des officiers royaux des bailliages et des sénéschaussées de 1328 à 1515*, 6 vols (Paris, 1942–61)

EHRENBURG, R., *Capital and finance in the age of the Renaissance. A study of the Fuggers and their connections*, trans. H.M. Lucas (London, 1928)

Die Eidgenössischen Abschiede aus dem Zeitraume von 1421 bis 1477, ed. A.P. Segesser, Amtliche Sammlung der älteren eidgenössischen Abschiede, II (Luzern, 1863)

Erens, A., 'Thierry van Tuldel et la commende en Brabant, 1470–1490', *Analecta Praemonstratensia*, 1 (1925) 321–56

Ernst, F., 'Über Gesandtschaftswesen und Diplomatie an der Wende vom Mittelalter zur Neuzeit', *AKG*, 33 (1950), 64–95

Escouchy, M. d', *Chronique*, ed. G. du Fresne de Beaucourt, Société de l'histoire de France, 3 vols (Paris, 1863–4)

Eubel, C., *Hierarchia catholica Medii Aevi*, 2 vols (Münster, 1913–14)

Excellente cronike van Vlaanderen (Antwerp, 1531)

Extrait d'une ancienne chronique commençant en 1400 & finissant en 1467, in P. de Commynes, *Mémoires*, ed. D. Godefroy and N. Lenglet du Fresnoy, 4 vols (Paris, 1747), II, 173–221

FANTONI, G.L., 'Un carteggio femminile del sec. XV: Bianca Maria Visconti e Barbara di Hohenzollern–Brandenburgo Gonzaga (1450–1468)', *Libri e documenti*, 7; 2 (1981), 6–29

Favier, J., 'Circulation et conjoncture monétaires au temps de Marie de Bourgogne', *Revue historique*, 272 (1984), 3–27

Ferguson, J., *English diplomacy 1422–1461*, Oxford Historical Monographs (Oxford, 1972)

Fernández Torregrosa, A., 'Aspectos de la política exterior de Juan II de Aragón', *Estudios de Historia Moderna*, 2 (1952), 99–132

Ferrand, H., *Jacques Valperga de Masin, chancelier de Savoye, et Philippe-sans-Terre, comte de Bresse. Les gentilshommes des pays de Savoye au XVe siècle* (Paris, 1862)

Ferrante I, king of Naples: see under *Regis*

Filelfo, F., *Cent–dix lettres grecques de François Filelfe publiées intégralement pour la première fois d'après le "Codex Trivulzianus 873"*, ed. and trans. E. Legrand, Publications de l'École des Langues Orientales Vivantes, 3rd ser., XII (Paris, 1892)

Filippi, G., *Il matrimonio di Bona di Savoia con Galeazzo Maria Sforza* (Turin, 1890)

Finot, J., *Étude historique sur les relations commerciales entre la Flandre et la république de Gênes au moyen âge* (Paris, 1906)

Flamini, F., 'Francesco Galeota, gentiluomo napolitano del Quattrocento e il suo inedito canzoniere', *GSLI*, 20 (1892), 1–90

Fobe, A.M., 'De Spaanse nalatenschap: de ontstaansredenen van de vroegste residerende gezantschappen vanuit de Nederlanden (1492–1506)', *TG*, 85 (1972), 171–9

Fonti aragonesi a cura degli archivisti napoletani, III, ed. B. Mazzoleni, Testi e documenti di storia napoletana pubblicati dall'Accademia Pontaniana, 2nd ser., 3 (Naples, 1953)

Fouw, A. de, *Philips van Kleve. Een bijdrage tot de kennis van zijn leven en karakter* (Groningen, 1937)

Fraknói, W., *Mathias Corvinus, König von Ungarn 1458–1490* (Freiburg im Breisgau, 1891)

Frati, L., 'Die Gründung des Abbreviatorenkollegs durch Pius II. und Sixtus IV.', in *Miscellanea in onore di Monsignor Martino Giusti, Prefetto dell'Archivio Segreto Vaticano*, Collectanea Archivi Vaticani, 5–6, 2 vols (Città del Vaticano, 1978), I, 297–329

Fryde, E.B., 'Lorenzo de Medici's finances and their influence on his patronage of art', in *Studi in memoria di Federigo Melis*, 5 vols (Naples, 1978), III, 453–67

Fubini, R., 'Osservazioni e documenti sulla crisi del ducato di Milano nel 1477 e sulla riforma del Consiglio segreto ducale di Bona Sforza', in *Essays presented to Myron P. Gilmore*, ed. S. Bertelli and G. Ramakus, Villa I Tatti Publications, 2, 2 vols (Florence, 1978), I, 47–103

Fubini, R., 'La figura politica dell'ambasciatore negli sviluppi di regimi oligarchici quattrocenteschi. Abbozzo di una ricerca (a guisa di lettera aperta)', *Annali della Facoltà di Scienze Politiche dell'Università di Perugia*, 16 (1979–80), 33–59

Fubini, R., 'Appunti sui rapporti diplomatici fra il dominio sforzesco e Firenze medicea. Modi e tecniche dell'ambasciata dalle trattative per la lega italica alla missione di Sacramoro da Rimini (1451–1473)', in *Gli Sforza a Milano e in Lombardia e i loro rapporti con gli stati italiani ed europei (1450–1535). Convegno internazionale, Milano, 18–21 maggio 1981* (Milan, 1982), 291–334

Fubini, R., 'I rapporti diplomatici tra Milano e Borgogna con particolare riguardo all'alleanza del 1475–1476', *PCEEB*, 28 (1988), 95–114

Fumagalli, E., 'Nuovi documenti su Lorenzo e Giuliano de' Medici', *IMU*, 23 (1980), 115–64

Fumi, L., 'Una farsa rappresentata in Parigi contro Bartolomeo Colleoni', in *Miscellanea di studi storici in onore di Antonio Manno*, ed. P. Boselli, 2 vols (Turin, 1912), II, 589–94

GABOTTO, F., *Un condottiere e una virago del secolo XV* (Verona, 1890)

Gabotto, F., *Lo stato sabaudo da Amadeo VIII ad Emanuele Filiberto II*, 3 vols (Turin–Rome, 1892–5)

Gachard, L.P., 'Analectes historiques. Troisième série', *BCRH*, 2nd ser., 7 (1855), 25–220

Gachard, L.P., 'Analectes historiques. Cinquième série', *BCRH*, 2nd ser., 9 (1857), 103–256

Gachard, L.P., 'Analectes historiques. Septième série', *BCRH*, 2nd ser., 12 (1859), 359–516

Gaier, C., *L'industrie et le commerce des armes dans les anciennes principautés belges du XIIIᵐᵉ à la fin du XVᵐᵉ siècle*, Bibliothèque de la Faculté de Philosophie et Lettres de l'Université de Liège, CCII (Paris, 1973)

Gallet-Guerne, D., *Vasque de Lucène et la Cyropédie à la cour de Bourgogne (1470). Le traité de Xénophon mis en français d'après la version latine du Pogge. Étude. Édition des Livres I et V*, Travaux d'humanisme et Renaissance, CXL (Geneva, 1974)

Gandilhon, R., *Politique économique de Louis XI* (Paris, 1941)

Ganz, M.A., 'Donato Acciaiuoli and the Medici: a strategy for survival in '400 Florence', *Rinascimento*, 2nd ser., 22 (1982), 33–73

Ghinzoni, P., 'La battaglia di Morat narrata dall'ambasciatore milanese presso il duca di Borgogna, testimonio oculare', *ASL*, 2nd ser., 9 (1892), 102–9

Giacomo, N., *Cronica di Napoli*, ed. P. Garzill (Naples, 1845)

Giannetto, N., 'Un'orazione inedita di Bernardo Bembo per Cristoforo Moro', *Atti dell'Istituto Veneto di scienze, lettere ed arti. Classe di scienze morali, lettere ed arti*, 140 (1981–2), 257–88

Giesey, R.E., 'Ernst Kantorowicz — scholarly triumphs and academic travails in Weimar Germany and the United States', *Leo Baeck Institute Yearbook*, 30 (1985), 191–202

Glorieux, P., 'Un chanoine de Saint Pierre de Lille, Jean Adourne', *Bulletin du Comité flamand de France*, 18 (1971), 295–324

Godard, J., 'Dans les Pays-Bas bourguignons: un conflit de politique commerciale', *Annales d'histoire sociale*, 1 (1939), 417–20

Goetstouwers, J.B., 'Notes sur les papiers d'affaires de Pierre de Hagenbach et spécialement une lettre d'indulgence accordée en 1472 par le nonce Lucas de Tolentis', *Analectes pour servir à l'histoire ecclésiastique de la Belgique*, 3rd ser., 7 (1911), 222–7

Gorissen, P., *De Raadkamer van de hertog van Bourgondië te Maastricht, 1473–1477*, Publications de l'Université Louvanium de Léopoldville, V (Louvain–Paris, 1959)

Grand, A., *Der Anteil des Wallis an den Burgunderkriegen* (Brig, 1913)

Gregory, W., *Chronicles of London*, in *The historical collections of a citizen of London in the fifteenth century*, ed. J. Gairdner, Camden Society, n.s. XVII (London, 1876), 55–239

Grunzweig, A., 'Un plan d'acquisition de Gênes par Philippe le Bon (1445)', *MA*, 42 (1931), 81–110

Guichenon, S., *Histoire généalogique de la royale maison de Savoie*, 4 vols, 2nd edtn (Turin, 1778–80)

Guillaume, H.L.G., *Histoire des bandes d'ordonnance des Pays-Bas*, Nouveaux mémoires de l'Académie royale de Belgique, XL (Brussels, 1873)

Gundersheimer, W.L., *Ferrara. The style of a Renaissance despotism* (Princeton, N.J., 1973)

HALE, J.R., 'International relations in the West: diplomacy and war', in *The new Cambridge modern history*, ed. G.R. Potter (Cambridge, 1962), 259–91

Hale, J.R., *Renaissance war studies* (London, 1983); contains, among others, 'Tudor fortifications: the defence of the realm, 1485–1558' (pp. 63–97; first published 1982), 'The military education of the officer class in early modern Europe' (pp. 225–46; first published 1976); 'Gunpowder and the Renaissance: an essay in the history of ideas' (pp. 389–420; first published 1966)

Handelingen van de Leden en van de Staten van Vlaanderen (1467–1477). Excerpten uit de rekeningen van de Vlaamse steden, kasselrijen en vorstelijke ambtenaren, ed. W.P. Blockmans, Publications in-quarto de la Commission royale d'histoire (Brussels, 1971)

Harsgor, M., 'Fidélités et infidélités au sommet du pouvoir', in *Hommages à Roland Mousnier. Clientèles et fidélités en Europe à l'époque moderne*, ed. Y. Durand (Paris, 1981), 259–77

Hatfield Strens, B., 'L'arrivo del trittico Portinari a Firenze', *Commentari*, n.s., 19 (1968), 315–19

Hautcoeur, É., *Histoire de l'église collégiale et du chapitre de Saint-Pierre de Lille*, 3 vols (Lille–Paris, 1896–9)

Hay, D., *Italian clergy and Italian culture in the fifteenth century*, Society for Renaissance Studies, Occasional Papers, I (London, 1973)

Hay, D., *The Italian Renaissance in its historical background. The Wiles Lectures given at the Queen's University, Belfast, 1960*, 2nd edtn (Cambridge, 1977)

Haynin, J. de, *Mémoires*, ed. D.D. Brouwers, 2 vols, 2nd edtn (Liège, 1905–6)

Heers, M.L., 'Les Génois et le commerce de l'alun à la fin du moyen âge', *Revue d'histoire économique et sociale*, 32 (1954), 31–53

Heimpel, H., 'Karl der Kühne und der burgundische Staat', in *Festschrift für Gerhard Ritter zu seinem 60. Geburtstag*, ed. R. Nürnberger (Tübingen, 1950), 140–60

Heitmann, K., 'Olivier de la Marche, "Le Debat de Cuidier et de

Fortune". Eine dichterische Meditation über den Untergang Karls des Kühnen', *AKG*, 47 (1965), 266–305

Hersey, G.L., *Alfonso II and the artistic renewal of Naples 1485–1495*, Yale Publications in the History of Art, 19 (New Haven–London, 1969)

Heymann, F.G., *George of Bohemia, king of heretics* (Princeton, N.J., 1965)

Hill, G.F., *A corpus of Italian medals of the Renaissance before Cellini*, 2 vols (London, 1930)

Höflechner, W., *Die Gesandten der europäischen Mächte, vornehmlich des Kaisers und des Reiches 1490–1500*, Österreichische Akademie der Wissenschaften, philosophisch–historische Klasse, historische Komission, Archiv für österreichische Geschichte (Vienna, 1972)

Hofmann, B., 'Barbara von Hohenzollern, Markgräfin von Mantua. Ein Lebensbild aus dem XV. Jahrh.', *Jahresberichte des historischen Vereins für Mittelfranken*, 41 (1881), 1–51

Hook, J., *Lorenzo de' Medici: an historical biography* (London, 1984)

ILARDI, V., 'The Italian League, Francesco Sforza and Charles VII (1454–1461)', *SR*, 6 (1959), 129–66

Ilardi, V., 'Fifteenth-century diplomatic documents in western European archives and libraries (1450–1494)', *SR*, 9 (1962), 64–112

Ilardi, V., 'France and Milan: the uneasy alliance, 1452–1466', in *Gli Sforza a Milano e in Lombardia e i loro rapporti con gli stati italiani ed europei (1450–1535). Convegno internazionale, Milano, 18–21 maggio 1981* (Milan, 1982), 415–47

Ilardi, V., and M.L. Shay, 'Italy', in *The new guide to the diplomatic archives of western Europe*, ed. D.H. Thomas and L.M. Case (Philadelphia, 1975), 165–211

Infessura, S., *Diario della città di Roma*, ed. O. Tommasini, Fonti per la storia d'Italia pubblicate dall'Istituto Storico Italiano, V: Scrittori, secolo XV (Rome, 1890)

Inventaire des chartes et cartulaires du Luxembourg, ed. A. Verkooren, Inventaire des archives de la Belgique, 5 vols (Brussels, 1914–31)

Inventaire sommaire des Archives Communales de la ville de Strasbourg antérieures à 1790. Sér. AA. Actes constitutifs et politiques de la commune, ed. J. Brucker, 4 vols (Strasbourg, 1878–86)

Inventaire sommaire des Archives Départementales antérieures à 1790, ed. A. Le Glay, M.A. Desplanque, C. Dehaisnes and J. Finot, 8 vols (Lille, 1863–1906)

Inventaire sommaire des Archives Départementales de la Côte d'Or. Série B, ed. C. Rossignol *et al.*, 6 vols (Dijon, 1863–94)

Isenburg, W.K. von, and F. von Loringhoven, *Stammtafeln zur Geschichte der europäischen Staaten (europäische Stammtafeln)*, 4 vols (Marburg, 1953–8)

JACOVIELLO, M., 'Relazioni politiche tra Venezia e Napoli nella seconda metà del XV secolo (dai documenti dell'Archivio Stato di Venezia)', *ASPN*, 96 (1978), 67–133

James, T.B., 'Chivalry: fact or fantasy?', *Literature and History*, 9 (1983), 102–5

J[amison], E.M., [Review of the original version of Croce's essay on Cola di Monforte], *EHR*, 51 (1936), 732–3

Jongkees, A.G., 'État et Église dans les Pays-Bas bourguignons: avant et après 1477', in *Cinq-centième anniversaire de la bataille de Nancy (1477). Actes du colloque organisé par l'Institut de recherche régionale en sciences sociales, humaines et économiques de l'Université de Nancy II (Nancy, 22–24 septembre 1977)*, Annales de l'Est, Mémoires, 62 (Nancy, 1979), 237–47

Jongkees, A.G., 'Charles le Téméraire et la souveraineté', *BMGN*, 95 (1980), 315–54

KAEGI, W., 'Ein Plan Jacob Burckhardts zu einem Werk über Karl den Kühnen', *BZGA*, 30 (1930), 393–8

Kaminsky, H., [Review of Vaughan, *Charles the Bold*], *Speculum*, 52 (1977), 175–7

Kantorowicz, E.H., *Selected studies*, ed. M. Cherniavsky and R.E. Giesey (Locust Valley, N.Y., 1965); contains, among others, 'The Este portrait by Roger van der Weyden' (pp. 366–80; first published 1939–40)

Keen, M.H., *The laws of war in the late Middle Ages* (London–Toronto, 1965)

Kendall, P.M., *Louis XI . . . "the universal spider" . . .* (London–New York, 1971)

Ker, N.R., *Medieval manuscripts in British libraries*, 5 volumes so far published (Oxford, 1969–2002)

Kervyn de Lettenhove, J.B.M.C., *Lettres et négociations de Philippe de Commines*, 3 vols (Brussels, 1867–8)

Kirk, J.F., *History of Charles the Bold, duke of Burgundy*, 3 vols (London, 1863–8)

Knebel, H., *Diarium/Tagebuch*, ed. W. Vischer and H. Boos, Basler

Chroniken herausgegeben von der Historischen und Antiquarischen Gesellschaft in Basel, II–III, 2 vols (Leipzig, 1880–7)

Kristeller, P., 'Barbara von Brandenburg, Markgräfin von Mantua', *Hohenzollern Jahrbuch* (1899), 66–85

Kristeller, P., *Andrea Mantegna*, trans. S.A. Strong (London, 1901)

Kristeller, P.O., *Iter Italicum. A finding list of uncatalogued or incompletely catalogued humanistic manuscripts of the Renaissance in Italian and other libraries*, 6 volumes so far published (London–Leiden, 1963–92)

Kurth, G., *La cité de Liège au moyen-âge*, 3 vols (Brussels–Liège, 1909–10)

LABANDE, L.H., *Avignon au XVᵉ siècle. Légation de Charles de Bourbon et du cardinal Julien de la Rovère*, Mémoires et documents publiés par ordre de S.A.S. le Prince Albert Iᵉʳ de Monaco (Monaco–Paris, 1920)

La Chauvelays, J. de, 'Mémoire sur la composition des armées de Charles le Téméraire dans les deux Bourgognes d'après les documents originaux', *Mémoires de l'Académie des sciences, arts et belles-lettres de Dijon*, 3rd ser., 5 (1879), 139–369

La Coste, M.E. de: see under Coste

La Marche, O. de, *Mémoires*, ed. H. Beaune and J. d'Arbaumont, Société de l'Histoire de France, 4 vols (Paris, 1883–8)

Lannoy, A. de, 'La garde de Charles le Téméraire à Nancy en 1477', *L'Intermédiaire des généalogistes*, 21 (1966), 120–6

Lee, E., *Sixtus IV and men of letters*, Temi e testi, 26 (Rome, 1978)

Lesellier, J., 'Une curieuse correspondance inédite entre Louis XI et Sixte IV', *MAHEFR*, 45 (1928), 21–37

Lettres de Louis XI, roi de France, ed. J. Vaesen, E. Charavay and B. de Mandrot, Société de l'histoire de France, 11 vols (Paris, 1883–1909)

Levati, L.M., *Dogi perpetui di Genova an. 1339–1528. Studio biografico* (Genoa, 1930)

Levi, E., 'Lo zibaldone di Bernardo Bembo', *Rassegna bibliografica della letteratura italiana*, 55 (1896), 46–50

Liagre, L., 'Le commerce de l'alun en Flandre au moyen âge', *MA*, 61 (1955), 177–206

Liebenau, T. di (von), 'Ueber eine geheime Mission des Gabriel Morosini', *Bollettino storico della Svizzera italiana*, 23 (1901), 96–100

Lightbown, R.W., *Mantegna: with a complete catalogue of paintings, drawings and prints* (Oxford, 1986)

Litta, P., *Famiglie celebri italiane*, 11 vols (Milan, 1819–85)

Lockwood, L., 'Dufay and Ferrara', in *Papers read at the Dufay*

Quincentenary conference, Brooklyn College, December 6–7, 1974, ed. A.W. Atlas (New York, 1976), 1–25

Lorraine et Bourgogne (1473–1478). Choix de documents, ed. J. Schneider (Nancy, 1982)

Lot, F., *L'art militaire et les armées au moyen âge en Europe et dans le Proche Orient*, 2 vols (Paris, 1946)

Louis XI, *Lettres*: see under *Lettres*

Lubkin, G.P., *A Renaissance court: Milan under Galeazzo Maria Sforza* (Berkeley, 1994) [published version of 'The court of Galeazzo Maria Sforza, duke of Milan (1466–1476), Ph.D. dissertation, University of California, Berkeley, 1982)]

Lunt, W.E., *Papal revenues in the Middle Ages*, Records of Civilisation: Sources and Studies, XIX, 2 vols (New York, 1934)

Lunt, W.E., *Financial relations of the papacy with England 1327–1534 (Studies in Anglo–papal relations during the Middle Ages II)*, Publications of the Mediaeval Academy of America, 74 (Cambridge, Mass., 1962)

Luzio, A., *L'Archivio Gonzaga di Mantova*, II = *La corrispondenza familiare, amministrativa e diplomatica dei Gonzaga*, Pubblicazioni della R. Accademia Virgiliana di Mantova, 1st ser.: Monumenti, II (Verona, 1922)

MACDOUGALL, N., *James III: a political study* (Edinburgh, 1982)

Maček, J., 'Le mouvement conciliaire, Louis XI et Georges de Poděbrady (en particulier dans la période 1466–1468)', *Historica* (Prague), 15 (1967), 5–63

Macquarrie, A.D., 'Anselm Adornes of Bruges: traveller in the East and friend of James III', *Innes Review*, 33 (1982), 15–22

Maes, L.T., and G. Dogaer, 'A propos de l'ordonnance de Thionville promulguée par Charles le Téméraire en 1473', *AB*, 45 (1973), 45–9

Magistretti, P., 'Galeazzo Maria Sforza prigionere nella Novalesa', *ASL*, 2nd ser., 6 (1889), 777–807

Malipiero, D., *Annali veneti dall'anno 1457 al 1500*, ed. P. Longo and A. Sagredo, Archivio storico italiano, VII/1 (Florence, 1843)

Mallett, M.E., 'Venice and its condottieri 1404–1454', in *Renaissance Venice*, ed. J.R. Hale (London, 1973), 121–45

Mallett, M.E., *Mercenaries and their masters. Warfare in Renaissance Italy* (London, etc., 1973)

Mallett, M.E., 'Some notes on a fifteenth-century *condottiere* and his library: Count Antonio da Marsciano', in *Cultural aspects of the Italian Renaissance. Essays in honour of Paul Oskar Kristeller*, ed. C.H. Clough (Manchester–New York, 1976), 202–15

Mallett, M.E., 'Preparations for war in Florence and Venice in the second half of the fifteenth century', in *Florence and Venice: comparisons and relations. Acts of the two conferences at Villa I Tatti in 1976–1977*, ed. S. Bertelli, N. Rubinstein and C.H. Smyth, Villa I Tatti Publications, 5, 2 vols (Florence, 1979), I, 149–64

Mallett, M.E., 'Diplomacy and war in later fifteenth-century Italy', *Proceedings of the British Academy*, 67 (1981), 267–88

Mancini, D., *The usurpation of Richard the Third. Dominicus Mancinus ad Angelum Catonem De occupations regni Anglie per Riccardum Tercium libellus*, ed. and trans. C.A.J. Armstrong, 2nd edtn (Oxford, 1969)

Mandrot, B. de, *Ymbert de Batarnay, seigneur du Bouchage, conseiller des rois Louis XI, Charles VIII et François Ier* (Paris, 1886)

Manfredi, M., 'Accrocciamuro, Ruggerone', *DBI*, I (1960), 123

Marche, O. de la: see La Marche, O. de

Marcora, C., 'Stefano Nardini, arcivescovo di Milano (1461–1484)', *Memorie storiche della diocesi di Milano*, 3 (1956), 257–488

Margny, J. de, *L'Aventurier*, ed. J.R. de Chevanne (Paris, 1938)

Marinis, T. de, *La biblioteca napoletana dei re d'Aragona*, 4 vols (Milan, 1947–52)

Martens, M., 'Les maisons de Médici et de Bourgogne au XVe siècle', *MA*, 56 (1950), 115–29

Martens, M., 'La correspondence de caractère économique échangée par Francesco Sforza, duc de Milan, et Philippe le Bon, duc de Bourgogne (1450–1466)', *BIHBR*, 27 (1952), 221–34

Martines, L., *Lawyers and statecraft in Renaissance Florence* (Princeton, N.J., 1968)

Matthew, D., *The medieval European community* (London, 1977)

Mattingly, G., *Renaissance diplomacy*, Bedford Historical Series, XVIII (London, 1962; first published 1955)

Matzenauer, M., *Studien zur Politik Karls des Kühnen bis 1474*, Schweizer Studien zur Geschichtswissenschaft, n.s., 11 (Zürich, 1946)

Maulde-La-Clavière, R.A. de, *La diplomatie au temps de Machiavel*, 3 vols (Paris, 1892–3; reprinted Geneva, 1970)

Medici, L. de', *Lettere*, ed. R. Fubini, N. Rubinstein and M. Mallett, 8 volumes so far published (Florence, 1977–2001)

Meersseman, G.G., 'La raccolta dell'umanista fiammingo Giovanni de Veris "De arte epistolandi"', *IMU*, 15 (1972), 215–81

Mémoires pour servir à l'histoire de France et de Bourgogne (attributed to Dom Des Salles), ed. L.F.J. de La Barre, 2 vols (Paris, 1729)

Mohler, L., *Kardinal Bessarion als Theologe, Humanist und Staatsmann*,

Quellen und Forschungen aus dem Gebiete der Geschichte, XX, XXII, XXIV, 3 vols (Paderborn, 1923–42)

Molinet, J., *Chroniques*, ed. G. Doutrepont and O. Jodogne, Académie royale de Belgique, Classe des lettres et des sciences morales et politiques, Collection des anciens auteurs belges, n.s., 3 vols (Brussels, 1935–7)

Mollat, M., 'Recherches sur les finances des ducs Valois de Bourgogne', *Revue historique*, 219 (1958), 285–321

Mollat, M., 'Une enquête à poursuivre: la situation financière de Charles le Téméraire dans les derniers temps de son règne', in *Cinqcentième anniversaire de la bataille de Nancy (1477). Actes du colloque organisé par l'Institut de recherche régionale en sciences sociales, humaines et économiques de l'Université de Nancy II (Nancy, 22–24 septembre 1977)*, Annales de l'Est, Mémoires, 62 (Nancy, 1979), 175–85

Moreau, R.E. de, *Histoire de l'Église en Belgique*, 5 vols (Brussels, 1940–52); IV (1949) = *L'église aux Pays-Bas sous les ducs de Bourgogne et Charles Quint, 1378–1559*

Morel, P., *Les Lombards dans la Flandre française et le Hainaut* (Lille, 1908)

Morselli, A., 'Vela e diamante', *Atti e memorie dell'Accademia di scienze, lettere e arti di Modena*, 5th ser., 9 (1950–1), 233–45

Motta, E., 'Musici alla corte degli Sforza. Ricerche e documenti milanesi', *ASL*, 2nd ser., 4 (1887), 29–64, 278–340, 515–61

Motta, E., 'Un documento per la battaglia di Nancy (1477)', *Bollettino storico della Svizzera italiana*, 10 (1888), 191–2

Motta, E., 'Spigolature d'archivio per la storia di Venezia nella seconda metà del Quattrocento (dall'Archivio di Stato milanese). I. Cassandra nel 1477?', *Archivio veneto*, 36 (1888), 377–8

Mugnier, F., 'La desconfiture de Charles le Téméraire', *Mémoires et documents publiés par la Société savoisienne d'histoire et archéologie*, 40 (1901), 145–69

NAGEL, R., 'Eine portugiesisch–klevische Heirat im Jahre 1453', *Aufsätze zur portugiesischen Kulturgeschichte. Portugiesische Forschungen der Görresgesellschaft. Reihe I*, 13 (1974–5), 320–7

Narducci, E., 'Intorno all'autenticità di un codice vaticano contenente il trattato di Boezio "De consolatione philosophiae" scritta di mano di Giovanni Boccaccio. Memoria seguita da un'appendice di documenti riguardanti le ambascerie di Bernardo Bembo', *Atti dell'Accademia Nazionale dei Lincei. Memorie della classe di scienze morali, storiche e filologiche*, 8 (1882), 243–63

Négociations diplomatiques de la France avec la Toscane, ed. A. Desjardins and G. Canestrini, Collection de documents inédits sur l'histoire de France, 1st ser., Histoire politique, 5 vols (Paris, 1859–86)

Nehring, K., *Matthias Corvinus, Kaiser Friedrich III. und das Reich. Zum hunyadisch–habsburgischen Gegensatz im Donauraum*, Südosteuropäische Arbeiten, 72 (Munich, 1975)

Neilson, G., 'A Venetian's commonplaces', *Athenaeum*, 3556 (21 December 1895), 871–2

Nolhac, P. de, *La bibliothèque de Fulvio Orsini. Contributions à l'histoire des collections d'Italie et à l'étude de la Renaissance*, Bibliothèque de l'École des Hautes Études, Sciences philologiques et historiques, 64 (Paris, 1887)

Noto, A., *Gli amici dei poveri di Milano. Sei secoli di lasciti e donativi cronologicamente esposti* (Milan, 1953)

Nuovi documenti per la storia del Rinascimento, ed. T. de Marinis and A. Perosa (Florence, 1970)

OFFLER, H.S., 'The heroic age', in E. Bonjour, H.S. Offler and G.R. Potter, *A short history of Switzerland* (Oxford, 1952), 107–40

Onofrio di Santa Croce: see Santa Croce, O. di

Oudenbosch, A. d', *Chronique. Nouvelle édition*, ed. C. de Borman, Publications de la Société des bibliophiles liégeois, 35 (Liège, 1902)

Ourliac, P., 'Louis XI et le cardinal Bessarion', *Bulletin de la Société archéologique du Midi de la France*, 3rd ser., 5 (1942), 33–52

Ourliac, P., 'Le concordat de 1472. Étude sur les rapports de Louis XI et de Sixte IV', *Revue historique de droit français et étranger*, 4th ser., 21 (1942), 174–223, and 22 (1943), 117–54 (translated, in slightly abbreviated form, as 'The concordat of 1472: an essay on the relations between Louis XI and Sixtus IV', in *The recovery of France in the fifteenth century*, ed. P.S. Lewis (London, 1971), 102–84, 370–93)

PALMER, J.J.N, 'English foreign policy 1388–99', in *The reign of Richard II. Essays in honour of May McKisack*, ed. F.R.H. du Boulay and C.M. Barron (London, 1971), 75–107

Palmer, J.J.N., 'England, France, the papacy and the Flemish succession, 1361–9', *JMH*, 2 (1976), 339–64

Palmieri, M., *Liber de temporibus*, ed. G. Scaramella, RSI, XXV/1 (Città di Castello, 1906)

Palumbo, P.F., *Medio Evo meridionale: fonti e letteratura storica dalle invasioni alla fine del periodo aragonese* (Rome, 1978)

Paparelli, G., *Callimaco Esperiente (Filippo Buonaccorsi)*, Collana umanistica, 4 (Salerno, 1971)

Paquet, J., 'Une ébauche de la nonciature de Flandre au XVᵉ siècle: les missions dans les Pays-Bas de Luc de Tolentis, évêque de Sebenico, 1462–1484', *BIHBR*, 25 (1949), 27–144

Paquot, J.N., *Mémoires pour servir à l'histoire littéraire des dix-sept provinces des Pays-Bas, de la principauté de Liège et de quelques contées voisines ...*, 18 vols (Louvain, 1763–70)

Paravicini, W., *Guy de Brimeu. Der burgundische Staat und seine adlige Führungsschicht unter Karl dem Kühnen*, Pariser historische Studien, 12 (Bonn, 1975)

Paravicini, W., 'Bemerkungen zu Richard Vaughan: Charles the Bold', *Francia* (Paris), 4 (1976), 757–73

Paravicini, W., 'Soziale Schichtungen und soziale Mobilität am Hofe der Herzöge von Burgund', *Francia* (Paris), 5 (1977), 127–82

Paschini, P., *Roma nel Rinascimento* (Bologna, 1940)

Pasquier, F., *Un favori de Louis XI. Boffille de Juge, comte de Castres, vice-roi de Roussillon. Publication d'après des documents inédits du chartrier de Léran (Ariège)*, Archives historiques de l'Albigeois, X (Albi, 1914)

Passero, G., *Storie in forma di giornali*, ed. V.M. Altobelli and M.M. Vecchioni (Naples, 1785)

Pastor, L., *The history of the popes from the close of the Middle Ages drawn from the secret archives of the Vatican and other sources*, trans. F.E. Antrobus *et al.*, 40 vols (London–St. Louis, Miss., 1923–53)

Pavanello, G., *Un maestro del Quattrocento (Giovanni Aurelio Augurello)* (Venice, 1905)

Paviot, J., *La politique navale des ducs de Bourgogne (1384–1482)*, Collection Economies et sociétés (Lille, 1995)

Pažout, J., 'König Georg von Böhmen und die Concilfrage im Jahre 1467. Ein Beitrag zur Geschichte von Böhmen', *Archiv für österreichische Geschichte*, 40 (1869), 323–71

Périnelle, G., 'Dépêches de Nicolas de' Roberti, ambassadeur d'Hercule Iᵉʳ, duc de Ferrare, auprès du roi Louis XI (novembre 1478–juillet 1480)', *MAHEFR*, 24 (1904), 139–203, 425–77

Perrens, F.T., *The history of Florence under the domination of Cosimo, Piero, Lorenzo de' Medicis, 1434–1492*, trans. H. Lynch (London, 1892)

Perret, P.M., 'Le manuscrit de Cicco Simonetta (Manuscrit Latin 10133 de la Bibliothèque Nationale)', *Notices et extraits des manuscrits de la Bibliothèque Nationale et autres bibliothèques*, 34 (1891), 323–63

Perret, P.M., 'Jacques Galéot et la republique de Venise', *BEC*, 52 (1891), 590–614

Perret, P.M., 'Boffille de Juge, comte de Castres, et la république de Venise', *Annales du Midi*, 3 (1891), 159–231

Perret, P.M., *Histoire des relations de la France avec Venise du XIIIᵉ siècle à l'avènement de Charles VIII*, 2 vols (Paris, 1896)

Persico, T., *Diomede Carafa, uomo di stato e scrittore del secolo XV, con un frammento originale dei "Doveri del principe", altri documenti inediti ed illustrazioni* (Naples, 1899)

Pescador del Hoyo, M. del Carmen, 'Tres documentos de Federico de Napoles en los fondos del Archivo Histórico Nacional de Madrid', in *Studi in onore di Riccardo Filangieri*, 2 vols (Naples, 1959), II, 249–60

Peter, J., *L'abbaye de Liessies en Hainaut depuis ses origines jusqu'auprès la réforme de Louis de Blois, 764–1566. Thèse présentée à la Faculté des Lettres de l'Université de Lille* (Lille, 1912)

Petrucci, F., 'Per un'edizione critica dei *Memoriali* di Diomede Carafa. Problemi e metodi', *ASPN*, 94 (1976), 213–34

Peyronnet, G., 'Riflessioni sul valore della storia militare a proposito di un recente lavoro', *ASI*, 109 (1951), 68–83

Peyronnet, G., 'La politica italiana di Luigi delfino di Francia (1444–1461)', *RSI*, 64 (1952), 19–44

Pfister, C., *Histoire de Nancy*, 3 vols (Paris, 1902–9)

Phillipps, T., 'Account of the marriage of Margaret, sister of King Edward IV, to Charles, duke of Burgundy, in 1468', *Archaeologia*, 31 (1846), 326–38

Pieri, P., 'Il "Governo et exercitio de la militia" di Orso degli Orsini e i "Memoriali" di Diomede Carafa', *ASPN*, 58 (1933), 99–212

Pieri, P., *Il Rinascimento e la crisi militare italiana*, Biblioteca di cultura storica, 45, 2nd edtn (Turin, 1952)

Pillinini, G., *Il sistema degli stati italiani 1454–1494*, Collana Ca' Foscari, Facoltà di Lingue e Letterature Straniere, Seminario di storia, Studi e ricerche, I (Venice, 1970)

Pisani, M., *Un avventuriero del Quattrocento. La vita e le opere di Benedetto Dei*, Biblioteca della "Rassegna", 5 (Genoa etc., 1923)

Plancher, U., *Histoire générale et particulière de Bourgogne*, 4 vols (Dijon, 1739–81)

Platt, C., *The castle in medieval England and Wales* (London, 1982)

Pontano, G.G., *Lettere inedite in nome de' reali di Napoli*, ed. F. Gabotto, Scelta di curiosità letterarie inedite o rare del secolo XIII al XIX, CCXLV (Bologna, 1893)

Pontieri, E., *Per la storia del regno di Ferrante I d'Aragona re di Napoli. Studi e ricerche*, 2nd edtn (Naples, 1969); contains, among others, 'Sulle mancate nozze tra Federico d'Aragona e Maria di Borgogna (1474–1476)' (pp. 161–208; first published 1939)

Porzio, C., *La congiura dei baroni del regno di Napoli contra il re Ferdinando Primo e gli altri scritti*, ed. E. Pontieri (Naples, 1958)

Prevenier, W., 'Financiën en boekhouding in de Bourgondische periode. Nieuwe bronnen en resultaten', *TG*, 82 (1969), 469–81

Prevenier, W., 'Officials in town and countryside in the Low Countries. Social and professional developments from the fourteenth to the sixteenth century', *Acta Historiae Neerlandicae*, 7 (1974), 1–17

QUELLER, D.E., *Early Venetian legislation on ambassadors*, Travaux d'humanisme et Renaissance, LXXXVIII (Geneva 1966)

Queller, D.E., *The office of ambassador in the Middle Ages* (Princeton, N.J., 1967)

RAPONI, N., 'Antonio d'Appiano', *DBI*, III (1961), 535–7

Recueil de choses advenues du temps et gouvernement de très haulte mémoire feu Charles, duc de Bourgogne, estant le seigneur du Fay gouverneur au pays de Luxembourg, in *Publications de la Société pour la recherche et la conservation des monuments historiques dans le Grand-Duché de Luxembourg*, III (Arlon, 1847), 85–153

Regis Ferdinandi Primi instructionum liber, ed. L. Volpicella, Società storica napoletana, Monumenti storici, II: Documenti (Naples, 1916)

Reiffenberg, F.A.F.T. de, *Histoire de l'Ordre de la Toison d'Or* (Brussels, 1830)

Rémy, F., *Les grandes indulgences pontificales aux Pays-Bas à la fin du moyen âge 1300–1531. Essai sur leur histoire et leur importance financière*, Université de Louvain, Recueil de travaux publiés par les membres des Conférences d'histoire et de philologie, 2nd ser., 15 (Louvain, 1928)

Reumont, A. von, *Della diplomazia italiana dal secolo XIII al XVI* (Florence, 1857)

Reumont, A. von, *Lorenzo de' Medici il Magnifico*, 2 vols (Leipzig, 1874)

Rey, M., and R. Fiétier, 'Le moyen âge du XIIᵉ au XVᵉ siècle', in *Histoire de Besançon*, ed. C. Fohlen, 2 vols, 2nd edtn (Besançon, 1981–2), I, 329–572

Richard, J., *La Papauté et les missions d'Orient au moyen âge (XIIIᵉ–XVᵉ siècles)*, Collection de l'École française de Rome, 33 (Rome, 1977)

Richard, P., 'Origines de la nonciature de France. Nonces résidents avant Léon X, 1456–1511', *Revue des questions historiques*, 88 (1905), 103–47

Roberti, G., S. *Francesco di Paola fondatore dell'Ordine dei Minimi (1416–1507). Storia della sua vita*, 2nd edtn (Rome, 1963)

Rochon, A., *La jeunesse de Laurent de Médicis (1449–78)*, Les Classiques de l'humanisme, Études, 9 (Paris, 1963)

Rogers, F.M., *The travels of the Infante Dom Pedro of Portugal*, Harvard Studies in Romance Languages, XXVI (Cambridge, Mass., 1961)

Roover, R. de, *Money, banking and credit in medieval Bruges. Italian merchant-bankers, Lombards and moneylenders. A study in the origins of banking*, Publications of the Mediaeval Academy of America, 51 (Cambridge, Mass., 1948)

Roover, R. de, *The rise and decline of the Medici bank 1397–1494*, Harvard Studies in Business History, XXI (Cambridge, Mass., 1963)

Rosi, M., 'La congiura di Gerolamo Gentile', *ASI*, 5th ser., 16 (1895), 176–205

Ross, C., *Edward IV* (London, 1974)

Rott, J., 'Note sur quelques comptes de collecteurs pontificaux du XVe siècle concernant la France', *MAHEFR*, 51 (1934), 293–327

Roye, J. de, *Journal connu sous le nom de chronique scandaleuse 1460–1483*, ed. B. de Mandrot, Société de l'histoire de France, 2 vols (Paris, 1894–6)

Ryder, A.F.C., 'Antonio Beccadelli: a humanist in government', in *Cultural aspects of the Italian Renaissance. Essays in honour of Paul Oskar Kristeller*, ed. C.H. Clough (Manchester–New York, 1976), 123–40

Ryder, A.F.C., *The kingdom of Naples under Alfonso the Magnanimous. The making of a modern state* (Oxford, 1976)

Ryder, G.F., 'La politica italiana di Alfonso d'Aragona (1442–1458)', *ASPN*, 77 (1958), 43–106

SABLON DU CORAIL, A., 'Les étrangers au service de Marie de Bourgogne: de l'armée de Charles le Téméraire à l'armée de Maximilien (1477–1482)', *Revue du Nord*, 84 (2002), 389–412

Sambin, P., 'Il Panormita e il dono d'una reliquia di Livio', *IMU*, 1 (1958), 276–81

Santa Croce, O. di, *Mémoire du légat Onufrius sur les affaires de Liège (1468)*, ed. S. Bormans (Brussels, 1885)

Santini, E., *Firenze e i suoi "oratori" nel Quattrocento*, Biblioteca "Sandron" di scienze e lettere (Milan, etc., 1922)

Santoro, C., *Gli uffici del dominio sforzesco (1450–1500)* (Milan, 1947)

Savy, P., 'A l'école bourguignonne. Rodolfo Gonzaga à la cour de Bourgogne (1469–1470)', *Revue du Nord*, 84 (2002), 343–66

Saxl, F., 'A Marsilio Ficino manuscript written in Bruges in 1475, and the alum monopoly of the popes', *JWCI*, 1 (1937), 61–2

Schaube, A., 'Zur Entstehungsgeschichte der ständigen Gesandt-schaften', *MIÖG*, 10 (1889), 500–52

Schaumburg, Wilwolt von: see Wilwolt von Schaumburg

Scheurer, R., 'Candida, Giovanni (Jean) di', *DBI*, XVII (1974), 774–6

Schiappoli, I., *Napoli aragonese: traffici e attività marinare*, Biblioteca di studi meridionali, 3 (Naples, 1972)

Schivenoglia, A., *Cronaca di Mantova dal MCCCCXLV al MCCC-CLXXXIV*, ed. C. d'Arco, in *Raccolta di cronisti e documenti storici inediti*, II (Milan, 1856), 121–94

Schlecht, J., *Andrea Zamometić und der Basler Konzilsversuch vom Jahre 1482*, Quellen und Forschungen aus dem Gebiete der Geschichte, 8, one volume only published (Paderborn, 1903)

Schneider, J., 'Un conseiller des ducs de Bourgogne: Georges de Bade, évêque de Metz (1459–1484)', in *Cinq-centième anniversaire de la bataille de Nancy (1477). Actes du colloque organisé par l'Institut de recherche régionale en sciences sociales, humaines et économiques de l'Université de Nancy II (Nancy, 22–24 septembre 1977)*, Annales de l'Est, Mémoires, 62 (Nancy, 1979), 305–38

Schneider, J., 'Campobasso en Lorraine', *Le pays lorrain*, 63 (1982), 5–24

Schryver, A. de, 'Notes pour servir à l'histoire du costume au XVe s. dans les anciens Pays-Bas et en Bourgogne', *AB*, 29 (1957), 29–42

Schulz, A.M., 'The Columba altarpiece and Roger van der Weyden's stylistic development', *Münchner Jahrbuch der bildenden Kunst*, 3rd ser., 22 (1971), 63–116

Schulz, W., *Andreaskreuz und Christusorden. Isabella von Portugal und der burgundische Kreuzzug*, Historische Schriften der Universität Freiburg, Schweiz, 1 (Freiburg, 1976)

Schwarzkopf, U., 'La cour de Bourgogne et la Toison d'Or', *PCEEB*, 5 (1963), 91–104

Scofield, C., *The life and reign of Edward the Fourth, king of England and of France and lord of Ireland*, 2 vols (London, 1923)

Sieveking, H., *Die Handlungsbücher der Medici*, Österreichische Akademie der Wissenschaften, Sitzungsberichte: Philosophisch-historische Klasse, CLI, Abhandlung 5 (Vienna, 1906)

Signorini, R., 'Lettura storica degli affreschi della "Camera degli Sposi" di A. Mantegna', *JWCI*, 38 (1975–6), 109–35

Signorini, R., '"Manzare poco, bevere aqua asai et dormire manco": suggerimenti dietetici vittoriniani di Ludovico II Gonzaga al figlio Gianfrancesco e un sospetto pitagorico', in *Vittorino da Feltre e la sua scuola: umanesimo, pedagogia, arti. Atti del Convegno di studi promosso dalla Fondazione Giorgio Cini, dai Comuni di Feltre e di Mantova e dall'Accademia Virgiliana di Mantova a conclusione delle celebrazioni del sesto centenario della nascita di Vittorino da Feltre, Venezia–Feltre–Mantova, 9–11 novembre 1979*, ed. N. Giannetto, Civiltà veneziana, Saggi, 31 (Florence, 1981), 115–48

Silvestri Baffi, R., 'Di Isabella del Balzo e del suo viaggio attraverso la Puglia', in *Studi di storia pugliese in onore di Giuseppe Chiarelli*, ed. M. Paone, 2 vols (Galatina, 1972–3), II, 321–51

Simonetta, C., *I Diarii*, ed. A.R. Natale, Acta italica B, one volume only published (Milan, 1962)

Simonetta, G., *Rerum gestarum Francisci Sfortiae Mediolanensium ducis commentarii*, ed. G. Soranzo, RSI, XXI/2 (Bologna, 1959)

Snieders, F., 'Bertino, Francesco', in *Dictionnaire d'histoire et de géographie ecclésiastiques* (Paris, 1912–), VIII (1935), col. 1613

Soldi Rondinini, G., 'Giovan Pietro Panigarola e il "reportage" moderno', *Archiv des historischen Vereins des Kantons Bern*, 60 (1976), 135–54

Soldi Rondinini, G., 'Condottieri italiens au service de Charles le Hardi, pendant les guerres de Suisse (1474–1477)', *PCEEB*, 20 (1980), 55–62

Soldi Rondinini, G., 'Milano, il Regno di Napoli e gli aragonesi (secoli XIV–XV)', in *Gli Sforza a Milano e in Lombardia e i loro rapporti con gli stati italiani ed europei (1450–1535). Convegno internazionale, Milano 18–21 maggio 1981* (Milan, 1982), 229–90

Solon, P.D., 'Popular response to standing military forces in fifteenth-century France', *SR*, 19 (1972), 78–111

Solsona Climent, F., 'Aspectos de la dominación angevina en Cataluña (1466–1472). La participación italiana y francesa en la revolución contra Juan II de Aragón', *Cuadernos de Historia J. Zurita*, 14–15 (1963), 31–54

Sora, V., 'I conti di Anguillara, dalla loro origine al 1465', *Archivio della Società romana di storia patria*, 29 (1906), 397–442; 30 (1907), 53–118

Soría, A., *Los humanistas de la corte de Alfonso el Magnánimo (según los epistolarios)* (Granada, 1956)

Sorricchio, L., 'Angelo ed Antonio Probi, ambasciatori di Ferdinando I d'Aragona (1464–1482)', *ASPN*, 21 (1896), 148–69

Sposato, P., 'Attività commerciali degli Aragonesi nella seconda metà del Quattrocento', in *Studi in onore di Riccardo Filangieri*, 2 vols (Naples, 1959), III, 213–31

Spufford, P., *Monetary problems and policies in the Burgundian Netherlands 1433–1496* (Leiden, 1970)

Stegmann, A., 'Commynes et Machiavel', in *Studies on Machiavelli*, ed. M.P. Gilmore (Florence, 1972), 267–84

Stein, H., *Olivier de la Marche, historien, poète et diplomate bourguignon* (Brussels–Paris, 1888)

Stein, H., *Charles de France, frère de Louis XI*, Mémoires et documents publiés par la Société de l'École des Chartes, X (Paris, 1919/21)

TALLONE, A., *Parlamento sabaudo . . .*, Atti delle assemblee costituzionali italiane dal medioevo al 1831. Ser. 1: Stati generali e provinciali, Sez. 5: Parlamenti piemontesi, 13 vols (Bologna, 1928–46) — IV/1 (1931) = 1458–72; V/1 (1932) = 1472–90

Taylor, F.L., *The art of war in Italy 1494–1529* (Cambridge, 1921)

Thelliez, C., 'A propos du testament de Jean de Bourgogne. Contribution à l'histoire du diocèse de Cambrai et de la maison de Bourgogne-Valois', *Anciens pays et assemblées d'états*, 62 (1973), 31–91

Thompson, C., and L. Campbell, *Hugo van der Goes and the Trinity Panels in Edinburgh* (Edinburgh, 1974)

Thomson, J.A.F., *Popes and princes, 1417–1517. Politics and polity in the late medieval Church*, Early Modern Europe Today series (London, 1980)

Tissoni Benvenuti, A., 'Un nuovo documento sulla "Camera degli sposi" del Mantegna', *IMU*, 24 (1981), 357–60

Tourneur, V., 'Jehan de Candida, diplomate et médailleur, au service de la maison de Bourgogne, 1472–1480', *Revue belge de numismatique*, 70 (1914), 381–411; 71 (1919), 7–48, 251–300

Tranchedino, F., *Diplomatische Geheimschriften. Codex Vindobonensis 2398 der Österreichischen Nationalbibliothek. Faksimileausgabe. Einführung Walter Höflechner*, Codices selecti phototypice impressi, XXII (Graz, 1970)

Truffi, R., *Giostre e cantori di giostre. Studi e ricerche di storia e di letteratura* (Rocca S. Casciano, 1911)

Tummulillis, A. de, da Sant'Elia, *Notabilia temporum*, ed. C. Corvisieri, Fonti per la storia d'Italia pubblicate dall'Istituto Storico Italiano, VII: Scrittori, secolo XV (Rome–Livorno, 1890)

UGHELLI, F., *Italia Sacra sive de episcopis Italiae et insularum adjacentium*, 10 vols, 2nd edtn (Venice, 1717–22)

Urkundliche Nachträge zur österreichischen–deutschen Geschichte im Zeitalter Friedrich III., ed. A. Bachmann, Fontes rerum Austriacarum, zweite Abteilung: Diplomataria et acta, XLVI (Vienna, 1892)

Uytven, R. van, 'Wereldlijke overheid en reguliere geestelijkheid in Brabant tijdens de late Middeleeuwen', in *Sources de l'histoire religieuse de la Belgique. Moyen âge et temps modernes / Bronnen voor de religieuze geschiedenis van België. Middeleeuwen en moderne tijden. Actes du Colloque de Bruxelles, 30 nov.–2 déc. 1967 (I^e et IIe sections)*, Bibliothèque de la Revue d'histoire ecclésiastique, 47 (Louvain, 1968), 48–134

VAL, M.I. del, *Isabel la Católica, princesa (1468–1474)*, Estudios y documentos del Instituto "Isabel la Católica" de historia ecclesiástica, 9 (Valladolid, 1974)

Vale, M.G.A., *Charles VII*, (Eyre Methuen) French Monarchs Series, I (London, 1974)

Vale, M.G.A., *War and chivalry. Warfare and aristocratic culture in England, France and Burgundy at the end of the Middle Ages* (London, 1981)

Valeri, D.G., 'Della signoria di Francesco Sforza nella Marca', *ASL*, 2nd ser., 1 (1884), 35–78, 252–304

Vander Linden, H., *Itinéraires de Charles, duc de Bourgogne, Marguerite d'York et Marie de Bourgogne (1467–1477)* (Brussels, 1936)

Vander Linden, H., *Itinéraires de Philippe le Bon, duc de Bourgogne (1419–1467), et de Charles, comte de Charolais (1433–67)* (Brussels, 1940)

Van Uytven, R,: see Uytven, R. van

Vaughan, R., *Philip the Bold. The formation of the Burgundian state* (London, 1962)

Vaughan, R., *John the Fearless. The growth of Burgundian power* (London, 1966)

Vaughan, R., *Philip the Good. The apogee of Burgundy* (London, 1970)

Vaughan, R., *Charles the Bold. The last Valois duke of Burgundy* (London, 1973)

Vaughan, R., *Valois Burgundy* (London, 1975)

Ventura, A., and V. Pecoraro, 'Bembo, Bernardo', *DBI*, VIII (1966), 103–9

Vespasiano da Bisticci, *Le Vite*, ed. A. Greco, 2 vols (Florence, 1970–6)

Vicens y Vives, J., *Fernando el Católico principe de Aragón, rey de Sicilia 1458–1478 (Sicilia en la política de Juan II de Aragón)*, Biblioteca "Reyes Católicos", Estudios, 3 (Madrid, 1952)

Vicens y Vives, J., *Juan II de Aragón (1398–1479). Monarquía y revolución en la España del siglo XV*, El hombre y su tiempo, I (Barcelona, 1953)

Vicens y Vives, J., *Historia crítica de la vida y reinado de Fernando II de Aragón*, Publicaciónes de la Institución "Fernando el Católico", 145 (Zaragoza, 1962)

Vigneulles, P. de, *Gedenkbuch aus den Jahren 1471 bis 1522*, ed. H. Michelant, Bibliothek des Litterarischen Vereins in Stuttgart, XXIV (Stuttgart, 1852)

Vigneulles, P. de, *Chronique*, ed. C. Bruneau, 4 vols (Metz, 1927–33)

Vocht, H. de, *History of the foundation and the rise of the Collegium Trilingue Lovaniense 1517–1550*, Humanistica Lovaniensia, 10–13, 4 vols (Louvain, 1951–5)

Volpicella, L., *Federico d'Aragona e la fine del regno di Napoli nel MDI* (Naples, 1908)

Volta, Z., 'Del Collegio Universitario Marliani in Pavia', *ASL*, 2nd ser., 9 (1892), 590–628

WALSH, R.J., 'The coming of humanism to the Low Countries: some Italian influences at the court of Charles the Bold', *Humanistica Lovaniensia*, 25 (1976), 146–97

Walsh, R.J., 'Charles the Bold and the crusade: politics and propaganda', *JMH*, 3 (1977), 53–86

Walsh, R.J., 'Music and Quattrocento diplomacy: the singer Jean Cordier between Milan, Naples and Burgundy in 1475', *AKG*, 60 (1978), 439–42

Walsh, R.J., 'Vespasiano da Bisticci, Francesco Bertini and Charles the Bold: an examination of an episode in the *Vite* as an illustration of Charles the Bold's relations with Italy', *European Studies Review*, 10 (1980), 401–27

Walsh, R.J., 'Diplomatic aspects of Charles the Bold's relations with the Holy See', *BMGN*, 95 (1980), 265–78

Walsh, R.J., 'Une citation inexacte de Lucain par Charles le Téméraire et Louis XI: de l'évaluation de l'instruction princière au quinzième siècle', *MA*, 86 (1980), 439–51

Walsh, R.J., 'Relations between Milan and Burgundy in the period 1450–1476', in *Gli Sforza a Milano e in Lombardia e i loro rapporti con gli stati italiani ed europei (1450–1535). Convegno internazionale, Milano, 18–21 maggio 1981* (Milan, 1982), 369–96

Walter, I., 'Bertini, Francesco', *DBI*, IX (1967), 540–2

Warburg, A.M., 'Flandrische Kunst und florentinische Frührenaissance', first published 1902, reprinted (1) in his *Gesammelte Schriften. Die Erneuerung der heidnischen Antike. Kulturwissenschaftliche Beiträge zur Geschichte der europäischen Renaissance*, ed. G. Bing, 2 vols (Leipzig–Berlin, 1932), 187–206 [the *Gesammelte Schriften* have now been published in English as *The renewal of pagan antiquity: contributions to the cultural history of the European Renaissance (texts and documents)*, trans. D. Britt (Getty Trust Publications, 2000)], and (2) in his *Ausgewählte Schriften und Würdigungen*, ed. D. Wuttke and C.G. Heise, Saecula spiritualia, 1 (Baden-Baden, 1980), 103–24

Waurin, J. de, *Anchiennes chroniques d'Engleterre*, ed. E. Dupont, Société de l'histoire de France, 3 vols (Paris, 1863)

Weinstein, D., *Savonarola and Florence. Prophecy and patriotism in the Renaissance* (Princeton, N.J., 1970)

Wellens, R., *Les États généraux des Pays-Bas des origines à la fin du règne de Philippe le Beau (1464–1506)*, Anciens pays et assemblées d'états, 64 (Heule, 1974)

Wielant, P., *Recueil des antiquités de Flandre*, ed. J.J. de Smet, in *Collection des chroniques belges inédits*, IV (Brussels, 1865), 1–442

Wiesflecker, H., *Kaiser Maximilian I. Das Reich, Österreich und Europa an der Wende zur Neuzeit*, 5 vols so far published (Munich, 1971–86)

Wilwolt von Schaumburg, *Die Geschichten und Taten*, ed. A. von Keller, Bibliothek des Litterarischen Vereins in Stuttgart, L (Stuttgart, 1859)

Wise, T., *Medieval warfare* (London, 1976)

Wolfe, M., *The fiscal system of Renaissance France*, Yale Series in Economic History (New Haven–London, 1972)

ZAMBARBIERI, T., 'Milano e la Borgogna tra il 1474 e il 1477: le loro relazioni diplomatiche nel contesto dell'Europa mediana', *Libri e documenti*, 8/1 (1982), 33–69; 8/2 (1982), 1–36

Zambotti, B., *Diario ferrarese dall'anno 1476 sino al 1504*, ed. G. Pardi, RSI, XXIV/7/ii (Bologna, 1934)

Zilverberg, S.B.J., *David van Bourgondië, bisschop van Terwaan en van Utrecht (1427–1496)*, Bijdragen van het Instituut voor Middeleeuwse Geschiedenis der Rijks-Universiteit te Utrecht, XXIV (Groningen–Jakarta, 1951)

Zippel, G., *Storia e cultura del Rinascimento italiano* (Padua, 1979);

contains, among others, 'L'allume di Tolfa e il suo commercio' (pp. 288–391; first published 1907)

Zorzi, G., 'Un vicentino alla corte di Paolo Secondo (Chierigino Chiericati e il suo Trattato della Milizia)', *Nuovo archivio veneto*, n.s., 30 (1915), 369–434

Unpublished theses and dissertations

Ditcham, B.G.H., 'The employment of foreign mercenary troops in the French royal armies — 1415–1470' (Ph.D. thesis, University of Edinburgh, 1978)

Fobe, A.M., 'De diplomaten van het Boergondische hof (1477–1506). De sociale en technische ontwikkelingsvormen van de moderne diplomatie in de Lage Landen, van Maria van Boergondië tot aan de dood van Filips de Schone', 3 vols ('Proefschrift ter verkrijging van een graad van Licenciaat in de Letteren en Wijsbegeerte', Rijksuniversiteit Gent, 1970)

Maeght, X., 'Les emprunts de Charles le Téméraire d'après les comptes de la recette générale de l'état bourguignon, et quelques comptes urbains' ('Mémoire principal pour le Diplôme d'Études Supérieures', Université de Lille, 1956)

Mangin, J., 'Guillaume de Rochefort, conseiller de Charles le Téméraire et chancelier de France. Notice sur Guy de Rochefort' ('Thèse de licenciat ès lois et lettres de l'École des Chartes', Paris, 1936)

Pesez, J.M., 'Chevaucheurs et courriers du duc de Bourgogne Charles le Téméraire' ('Thèse de Diplôme d'Études Supérieures soutenue devant la Faculté des Lettres', Université de Lille, 1954)

Schmidt-Sinns, D., 'Studien zum Heerwesen der Herzöge von Burgund 1465–1477' (dissertation, Georg-August Universität, Göttingen, 1966)

Taparel, H., 'Le duché Valois de Bourgogne et l'Orient ottoman au XIV et XV° siècle' ('Thèse de 3° cycle, Université de Toulouse le Mirail, U.E.R. d'Histoire, année 1981–2')

Walsh, R.J., 'Charles the Bold, last Valois duke of Burgundy 1467–1477, and Italy' (Ph.D. thesis, University of Hull, 1977)

APPENDIX: Earlier publications of Richard J. Walsh relating to Charles the Bold

'The coming of humanism to the Low Countries: some Italian

influences at the court of Charles the Bold', *Humanistica Lovaniensia*, XXV (1976), 146–97

'Charles the Bold and the Crusade: politics and propaganda', *The Journal of Medieval History*, III (1977), 53–86

'Music and Quattrocento diplomacy: the singer Jean Cordier between Milan, Naples and Burgundy in 1475', *Archiv für Kulturgeschichte*, LX (1978), 439–42

'Vespasiano da Bisticci, Francesco Bertini and Charles the Bold: an examination of an episode in the *Vite* as an illustration of Charles the Bold's relations with Italy', *European Studies Review*, X (1980), 401–27

'Diplomatic aspects of Charles the Bold's relations with the Holy See', *Bijdragen en mededelingen betreffende de geschiedenis der Nederlanden*, XCV (1980), 265–78

'Une citation inexacte de Lucain par Charles le Téméraire et Louis XI: de l'évaluation de l'instruction princière au quinzième siècle', *Le Moyen Age*, LXXXVI (1980), 439–51

'Relations between Milan and Burgundy in the period 1450–1476', in *Gli Sforza a Milano e in Lombardia e i loro rapporti con gli stati italiani ed europei (1450–1535)* (International Conference, Milan, 1981) (Milan, 1982), 369–96

'Charles the Bold and the "monstrous ransom" story', in *The Bulletin of the Society for Renaissance Studies*, V (1988), 1–13

Bibliographical Supplement

Werner Paravicini

Over thirty years ago, in 1973, Richard Vaughan announced in his *Charles the Bold* that a pupil, Richard Walsh, was engaged upon a doctoral thesis at Hull University entitled 'Charles the Bold and Italy'. I then wrote that 'maybe here was the most exciting theme which Burgundian historiography still had to offer' (*Francia*, 4, 1976, 762) — a verdict the reader will now find fulfilled and justified. In October 1977 the thesis (comprising 937 pages) was submitted and the following year was approved. Since then the text has been available to scholars on microfilm and on microfilm-print. Moreover, Richard Walsh has subsequently developed themes from it in a number of important published articles, and these touch on certain key aspects (see the list of Walsh's publications in the Appendix to his Bibliography). Yet the thesis itself has remained unpublished. It ought to have been printed shortly after completion, and why this did not happen I shall never understand. The subject is magnificent, the study supported with archival research of exceptional breadth and depth, its mastery virtually perfect. My only personal regret remains that a prosopographical list of the Italians in Burgundian service does not enrich it.

But here, at last, is the thesis itself, slightly reduced in length and revised. It is published thanks to the insight and stubborn insistence of Dr Cecil Clough. In March 1996 he and I met in Paris at the Conference 'Les Princes et l'Histoire', where over a dinner we chatted about 'cabbages and kings'. Incautiously I remarked that unfortunately Richard Walsh's thesis remained unpublished. He told me of a failed 1985 attempt with a draft here only slightly amended. He nailed me down, stressing the necessity of my doing something to promote publication, namely by reading the draft, and revising it in the light of over a decade's published researches, by contributing *addenda et corrigenda*. This, he stressed, I uniquely could do, given my specialist knowledge, whereas Richard Walsh could not, since the obligation of employment had necessitated his turning to other matters in the mid-1980s. Alas! such a task in detail was what I could not and cannot do: *ars longa, vita brevis*. However, fortunately, there was no need to rework the text. Being based almost entirely on primary sources, it has proved remarkably resistant to ageing — contrary to the common fate of scholarship that is based largely on secondary material. Accordingly, I merely provide below a listing of supplementary bibliographical material, essentially secondary at that, including certain works in preparation, in progress, or forthcoming, together with just a little on untapped archival sources. Having neither the intention nor the possibility of doing more, I stress that this Postscript has no pretensions towards completeness.

Printed primary and secondary works: recent and forthcoming

1 On Charles the Bold
New documentary material is provided by two repertories: one of the correspondence of Charles the Bold, the other of his charters and acts, in part published recently, in part forthcoming, neither being yet complete. (1) *Der Briefwechsel Karls des Kühnen (1433–1477). Inventar*, ed. W. Paravicini, with assistance from S. Dünnebeil and H. Kruse, commentary, notes and indices by S. Baus, S. Dünnebeil, J. Kolb, H. Kruse, H. von Seggern and T. Sgryska, Kieler Werkstücke, D.5, 2 vols. (Frankfurt-am-Main, 1995); (2) H. Stein, *Catalogue des actes de Charles le Téméraire (1467–1477). Mit einem Anhang: Urkunden und Mandate Karls von Burgund, Grafen von Charolais (1433–1467)*, ed. S. Dünnebeil, Instrumenta, German Historical Institute, Paris, D.3 (Sigmaringen, 1999). Material held in the National Library at Paris has been partially calendared (not always correctly) in Anne Le Cam, *Charles le Téméraire: les actes et les lettres conservéees à la Bibliothèque Nationale*, unpublished M.A. thesis, University of Paris IV, ca. 1990.

For Charles the Bold's relations with Louis XI, see J.-M. Cauchies, *Louis XI et Charles le Hardi: De Péronne à Nancy (1468–1477). Le conflit*, Bibliothèque du moyen âge, 8 (Brussels 1996). For his library, see

Charles le Téméraire, 1433–1477, Exhibition Catalogue, Royal Library, Brussels (Brussels, 1977). Burgundian historiography in general for the period of Charles's rule is dealt with in M. Zingel, *Frankreich, das Reich und Burgund im Urteil der burgundischen Historiographie des 15. Jahrhunderts* (Sigmaringen, 1996). On the Burgundian Netherlands in general, see W. Prevenier and W. Blockmans, with picture research by A. Blockmans-Delva, *Les Pays-Bas bourguignons* (Antwerp, 1984), English translation *The Burgundian Netherlands* (Cambridge, 1986); *Le Prince et le Peuple. Images de la société du temps des ducs de Bourgogne (1384–1530),* ed. W. Prevenier (Antwerp, 1999); B. Schnerb, *L'État bourguignon 1363–1477* (Paris, 1999).

For Commynes — on whose importance and treason new light is shed by Walsh (Chapter 7, note 116) — see J. Blanchard, *Commynes l'Européen: L'invention du politique* (Geneva, 1996). Blanchard has now edited both Commynes' *Lettres. Édition critique,* Textes littéraires français, 534 (Geneva, 2001), and his *Mémoires,* Lettres gothiques, 4564 (Paris, 2001). See also J. Dufournet, *Philippe de Comynes: Un historien à l'aube des temps modernes* (Brussels, 1994). In relation to Georges Chastellain, there has appeared a recently identified portion of his *Chronique: Les fragments du livre IV,* ed. J.-C. Delclos (Geneva, 1991). This covers the years 1456–1457 and 1459–1461, and in particular it provides a detailed account of the Burgundian delegation's participation at the Congress of Mantua in 1459. The standard work on Chastellain is G.P. Small, 'The Chronicle and Career of George Chastelain [*sic*], *c.*1415–1475: A study in the political and historical culture of the Court of Burgundy' (Ph.D. thesis, Edinburgh University, 1994), published as *George Chastelain and the shaping of Valois Burgundy,* Royal Historical Society Studies in History (Woodbridge, 1997). For Jean Molinet, Chastellain's pupil and successor as official ducal historiographer, see J. Devaux, *Jean Molinet: Indiciaire bourguignon* (Paris, 1996).

Details of the Burgundian central institutions are admirably provided in J. van Rompaey, *De Grote Raad van de hertogen van Boergondië en het Parlement van Mechelen* (Brussels, 1973). Biographical notices of Charles the Bold's secretaries, including the Italian ones, are to be found in P. Cockshaw, *Prosopographie des secrétaires des ducs de Bourgogne (1384–1477),* Instrumenta, German Historical Institute, Paris (Sigmaringen, forthcoming). For the state's financial organisation — the amount of its income and expenditure having been much greater than previously thought — see C. Albrecht, 'Die Monatsrolle des burgundischen Argentiers Nicolas de Gondeval für den Oktober 1475. Teil I:

Einführung und Edition', *Francia*, 22/1 (1995), 79–127; and 'Eine reformierte Zentralfinanz: Die Finanzverwaltung während der Herrschaft Karls des Kühnen untersucht anhand der Rechnungsüberlieferung des burgundischen Argentiers', in *Finances publiques et finances privées au bas moyen âge*, ed. M. Boone and W. Prevenier (Louvain–Apeldoorn, 1996), 219–37.

Much has recently been published concerning the Order of the Golden Fleece: D'A.J.D. Boulton, *The Knights of the Crown: The Monarchical Orders of Knighthood in Later Medieval Europe, 1325–1520* (Woodbridge, 1987; revised 2nd edn 2000), 356–96; *Les chevaliers de l'Ordre de la Toison d'Or au XVᵉ siècle: Notices bio-bibliographiques*, ed. R. de Smedt, Kieler Werkstücke, D.3 (Frankfurt-am-Main, 1994; revised 2nd edn 2001); *L'Ordre de la Toison d'Or, de Philippe le Bon à Philippe le Beau (1430–1505): Idéal ou reflet d'une société?*, Exhibition Catalogue, Royal Library, Brussels (Turnhout, 1996); F. de Gruben, *Les chapitres de la Toison d'Or à l'époque bourguignonne (1430–1477)* (Louvain, 1997).[1]

Several individuals of importance for an appreciation of the formation of Charles the Bold's character have recently received attention. On Charles's beloved mother (d. 1471), see Monique Sommé, 'Isabelle de Portugal, duchesse de Bourgogne: Une femme au pouvoir au XVᵉ siècle' (Thèse des Lettres, University of Lille, 3 vols., 1995), published version, same title (Villeneuve d'Asq, 1998); 'Les Portugais dans l'entourage de la duchesse de Bourgogne, Isabelle de Portugal', *Revue du Nord*, 77 (1995), 321–43; and 'Une mère et son fils: Isabelle de Portugal, après son départ de la cour (1457–1471) et Charles le Téméraire', in *Autour de Marguerite d'Écosse. Reines, princesses et dames du XVᵉ siècle*, ed. G. and P. Contamine (Paris, 1999), 99–121.[2] An important related sourcebook is *Portugal et Bourgogne au XVᵉ siècle (1384–1482): Recueil de documents extraits des archives bourguignonnes*, ed. J. Paviot (Lisbon–Paris, 1995), which is complemented by the same author's 'Les Portugais à Bruges au XVᵉ siècle', *Arquivos do Centro Cultural Calouste Gulbenkian*, 38 (Paris, 1999), 1–122. Another family figure has been studied in C. van de Bergen-Pantens, 'Héraldique et bibliophilie: le cas d'Antoine, Grand Bâtard de Bourgogne (1421–1504)', in *Miscellanea Martin Wittek* (Louvain–Paris, 1993), 323–54.

For leading church dignitaries associated with Charles the Bold, see C. Märtl, *Kardinal Jean Jouffroy (obit 1473): Leben und Werk* (Sigmaringen, 1996); and *Le Pontifical du cardinal Ferry de Clugny, évêque de Tournai*, ed. A. De Schryver, M. Dykmans and J. Ruysschaert, Collezione paleografica vaticana, 3 (Vatican City, 1989), which provides a detailed biography of Ferry de Clugny. For Guillaume Fillastre the Younger, see now M. Prietzel, *Guillaume Fillastre der Jüngere (1400/07–1473). Kirchenfürst und herzoglich-burgundischer Rat*, Beihefte der Francia, 51 (Stuttgart, 2001); see also his 'Guillaume Fillastre d.J.: über Herzog Philipp den Guten von Burgund. Text und Kommentar', *Francia*, 24/1 (1997), 83–121;[3] and A. and W. Paravicini, 'L'arsenal intellectuel d'un homme de pouvoir: Les livres de Guillaume Hugonet, chancelier de Bourgogne', in *Penser le pouvoir au Moyen Age. Études offertes à Françoise Autrand*, ed. D. Boutet and J. Verger (Paris, 2000), 261–325 [reprinted in W. Paravicini, *Menschen am Hof der Herzöge von Burgund. Gesammelte Aufsätze*, ed. K. Krüger, H. Kurse and Andreas Ranft (Sigmaringen, 2002), 143–208], which notes that there were many legal manuscripts of Italian origin in the chancellor's possession.[4]

On military and naval matters, see: J. Paviot, *La politique navale des ducs de Bourgogne, 1384–1482* (Villeneuve d'Asq, 1995); W. Paravicini, 'Kleve, Geldern und Burgund im Sommer 1473. Briefe aus einer verlorenen Korrespondenz', *Francia*, 23/1 (1996), 53–93 (reprinted in Paravicini, *Menschen . . .*, 621–69); A. Esch, 'Alltag der Entscheidung. Berns Weg in den Burgunderkrieg', *Berner Zeitschrift für Geschichte und Heimatskunde*, 50 (1988), 3–64; also, elaborated, in his *Alltag der Entscheidung. Beiträge zur Geschichte der Schweiz an der Wende vom Mittelalter zur Neuzeit* (Bern, 1998), 9–86; C. Sieber-Lehmann, *Spätmittelalterlicher Nationalismus. Die Burgunderkriege am Oberrhein und in der Eidgenossenschaft* (Göttingen, 1995) and 'Der türkische Sultan Mehmed II. und Karl der Kühne, der "Türk im Occident"', *Zeitzchrift für Historische Forschung*, Beiheft 20 (1997), 13–28; *Die Murtenschlacht: La Bataille de Morat, 1476–1976* (Fribourg–Bern, 1976). For an interesting discussion of Charles's army as a means of power, see P. Contamine, 'L'armée de Charles le Téméraire: expression d'un État en devenir ou instrument d'un conquérant?', in *Aux armes, citoyens! Conscription et armée de métier de Grecs à nos jours*, ed. M. Vaïsse (Paris, 1998), 61–77.[5] Regrettably, there is no modern monograph on the fighting techniques of Charles the Bold's soldiers or on the composition of his armies, considerations of importance for appreciating his Italian connections.

2 On Burgundy and Italy generally

Brought to completion after fifty years' work is the invaluable annotated compendium of P.O. Kristeller: *Iter Italicum: A Finding List of Uncatalogued or Incompletely Catalogued Humanistic Manuscripts of the*

Renaissance in Italian and other Libraries, I–VI (London–Leiden, 1963–1992), *Cumulative Index* (Leiden, 1997), now available on CD. For tracing source material, we also have V. Ilardi, 'The Ilardi Microfilm Collection of Renaissance Diplomatic Documents, ca. 1450–ca. 1500' [held at the Sterling Memorial Library, Yale University], in *The French Descent into Renaissance Italy, 1494–95: Antecedents and Effects*, ed. D. Abulafia (Aldershot, 1995), 405–83. Of related interest are the collected papers of V. Ilardi: *Studies in Italian Renaissance Diplomatic History* (London, 1986).

For a useful general study, see N. Rubinstein, 'Das politische System Italiens in der zweiten Hälfte des 15. Jahrhunderts', *Zeitschrift für Historische Forschung*, Beiheft 5: *'Bündnissysteme' und 'Aussenpolitik' im späteren Mittelalter* (Berlin, 1988), 105–19. Perceptive is R. Fubini, 'Federico da Montefeltro e la congiura dei Pazzi: Politica e propaganda alla luce di nuovi documenti', in *Federico di Montefeltro: Lo stato, le arti, la cultura*, ed. G. Chittolini, G. Cerboni Baiardi and P. Floriani, 3 vols. (Rome, 1986), I (*Lo stato*), 357–470; later reprinted, but without the seven documents (446–70), as 'Federico da Montefeltro e la congiura dei Pazzi: immagine propagandistica e realtà politica', in R. Fubini, *Italia quattrocentesca: politica e diplomazia nell'età di Lorenzo il Magnifico* (Milan, 1994), 253–326. Not yet printed is the doctoral thesis of Petra Ehm, 'Burgund und das Reich. Spätmittelalterliche Aussenpolitik am Beispiel der Regierung Karl des Kühnen (1465–1477)', University of Bonn, 2000, where special attention is paid to gift-giving in the duke's foreign policy, a striking feature of his relations with Italian powers.

For intellectual considerations in general, see A. Vanderjagt, 'Classical learning and the building of power at the fifteenth-century Burgundian Court', in *Centres of Learning*, ed. J.W. Drijvers and A.A. MacDonald (Leiden, 1995), 267–77. A notable study relating to an outstanding intellectual is D. Robin, *Filelfo in Milan: Writings 1451–1477* (Princeton, N.J., 1991). An important Bruges merchant of Genoese origin has been the subject of several publications: *Itinéraire d'Anselme Adorno en Terre Sainte (1470–1471)*, ed. J. Heers and G. de Groër (Paris, 1978); *Adornes en Jeruzalem: Internationaal leven in het 15de en 16de eeuwse Brugge*, ed. N. Geirnaert and A. Vandewalle, Exhibition Catalogue, Bruges (Bruges, 1983); N. Geirnaert, *Het archief van de familie Adornes en de Jeruzalemstichting te Brugge*, I, *Inventaris*, II, *Regesten van de oorkonden en brieven tot en met 1500*, 2 vols (Bruges, 1987–89). Information about two bastard sons of Duke Philip the Good with Italian connections, and successively bishops of Utrecht, is furnished in *L'art en Hollande au temps de*

David et Philippe de Bourgogne: Trésors du Musée National, Het Catharijneconvent à Utrecht, ed. H.C.M. Defoer and W.C.M. Wüstefeld, Exhibition Catalogue, Paris–Dijon (Zwolle, 1993). For a Flemish bibliophile of the period see A. Derolez, *The Library of Raphael de Mercatellis, Abbot of St Bavon's, Ghent (1473–1508)* (Ghent, 1979); A. Arnoul, 'The art historical content of the library of Raphael de Mercatellis' (doctoral thesis, University of Ghent, 1992); also *Vlaamse miniaturen voor vorsten en burgers 1475–1550*, ed. M. Smeyers and J. Van der Stock, Exhibition Catalogue, Museum voor Schone Kunsten, Antwerp (Ghent, 1997). Certain recently discovered documents relating to Duke John of Cleves and Jean de Croy, heads of the Burgundian embassy sent to the Congress of Mantua of 1459, are published by A. Sottili, 'Die Universität Pavia im Rahmen der Mailänder Aussenpolitik: Der Italienaufenthalt von Johann I. von Kleve und Jean de Croy und andere Anekdoten über die Universität Pavia', in *Miscellanea Domenico Maffei dictata*, 2 vols. (Goldbach, 1995), II, 457–89.[6] Important for cultural and political relations in general is E. Lecuppre-Desjardins, 'L'art au service de la persuasion politique: les cérémonies urbaines italiennes et bourguignonnes au XVᵉ siècle', in *Rapporti e scambi tra l'umanesimo italiano e l'umanesimo europeo*, Atti di un convegno, Cianciano-Pienza, 19–22 luglio, 1999, forthcoming.

3 On Milan

Undoubtedly the first item to mention is *Carteggi diplomatici fra Milano sforzesca e la Borgogna*, ed. E. Sestan, 2 vols. (Rome, 1985–87), now cited in Walsh's notes. This work has published the very important 'Borgogna filza' of the Archivio di Stato, Milan. The 'Francia filza' from 1450 to 29 June 1466 has been published in English translation: *Dispatches with Related Documents of Milanese Ambassadors in France and Burgundy (1450–1483)*, ed. P.M. Kendall and V. Ilardi, 3 vols. to date (Athens, Ohio, 1970–81); while the section of the Milan–France correspondence covering from 18 August 1450 to 26 December 1456 has appeared in *Carteggi diplomatici fra Milano sforzesca e la Francia* [numbered I, but the only volume published to date], ed. E. Pontieri (Rome, 1978). Hence for the period of Charles the Bold's rule the *'Francia filza'* is still largely unpublished, while the various *'filza'* for Savoy and the other Italian states, which exist in the Milanese archives and were cited by Walsh from the originals, remain entirely unpublished. They certainly still contain much untapped relevant material.

For diplomacy and diplomats in general, I underline the importance of W. Schott, 'Untersuchungen zur italienischen Diplomatie vom 13. bis zum 15. Jahrhundert, unter besonderer Berücksichtigung des Agentenwesens' (doctoral thesis, University of Heidelberg, 1955). The more up-to-date studies on the subject include L. Cerioni, *La diplomazia sforzesca nella seconda metà del Quattrocento e i suoi cifrari segreti* (Rome, 1970); T. Zambarbieri, 'I rapporti tra il dominio sforzesco e il ducato di Borgogna tra il 1474 e il 1477 attraverso le relazioni degli ambasciatori milanesi', 'Tesi di laurea', University of Milan, 1980; 'La partecipazione milanese alla guerra del Bene Pubblico (1465): allestimento e realizzazione dell'impresa militare', *Nuova rivista storica*, 69 (1985), 1–30; the thesis later revised in French translation as *Milan et les États bourguignons: deux ensembles politiques princiers entre Moyen Age et Renaissance*, Publications du Centre Européen d'Études Bourguignonnes, 28 (Basel, 1988) [and reviewed by L. Pesavento, *Nuova rivista storica*, 72 (1988), 161–8]; later reprinted in Italian as *Milano e Borgogna: Due stati principeschi tra Medioevo e Rinascimento* (Rome, 1990); G. Soldi Rondinini, 'Giovan Pietro Panigarola e il "reportage" moderno', in *Die Murtenschlacht: La Bataille de Morat, 1476–1976* (Fribourg–Bern, 1976), 135–54; 'Aspects de la vie des cours de France et de Bourgogne par les dépêches des ambassadeurs milanais (seconde moitié du XVᵉ siècle)', in *Adelige Sachkultur des Spätmittelaters*, Conference papers, Krems an der Donau, 1980 (Vienna, 1982), 195–214; later reprinted in Italian with minor modifications as 'Le relazioni degli ambasciatori milanesi quali testimonianze della vita nelle corti di Francia e di Borgogna (seconda metà del secolo XV)', in her *Saggi di storia e storiografia visconteo-sforzesche* (Bologna, 1984), 65–81; P. Savy, 'Les ambassadeurs milanais à la cour de Charles le Téméraire', 'Mémoire de Maîtrise', University of Paris X –Paris IV, 1996; 'Les ambassadeurs milanais à la cour de Charles le Téméraire', *Annales de Bourgogne*, 68 (1996), 35–56;[7] R. Fubini, 'I rapporti diplomatici tra Milano e Borgogna con particolare riguardo all'alleanza del 1475–1476', in *Milan et les États bourguignons* [cited above] (Basel, 1988), 95–114; also in *Nuova rivista storica*, 72 (1988), 23–46; later reprinted, shortened, in *Milano e Borgogna: due stati principeschi tra medioevo e rinascimento*, ed. J.-M. Cauchies and G. Chittolini (Rome, 1990), 95–131; later reprinted in R. Fubini, *Italia quattrocentesca: politica e diplomazia nell'età di Lorenzo il Magnifico* (Milan, 1994), 327–50.

Fundamental for the various aspects of Milanese culture at the time of Charles the Bold are the following: G. Lubkin, *A Renaissance Court: Milan under Galeazzo Maria Sforza* (Berkeley–Los Angeles–London,

1994); and E.S. Welch, *Art and Authority in Renaissance Milan* (New Haven–London, 1995).

4 On Venice

For an ambassador of the Republic to the Burgundian court, see N. Giannetto, *Bernardo Bembo. Umanista e politico veneziano*, Civiltà veneziana. Saggi, 34 (Florence, 1985). An essential guide for the Italians in Charles's military service is B. Schnerb, 'Troylo de Rossano et les Italiens au service de Charles le Téméraire', *Francia*, 25/1 (1999), 103–28. On Bartolomeo Colleoni, Venice's leading general, whom Charles the Bold, in concurrence with others, notably Louis XI and Duke René d'Anjou, tried vainly to attract into his service see M.E. Mallett, 'Colleoni, Bartolomeo', *Dizionario biografico degli italiani*, XXVII (1982), 9–19; D. Erben, *Bartolomeo Colleoni: Die künstlerische Repräsentation eines Condottiere im Quattrocento* (Sigmaringen, 1996); P. Boucheron, *Les condottieri italiens de la fin du moyen âge* (Paris PUF, 1999).[8]

5 On Florence

As regards Florence, perhaps the most important development of the past two decades has been the publication of the correspondence of Lorenzo de' Medici, in *Lettere*, ed. R. Fubini, N. Rubinstein and M.E. Mallett, 7 vols to date (Florence, 1977–98), the published volumes covering the years of Charles the Bold's rule. A preliminary work, P.G. Ricci and N. Rubinstein, *Censimento delle lettere di Lorenzo di Piero de' Medici* [*Checklist of the Letters of Lorenzo de' Medici*] (Florence, 1964), had indicated the project's potential. The fifth centenary of Lorenzo's death in 1992 provided the incentive for the publication of many valuable related studies and associated exhibition catalogues. The papers of many of the international conferences have appeared in print: *Lorenzo de' Medici: New Perspectives*, ed. B. Toscani (New York–Bern, 1993); *La Musica a Firenze al tempo di Lorenzo il Magnifico*, ed. P. Gargiulo (Florence, 1993); *Lorenzo il Magnifico e il suo mondo*, ed. G.C. Garfagnini (Florence, 1994); *Lorenzo der Prächtige und die Kultur in Florenz des 15. Jahrhunderts*, ed. H. Heintze, G. Staccioli, B. Hesse (Berlin, 1995); *Lorenzo the Magnificent: Culture and Politics*, ed. M.E. Mallett and N. Mann (London, 1996); *La Toscana al tempo di Lorenzo il Magnifico. Politica, economia, cultura, arte*, 3 vols. (Pisa, 1996). Of the many useful exhibition catalogues I single out *'Le temps revient': Il tempo si rinuova. Feste e spettacoli nella Firenze di Lorenzo il Magnifico*, ed. P. Ventrone (Florence, 1992).[9] The centenary spawned a number of biographies of which perhaps the best is M.M. Bullard, *Lorenzo il Magnifico: Image and Anxiety, Politics and Finance* (Florence, 1994).

Tommaso Portinari's correspondence up to 1464, but only from the Bruges branch of the Medici Bank to the head office in Florence, was long ago published as *Correspondance de la filiale de Bruges des Medici. Part I*, ed. A. Grunzweig (Brussels, 1931) — the completion of this project should now be given some priority. A valuable essay on this most interesting person and his creditor Charles the Bold has just appeared: M. Boone, 'Apologie d'un banquier médiéval: Tommaso Portinari et l'État bourguignon', *Le Moyen Age*, 105 (1999), 31–54; see also M. Boone and J. Dumolyn, 'Les officiers-créditeurs des ducs de Bourgogne dans l'ancien comté de Flandre: aspects financiers, politiques et sociaux', *Publications du Centre européen d'études bourguignonnes*, 30 ('Crédit et société: les sources, les techniques et les hommes (XIVᵉ –XVIᵉ s.') (Neuchâtel, 1999), 225–41. For Portinari's altarpiece with shutters of 'The Last Judgement' attributed to Hans Memling (now in Gdańsk, formerly Danzig), see D. De Vos, D. Marechal and W. Le Loup, *Hans Memling. Catalogue*, Exhibition, Bruges, August–November 1994 (Antwerp, 1994), 34–41; however, the theme merits a more definitive investigation, and to this end I plan a contribution. For Bruges' importance as an artistic centre, see *Brugge en de Renaissance: van Memling tot Pourbus*, ed. M.P.J. Martens, 2 vols (Bruges, 1998), Volume 1, *Catalogus*; Volume 2, *Notities*; with a reduced version of the catalogue in English.

For the exceptionally interesting artistic relations between Flanders and Florence, see particularly M. Rohlmann, *Auftragskunst und Sammelbild: Altniederländische Tafelmalerei im Florenz des Quattrocento* (Alfter, 1994) (in origin a doctoral thesis, University of Cologne, 1993). An exhibition, 'Hans Memling: Five Centuries of Fact and Fiction' (Bruges, 1994), was supported by both a *Catalogue* (as noted above) and a volume of *Essays*, ed. D. De Vos, 2 vols (Bruges for the English text, and Antwerp for the French text, 1994). Likewise published in conjunction with an exhibition was N.W. Ainsworth and M.P.J. Martens, *Petrus Christus: Renaissance Master of Bruges* (New York, 1994). The papers of a symposium at the National Gallery, London, have been published as *Robert Campin: New Directions in Scholarship*, ed. S. Foister and S. Nash ([Turnhout], 1996). There is now a general introduction to Burgundian art: *Die Kunst der burgundischen Niederlande. Eine Einführung*, ed. B. Franke and B. Welzel (Berlin, 1997). Finally, not to be overlooked is the magnificent catalogue of the

Royal Academy Winter Exhibition of 1992: *Andrea Mantegna*, ed. J. Martineau (London, 1992). Two related important contributions are *From Van Eyck to Bruegel: Early Netherlandish Painting in the Metropolitan Museum of Art*, ed. M.W. Ainsworth and K. Christiansen (New York, 1998), and L. Campbell, *National Gallery Catalogues: The Fifteenth-Century Netherlandish Paintings* (London, 1998).

Archive sources recently (or soon) more available

Richard Walsh did not utilise Charles the Bold's Household Ordinances, and could make only limited use of the daily accounts (*écroes*). Most of the ducal officers of Italian birth figure in both sources, with specifications of post and salary. In the near future this material will become more available to scholars. The Household Ordinances, edited by Dr Anke Greve and myself, are to be published; and the *écroes* will be available on a database created by a group working at the German Historical Institute in Paris, of which Dr Hanno Brand and Dr Holger Kruse are the principal members. For the Court's organisation, see W. Paravicini, 'The Court of the Dukes of Burgundy: A Model for Europe', in *Princes, Patronage and the Nobility: The Court at the Beginning of the Modern Age, c.1450–1650*, ed. R.G. Asch and A.M. Birke (London, 1991), 69–102 (reprinted in Paravicini, *Menschen . . .*, 507–34); H. Kruse, *Hof, Amt und Gagen. Die täglichen Gagenlisten des burgundischen Hofes (1430–1467) und der erste Hofstaat Karls des Kühnen (1456)* (Bonn, 1996); H. Kruse, 'Die Hofordnungen Philipps des Guten von Burgund', in *Höfe und Hofordnungen 1200–1660*, ed. H. Kruse and W. Paravicini (Bonn, 1996), 141–65; W. Blockmans, A. Janse, H. Kruse and R. Stein, 'From territorial courts to one residence. The Low Countries in the Middle Ages', in *La cour comme institution économique*, ed. M. Aymard and M.A. Romani (Paris, 1998), 17–28; and W. Paravicini, '*Ordre et règle*. Charles le Téméraire en ses ordon-nances de l'hôtel', in *Comptes-rendus des séances de l'Académie des Inscriptions et Belles-Lettres, 1999* (Paris, 2000), 307–55 (reprinted in Paravicini, *Menschen . . .*, 671–713). The papers of a section at the Congress of German Historians meeting at Aachen in September 2000 will be published as *Der berühmteste Hof Europas: Das Machtzentrum des burgundischen Staates im 15. Jahrhundert*, ed. W. Paravicini.[10]

As for the presence of Italian resident ambassadors and visiting envoys at the Burgundian court, H. van der Linden's *Itinéraires de Charles, duc de Bourgogne (1467–1477)* (Brussels, 1936) was based largely on Jean Godefroy's unpublished manuscript, compiled about 1720 from the now-lost household accounts of the *Maître de la Chambre aux deniers.* Godefroy's precious volume still exists in Lille (Archives départementales du Nord, shelf number: B.19.561), and its lists are considerably more extensive than those provided by van der Linden; moreover, Godefroy sometimes added extracts from the now-lost accounts of the ducal *Argentier.*[11] Walsh acknowledges (Chapter 2, note 2) that he was not able to examine the immense quarry of relevant documentary materials in the Vatican Archives and it is here, if anywhere, that significant future discoveries will most likely be made.

*   *   *

I conclude with a profound sigh of relief now that this important study of political, diplomatic and military history is at last published. It is a commonplace that Louis XI and Commynes were fascinated by the world of the Italian peninsula of their day; now we have discovered that Charles the Bold was much more Italianate than we had supposed. In consequence a new poignancy is given to the key question dear to the hearts of Aby Warburg and Ernst Kantorowicz: What was the nature of the relationship — economic, intellectual and artistic — between the Italian Renaissance and its mirroring in the Burgundian North? This fascinating challenge awaits a dedicated and imaginative scholar.

Paris, St Jules, 2000

Notes

1. An edition of the records of the chapters of the Order covering the period of Charles the Bold's rule is being prepared by S. Dünnebeil of Vienna for publication in the series Instrumenta, German Historical Institute, Paris [now published: *Die Protokollbücher des Ordens vom Goldenen Vlies, 2: Das Ordensfest 1468 in Brügge unter Herzog Karl dem Kühnen,* Instrumenta, 12 (Ostfildern, 2003)].
2. Monique Sommé is preparing for publication, in the series Instrumenta, German Historical Institute, Paris, an edition of Isabelle of Portugal's correspondence, material of notable importance since she was very active in politics.
3. The *Ausgewählte Werke* of the cardinal are in process of being edited by the same author [now published: *Guillaume Fillastre d.J. Ausgewählte Werke,* Instrumenta, 11 (Ostfildern, 2003)].
4. Gérard Desmedt of Lille is engaged on a study of an individual of notable political authority who had considerable influence on Charles the Bold, Guillaume de Bische.

5. Franck Fusibet of Paris is engaged on preparing a comprehensive edition of the military ordinances of Charles the Bold.

6. For the Congress in general, see Jocelyn G. Russell, 'The Humanists Converge: The Congress of Mantua (1459)', in her *Diplomats at Work: Three Renaissance Studies* (Stroud, 1992), 51–93, and the papers presented at the Mantuan Congress entitled 'Il sogno di Pio II e il viaggio da Roma a Mantova', organised in April 2000 by the Centro Studi Leon Battista Alberti.

7. Which makes clear this scholar's intention to research further on the theme — he is preparing a thesis on the del Verme family, while a paper of his on Rodolfo Gonzaga at the court of Burgundy (1469–70) will appear in *Les étrangers à la cour de Bourgogne*, ed. W. Paravicini and B. Schnerb, in preparation [now published: see above, Chapter 6 note 50].

8. I myself am preparing a number of papers on Charles the Bold and Colleoni: see 'Ein Spion in Malpaga. Zur Überlieferungsgeschichte der Urkunden des René d'Anjou und Karls des Kühnen für Bartolomeo Colleoni', in *Italia et Germania. Liber Amicorum Arnold Esch*, ed. H. Keller, W. Paravicini and W. Schieder (Tübingen, 2001), 469–87; the Parisian Colleoni documents will be published in *Francia*, 27/1; and at a later date a general study of 'Colleoni und Karl der Kühne' will appear.

9. Of allied interest is a monograph on chivalric tournaments: L. Ricciardi, *Col senno, col tesoro e colla lancia: Riti e giuochi cavallereschi nella Firenze di Lorenzo il Magnifico* (Florence, 1992).

10. And A. Greve (Paris) is preparing a book on the contemporary and subsequent myth of the Burgundian court.

11. Cf. W. Paravicini, 'Kleve, Geldern und Burgund im Sommer 1473. Briefe aus einer verlorenen Korrespondenz', in *Francia*, XXIII, i (1996), 53–93 (81–2), and also W. Paravicini, 'L'embarras de richesse: Comment rendre accessibles les archives financières de la maison de Bourgogne-Valois', in *Bulletin de la Classe des Lettres et des Sciences morales et politiques de l'Académie royale de Belgique*, series vi, VII, 1996 (published Brussels, 1997), 21–68, where pages 55–9 present a provisional list of these accounts. The three full years of the extant accounts, 1468, 1469 and 1470, are being prepared for publication by E. Lebailly and A. Greve at the German Historical Institute, Paris.

Index